NEAR EASTERN STUDIES

# NEAR EASTERN STUDIES IN HONOR OF WILLIAM FOXWELL ALBRIGHT

EDITED BY HANS GOEDICKE

THE JOHNS HOPKINS PRESS BALTIMORE AND LONDON

The Johns Hopkins Press, Baltimore, Maryland 21218
The Johns Hopkins Press Ltd., London

Library of Congress Catalog Card Number 70–142817

International Standard Book Number 0–8018–1235–6

*To*

WILLIAM FOXWELL ALBRIGHT

*dedicated on the occasion of his eightieth birthday*

*May 24, 1971*

*by friends, pupils, colleagues, admirers, and the*

*Department of Near Eastern Studies of*

*The Johns Hopkins University*

# Contents

# Preface

FEW scholars have received as many and as varied honors as William Foxwell Albright, but few deserve them as fully. He is the holder of numerous honorary degrees from universities of the Western and Eastern hemispheres. He is a member of a number of learned societies and academies reflecting his influence on the development of Near Eastern Studies.

His career has always been closely connected with The Johns Hopkins University. He received his doctorate at Hopkins in 1916. After becoming Director of the American Schools of Oriental Research in Jerusalem from 1920 to 1929, he returned to Baltimore and was appointed W. W. Spence Professor for Semitic Studies in 1929. For almost thirty years he held this position, until his retirement in 1958. During these years he trained and educated many students in various fields of Near Eastern studies. He succeeded in conveying to them his lively and relevant approach to scholarship, and many of them now occupy leading positions in academic life as representatives of what has come to be recognized as the Albright school.

Even in his retirement he has continued his active participation in all matters pertaining to Near Eastern studies and gives freely of his knowledge and experience. This applies not only to those who have the advantage of personal contact with him but also to those with whom he entertains a voluminous correspondence. His lively interest, his enthusiasm, and his generous advice are equally precious to all.

This volume, made possible by the munificence of Wendell Phillips, attempts to honor Dr. Albright on his eightieth birthday in recognition of his paramount role in Near Eastern studies, which he began and fostered at The Johns Hopkins University.

# Abbreviations

| | |
|---|---|
| A | Aḥiqar |
| *AANL* | *Atti della Accademia Nazionale dei Lincei*, Roma |
| *AASOR* | *Annals of the American Schools of Oriental Research*, New Haven |
| *AbhPAW* | *Abhandlungen der Preussischen Akademie der Wissenschaften*, Berlin |
| *AD* | G. R. Driver, *Aramaic Documents of the Fifth Century*, rev. ed.; Oxford, 1957 |
| *ÄF* | *Ägyptische Forschungen* |
| *AfO* | *Archiv für Orientforschung*, Graz |
| *AHDO* | *Archives d'histoire du droit oriental* |
| *AHW* | W. von Soden, *Akkadisches Handwörterbuch* |
| *AIPHOS* | *Annuaire de l'institut de philologie et d'histoire orientales et slaves* |
| *AJSL* | *American Journal of Semitic Languages and Literatures* |
| *ABAT* | *Altorientalische Bilder zum Alten Testament* |
| *ANEP* | *The Ancient Near East in Pictures Relating to the Old Testament*, ed. by J. B. Pritchard, Princeton, 1954 |

| | |
|---|---|
| *ANET* | *Ancient Near Eastern Texts Relating to the Old Testament*, ed. by J. B. Pritchard, Princeton 1950; 2nd ed., 1955 |
| ANL | Accademia Nazionale dei Lincei, Roma |
| *AP* | A. Cowley, *Aramaic Papyri of the Fifth Century* B.C., Oxford, 1923 |
| *APA* | *Aramaic Papyri Discovered at Assuan*, London, 1906 |
| *ARM* | *Archives Royales de Mari* |
| *ArOr* | *Archiv Orientální* |
| *ASAE* | *Annales du Service des Antiquités de l'Égypte*, Le Caire |
| *ASAW* | *Abhandlungen der Sächsischen Akademie der Wissenschaften* |
| *ATD* | *Das Alte Testament Deutsch* |
| *'Atiqot* | *'Atiqot. Journal of the Israel Department of Antiquities*, Jerusalem |
| *BA* | *The Biblical Archaeologist*, New Haven |
| *BAL* | *Berichte über die Verhandlungen der Sächsischen Akademie der Wissenschaften zu Leipzig*, Berlin |
| *BASOR* | *Bulletin of the American Schools of Oriental Research* |
| *BBB* | *Bonner Biblische Beiträge*, Bonn |
| *BHSt* | *Biblia Hebraica Stuttgartensia* |
| *BHTh* | *Beiträge zur Historischen Theologie*, Tübingen |
| *BIFAO* | *Bulletin de l'Institut Français d'Archéologie Orientale* |
| *BiOr* | *Bibliotheca Orientalis* |
| *BJRL* | *Bulletin of the John Rylands Library*, Manchester |
| *BK* | *Biblischer Kommentar*, Neukirchen |
| *BMAP* | E. G. Kraeling, *Brooklyn Museum Aramaic Papyri: New Documents of the Fifth Century* B.C. *from the Jewish Colony at Elephantine*, New Haven, 1953 |
| Brockel *GVGSS* | C. Brockelmann, *Grundriss der vergleichenden Grammatik der Semitischen Sprachen* |
| *BWANT* | *Beiträge zur Wissenschaft vom Alten und Neuen Testament*, Stuttgart |

| | |
|---|---|
| *BZ* | *Biblische Zeitschrift*, Paderborn |
| *BZAW* | *Beihefte zur Zeitschrift für die Alttestamentliche Wissenschaft*, Berlin |
| *CAD* | *Chicago Assyrian Dictionary* |
| *CBQ* | *Catholic Biblical Quarterly*, Washington |
| *CIS* | *Corpus Inscriptiorum Semiticarum* |
| Cooke *NSI* | Cooke, *North Semitic Inscriptions* |
| *CRAIBL* | *Comptes Rendus de l'Académie des Inscriptions et Belles-Lettres*, Paris |
| *DISO* | C. F. Jean and J. Hoftijzer, *Dictionnaire des inscriptions sémitiques de l'ouest*, Leiden |
| Donner-Rollig, *KAI* | *Kanaanäische und Aramäische Inschriften*, Wiesbaden |
| *EB* | *Études Bibliques*, Paris |
| *Ephemeris* | M. Lidzbarski, *Ephemeris für semitische Epigraphik*, Giessen |
| *EThL* | *Ephemerides Theologicae Lovanienses*, Louvain |
| *EvTh* | *Evangelische Theologie*, München |
| *FRLANT* | *Forschungen zur Religion und Literatur des Alten und Neuen Testaments*, Göttingen |
| *Greg.* | *Gregorianum* |
| *HbzAT* | *Handbuch zum Alten Testament* |
| *HermWPap* | *Papyri of Hermopolis West* (E. Bresciani and M. Kamil, Le lettere aramaiche di Hermopoli, ANL, *Memorie*, *Cl. di. sc. mor.*, 8/12, fasc. 5) |
| *HS* | *Die Heilige Schrift des Alten Testaments* |
| *HThR* | *Harvard Theological Review*, Cambridge |
| *HUCA* | *Hebrew Union College Annual*, Cincinnati |
| *IB* | *The Interpreter's Bible*, New York |
| *ICC* | *The International Critical Commentary*, Edinburgh |

| | |
|---|---|
| *IEJ* | *Israel Exploration Journal*, Jerusalem |
| *IPN* | M. Noth, *Die israelitischen Personennamen im Rahmen der gemeinsemitischen Namengebung*, Stuttgart |
| *JAOS* | *Journal of the American Oriental Society*, New Haven |
| *JbDAI, ArAnz* | *Jahrbuch des Deutschen Archäologischen Instituts*, Archäologischer Anzeiger, Berlin |
| *JBL* | *Journal of Biblical Literature*, New York |
| *JCS* | *Journal of Cuneiform Studies*, New Haven |
| *JE* | *Jewish Encyclopedia* |
| *JEA* | *Journal of Egyptian Archaeology*, London |
| *JNES* | *Journal of Near Eastern Studies*, Chicago |
| *JPOS* | *Journal of the Palestine Oriental Society*, Jerusalem |
| *JQR* | *Jewish Quarterly Review*, Philadelphia |
| *JRAS* | *Journal of the Royal Asiatic Society of Great Britain and Ireland*, London |
| *JSS* | *Journal of Semitic Studies*, Manchester |
| *KAI* | H. Donner and W. Röllig, *Kanaanäische und aramäische Inschriften*, Wiesbaden |
| *KAT* | *Kommentar zum AT*, Gütersloh |
| *KIT* | *Kleine Texte für theologische und philosophische Vorlesungen* |
| *LFAA* | P. Leander, *Laut- und Formenlehre des Ägyptisch–Aramäischen*, Göteborgs Högskelas Årsskrift 34, 1928, nr. 4 |
| *MAOG* | *Mitteilungen der Altorientalischen Gesellschaft*, Leipzig |
| *MGWJ* | *Monatsschrift für Geschichte und Wissenschaft des Judentums*, Breslau |
| *MUSJ* | *Mélanges de l'Université Saint-Joseph* |
| *MVAeG* | *Mitteilungen der Verderasiatisch–Äegyptischen Gesellschaft*, Leipzig |
| *NTT* | *Norsk Teologisk Tidsskrift*, Oslo |
| *OLZ* | *Orientalische Literaturzeitung*, Berlin |

| | |
|---|---|
| *Or* | *Orientalia* |
| *OrAn* | *Oriens Antiquus* |
| *OTS* | *Oudtestamentische Studien*, Leiden |
| *OTWSA* | *Die Oud Testamentiese Werkgemeenskap in Suid-Afrika*, Pretoria |
| *OuTWF* | *Die Oud Testamentiese Werkgemeenskap*, Pretoria |
| *PEQ* | *Palestine Exploration Quarterly*, London |
| *PJ* | *Preussische Jahrbücher*, Berlin |
| *PRU* | *Le Palais Royal d'Ugarit*, Paris |
| *PSBA* | *Proceedings of the Society of Biblical Archaeology*, Bloomsbury |
| *RA* | *Revue d'Assyriologie et d'Archéologie Orientale*, Paris |
| *RB* | *Revue Biblique*, Paris |
| *RCHL* | *Revue critique de l'histoire et de littérature* |
| *RHA* | *Revue Hittite et Asianique*, Paris |
| *RHR* | *Revue de l'Histoire des Religions*, Paris |
| *RLA* | *Reallexikon der Assyriologie*, hrsg. von Ebeling und Meissner, Berlin |
| *RSO* | *Rivista degli Studi Orientali* |
| *RSV* (*RV*) | Revised Standard Version of the *Bible* |
| *SAB* | *Sitzungsberichte der Deutschen (Preussischen) Akademie der Wissenschaften zu Berlin*, Berlin |
| *Sem* | *Semitica* |
| Sf | Sefîre Inscriptions (see KAI no. 222–24) |
| *StBFr* | *Studii Biblici Franciscani* |
| *StSem* | *Studi Semitici* |
| *SVT* | *Supplements to Vetus Testamentum*, Leiden |
| *Syria* | *Syria. Revue d'Art Oriental et d'Archéologie*, Paris |
| *TA* | N. Aimé-Giron, *Textes Araméens de l'Égypte*, Le Caire |

| | |
|---|---|
| *TGI* | *Texte für die Geschichte Israels* |
| *ThLZ* | *Theologische Literaturzeitung*, Berlin |
| *ThWNT* | *Theologisches Wörterbuch zum Neuen Testament* |
| *ThZ* | *Theologische Zeitschrift*, Basel |
| *UT* | *Ugaritic Text* |
| *VT* | *Vetus Testamentum*, Leiden |
| *VTS* | *Vetus Testamentum Supplementum* |
| *WdO* | *Die Welt des Orients. Beiträge zur Kunde des Morgenlandes* |
| *WMANT* | *Wissenschaftliche Monographien zum Alten und Neuen Testament*, Neukirchen |
| *WZKM* | *Wiener Zeitschrift für die Kunde des Morgenlandes*, Wien |
| *ZA* | *Zeitschrift für Assyrologie*, Berlin |
| *ZAW* | *Zeitschrift für die Alttestamentliche Wissenschaft*, Berlin |
| *ZDMG* | *Zeitschrift der Deutschen Morgenländischen Gesellschaft*, Wiesbaden |
| *ZDPV* | *Zeitschrift des Deutschen Palästina-Vereins*, Wiesbaden |
| *ZThK* | *Zeitschrift für Theologie und Kirche*, Tübingen |

# William Foxwell Albright: A Personal Appreciation

WENDELL PHILLIPS

It was early in the winter of 1943, while visiting two student friends at Princeton Theological Seminary, that I picked up the copy of Professor Albright's *From the Stone Age to Christianity*, which enticed me to visit the author. My unexpected visit to Professor Albright's office was met with warmth, kindness, and generosity. This first visit terminated with the Professor autographing a copy of the book which had first directed me to him. Several years later, after wartime invasions and battles, I ended up with polio in the Marine Hospital in Baltimore, where every afternoon, unrecognized by the staff, Professor Albright devoted one of his precious hours to keeping up the spirits of one very sick young man who might never walk again.

In 1946, I organized the University of California African Expedition, which conducted research in over two dozen countries from Cairo to Capetown during the next three years from 1947 to 1949. While I possessed nothing at the time except youthful enthusiasm, Professor Albright lent to me and my project his enormous worldwide prestige, which contributed so much to the actual success of the expedition. One of the most significant contributions made by our expedition to Southern Sinai was the discovery by Professor Albright of a small Egyptian seaport in the Merkhah region, south of Abu Zeneimeh. It had long been known that Egyptian expeditions used to cross the Gulf of Suez to mine in Sinai the turquoise with which the Pharaohs and their ladies were adorned. Now this seaport, situated only 100 meters from the waterline and about 5 meters above the mean Red Sea level, had obviously served as the outlet for ancient Egyptian mining expeditions from Serabit el-Khadim. Broken pottery was distributed over an area of 50 × 100 meters and was later dated about 1500 B.C., in the period of Hatshepsut and Tuthmosis III. Soundings were made which clearly demonstrated that the debris of occupation had been almost completely removed by erosion. "Heavens!" exclaimed Professor Albright, after careful examination of the mound and the fragments of crude dark pottery. "This is the site that Petrie and others have been looking for all these years!"

During our last days in Sinai we made a difficult drive to the foot of Serabit el-Khadim to visit the Egyptians' ancient turquoise mines and examine the inscriptions on the rocks. For this final phase of the archaeological and anthropological reconnaissance of Sinai, we had been joined by Drs. William H. Brownlee and John C. Trevor (both of subsequent Dead Sea Scroll fame) and William A. Beling, all of the American Schools of Oriental Research in Jerusalem.

We were, therefore, quite an expedition as we started our ascent of Serabit el-Khadim. We were strung out along the face of the cliff, often hanging by our eyelashes with a steep 500-foot drop below our feet. After nearly two hours of hard climbing we reached the summit. Here Egyptian miners of turquoise had built a temple with elaborately carved stelae, a sanctuary, and cubicles for sleepers. Since many archaeological expeditions have studied the site for more than a century, we did not expect to make any significant contribution during the short stay allotted. While in the Sinai Peninsula Professor Albright made the extremely difficult climb with us up the 3,500 steps to the top of Mount Sinai.

The eventful and successful phase of our Egyptian operation concluded with a dinner party given in our honor by the late Nokrashi Pasha, then Prime Minister of Egypt and soon to fall before an assassin's bullet. During the dinner, Professor Albright won a debate with the Prime Minister on the use of various grammatical forms of Egyptian Arabic.

After the successful completion of the African expedition, with its termination in Capetown, I spent a delightful night at the Albright's home in Baltimore, during the winter of 1949. On this occasion the Professor and I decided to establish a nonprofit foundation specializing in archaeological work, the American Foundation for the Study of Man. During the years 1950 and 1951, Professor Albright, as first Vice President of the American Foundation, served as chief archaeologist on the two initial expeditions into little-known South Arabia.

While the first party of Americans advanced to the Wadi Hadhramaut, Professor Albright stayed behind at the City of Seyun to recover from an illness incurred as we had labored up slopes and through precipitous gorges past the village of Ma'adi and up a long series of breathtaking hairpin turns that lifted us onto the enormous tableland called the Djol, where it was below freezing at night. When Professor Albright reached Timna, capital of the ancient kingdom of Qataban, sooner than we had expected, he was somewhat disappointed to learn that we had not already taken care of all diplomatic formalities. Nevertheless, he enjoyed as much as the rest of us the visit we paid to Sherif Hussein, Ruler of Beihan, about seventeen miles south of Timna. After dinner we moved to a large room where Sherif Hussein made a somewhat lengthy speech, which was translated by Professor Albright.

Finally, in a large open courtyard, two dancing girls from Yemen entertained us. After two hours, all one could admire was the girls' endurance. As Professor Albright was obviously the oldest man present and the girls had been told by fun-loving Henry Field that he was loaded with piasters, the dancers directed most of their activities in his direction. It was quite a scene, with our Professor sitting there, Gladys Terry perched on the arm of his chair, and the gypsies dancing as close as possible to him. The Professor's face became redder and redder, and his one comment on the performance was, "My, what marvelous control!"

While making the difficult return trip to Timna we viewed the huge occupation mound of Hajar bin Humeid, where erosion had exposed a stratified face of about 50 feet. The digging at Hajar bin Humeid was slow and difficult, and worst of all, there were few pottery fragments in the spot that we attacked. The more difficult and discouraging the work became the harder Professor Albright labored. Under the best of circumstances, he was a tireless dynamo of energy, and when challenged by a tempting mound like Hajar bin Humeid, he tried to double his labor output. Professor Albright's reputation was such that Bedu traveled from miles around to marvel at the elderly Sahib without hair who never ceased working from morning till night. Now, as the season neared its end, the Professor would have worked through the night as well if he had been able to see and if there had been human beings capable of matching his efforts, even in two shifts.

Doing archaeological work alongside Professor Albright was no mean task, for he was always up and cheerful at five in the morning. Within a few minutes, in his eagerness to get everything assembled for the day's work, he managed without fail to rouse the entire expedition into an unwelcome state of wakefulness. On top of this, being a charter member of the old school, he believed that any equipment beyond the barest necessities was a sign of inherent weakness.

An old man had worked three days on Professor Albright's dig at Hajar bin Humeid before I noticed that he was totally blind. He was so industrious and careful an excavator that we wanted to keep him, but his blindness was certain to make him cause trouble with the shovel in time. The Professor finally put him to work with a stick cleaning around the stone blocks of new walls as they were uncovered, where care had to be exercised to prevent damage to ancient materials. This was an excellent idea, but one day he industriously cleaned all the supporting sand from the base of a sagging stone wall, nearly bringing the whole structure down on top of us.

During the end of our first season of work, Professor Albright came to Hajar bin Humeid, and as he was looking approvingly at the walls of Stratum D, he pounced eagerly on an exposed fragment of pottery. "Thank Heaven! We have it!" he shouted happily, for many of the sherds bore inscriptions. This was the pottery he had been hoping to find, for the script was the same as that found in earlier tombs in the area and he could thus establish an accurate date in the third century B.C.

The Professor was so pleased with this result that he agreed, though reluctantly, that work at Hajar bin Humeid could be closed down for the season. He nevertheless looked longingly at the remaining thirty-five feet of the mound, which contained at least seven strata that might carry us back well into the second millennium B.C. "Next season," I said comfortingly, and the Professor nodded his head.

In the December 1969 issue of the *Scientific American*, Dr. Gus Van Beek, an Albright student, who was in charge of the Hajar bin Humeid excavations for the second season, summarized the work, noting that over twenty successive levels of occupation could be traced beginning with the eleventh or tenth century B.C. The excavation of this site had established a frame of reference for all future archaeological work in South Arabia.

Among the many problems that were neither archaeological nor medical with which we had to cope, the most distracting was the invasion of the spiders. A new word should be invented for these creatures in Beihan, for the word "spiders" calls to mind something from a quarter of an inch to two inches, at most, in diameter. Our spiders were not of this size. Several proved to be more than seven and a half inches across. Their bodies were round, fat, and hairy. Their legs were the size of matchsticks—the big kind! And there were scores of them.

One evening several of us were talking in one of the large rooms of our palace, while Professor Albright was working at a desk nearby. Suddenly someone saw one of these huge spiders on the wall and let out the yell that usually came with such a sight. From the shadows an Arab boy, Naser, appeared, made a running leap through the air, and with his bare left foot smashed the spider against the wall. The rest of us felt somewhat shattered by the experience, but the Professor was so absorbed in his work that he did not even look up. Professor Albright was singularly unconcerned with the spiders, especially when he had removed his glasses. At such times, they disappeared from view, which was perhaps the most effective way of handling the whole situation. But it was hard on the rest of us.

Excavation at the South Gate of Timna was from the beginning most exciting and rewarding work. By the second season of work, many of our workers were well trained. Salim, our native truck driver hired in Mukalla, had recently been promoted by Professor Albright to straw boss over a group of diggers in the South Gate area and proved himself more capable every day.

One day, I wearily went up to my room, where I had hoped to do some essential writing before going back to work at the South Gate. But our head Somali, Jama Ishmail, rushed by shouting something important and exciting in a mixture of Arabic, Somali, and English. I staggered out on the landing, and there I found Salim, half standing, half sitting, and apparently about to drop from exhaustion. But I could scarcely see Salim because of something he held in his arms, something that looked like a green lion with a creature riding on its back. Salim began to slump toward the floor saying, "Sahib, Sahib Phillips," followed by something completely unintelligible in Arabic. The green lion and rider were still in Salim's arms, and I knew that a great find had been made. "Where did you get it?" I gasped in Arabic. "By House Yafash, Sahib," said Salim.

I helped Salim set the green figure on a nearby army cot. Then I ran to get Professor Albright out of bed, where he had been confined by illness. We stood and stared at the figure that lay before us. Then Professor Albright threw a bit of cold water on my excitement by asking how the lion happened to be lying on a cot in my room. When I told him that Salim had carried it in, the Professor shook his head in disapproval. "Very bad archaeological practice," he muttered. After getting the matter of bad archaeological practice out of the way, we could all look at the statue with more appreciative eyes.

It was a bronze lion, and on its back sat a fat cupid holding in one hand a dart and in the other a broken chain leading to a collar fastened around the lion's neck. At the base of the statue there was a complete inscription in ancient Qatabanian characters. Professor Albright slowly straightened up with words I shall never forget: "Wendell, we've done it. By Heaven, we've got it!" I had never seen Professor Albright so excited. "Got what, Professor?" I asked. "A date. Look!" He leaned over and pointed to the inscription on the base of the figure. Slowly he read it aloud. "Thuwaybum wa 'Aqrabum dhuway Muhasni'im shayyamu Yafash." "That means," he continued, "that Thuwaybum and 'Aqrabum, members of the family of Muhasni'im, who decorated the House Yafash, also made these lions, or had them made." "So?" I timidly inquired. "So this discovery is unique in the annals of South Arabian archaeology and will straighten out our chronology, help fix the dates of the kings of Qataban, and enable us to date our masonry with reference to the development of civilization in South Arabia." I took a deep breath and hesitantly inquired, "How?" "This lion is a copy of a Hellenistic original and couldn't have been copied much before 150 B.C. because the Greeks were not making them long before that. If King Shahr Yagil Yuhargib had the House Yafash redecorated, as we believe we have learned, he also had this lion installed, because the same two craftsmen did both jobs. So Yuhargib lived in the second or first century before Christ, and not the fifth, sixth, seventh, and eighth, as has been thought. This clears up our main lines of history in South Arabia."

About four in the afternoon Abdullah, one of our best workmen, cried, "Baksheesh, baksheesh, ya sahib!" I walked slowly over to him, sure that nothing else of importance would be found on such a day of days and expecting the usual small inscription or corroded bracelet. Abdullah was pointing to a bit of green metal which appeared through a burned layer a few feet from the spot at which the bronze lion had been discovered.

What was uncovered in the next few minutes were many narrow ridges of green metal leading off in all directions. The size and shape seemed about right for another lion, but it looked nothing like the lion we had found. The reason, of course, was that it was buried face down and all we saw were the ridges of bronze on the back of the statue, where it was originally affixed to the wall. When lifted carefully from its centuries-old bed, it was indeed another lion and cupid, identical with the first except that it faced in the opposite direction. The cupid had broken from his place, and there was other damage, but it was all there, complete and beautiful. This was indeed the expedition's day of triumph.

That evening Professor Albright repeated for the other members of our staff the significance of the lions. Along with other finds, they proved that the king under whom they were constructed could not have lived before about 150 B.C., although he had previously been dated as early as 700 B.C. Ancient

Arabia was slowly showing itself through the sands of time and neglect. Our knowledge of the history of the civilization of early South Arabia was on firm ground for the first time. By the season's end Professor Albright was able to correlate the various types of masonry and script so well that he could give approximate dates to new buildings and inscriptions as they appeared.

"Wendell, I consider this our most important find to date—even more important than the lions." It was Professor Albright speaking, after our small group returned from Mablaqa Pass. He was obviously excited and elated over a discovery made during our absence. So excited that he neglected to tell us what had been found and where. "It will also add a great deal to our knowledge of mortuary practices and offerings to the dead," he announced triumphantly. "Wonderful!" I said. "But, Professor, even though I do not want to appear unduly impatient, can you tell me what you have found?" "Oh, yes, of course," the Professor replied. "Well, you will recall that we found no objects of major importance in the upper two strata of House Yafash." By this time the House Yafash had been unearthed. We had been delighted to find three rooms along its east side completely intact—the first such instance in South Arabian excavations—giving us an excellent idea of the inside appearance of an ancient Qatabanian house. Many objects had been found which were very revealing and instructive, including bronze mirrors and incense boxes, but nothing of significance comparable to the lions of Timna.

"You will also recall," he continued, "that when we began clearing House Hadath I suggested that we carefully check the stratification for comparison with that of House Yafash, across the street." House Hadath had been discovered near the end of the first season and its outer wall exposed to view. For some time the work of clearing the interior had been going on. "Well," Professor Albright went on, "yesterday morning at 11:30 I was below the wall of House Hadath taking notes from the street when Rais Gilani—our Egyptian foreman—called me, saying 'Etla' ('come up'). I went to him and looked at the object he pointed out. There, to my astonishment, I saw the back of a bronze statue seated on a stone pedestal. It was lying face down on the floor of the cellar room of House Hadath. I saw in one corner that some of the original plaster floor had been preserved by surrounding mud. It was obvious, upon closer examination, that this statue had fallen from an upper story during the destruction of Timna. Since the weight of the statue and stone pedestal was so great, the pedestal sank several centimeters into the mud floor adjacent to the original plaster, leaving the face without serious damage just above the level of the plaster, without striking or penetrating it. We devoted the next hour and a half to removing and cleaning the statue, using knives and then soft brushes to clear away the earth and corrosion. One arm had fallen off when the statue originally fell, but it was lying nearby. The other came off when we first touched it, but the figure is easily restored and is complete."

We examined the bronze statue which the Professor pronounced our most important find. It was the figure of a lady, seated upon a stone, altogether about three feet high. Our lady possessed an aristocratic dignity that was impressive, and one felt immediately she was of high birth in ancient Qataban. The Hellenistic influence was apparent not only in the statue but in the lady herself, for her coiffure was an elaborate coiled and braided affair popular in the Greek world in the first century B.C. As we were looking at the site, the local Wali called Professor Albright's attention to numerous mason's marks found on the face of some paving slabs in the northeast corner of the colonnade running around three sides of the low central court. Although such marks had been recorded by the score from detached facing slabs, this was the first time they had been noted on slabs in situ. This was a discovery of the first importance.

Although Professor Albright was scheduled to return to Baltimore, we had hoped that he might join us on an exploratory trip to Yemen. Much as he was tempted, however, he decided that there were too many chances of his being delayed and he went on to the United States after going with the rest of us as far as Aden.

Although we were never privileged to have Professor Albright again with us in Arabia, his archaeological work was brilliantly continued by a former student, Dr. Frank P. Albright, when the expedition moved in 1951/52 to Marib, the capital of the ancient Sabean Kingdom. In 1958 Professor Albright's pioneer work was extended farther east to the Batinah Coast of Oman, north of Muscat, where another of his students, Dr. Ray L. Cleveland, excavated the traditional home of Sinbad the Sailor at Sohar.

It is impossible to divide a man into his scholarly and personal components. Professor Albright is an example of this. His religious training, which began before he could walk, became his career; the Bible has been the center of all his research, particularly the Old Testament, which made such a vivid impression on him as a boy. It was his real world more than the modern world in which he lived. He believed in it as history and he identified himself with it, just as he identified himself with the Old Testament warriors and kings.

NEAR EASTERN STUDIES

# Passive and Ergative in Hebrew

FRANCIS I. ANDERSEN

AMONG the many contributions of transformational grammar to linguistic theory has been its recognition of the utility, indeed the necessity, of mutually defining related categories.[1] The concepts of "active" and "passive" are such a pair of correlatives. Some elementary grammars, which base their treatment of syntax on the morphological contrasts exhibited by the verb system, sometimes find it useful to present both together, for pedagogical reasons.[2]

A clause like *τότε ὁ 'Ιησοῦς ἀνήχθη εἰς τὴν ἔρημον ὑπὸ τοῦ πνεύματος* (Matthew 4:1) can be described as a transformation of the clause **τότε τὸν 'Ιησοῦν ἀνήγαγεν εἰς τὴν ἔρημον τὸ πνεῦμα* (compare Luke 2:22).

The mutual relationships between two such clauses may be expressed as an optional transformation:

$$T^{Op} - 1: SA + VA + OA \rightarrow SP + VP + AgP$$

Each clause has the same three referents, an activity (verb), a performer of the activity (agent), a recipient of the activity (victim).[3] Each of these is

1. See Noam Chomsky, *Aspects of the Theory of Syntax* (Cambridge: M.I.T. Press, 1965); idem, "Introduction to the Formal Analysis of Natural Languages," *Handbook of Mathematical Psychology*, ed. R. Duncan Luce, Robert R. Bush, and Eugene Galanter (New York: John Wiley and Sons, 1963), vol. II, pp. 269–321; Emmon Bach, *An Introduction to Transformational Grammars* (New York: Rinehart and Winston, 1964).

2. See, for example, Eugene Van Ness Goetchius, *The Language of the New Testament* (New York: Charles Scribner's Sons, 1965), pp. 92–97.

3. This term, suggested by Martin Joos (*The English Verb: Form and Meanings* [Madison and Milwaukee: The University of Wisconsin Press, 1964], p. 93), has the advantage of reserving "object" for a strictly grammatical category.

expressed by a pair of formally contrasting tagmemes in the active and passive clause. The transformation $T^{op} - 1$ involves three constituent transformations between these corresponding pairs: (i) the object (OA) of the active verb (VA) becomes the subject (SP) of the passive verb (VP), with a change from accusative to nominative *case*; (ii) the *form* of the verb changes from active (VA) to passive (VP) *voice*; (iii) the subject of the active verb (SA) becomes the agentive tagmeme of the passive verb (AgP), with a change from nominative to genitive *case*, together with the additional feature of the use of the preposition *ὑπό* to signal the agential relationship of the agent to the passive verb. Possible changes in word sequence have been ignored as marginal to clause structure as such.[4] Furthermore, grammatical concord between subject and verb may require a change in the *number* of the verb (not needed in the example above).

The array of formal contrasts in the transformation is thus almost maximal. The only feature found in both clauses is the use of nominative case for the subject, whether of an active or of a passive verb. This case accordingly does not distinguish the agent from the victim. But the other cases are unequivocal in this regard, the genitive, as the signal of agent, being supplemented by the (redundant) preposition.

The semantic equivalence between the two clauses implies that the choice of one or other in the optional transform depends on what one wishes to bring into prominence as theme or topic—the agent or the victim. The nominative case identifies what has been selected as the topic of discourse (answering questions corresponding to English *Who?*), and is neutral in the matter of agent and victim.

The active-passive transformations in English depend on tagmeme sequences rather than cases to distinguish agent and victim, but negatively. The situation is complicated further by the fact that items in the predicate apart from the victim (direct object) can be transposed into the position of subject. The equivalent clauses:

*The teacher gave the boy the book.* (1)
*The teacher gave the book to the boy.* (2)

are open to the transformations:

*The book was given to the boy by the teacher.* (3)
*The boy was given the book by the teacher.* (4)

4. For a study of the typology of transformations of this kind see B. A. Uspenskiĭ, "Opyt transformatsionnogo issledovaniya sintaksicheskoĭ tipologii," *Issledovaniya po struckturnoĭ tipologii*, ed. T. N. Moloshnaya (Moskva: Akademiya nauk S.S.S.R., 1963), pp. 52–60.

Since agential *by* occurs only with a passive verb, it is really redundant, so long as the victim as subject is always identified by its preverbal position. The nouns with the active verbs, on the other hand, rely entirely on sequence as the grammatical signal of their identity as agent or victim.

It is even possible for a noun in an adverbial prepositional phrase[5] to be transformed into the subject of a passive verb:

*The chair was sat in by every person in turn.* (5)

The specification of the agent distinguishes such a clause from the stative use of passive forms:

*The bed has been slept in.* (6)

The differences between (1), (2), (3), and (4) are matters of focus rather than of information. The contrast between (5) and (6) suggests that the latter is resorted to when the agent is not known or when his identity is irrelevant.[6]

After discussing such data, Joos concludes that in English "the meaning of the passive is that the subject does not designate the actor"[7] and proceeds to distinguish three categories of passival construction.

Other languages are less permissive in their transformational possibilities. An example close to English is supplied by Jamaican Creole, in which related "active" and "passive" clauses are:

| | | |
|---|---|---|
| *dem sel-aaf di bota,* | "they have sold all the butter" | (7) |
| *di bota sel-aaf,* | "the butter has all been sold" | (8)[8] |

$$T^{op} - 2\colon SA + V + OA \rightarrow SP + V$$

Here there are no changes in the forms (case) of the nouns; the transformation of OA to SP involves transposition only. There is no change in verb form (voice). Furthermore, "no expression of the agent is possible in such constructions in Creole."[9] $T^{op} - 1$ is not realized. If $T^{op} - 1$ is definitive of the active-passive co-categories, then the category of "active" (and with it "passive") has no status in a language which admits only $T^{op} - 2$. It is

5. This analysis can be avoided by describing a construction like "sit in" as a ve (phrase). Equivocation in the assignment of an item like "in" in such clauses constitute major defect in Immediate Constituent Analysis; and substitution tests can lead to e result.

6. Joos, *The English Verb*, pp. 91–98, where more examples may be found.

7. Ibid., p. 95.

8. Beryl Loftman Bailey, *Jamaican Creole Syntax: A Transformational Approach* (Ca University Press, 1966), pp. 33–34.

9. Ibid., p. 81.

enough to say that the verb has a subject, which may be either the agent or the victim of the action, but must be the agent when the agent is specified. The preverbal position for the subject is obligatory, so it is the lack of a post-verbal tagmeme that identifies the subject as victim.

Typologically this bears a resemblance to Arabic, where a similar restriction obtains; at least in this, that the agent of an action described by a passive-form verb is never specified. The reason for the choice of such a construction is either that the focus is on the victim or because the identity of the agent is suppressed through ignorance or as tabu.[10] (St. Mark's frequent passives may rest on an Aramaic substratum with the same trait, using the passive when the agent is not specified; but St. Matthew's transformation of St. Mark's actives to passives may betray the further influence of a convention that speaks thus indirectly about acts of God.)[11]

But Arabic differs from the Creole in two respects. Passive verbs display a contrast in form with their active counterparts; and the verb need not have an explicit subject. When neither agent nor victim is identified, the verb as such may be viewed as the topic. Other nouns may be predicative, so that the verb in such a construction is sometimes described as "impersonal." A passive form of the verb is used when generating a clause in which the verb has no grammatical subject.

To sum up. If the normative feature of active/passive is agent as grammatical subject/agent as part of grammatical predicate, then this is not realized when the "passive" clause represses the agent. If the normative feature of active/passive is agent as subject/victim as subject, then this is not realized when the "passive" clause has no subject. If the only feature of $T^{op} - 1$ present is a contrast in the forms of the verbs, it does not follow that these must correspond to active/passive. It is better to restrict these terms to clause types.

And other categories may need recognition. Compare clauses (1)–(6) with

*This bread cuts easily.* (9)
*This bed sleeps two persons.* (10)[12]

The descriptive names for the grammatical categories of Indo-European

10. Acts of God are frequently described with the aid of the passive voice (W. Wright, *A Grammar of the Arabic Language*[3] [Cambridge: University Press, 1896], vol. I, p. 50).

11. For notes on this point, see F. Blass and A. Debrunner, *A Greek Grammar of the New Testament*, trans. Robert W. Funk (Chicago, 1961), pp. 72, 164, 176.

12. John Anderson,, "Ergative and Nominative in English," *Journal of Linguistics* 4 (1968): 1–32. John Lyons, *Introduction to Theoretical Linguistics* (Cambridge, 1968), pp. 350–71.

("passive" and "active" for verb forms, "nominative" [agent] and "accusative" [victim] for noun cases) may be inapplicable to the structural relationships of other languages. This typological variety is illustrated by the diverse functions of the oblique case in Kurdish.[13]

*ez khytêbê dyxunym*, "I [direct case] a book [oblique case] am-reading" (11)
*myn khytêb xwend*, "I [oblique] a book [direct] read [past]" (12)

The clause constructions are in complementary distribution with the verb tense. They are not described by $T^{op} - 1$, but by an obligatory transformation:

$$T^{Ob} - 3\text{: SA + OA + VA(pres.)} \rightarrow \text{AgP + SP + VP(past)}$$

The identification of "I" as SA in (11) and of "book" as SP in (12) relies on the coexistence of two features—the case of the noun, the concord of the noun with the verb. But the analysis, and the validity of $T^{Ob} - 3$, relies on a rule that all present tense verbs are active and all past tense verbs are passive. This is not efficient; two grammatical categories are invoked for one formal contrast; there is no minimal contrast for each.[14] The victim is oblique case when the verb is present (also future); the agent is oblique case when the verb is past.

Similar typological features are met in Georgian. Alf Sommerfelt has pointed out how inappropriate it is to use the ideas of "subject" and "object" when describing the use of the narrative (or ergative) rather than the nominative case when the predicate contains a perfect verb.[15] There is no need to say that the perfect is passive; rather one should recognize that the verb is neutral.[16] The contrastive signals are not in the verb forms (active versus passive) but in the noun cases (nominative versus ergative).[17] In the usage of some scholars "ergative" is precisely the name of the case of the

13. K. K. Kurdoyev, *Grammatika kurdskogo yazyka* (*Kurmandzhi*) (Moskva–Leningrad: Akademiya nauk, 1957), pp. 62ff.

14. On the problem of terminology for describing these relationships, see I. I. Tsukerman, "K utochneniyu ponyatiya passivno-obʾyektnogo spryazheniya v severnom narechii kurdskogo yazyka (Kurmandzhi)," *Palestinskiĭ Sbornik* 15 (78) (1966): 197–200. He recommends "passive-objective" rather than "ergative."

15. Alf Sommerfelt, "Sur la notion du sujet en Géorgien," *Diachronic and Synchronic Aspects of Language* (The Hague: Mouton, 1962), pp. 66f.

16. See the note on this point in the Russian translation of J. Marouzeau, *Lexique de la terminologie linguistique—Slovarʾ lingvisticheskikh terminov*, trans. N. D. Andreyev (Moskva: Izdatel'stvo inostrannoĭ literatury, 1960), p. 347, n. 1.

17. I. I. Meshchaninov, *Struktura predlozheniya* (Moskva–Leningrad: Akademiya nauk S.S.S.R., 1963), pp. 79–81.

agent when the verb is passive.[18] But if the language lacks $T^{Op} - 1$, this may be a misnomer, since the passive status of the verb has already been inferred by arguing that the agent tagmeme, being inflected, is not the subject, and the status of the victim tagmeme as subject has been inferred from its concord with the verb. But it is not axiomatic that a verb always agrees with its subject rather than its object. Even in Indo-European an object verb conjugation in contrast to the familiar subject conjugation has been conjectured.[19]

The term "ergative" is more serviceable if it is used to describe several related linguistic features of clause structure, including morphology (the ergative case of a noun with an ergative suffix), syntax (the ergative construction realizing the agent-action relationship between a noun and a verb), and deep structure (when this is disclosed by transformations). There is now a considerable literature on the typological variety of ergative clauses.[20]

The ergative construction is one of the typological features that the Hurrian[21]–Urartian[22] family has in common with certain Caucasian languages.[23] A genetic relationship has been inferred from this fact, but not decisively.[24] For one thing, the syntax of the ergative varies considerably within the Caucasian family. In Khinalug, for instance, unlike Georgian, it is used with all tenses.[25] In others, like Akhvakh[26] and Batsbian,[27] it has instrumental as

18. O. S. Akhmanova, *Slovar᾽ lingvisticheskikh terminov* (Moskva: Sovetskaya entsiklopediya, 1966), p. 528.

19. L. A. Pireĭko, *Osnovniye voprosy ergativnosti na materiale indoiranskikh yazykov* (Moskva: Nauka, 1968), p. 6.

20. In addition to the bibliography with Anderson's article (note 12), see I. I. Meshchaninov, *Ergativnaya konstruktsiya v yazykakh razlichnykh tipov* (Leningrad: Nauka, 1967), for a full-scale study, and V. M. Zhirmunskiĭ, *Ergativnaya konstruktsiya predlozheniya v yazykakh razlichnykh tipov* (Leningrad: Nauka, 1967), for a wide range of articles.

21. E. A. Speiser (*Introduction to Hurrian*: *AASOR*, vol. XX [New Haven, 1941], p. 108) declined to use the term "ergative" for the agentive so as not to beg the question of generic connection with any Caucasian language.

22. G. A. Melikishvili, *Urartskiye klinoobrazniye nadpisi* (Moskva: Akademiya nauk, 1960), p. 55; I. I. Meshchaninov, *Grammaticheskiĭ stroĭ urartskogo yazyka* (Moskva–Leningrad: Akademiya nauk, 1958), pp. 120–23; G. A. Melikishvili, *Urartskiĭ yazyk* (Moskva: Nauka, 1964), pp. 32 f.

23. For a survey of this family, with bibliography, see V. V. Vinogradov, ed., *Yazyki narodov SSSR IV: Iberiĭsko-kavkazskiye yazyki* (Moskva: Nauka, 1967).

24. I. I. Meshchaninov, *Grammaticheskiĭ stroĭ urartskogo yazyka* (note 22), part 2 (1962), pp. 54–72; idem, "Ergativnaya konstruktsiya v Iberiĭsko-kavkazskikh yazykakh i yeyo kharakterniye osobennosti v Biaĭnskom (Urartskom) yazyke," *Voprosy izucheniya Iberiĭsko-kavkazskikh yazykov*, ed. E. A. Bokarev (Moskva: Akademiya nauk, 1961), pp. 5–13.

25. Yu. D. Desheriyev, *Grammatika Khinalugskogo yazyka* (Moskva: Akademiya nauk, 1959), p. 23.

26. Z. M. Magomedbekova, *Akhvakhskiĭ yazyk* (Tbilisi: Metsniyereba, 1967), p. 53.

27. Yu. D. Desheriyev, *Batsbiĭskiĭ yazyk* (Moskva: Akademiya nauk, 1953), p. 63. This language has twenty-two cases.

well as agentive meaning; while in Kabardino–Cherkes it has a wide range of functions.[28] The many relationships that have been suggested are reviewed by Dyakonov.[29] It has even been possible to argue for a remote connection between Urartian and Indo-European;[30] the ergative of the former, which has generally been taken as evidence that there is no relationship, being identified as an archaic link with the objective conjugation supposed by Kretschmer for Proto-Indo-European.[31]

The characteristic features of the ergative construction in Urartian may be illustrated by these typical clauses:

> $^{\mathrm{URU}}$ar-di-ni-di nu-na-a-li $^{\mathrm{I}}$iš-pu-ú-i-ni-ni $^{\mathrm{I\ DINGIR}}$ sar$_5$-dur$_6$-e-ḫé $^{\mathrm{I}}$me-nu-a $^{\mathrm{I}}$iš-pu-ú-i-ni-ḫé,
> "Ishpuini (nom.), son of Sarduri, and Menua (neut.), son of Ishpuini, came to the city of Ardini" [19:26f.] (13)
> $^{\mathrm{I}}$me-nu-a-še $^{\mathrm{I}}$iš-pu-u-i-ni-ḫi-ni-še i-ni pi-i-li a-gu-ni,
> "Menua (erg.), son of Ishpuini, this canal (nom.) constructed" [44:1–3][32] (14)

In (13) the subject of the intransitive verb is in neutral or nominative case; in (14) the victim of the action is nominative, the agent ergative. When the ergative construction is realized, the verb agrees with the noun in the ergative case. In the absence of a transformation like $T^{Op} - 1$, it is unwarranted to call the verb in (14) passive.

The so-called "passive" verbs are an innovation in Semitic.[33] In West Semitic a process of inner flexion[34] gave rise to a passive *qutila* present already in Ugaritic.[35] In ancient Hebrew it extended by analogy to D and *h*– forms, but later became otiose in G after secondary doubling (to save the distinctive short vowel –*u*–) made G-passive identical with D-passive. Furthermore, in Hebrew the potentiality of G-passive was quenched by the extension of N, strictly middle at first, to "passive" constructions, so that grammarians

28. M. L. Abitov, et al., *Grammatika Kabardino-cherkesskogo literaturnogo yazyka* (Moskva: Akademiya nauk, 1957), pp. 48f.

29. I. M. D'yakonov, *Yazyki drevneĭ peredneĭ Azii* (Moskva: Nauka, 1967), pp. 163–65.

30. G. B. Dzhaukyan, *Urartskiĭ i indoyevropeĭskiye yazyki* (Erevan: Akademiya nauk Arm.-S.S.R., 1963), especially pp. 56, 87.

31. Note 19.

32. References are to the Melikishvili corpus (note 22). Johannes Friedrich, "Zum Ausdruk unseres Subjekts und Akkusativobjekts im Chaldischen," Beiträge zu Grammatik und Lexikon des Chaldischen, *Caucasia* 7 (1931): 53–61.

33. Frank R. Blake, "The internal passive in Semitic," *JAOS* 22 (1901): 45–54.

34. K. Petráček, "Die innere Flexion in den semitischen Sprachen," *ArOr* 28 (1960): 547–606; 29 (1961): 513–45; 30 (1962): 361–408.

35. Cyrus H. Gordon, *Ugaritic Textbook* (Rome, 1965), p. 73.

described it as the passive of G. In Aramaic passives developed much later, and from different patterns, originally reflexive in meaning.[36]

Arabic has developed the fullest repertoire of passive forms. Only the ninth and eleventh forms lack them. Besides the syntactic limitations already noted, the gaps in the array of verb forms are instructive. There are no imperatives. Yet intransitive verbs also have "passive" forms. By the criterion of $T^{Op} - 1$ this is a misnomer. The established terminology is the result of reading Semitic through Indo-European spectacles. Arabic "passives" are used in clauses in which the agent is not specified. This is precisely how the Arabic grammarians themselves described the facts.[37]

If the term "passive" is used more strictly for describing a set of clauses each of which may be related by $T^{Op} - 1$ to members of a set of "active" clauses, without remainder, then it is not appropriate for Hebrew either. The facts may be illustrated by the verbs describing birth based on the root *y–l–d*. Three persons are involved in this activity—the father (F), the mother (M), and the child (C). Four, if the midwife be included. The noun *məyalledet* occurs only in Gen. 35:17; 38:28 and Exod. 1. It is never used in a clause with a verb *y–l–d*; it is always used absolutely, it never has an object, for instance. The one occurrence of the corresponding D verb is the infinitive in Exod. 1:16, meaning "perform the services of a midwife." The object is the mother. All other forms traditionally called *puᶜal* are not D but *qal* passive ($G_p$).

The following clause types are met:

$$\text{Cl} - 1:\ V(G_a, H_a) + S_F \pm O_C \qquad (15)$$

Clause-set 1 consists of clauses with an active verb (which may be *qal* or *hipᶜîl*), an obligatory subject which indicates the father, and an optional object indicating the child.

$$\text{Cl} - 2:\ V(G_a) + S_M \pm O_C \pm R_F \qquad (16)$$

$$\text{Cl} - 3:\ V(G_p, N) \pm S/O_C \pm R_F \qquad (17)$$

These formulae generate the following subsets of clauses. From (15):

$$V(G_a) + S_F \qquad (18)$$

Example: *wəlōᵓ yālād*, "and he did not engender" (Jer. 17:11). The apparently masculine subject is implicit in the verb. But it is probably epicene

36. Giovanni Garbini, *Il Semitico di Nord-Ovest* (Napoli, 1960), pp. 126–35.

37. B. M. Grande, *Kurs arabskoĭ grammatiki v sravnitel'noistoricheskom osveshchenii* (Moskva: Vostochnaya literatura, 1963), pp. 168–72.

(compare [22]), and the verb, which means here "lay [eggs]" is probably transitive, the pronoun object lacking by brachylogy.

$$V(G_a) + S_F + O_C \quad (19)$$

Example: *wəyālad šāqer*, "and he engendered lies" (Ps. 7:15); *wəkūš yālad ʾet-nimrōd*, "and Kush engendered Nimrod" (Gen. 10:8). O may be a pronoun suffix (Deut. 32:18; Ps. 2:7; Prov. 23:22; Job 38:29).

$$V(H_a) + S_F \quad (20)$$

Example: *wəšaḥărayim hôlīd biśdē môʾāb*, "and Shaharayim had children in the land of Moab" (1 Chron. 8:8). Compare Isa. 66:9.

$$V(H_a) + S_F + O_C \quad (21)$$

Example: *wayyōled bānīm ūbānōt*, "and he engendered sons and daughters" (Gen 5); *ʾabrāhām hōlīd ʾet-yiṣḥāq*, "Abraham engendered Isaac" (Gen. 25:19). Clauses of the latter type are common, and always with sequence S–V–O. From (16):

$$V(G_a) + S_M \quad (22)$$

Example: *wəlōʾ yālədā*, "and she did not bear" (Judges 13:2,3; compare Isa. 23:4; 54:1). The same construction occurs with prefixed verb (Gen. 18:13), co-ordinated prefixed verb (Gen. 30:3); consecutive prefixed verb (1 Kings 3:17), infinitive construct (Gen. 25:24; Isa. 26:17), a suffixed pronoun being always $S_M$.

$$V(G_a) + S_M + O_C \quad (23)$$

Example: *wəhaṣṣəʿīrā gam-hīʾ yālədā bēn*, "and the older one too bore a son" (Gen. 19:38; compare 30:21); *ūbāśəmat yālədā ʾet-rəʿūʾēl* (Gen. 36:4; compare 6:5; 1 Chron. 2:17; Isa. 66:8). O may be a pronoun suffix (Jer. 20:14), or a pronoun with *nota accusativi* (1 Kings 1:6). A similar construction is realized in relative clauses like *ʾăšer yālədā hāgār* (Gen. 16:15) if *ʾăšer* is O. This clause type occurs with prefixed verb (Gen. 3:16), consecutive affixed verb (Judges 13:3), consecutive prefixed verb (numerous examples), participle (Isa. 7:14), infinitive absolute (Job 15:35).

$$V(G_a) + S_M + R_F \quad (24)$$

Example: *wəśāray ʾēšet ʾabrām lōʾ yālədā lō*, "and Sarai, Abram's wife, had not borne for him" (Gen. 16:1; compare 30:1)

$$V(G_a) + S_M + O_C + R_F \quad (25)$$

Example: *wattēled hāgār lǝʾabrām bēn*, "and Hagar bore a son for Abram" (Gen. 16:15; compare 21:2). See also Gen. 22:23; 29:34; 30:20; 44:27; Deut. 21:15; Judges 8:31. This clause type is realized also in a relative clause like *ʾăšer yālǝdā-llō śārā* (Gen. 21:3), if *ʾăšer* is O. Compare Gen. 24:47; 25:12; 41:5; 2 Sam. 12:15; Ruth 4:12; and Ugaritic Accadian: *ana mărî*^M^ *ša tullad* ^SAL^*pidaya ana rašapabu* (RS. 17:33, l. 6′). The feminine S may be implicit in the verb suffix (Gen. 21:9; 24:24; 34:1; 46:15). This throws suspicion on the pleonastic object *ʾōtāh* in Num. 26:59 and suggests that this is an ergative O of a $G_p$ verb **yullǝdā*—"Jokebed bat-Lewi, who was born to Lewi in Egypt."

*wattēled ʿādā lǝʿēśāw ʾet-ʾĕlīpāz*, "and Ada bore Elipaz for Esau" (Gen. 36:4). From (17):

$$V(G_p)\ [+\ S/O] \qquad (26)$$

Example: *hayyōm ʾăšer yulladtī bō*, "the day on which I was born" (Jer. 20:14; compare 22:26; Job 3:2). The identity of the child is signalled only by the pronoun suffix subject of the verb. There is no mention of either parent.

$$V(G_p) + S/O_C \qquad (27)$$

Example: *ze yullad-šām*, "this one was born there" (Ps. 87:4,6).

$$V(G_p) + R_F \qquad (28)$$

Example: *ūlǝšēm yullad*, "and [children] were born for Shem" (Gen. 10:21).

$$V(G_p) + S/O_C + R_F \qquad (29)$$

Example: *yeled yullad-lānū*, "a child has been born for us" (Isa. 9:5; compare Gen. 6:1); *ūlǝyōsēp yullād šǝnē hānīm*, "and to Joseph was(!) born two sons" (Gen. 41:50; compare Gen. 4:26 with use of N in 4:18). See also (with discord) Gen. 10:25; 1 Chron. 1:9. There may be a reference to the father ($R_F$) when $G_p$ is used, but there is no mention of M in any extant example. When C is specified, it is always indefinite. In the absence of an explicit definite $S/O_C$, the issue of the use or nonuse of *ʾet–* remains unresolved. Similar constructions in relative clauses are in Gen. 35:26; 36:5; 46:22,27; 50:23.

$$V(N)\ [+\ S/O] \qquad (30)$$

Example: *nōlad*, "he was born" (Ecc. 4:14; compare Job 3:2). This absolute use, without even a referential, is rare; see Ps. 22:32; 78:6.

$$V(N) + S/O_C \qquad (31)$$

Example: *ʾim-yiwwālēd gōy paʿam ʾeḥāt*, "can a people be born at one stroke?" (Isa. 66:8). In a relative clause, Deut. 15:19.

$$V(N) + R_F \tag{32}$$

Example: *halləben mēʾā-šānā yiwwālēd*, "will [a son] be born to a person one hundred years old?" (Gen. 17:17).

$$V(N) + S/O_C + R_F \tag{33}$$

Example: *wəʾāḥ ləṣārā yiwwālēd*, "and a brother is born for distress" (Prov. 17:17); *wayyiwwālədū* (Q) *lədāwīd bānīm bəḥebrōn*, "and sons were born for David in Hebron" (2 Sam 3:2); *wayyiwwālēd laḥănōk ʾet-ʿīrād*, "and Irad was born to Hanok" (Gen. 4:18).

Clauses like (32) and (33) are commoner than ones like (30) and (31). In other words, V(N) is characteristically used with a reference to F, but not to M. The *nota accusativi* is always used when $S/O_C$ is a personal name.[38]

To complete the list of verb forms, we may note that $H_p$ infinitive *hulledet* occurs three times, always with *ʾet–* + $S/O_C$ (Gen. 40:20; Ezek. 16:4,5). The term for "parent" is the G participle, masculine (Jer. 30:6; Prov. 17:21; 23:24; etc.) or feminine (Jer. 50:12; Prov. 17:25, etc.). The latter seems to be restricted to a woman in labor, as in the common simile for extreme pain (Jer. 30:6). The G passive participle is used as an equivalent of *yeled* (1 Kings 3:26f.) or *ben* (Job 14:1; 15:14; 25:4), generally in relationship to the mother.

This complete list of attested clause types shows that all imaginable patterns are not realized.

Most realizations of (18), (22), and (24) are negated. An absolute use without negation is Exod. 1:19; Ezek. 31:6; Mic. 5:2; but it could be argued that an object is implied. *Yālədā* in Isa. 66:7 is not absolute, since *zākār* is a double duty object. It is better to regard *yālədā* in Jer. 14:5 and *yālādtī* in 1 Chron. 4:9 as elliptical realizations of (23).

Remarks about the variety of tenses used for some clause types are included in order to show that the choice of one construction rather than another does not correlate with tense as in Georgian and Kurdish. Nor does there seem to be any restriction of any verb person to any one clause type. It should be noted, however, that consecutive perfect verbs show a strict distribution: $S_F$ always has $H_a$; $S_M$ has $G_a$, but other forms of $G_a$ occur with either $S_F$ or $S_M$.[39]

38. K. Albrecht, "אֵת vor dem Nominativ und beim Passiv," *ZAW* 47 (1929): 274–84.

39. On the use of these data in source criticism see U. Cassuto, *The Documentary Hypothesis* (Jerusalem: Magnes, 1961), pp. 42–54.

In the formulae generated by (15), (16), and (17) no attention has been given to the sequence of tagmemes. The preferred patterns for (25) are

V S R O
O V S R
S V R

These are congruent. R is preverbal only in interrogation. The most important variant is V R S O (1 Kings 11:20; 1 Chron. 4:6), preferred when R is a pronoun. The sequence V O R in Gen. 46:18,25 similarly places the pronoun object near the verb. This is normal for Hebrew syntax. But not, apparently, for Ugaritic, where V O R holds, even when R is a pronoun; for example, *wld.bn.lh* (Herdner 15:20), *wld.bnm.lh* (15:21), *wld.špḥ.lkrt* (14:152). It is not clear whether these patterns are (25) or (33).[40] But *tld.šbᶜ.bnm.lk* (15:23) and *k.yld.bn.ly* (17:II:14) are (25) and (33) respectively. The apparent sequence V S O R (Gen 24:36), which departs from the Hebrew norm, is then either a Canaanism or else an indication that *bēn laʾdōnī* is a phrase; contrast Gen. 21:2. But in Gen. 30:5,10,17 (R before O) and Gen. 30:7,12,19 (O before R) the Hebrew and the Ugaritic norms alternate.

The most important restrictions in the repertoire of clause types are:

(i) F or M as agent are realized only as S (Cl − 1, Cl − 2).

(ii) When F is realized as agent, M is not specified (Cl − 1). That is, a clause that says "F engendered C out of M" is rare. In fact, *šəlōšā nōlad lō mibbat-šūᶜ hakkənaʿănīt*, "three was(!) born for him from Bath-Shua the Canaanitess" (1 Chron. 2:3), is unique. It could be that M appears as R in Isa. 49:21; but this is another unique construction—the only occurrence of a masculine verb in a (25) clause—and parenthood does not seem to be involved. Compare Ezra 10:3, where *mēhem* refers to fathers. (This limitation is not present in Accadian, where it is possible to speak of engendering children "from" a woman: *ultu aššati šaniti*, "from a second wife" [RS. 17:33, l. 3′].)[40a]

(iii) When F and M are both specified—(24) and (25)—F is referential, not agential. *Yullad-bēn lənoᶜŏmī*, "a son is born for Naomi" (Ruth 4:17) is the only example of female referential (but see Isa. 49:21), who is not M but a stand-in for the deceased levirate father.

40. On the morphology of these verbs, see the writer's paper "Biconsonantal byforms in Hebrew," to be published in *ZAW*.

40a. But compare *zeraᶜ min-hāʾiššā hazzōʾϑ* "seed from this woman" (I S. 2:20), and Ruth 4:12.

This raises the question whether there is a proper agential tagmeme in the Hebrew verb clause. Various occurrences of *b–*, *min–*, and *l–* have been classified as agential in function. I believe it is possible to show that all such cases are better explained as instrumental (*b–*, *min–*) or referential (*l–*), but detailed demonstration is outside the scope of this paper.

(iv) No clause occurs in which the production of a child is described as the joint action of both parents.

(v) There seem to be no semantic differences between $G_a$ and $H_a$ in Cl – 1 and $G_p$ and N in Cl – 3.

The stage is now set to raise the prime question of the transformational relationships between these clause types. *No transformations without remainder are possible between any pairs of members of the three sets.* Specifically, $T^{Op}$ – 1 does not occur, so by this criterion there is no proper passive construction in Hebrew. The three clause types represent a choice of F, M, or C as topic of discourse.[41] Well-formed transformations between any of them are prevented by the restrictions that M is never specified in Cl – 1 or Cl – 3, so neither of these can be a transform of Cl – 2; and F is realized in Cl – 2 and Cl – 3 only as R, so neither of these can be a transform of Cl – 1.

The feature that F = R, common to Cl – 2 and Cl – 3, invites study of possible transformations between them. Cl – 3 can be regarded as a transform of Cl – 1 only if $R_F$ in Cl – 3 is considered as agential. We have already expressed doubts as to the existence of such a tagmeme in Hebrew; but in any case $R_F$ in Cl – 2 is not agential, and it is better to classify it as referential in both cases, rather than multiply categories needlessly.

Cl – 3 is then a restrictive transform of Cl – 2, with suppression of M. This result is supported by the restriction of V in Cl – 3 to $G_p$,N; there is no $H_p$ to match $H_a$ of Cl – 1. $R_F$ is unchanged in the transformation. $R_F$ is rarely lacking from Cl – 3.

It is not only the failure of $T^{Op}$ – 1 that calls into question the traditional description of Cl – 3 with C as S of $V_p$. The syntactic relationships of C to the verb are the same in Cl – 2 and Cl – 3; C is the object in both cases. The *only* change in Cl – 2 → Cl – 3 is the suppression of the subject. Cl – 3 could be described as clauses without subjects.

The reason for regarding C as S in Cl – 3, in spite of the consistent use of *nota accusativi*, is concord between V and C. This, however, often fails, a fact

41. On the contrastive information-bearing functions of such correlative clauses see the discussion of the linguistic theory of Vilem Mathesius by Paul L. Garvin in *Linguistics Today*, ed. Archibald A. Hill (New York–London: Basic Books, 1969), pp. 233ff.

generally accounted for by the doctrine of an "impersonal" passive.[42] In so far as concord is realized, it shows that C is S only if supported by a rule that what V agrees with is S. The argument is circular.

Here the typology of the ergative construction is suggestive. In Urartian it is confusing to call nominative the case of S of intransitive but of O of transitive verbs. If "ergative" is the case of agent and "nominative" the case of nonagent, the categories of nominative and accusative are inappropriate; for in Urartian "nominative" is used for what is called object, while in Hebrew "accusative" is used for what is called subject. If "nominative" is considered a neutral case, then in Urartian the ergative differentiates agent from nonagent (victim) when both are specified; in Hebrew *nota accusativi* distinguishes victim from agent when both are specified, or rather when they need to be distinguished to avoid ambiguity.[43]

Apparent inconsistencies in the use of *ᵓet–* in Hebrew can be accounted for in these terms. In Moabite it seems as if *ᵓet–* differentiates victim from agent only when both are specified in sequence *after* the verb, whereas in sequence S V O, S and O are not distinguished by overt markers.[44]

The same facts can then be stated differently if V agrees with O when S is suppressed. Hebrew does have constructions which support this; for example, *bəhimmōlō ᵓēt bəśar ᶜorlātō*, "when the flesh of his foreskin [it] was circumcised" (Gen. 17:24). Compare *wattirᵓēhū ᵓet-hayyeled*, "and she saw [him] the boy" (Exod. 2:6).

This construction in Hebrew thus has some typological resemblance to the passive-objective construction of Kurdish, and to Kretschmer's "objective conjugation" in Indo-European, where the verb agrees with the agent in an oblique case.

Speiser has pointed out that Nuzi Accadian often follows the normal Hurrian sequence of Victim—Agent—Action.[45] Alalakh Accadian similarly

42. On the passive as impersonal, see F. Giesebrecht, "Zur Hexateuchkritik," *ZAW* 1 (1881): 263–65. The peculiarities of the alleged impersonal passive give rise to some strained supporting arguments. "The construction itself can only be explained by supposing that while using the passive form the speaker at the same time thinks of some author or authors of the action in question . . ." (E. Kautzsch, *Gesenius' Hebrew Grammar*,[28] trans. A. E. Cowley[2] (Oxford: Clarendon, 1910), p. 387, n. l.

43. D'yakonov (in Zhirmunskii, *Ergativnaya konstruktsiya* [note 20], p. 99) points out that nouns in Hurrian which are called S of stative and O of transitive verbs constitute a single grammatical category, since there are no morphological or syntactical differences between them. By the same token the realizations of $R_F$ are the same category in Cl − 2 and Cl − 3; and the realizations of $O_C$ are the same category in Cl − 2 and Cl − 3.

44. See the writer's discussion in "Moabite Syntax," *Or* 35 (1966), pp. 117ff. Compare also *wəyahwe sāgar raḥmāh*; *kī sāgar yahwe baᶜad raḥmāh* (I Sam. 1:5,6).

45. Speiser, *Introduction to Hurrian* (note 21), p. 206.

exhibits some abnormal clause types. While in terms of morphology the passive forms are a development peculiar to West Semitic, in terms of syntax the Hurrian substratum seems to have exerted pressure on Semitic precisely in the matter of the ergative. It is interesting to speculate whether the syntax of the passive in North-West Semitic owes anything to such an influence.[46]

46. Dr. Anne Kilmer has kindly drawn my attention to the form *pu-li-il-šu* in a Middle Babylonian text from Alalakh (No. 87, line 7), which Wiseman (p. 53) took to be a noun. It is an excellent North-West Semitic passive, but the syntax is extraordinary. The agent (Kabiya) is explicit as S; there is an object ("his house, etc.") and an indirect object, grammatically direct (Tubbi-AN MEŠ), resumed by the suffix *-šu*, as if the verb were active and transitive.

# Altisraelitische Erweckungsbewegungen

HANS BARDTKE

Der Gegenstand der nachfolgenden Untersuchung gehört in den Bereich der Religionsphänomenologie.[1] Erweckungen und daraus resultierende Erweckungsbewegungen sind dann und wann auftretende Erscheinungen innerhalb festgefügter religiöser Gemeinschaften oder größerer religiöser Bereiche. Derartige Erweckungen lassen sich häufig feststellen und sind insbesondere in christlich bestimmten Religionsbereichen Gegenstand kirchengeschichtlicher Forschungen geworden.[2] Auch für Altisrael können solche Erweckungen und daraus sich ergebende Bewegungen angenommen werden. Es wäre sonderbar, wenn ein in religiöser Hinsicht so hervorragend begabtes Volk wie Altisrael keine

1. Siehe z.B. die Religionsphänomenologie von G. van der Leeuw, Phänomenologie der Religion (Neue Theologische Grundrisse, herausgegeben von Rudolf Bultmann) Tübingen, 2. Auflage, 1956, S. 297, 604f, 701f. Ferner: Friedrich Heiler, Erscheinungsformen und Wesen der Religion (Die Religionen der Menschheit. Herausgegeben von Christel Matthias Schröder Band I), Stuttgart, 1961, S. 274f, 282f, 304f, 499, 554.

2. Reiche Literaturangaben enthält das von E. Beyreuther bearbeitete Stichwort "Erweckung" in RGG II, 3. Auflage, 1958, 621–29. Phänomenologisch wichtig ist ebenda das Stichwort "Erweckungen in der Mission" Spalte 629–31 von W. Freytag. Ich zitiere aus letzterem Artikel: "Erweckungen treten nach den bisherigen Beobachtungen frühestens etwa 30 Jahre nach dem Entstehen einer Kirche auf, gehören also einer bestimmten Altersstufe an. Bei den Erweckten ist es ein Vorgang der Individuation, ein Erfassen der Botschaft auf tieferer persönlicher Ebene . . . Zugleich lernt man zwischen der empirischen Kirche und der "Kirche in den Kirchen" unterscheiden. Damit wacht ein eschatologisches Verständnis der Kirche auf, wie es der ersten Generation nicht gegeben ist."

Aus der nordamerikanischen Erweckungsbewegung verweise ich auf das materialreiche Werk von C. C. Goen, Revivalism and Separatism in New England, 1740–1800, New Haven and London, 1962.

Erweckungsphänomene aufgewiesen hätte. Eine andere Frage ist es, ob derartige religiöse Phänomene wie Erweckungen dem antiken Israel als besondere Größen bewußt geworden sind, so daß es dafür sogar eigengeprägte Begriffe schuf. In der Regel ist erst der Historiker in der Lage, eine solche religiöse Bewegung als Erweckung zu bezeichnen, indem er die Erscheinung als Ganze in sich und in ihren geistigen und dynamischen Auswirkungen auf einen größeren regionalen und zeitlichen Bereich zu überschauen und zu werten vermag.

Diese religionsphänomenologische Fragestellung ist für das Alte Testament und für Altisrael bisher noch kaum aufgegriffen worden abgesehen von einigen mehr zufälligen Bemerkungen in wissenschaftlichen Abhandlungen. Wenn sie hier in dieser Festschrift aufgenommen wird, so geschieht das in dem Bewußtsein, daß der verehrte Jubilar, dem diese Untersuchung gewidmet ist, für derartige Fragestellungen Sinn und Interesse hat,[3] wie seine zahlreichen Arbeiten auf dem Gebiet der Religionsgeschichte Israels ausweisen, die ihn zur Beschäftigung nicht nur mit religionspsychologischen Problemen, sondern auch zu religionsphänomenologischen Fragestellungen führten.

## I

Der Begriff der Erweckungsbewegung bedarf vorerst einiger einschränkender Abgrenzungen. Die sogenannte Heilserwartungsbewegung, die in den letzten zwanzig Jahren mehrfach der Gegenstand ausgedehnter Untersuchungen[4] wurde, scheidet aus dem Kreis der Untersuchung aus. Einmal haben die modernen Erscheinungen solcher Heilserwartungsbewegungen, wie sie innerhalb der Kolonialvölker gelegentich auftauchten—etwa in Gestalt des Cargo-Kultes oder verwandter Erscheinungen—einen ganz anderen Ursprung als ähnlich geartete Vorgänge in Altisrael, die man als Heilserwartungsbewe-

3. Ich verweise auf sein Selbstbekenntnis in seinem auch in deutscher Sprache vorliegenden Werk "Die Religion Israels im Lichte der archäologischen Ausgrabungen," München/Basel, 1956, S. 15f: "Der Verfasser hat in den letzten zwölf Jahren eine ausgedehnte Literatur auf dem Gebiet der modernen Psychologie durchgearbeitet, einem früheren Plane zufolge, intensives Studium der Psychologie mit der Erforschung des Lebens und Denkens im alten Nahen Orient zu verbinden." Der Titel der Originalausgabe lautet "Archaeology and the Religion of Israel," übersetzt von Friedrich Cornelius.

4. Z. B. Guglielmo Guariglia, Prophetismus und Heilserwartungsbewegungen als völkerkundliches und religionsgeschichtliches Problem 1959. Wilhelm E. Mühlmann, Chiliasmus und Nativismus. Studien zur Psychologie, Soziologie und historischen Kasuistik der Umsturzbewegungen. Berlin, 1961. Vom letzterem Werk ist besonders der erste Teil S. 17–240 zu vergleichen, darunter ein instruktiver Aufsatz über "Die Cargo-Kulte in Neuguinea und Insel-Melanesien" von Helga Uplegger und dem Herausgeber.—Auch das Buch von Bengt G. M. Sundkler, Bantupropheten in Südafrika (Titel der englischen Originalausgabe "Bantu prophets in South Africa"), Stuttgart, 1964, muß hier genannt werden.

gung bezeichnen könnte. Als eine solche könnte man etwa nennen die Erwartung der 597 nach Babel exilierten Judäer, denen Propheten in Babel als Heilserwartung die baldige Rückkehr besonders nahelegten, aber auch diese Heilserwartung war auf Jahwe gerichtet und gründete sich auf die alten Heilsverheissungen und die Bundesvorstellung, also auf den alten religiösen Besitzstand Israels.[5]

Auch die revolutionären Bewegungen bleiben aus unserer Untersuchung ausgeklammert. Die kollektiven Phänomene solcher Bewegungen werden als eine gesteigerte kollektive Mobilität geschildert, als ein plötzliches In-Bewegung-kommen bis dahin ruhiger und harmloser Menschen, die von einer Stimmung—"es muß anders werden"—beseelt sind, d.h. sie sind in ihrer Bewegtheit von einer psychischen Tiefenschicht beherrscht, während bei Nachlassen der Bewegung und hervortretender Ernüchterung die Rationalschicht bestimmend wird.[6] Daher werden in unserer Untersuchung die alttestamentlichen Berichte über Revolutionen in Altisrael[7] nicht berücksichtigt, wenn auch bei revolutionären Erscheinungen unter Umständen die Triebkräfte religiöser Erweckungsbewegungen sich auswirken können. Das scheint mir bei der Trennung des Nordreiches vom Südreich (1 Kön. 12) und bei der Revolution des Jehu (2 Kön. 9:10) der Fall gewesen zu sein. Bei ersterer wirkt die Erweckungsbewegung der Samuelzeit[8] nach, bei letzterer die Erweckung unter Elia.[9]

## II

Der Gedanke, daß im Alten Testament auch Erweckungsbewegungen bezeugt werden, ist in der Literatur über Erweckungsbewegungen schon

5. Jer. 29:15, 21–32. Die modernen Heilserwartungsbewegungen sind eine Größe für sich, die mit alttestamentlichen Befunden nicht in Beziehung gesetzt werden können.

6. Mühlmann, a.O. S. 261f.

7. Ich habe hier im Blickfeld den Aufstand des Absalom gegen David (2 Sam. 14–19:9) sowie den Aufstand des Scheba zur Davidzeit (2 Sam. 20:1–22). Kollektive Symptome, d.h. Bewegung und Erregung sowie Teilnahme größerer Gruppen sind bei diesen Revolutionen wohl nachzuweisen, z.B. 2 Sam. 17:11. Der Ratschlag, den Husai dem Absalom erteilt, spricht vom Aufgebot ganz Israels von Dan bis Beer Scheba, "so massenhaft wie der Sand, der am Meer liegt." Ähnlich 2 Sam. 20:2; an welcher Stelle vom Abfall der Nordstämme zu Scheba gesprochen wird. Im Aufstand des Jehu steht die Masse des Heeres auf seiner Seite.

8. Zu diesen möglichen Nachwirkungen siehe meinen Aufsatz "Samuel und Saul. Gedanken zur Entstehung des Königtums in Israel" (*BiOr* 25 [1968]: 289–302).

9. Über Elia werde ich noch eine gesonderte Untersuchung vorlegen, die die von ihm entfesselte Bewegung im Licht einer echten religiösen Erweckungsbewegung zeigt. Über Erweckungsphänomene in der exilisch-nachexilischen Zeit und deren Literatur innerhalb des Alten Testaments habe ich mich in der Festschrift für Otto Eissfeldt, "Von Ugarit nach Qumrān," Berlin, 1958, S. 9–24 geäußert.

ausgesprochen worden.[10] Bei der hohen Einschätzung, die eine solche Bewegung genießt, ist das nicht verwunderlich—führte doch beispielsweise der Evangelist Finney[11] alles, was an geistlich-christlichem Leben in der Welt vorhanden sei, ursprunghaft auf eine Erweckungsbewegung zurück. So ist es verständlich, daß man im Alten Testament die Figuren eines Mose und eines Josua, eines Samuel und eines Elia, eines Hiskia und eines Josia, eines Esra und eines Nehemia als Erwecker und die von ihnen ausgegangenen Wirkungen als Erweckungsbewegungen kennzeichnete, freilich mit dem charakteristischen Sprachgebrauch, der lieber den Begriff der Bußbewegung[12] verwendete, um den Begriff der Erweckung nur christlichen Erscheinungen vorbehalten zu können. Freilich sind das keine historischen, sondern Glaubensurteile, wie die Reihe jener eben genannten Figuren ausweist.

Um nun die Fragestellung nach altisraelitischen Erweckungsbewegungen beanworten zu können, ist es notwendig darzulegen, was begrifflich unter "Erweckung" und "Erweckungsbewegung" verstanden wird.

(1) Eine religiöse Erweckungsbewegung tut sich in einem zentralen, auf Erfahrung gegründeten religiösen Erleben kund, das ein einziger Mensch oder auch—wenn faßbar—ein kleinerer Kreis von Menschen gleichen Glaubens und gleicher religiöser,[13] sozialer und ethnischer Gemeinschaft gehabt hat.

(2) Dieses religiöse Erleben ergreift durch verschiedene Umstände und mittelnde menschliche Größen einen kleineren oder größeren Menschenkreis des gleichen oder gleichgearteten religiösen Glaubens und teilt sich ihm in starker religiöser Triebkraft, dem religiösen Impetus, mit.

(3) Unter Hintanstellung aller anderen Werte und Rücksichtnahmen treibt dieses zentrale religiöse Erlebnis spontan zu verschiedenen religiösen Handlungen an, z.B. gesteigerte Teilnahme am Kultus und völlig gewandelte

10. J. W. van Zeijl, Wenn Gottes Winde wehen. Erweckungen in aller Welt. Übersetzt aus dem Holländischen, 1955—Theodor Brandt, Im Aufbruch. Gestalten der Erweckung, 1951. —Hans Bruns, Feuer vom Himmel. Seelsorgerliche Gedanken über Erweckungen in der Bibel. Stuttgart, 1950.—Georg F. Vicedom, Ein Volk findet Gott. Erweckkung in Formosa. Bad Salzuflen, 1962.

11. J. W. van Zeijl, a.O. S. 11.

12. J. W. van Zeijl, a.O. S. 15 bezeichnet diese Erweckungen als merkwürdig. "geistliche Erweckung ist das aber nicht" . . . "Es waren mehr oder weniger tiefgehende Bußbewegungen, in denen das Verlangen nach einem heiligen Lebenswandel geweckt wurde."

13. Der Gedanke des Vorhandenseins der gleichen religiösen Bindung legt sich nahe durch den Gedanken der Erweckung. Die gleiche gewohnheitsmäßige Haltung gegenüber dem überlieferten Glaubensgut ist bei allen Erweckten vorhanden gewesen. Die gleiche ethnische Bindung ist nahegelegt durch die Erfahrungen der Mission. Grundsätzlich möglich ist natürlich, daß ein religiöser Glaube auch ethnische Schranken überwindet.

innerliche Einstellung zum Kultus,[14] intensive Pflege persönlicher Frömmigkeit und deren Äußerung in Liedern, Gebeten und Bekenntnissen.

(4) Aus einer echten religiösen Erweckung kann es oft zur Bildung neuer Gemeinschaften kommen.[15]

(5) Eine führende Gestalt, ein Erwecker, kann vorhanden sein. Ist die Erweckung ein Kollektivphänomen, können mehrere führende Gestalten heraustreten und für den weiteren Bestand und die weitere Ausbreitung der Bewegung und der von ihr gebildeten Gemeinschaft Sorge tragen.

(6) Eine solche Erweckungsbewegung hat prinzipiell ihren Höhepunkt in dem Erleben und Erfahren der ersten Generation[16] und fällt von diesem Höhepunkt ab in den folgenden Generationen, sofern in diesen nicht wieder eine Erweckung sich vollzieht.

(7) Charakteristisch für eine Erweckung ist ihre oft rasche Ausbreitung in einem Territorium, ihr Überspringen auf andere Territorien und andere religiöse Gemeinschaften sowie ihre Verpflanzung durch Sendboten.

(8) Für eine religiöse Erweckungsbewegung können vorhandene nationale, soziale und politische Verhältnisse unter Umständen sehr förderlich sein.

Aus diesen Gesichtspunkten ergibt sich, daß Erweckungen und Erweckungsbewegungen nicht künstlich gemacht oder gar durch geschickte

14. Das wird in zahlreichen Darstellungen von Erweckungen geschildert. Auch Rafael Gyllenberg, Kultus und Offenbarung (Mowinckel-Festschrift, "Interpretationes ad Vetus Testamentum pertinentes," Oslo, 1955, S. 72–84) weist daraufhin, besonders S. 83: "Es mag hier genügen darauf hinzuweisen, daß ein echter, lebendiger Kult wenigstens durch die zahlreichen religiösen Erweckungsbewegungen des letzten Jahrhunderts in den nordischen Ländern ins Leben gerufen wurde."

15. Und zwar insbesondere dann, wenn etwa die religiöse Erweckung nicht auf alle soziologischen Bereiche und Strukturen übergreift, sondern eine Volksgruppe unerweckt bleibt, so daß es zu einem Gegenüber für die Erweckten kommt. Darauf hat Vicedom a.O. S. 106 hingewiesen. Siehe auch G. van der Leeuw, a.O. S. 701.

16. Diese merkwürdige und nie genügend berücksichtigte Tatsache erklärt sich aus dem zentralen religiösen Ersterlebnis, das auf eigener Erfahrung beruhte. Diese Erfahrung kann den Kommenden nur im Zeugnis vermittelt werden, ohne daß die einst von der ersten Generation gemachten tiefen Erfahrungen und Erlebnisse sich auch bei der nächsten Generation einstellen. Die oben unter Punkt 8 erwähnten Umstände spielen gewiß dabei eine sehr wesentliche Rolle. Die Erweckung hängt auch ab von den unwiederholbaren geschichtlichen Zeitumständen und geistigen Konstellationen. In diesem an der Erweckung sichtbar werdenden Tatbestand wird das Problem deutlich, das Jean-Louis Leuba, Institution und Ereignis. Gemeinsamkeiten und Unterschiede der beiden Arten von Gottes Wirken nach dem Neuen Testament, Göttingen, 1957, ausführlich behandelt hat. Er stellt mit Recht einen Dualismus von Institution und Ereignis heraus. Dieser ist auch feststellbar in dem Wechsel von Erweckung und kultisch-gemeindlichen, institutionalisierten, religiösen Übungen.

Organisation hervorgerufen werden können.[17] Es ist möglich, daß in erregten, nervlich sehr gespannten Zuständen sich Ekstasen, Verzückungen, Glossolalie und andere Phänomene zeigen können, die rasch wieder abklingen, ohne eine nennenswerte Wirkung zu zeigen.[18] Diesen Phänomenen gegenüber, die häufig zu Verwechslungen mit echten Erweckungsbewegungen führen, ist hier ausdrücklich der auf religiöser Erfahrung gegründete Erlebnisakt als die entscheidende Ursache für eine Erweckung betont. Gleichzeitig aber wird auch der Akzent auf den Menschen gesetzt, wie er auf den dynamischen Eindruck des religiösen Erlebens reagiert und was er unter dem Zwang der religiösen Erweckung tut. Die Selbsttätigkeit des Menschen ist in der Erweckung nicht ausgeschaltet, sondern gerade angereizt. Diese ausgelöste Selbsttätigkeit des Menschen ist der Gegenstand der religionsphänomenologischen Untersuchung. Von diesen Beobachtungen aus treten wir nun an das alttestamentliche Material heran.

## III

Die erste Stelle, in der m.E. klar von einer Erweckungsbewegung als Phänomen gesprochen wird, ist Am. 8:11–12:

"Siehe, es kommen die Tage, spricht der Herr Jahwe, da will ich senden einen Hunger ins Land,/

keinen Hunger nach Brot, keinen Durst nach Wasser, sondern (Hunger danach,) Jahwes Wort zu hören./

Von West nach Süd irrt man umher, von Nord nach Ost schweift man umher, Jahwes Wort zu suchen, und findet es nicht/."

17. L. Casutt, Erweckung (LThk III Spalte 1063, 2. Auflage, 1959) schreibt: "Im Sprachgebrauch der evangelischen Theologie und Frömmigkeit bezeichnet Erweckung die relativ plötzliche und intensive Bekehrung eines Sünders oder relativ Gleichgültigen zu einem lebendigen christlichen Leben. Wo diese Erweckung methodisch organisiert wird (eine Spitze gegen die Aufklärungstheologie hat) und religionssoziologisch zum Massenphänomen wird, spricht man hier von Erweckungsbewegungen." Es mag sein, daß es in der Kirchengeschichte hier und da derartige methodisch organisierte Erweckungen gegeben hat—ich brauche hier keine Beispiele zu nennen—aber derartige Phänomene werden in unserer Untersuchung nicht ins Auge gefaßt.

Desgleichen muß ich mich von der Grundhaltung des Buches von William Sargant, Der Kampf um die Seele. Eine Psychologie der Konversionen, München, 1958 distanzieren (Titel der Originalausgabe: The Battle for the Mind, London, 1957). Es genügt darauf hinzuweisen, daß die alttestamentlichen Propheten sich nicht nur an den Intellekt gewendet haben mit ihrer Verkündigung, wie es die moderne Predigt des Protestantismus weithin tut. Dieser erwecklich-prophetischen Verkündigung gilt es nachzuspüren, ohne daß man dabei in den Verdacht gerät, eine Erweckung künstlich herbeiführen zu wollen.

18. Auf diese Phänomene wird in den religionsphänomenologischen Veröffentlichungen als Begleiterscheinungen der Erweckungen hingewiesen. Wie rasch es zu einer ekstatischen Bewegung kommen kann, hat Gerhard Hauptmann in seinem Roman "Der Narr in Christo Emanuel Quint," Berlin, 1910, S. 325ff gezeigt, freilich hat er auch ihr rasches Abklingen dargetan.

Die notwendigen Tilgungen sind hier mitübersetzt. Vorgeschlagen zur Streichung wird *neʾūm ʾadōnaj JHWH* und *weloʾ ṣāmāʾ lammajim*. Für *dibrē* ist einfach wie in V. 12 *debar* zu lesen.[19]

Die Abgrenzung der literarischen Einheit gegenüber dem Vorhergehenden ist nach der Parascheneinteilung des textus receptus, wie er noch der zweiten Auflage der hebräischen Bibelausgabe von Kittel zugrunde lag, durch Setzung einer *setūmā* gesichert sowie aus sachlichen Gründen. Gegenüber den folgenden Versen 13 und 14 hat der einstige Paraschenabteiler keine Notwendigkeit einer Abgrenzung gesehen, doch enthalten die folgenden Verse andere Gedanken, die sich nicht sachlich mit dem Inhalt von 11–12 verbinden lassen, so daß für unsere Beobachtungen nur diese Verse genügen müssen.[20]

Julian Morgenstern hat diese Verse 1961 für eine spätere Glosse erklärt, die kein genuines Jahwewort enthalten.[21] Reinhart Fey dagegen hat zwei Jahre später die Echtheit wieder verteidigt.[22] Auch Theodore H. Robinson ist für die Herleitung von Amos eingetreten in seinem Zwölfprophetenkommentar.[23] Fey hat die gattungsmäßige Bestimmtheit der Verse mit Recht als ein Drohwort ohne Begründung bezeichnet.[24]

Es gibt eine verwandte Stelle im Amosbuch im Kehrversgedicht 4, 6–13: "Und ihr seid nicht zu mir zurückgekehrt." Dort heißt es in V. 8: "Und zwei, drei Städte irrten zu einer (anderen) Stadt, um Wasser trinken zu können, und sie wurden nicht satt, ihr aber seid nicht zu mir zurückgekehrt."

Die Bewegung im Land, die durch das Suchen nach Wasser entsteht, hat der Prophet ins Geistige erhoben[25] und damit eine Schilderung einer religiösen Erweckungsbewegung gegeben.

Aber das Verhältnis beider Stellen zueinander bedarf noch der Beleuchtung. In 4, 8 ist die Ursache für das Aufsuchen von Quellen anderer Städte der vorhandene Wassermangel in der eigenen Stadt und zugleich die Notwendigkeit, den eigenen Dursttrieb befriedigen zu müssen. Von dieser

19. M. Bič, Das Buch Amos, Berlin, 1969, zur Stelle, verzichtet auf diese Korrekturen und behandelt den masoretischen Text im Wortlaut.

20. Diese Trennung wird wohl von den meisten Exegeten vollzogen. Bič bleibt auch hier bei dem überlieferten Textzusammenhang, wobei ich ihm nicht zu folgen vermag.

21. Amos Studies (Part Four), *HUCA* 32 (1961): S. 295–350, speziell S. 327. Er leitet diese Verse aus der nachexilischen Zeit her.

22. Amos und Jesaja. Abhängigkeit und Eigenständigkeit des Jesaja, *WMANT* 12 (1963): S. 40 Anm. 2.

23. *HbzAT*, Die zwölf kleinen Propheten von Th. H. Robinson und F. Horst. 2. Auflage, Tübingen, 1954 zur Stelle.

24. a.O. S. 132.

25. Diese Transponierung ins Geistige kann keine Ursache für irgendeine Unechtheitserklärung dieser Stelle in 8, 11–12 bilden. Dem Propheten stand es frei, mit seinem literarischen Material frei umzugehen und es in verschiedener Weise zu verwenden. Beispiele lassen sich zahlreich aus der prophetischen Literatur erbringen.

Befriedigung des Dursttriebes an anderen Stadtquellen wird gesagt: "Sie wurden nicht satt," d.h. sie haben wohl getrunken, aber nicht bis zur völligen Löschung des Durstes. Es ist nicht völliges Versagen des Wassers, sondern nur Vorenthaltung der für die Durstlöschung notwendigen Wassermenge. Hier erscheint der Mangel als Phänomen der Bekehrungsbemühungen Jahwes gegenüber seinem Volk. Demgegenüber ist in 8, 11f die Situation verschärft. Dem triebhaft erweckten Verlangen, Gottes Wort hören zu wollen, wird selbst die geringe, vorübergehende Sättigung versagt. Darin liegt zweifellos die Absicht des Propheten, das Gericht, das in der Verweigerung des Wortes Gottes besteht, gegenüber der strafenden, aber werbenden Züchtigung (4, 8) abzuheben.

Aber noch ein anderer Unterschied läßt sich feststellen. Während der Dursttrieb zum geschöpflichen Bestand des Menschen gehört, ist das Verlangen, Gottes Wort zu hören, anderen Ursprungs. Es geht direkt auf Jahwes Veranlassung zurück, auf seine Sendung, wobei offenbleibt, wie dieses Verlangen nun erweckt wird, ob durch besondere Lebensumstände, durch Propheten, durch kultische Erfahrungen und Ereignisse. Dieser Hunger, diese Sehnsucht nach Gott und seinem Wort sind, wenn wir auf die Begriffsbestimmung der Erweckung zurückgreifen,[26] das zentrale religiöse Erlebnis, das sich sogar einem ganzen Land und seiner Bevölkerung[27] mitteilen soll. Die unter 1 and 2 genannten Gesichtspunkte sind demnach von diesem Text aus gegeben. Auch der dritte Gesichspunkt der vom religiösen Erleben verursachten spontanen Handlungen liegt vor. Die Menschen verlassen ihre Heimat, die soziologischen Formen der eigenen bisherigen Existenz, das Haften am heimatlichen Boden, an Familie, Sippe und Stamm, ja an dem Staat, dessen politischen Schutz sie genießen.[28] Quer durch Palästina ziehen sie—vom Mittelmeer zum Golf von Aqaba, von Galiläa nach Osten in das Ostjordanland, in den Steppengürtel und in die Wüste.[29] Das Hören und

26. Siehe oben S. 20 f die Gesichtspunkte für eine begrifflich scharfe und umfassende Erfassung der Erweckung.

27. In 8, 11 wird sich bāʾāreṣ auf Palästina, zumindest auf das Territorium des Nordreiches beziehen. Damit wäre auch der Gesichtspunkt 7 erfüllt hinsichtlich der territorialen Ausdehnung einer Erweckungsbewegung.

28. In diesem Zusammenhang darf darauf hingewiesen werden, wie die Perikope Am. 8:11f einen schönen Beleg liefert für die Formulierung, die van der Leeuw bei seiner Schilderung der Phänomene einer Erweckungsbewegung gebraucht: "Erweckung . . . besteht jedenfalls in einer Lockerung der Lebensmächtigkeiten, die sich alle, ohne Hemmungen und frei von dem Zwang der geregelten Begehung, auf den religiösen Zweck stürzen" (a.O. S. 701).

29. Die Kommentatoren sind in der Ausdeutung der Richtungsangaben oft sehr verschiedener Meinung. Auch der letzte Kommentator M. Bič sieht in der Wendung "Von Meer zu Meer" die ganze Erde umschrieben, indem er sich auf den Kommentar von Nowack beruft, während er in der Richtungsangabe von Nord nach Ost eine Anspielung auf den Götterberg (Jes. 14:13) und auf das Paradies (Gen. 2:8) findet. Entsprechend meiner Deutung auf eine religiöse Erweckungsbewegung kann ich die Richtungsangaben nur ganz konkret fassen.

Zugesprochenbekommen des Wortes Jahwes ist plötzlich die übergeordnete Macht in ihrem Leben geworden. Man wird sich diese Wanderer vorstellen dürfen, wie sie mit Kultgesängen und Wallfahrtsliedern auf den Lippen dahinziehen, die Hoffnung auf Jahwe und sein Wort im Herzen. So wie Wallfahrer eine Gemeinschaft bilden, um zu einem Heiligtum zu gelangen, so bilden auch diese nach Jahwes Wort Verlangenden eine Sehnsuchtsgemeinschaft, eine Wandergemeinschaft. So würde auch der vierte Gesichtspunkt für eine Erweckungsbewegung auf das hier beschriebene Phänomen zutreffen.

Ein Prophet als mittelnde Größe wird nicht erwähnt, desgleichen auch kein Heiligtum. Beide sind aber vorausgesetzt, wenn es sich um die Sehnsucht nach dem Wort Gottes als Eigenart der hier geschilderten Erweckungsbewegung handelt. Sicher würde Amos bei seiner Hochschätzung der Prophetie[30] einen Propheten als mittelnde Größe angenommen haben, doch selbst, wenn diese Menschen nun Propheten aufsuchen würden, würden sie für die Wanderer kein Wort Jahwes haben, könnten ihrer Erwecktheit nicht entsprechen, wenn sie zu ihnen sprächen.

Aus diesen vorstehend geschilderten Phänomenen der von Amos skizzierten Erweckungsbewegung schließe ich, daß Amos entweder selbst solche Erweckungsbewegungen gekannt hat oder in der ihm vorliegenden Tradition solche Erweckungsbewegungen bezeugt fand. Daß er hier an eine Wallfahrt denkt, ist durch nichts nahegelegt. Eine Wallfahrt ist etwas Gewohnheitsmäßiges, ein der religiösen Routine und Sitte entsprechendes Phänomen, sicher von starken Kräften persönlicher und sippenhafter Frömmigkeit getragen, aber nicht vom Impetus des Verlangens nach dem Wort Jahwes bestimmt.[31] Hat aber Amos derartige Erweckungsbewegungen gekannt, tritt die ganze Härte des Gerichtes Gottes heraus, der erweckt, aber dem Erweckten nur im göttlichen Gericht sich konfrontiert, nicht aber in dem lebengewährenden, starken und neu ausrichtenden Wort. Es mag als sicher gelten, daß diesem Gerichtswort von einem Späteren eine Begründung in Gestalt der Verse 8, 13f zugefügt wurde, um die Härte und Ausweglosigkeit dieses Gerichtes mit dem Abfall zu anderen Göttern zu begründen.

Ich hoffe, mit diesen phänomenologischen Beobachtungen, die eine nur auf Form und theologische Tradition gerichtete Auslegung[32] nicht in den

30. Siehe die Stellen Am. 2:11f und 3:7.

31. Ein solcher Impetus ist ja gerade durch Jahwe in den Herzen der Israeliten geschaffen worden. Das Suchen nach dem Wort Jahwes steht von Anfang an unter einem anderen Motiv als eine Wallfahrt.

32. Siehe die einzelnen Kommentare zu Amos. Am stärksten hat noch A. Weiser das Phänomen einer Erweckungsbewegung in Am. 8:11f gespürt, wenn er in seinem Kommentar (ATD 24, 3. Auflage, 1959, S. 197) schreibt: "Zunächst könnte es scheinen, als ob dieser Hunger nach Gottes Wort ein gutes Zeichen religiöser Lebendigkeit im Volk wäre."

Blick bekommt, nicht nur gezeigt zu haben, daß Amos Erweckungsbewegungen gekannt hat, sondern daß er auch auf das *lōʾ tinnābᵉūʾ* von 2, 12b in diesem Gerichtswort eine Antwort zu geben weiß.

Mit diesem Gerichtswort des Amos hängt nun m.E. eine andere Perikope zusammen, Jes. 2:2–4, die in den Schilderungen der Phänomene einer Erweckungsbewegung homogen mit dem eben besprochenen Amoswort ist. Auch hier gilt es auf die Phänomene zu achten. Die theologisch-traditionsgeschichtliche sowie die formkritische Auslegung hat sehr schön herausgestellt, daß es sich hier um eine eschatologische Wallfahrt der Völker zum Zion handele und es hier um eine "Rechtsaufrichtung" durch Jahwe geht, so daß "vom Zion wieder belehrende Weisung, schlichtendes Wort Jahwes zum Heil aller Welt ausgehen."[33] Die Völker und Sippen der Welt kommen zum Zion, um Recht und Weisung zu erbitten. Das entwickelte Bild ist groß und kühn, man kann als Quelle eine dichterische Intuition vermuten. Näher liegt es, hier eine Berührung zu Am. 8:11f zu finden. Auch Jesaja wird entweder selbst solche Erweckungen gekannt haben oder in der Tradition bezeugt gefunden haben. An das Bild der Wallfahrt ist auch hier nicht aus den schon weiter oben angegebenen Gründen zu denken. Ebenfalls ist hier die Erkenntnis zu gewinnen, daß Jahwe die Erweckung gewirkt hat, denn die Erhöhung des Berges Jahwes ist offensichtlich seine Tat. Mit dieser Erhöhung gibt er das Signal, hebt er das Panier hoch, auf dessen Wirkung hin die Völker sich auf den Weg machen. Auch die ausdrückliche Erklärung der betroffenen Völker, sie wollten auf Jahwes Wegen wandeln, zeugt von der Auswirkung einer religiösen Erweckung auf sie. Schön ist hier die kollektive Erweckung[34] skizziert. Von der Bildung neuer Gemeinschaftsformen wird nichts gesagt. Es ist vorausgesetzt, daß die ethnischen Ordnungen, die Einteilung der Völker und Staaten erhalten bleiben. Die unter 7 und 8 verzeichneten Gesichtspunkte kommen hier zur Geltung. Ich glaube, diese Perikope als das positive Gegenstück zu Am. 8:11f ansehen zu dürfen.[35] Der positiven Erweckung durch Jahwe entspricht nun auch das Zugesprochenwerden der

33. Die Formulierung nach R. Fey, a.O. S. 77. Fey verweist auch auf den schönen Aufsatz von G. von Rad, Die Stadt auf dem Berge (*EvTh* 8 (1948/49): S. 439–47, jetzt in "Gesammelte Studien zum Alten Testament." Theol. Bücherei, 8, München, 1958, S. 214–24).

Merkwürdigerweise hat R. Fey den Zusammenhang zwischen Am. 8:11f und Jes. 2:2–4 in seiner so verdienstlichen Untersuchung nicht beachtet.

34. Vergleiche die Wendungen in Jes. 2,2b.3a *kol haggōjīm* und *ʿammīm rabbīm*. Als Urheber dieser Erweckung erscheint hier wieder Jahwe, der mit der Verwandlung des Zion in den höchsten Berg die Erweckung auf geheimnisvolle und unwiderstehliche Weise vollzieht.

35. Diese Feststellung nimmt ein wenig den Schrecken von der Amosperikope. Auch Jesaja muß diese abschreckende und abstoßende Art des Gerichtsvollzuges–Erweckung durch Jahwe, aber das Vorenthalten des Wortes-empfunden haben.

Rechtsordnungen und Forderungen Jahwes, die das Heil unter den Völkern schaffen.

Die letzte der drei Stellen, die phänomenologisch für eine Erweckung auszuwerten ist, ist Num. 11:24–30. Der Inhalt der Perikope besagt, daß Jahwe von dem Geist (*rūach*) der auf Mose ist, etwas nimmt[36] und auf die Ältesten des Volkes überträgt. Jahwe benutzt also einen bereits durch seinen Geist erweckten Menschen, um die Erweckung weiterzutragen. Der Vorgang vollzeiht sich am *ʾŌhel Mōʿēd*, also an einem Heiligtum. Die Perikope wird allgemein der elohistischen Quellenschicht[37] zugeschrieben.

Im gleichen Zusammenhang wird berichtet, daß zwei Älteste, die sich nicht am *ʾŌhel Mōʿēd* befanden, ebenfalls in diese religiöse Bewegung hineingeraten. Auch an ihnen erweist sich die durch Jahwe erfolgte Geistgabe wirksam. Als Hintergrund dieser Erzählung, die als eine Legende angesehen werden muß, da sie sich an die Gestalt des Mose anschließt, anderseits aber auch Züge der Sage an sich trägt, da sie von einem Heiligtum berichtet (*ʾŌhel Mōʿēd*), sehe ichine von einem Heiligtum ausgehende Erweckungsbewegung, die sich auch im Volk, auch in den einzelnen Dörfern, fernab von dem Jahweheiligtum manifestiert.[38] Die Erweckungsbewegung hat offenbar rasch um sich gegriffen (Punkt 7).

Zum Kreis der Erweckten gehören die Ältesten und, da es sich um ein Heiligtum handelt, wohl auch die Priester.[39] Die zwei Ältesten zeigen an sich das Phänomen einer Erweckung auch außerhalb des Heiligtums, außerhalb kultischer Vorgänge in der profanen Sphäre. Der Widerspruch gegen eine im Land sich verbreitende Erweckungsbewegung zugunsten des Prioritätsanspruches einer am Heiligtum geschehenen Erweckung hat sich in der Figur des sich ereifernden Josua erhalten. In der Einstellung des Mose zu diesem Widerspruch tut sich noch die Meinung des Erzählers kund, daß eine solche außerhalb des Heiligtums geschehene Erweckung nicht gehindert

36. Die Auslegung, die Noth (Überlieferungsgeschichte des Pentateuch, Stuttgart, 1948, S. 141f) dieser Perikope gibt, schließt sich an das prophetische Phänomen an, an "die Massenerscheinung des ekstatischen Nabitums." Außerdem rechnet er mit dem Phänomen der Ekstase. Mose erscheint nach seiner Meinung in einer Art von "Über-Prophet-Sein." Diese Fragen bedürfen einer neuen Bearbeitung, da sie sehr eng mit dem Verständnis der Wurzel *nbʾ* zusammenhängen.

37. Siehe O. Eissfeldt, Hexateuch-Synopse, Leipzig, 1922, S. 162f.

38. Durch den Gesichtspunkt der Erweckungsbewegung liefert diese Perikope einen guten Beitrag zu dem Problem von Kultus und Erweckung. Ich hatte schon in dem dritten Gesichtspunkt für die Phänomene einer Erweckung darauf hingewiesen, auch in Anmerkung 14. Unsere obige Perikope bietet nunmehr in dem von mir vorgeschlagenen Verständnis einen guten Beleg. Außerdem tritt die Debatte über die Stellung der Propheten zum Kult ihrer Zeit durch den Gesichtspunkt der Erweckungsbewegungen in ein neues Licht.

39. Sie werden nicht erwähnt, können aber erschlossen werden aus dem vorausgesetzten Heiligtum, das in der Perikope *ʾŌhel Mōʿēd* genannt wird.

werden dürfe. Wer einer solchen Erweckungsbewegung hinderlich in den Weg tritt, hindert Jahwe selbst, denn von ihm allein gehen solche Erweckungen aus.

Das zentrale religiöse Erlebnis zeigt sich in einer Treue zu Jahwe gegenüber den Abfallstendenzen des Volkes. Außerdem wird in dieser Perikope etwas über den Zustand der Erweckten gesagt. Nach der Lesart des Targum Onkelos, Jonathan und Vulgata soll in V. 25 gelesen werden "*lōʾjāsūphū* = sie fanden kein Ende" oder "sie nahmen kein Ende,"[40] d.h. der Erweckungszustand hörte nicht auf. Dieser Erweckungszustand—auch das besagt die Perikope an dieser Stelle—muß als solcher für die Betroffenen selbst kenntlich und spürbar gewesen sein, ebenso auch für die anderen Menschen ihrer Umgebung. Hier pflegt der überwiegende Teil der Forscher an ekstatische Zustände zu denken.[41] Aber jede Ekstase muß einmal abklingen und dem klaren Bewußtsein Raum geben, denn Ekstase ist Entleerung des Bewußtseins,[42] während Erweckung und Erwecktsein gerade ein neues Erfülltsein des Bewußtseins mit gänzlich unerwarteten religiösen Inhalten bedeuten. Es ist auch kaum annehmbar, daß ein Erzähler, der um die Wirklichkeit der Ekstase Bescheid wußte, dem Mose diesen Wunsch in den Mund gelegt haben würde, das ganze Volk möchte aus solchen schwer verständlichen, zu einer klaren Verkündigung gar nicht fähigen Ekstatikern bestehen.[43] Von religiös Erweckten ist dieser Wunsch aber gut zu begreifen. Man muß also bei *hithnabbēʾ* an den auch äußerlich wahrnehmbaren Zustand des religiös erweckten Menschen denken, wie das kürzlich Ph. Seidensticker in einer Arbeit behauptet hat.[44] Es ist ein oft beobachtetes Phänomen, daß ein Erweckter auch in Gang und Haltung, in Gesichtsausdruck und Stimmung seine gewandelte Wesensart, seinen Zustand der Erweckung zum Ausdruck bringt, unwillkürlich, ohne Zwang und ohne Absicht.[45]

Im Hinblick auf diese Perikope würden also die unter 1–3, 5, und 7 genannten Gesichtspunkte maßgeblich erfüllt sein. Die Frage, ob es zur Bildung

40. Als Konjektur auch bei Köhler-Baumgartner im hebräisch-aramäischen Lexikon sub voce vorgeschlagen.

41. Ich verweise auf Anmerkung 36 und das dort über Noths Auffassung Gesagte. Durch Verwendung des Hithpaʿelstammes von *nbʾ* und die Analogie zu den Prophetenscharen der Samuel-Saul-Zeit ist diese ekstatische Deutung nahegelegt, wenn man nicht dem Stamm eine andere Bedeutung zuschreiben will.

42. Abraham Heschel, Die Prophetie, Krakow, 1936, S. 34ff.

43. Heschel S. 36: "Betrachtet man die Beschreibungen und Berichte der Ekstatiker, so stellt man fest, daß ihr positiver Erkenntnisertrag unbeträchtlich ist."

44. "Prophetensöhne-Rechabiter-Nasiräer," (*StBFr* 10 [1959/60]: S. 77). Siehe auch den in meiner Anmerkung 8 genannten Aufsatz S. 297 und Anmerkung 64 daselbst.

45. Ich muß es mir versagen, aus zahlreichen Biographien Beispiele anzuführen. Selbst für Afrika gibt es derartige Beispiele, z.B. Gerhard Günther, Erweckung in Afrika. Vom Aufbruch junger Kirchen im östlichen Afrika. Stuttgart, 1959 S. 28.

neuer Gemeinschaften kommt, kann von dieser Perikope und ihrem jetzigen literarischen Ort nicht beantwortet werden. Aber der unter 8 genannte Gesichtspunkt könnte in diesem Zusammenhang als erfüllt angesehen werden.

## IV

Hat also Altisrael solche Erweckungsbewegungen gekannt, muß an die Quellen des Alten Testaments die Frage gerichtet werden, welche geschichtliche Erscheinungen als Erweckungsbewegungen angesprochen werden können, wobei jede einzelne als ein eigenständiges, historisches und religionsphänomenologisch erfaßbares Ereignis betrachtet werden muß, ehe Verbindungslinien zwischen den einzelnen Erweckungsbewegungen ausgezogen werden können.

In diesem Zusammenhang ist die Auswanderung aus Ägypten unter einem religiös bestimmten Führer, Mose, ausdrücklich zu nennen. Die Berufung durch Jahwe wird von ihm ausdrücklich ausgesagt (Ex. 3). Seine Sendung zu der ägyptischen Israelgruppe geschieht im Namen dieses Gottes, wodurch die Annahme eines vormosaischen Jahwismus[46] nahegelegt wird. Dieser vormosaische Jahwismus mag im 15. Jahrhundert v.Chr. von Qadesch aus seinen Weg nach Palästina in die späteren Israelstämme gefunden haben.[47] Die Phänomene der Erweckung tun sich kund im religiösen Ursprungserlebnis der führenden Persönlichkeit (Punkt 1, 5) sowie in der Übertragung dieses Erlebens auf die ägyptische Israelgruppe (Punkt 2), denn diese leistet ihm unter diesem Gott Gefolgschaft und erweist ihm Gehorsam und meistert mit ihm gefährliche Situationen (Punkt 3) wie die Verfolgung durch die ägyptische Polizeitruppe (Ex. 14), wie Hunger und Durst (Ex. 15:22–27; 16:1–17,7) sowie Kämpfe (Ex. 17:8–16). Ein sozialrevolutionäres Element mag sich dieser Erweckung mitgeteilt haben, indem die Rechtsstellung der Zwangsar-

46. Die Annahme eines vormosaischen Jahwismus ergibt sich im Zusammenhang der von uns entwickelten Erweckungsanschauung aus der Voraussetzung gleichen Glaubens (Punkt 1 und 2). Zum Jahwismus und vormosaischen Jahwismus siehe die bei Gerhard von Rad angegebene Literatur, Theologie des Alten Testaments I, 1957, S. 20ff. Ferner S. Herrmann, Der alttestamentliche Gottesname (*EvTh* 26 [1966]: S. 281–93). Siehe auch die reichen Literaturangaben im Artikel "Jahwe" von P. van Inschoot und H. Haag in der zweiten Auflage des Bibel-Lexikon 1968, Spalte 796-98.

47. Siehe H. H. Rowley, From Joseph to Joshua. Biblical Traditions in the Light of Archaeology, London, 1952, speziell dort S. 164 Summary of Dates. Ferner: Manfred Weippert, Die Landnahme der israelitischen Stämme in der neueren wissenschaftlichen Diskussion S. 71 und Anmerkung 451 in der maschinenschriftlichen Wiedergabe. Die Druckausgabe war mir nicht zugänglich.

beiter abgeschüttelt wurde und die Flucht in die Freiheit mit ungewissem Schicksal gewählt wurde (Ex. 14:11ff) (Punkt 7 und 8).

Nach der These von Mendenhall[48] soll diese ägyptische Gruppe einer in Palästina gegen die Stadtstaaten zum Ausbruch gekommenen Sozialrevolution der Landbevölkerung den religiösen Charakter und den religiösen Impetus verliehen haben. Daraus ergab sich die Schaffung der normativen Traditionen,[49] die Auswanderungs- und Errettungstraditionen. Neben dieser starken, von der jahwistisch-mosaischen Erweckungsbewegung ausgehenden Traditionsbildung steht die Schaffung einer neuen Gemeinschaft, nämlich des Stämmebundes, der Amphiktyonie.[50] Der eigentliche Erretter aus der sozialen Not in Ägypten und in der Wüste und der Geber des Kulturlandes ist Jahwe, er wird der Herr und der König dieser neuen Stämme-Bund-Gemeinschaft.[51]

Das zweite geschichtliche Beispiel einer religiösen Erweckung in Altisrael schließt sich an die soeben genannte Amphiktyonie an, die in der Schlacht mit den Philistern bei Aphek zum Erliegen kommt.[52] Die Philister bemächtigen sich eines großen Teils des Territoriums der Amphiktyonie und üben eine Oberherrschaft über die Israeliten aus. In dieser Zeit kommt es zu einer religiösen Erweckung, die wiederum ein kollektives Phänomen aufweist, nämlich die Prophetenscharen, die im Zusammenhang mit Samuel und seiner Zeit genannt werden.[53] Sie werden uns so geschildert, daß sie das Land durchzogen haben mit Musik und Gesang, so daß Martin Buber sie die "patriotischen Wandersänger" nennen konnte.[54] Samuel weist im Zusammenhang mit Saul und seiner Kürung zum König so auf sie hin, daß man den Rückschluß vollziehen muß, sie seien schon vorhanden gewesen und stellten eine damals bekannte und vertraute Erscheinung dar. Die Frage nach ihrer Verkündigung, die sie in ihrem Auftreten übten, kann gar nicht anders beantwortet werden als mit dem Hinweis auf die vorhin genannten norma-

48. The Hebrew Conquest of Palestine (*BA* 25 [1962]: 66–87).

49. So Bright bei John L. McKenzie, S. J., *The World of the Judges* (London, 1967), S. 109. Gegen Mendenhall würde ich zusammen mit McKenzie noch stärker das Element der Einwanderung betonen.

50. Obwohl der Begriff in der jüngsten Forschung nicht mehr unbestritten ist, sei er hier verwendent. Die religionsphänomenologische Betrachtungsweise muß hier eine neue Gemeinschaft konstatieren, ganz gleich wie sie genannt wird.

51. Siehe Martin Buber, Königtum Gottes, 3. Auflage, Heidelberg, 1956.

52. Dieses Erliegen bestätigt den Punkt 6 der Merkmale einer Erweckungsbewegung. Die Amphiktyonie hat nicht die alte Höhe und Begeisterungsfähigkeit erhalten. Die Generation der Schlacht von Aphek hat die Kraft des religiösen Ersterlebnisses nur im Zeugnis empfangen. Eine Erweckung scheint zwischendurch die Glieder der Amphiktyonie nicht erreicht zu haben.

53. 1 Sam. 10:5–6, 10–13; 19:20–24.

54. Die Erzählung von Sauls Königswahl (*VT* 6 [1956]: S. 134 Anmerkung 2).

tiven Traditionen der gelungenen Befreiung aus Ägypten, die als Jahwes Tat ebenso verkündigt worden ist wie die Errettung aus mancherlei Nöten der Wanderung nach Palästina. Diese zum damaligen Zeitpunkt (um 1050) zweihundert Jahre alten Glaubenszeugnisse der Mose-Erweckungsbewegung werden jetzt zum Instrument neuer Jahweerweckung durch die Wanderpropheten. Diese Wanderpropheten sind das Kollektivphänomen, die zugleich eine Wandergemeinschaft bilden, und diese Wandergemeinschaft (Punkt 4) ist zugleich eine Verkündigungsgemeinschaft, die am jahwistischen Kult teilnimmt und unter den Augen der philistäischen Besatzungsmacht zu agieren wagt im genuin israelitisch-jahwistischen Sinn.[55]

Diese prophetische Erweckung gewinnt an Breite gegen Ende der Philisternot, als die Kürung eines Königs an Samuel herangetragen wird. Die Tradition von 1 Sam. 8, der zufolge Samuel sich gegen dieses Ansinnen stellt, ist vordeuteronomisch.[56] Der beherrschende Gedanke dieser sich verbreiternden Erweckungsbewegung ist der Glaube, daß Jahwe der einzige, wahre König Israels ist. Diese Erweckungsbewegung unter Samuel hat keinen politischen Erfolg gehabt. Der irdische König ist eingesetzt worden, wenn auch mit gewissen Sicherungen, die aber auf das Ganze gesehen keine praktische Bedeutung erlangt haben. Das Königtum wurde rasch absolutistisch.

Als eine Erweckunsbewegung muß selbstverständlich, wie schon oben[57] bemerkt wurde, auch Elia und sein Widerstand gegen die wachsende Baalisierung des Jahweglaubens zur Zeit der Omridendynastie gerechnet werden. Die Prophetenscharen, die die Heiligtümer besetzt halten, sind eine lebendige Auswirkung und Darstellung der Kraft jener Erweckungsbewegung unter Elia. Damit sind die einzelnen Phänomene, die wir unter 1–5 und 8 anführten, gegeben. Sie brauchen hier nicht im Einzelnen angeführt zu werden. Das Ursprungserleben des Elia muß erschlossen werden und erscheint widergespiegelt in 1 Kön. 19. Auch die Auswirkung auf die jahwetreuen Kreise ist vorhanden. Siehe in 1 Kön. 19:18, jene siebentausend Israeliten, die nicht den Baal gehuldigt haben. Seltsam bleiben in diesem Zusammenhang die Versammlungen der Propheten an den verschiedenen Heiligtümern im Süden des Reiches Israel. G. von Rad hat sehr ansprechend vermutet,[58] daß der Asylcharakter des Heiligtums zu der Bildung dieser Prophetengenossenschaften beigetragen hätte. Die Propheten hätten sich aus den deklassierten

55. Siehe zu den Einzelheiten meinen in Anmerkung 8 genannten Aufsatz S. 295–98.

56. Im Anschluß an Mendelssohn, Samuel's Denunciation of Kingship in the Light of the Akkadian Documents from Ugarit (*BASOR* 143, 1956, S. 17–22) gegen Noth und andere Forscher.

57. S. 2 und Anmerkung 9.

58. Theologie des Alten Testaments II, 1960, S. 39.

Elementen der Bevölkerung gebildet, die die wirtschaftliche Gesamtlage zum Ruin geführt hätte. Diese Vermutung klärt sicher eine Komponente, die zu der Entstehung dieser Prophetengruppen geführt hat. Unter den phänomenologischen Gesichtspunkten einer Erweckung wird noch eine andere Einsicht erzielt, daß es sich nämlich in diesen Prophetenkolonien um eine Form der Gemeinschaftsbildung handelt, zu denen eine Erweckung führen kann, und die keineswegs immer bezeugt wird. Gegenüber den Wandergemeinschaften der Propheten der Samuelzeit ist hier die Prophetenkolonie an den Heiligtümern das Ergebnis jener am Widerstand gegen den Baalismus der Omridendynastie geprägten Erweckungsbewegung zu bemerken. An den Heiligtümern selbst dürften sie auf den Kult geachtet haben, auf seine genuine jahwistische Durchführung und auf die Verkündigung des Jahwerechtes, wie G. von Rad im gleichen Zusammenhang hervorhebt.[59] Reizvoll erscheint in diesem Gedankenkreis auch die erwägenswerte Möglichkeit, daß die Heiligtümer Quellorte jener Erweckung gewesen sind, also die Eliazeit ein neues Beispiel für den Zusammenhang zwischen Kult und Erweckung liefern würde.

Zuletzt soll die Frage aufgeworfen werden, ob diese phänomenologischen Gesichtspunkte nicht auch anwendbar sind auf die Propheten, die wir als Schriftpropheten zu bezeichnen pflegen? Alle erforderlichen Phänomene sind tatsächlich nachzuweisen, z.B. die führende Persönlichkeit, das Ursprungserlebnis derselben, die Auswirkung auf die Menschen- und Anhängergruppe, die sich um den Propheten bildete, die religiösen Handlungen, die von jenen erweckten Kreisen ausgehen und geübt werden. Berufung und Sendung des Propheten erweisen das Phänomen, daß die Erweckung von Jahwe ausgeht.[60] Für die vorexilische Prophetie mag dieses Urteil allgemein gelten, wobei freilich bei Nahum und Habakkuk Fragezeichen zu setzen sind.

Man wird gegen diese These einwenden können, daß die Anhänger der Propheten, die von ihnen erweckten Volkskreise gar nicht oder nur in geringen Spuren und dann nicht eindeutig als Erweckte,[61] sondern als Wohlwol-

59. a.O. S. 40.

60. Ich bin mir des Wagnisses einer solchen Anwendung der Erweckungsphänomene auf die Schriftpropheten des Alten Testaments durchaus bewußt. Es ist selbstverständlich, daß ich diese Frage nicht im Rahmen eines Aufsatzes beantworten kann. "Israels Propheten als Erwecker" ist ein Thema, das zu seiner Behandlung größeren Raum beanspruchen muß.

61. Bei Jesaja läßt sich ein solcher Kreis vermuten in seinen Schülern, Jes. 8:16 und Jes. 8:18, wobei die jelādīm vielleicht nicht nur die leiblichen Kinder des Propheten betreffen könnten. Bei Jeremia könnten möglicherweise auch die Rekabiter zu seinen Anhängern gehört haben (Jer. 35), ferner die königlichen Beamten, sofern sie Sympathie für ihn zeigten, dann jener Ebed-Melech, der ihn aus der Zisterne errettete (Jer. 38:7–13). Jeremia wird auch

lende, Hilfsbereite und Schutzgewährende erscheinen. Letzteres Phänomen tritt besonders bei Jeremia und den Persönlichkeiten, die ihm Schutz angedeihen lassen, hervor. Gegen diesen Einwand ist zu antworten, daß die Bewahrung der prophetischen Verkündigung in den unter ihrem Namen gehenden Büchern von dem einstigen Vorhandensein solcher erweckten Kreise zeugt. Aus diesem Vorhandensein kann geschlossen werden auf ein häufig nicht mehr wahrnehmbares Verbindungsglied zwischen lebendiger Prophetie und ihrer schriftlichen Tradition, eben jene erweckten Kreise, die die Worte der Propheten hörten, sammelten und weitergaben. Karl Budde hat einmal auf eine Redaktion der Prophetenbücher geschlossen, bei der alle Berichte über den Erfolg und den Verlauf der Prophetentätigkeit getilgt worden seien.[62]

Aber auch bei den Propheten läßt sich die Beobachtung machen, die sich schon in der Betrachtung der Samuelerweckungsbewegung ergab, daß nämlich keineswegs eine Erweckungsbewegung sich immer erfolgreich durchsetzen muß. So bildet sich der Restgedanke heraus, daß nur ein Teil des Volkes durch das Gericht gerettet werden kann.[63] Otto Procksch hat dafür aus dem Neuen Testament die Unterscheidung von Israel *kata pneuma* und Israel *kata sarka* eingeführt.[64] Das Israel *kata pneuma* nimmt die Verkündigung der Prophetie an, das andere Israel sperrt sich dagegen. Trotz dieses Mißerfolges bricht die Kette der Prophetie nicht ab, sondern setzt sich fort. Israel hat stets die Gnade fortwirkender Prophetensendungen erfahren. Unter dem Gesichtspunkt sich wiederholender Erweckungen kann seine Geschichte nicht als eine *historia calamitatum* bezeichnet werden.

Die reizvolle Aufgabe bleibt noch, die erhaltene Verkündigung der Schriftpropheten unter dem Gesichtspunkt der Erweckungspredigt neu zu interpretieren, inhaltlich wie auch formal. Die aufgezeigten phänomenologischen Gesichtspunkte wollen dazu verhelfen, stärker frömmigkeitsgeschichtliche Gesichtspunkte in die Prophetenforschung einzubringen. Daß das

---

unter den 597 nach Babel Verbannten seine Anhänger gehabt haben, an die sein Brief (Jer. 29) gerichtet gewesen sein dürfte. Das Jeremiabuch dürfte im Exil dem Deuterojesaja bekannt gewesen sein. Auch Ezechiel erweist sich von Jeremia abhängig (J. W. Miller, *Das Verhältnis Jeremias und Hesekiels sprachlich und theologisch untersucht*, Assen, 1955).

62. Unter diesen Berichten müßten auch Mitteilungen über die Anhänger, die vom Propheten erweckten Volkskreise enthalten gewesen sein. Diese müßten aber, wenn Budde recht haben sollte, zahlenmäßig nicht ins Gewicht gefallen sein gegenüber den Leiden und Verfolgungen der Propheten. Andernfalls verstünde man nicht die Tilgung der Mitteilung über die Anhänger. Karl Budde, Eine folgenschwere Redaktion des Zwölfprophetenbuches (*ZAW* 39, 1921/22, S. 218–29).

63. Werner E. Müller, Die Vorstellung vom Rest im Alten Testament. Diss. theol. Leipzig, 1939.

64. *Theologie des Alten Testaments*, Gütersloh, 1949, S. 190ff.

Problem der Tradition durch die phänomenologische Erfassung religiöser Erweckungen einen neuen Aspekt erhält, soll hier zum Schluß nur angemerkt werden. Die letzte Konsequenz würde dann darin bestehen, die alttestamentliche Religion als eine Erweckungsreligion aufzufassen, zu erforschen und darzustellen.

# Josua und Retterideal

M. A. BEEK

DER Name Josua bin Nun kommt ausser im Hexateuch und im Anfang des Richterbuches nur noch Neh. 8:14–18, I Kön. 16:34 und I Chr. 7:20–27 vor. Es könnte für die Forschung des Josuabuches und die Feststellung seiner Funktion in der Darstellung der israelitischen Heilsgeschichte wichtig sein, gerade diesen Stellen eine Exegese, wenn möglich in gegenseitiger Beleuchtung, zu widmen.

Neh. 8:14–18 bietet eine lebendige Beschreibung der Feier des Laubhüttenfestes, nachdem in der Thora eine sich auf das Datum (den siebenten Monat) und Riten beziehende Vorschrift entdeckt wurde. Ohne Zweifel spricht der Text von Jehoschu'a bin Nun, obwohl es auffällt, dass er hier Jeschua genannt wird. Man hat vorgeschlagen, mit IMS$^{K}$ das "bin Nun" zu streichen, und diesen Jeschua mit dem Hohenpriester Josua, der ein Zeitgenosse Serubabels war, zu identifizieren, aber überzeugend ist das nicht.

Nachdrücklich sagt der Text, dass das Laubhüttenfest seit den Tagen von Jeschua bin Nun bis zu jenem Tag—d.h. dem Tag, an dem Esra in Jerusalem aus dem Buche der Thora las—nicht so gefeiert wurde. Die Vorschriften wurden in der Thora, die JHWH durch Moses gegeben hatte, gefunden. Nach der Vorstellung des Nehemiabuches gehen die Vorschriften auf Moses zurück und hat die richtige Feier des Laubhüttenfestes erst in den Tagen Josuas angefangen. Hiernach wurde es nicht mehr in dieser Art gefeiert, bis Esra im siebenten Monat auf dem Platze vor dem Wassertor aus dem Buche der Thora Moses vorlas. Man darf also fragen, was nach der Vorstellung des

Nehemiabuches mit der Feier z.Z. Josuas oder in der Periode kurz nach Josuas Auftreten vergleichbar war.

Die Zusammenfassung der Riten nach Neh. 8:15 gibt keine befriedigende Antwort. Das Baumaterial für die Laubhütten muss aus dem Gebirge geholt werden. Die gebrauchten Worte stimmen inhaltlich mit denen in Lev. 23:40 überein und betonen die Freude als Kennzeichen des Festes. Der Autor des Nehemiabuches fühlte sich nicht zur wörtlichen Wiedergabe der uns bekannten Thoravorschrift verpflichtet. Für die Lösung des aufgeworfenen Problems liefert diese Dissimilation keinen Beitrag.

Auch die übrigen Texte, die sich auf das Laubhüttenfest beziehen, erklären nicht, warum die Feier nach dem Auftreten Esras anders war als seit den Tagen Josuas üblich war (vgl. Deut. 16:13–17; Ex. 23:16; 34:22; Num. 29:13–34). Wenn also das Andere und Abweichende nicht in den Riten lag, über die Nehemia dürftige Information gibt, scheint es nützlich, die Aufmerksamkeit auf die Situation, in der das Fest gefeiert wurde, zu richten.

Was die Situation betrifft, berichtet Neh. 8:17, dass das Fest von der *ganzen* Gemeinde der aus der Gefangenschaft Heimgekehrten gefeiert wurde. Das Wort "ganz" hat in Neh. 8 einen starken Nachdruck, es wird 11 mal von כל־העם gesprochen, ausserdem von וכל מבין, בכל־עריהם und כל־קהל.

Dieses כל ist ebenfalls ein Motivwort des Josuabuches. Der Eingang des Josuabuches ist das Zeugnis eines ganzen Volkes das in das eine Land geführt wurde, das JHWH ihm verheissen hat und ihm schenkt (1:2). Nach Jos. 24:1 versammelt Josua כל־שבטי ישראל und spricht אל־כל־העם (24:2); dasselbe tut er noch einmal beim Aufrichten des grossen Steins (24:27). In derselben Weise spricht Neh. 8 von einem ganzen Volk, das als eine Gemeinde aus der Gefangenschaft heimgekehrt ist.

Das Volk wurde von Josua um eine Thora, die Moses geboten und die in einem Buche niedergelegt war, versammelt (1:3,8; 8:31,32,34; 23:6, und 24:26). Genau dieselben Ausdrücke mit denselben Nuancierungen kommen Neh. 8:1,2,3,7,8,9,13,14, und 18 vor. Sowohl in Neh. 8 als in Josua wird von einem *ganzen* Volk gesprochen, das aus der Gefangenschaft heimgekehrt ist und sich dem Buch der Thora Moses oder Gottes zum Gehorsam verpflichtet.

Während der Parallelismus Josua und die Landnahme einerseits—das Auftreten Esras andererseits auf der Hand liegt, bleibt unklar, warum Josua in Neh. 8 im Zusammenhang mit dem Laubhüttenfest erwähnt wird. Das Wort סכת kommt im Josuabuch nicht vor; mit Ausnahme von Neh. 8 wird nie auf eine Beziehung zwischen Josua und diesem Fest angespielt. Das Josuabuch berichtet von einem Pesachfest, das nach Vollziehung der Beschneidung bei Gilgal בערבות יריחו gefeiert wurde. Dass Pesach gerade hier einen sinnvollen Platz gefunden hat, ist ohne weiteres verständlich. Die Beschneidung folgte nach dem Durchzug durch den Jordan und dieser wurde wie eine Wiederholung durch das Schilfmeer beschrieben. Als die Lade durch den Jordan getragen wurde, wurden die Gewässer des Jordans "abgerissen" (4:7).

Nun bietet II Kön. 23:21f einen stilistisch mit Neh. 8:18 verwandten Text. Josia hat geboten, das Pesachfest neu zu feiern. Der König hat כל־העם befohlen, in Übereinstimmung mit dem zu handeln, was im Bundesbuch geschrieben stand. Es wurde nicht mehr in dieser Art seit den Tagen der Richter gefeiert. Wenn wir annehmen, dass die Restauration im Rahmen der josianischen Reformation als ein in Jerusalem zentralisiertes Geschehen betrachtet wurde, ist der Ausdruck "seit den Tagen der Richter" unverständlich. Jerusalem ist erst in den Tagen Davids ein politisches und religiöses Zentrum geworden.

Diese Schwierigkeit kann man auch in Neh. 8 beobachten. In der Beschreibung wird vor allem die Feier in Jerusalem betont: die Laubhütten wurden in den Höfen des Tempels, auf dem Platze des Wassertores und auf dem Platze des Ephraimtores gemacht. Aber auch in den Tagen Josuas konnte Israel sein Pesach nicht in Jerusalem feiern. II Chr. 30:26 berichtet, dass unter Hiskia ein Pesachfest gefeiert wurde, wie es seit Salomo nicht geschah. Dieser Text stellt uns nicht vor das Problem, das Neh. 8 und II Kön. 23 bieten.

Es kann nur gelöst werden, wenn wir die historisierte Bedeutung, die später dem Laubhüttenfest gegeben wurde, in Betracht ziehen. Daraus ergibt sich, dass es als ein zweites Pesachfest im Herbst aufgefast wurde. Wenn nach Lev. 23:42–43 כל־אזרח בישראל in Hütten zu wohnen verpflichtet ist, wird das begründet: "damit eure Geschlechter wissen, dass ich in Hütten die Israeliten wohnen liess, als ich sie aus Ägypten führte." Genau genommen ist das nicht richtig, da die Nomaden der Wüste in Zelten und nicht in Laubhütten zu wohnen pflegen. Der Kommentator war auch nicht darauf aus, auf die sichtbaren Hütten hinzuweisen, sondern auf den unsichtbaren Schutz Gottes, dessen Symbol die Hütte ist, wie der Psalmendichter singt: "du birgst sie in einer Hütte vor dem Streit der Zungen" (Ps. 31:21b, vgl. auch Jes. 4:6a). Das Buch Jona betont am Schluss den relativen Wert der Hütte, die ein Mensch sich gebaut hat. Gott bestimmte einen Wunderbaum, der besser war als die Hütte, die Jona aufgerichtet hatte. Nachdem der Wunderbaum verdorrt war, spielt die Hütte keine Rolle mehr. Der schweigende Chamsin steckt das Haupt Jonas und trotz seiner Hütte begehrt der Prophet zu sterben.

Das Laubhüttenfest ist nach der historisierenden Interpretation eine Erinnerung an den göttlichen Schutz, den Israel während Auszug und Durchzug erfahren hat. Das Fest des Einsammelens (Ex. 23:16 und 34:22) wurde nach der Ernte von Oliven und Trauben gefeiert und hat dem jährlich wiederkehrenden Naturfest seine Riten entlehnt. Diese konnten aber erst, nachdem das *ganze* Volk sich im Kulturland angesiedelt hatte, als ein zweites Pesach gefeiert werden. In einer zweiten Phase wurden diese Riten vom Lande nach der Stadt Jerusalem, wo sie ursprünglich nicht hingehörten, verlegt.

Beide Feste, Laubhütten und Pesach, heissen auch חג יהוה. Appellierend an ein solches Fest bittet Moses den Pharao um Zustimmung für einen Auszug (Ex. 10:9). Richter 21:19 erwähnt ein Fest im Herbst, an dem die Mädchen in den Weinbergen Reigentänze reihen und nennt es ein חג יהוה. Mit demselben Ausdruck spricht Hos. 9:5 von einem Fest im Herbst, das nur mit Laubhütten identifiziert werden kann. Lev. 23:41 betont dieses Kennzeichen mit den Worten וחגתם אותו חג ליהוה. Beide Feste hatten nach der Vorstellung des biblischen Autors ihre wesentliche Bedeutung und Form bekommen, nachdem das *ganze* Volk in dem einen Land unter den Schutz des einen Gottes zusammengebracht worden war.

Der zweite Text, der in diesem Zusammenhang Aufmerksamkeit erfordert, ist I Kön. 16:34. Die Worte schliessen einige Berichte über das Auftreten Achabs ab und leiten in die Elia- und Elisa-erzählungen ein, welche sich dann und wann in Jericho abspielen (II Kön. 2:4ff., 19–22). I Kön. 16:34 hat eine Funktion, die dem Bericht I Kön. 16:25 über die Gründung Samariens durch Omri vergleichbar ist. Auch in dieser Stadt werden nachher wichtige Ereignisse, bei denen Elia und Elisa ihre grosse Rolle spielten, lokalisiert (I Kön. 20:22; II Kön. 2:25; 6:24–7,20).

Die Frage, ob I Kön. 16:34 auf die Verfluchung Jerichos durch Josua nach Jos. 6:26 zurückgreift, oder umgekehrt, ist kaum zu beantworten. Noth hat I Kön. 16:34 als eine ursprüngliche Information bezeichnet. Der Josuatext wäre dann als eine Hinzufügung auf Grund historischer oder legendarischer Berichte über Hiel und seine Söhne Abiam und Segub zu betrachten. Fest steht nur, dass der Erzähler des Elia- und Elisazyklus den Namen Josua bin Nun mit der Verfluchung Jerichos verbunden hat. Diese Verfluchung hätte sich dann in einem katastrophalen Ereignis erfüllt, wobei die Söhne Hiels umkamen oder, wie man früher wohl meinte, als Bauopfer dargebracht wurden.

Welche Rolle hat Jericho in der israelitischen Heilsgeschichte gespielt?

Angesichts der sehr beschränkten Information kann die Antwort einfach sein. Mit Ausnahme von Josua und II Kön. 2 ist Jericho nicht mehr als ein geographischer Anknüpfungspunkt. So kommt in Num. der Ausdruck בערבות מואב מעבר לירדן יריחו 8 mal vor (vgl. auch Jer. 39:5 = 52:8; II Sam. 10:5 = I Chr. 19:5). Esra 2:34 = Neh. 7:36 erwähnt Männer aus Jericho, die beim Wiederaufbau Jerusalems mithalfen. II Kön. 2 wird Jericho wichtiger als Wohnsitz der Prophetensöhne. Ausserdem ist Jericho die Stadt in der Nähe des Jordan. In diesem Fluss wurde noch einmal der wunderbare Durchzug wiederholt: der Mantel Elias ist das Mittel, das Elisa befähigte, trocknen Fusses den Jordan zu überqueren.

Im Josuabuch kommt Jericho 27 mal vor, hauptsächlich im Zusammenhang mit der Eroberung der Stadt. Diese Erzählung von dem mirakulösen Fall der Stadtmauer hat manchen Erklärer vom Kern der Verkündigung abgelenkt. Abel[1] hat mit Recht darauf hingewiesen, dass die Jerichoerzählung gemeint ist als eine Illustration der Auffassung, die Israel vom "Bann" hatte. Um den חרם herum sind drei Gruppen zu unterscheiden: die Familie der Rachab, die von Achan und die Gibeoniter. Rachab ist zu vergleichen mit Abigail. Wie diese das Königtum Davids vorhersah und im Hinblick darauf ihre Massnahmen traf, so sah Rachab den Sieg des Gottesvolks und rechnete damit. Die Familie der Rachab entging dem Bann, obwohl sie Israel nicht angehörte, Achan vergriff sich am gebannten Gut und ging mit seiner Familie zugrunde, obwohl er ein Israelit war. Die Gibeoniter entzogen sich dem Bann durch Betrug und gerieten in eine untergeordnete Stellung.

In der Jerichoerzählung ist die Stadt als ein pars pro toto zu betrachten. Jericho erkunden heisst das Land erkunden, die Stadt erobern heisst das ganze Land erobern. Stadt und Land stehen unter dem Bann, sie gehören JHWH an und das Ihm zugehörige Gebiet ist heiliger Boden.

So ist auch die geheimnisvolle Perikope Jos. 3:13–15 zu erklären. Josua befindet sich—in einem Traumgesicht—in Jericho und sieht einen Mann, der gezogenen Schwertes ihm gegenüber steht und sich als שר־צבא יהוה zu erkennen gibt.

Er befiehlt, die Schuhe von den Füssen zu streifen, da der Boden, auf dem Josua steht, heilig ist. Das Intermezzo endet, als Josua getan hat, was ihm gesagt war. Mehr zu erzählen, wäre auch überflüssig: das Jerichogebiet ist heilig, es gehört dem Volke JHWH's an. Bald muss sogar die Rachabsfamilie sich ausserhalb des Lagers aufhalten (Jos. 6:23). Der Text I Kön. 16:34

1. F.-M. Abel, "L'Arathème de Jéricho et la maison de Rahab," *RB* 64 (1957): 321–30. C. H. W. Brekelmans, *De Ḥerem in het Oude Testament* (Njnnegen, 1959), hat die theologische Bedentung des ḥerems stark betont.

lässt auf den Elia-Elisa-zyklus anklingen und verknüpft diese Erzählungen in sinnvoller Weise mit Josua bin Nun und der in der Nähe des Jordan gelegenen Stadt Jericho. Das Manna fiel nicht mehr aus dem Himmel, die ungesäuerten Kuchen wurden von der Ernte des Landes gebacken und der Weg nach dem Laubhüttenfest war gebahnt. Josuas Name wurde in die Genealogien von I Chr 7 aufgenommen. Nach. 7:20–27 ist er ein Abkömmling Ephraims in der vierzehnten Generation. Mit Recht bemerkt der ICC zur Stelle "This is the only record of Joshua's line of descent and its late and artificial character reveals itself at once." Rudolph gibt in seinem Kommentar[2] derselben Verlegenheit Ausdruck, wenn er von einem "durch das Zusammenleimen zweier verschiedener Stammbäume" hervorgerufenen idealen Stammbaum spricht. Die Genealogie erzählt Merkwürdigkeiten über Ephraim, dessen Söhne Ezer und Elad, die durch Männer aus Gath getötet worden waren, auch über einen gewissen Beria und eine Tochter Seïra, aber über Josua und seinen Vater Nun war scheinbar nichts zu erwähnen. Man kann nicht einmal sagen, dass der Inhalt des Josuabuches als bekannt vorausgesetzt wurde.

In den Büchern Esra, Nehemia, Haggai und Sacharja kommt Josua als Name 21 mal und in der verkürzten Form ישוע noch 20 mal vor. I Sam. 6:14 und 18 erwähnen einen Mann aus Beth Schemesch und II Kön. 23:8 einen שר העיר, der diesen Namen trägt. Den Namen הושע, der nach Num. 13:8,16 und Deut. 32:44 ein zweiter Name Josuas war, trug auch der letzte König des Nordreiches (II Kön. 15–18) und ein Prophet, der um die Mitte des 8. Jahrhunderts im Nordreich predigte. Obwohl der Name mit dem Verbum ישע zusammengestellt ist, wird nie expressis verbis gesagt, dass man einen tieferen Zusammenhang zwischen Josua und "retten" spürte, mit Ausnahme von Sir 46,1 Von *Ιησους Ναυη* sagt der Text "*ὅς ’εγενετο χατα το ὀνομα αὐτου μεγας ’επι σωτηριᾳ ’εχλεχτων αὐτου.*" Der hebräische Text liest בימיו statt כשמו, was zu erwarten wäre, aber hat doch die griechische Übersetzung vorbereitet, wo es heisst, dass יהושע die תשועה gebracht hat.

Und doch ist es möglich, dass ein gewisser יהושע, Sohn eines Vaters mit einem seltsamen und geheimnisvollen Namen (Nun = Fisch?), gerade seinem Namen die charakteristische Funktion, die er im Ganzen der israelitischen Heilsgeschichte einnimmt, zu verdanken hat. Auffallend ist, dass der Hiphil von ישע so manchmal im Richterbuch vorkommt. Das Motivwort ist mit 2, 18a gegeben: JHWH lässt einen Richter aufstehen, Er ist mit dem Richter und rettet Sein Volk aus der Hand seiner Feinde alle Tage des Richters.

2. W. Rudolph, "Chronikbücher," *HbzAT* (Tübingen, 1955) z. St.

Wieder und wieder lässt JHWH einen Retter aufstehen: Othniel (3:9), Sjamgar (3:31), Gideon (6:14,15,36,37; 7:2,7; 8:22), Thola (10:1). Von Simson heisst es והוא יחל להושיע את־ישראל מיד פלשתים. Auch JHWH selbst tritt als מושיע auf (10:12f.).

Sawyer hat neuerdings die Bedeutung des מושיע einer tiefgehenden Forschung unterworfen und folgerte, dass "there was a place in ancient Israel for an advocate or a witness for the defence and also for a witness for the prosecution."[3] Er meint einen "forensic root" für den Stamm ישע annehmen zu dürfen und suggeriert eine Entwicklung "from a definite office within a definite sphere of life, and from there to a title of God in any general context." Seine Argumente sind überzeugend, wenn er sich auf Stellen wie Deut. 22:27; I Sam. 25:26,31,33; II Sam. 17:4 und II Kön. 6:26 bezieht. Auch seine These, dass "the meaning of advocate or witness for the defence fits well and adds something to the passage" hat ihren exegetischen Wert für die Hintergründe von Jes. 43:3,11 und 45:2ff. Die andere These, dass "there are no cases in the OT where a forensic meaning is impossible," wird aber durch die Exegese der betreffenden Stellen im Richterbuch widerlegt.

Hier hat das Wort מושיע eine theologische Bedeutung. Die Richter haben Israel gerettet, aber sie waren nur durch die Hilfe JHWH's dazu imstande. Am stärksten wurde das in der Gideonsgeschichte zum Ausdruck gebracht. Israel darf nicht sagen: ידי הושיעה לי. Eine Fortsetzung dieses grundliegenden Bekenntnisses findet man I Sam. 14:6,23,39 und 17:47.

So ist im Josuabuch der Name der Hauptperson ein Programm und somit füllt das Buch eine Lücke zwischen Thora und Richterbuch. Der Name Josuas sagt aus, dass die Rettung nur durch die Macht JHWH's zu erwarten sei und in Übereinstimmung mit diesem Namen wird durch Josua gehandelt. Die Initiativen kommen immer von JHWH und Josua ist das Beispiel des Gehorsamen. Er leitet die Befehle weiter oder erledigt die göttliche Aufträge (Jos. 1:1ff.; 3:7,4,1b, 15–17; 5:2,9,14f.; 6:2–6; 7:10–15; 8:1–3,18; 9:14; 10:8; 11:6; 13:1b; 20:1; 24:2). Wenn er gehorcht, haben seine Unternehmungen Erfolg, wenn er in einer schwierigen Lage versäumt, vorher JHWH zu befragen, folgt ein Misslingen. Dies wird mit der gelungenen List der Gibeoniten illustriert. Der Autor des Josuabuches gibt ein Beispiel des wahren Retters und damit ist die Funktion des Buches gegeben. Es füllt nicht nur eine Lücke, sondern ist auch Vorbereitung auf eine heilshistorische Erzählung, die mit den Richtern einen neuen Anfang macht.

3. J. Sawyer, "What was a mošia<sup>c</sup>?" *VT* 15 (1965): 475–86.

Die Frage nach der Geschichtlichkeit, historischen Hintergründen oder Zusammenhängen zwischen ätiologischen Sagen und Geschichtlichkeit können wir auf sich beruhen lassen, wenn wir die Funktion des Josuabildes in der Heilsgeschichte festzustellen versuchen.[4] Eissfeldt sagt, dass die Erzählungen um Josua "weithin sagenhafter Art sind und nur durch behutsam kritische Prüfung historisch ausgewertet werden können." Aber er lässt auch Worte fallen wie "zuverlässige Erinnerungen," "geschichtliche Gestalten," "Angaben, wenigstens ihrer Grundlage nach geschichtlich."[5] Damit spielt er auf eine Forschung an, in der Intuition mehr als Tatsachen den Weg gewiesen haben, während archäologische Materialien keine überzeugenden Beweise liefern konnten.

Segal hat festgestellt, dass das Josuabuch nie ein integraler Teil des Pentateuch gewesen ist.[6] Damit hat er recht und doch spricht man nicht ohne Grund vom Hexateuch. Die Namen Moses und Josua, die ausserhalb des Hexateuch so auffallend selten vorkommen, sprechen deutlich für die literarische Einheit des Hexateuch. Dass die Redaktion bei Josua einen neuen Anfang gemacht hat und das Buch zu den "früheren Propheten" rechnete, muss daraus erklärt werden, dass die Thora in ihrem ersten Entwurf vollendet war, bevor das Josuabuch komponiert wurde. Segal meinte, die Entstehungszeit in einer Periode der politischen Stabilität und Wohlfahrt ansetzen zu können, z.B. während der Regierung der Omriden im Nordreich.

Was wir gefunden haben, weist hin auf einen jungen Ursprung in einer Periode der Ordnung nach einem neuen Anfang.[7] Damals nach dem Exil war die Zeit reif für den Entwurf des idealen מושיע, und er wurde in die Gestalt des יהושע hinein projiziert. Er hatte ein ganzes Volk in einem Land um eine Thora versammelt und er hatte es vermocht, mit Hilfe von und in Gehorsamkeit an JHWH.

4. G. E. Mendenhall, "The Hebrew Conquest of Palestine," *BA* 25 (1962): 66–87, hat m. E. mit Recht die traditionelle Vorstellung der Landnahme bezweifelt und überzeugend die These verteidigt: In summary, there was no real conquest of Palestine at all; what happened instead may be termed, from the point of view of the secular historian interested only in sociopolitical process, a peasant's revolt against the network of interlocking Canaanite city states. Vgl. jetzt auch M. Weippert, "Die Landnahme der israelitischen Stämme in der neueren wissenschaftlichen Diskussion. Ein kritischer Bericht," *FRLANT* 92 (Göttingen, 1967).

5. O. Eissfeldt, *Israels Führer in der Zeit vom Auszug bis zur Landnahme*, Studia Bibl. et Sem. Th. Chr. Vriezen dedicata (Wageningen, 1966) pp. 62–70.

6. M. Segal, "YHWH and Elohim in the Book of Joshua," in *The Pentateuch and Other Biblical Studies* (Jerusalem, 1967), pp. 117–19.

7. J. G. Vink, "The date and origin of the Priestly Code in the Old Testament," *OTS* 15 (1969): 63–80, hat sehr richtig den Zusammenhang zwischen Josuatext und dem Auftreten von Esra und Nehemia gesehen und kommt in Bezug auf Jos. 8:30–35 auf einem anderen quellenkritischen Wege zu einer späten Datierung.

# The Identity and Date of the Unnamed Feast of John 5:1

JOHN BOWMAN

EVERY feast of the Jewish liturgical year has been, at some time or other, suggested to fill the role of this unnamed feast. The present writer suggests Purim and in so doing is well aware that this is not in the least novel. But, what is *new* is how we arrive at this conclusion.

We are aware that by postulating disarrangement of the text, the feast of Jn. 5:1 can become Passover. While that may be desired on other grounds, if the order of the text is left as it is, the teasing question remains as to what the feast in Jn. 5:1 is.

The answer may be provided by turning one's attention to Jn. 4 and in particular v. 35: "Do you not say: 'There are yet four months, and then the harvest comes.'" It is possible to say this is a proverbial saying. But, if so, why "four months"? The harvest, presumably, is the grain harvest at the Feast of Weeks (Pentecost), fifty days after Passover, if we adopt the Pharisaic[1] Jewish dating of commencing the *Sefirath ha-Omer*, i.e., of counting the fifty days from the morrow of the Passover, this latter being understood as a Sabbath even if actually a week day. Four months is either 116 days or 120 days, depending on whether one understands a month to have been of twenty nine or thirty days. If we understand the Fourth Gospel to have been written in the last decade of the first century A.D., the Judaism it reflects is that of its own period. This would mean that the months are Jewish months. The lunar

1. Cf. T. B. Men, 65b.

year consists of twelve months or 354 days, 8 hours, 876 parts [of an hour].[2] The moon passes through her different phases in 29 days,[3] 12 hours, 793 parts [of an hour]. But, since months are reckoned by full days and start from the beginning of the night (when the moon is seen), months are either twenty nine or thirty days. If the former, deficient by half a day. If the latter, half a day over. Four Jewish months would have been 118 days, approximately. Four months before Pentecost would be sixty-seven days before Passover, then comes Passover itself and fifty days from the morrow of Passover to Pentecost. Sixty-seven days (or two months, eight days), before Passover would bring one to about one week before the New Year for Trees, which was on the 15th of Shebat.[4] However, if that year were a leap year and a second month of Adar had been intercalated, sixty-seven days before Passover would be at the end of the first week of the first month of Adar. Neither of these dates that we thus arrive at have any significance for Jews. But this is what we may rightly expect. Jesus was, in Jn. 4, among the Samaritans. He had chosen to go at this time to the Samaritans. He had, at Jacob's Well, met the Samaritan woman who represents the Samaritan community. The woman perceived He was a prophet (Jn. 4:19). Jesus told her plainly that salvation is from the Jews. This statement not only makes plain whence salvation comes but is an announcement that it is coming. This is plain in the verse that follows. But the hour comes and now is, when the true worshippers shall worship the Father in spirit and truth. Religion then will be a source of life. In Jn. 4:25 the woman senses the meaning of the announcement made at the end of Jn. 4:22 and says: "I know that Messiah comes, when he is come he will declare to us all things." This last could be a reference to Dt. 18:18 and be her paraphrase of Yahweh's promise to raise up a prophet from among their brethren, like to Moses; Yahweh would put His words in his mouth and the prophet like Moses would speak to them all that Yahweh commanded him.

Jesus, in Jn. 4:26 says: "It is I who speak to you." This could be interpreted as saying He is the Messiah, or it could be a declaration of being Yahweh. We must remember that the Fourth Gospel deals with the Jesus of faith, who is LORD. There seems little doubt that the early church identified Yahweh and Jesus, cf. Justin Dial. ch. CXXVII; cf. also Thomas's statement of faith (Jn. 20:28) "My Lord and My God" (while it is true one did not say My Yahweh, one did say My Lord and mean Yahweh). Jesus' reply merely

2. Cf. *JE*, vol. 3, art Calendar, p. 503.
3. Cf. ibid., p. 502.
4. Cf. M. Rosh ha-Shanah 1:1.

highlights the basic problem of communication. She uses the term Messiah, which a Samaritan would not apply to their Taheb. It is true that later the Samaritans in their own works[5] refer to Jesus as the Messiah, just as the Muslims do. However, by the time this Gospel was written there was a Samaritan Christian Church and the term Messiah would even then not be unfamiliar to Samaritans. In fact the phrase "the Messiah comes (who is called Christ)" sounds very much like the parroting of the Christian confession of hope of His return. This Gospel proclaims that salvation sprang from the Jews—and not the Samaritans—but it does not copy or foster Jewish Messianic views.

The Samaritans called their hoped-for Savior the Taheb who, while possibly the Returning One, is as well the Restorer. But who, and of what? The biblical basis for the hope is assumed to be Dt. 18:18: "The prophet like Moses whom Yahweh will raise up." Dt. 34:10 states that there has not arisen a prophet since in Israel like Moses, though in Dt. 34:9 we are told that Joshua the son of Nun was full of the spirit of wisdom, for Moses had laid his hands upon him, cf., Num. 27:18,23. According to the Hebrew Mass. text Joshua is not the Taheb. In the Sam. Heb. the statement in Dt. 34:10 is: "there will not arise one like Moses" which rules out any future prophet like Moses. But this did not rule out Joshua. Actually in the early Samaritan priestly sources there is no doctrine of the Taheb. By priestly sources one means the Hebrew Torah and the Targum, and the halakhic works like the *Kafi* of Yusuf b. Salama, the *Kitab at-Tabakh* of Hassan As-Suri, the *Tolidah*, or Chain of High Priests, which latter work contains also doctrine. Liturgy must be approached with caution. It is priestly, but after the fourteenth century, Dosithean doctrines enrich priestly Samaritanism with what was to them a new theology. This led to a stupendous blossoming of liturgical expression of their new theology. Dositheism was not new. It could go back to the Persian period, but is more likely to have sprung up in the Hasmonean, as an anti-priestly, antisacrificial movement, after the Temple on Mt. Gerizim was destroyed. But it is in Dositheism and its subsects that we find Samaritan Messianism. This is where the doctrine of the Taheb develops. Dusis himself may have claimed to be Moses returned, but this is not at all clear.[6] What is certain is that Dositheism would have had *no* inhibition in applying Dt. 18:18 to Joshua as successor of Moses. Modern Western scholars have assumed too much on the basis of Dt. 18:18 that the prophet like Moses is Moses himself returned.

5. *Abu'l Fath*, ed. Vilmar, vol. II, p. 107.
6. Cf. ibid., p. 156ff.

Josephus Ant. III. II. 3 states that Joshua was "indeed made, like another Moses, a teacher of piety towards God." Further, Josephus Ant. IV. VII. 2 affirms that Moses appointed Joshua as his successor, "both to receive directions from God as a prophet, and for a commander of the army, if they should at any time stand in need of such a one; and this was done by the command of God, that to him the care of the public should be committed. Now Joshua had been instructed in all kinds of learning which concerned the laws and God Himself and Moses had been his instructor." In Num. 27:19–23 and Dt. 31:14 it is clear that Joshua was Moses' divinely appointed successor. Dt. 34:9 states that Joshua was full of the spirit of wisdom because Moses had laid his hands upon him. But the very next verse (Dt. 34:10) asserts that there has not arisen a prophet since in Israel like Moses, whom Yahweh knew face to face. Early priestly Samaritanism regarded Moses as the one and only prophet. The fact that their Bible was only the Pentateuch guaranteed the uniqueness of Moses as a prophet, and even as a leader of his people. But is there really any necessary connection between the Taheb doctrine and Moses? Since Dt. 34:10 claims the uniqueness of Moses and yet Dt. 18:18 promises a prophet like Moses, it has been assumed, mainly by modern Western scholars, that the Taheb or Samaritan Messiah is Moses Redivivus. But priestly Samaritanism before the fourteenth century did not hold any view about the Taheb.[7] It did know of the loss of the Tabernacle (cf., the Tolidah). It is not clear that early priestly Samaritanism divided its sacred history into periods of Divine Favor (*Rahutha*) and Divine Disfavor (*Panutha*). However, if Abuᵓl Fath, the historian of a reunited Samaritanism of the fourteenth century, does know of such epochs in its *heilgeschichte*, he derives the concept from the Samaritan Book of Joshua.[8] The Samaritan Bible is the Torah. The Samaritan Book of Joshua was not a rival to the Heb. Mass. Joshua, for the latter was never accepted by the Samaritans. The problem is who among the Samaritans, and when, used the Samaritan Book of Joshua and, in any case, what was it? The Book of Joshua 5:10,11 does tell of the first Passover (that at Gilgal) in the land of Israel. It seems possible that the Samaritans read their Book of Joshua during the seven days of Passover just as the Jews then read the Megillah of Shir ha-Shirim. The Samaritans read the Molad Mosheh (The Birth of Moses) at Tabernacles, just as the Jews read the Megillah of Koheleth then.

7. The present writer does not regard Marqa, who wrote in the time of Baba Rabba's attempted reunion of priestly Samaritanism and Dositheism, as representing the orthodox priestly position. Rather Abuᵓl Hasan As-Suri, though later, is more typical.

8. Cf. *Abuᵓl Fath*, ed. Vilmar, vol. II, p. 4.

The Samaritan Book of Joshua seems best represented by the Scaliger Leiden MS. This includes matters relating to Joshua in Numbers, Deuteronomy, as well as a considerable part of the Hebrew Book of Joshua. In addition, there are tales of unheard of wars of Joshua. The work also contains the story of the beginning of Panutha (Divine Disfavor) under Eli; then in the last few chapters it gives a quick résumé of the era of Samaritan history, ending with Baba Rabba.

Great and unique as Moses is for the Samaritans, Joshua is he who took them into the land, partitioned it out among the tribes, and, with the priest Eleazar, established the Tabernacle on Mt. Gerizim, the place which for them God had chosen, the very house of God; that Mt. Gerizim is such is an essential item in the Samaritan Creed. This was the period of Rahutha (Divine Favor). Now Baba Rabba, with whom the Book of Joshua (Scaliger MS) ends, established the Temple on Mt. Gerizim and divided up the land among the Samaritans. He was, as it were, a second Joshua. Like Juynboll,[9] I hold to the essential unity of the Leiden Book of Joshua. There are other versions, either more like the biblical Book of Joshua in length, or more like a chronicle of the Samaritans of which Joshua is but a part. Each in its own manner reflects different attitudes to the uniqueness of Joshua. It seems to me that the Leiden Samaritan Joshua is the earliest source giving descriptions of the period of Divine Favor and that of Divine Disfavor and blaming Eli for the coming of the latter. It would appear that the above work intends one to draw the following conclusions: (a) that Baba Rabba was Joshua Returned (i.e., Taheb) and (b) that Rahutha was restored while Baba Rabba ruled. In Samaritan sources the identity of the Taheb is vague. If some felt it could only be Moses, there were those who would feel that Joshua, as establisher of the house of God on Mt. Gerizim and as conqueror and partitioner of the land, was better equipped for the task of restoring what he himself had established. Moses was unique, just as the Torah he had revealed was unique. Orthodox priestly Samaritanism stood solidly behind Moses. Even Baba Rabba, who achieved a union (temporary though it was to be) between the priestly and the Dositheans who were antipriestly, though he acted as a Joshua, could not claim to be so. There is a pall over Baba's end. If he did not become Christian, his son did (cf. Abuʾl Fath).[10]

The Samaritans make much of the Balaam pericope, especially Num. 24. For their doctrine of the Taheb it is fundamental, as indeed it is for Judaism if one seeks a Pentateuchal basis for the Messianic hope. Num. 24:20 is

9. *Chronicon Samaritanum* (Leiden, 1848), op. cit.
10. Cf. *Abuʾl Fath*, ed. Vilmar, vol. II, pp. 147, 148.

directed at Amalek in a manner implying, as actually the Midrash understood, that Amalek was present with Balak. Perhaps more noteworthy even is the reference in Num. 24:7 to Agag who was the leader of Amalek of the time of Samuel and Saul. But both the Samaritan Hebrew and the LXX render Agag of Num. 24:7 by Gog. One need not postulate that Ezekiel's Gog is Agag, or even that he meant one to associate the working out of the doom on Amalek with the overthrowing of Gog, as the prelude to the Messianic Age. But the latter is clearly the intention of the LXX, the Samaritan has followed. Ezekiel's *Nasi* seems to have been drawn on to provide the Samaritan pattern of the Taheb (cf. Bowman, J., *Ezekiel and the Zadokite Priesthood*, *TrGUOS*, vol. 16 [1955–56], p. 13). Actually, apart from the Davidic descent of the *Nasi*, one is reminded, even in Ezekiel's account, of the work of Joshua in setting up the Tabernacle and dividing the land. "Balaam" in Jewish sources, cf. Targum Pseudo-Jonathan on Num. 22:5 and T. B. Sanh. 105b is understood as "he who sought to swallow up the people of the house of Israel." M. Gaster, in *The Asatir*, R.A.S. (London, 1927), p. 94, points out that *'Ερεμηλάος* as a translation of Balaam is based on the above-mentioned Jewish interpretation; and, if so, Balaam is the prototype of *Armilos*, the antagonist of the Messiah, mentioned in the Targum to Isa. 11:4 and in the Targum Pseudo-Jonathan on Dt. 34:3. But the important thing about the Samaritan and LXX identification of Agag with Gog in Num. 24 is that it brings together on the one hand Amalek/Edom, seen as the enemy of Israel from the wilderness days to those of the Exile, with the lives of Esther and Mordecai and the Jews threatened by Haman, Amalek's descendant through Agag and, on the other hand, Gog of the land of Magog, and the hosts of the North-East who assail the people of Israel in their land. Amalek does not seem to have been for the Samaritans, as for the Jews, the type par excellence of the antagonist of Israel and Joshua. In the Samaritan Book of Joshua as much attention is given to the slaying of five kings of Midian and Balaam and much more to the battle with Shaubak the son of Hamam than to Amalek. It may be significant, however, that Hamam was King of Persia. Kohler in his article on Shobach, *JE*, vol. 11, pp. 300–1, describes Shobach as son of Haman, son of Put, son of Ham, son of Noah. It is not impossible that the Samaritans, with only their Book of Joshua to serve as a substitute for the rest of the Hebrew Jewish Canon other than the Law, sought to make their Joshua also the equivalent of Mordecai and his deliverance of the Jews from Haman.

If the practice was to read the Book of Joshua as a Megillah during the week of the Passover, it is possible that the Ẓimmuth Pesaḥ did not only tell of Moses coming to deliver Israel but rather among the Dositheans, who saw Joshua as the one like Moses and hoped for his return, it was a memorial of the work of Joshua who led them across Jordan and celebrated with them the first Passover in the land of Israel at Gilgal. He who had routed their enemies, built their Tabernacle on Mt. Gerizim, and divided the land among the Tribes was the one they looked for, not Moses.

Now, what has this to do with Jn. 4? It is possible that the woman at Jacob's Well did not think of Jesus as Moses returned, but Joshua who would restore the Temple on Mt. Gerizim, recapture the land and divide it among the Samaritans as the true Israel.

What would make her and the Samaritan men to whom she brought Him more receptive was that He should come when He did, four months before the harvest, for then was the Samaritan minor feast of Ẓimmuth Pesaḥ, presumably the Sabbath, nearest to the vernal conjunction of sun and moon. Four months before Pentecost, as we saw above, is sixty-seven before Passover, i.e., nine weeks, four days. We must remember that the Jewish Passover and the Samaritan did not usually coincide.

The Ẓimmuth Pesah is a minor feast of the Samaritans, similar in purpose to Purim among the Jews. It fixes when Passover will fall. In fact Ẓimmuth Pesaḥ is called the gate of festivals (cf. J. Van Goudoever, *Biblical Calendars* (Leiden, Brill, 1959), p. 82). Each has been given a religious connotation of its own. In the Samaritan Liturgy, Ẓimmuth Pesaḥ is the anniversary of Moses, commissioned by Yahweh at the Burning Bush, meeting Aaron and telling him of the coming salvation of Israel. If Jesus comes on the day the Samaritans are having their annual memorial of this auspicious event, then His claims would the more easily be grasped by the woman at the well and her co-religionists. The fact that Moses had come to announce deliverance does not mean that the Taheb must be Moses. Some Samaritans would understand Him to be Joshua. Others might understand Him to be their God Himself. It was a positive response, cf. Jn. 4:42 "we know that this is indeed the Savior of the world."

We should remember that the Fourth Gospel is presenting the Jesus of the Church of the end of the first century to Samaritans of that period. It is, therefore, logical to see it as envisaging Samaritans infected by the claims and teachings of Simon Magus (classed by Abu'l Fath[11] the Samaritan: as among the Dositheans-style sects). One recalls the claim of Simon Magus to be the Standing One ὁ ἑστώς[12] which is a literal translation of

11. Cf. ibid., p. 157ff.
12. Hipp. Phil. VI: 17.

*Kawam*[13] participle of קום standing, but a Samaritan epithet of God as The Existing One.

The comparable minor feast to Ẓimmuth Pesaḥ in Judaism is Purim. The reading of Esther on the 15th Adar, telling of the latter day deliverance of the Jews by Mordecai and Esther, was a clear indication that Passover was thirty days later. If it were not read on the 15th Adar, that was a clear sign that Passover was sixty days off and a second Adar would be intercalated that year. Purim celebrates the victory over Haman, descendant through Agag of Amalek, in not only having Haman's decree against the Jews reversed but Haman and his sons hung and his supporters massacred. Mordecai and Esther were held to be seeking to carry out what is mentioned in Ex. 17:14 "And Yahweh said to Moses, 'Write this for a memorial in a book, and rehearse it in the ears of Joshua: that I will utterly blot out the remembrance of Amalek from under heaven.'"

To this day the parashah "Remember what Amalek did to you" (Dt. 25:17–19) is read in the Synagogue on the Sabbath preceding Purim. This section refers to Ex. 17:8–15 and the battle which the Israelites, led by Joshua, fought with Amalek.

The Jews have made much of Amalek. As the first nation to attack Israel, Amalek has become the symbol of the anti-Jewish oppressor, or opponent, and even the Devil. With them Joshua was kept in the shadow of Moses. There was the complaint too that "the Christians apply to Jesus (=Joshua) the son of Joseph what the Jewish Haggadah claims for Joshua the son of Nun" (L. Ginzberg, *The Legend of the Jews*, vol. VI, p. 93, n. 505). The Samaritans do not make much of Amalek. In the Memar Marqa, Amalek is regarded as having been an enemy who was completely destroyed (the Samaritans have only the reference to Amalek in the Torah and *not* those in Jud. 3:13, 5:14; I Sam. 15:2,3,5,20; I Sam. 28:18; 2 Sam. 8:12; I Chr. 18:11; Ps. 83:7). However, the Ẓimmuth Pesaḥ looks forward to a deliverer who could be a second Joshua and re-establish their Temple on that mountain where their fathers worshipped (cf., Jn. 4:20) and give them back the land that Joshua gave to them. Purim remembers Amalek and knows that he was not rooted out then or under Saul or by David, Hezekiah, or even Mordecai and Esther. But Purim centers around the Book of Esther, that tale of self-help and national self-confidence.

Justin of Neapolis (Nablus) had been a Samaritan. In his dialogue with Trypho the Jew it is interesting to note how he seizes on Ex. 17:14. Joshua was victorious over Amalek because he had been given the name of Jesus

13. Cf. A. E. Cowley, *The Samaritan Liturgy*, 2 vols. (Oxford, 1909), vol. II, p. LXVII.

(Joshua). Jesus was the name of Him who spoke from the Bush, cf., Dial. LXXXV. Joshua, first called Hoshea, is (Num. 13:16) called by this name (Jesus). It is the name of Him who said to Moses "for My name is in him" cf., Dial. CXXVII. Justin Dial. CXXXI interprets Ex. 17:14 without specific reference (a) to writing (b) to a book. The memorial of Amalek was to "be recorded and the name of Jesus laid up in your understanding, saying that this is He who would blot out the memorial of Amalek from under heaven." The memorial of Amalek remained after the son of Nun, but it is through Jesus that demons were destroyed dreading His name; and those who believe in Him, out of all the nations, would be shown as God-fearing and peaceful men. Amalek was identified by the Jews at the end of the first century as Rome which was also called Edom. The destruction of Edom was an essential prerequisite of the (Jewish) Messianic Age, but for the Christian it would be real destruction of the memorial of Amalek if Amalek himself were changed.

We note that Justin either knows nothing of Esther and Mordecai or ignores them. But he is aware of the significance given to Amalek as both a demonic power and a world power of the moment against the Jews. I do not know of either significance given to Amalek in Samaritan literature. In Jewish, Amalek is the world power of the moment; yes, but he is not depicted as a demonic power, not earlier in Judaism than the mediaeval Cabbala. Christianity here anticipated Judaism. As to the Messiah or Taheb being a second Joshua, cf. our remarks above on the Samaritan Book of Joshua. As to Jesus (Joshua) being for Justin the "Name of the God of the Hebrews" this, on the one hand, reflects the Jewish Mystery of the *Shem ha-Meforash* Christianized; but, on the other hand, it bears witness to the faith of the Christian church to which Justin belonged, that Yahweh Savior God of the Psalms and Isaiah has revealed Himself in the flesh as Jesus.

Jn. 5:1 "After these things there was a feast of the Jews." Between Jesus' saying "There are yet four months to harvest" and His going up to Jerusalem to this feast of the Jews there are two days with the Samaritans. Jn. 4:40,43: "on the third day He goes to Galilee." There is no indication of how long He was in Galilee. Perhaps it is intended to be a brief visit, cf. vv. 45, 46. We have no way of telling. What is certain is that the gospel writer indicates that this feast of the Jews comes after the occasion when Jesus and His claims for Himself were received by the Samaritans. Remembering that this Gospel is obviously directing itself at the Samaritans as well as the Jews, it is but natural to describe the feast that follows, as indeed all the feasts in the Fourth Gospel, as "of the Jews." It was not of the Samaritans. If Jesus' coming to the Samaritans fell on Ẓimmuth Pesaḥ, it would be all the more natural, having

Samaritan readers in view, to refer to Purim, which comes after the Samaritan Zimmuth Pesah as "a feast of the Jews." It was not a Pentateuchal feast. Nor indeed was Hanukkah also mentioned in this Gospel. But, even the feast of Tabernacles was not kept according to the regulations of the written Torah but according to Jewish tradition. Samaritans could not keep the feast of Tabernacles or Passover after the Jewish manner.

If it is felt that the time period between the occasion when Jesus was with the Samaritans and a feast of the Jews is intended by the Fourth Gospel to be but of a few days, one could argue that the Jews had intercalated that year. Then "a feast of the Jews" would be the incomplete celebration of Purim in First Adar, only to be fulfilled fully with the reading of Esther at Purim in Second Adar. If, however, it were pressed that in Jn. 4:35 Jesus said "the fields are white already to harvest" there would be no need for intercalation that year. However, *Μετὰ ταῦτα* "after these things" does not necessarily mean immediately after.

"A feast of the Jews" Purim was not a pentateuchal feast; was it even a biblical feast? The answer depends on the state of the biblical Canon when this Gospel was written. In the last decade of the first century the Book of Esther was declared to be canonical, chiefly by the advocacy of R. Akiba. Part of the argument for the Book of Esther's inclusion in the Canon and holy scripture, was the identification of it with the book mentioned in Ex. 17:14: "Write this for a memorial in a book. . . ." The same verse also mentioned Yahweh's statement: "I will utterly blot out Amalek. . . ." In Esth. 3:1 Haman's genealogy includes Agag (the Amalekite king of David's time). It was thereby possible to connect Haman with Amalek and the Torah and Yahweh's promise of extirpation. Since the reading of Esther is the fundamental thing about Purim, this feast could not have been recognized by the Rabbis until they had managed to put Esther in the Canon. The man who lay thirty-eight years at the pool Bethesda, with its five porches, typifies Israel in the Wilderness. He was still in his infirmity.

Thus does the writer of the Fourth Gospel assess the Jews of his time. Jesus has first to establish that the man wants to be made whole (Jn. 5:6). The man (Jn. 5:7) does not categorically say "Yes" but excuses himself that he has "no man" to help him. "Man," incidentally, was used (cf. A. Marmorstein, *The Old Rabbinic Doctrine of God*, vol. I [Oxford 1927], pp. 65ff.) as a name of God. Jesus tells the man: "Arise, take up your bed, and walk." Güdemann[14] held that, in Aramaic, this would have been פּוּרְיָא and that

14. Cf. Frankel's Monatschrift, 37. Jahrgang, Das IV. (Johannes–), Evangelium und der Rabbinismus, p. 298.

this word for litter was a pun on Purim פּוּרְיָא in Aramaic. The Aramaic word is probably a loan word from the Greek *φορεῖον*. The Greek word, however, which the Fourth Gospel uses, is *κράβατος*. Güdemann held that the "feast of the Jews" (in Jn. 5) is Purim. There was in this gospel another non-pentateuchal feast, Hanukkah, which was only established in Rabbinic Judaism about the same time as Purim. In fact, by then there were five feasts: Purim, Passover, Weeks (Pentecost), Tabernacles, and Hanukkah (the Winter Tabernacles). Purim was a sort of latter-day Passover, self-help variety. If, however, Rosh ha-Shanah and Yom Kippur are included, though not feasts, there were seven. In considering the pool Bethesda with its five porches, we should carefully distinguish between the pool and the five porches. The pool (=water, cf. Jn. 5:7) presumably is an allegorical expression for the Torah.[15] The five porches have, in the past, been interpreted as the Five books of the Law. While this might be justified, with difficulty, as setting form (the five porticoes) as over against content (the teaching itself), one must remember in dealing with the Fourth Gospel that the writer knew the living issues of Judaism of his time. One of these was biblical canon. Most of the discussion centered on the Hagiographa, e.g., Song of Songs, Ecclesiastes, Esther. These, along with Ruth and Lamentations, form the five Megilloth or Scrolls. Eventually each of these Megilloth came to be individually associated with some festive or sacred occasion. Song of Songs at Passover, Ruth at Pentecost, Lamentations at the 9th of Ab, Ecclesiastes at the Feast of Tabernacles. Esther was already definitely associated with Purim. It could be that this story of the paralytic in the five porches at Bethesda, who never reached the water in the pool, is attacking the use of the five Megilloth on festive and sacred occasions and Esther, in particular, as keeping people away from the Torah and the possibility of hearing it speak for itself. Actually Esther was in a class by itself as at this period, and for long thereafter only it was read publicly, the others privately. The Samaritan use of their book of Joshua may also indirectly be criticized in passing.

Purim could fall on a Sabbath, though the Scroll would be read earlier and the Purim festive meal be on the morrow. On the Sabbath itself the Parashah of Amalek is read. Jesus told the man to rise up and take up his bed and walk, and the Jews (v. 10) said: "It is the Sabbath and it is not lawful for you to take up your bed." There is no recognition that the paralytic of thirty-eight years was now healed; that the Sabbath and the Law was being broken was more significant. It is all the more ironical in that when Mordecai (and Esther) decided to act on behalf of their people, they transgressed the

15. Cf. M. Shir. R. i. 2: "As water refreshes the body so does the Torah refresh the soul."

Torah in fasting at the Festival of Passover. Jn. 5:15–18 sums up the two significant areas of conflict between Jesus and the Jews, i.e., early Christianity and Judaism—(a) attitude to the Law; (b) who Jesus is. It is significant that it is from this feast, Purim, that the Fourth Gospel made the Jews seek to kill Jesus. The Evangelist must have attached very considerable importance to this feast. But so did the Jews. Later it was held that of the Bible only the Torah and the Scroll of Esther will remain in the world to come,[16] when only Purim and Yom Kippurim will remain of the feasts.[17]

In Jn. 5 Jesus cites God His Father as witness as to who He is, ibid. and in v. 38 tells His opponents that they have not God's word abiding in them since they do not believe Him (Jesus). In v. 39 He says that they search the scriptures because they think that in them they have eternal life. But these very scriptures testify of Him. Scriptures could be taken in the Jewish technical sense of Kethubim the third section of the Jewish Canon of the O.T. which was under discussion in A.D. 90 and to which the Five Megilloth (see above) belonged. Eternal life cannot mean eternal life in a Johannine sense but life in the Messianic Age. Jesus says these very Kethubim bear witness of Him. Where could the Book of Esther be understood as so doing? Possibly Mordecai's words to Esther (Esth. 3:14) prior to her resolve to go in and beard Ahasuerus in his den. "For if you altogether hold your peace at this time, then shall relief and deliverance arise to the Jews from another place." "From another place" could mean God, vf. *Maqom*, as a name of God. The Targums do insert "God" here. The Psalms were, along with the five Megilloth in the third section of the Canon, the Hagiographa. Further (Ps. 22) is in T. B. Meg. 15b and in M. Psalms (Ps. 22) associated with Esther. In all four gospels it forms the basis for the haggadic midrash of the crucifixion of Jesus. It is not that Esther did not go in to Ahasuerus, it is not that she did not confound Haman's devilish schemes, but she did not, even so, finish Amalek. This the Jews, smarting from defeat and destruction at the hands of Rome (whom they now called Amalek), did not recognize. Certainly they did not realize that her methods were not enough. Jesus (v. 43) especially castigates them for not receiving Him who had come in His Father's name, whereas "if another came in his own name, him you will receive." If this feast is Purim, this is a cut at Mordecai and Esther who, admittedly, acted on their own initiative. In v. 44ff. there appears to be an attack on Rabbinism and the Oral Law, cf. also v. 47, cf. "if you do not believe his writings." However, Jesus will not accuse them, Moses will do that. If this feast is Purim, this last

16. Cf. T. J. Meg. 1, 70d.
17. Cf. M. Mishle 9, 61.

verse (v. 45) becomes the more comprehensible. The scroll of Esther had very recently been declared Holy Writ, mainly by the advocacy of Rabbi Akiba. It was written in the same manner as the Law and was read like the Law. The main argument for its inclusion had been what Yahweh said to Moses. Ex. 17:14: "Write this for a memorial in a book and rehearse it in the ears of Joshua." We have seen above how Justin interpreted this. The Epistle of Barnabas, ch. XII, has "What, again, says Moses to Jesus (Joshua) the son of Nave, when he gave him this name, as being a prophet, with this view only that all the people might hear that the Father would reveal all things concerning His son Jesus to the son of Nave?" Whereas the Epistle of Barnabas (ibid.) does not associate the victory by Joshua over Amalek with his having the name of Jesus, as does Justin, he does associate (Ex. 17) Jesus and the ultimate victory over Amalek. The Epistle of Barnabas (ibid.) continues: "This name (Jesus) then being given him when he sent him to spy out the land, he said: "Take a book into thy hands, and write what the Lord declares, that the Son of God will in the last days cut off from the roots all the house of Amalek."

This is specifically referring, however, to Ex. 17:14, the verse used to justify the inclusion of the Book of Esther in Holy Writ. It is significant too that in the Targum Jerushalmi to Ex. 17:14, as apparently part of Yahweh's oath (Ex. 17:16) "the first king who will sit upon the throne of the kingdom of the sons of Israel, Saul, the son of Kish, will set the battle in array against the house of Amalek and will slay them: and those of them that remain will Mordecai and Esther destroy. The Lord has said by His Word that the memory of Amalek shall perish to the age of ages." Targum Pseudo-Jonathan, on the same verse: "Because the Word of the Lord has sworn by the throne of His glory, that He by His Word will fight against those of the house of Amalek, and destroy them to three generations: from the generation of this world, from the generation of the Messiah, and from the generation of the world to come." These two Targums show a significant difference in interpretation of this verse. Targum Jerushalmi shows how it was referred to Mordecai and Esther. The Epistles of Barnabas and Justin show how the early Christians referred it to Jesus. It has been customary to see Jn. 5:46 "for he (Moses) wrote of me" as referring to Dt. 18:18 and Num. 21:9, cf. also Jn. 3:14, but one would submit that Ex. 17:14 is specifically here intended and is the more apposite.

Note in particular the command of Yahweh to Moses in that verse: "Write this for a memorial in a book and rehearse it in the ears of Joshua (Jesus)" LXX and the statement in Jn. 5:46: "for he (Moses) wrote of me."

We have seen that Jesus' visit to the Samaritans would fall at their Ẓimmuth Pesaḥ. The "feast of the Jews" mentioned after that would, calendarwise, be Purim. M. Ps. 57. 2 and T. B. Meg. 7a state that Heaven (i.e. God) approved the Rabbis' decision after they had declared Esther Holy Writ.

They were not lacking in self-confidence. Is Jn. 5:15, 43, 44 written criticizing such procedure? The Written Law and Moses seemed to be set aside, or so the argument ran. And it was because they thought more of their own opinions than either the expressed word of God or that of Moses that they could not, or would not, recognize Jesus' claim to be Son of God sent by His Father. The then current or very recent Rabbinic approval of the canonicity of Esther and its injunctions (now as word of God) to celebrate Purim annually must have worried quite a few Jews. It showed the power of the Rabbis and it seemed to encroach on Passover. If Moses had meant it to be, he would have spelled it out. Where did he write of Esther or Mordecai? The situation was an opportunity for the Christian apologist and that was what the Fourth Evangelist was.

For the full implications of the above, vis-à-vis the Fourth Gospel as a whole, see my forthcoming book, *The Fourth Gospel and the Jews.*

# Le Cadre Littéraire de Michée V:1–5

J. COPPENS

PARMI les textes généralement considérés comme se rapportant au roi sauveur de l'avenir, c'est-à-dire au roi messianique, l'oracle de Mich. V:1–5 occupe une place privilégiée.[1] Toutefois son interprétation soulève pas mal de difficultés. En particulier, l'intégrité de la péricope et son contexte littéraire font l'objet de discussions. Il convient en particulier de se demander s'il y a une connexion littéraire entre Mich. IV:14 et V:1–5, puis s'il importe de maintenir comme parties intégrantes de la péricope les vv. 4–5 et 2.[2]

Le verset 14 du chapitre IV est d'une interprétation difficile. Aucune version satisfaisante ne s'impose. Il semble bien que l'hagiographe vise une situation pénible où se trouve Sion, la ville royale. Si la cité n'est pas déjà occupée par des étrangers, elle est pour le moins assiégée ou menacée de l'être. Les belligérants humilient le juge d'Israël.[3] Mais quelle que soit la version du verset en cause, il faut convenir qu'il se présente bien comme une introduction à l'oracle de Mich. V:1–5. A l'humiliation du *šōphét* de Jérusalem,[4] l'hagiographe oppose le glorieux destin du souverain de l'avenir à naître de la souche d'Isaï à Bethléem.

1. Lire sur le messianisme, J. Coppens, *Le messianisme royal. Les origines. Son développement. Son accomplissement*, dans *Lectio Divina*, Paris, 1969.

2. Voir le dernier article sur l'oracle en discussion: J. T. Willis, *Micah IV:14–V,5–a Unit*, dans *VT* 18 (1968): 529–47.

3. Le "juge d'Israël" est à identifier vraisemblablement avec le "roi" de Jérusalem. C'est l'opinion défendue par A. Weiser, *Das Buch der zwölf Kleinen Propheten*, t. I, 5e édit., dans *ATD*, Goettingen, 1907, p. 272, n. 1 et par J. T. Willis, art. cit., p. 533, n. 1.

4. Il n'est pas requis de supposer avec S. Mowinckel que Jérusalem est de fait occupée par les troupes ennemies et dès lors que le texte nous transpose après l'exil: cfr. *Det Gamle*

Selon d'aucuns, cette interprétation du v. 14 se confirme par la structure des chapitres IV et V de Michée, qui se composeraient de sept péricopes comprenant toutes deux éléments, à savoir une allusion à une situation de malheur et l'annonce d'un salut plus ou moins imminent.[5] Quoiqu'il en soit de cette structuration, la connexion de III: 14 et V:1–5 nous semble devoir être maintenue conformément d'ailleurs à l'avis exprimé entre autres par H. Oort, E. Stave, J. Ridderbos, W. Beyerlin, S. Mowinckel.[6] Pour sa part, Albin Van Hoonacker proposa la même connexion,[7] et A. George l'a suivi.[8]

En ce qui concerne l'intégrité de la péricope, il importe de se demander en premier lieu si les versets 4–5 lui appartiennent. Pas mal d'auteurs le contestent et à cet effet ils font valoir diverses raisons. Il n'y a pas de suite logique entre 1–3 et 4–5; au contraire, quelques antinomies frappantes se font jour: (1) alors qu'en 1–3 Yahvé est censé devoir sauver le pays sans recours à une force militaire quelconque, en 4–5 l'épée assurera la victoire; (2) tandis que 1–3 entrevoient l'extension du royaume du souverain de l'avenir jusqu'aux confins de la terre, les versets 4–5 ne songent qu'à une victoire sur l'Assyrie; (3) en 1–3, le roi-sauveur est un monarque à naître de la race de David; en revanche, les versets 4–5 ne font pas mention d'un davidide; au reste ils ne font pas appel à un seul sauveur mais à "sept pasteurs"; (4) enfin, c'est Yahvé lui-même qui suscite le roi sauveur en 1–3, tandis que l'initiative d'installer sept pasteurs dérive du peuple.

Ces difficultés, observe-t-on, concernent surtout les versets 4b–5ab. En revanche, puisque dans 4a et 5cde le sujet est au singulier, rien n'empêche qu'à la rigueur ces deux bouts de phrase se rapportent au monarque idéal entrevu dans 1–3. Dans ces conditions on traduirait 4a + 5cde: "Et il sera la paix, et il (nous) délivrera d'Assur quand celui-ci viendra dans notre pays et foulera aux pieds nos frontières."

Mais à ce sauvetage de 4a + 5cde s'opposent diverses difficultés. D'abord la traduction de 4a soulève des problèmes. Lire avec É. Dhorme:[9] "Et c'est

---

*Testamente. De senere Profeter*, Oslo, 1944, p. 686. S. Mowinckel interprète Mich. IV:14 comme impliquant l'absence de roi à Jérusalem. L'hagiographe viserait selon lui le gouverneur civil de la cité ou peut-être le grand prêtre.

5. J. T. Willis, art. cit., p. 532. Voir aussi B. Renaud, *Structure et attaches littéraires de Michée IV–V*, dans *Cahiers RB*, Paris, 1964, ouvrage dont les conclusions ne me paraissent pas s'imposer.

6. Cités ibid., p. 535, n. 1.

7. A. Van Hoonacker, *Les Douze Petits Prophètes traduits et commentés*, dans *EB*, Paris, 1908, p. 388.

8. A. George, *Michée, Sophonie, Nahum*, 2e éd., dans *La Sainte Bible de Jérusalem*, Paris, 1958, p. 35.

9. É. Dhorme, *La Bible. L'Ancien Testament*, t. II, Paris, 1959, p. 784.

lui qui sera la paix," c'est supposer dans le texte hébreu la présence du pronom *hû* alors que nous y lisons *zèh.*[10] Puis la reprise de 4b en 5d: "Quand Assur viendra dans notre pays" paraît indiquer que nous sommes en présence d'une inclusion rédactionnelle,[11] encadrant une parole prophétique primitivement indépendante.[12] C'est à cette solution que se résout S. Mowinckel, qui traduit l'oracle en ces termes:

*Quand Assur entrera dans notre pays,*
*et quand il foulera notre sol,*
*alors nous susciterons sept pasteurs,*
*voire huit préposés d'hommes contre lui.*
*Ils raseront Assur avec l'épée*
*Et le pays de Nimrod avec un glaive affilé.*[13]

Albin Van Hoonacker parle également d'une glose,[14] mais, se rendant compte de la valeur de *zèh* en Mich. V:4a, il interprète le passage comme un lemme introduisant l'oracle: "Et la paix se fera ainsi". Quant à Mich. V: 5cde, il rapporte cette phrase au prince idéal de l'avenir.

A mon avis les objections soulevées contre l'authenticité michéenne de Mich. V:4–5 sont valables. Rallions-nous pour l'incipit provisoirement à la version de Van Hoonacker: "Et ainsi viendra la paix,"[15] mais, en désaccord avec lui, incluons Mich. V:5cde parmi les additions. Ce bout de phrase est un élément rédactionnel, tout comme V:4a.[16]

10. Cfr. A. Van Hoonacker, op. cit., p. 391.
11. Cfr. S. Mowinckel, op. cit., p. 687. L'auteur attribue à R les vv. 4a et 5 cde.
12. Ibid., p. 686, note: "Er oprinnelig et selvstendig profetord."
13. Ibid., p. 867. Nous rendons par "glaive affilé" les mots "med kvasse 'odd'" de S. Mowinckel. A. Van Hoonacker proposait de corriger et de traduire "glaive dégâiné." Reprenant une suggestion de Ehrlich (*Randglossen,* p. 284), K. J. Catcart suggère de lire בִּפְתִחֶיהָ "with its own drawn weapon." Les "sept pasteurs" ravageront l'Assyrie avec les propres armes de ce pays dont sans doute ils sont censés s'être emparés: *Notes on Micah 5:4–5,* dans *Bibl.* 49 (1968), pp. 511–14.
14. Op cit., pp. 391–92.
15. Ibid., p. 391.
16. Cfr. S. Mowinckel, op. cit., p. 687. Dans *Notes on Micah 5:4–5* (*Bibl.* 49 [1968]: 511–14), Kevin J. Catcart, faisant appel à l'ougaritique, où *d/dt* peut avoir le sens d'un relatif ou d'un déterminatif (ibid., p. 512), propose de traduire *zèh šālôm,* "the One of Peace," "and He will be the One of Peace." Si l'on accepte cette version, on peut garder notre hypothèse, tout en la modifiant légèrement. Dans ces conditions, 5a s'intègre à la péricope touchant le roi de l'avenir:

5a. *et il sera Celui de la paix,*
5cde. *et il nous délivrera d'Assur,*
*quand celui-ci entrera dans notre pays*
*et foulera nos frontières.*

Dès lors l'oracle de Michée comprendrait les versets 1, 3, 4a, 5cde. Il reste toutefois que les versets 4a et 5cde peuvent avoir été ajoutés à l'oracle primitif pour l'actualiser par rapport à l'Assyrie. Il se peut aussi que cette actualisation ait comporté seulement 5cde. Seul 4a serait dès lors à rattacher à l'oracle primitif.

Pour maintenir l'authenticité de Mich. V:4–5, on a appelé l'attention sur la structure de la péricope qui comprendrait trois membres dont le premier et le troisième se correspondraient.[17] Souscrivons à cette remarque mais n'en déduisons pas la même conclusion. Cette facture harmonieuse prouve tout simplement que le rédacteur-interpolateur procéda avec un sens artistique à l'amplification du texte.

Il reste à considérer le verset 2 que Van Hoonacker traduisait: "Il les livrera donc jusqu'au temps où celle qui doit enfanter ait enfanté. Et le reste de ses frères reviendra aux enfants d'Israël."[18] Les obscurités et les anomalies ne manquent pas. D'abord il importe de suppléer un sujet.[19] Puis il s'agit pour d'aucuns de comprendre "donner" au sens "d'abandonner."[20] Probléme plus grave: qui sont "les frères" visés par le prophète? Enfin comment identifier la mystérieuse personne dont la maternité est envisagée et proclamée comme le terme du salut?

On observe que les "frères" peuvent s'entendre soit d'autorités dispersées, soit de membres de la dynastie davidique déportés en Babylonie, soit des habitants exilés du royaume du Nord.[21] La première hypothèse n'est guère retenue. A. Van Hoonacker préfère la troisième en insistant non seulement sur le retour matériel des "frères" mais sur leur conversion à Yahvé.[22] S. Mowinckel opine résolument pour la deuxième.[23] Il semble en effet peu vraisemblable de désigner les habitants du Nord comme "frères" du roi idéal de l'avenir. S'ils étaient visés, pourquoi ne pas les appeler de leur nom et parler clairement d'un retour d'Israël à Juda?

Quant à la *yôlēdāh*, un article récent étudia tous les textes qui présentent une certaine accointance.[24] Sur la base de cet examen, l'auteur estime que la *yôlēdāh* n'est pas à interpréter en fonction d'Is. VII:14. Elle ne viserait ni la mère du roi idéal, ni la ville d'où il sera originaire, ni sa tribu ou sa souche. L'expression concerne plutôt la *yôlēdāh* dont il est explicitement question dans un contexte relativement proche, à savoir Jérusalem (IV:10). Entendue

17. J. T. Willis, *art. cit.*, p. 543.
18. Op. cit., pp. 390–91.
19. E. Dhorme, op. cit., p. 784, n. 2.
20. C'est la version de É. Dhorme, op. cit., p. 784. A. Van Hoonacker et S. Mowinckel choisissent un terme plus fort et plus exact: "il les livrera." Cfr. aussi *The Bible. An American Translation. The Old Testament under the Editorship of J. M. Powis Smith*, ~~10 éd.~~, Chicago, 1946, p. 855: "he will give them up."
21. Cfr. S. Mowinckel, op. cit., p. 686, en note.
22. Op cit., p. 390.
23. Op. cit., p. 686, en note.
24. Th. Lescow, *Das Geburtsmotiv in den messianischen Weissagungen*, dans *ZAW* 67 (1967): 172–207. Cfr. J. Coppens, *Le messianisme royal*, pp. 23–31.

de Jérusalem, l'expression peut signifier soit le temps de détresse que la ville aura à subir et à traverser, soit le temps qui suivra la période de malheur, temps auquel elle pourra enfanter sans douleurs (Is. LXVI:7). Comme le passage du Trito-Isaïe, passage à rapprocher d'Is. LIV:1–6, apparaît dans une collection d'oracles, qui envisagent également le retour des exilés (Is. LX:4), il n'est pas absolument interdit de penser que l'auteur de Mich. V:2, surtout s'il agit d'un glossateur tardif, vise la période de restauration de la Ville sainte et du Peuple élu. Toutefois on n'est pas en droit d'exclure, vu la proximité de Mich. V:10, que l'hagiographe puisse également songer aux détresses de la captivité.[25] Dans ce dernier cas, le texte signifierait que le roi idéal ne viendra pas avant que Jérusalem n'ait traversé les souffrances de l'exil babylonien (cfr. Mich. IV:10). C'est au moment et à partir de cet exil que le salut viendra et que la restauration de la lignée davidique se réalisera. Alors, les davidides exilés regagneront leur patrie et ils se rallieront autour du rejeton de leur race que Yahvé aura suscité pour leur salut et celui de toute la nation.[26]

Nous estimons donc que le verset 2 constitue une glose qu'il est difficile de dater. Ce caractère de glose explique, ce nous semble, l'absence de sujet et celle de précision touchant le pronom suffixe du verbe "donner." Pour le glossateur, il allait de soi qu'il s'agissait de "Dieu" livrant les "enfants d'Israël" à la détresse jusqu'à la venue du Sauveur.

Traduisons donc l'oracle comme suit:

IV:14 *Et maintenant, lacère-toi,*
*Fille habituée à être assiégée!*[27]
*Le siège, on l'a dressé contre nous.*
*Ils frappent de la verge sur la joue*
*le Juge d'Israël.*[28]
V:1 *Mais quant à toi, Bethléem, Ephrata,*
*trop petite pour être comptée*
*parmi les unités militaires de Juda,*[29]

25. C'est la solution à laquelle nous nous rallions finalement: *Le messianisme royal*, p. 88.

26. Signalons à titre de curiosité une exégèse bien curieuse de Dom Augustin Calmet, *Les XII Petits Prophètes*, dans *Commentaire littéral sur tous les Livres de l'Ancien et du Nouveau Testament*, Paris, 1719, pp. 364–65. Lui aussi songe aux détresses de l'exil babylonien, mais la *yôlēdāh*, n'est pas Israël en travail d'enfant, mais Babylone appelée à rendre la liberté aux captifs "qu'elle tenait comme enfermés dans son sein." L'exégète bénédictin semble donc avoir entrevu une part de l'interprétation qui nous paraît pour l'instant la meilleure.

27. Nous avons déjà noté qu'aucune version n'est réellement suffisante. Pour "habituée à être assiégée," cfr. É. König, *Hebräisches und aramäisches Wörterbuch zum Alten Testament*, 2e et 3e éd., Leipzig, 1922, p. 55a: "du angriffsgewöhnte . . ."

28. On a songé aux ennemis qui s'apprêtent à fouler aux pieds les assiégés.

29. D'autres traductions sont proposées, par exemple "clans" (Van Hoonacker, American Version, A. George, É. Dhorme, A. Weiser).

*de toi il sortira pour moi*[30]
*celui qui deviendra souverain en Israël,*
*et dont les origines sont de toute antiquité,*
*depuis les jours d'antan,—*
2 *c'est pourquoi (dans l'entretemps)*
*il les abandonnera*
*jusqu'à l'époque*
*où celle qui doit engendrer aura engendré,*
*et (alors) le reste de ses frères*
*reviendra vers les fils d'Israël,*[31]*—*
3 *Il se tiendra debout et fera paître*
*par la puissance de Yahvé,*
*par la gloire du nom de Yahvé son Dieu,*
*et ils pourront s'établir*[32]
*alors qu'il grandira*
*jusqu'aux confins de la terre.*

A accepter notre interprétation du verset 2 et notre version, Mich. V:1–3 ne peut plus servir à jeter quelque lumière sur la figure de la ᶜ*almah* d'Is. VII:14 et sur la naissance d'Emmanuel y envisagée.[33] De même, il n'y a plus lieu, semble-ti-il, de faire appel aux prétendus parallèles ougaritiques pour expliquer la *yôlēdāh*.[34] Que ces textes puissent avoir une certaine importance pour le texte isaïen est un problème distinct que le présent article n'a pas à résoudre.[35]

30. L'affirmation et la construction offrent quelques difficultés. D'où les tentatives de corriger le texte: cfr. S. Mowinckel, loc. cit., p. 686. E. Sellin, *Das Zwölfprophenbuch*, 3e éd., Leipzig, 1929. J. A. Fitzmyer, *L as a Preposition and a Particle in Micah 5:1*, dans *CBL* 18 (1956): 12–13. S. J. Schwantes, *A Critical Study of the Text of Micah.* Unpublished dissertation, Johns Hopkins University, Baltimore, 1962.

J. T. Willis, *Mmk ly yṣ*ᵓ *in Micah 5:1*, dans *JQR* 58 (1968): 317–22, maintient le texte masorétique. Selon lui, l'intention de l'hagiographe est d'indiquer que le roi idéal de l'avenir acceptera le statut de vassal de Yahvé. Willis confirme sa manière de voir par un examen du sens qui revient à *yāsa*ᵓ dans divers passages.

31. Quelle que soit l'interprétation adoptée: que l'on songe à Israël–Sion qui arrive au bout des douleurs de l'enfantement exilique ou que l'on préfère songer à Israël–Sion dotée par le Seigneur au lendemain de l'exil d'une fécondité merveilleuse, le glossateur songerait à la captivité babylonienne.

32. On sous/entend généralement "en sécurité."

33. C'est pourtant l'opinion la plus répandue: cfr. A. Weiser, op. cit., p. 274, et. S. Mowinckel, op. cit., p. 685, en note: "Både denne tanken (à savoir qu'une naissace mystérieuse est proche et qu'elle marquera la fin de la détresse du peuple de Dieu) og det mysteriøst-antydende uttrykk "fødersken" viser at vi her har å gjøre med en form av det samme forestillingskomplekset som i Jes. 7:10-17."

34. A. Weiser (op. cit., p. 274) renvoie à Ringgren, *ZAW* 64 (1952): 131, 136. W. Vischer, *Die Immanuelbotschaft im Rahmen des königlichen Zionfestes*, dans *Theol. Studien*, 1955, fasc. 45, p. 47 ss. W. Beyerlin, *Die Kulttraditionen Israels in der Verkündigung des Propheten Micha*, 1959, p. 78 ss.

35. Cfr. J. Coppens, *La prophétie de la* ᶜ*Almah*, dans *EThL* 52 (1952): 648–78, surtout, pp. 656–57, 664–65, 668–71. Le Même, *Le Messianisme royal*, pp. 69–76.

# Phoenician Elements in Isaiah 52:13–53:12

MITCHELL DAHOOD, S.J.

Few biblical passages teem with as many textual and exegetical difficulties as The Fourth Servant Song—or can display a longer bibliography. Since progress in interpretation must be preceded by improved understanding of the text and its grammar, this brief study will seek to clarify some grammatical points by assuming that the author of this song was a diaspora Jew living in Phoenicia. Already in his commentary on Isaiah, Bernhard Duhm[1] suggested that the author of chapters 40–55, with the exception of later additions, composed his work around 540 B.C. some place in the Lebanon or Phoenicia. Duhm considered the object of the present study to be a later insertion and, presumably, not composed in the Lebanon or Phoenicia. By assuming, contrary to Duhm, a Phoenician provenance of this poem, we may submit the following translation:

13 Behold the Exalted and Sublime and Most Lofty
will prosper his servant,
14 though full many were aghast at him.
Truly was his countenance disfigured by men,
and his comeliness by the sons of men.
15 Truly he startled mighty nations,
before him kings shut their mouths,
For they saw what had never been told to them,
and what they had never heard they pondered.

1. *Das Buch Jesais übersetzt und erklärt* (3rd rev. ed.; Göttingen, 1914), p. XV.

1 Who has believed what we have heard,
and Yahweh's arm—before whom has it been bared?
2 Yet he shot up like a sapling in his presence,
and like a root out of parched soil.
No comeliness was his nor majesty that we should envy him,
no composure that we should desire him.
3 He was despised as the most stupid of men,
a man of sorrows and known by disease.
And since he turned his face from us,
we considered him a despicable cipher.
4 Yet our diseases he himself bore,
and our sorrows he carried,
While we considered him stricken,
smitten by God and afflicted.
5 But he was pierced for our rebellious deeds,
crushed for our iniquities.
The penalty we should have paid fell upon him,
and by his stripes we were healed.
6 All of us had strayed like sheep,
each of us had gone his own way,
While Yahweh made light upon him
the guilt of us all.
7 He was harshly treated, but he submitted,
and opened not his mouth.
Like a lamb he was led to the slaughter,
and like a ewe before her shearers;
He was silent and opened not his mouth.
8 Without restraint and without moderation he was taken away,
and who gave his life a thought?
For he was cut off from the land of the living,
for the rebellion of his people he was struck from them.
9 His grave was put with the wicked,
and with the rich his burial mound,
Even though he had not done violence,
nor was there falsehood from his mouth.
10 But Yahweh willed to crush him and to pierce him;
certainly was his life made a guilt offering.
Still he will see offspring, prolong his days,
and Yahweh's will shall advance because of him.
11 With the anguish of his soul he was sated,
he was soaked by his sweat,
But the Just One will vindicate his servant before the great,
since he himself carried their iniquities.
12 Therefore I will give him a share with the great,
and with the powerful he shall divide spoil,
Because he exposed himself to death,
and with the rebellious was counted.
It was he who bore the sins of many,
and made entreaty for the rebellious.

13. *the Exalted and Sublime and Most Lofty*. That *yārûm wᵉniśśāʾ wᵉgābah mᵉʾōd* should be understood as divine appellatives is suggested by Isa. 57:15a, *kî kōh ʾāmar rām wᵉniśśāʾ*, "For thus speaks the Exalted and Sublime." It probably follows that *yārûm wᵉniśśāʾ* in our verse are also divine appellatives, the former deriving from *yrm*, a by-form of *rwm*, discussed by me in *Psalms I*, pp. 118, 168; *Psalms II*, pp. 85, 106. The root of the third appellative *gābah mᵉʾōd*, "Most Lofty," is discussed in *Psalms I*, p. 62; see also R. Gordis, *The Book of God and Man: A Study of Job* (Chicago, 1965), p. 329, who points out that the very common title *gābōʾāh*, "the Lofty," in rabbinic literature is probably a development of the usage in Ps. 138:6.

*will prosper his servant*. Once God is identified as the subject of *yaśkîl*, the suffix of *ʿabdî* parses as the Phoenician suffix of the third person singular;[2] five other instances of this suffix will be identified in vss. 14, 8, 9, 10, 11. Thus *yaśkîl ʿabdî* may semantically be compared with vs. 11, *yaṣdîq ṣaddîq ʿabdî*, "The Just One will vindicate his servant."

14. *full many were aghast at him*. Dividing consonantal *šmmw ʿlyk rbym* to read *šāmᵉmû ʿālēy kī rabbîm*, and parsing *ʿālēy* as another Phoenician form (cf. Kilamuwa 8, *ʿly*, "before him"), *kī* becomes emphatic as in Ps. 32:9–10, *kī rabbîm*, "How many!"[3]

*Truly*. The force of *kēn* seems to be emphatic, as also in vs. 15.

*disfigured by men*. Repointing MT *mišḥat* to hophal participle *mošḥat*, attested in Prov. 25:26, with *mēʾîš* expressing the agent; (cf. Brown-Driver-Briggs, *Lexicon*, p. 580a, and *Psalms III* on Ps. 102:5). This line echoes Isa. 50:6, "I gave my back to the smiters, and my cheeks to the pluckers."

15. *he startled*. The preceding *qtl* verb *šāmᵉmû*, "were aghast," and the following *qtl* verb *rāʾû*, "they saw," suggest that the *yqtl* form *yazzeh* likewise describes a past event. Second Isaiah frequently employs *yqtl* verbs in descriptions of the past; e.g., 40:26; 42:19,23; 43:2,9,17; 50:2-3; 51:2; 53:7, 12; 54:6.

*before him*. For this meaning of *ʿālāyw*, see P. Suárez, *Verbum Domini* 42 (1964): 71–80, and *Psalms II*, p. 120, on Ps. 66:5, *nôrāʾ ʿᵃlîlāh ʿal bᵉnê ʾādām*, "terrifying in action before men." This meaning recurs in Isa. 53:1.

2. Consult *Psalms I*, pp. 10–11; L. Sabottka, *BZ* 13 (1969): 242, 244. Failure to recognize the nature of this suffix may serve to explain the variety of translation proposed for this line; another new version has been submitted by G. R. Driver in *In Memoriam Paul Kahle*, eds. M. Black and G. Fohrer, *BZAW* 103 (Berlin, 1968): p. 103, "Lo! My servant shall be bound and lifted up, he shall be raised aloft very high."

3. As read and parsed in *Psalms I*, p. 197. Cf. also Ps. 131:2, *kaggāmūl ʿālēy* (MT *ʿālay*) *napšî*, "Like the weaned child before him is my soul," and Mal. 2:15, *ûbᵉʾēšet nᵉʿûrēy kī* (MT *nᵉʿûrekā*) *ʾal yibgōd*, "And let no one ever be faithless to the wife of his youth," as read and analyzed in *Bibl.* 49 (1968): 365.

*shut their mouths.* Continuing the description of *yazzeh*, the *yqtl* verb *yiqpeṣû* states a past event; 1QIs[a] seems to have experienced some difficulty with this verb, reading *wqpṣw* for MT *yqpṣw*. The gesture described here may be compared with Job 21:5, "Look at me and be aghast, and lay your hand upon your mouth,"[4] and Job 29:9, "Princes refrained from speech, and laid their hand upon their mouth."

1. *and Yahweh's arm.* A neat instance of *casus pendens* which is obliterated in, say, RSV, "And to whom has the arm of the Lord been revealed?"

*before whom.* Both 1QIs[a] and 1QIs[b] read *ʾl my* for MT *ʿl my*, an indication that the true force of *ʿl* escaped them. As in 52:15, *ʿal* carries the meaning "before"; compare Isa. 52:10, *ḥāśap yhwh ʾet zerōaʿ qodšô leʿênê kol haggôyīm*, "Yahweh has stripped his holy arm before the eyes of all the nations."

2. *a root . . . comeliness.* This biblically unique collocation of *šōreš* and *tōʾar* recurs in the contemporary sixth-century Phoenician Inscription of Eshmunazor, 11–12, *ʾl ykn lm šrš lmṭ wpr lmʿl wtʾr bḥym tht šmš*, "May they have no root down below and no fruit up above, nor comeliness among the living under the sun!"[5] This rapprochement assumes even greater significance by reason of the typically Phoenician plural *ʾîšîm* in the next verse.

*that we should envy him. Psalms I*, p. 302, documents this meaning of *nirʾēhû*, which receives the *athnach* rather than *hādar*, as in MT. The suspicion that *wenirʾēhû* might be an addition (BHK) is laid to rest by both 1QIs[a], which, however, reads *nrʾnw* with the energic ending, and 1QIs[b].

3. *the most stupid of men.* P. J. Calderone (*CBQ* 24 [1962]: 418–19) discusses this translation of *ḥadal ʾîšîm.*

*men.* Phoenician plural *ʾîšîm* occurs elsewhere in Ps. 141:4 and Prov. 8:4, both heavily Phoenicianizing texts; *Psalms III*, (*ad loc.*), examines the Phoenician terms in Ps. 141, and my article, "Proverbs 8, 22–31: Translation and commentary," in *CBQ* 30 (1968): 512–21, examines this passage in the light of Albright's insight that Proverbs 8–9 are based on an original Canaanite text.[6] Our text equally teems with Phoenician spellings and forms. Duhm, *Jesaia*, p. 368, finds the sequence *ʾîšîm ʾîš* "hässlich," and accordingly emends the Phoenician plural *ʾîšîm* to *ʾanāšîm*. What would Duhm have done to UT,

4. On the significance of this gesture, see Dahood in *The Bible in Current Catholic Thought* (*Gruenthaner Memorial Volume*; New York, 1962), p. 64; M. H. Pope, *Job* (The Anchor Bible, vol. 15; Garden City, N.Y., 1965), p. 144.

5. In the revised edition of *ANET* (1955), Franz Rosenthal tentatively translates *wtʾr bḥym*, "and *may they be cursed* among the living," with the note "Or perhaps: 'may they not have any stately appearance'" (p. 505). The biblical collocation of *šōreš* and *tōʾar* clearly sustains the footnote translation.

6. Cf. *From the Stone Age to Christianity* (Baltimore, 1940), p. 283.

69:11–12, *šmk at ygrš ygrš grš ym grš ym lksih,* "Your own name is Driver; Driver, drive Yamm, drive Yamm from his throne"?

*sorrows.* Here the prophet employs the feminine plural *makʾōbôt,* but in the next verse he uses masculine *makʾōbênû* with no appreciable difference of meaning. 1QIs[b] found this variation irksome and read both as masculine plural, *mkʾbym* here and *mkʾbyw* in vs. 4. But this levelling does not commend itself in view of the numerous nouns in Northwest Semitic exhibiting both masculine and feminine plurals. For present purposes, an instructive parallel is supplied by UT, 2001:rev:5–6, where the masculine plural *kbkbm,* "stars," is followed in the next line by the feminine plural *kbkbt.*

*known by disease.* Frequently translated "acquainted with sickness," a version not reflecting the qal passive participle *yᵉdûaᶜ* (1QIs[a] reads active participle *ywdᶜ* and 1QIs[b] has *ydᶜ*), the phrase *yᵉdûaᶜ ḥōlî* becomes more intelligible when compared with UT, 127:35–36, *km aẖt ᶜrš mdw anšt ᶜrš zbln,* "Thus you have made the bed of illness your brother, you have made the bed of disease a companion." In the Kirta Legend the king brought sickness upon himself by his malfeasance—hence the active verbs—but the Servant was made acquainted with sickness through no sin of his own, hence the passive participle.

*he turned.* MT *mastēr,* which looks anomalous, may be due to *scriptio defectiva,* and ought to be repointed hiphil participle *mastīr.* 1QIs[a] reads hiphil participle *mstyr.* Most versions translate singular *mastīr* as plural (cf. Driver, "An object from which men turn their gaze"[7]). Aware of his personal ugliness and disfigurement, the Servant turned his face from his fellowmen.

*from us.* When the Servant is construed as the subject of *mastīr,* ambiguous *mimmennû,* "from him/us," assumes the latter meaning.

*we considered him.* Defectively spelled *ḥᵃšabnūhû* (cf. 1QIs[a] *ḥšbnwhw*) agrees with other instances of defective spelling in this song.

*a despicable cipher. nibzeh wᵉlōʾ* may be construed as hendiadys when *lōʾ* is parsed as a substantive "nothing, cipher," as proposed in *Biblica* 47 (1966): 408. Thus *nibzeh wᵉlōʾ ḥᵃsabnūhû* may be compared with Isa. 40:17, *kol haggôyīm kᵉʾayin negdô-m ʾepes wātōhû neḥšᵉbû lô,* "All the nations are as nothing before him; a blank cipher are they considered by him."

4. *our diseases.* The *scriptio defectiva* of plural *ḥᵒlāyēnû* (cf. 1QIs[a] *ḥlyynw* with the second *y* written above the first *y*) accords with Phoenician orthographic practice. A similar instance of defective spelling recurs in the next verse.

*he carried.* The longstanding proposal, based on some twenty manuscripts

7. See *In Memoriam Paul Kahle,* p. 103. Driver apparently construes *mastēr* as an infixed *-t-* form of *sûr,* against which he inveighed in *JSS* 10 (1965): 113.

as well as on the Syriac and Vulgate, to insert *hûʾ* before *sᵉbālām* is not sustained by either 1QIs[a] or 1QIs[b].

*we considered him.* As in vs. 3, *ḥᵃšabnūhû* is spelled defectively, and 1QIs[a] again supplies the full spelling *ḥšbnwhw*.

5. *our rebellious deeds.* MT plural *pᵉšāʿēnû* is a further example of *scriptio defectiva*; both 1QIs[a] and 1QIs[b] supply the expected *mater lectionis y*, reading *pšʿynw* for MT *pšʿnw*. Why Mandelkern's *Concordance* cites our text with *plene* written *pᵉšāʿênû* is not clear to me. Parallelism with plural *ʿᵃwōnōtênû*, "our iniquities," indicates that the plural vocalization is correct, and urges against the singular translation "our transgression" proposed by Driver, op. cit., p. 103.

*The penalty we should have paid.* The ambiguity of the hapax-legomenon expression *mûsar šᵉlômēnû* (1QIs[b] offers the interesting variant spelling *šlmnw* which points to a defectively spelled original) can perhaps be circumscribed by detecting here a judicial metaphor developing the statements of the first two cola. On this hypothesis, consonantal *šlmnw* (cf. 1QIs[b]) would be pointed as piel infinitive construct.

*upon him.* Or "to his debit," a nuance of *ʿālayw* identifiable in Ugaritic *ʿl*; Gen. 30:28, 34:12; II Kings 15:20; Job 6:27, 13:26 etc.; cf. *Gruenthaner Memorial Volume*, pp. 59–60.

*his stripes.* Singular *ḥᵃbūrātô* is commonly interpreted as a singular form with a collective meaning, but 1QIs[a] *ḥbwrtym* is a curious blend of singular noun (1QIs[a] normally writes feminine plural nouns fully) followed by the third singular suffix *-yw* that follows plural nouns. One should infer, then, that MT *ḥᵃbūrātô* is due to *scriptio defectiva* of the original and should be repointed to *ḥᵃbūrōtāw*, "his stripes."

7. *to the slaughter.* One should register here the variant *lṭbwḥ* of 1QIs[a] and 1QIs[b], which shows that they construed it similarly to Jer. 11:19, *kᵉkebeś ʾallûp yûbal liṭbôaḥ*, "like a gentle lamb led to be slaughtered."

*he was silent.* MT *neʾᵉlāmāh* parses as the archaic third singular masculine *qatala* verb, discussed in *Psalms I*, p. 26; *Ugaritic-Hebrew Philology*, p. 20, and *Biblica* 48 (1967): 434. Thus there is no need to emend it to *neʾᵉlam*, as proposed by *The Confraternity of Christian Doctrine Version* (CCD). Another instance of archaic *qatala* in Second Isaiah occurs in 40:2b, *mālᵉʾāh ṣᵉbāʾāh*, "her warfare is ended"; elsewhere *ṣābāʾ* is always masculine, so *mālᵉʾāh* must also be masculine. The needs of rhyme and assonance convincingly explain its choice.

*opened not.* As in the second colon of this verse, the *yqtl* verb *yiptaḥ* expresses a past event; this becomes doubly clear from 1QIs[a] *ptḥ*, a significant variant not registered by D. Winton Thomas, *Liber Jesaiae* (*BHSt.* 7; 1968). Instead

Professor Thomas recommends the deletion of *wᵉlōʾ yiptaḥ pîw*, a recommendation which finds no support in 1QIs^a and 1QIs^b, and which should firmly be rejected. The text-critical apparatus, it may be submitted, is not the proper place for literary criticism.

8. *without moderation.* The apparent synonymy with *mēᶜōṣer* suggests this nuance of *mišpāṭ*, which is witnessed in such texts as Prov. 13:16, 28:5; Eccles. 8:5–6. The prophet contrasts the lamb-like meekness of the Servant with the ruthlessness of his executioners. The repetition of this idea by the two terms *mēᶜōṣer ūmimmišpāṭ* corresponds to the repeated stressing of the Servant's gentleness in the preceding verse. Compare Ecclus. 16:23 (25), *bmšql . . . wbhṣnᶜ*, "without weighing . . . without reservations," as proposed in *Biblica* 48 (1967): 435. The recent proposal of G. W. Ahlström (*BZ* 13 [1969]: 97), to translate this colon, "He is cut off from his just position of power," does not carry conviction. A similar translation has also been proposed by P. R. Ackroyd (*JSS* 13 [1968]: 7), "From (royal) power and administration he is removed."

*his life.* Ascribing to much-disputed and emended *dôrô* the shade of meaning attested in Isa. 38:12, where *dôrî* is parallel to *ḥayyay*.

*he was cut off from the land of the living.* It is impossible to accept the opinion of Driver (op. cit., pp. 95, 104), that this clause does not imply the death of the Servant, but may refer only to solitary confinement away from the society of men. Comparison of *nigzar mēʾereṣ ḥayyîm* with Ps. 88:6, *miyyādᵉkā nigzārû*, "cut off as they are from your love,"—a description of the dead in Sheol—notably clarifies what the prophet had in mind when using this expression. As pointed out by H. S. Nyberg (*ZDMG* 92 [1938]: 332, n. 1), King Eshmunazor of Sidon, to describe his premature death, employed the cognate verb *gzl*: *ngzlt bl ᶜty*, "I have been snatched away before my time" (lines 2–3). The further identification of Phoenician factors in this poem lends greater weight to Nyberg's comparison of *nigzar* with *ngzlt* and at the same time weakens Driver's position. Cf. also Ahlström (loc. cit., p. 97, n. 17).

*his people.* That the suffix of *ᶜammî* must be the Phoenician third-person *-y* is evident from its frequent emendation to *-ô* (*ᶜammô*), an emendation buttressed by 1QIs^a *ᶜmw*, but still unnecessary when the poem is studied against a Phoenician background. 1QIs^b reads *ᶜmy*, so we must come to terms with this reading.

*he was struck from them.* Usually considered corrupt, *negaᶜ lāmô* can be salvaged into sense when *negaᶜ* is repointed niphal preterit *niggaᶜ* or qal passive *nūgaᶜ*, a repointing that harmonizes with 1QIs^a *nwgᶜ*. If strict parallelism with *nigzar mēʾereṣ ḥayyîm* is assumed, *niggaʿ lāmô* may be rendered "he was struck from them," namely, from the living; grammatically this is viable since *la* in Northwest Semitic often denotes "from."[8]

9. *was put.* MT *yittēn* parses more satisfactorily when repointed as qal passive *yuttan*, as proposed by Albright (*VTS* 4 [1957]: 245).

*and with the rich.* Just what *ʿāšîr* means in this context cannot be made out with certainty,[9] but its parallelism with *r*$^{e}$*šāʿîm* sustains the widely held view that it connotes the godless. In *Psalms I*, p. 296, and *Biblica* 47 (1966): 277–78, the writer has discussed Ps. 49:3; Job 24:6; Prov. 11:7, and Eccles. 8:8, where *rāšāʿ*, "the wicked," and *ʿāšîr*, "the rich man," seem to be interchangeable terms. And one is hardly free to emend *ʿāšîr* (see McKenzie, *Second Isaiah*, p. 130) in view of the observation that it contains the same consonants, although in a different order, as *rāšāʿ*. Cf. Isa. 43:2, *tʿbr . . . tbʿr*; 54:7, *rgʿ . . .* 9. *gʿr*; 61:3, *pʾr . . . ʾpr*; 65:11, *ʿrkm . . .* 12. *tkrʿw*. From the numerous Phoenician elements in these verses one may hazard the opinion that the exegetical problem will be solved when Phoenician social structures and practices become better understood.

A further stylistic comment may preserve singular *ʿāšîr* against its alteration to plural *ʿ*$^{a}$*šîrîm* with the LXX and 1QIs$^{a}$, where someone, however, attempted to erase the plural ending *-ym*. Hebrew poetry affords many examples of parallelism between plural and singular (albeit with collective meaning) nouns: e.g., Isa. 52:14, *ʾîš/b*$^{e}$*nê ʾādām*; Job 20:5, *r*$^{e}$*šāʿîm/ḥānēp*; Prov. 14:33, *nābôn/k*$^{e}$*sîlîm*; 14:34, *gōy/l*$^{e}$*ummîm*. That this practice goes back to the Late Bronze Age can be gathered from UT, *ʿnt*: II:27–28, *kbrkm tǵll bdm ḏmr ḥlqm bmmʿ mhrm*, "Then to her knees she wades in the blood of troops, to her neck in the gore of soldiers." Here singular *ḏmr/mhrm* illustrates Isaianic *r*$^{e}$*šāʿîm/ʿāšîr*.

Though 1QIs$^{a}$ reads *ʿm* in the second colon for MT *ʾet*, and Albright, *VTS* 4, 245, considers this an improvement, the numerous Ugaritic–Hebrew examples of the same word or preposition repeated in both halves of a bicolon discountenance the adoption of *ʿim* against MT *ʾet*.

*his burial mound.* MT *b*$^{e}$*mōtāyw* may be traced back to a defectively written

8. W. F. Albright in *Hebrew and Semitic Studies Presented to Godfrey Rolles Driver*, eds. D. W. Thomas and W. D. McHardy (Oxford, 1963), p. 4.

9. G. W. Ahlström, *BZ* 13 (1969): 97, considers a possible identification of *ʿāšîr* with Ugaritic *ʿšr*, "to pour out"; *ʿāšîr* would then be a person belonging to a class of service men, a kind of servant. But he does not press the point, and reverts to the common interpretation that *ʿāšîr* designates someone corrupt, as is clear from the parallelism. Ahlström (p. 98, n. 25) seems to have misunderstood my point when taxing me with emending *rāšāʿ* to *ʿāšîr* in Job 24:6. Of course, I made no such emendation as can be ascertained by consulting *Biblica* 47 (1966): 277–78.

*bmty*, because 1QIs^a reads singular *bwmtw*. Hence one may vocalize *bōmātî*, the singular noun followed by the Phoenician suffix *-y*, and attach the final *-w* to the next verse. The balance of suffixes witnessed in *qibrô/bōmātî* recurs in vs. 11. Cf. *Psalms I*, p. 112, and *Psalms III* on Ps. 105:6.

10. *to crush him and to pierce him.* Repointing *dakkeʾô wehāḥillî*; the final *-w* of *dkʾw* is taken as a singly written consonant to be shared by the next word. Cf. W. Watson, "Shared Consonants in Hebrew," in *Biblica* 50 (1969). That the root *ḥll*, "to pierce," underlies consonantal *hḥly* is inferred from vs. 5b, *meḥōllāl/medukkāʾ*.[10] But what is the form? Consonantal *hḥly* may be analyzed as the hiphil infinitive construct followed by the third person suffix *-y*; hence vocalize *hāḥillî*. Thus both infinitives construct depend upon *ḥāpeṣ*, a usage elucidated by comparison with Job 33:32. 1QIs^a *wyḥllhw*, "and he pierced him," sustains our translation which, however, preserves the consonantal text. The emergent parallelism between the suffixes *-ô/î* accords with the same balance in vs. 9a and b.

*certainly was (his life) made.* MT second person *ʾim tāśîm* scarcely harmonizes with the third person of the first colon, but the text becomes congruent when read *ʾemet śîmā*, "certainly was (his life) made." On emphatic *ʾemet*, which recurs in Isa. 42:3, 43:9, see *CBQ* 22 (1960): 406; R. de Vaux, *Les sacrifices de l'Ancien Testament* (Paris, 1964), p. 100, n. 1; *Psalms I*, p. 188; W. Baumgartner, *Lexikon*, 3rd ed., p. 67a. Pointed *śîmā*, this verb would parse as qal passive feminine singular whose subject is *napšô*. Other instances of qal passive *śîm* occur in II Sam. 14:7; Job 20:4; Obad. 4; Phoenician *śm* in Eshmunazor, line 5, and have been studied in *Gruenthaner Memorial Volume*, p. 64.

*But he will see offspring.* Though the servant has been slain for the guilt of others, he will be raised up by God to see that his sacrificial death has not been in vain. The prophet firmly expresses his belief in the resurrection, a belief which accords with that of some psalmists; cf. the Introduction to *Psalms III*. McKenzie, *Second Isaiah*, p. 135, intuits the sense of vs. 10, but cannot account for it because of his mistaken notion that resurrection is a late belief in Israel. He writes, "Delivery from death is a paradoxical element in a poem which is earlier than any attested belief in the resurrection. . . . The prophet must therefore be expressing without explanation or rationalization his faith that the saving work of the Servant cannot end in the total defeat of death. Unless he is vindicated in some way and knows that he is vindicated, justice would not be achieved." In view of the forty-odd texts, old and recent, from Psalms and Proverbs attesting a belief in an afterlife or a resurrection

10. The attempt of Driver, op. cit., p. 96, to explain *dkʾ* as Aramaizing for *zkh*, "to be pure, innocent," appears to be misplaced.

that are examined in the Introduction to *Psalms III*, there appears to be no reason for withholding this belief from the prophet when the context so clearly demands it. The basis for the prophet's belief in resurrection can be seen in his description of Yahweh in vs. 11 as *ṣaddîq*, "the Just One."

*shall advance.* The verb *yiṣlaḥ* reprises the theme announced in the opening clause, *hinnēh yaśkîl ᶜabdî.*

*because of him.* Literally "in his hand," *bᵉyādô* seems to bear the idiomatic sense recurring in Isa. 64:6, *bᵉyad ᶜᵃwōnēnû*, "because of our iniquity," Jer. 41:9, *bᵉyad gᵉdalyāhû*, "because of Gedaliah," and elsewhere.[11]

11. *he was sated.* For this definition of *yirᵓeh* (possibly to be vocalized *yurᵓā*), cf. my *Proverbs and Northwest Semitic Philology*, p. 23, and Driver, op. cit., p. 97. When the first colon is construed thus, there is no need to suppose the haplography of *ᵓôr*, "light," which critics have restored with the aid of the LXX, a restoration now supported by both 1QIsᵃ and 1QIsᵇ.

*he was soaked by his sweat.* If the arrangement of this bicolon is recognized as chiastic, *bdᶜtw* becomes the counterpart of *mᶜml npšw*, "with the anguish of his soul." Hence consonantal *dᶜtw* may be explained as a Canaanite (cf., Ugaritic *dᶜt*, "sweat") form of *zēᶜāh*, "sweat." This etymology, proposed in *Greg.* 43 (1962): 63–64, has been adopted by Baumgartner *Lexikon*, 3rd ed., p. 220a.

*But the Just One will vindicate his servant.* MT *yaṣdîq ṣaddîq ᶜabdî* yields sense when *ṣaddîq* is interpreted as a divine appellative,[12] and *ᶜabdî* parsed as the direct object with the third person suffix *-y*, precisely as in Isa. 52:13, *hinnēh yaśkîl ᶜabdî.*

*he . . . carried.* In vs. 4 the prophet employed the *qtl* form *sᵉbālām* to express this idea, but here, to achieve stylistic variation, he uses *yisbōl*. Similarly, in vs. 6 he uses the *qtl* verb *hipgîaᶜ* but *yqtl yapgîaᶜ* in vs. 12.

12. *who bore . . . made entreaty.* The *qtl-yqtl* sequence seen in *nāśāᵓ* . . . *yapgîaᶜ* has Canaanite antecedents in Ugaritic.

*the sins.* The fact that MT has singular *ḥēṭᵓ*, while both 1QIsᵃ and 1QIsᵇ read plural construct *ḥṭᵓy*, may be attributable to the *scriptio defectiva* of the original poem. See the next comment.

*made entreaty.* Another indication that *scriptio defectiva* characterized the autograph is furnished by the variant *ypgᶜ* of 1QIsᵃ against MT hiphil *yapgîaᶜ*. Qumranic *ypgᶜ* can scarcely be the qal form, which does not give the

11. Cf. *Biblica* 44 (1963): 301–2; *Mélanges E. Tisserant*, I. p. 90; Z. Rin, *BZ* 7 (1963): 33; C. Westermann, *Das Buch Jesaja* (Göttingen, 1966), p. 311, n. 10; T. F. McDaniel, *Biblica* 49 (1968): 200–1.

12. For other texts with this appellative, consult *Psalms I*, pp. XXXVII, 69; *Psalms II*, p. 216, and *Psalms III* on Pss. 112:4, 141:5.

desiderated meaning in this context; hence it must be a defectively spelled hiphil form. If this inference is correct, we have a remarkable instance of *scriptio defectiva* in 1QIs[a], which normally employs many more *matres lectionis* than MT.

In summary, the typically Phoenician elements which have been identified in this poem are the following:

(1) *scriptio defectiva:* vss. 3, *ḥšbnhw, mstr;* 4, *ḥšbnhw, ḥlynw;* 5, *pšʿnw;* 10, *śm;* 12, *ḥṭʾ*.

(2) third person singular suffix *-y*: vss. 13, *ʿbdy*; 14, *ʿly*; 8, *ʿmy*; 9, *bmty*; 10, *hḥly*; 11, *ʿbdy*.

(3) morphology: vs. 3, *ʾîšîm*.

(4) collocation: vs. 3, *šōreš . . . tōʾar*.

Twenty years ago the writer completed his dissertation, "Canaanite-Phoenician Influence in Qoheleth," under the direction of Professor Albright. Today it is no less a pleasure to contribute this article to honor a scholar who has taught us that, "There can no longer be any doubt that the Bible has preserved some of the best in Phoenician literature, especially lyric and gnomic poetry. Without the powerful influence of the Canaanite literary tradition, we should lack much of the perennial appeal exerted by Hebrew poetic style and prosody, poetic imagery, and vivid description of natural phenomena. Through the Bible the entire civilized world has fallen heir to Phoenician literary art."[13]

13. *The Bible and the Ancient Near East: Essays in Honor of William Foxwell Albright*, ed. G. Ernest Wright (Garden City, N.Y., 1961), p. 351.

# Bemerkungen zum Verständnis zweier aramäischer Briefe aus Hermopolis

HERBERT DONNER

Das Corpus der 1945 in Ṭūna el-Gebel (Hermopolis-West) gefundenen, jedoch erst 1966 veröffentlichten reichsaramäischen Privatbriefe aus der Mitte des 5. Jahrh. v. Chr.[1] hat bislang geringere wissenschaftliche Aufmerksamkeit gefunden, als es verdient. Immerhin sind zwei beachtliche Studien erschienen, die das sprachliche und inhaltliche Verständnis der Texte gefördert haben: eine Darstellung von monographischer Breite aus der Feder des Orientalisten J. T. Milik[2] und eine Gemeinschaftsarbeit von B. Porten und J. C. Greenfield.[3] Darüberhinaus wird noch vieles an Interpretationsarbeit zu leisten sein. Denn der bescheidene Inhalt der Briefe—Mitteilungen über Familienangelegenheiten und Rechtsgeschäfte—darf nicht darüber hinwegtäuschen, daß es sich um eine Quellensammlung von höchstem Interesse handelt: nicht nur für den Aramaisten, dessen Material für die Kenntnis des Ägyptisch-Aramäischen[4] vermehrt wird, sondern auch für den Religionshistoriker und vor allem für den, der sich die Erforschung der Rechts- und Sozialverhältnisse der in

1. E. Bresciani—M. Kamil, "Le lettere aramaiche di Hermopoli," *AANL*, CCCLXIII, Memorie, Classe di Scienze morali, storiche e filologiche, Ser. VIII, Vol. XII, fasc. 5 (1966): 359–428.

2. J. T. Milik, "Les papyrus araméens d'Hermoupolis et les cultes syrophéniciens en Égypte perse," *Bibl.* 48 (1967): 546–622.

3. B. Porten—J. C. Greenfield, "The Aramaic Papyri from Hermopolis," *ZAW* 80 (1968): 216–31; vgl. auch E. Hammershaimb, "Some Remarks on the Aramaic Letters from Hermopolis," *VT* 18 (1968): 265–67.

4. Vgl. noch immer P. Leander, *Laut- und Formenlehre des Ägyptisch-Aramäischen* (1928).

Ägypten lebenden nichtjüdischen Semiten aramäischer Zunge zur Aufgabe gemacht hat. Ganz besonders dem Letzteren wird das Briefcorpus willkommen sein; denn er leidet unter notorischem Quellenmangel und sieht sich obendrein der Schwierigkeit gegenüber, daß die Hauptmasse ägyptisch-aramäischer Texte aus der jüdischen Militärkolonie von Elephantine stammt, deren Sonderverhältnisse jeweils mit in Anschlag gebracht werden müssen. Gleichwohl leisten die Elephantine-Papyri Deutungshilfe für die aramäischen Briefe aus Hermopolis, nicht zuletzt deswegen, weil beide Corpora in großer zeitlicher und räumlicher Nähe zueinander stehen. Von den acht erhaltenen Briefen sind vier (Nr. 1–4) von Memphis nach Syene/Assuan gerichtet, drei (Nr. 5–7) nach Ophis/Luxor; bei einem (Nr. 8) ist die Adresse nicht mehr erkennbar. Aus unbekannten und zur Erfindung romanhafter Umstände anreizenden Gründen hat keiner der Briefe seinen Bestimmungsort erreicht. Niemand vermag zu sagen, wie sie in die unterirdische Galerie des Ibieions von Hermopolis–West gelangt sind, wo sie 1945 während ägyptischer Grabungen unter der Leitung von Sami Gabra gefunden wurden.[5]

Die folgenden Erörterungen betreffen schwer verständliche Einzelheiten rechtlicher Art aus den Briefen 1 und 2. Allseits befriedigende Lösungen können hier allerdings nicht angeboten werden. Dem steht nicht zuletzt der Charakter der Texte als Privatbriefe entgegen, deren andeutende und für den Adressaten verständliche Formulierung die gemeinten Rechtsverhältnisse und Geschäftsgänge nicht immer genau erkennen läßt. Das entbindet jedoch nicht von der Pflicht, sich um Erklärungen von möglichst hohem Wahrscheinlichkeitsgrad zu bemühen, in der Hoffnung, es möchten sich zukünftig Bestätigungen oder Widerlegungen dafür finden lassen.

## I

Hermopolis 1 ist von einem Manne namens MKBNT[6] an seine in Syene lebende Schwester RʿYH gerichtet. Er behandelt im ersten Teile (Z. 1–9) Familienangelegenheiten, hauptsächlich das Befinden des Bruders ḤRWṢ, der sich zusammen mit MKBNT und unter dessen Obhut in Memphis befindet. In Z. 9–10 steht, ohne erkennbaren Zusammenhang nach vorn und hinten, der Satz: *wkʿt hn ʾt ʿrb ʿlyky ʾtyk ltpmt*. Problematisch ist dabei das Verständnis des Wortes *ʿrb*. Bresciani–Kamil übersetzen: "E ora, se c'è presso di te un

5. Bibliographie der Vorberichte bei Porten—Greenfield, a.a.O., S. 216, Anm. 1–5.

6. Der Name entspricht einem gemeinsemitischen Namenstyp, der z.B. akkadisch in der Form *Mannu(m)-kī(ma)-*$^{d}$*NN* vielfach belegt ist; vgl. J. J. Stamm, *MVAeG* 44 (1939): §33, la. Nach Analogie des westsemitischen Vokalismus empfiehlt es sich jedoch, gegen das "Makkibanit" der Bearbeiter, "Makkabanit" zu vokalisieren.

pegno, mandalo a Tpmt"; sie rechnen also mit der Bedeutung "Pfand," und dieses Pfand soll an die in Memphis ansässige Dame mit dem ägyptischen Namen *Tꜣ-pꜣ-Mw.t*[7] geschickt werden. Man fragt sich: warum? Denn der Absender weiß anscheinend nicht, ob seine Schwester ein Pfand besitzt; er versucht, im Falle des Vorhandenseins eines Pfandes, dessen Überstellung an TPMT zu veranlassen. Das Pfand aber ist Vertreter eines Schuldgegenstandes; also muß ein Schuldverhältnis einer nicht genannten Person gegenüber RᶜYH angenommen werden, dessen Beendigung die Ablösung des Pfandes zur Folge haben würde. TPMT kann nicht Pfandschuldnerin sein, weil MKBNT das wissen müßte und dann nicht konditional zu formulieren brauchte. So bleibt allenfalls die Annahme eines Verfallpfänders, der nach Verfall Teil des Vermögens der RᶜYH sein würde und den sie dann nach Belieben verwenden könnte. Wenn aber nicht mehr ausgesagt werden soll, als daß RᶜYH eine Schuld gegenüber TPMT zu begleichen hat, warum dann der Terminus *ᶜrb*? Diese Schwierigkeiten hat Milik gesehen. Er übersetzt: "Et maintenant, s'il y a chez toi quelque cadeau, fais-le parvenir à Tapamut." Dabei wird *ᶜrb* aus akkad. *irbu* (*erbu*, *urbu*) erklärt, das nicht "Pfand," sondern "Einkommen, Summe, Wert, Gabe, Einfuhrzoll u.ä." bedeutet.[8] In diesem Falle würde es sich einfach um eine Gabe an TPMT handeln, vielleicht aus Erkenntlichkeit wegen der Fürsorge, die sie nach Z. 5 zusammen mit ʾḤTSN dem ḤRWṢ angedeihen läßt. Es fragt sich allerdings, ob das westsemitische Bedeutungsfeld der Wurzel *ᶜrb* und ihrer nominalen Derivate dieser Auffassung entspricht. Porten—Greenfield[9] schließlich deuten *ᶜrb* im Sinne von "Bürge": "And now, if a guarantor has a claim against you, send him to Tapamut." Dahinter stünde dann die Annahme des MKBNT, seine Schwester könne einem Bürgen verpflichtet sein, entweder weil dieser für eine fällig gewordene Schuldsumme bereits eingetreten ist, oder auf Grund einer vertraglichen Abmachung zwischen Gläubiger und Schuldner. Bei dieser Interpretation, die den Satz wie Bresciani-Kamil aus dem Kreditwesen erklärt, bleibt freilich völlig unverständlich, weshalb der Bürge [sic!] zu TPMT geschickt werden soll, womöglich von Syene nach Memphis. Was soll der Bürge bei TPMT? Man könnte sich allenfalls denken, daß er dort seine Bürgschaft erstattet bekommen soll. Das aber würde eine Schuldverbindlichkeit der TPMT gegenüber RᶜYH voraussetzen; TPMT wäre es, die zu zahlen hätte, und der Satz müßte lauten: "Wenn ein Bürge (einen Anspruch) gegen dich hat, schicke TPMT zu ihm!"

7. Vgl. Z. 5.
8. Milik, a.a.O., S. 550, Vgl. CAD 7 [I/J] 173–76.
9. A.a.O., S. 226, 228.

Soll hier ein Schritt vorwärts getan werden, dann muß man sein Augenmerk auf das westsemitische Wortfeld der Wurzel *ᶜrb* richten. Es empfiehlt sich, mit dem Alten Testament zu beginnen. Das Verbum *ᶜrb* ist in den alttestamentlichen Rechtscorpora nicht belegt, wohl aber außerhalb derselben, und zwar in doppelter Bedeutung: "Bürgschaft leisten" und "verpfänden." Die Bürgschaftsleistung,[10] nicht selten verbunden mit einem altertümlichen Handschlagritus, begegnet in rechtlichem Sinne: Prov. 6:1; 11:15; 20:16; 22:16; 27:13; einmal mit dem nominalen Derivat *ᶜrbh* "Bürgschaft" Prov. 17:18. Daneben gibt es Stellen, an denen übertragener Gebrauch vorliegt: "für jm. verantwortlich sein, sich für jm. einsetzen" Gen. 43:9; 44:32; Jes. 38:14; Ps. 119:122; Hi. 17:3. Der Schuldner steht im Akkusativ, kann aber auch mit den Präpositionen *l* (Prov. 6:1) oder *lpny* (Prov. 17:18) eingeführt werden; die Angabe des Gläubigers erfolgt einmal mit der zusammengesetzten Präposition *mᶜm* (Gen. 44:32). Will man den "Bürgen" bezeichnen, dann geschieht das einfach durch Verwendung des part. act. Qal der Wurzel *ᶜrb*. Verbaler Gebrauch von *ᶜrb* im Sinne von "verpfänden" begegnet *strictu senso* nur Neh. 5:3; hinzu kommt ein vereinzelter Beleg für metaphorischen Gebrauch "sein Herz verpfänden = sein Leben wagen" Jer. 30:21. Mit den nominalen Derivaten der Wurzel *ᶜrb* verhält es sich ganz ähnlich. *ᶜrbwn* im Sinne von "Pfand," genauer "Pfandgegenstand," ist Gen. 38:17f., 20 bezeugt: Juda hat an die sich prostituierende Thamar ein Ziegenböckchen als Kaufpreis zu zahlen. Da ihm ein solches nicht zur Hand ist, gibt er Thamar seinen Siegelring, seine Schnur (Amulettgehänge?) und seinen Stab als *ᶜrbwn* = Übergabepfand.[11] In übertragener Bedeutung kommen ferner vor: *ᶜrbh* "Unterpfand" in 1 Sam. 17:18 und *ᶜrbh* juristisch exakt als "Bürgschaft" in Prov. 17:18.

Hebräischem *ᶜrbwn* "Pfandgegenstand" entspricht reichsaramäisch *ᶜrbn* in den Elephantine—Papyri.[12] Darüber herrscht Einverständnis; es genügt, die Belege aufzuführen. In Betracht kommt hauptsächlich die Darlehensurkunde Cowley 10 aus dem 9. Jahre Artaxerxes I. (456 v.Chr.), deren Pfandklausel (Z. 7–11) lautet: ". . . Und wenn das 2. Jahr gekommen ist,

10. Vgl. A. Abeles, Der Bürge nach biblischem Recht. *MGWJ* 46 (1922): 279–94; 47 (1923): 35–53; R. de Vaux, Das Alte Testament und seine Lebensordnungen 1 (1960): 278f.

11. Daneben sind andere termini technici für "Pfand" geläufig, die hier nicht in Betracht kommen. Vgl. zum israelitischen Pfandrecht H. M. Weil, Gage et cautionnement dans la Bible. *AHDO* 2 (1938): 171–240; M. David, Deux anciens termes bibliques pour le gage, *OTS*, 2 (1943): 79–86; R. de Vaux, a.a.O., S. 276–78.

12. Die Belege in *DISO* 221. Zur Sache vgl. R. Yaron, Introduction to the Law of the Aramaic Papyri (1961) 96f.; A. Verger, Ricerche giuridiche sui Papiri aramaici di Elefantina, StSem 16 (1965): 137–40.

und ich dir dein Geld und seine Zinsen, die in dieser Urkunde festgelegt sind, nicht zurückgezahlt habe, dann haben du, Mešullām, und deine Kinder das Recht, jeden Pfandgegenstand, den du bei mir finden kannst, zu nehmen . . . bis du mit deinem Geld und seinen Zinsen bezahlt bist." Der Tatbestand des Vertragspfandes wird in der Klageverzichtsklausel (Z. 12–14) wiederaufgenommen: "Ich darf gegen dich vor dem Gerichtsherrn keine Klage erheben und keinen Prozeß anstrengen mit der Begründung: Du hast von mir Pfand genommen! während diese Urkunde in deiner Hand ist." Schließlich ist die Vererbbarkeit des Schuldverhältnisses vorgesehen (Z. 15–17): "Und wenn sie (d.h. die Kinder des Schuldners) dir dieses Geld und seine Zinsen nicht zurückzahlen, dann hast du, Mešullām, das Recht, dir jede Deckung und jeden Pfandgegenstand, den du bei ihnen finden kannst, zu nehmen." Diese letztere Klausel begegnet auch, geringfügig variiert, in der Darlehensurkunde Kraeling 11 aus dem 4. Jahre Artaxerxes II. (401 v.Chr.), Z. 9–12. Da der Text nicht ganz eindeutig ist, empfiehlt sich die Transskription: (9) . . . *whn lʾ šlmw lk bny wʾdrngy* (10) *kspʾ znh zy mnʿl ktyb ʾḥr ʾnt pḫnwm šlyṭ bʿrbny*[13] *lmḥd*[14] *wtlqḥ lk mn* (11) *by zy lbnn . . . ʿd tšlm bkspk zy mnʿl* (12) *ktyb* "Und wenn meine Kinder und mein *ʾdrng*[15] dir dieses Geld nicht zurückzahlen, das oben festgesetzt ist, dann hast du, Pachnum, das Recht, Pfand von mir zu nehmen (?) und darfst dir aus dem Hause der Kinder nehmen . . . bis du mit deinem Geld, das oben festgesetzt ist, bezahlt bist." Den beiden noch verbleibenden Belegen für *ʿrbn*[16] ist wegen des schlechten Erhaltungszustandes der Texte nichts Sicheres zu entnehmen: Cowley 42, 5; 68, Nr. 10, Obv. 3. Immerhin ist die Wahrscheinlichkeit groß, daß *ʿrbn* auch hier "Pfand" bedeutet.

Darüberhinaus gibt es vier schwer verständliche Belegstellen für *ʿrb* ohne die Nominalendung *–ān*, hebr. *–ōn*. Bei keiner von ihnen ist die Bedeutung des Wortes zweifelsfrei zu ermitteln.

1. *CIS II, 65:* Aramäische Beischrift zu einem babylonischen Vertrag über die Mietung eines Bronzegefäßes aus dem 17. Jahre des Darius (504 v. Chr.).[17] Der Text ist rätselhaft: (1) *ʿrbʾ zy qdm* (2) *kyšwš ʾt bytʾ* (3) *ʾ? lh ?*

13. So statt *bʿd bny* mit H. L. Ginsberg, *JNES* 18 (1959): 148f.; R. Yaron, *JNES* 20 (1961): 127f.

14. Nicht ganz sicher. Kraeling: *lmḫr*; Yaron: *lmḥd* als inf. cstr. Peal von *ʾḥd* "nehmen" mit Präposition *l*. Dieser Infinitiv lautet Cowley 2, 17 *mʾḥd*; auch sonst sind Formen der Wurzel mit Elision des Anlautkonsonanten nicht belegt.

15. Vgl. E. G. Kraeling, The Brooklyn Museum Aramaic Papyri (1953) 243.

16. *DISO* 221 verweist mit Fragezeichnen auf E. Ebeling, Das aramäisch-mittelpersische Glossar Frahang-i-Pahlavik im Lichte der assyriologischen Forschung, *MAOG* XIV, 1 (1941) XVII, 1. Für die hier beschäftigende Problematik ist daraus nichts zu gewinnen.

17. Vgl. H. Petschow, Neubabylonisches Pfandrecht. *ASAW* 48, 1 (1956) Anm. 158, 161.

*6.*[18] Denn *kyšwš* = *Kī-ᵈŠamaš* ist in der babylonischen Urkunde einer der Mieter des Gefäßes, seine Vertragsposition die eines Mietzinsschuldners. Damit scheidet die Bedeutung "der Bürge" oder "die Bürgschaft" für *ʿrbʾ* aus. Aber auch "Pfand" ergibt keinen rechten Sinn; es sei denn, man nimmt an, daß der Mieter für den Fall der Nichtübereignung des gemieteten Gegenstandes[19] ein Pfand behalten darf. Dann entspräche *qdm* der Formel *ina pāni* babylonischer Mietverträge; das Pfand bestünde vermutlich in *ʾt bytʾ* "Hausmiete (?),"[20] und es wäre zu übersetzen: "Das Pfand, das zur Verfügung des Kī-ᵈŠamaš ist, (beträgt) eine Hausmiete von 6 . . . (unleserlich).[21]

2. *Berytus 5 (1938) 133:* Palmyrenische Türinschrift vom Grabe des ʿAbdʿastôr.[22] Der Text lautet: *mnw dy yzbn ʿrbʾ dy qdm mʿrtʾ ʿl npšh ḥṭʾ* "Wer den *ʿrbʾ* verkauft, der vor dem Grabe ist, sündigt gegen sich selbst." *ʿrbʾ* im Zusammenhang mit einem Verkaufsverbot könnte hier bedeuten: (a) den allgemeinen Rechtsanspruch der Familie auf das Grab; (b) das Pfandrecht, das Gläubiger bei allfälligen Restaurationsarbeiten an der Grabanlage dann haben könnten, wenn die Familie zahlungsunfähig ist. Im letzten Falle würde *ʿrbʾ* "Pfandrecht" und nicht "Pfandgegenstand" heißen—verkauft werden kann das Recht, hier aber wohl nicht das Grab. Wiederum scheiden die Bedeutungen "Bürge, Bürgschaft" aus.

3. *KAI*, 60, 5f.: Phönikische Kranzinschrift von Sidon aus dem Jahre 96 v.Chr. (?). Der Beschluß der sidonischen Gemeinde über die "Bekränzung" eines ihrer Honoratioren soll auf einer Stele (*mṣbt*) festgehalten werden, für die die Gemeinde *ʿrb* ist: (5) . . . *lknt gw* (6) *ʿrb ʿlt mṣbt z* ". . . die Gemeinde zum *ʿrb* über diese Stele zu ernennen." Das Wort *ʿrb* kann hier nicht "Pfand" bedeuten, aber auch nicht "Bürge"; denn die Gemeinde ist selbst Schuldner der Steinmetzen. Für wen sollte sie bürgen? Schwerlich für die "Vorgesetzten über das Gotteshaus" (Z. 4f. *hʾdmm ʾš nśʾm ln ʿl bt ʾlm*), denn diese sind Beauftragte der Gemeinde. Es ist zu vermuten, daß *ʿrb* mit "Zahlungspflichtiger" übersetzt werden muß.

4. *RB* 61 (1954): 183[23]: Jüdisch-aramäische Grundstücksverkaufurkunde aus der Gegend des Toten Meeres; Jahr 134 n.Chr. Die einschlägige

18. Die beiden mit Fragezeichen als unsicher qualifizierten Buchstaben sind auf der photographischen Tafel nicht zu erkennen. Hier könnte nur eine Kollation mit dem Original weiterhelfen.

19. Die babylonische Urkunde verbindet die Vertragsausfertigung nicht mit der *traditio corporalis* des Mietgegenstandes; vgl. H. Petschow, a.a.O., S. 55f.

20. Nach babylon. *idī bīti*; *CAD* 7 [I/J] 16–20. So schon *CIS*; vgl. *DISO* 29.

21. *DISO* 221 "gage . . . donné à K. comme garantie, au lieu de rente arriéré" ist nach dem Sachzusammenhang sinnlos.

22. Aus: H. Ingholt, Inscriptions and Sculptures from Palmyra II.

23. J. T. Milik, ebenda S. 182–90.

Klausel ist leider sehr schlecht erhalten und inhaltlich kaum verständlich: (11) *wʾn̊h ʾh̊ẘy ʿrb̊ x̊ [bz]b̊n bth dk mn ymh dnh* (12) *wlʿlm*[24] "Und ich werde Bürge sein (?) [für] dieses [erwor]bene Grundstück von jetzt an bis auf immer." Voraus geht, wenn nicht alles täuscht, eine Vindikationsklausel gegen den Verkäufer, dem die Geltendmachung von Rechten auf das verkaufte Grundstück durch den Käufer untersagt wird. Keine der Bürgschaftsformen (Ersatzbürgschaft, Zahlbürgschaft usw.) erscheint sinnvoll, da von einem wie immer gearteten Schuldverhältnis in der Urkunde nicht die Rede ist. Die Bedeutungen "Pfand, Pfandnehmer oder -geber" kommen nach allem, was sich erkennen läßt, nicht in Frage. Die Sache muß unentschieden bleiben.

Schließlich ist noch darauf hinzuweisen, daß das Verbum *ʿrb* "als Bürgschaft eintreten" und das Nomen *ʿrbn* "Bürgschaft"[25] auch im Ugaritischen vorkommen.[26] *PRU* II, 161: *spr ʿrbnm dt ʿrb b mtn bn ayaḫ b ḫbṯh ḥwt ṯth w mnm šalm dt tknn ʿl ʿrbnm hn hmt tknn* . . . (Namen). Nach dem Zusammenhang muß *ʿrbn* "Bürgschaft" und nicht—wie gewöhnlich übersetzt—"Bürge" heißen; denn der zweite Satz ist so formuliert, daß bei der Bedeutung *ʿrbn* = Bürge die Namen der Bürgen fehlen würden. Sie fehlen aber keineswegs; es sind die *ʿl ʿrbnm*. Also ist zu übersetzen: "Liste der Bürgschaften, die eingetreten sind für Mtn, den Sohn des Ayaḫ, für seinen ḫubšu . . .[27] Und wer immer nach denen fragt, die über den Bürgschaften sind, es sind die folgenden: . . . (Namen)."

Das Ergebnis ist zusammenzufassen. Die Verbalwurzel *ʿrb* hat westsemitisch—soweit es die Rechtsterminologie betrifft[28]—zwei Bedeutungen: 1. Bürgschaft leisten, 2. verpfänden. An nominalen Derivaten kommen vor: *ʿrbn* 1. Bürgschaft, 2. Pfand, Pfandgegenstand; *ʿrb* 1. Zahlungspflichtiger (?), 2. Pfand, Pfandrecht (?); *ʿrbh* 1. Bürgschaft, 2. Unterpfand. Nicht berücksichtigt sind Cowley 42, 5; 68, Nr. 10, Obv. 3; *RB* 61 (1954): 183. Der Sprachgebrauch läßt das Wort mit voller Deutlichkeit als terminus technicus des Kreditwesens erkennen. Bereits diese Beobachtung macht Miliks Interpretation[29] von Hermopolis 1, 9f. unwahrscheinlich; denn akkad. *irbu* ist im Kreditwesen nicht gebräuchlich. So bleiben Bürgschaft und Pfand als

24. Die Transskription Miliks *ʾhn wʿrb* ergibt keinen Sinn; Milik läßt beide Wörter unübersetzt. Die in *DISO* 11 mit Literaturverweisen vorgeschlagene Lesung *ʾḥry ʿrb* ist paläographisch ausgeschlossen. Der obige Lesungsversuch nach *Birnbaum*, *PEQ* (1957): 114.127.130.

25. *PRU* III, 220: *ú-ru-ba-nu*.

26. J. Aistleitner, WUS 2094; C. H. Gordon, UT 1915.

27. Mit *ḥwt* "Leben" (?) und *ṯt* "zwei, zweiter" (?) ist nichts anzufangen.

28. Die Grundbedeutung "eintreten" kann vorerst außer Betracht bleiben. Vgl. akkad. *erēbu*, das auch "als Pfand eintreten" bedeuten kann; *CAD* 4 [E] 262.

29. S.o.S...

mögliche Deutungen übrig. Beiden ist mit Blick auf die Grundbedeutung der Wurzel *ᶜrb* gemeinsam, daß sie Vorgänge des "Eintretens" bezeichnen. Der Bürge tritt für den Schuldner ein: Er haftet für das Verbleiben des Schuldners am Erfüllungsort (Stillesitzbürgschaft), für die Gestellung des Schuldners zur Personalexekution (Gestellungsbürgschaft) oder—in späterer entwickelter Form—mit seinem Vermögen für die Erfüllung der Zahlungspflicht des Schuldners (Ersatzbürgschaft, Zahlbürgschaft).[30] Das Pfand tritt für den Schuldgegenstand ein: Der Gläubiger nimmt es als dingliche Sicherheit für die späterhin zu leistende Erfüllung der Schuld oder er sichert sich ein Pfandrecht am Vermögen des Schuldners für den Fall der Nichterfüllung.[31] Daß *ᶜrb* in Hermopolis 1. 9f. "Bürgschaft" oder "Bürge" heißen könne, ist nicht anzunehmen; es bliebe unverständlich, wie der *ᶜrb* zu TPMT geschickt werden soll.[32] Aber auch gegen die Bedeutung "Pfand" bestehen starke Bedenken.[33] Die Untersuchung scheint in einer Sackgasse zu enden. Nun ist allerdings darauf zu achten, daß sich der *ᶜrb* "auf" RᶜYH befindet (*ᶜlyky*). Die Präposition *ᶜl* aber wird in aramäischen Rechtsurkunden gewöhnlich zur Qualifikation von Schuldverhältnissen verwendet[34]; sie entspricht also den Präpositionalausdrücken *eli, ana muḫḫi* "zu Lasten von" in babylonischen Verpflichtungsscheinen (*uʾiltu*) oder *ina* (*ana*) *pāni* "zur Verfügung von" in babylonischen sog. ina-pāni-Realverträgen.[35] Dabei ist der den Präpositionen folgende Name der des Schuldners, für den—jedenfalls nach den genauen Differenzierungen im Keilschriftrecht—das neutrale Bestehen einer Schuldverbindlichkeit (Verpflichtungsschein) oder die tatsächlich vollzogene Übergabe des Schuldgegenstandes (Realvertrag) beurkundet wird. Ob juristische Unterscheidungen dieser Art auch für das ägyptische Kreditwesen des 5. Jahrh. v.Chr. angenommen werden dürfen, wissen wir nicht. Es ist für das Verständnis von Hermopolis, 1. 9f. von geringer Bedeutung. Die Interpretation des Satzes würde jedenfalls auf der Basis der vorausgegangenen Erörterungen zu folgendem Ergebnis führen: RᶜYH hat eine Pfandschuld (*ᶜrb*) gegenüber einem nicht genannten Gläubiger (NN)—oder könnte sie doch haben, MKBNT weiß es nicht genau[36]—; d.h. der Gläubiger hat seine Forderung an RᶜYH durch Pfandrecht vertraglich gesichert. Es besteht aber

30. Vgl. H. Petschow, a.a.O., Anm. 242.
31. H. Petschow, a.a.O., S. 52ff. Der Sprachgebrauch weicht von dem des Keilschriftrechtes ab; abgesehen von älteren Ausdrücken begegnet in der Masse der neubabylonischen Urkunden hauptsächlich *maškānu* von *šakānu* "deponere," also "Hingelegtes."
32. S.o.S . . . zu Porten—Greenfield.
33. S.o.S . . . zu Bresciani—Kamil.
34. Vgl. z.B. *KAI* 234–36 und die Erörterung Bd.2, S. 293f.
35. Vgl. H. Petschow, a.a.O., S. 9ff.
36. Daher der Konditionalsatz!

noch ein zweites Schuldverhältnis, das MKBNT, weil am Orte befindlich, genau kennt: RᶜYH ist Gläubigerin der TPMT. MKBNT teilt nun seiner Schwester mit, daß TPMT zur Schuldübernahme bereit wäre. Dabei müßte die Verbindlichkeit der RᶜYH gegenüber NN auf TPMT übertragen werden (*ʾtyh ltpmt*); TPMT würde die Forderung des NN erfüllen und damit zugleich das Pfandrecht des NN am Vermögen der RᶜYH erlöschen lassen. Hatte Pfandnahme stattgefunden, d.h. befand sich ein Pfandgegenstand im Besitz des Gläubigers NN, dann würde das Pfand durch dieses Rechtsgeschäft abgelöst werden; es fiele an RᶜYH zurück. Gleichzeitig wäre die Forderung der RᶜYH an TPMT ganz oder teilweise befriedigt. Die darüber hinaus denkbaren Besonderheiten des Rechtsgeschäftes können auf sich beruhen bleiben; der Satz ist zu kurz, als daß er weitere Rekonstruktion gestattet. Hermopolis 1. 9f. kann nach alledem so übersetzt werden: "Und ferner: Wenn eine Pfandschuld zu deinen Lasten besteht, dann übertrage sie auf TPMT!"

## II

Hermopolis 2, von MKBNT an seine Schwester oder Gattin[37] TŠY geschrieben, lautet Z. 4–6 wie folgt: (4) . . . *wkᶜt hlw mst ksph zy* (5) *hwh bydy nttn wpr/dt lbntsr br tby ʾḥt* (6) *nbwšh ksp š 6 wzwz ksp zwz*. Bresciani—Kamil übersetzen: "E ora, ecco, la somma d'argento che era in mano mia (l')avete data e ha fruttato a Bntsr figlio di Tby sorella di Nbwšh argento 6 š(qln) e 1 zūz, zūz d'argento." Das 4. Wort der 5. Zeile ist *wprt* gelesen und als 3. Pers. fem. sing. perf. des Grundstammes von *pry* "fruchtbar sein, Frucht bringen"[38] aufgefaßt; gemeint ist "Frucht" im Sinne von "Zinsen."[39] Diese Bedeutung ist freilich nirgendwo belegt; vielmehr heißt "Zinsen bringen" im Ägyptisch-Aramäischen der Elephantine-Papyri *rby*[40] und "Zins" *mrby*.[41] Es kommt hinzu, daß die Lesung *wpdt* wahrscheinlicher ist als *wprt*. Das führt Milik[42] zu folgender Übersetzung: "Et maintenant voici, une partie de l'argent dont je dispose, je l'ai donnée, à intérêt (?), à Banitesar, fils de Tabî, soeur de Nabôšeh: la somme de 6 sicles et un zûz, (en pièces ?) de zûzs d'argent." Dabei ist zunächst die Form *nttn* falsch interpretiert: als 1. Pers. comm. sing. perf. G von *ntn* mit Suffix der 3. Pers. masc. sing. (!) und *n—energicum*. Diese Form

37. Vgl. Milik, a.a.O., S. 547–49.
38. Hebr. *prh*, jüd.-aram. *prʾ*.
39. Bresciani—Kamil, a.a.O., S. 387.
40. *DISO* 272.
41. *DISO* 167.
42. A.a.O., S. 551.582.

kommt nicht in Frage, da *n-energicum* nur beim Imperfekt stehen kann.[43] *nttn* ist vielmehr 2. Pers. fem. plur. perf. G.[44] Das rätselhafte Wort *wpdt* soll ein aus dem Persischen entlehntes Substantiv sein, über dessen Etymologie Milik freilich keine Angaben macht. Es fragt sich aber, ob man *wpdt* nicht doch semitisch erklären kann: als 3. Pers. fem. sing. perf. G. von der Wurzel *pdy* "loskaufen, auslösen"[45] mit kopulativem *w*–. Dabei müßte allerdings der mißliche Umstand in Kauf genommen werden, daß die Wurzel *pdy* im Aramäischen bisher nicht belegt ist. Das kann Zufall sein, ebenso wie es Zufall ist, daß *yṣp* "sich sorgen um" in den Hermopolis-Papyri ungewöhnlich häufig vorkommt, in der weit gestreuten reichsaramäischen Literatur sonst aber fehlt. Größere Schwierigkeiten bereitet die Akkusativrektion des Verbums *pdy*: das Loszukaufende oder Losgekaufte steht—wenn es überhaupt genannt ist—im Akkusativ. Man müßte also annehmen, daß nicht BNTSR losgekauft worden ist, sondern ein nicht genanntes Objekt zugunsten von BNTSR, des Sohnes der TBY. Dann wäre Hermopolis 2, 4–6 zu übersetzen: "Und ferner: Siehe, den Geldbetrag, der mir gehört, habt ihr gezahlt, und er hat losgekauft zugunsten von BNTSR, des Sohnes der TBY, der Schwester der NBWŠH: 6 Silbersekel und 1 zūz, 1 Silberzūz."[46] Der Vorzug dieser Deutung bestünde darin, daß sie ausgezeichnet zum Text der Z. 6–10 passen würde: "Und ferner: Sende Botschaft an TBY, daß sie dir Wolle von ihrem Anteil im Werte von 1 Silbersekel schicke! Und ferner: Wenn sie (man) dir ein Schaf mit seinem Wollvließ[47] bringt, sende mir Botschaft! Und wenn sie (man) dir die Wolle bringt, die dem (der) MKY gehört,[48] sende mir Botschaft! Und wenn sie (man) dir nichts bringt, sende mir Botschaft, damit ich hier gegen sie Klage erheben kann!" Der Zusammenhang könnte so interpretiert werden: Mit dem Gelde des MKBNT erfolgte der Loskauf eines nicht genannten Objektes zugunsten des BNTSR, dessen Familie, repräsentiert durch die Mutter TBY, dadurch gegenüber MKBNT verschuldet war. Vielleicht war von Anfang an die Lieferung von Wolle als Gegenleistung vereinbart worden, und zwar in Raten, da die Summe von Z. 7 geringer ist als die von Z. 6. MKBNT möchte von der

43. Die von Milik genannte Parallelstelle Hermopolis 4, 5 hat denn auch imperf. *ʾtnnh* "ich gebe sie (es)."

44. Bresciani—Kamil im Glossar S. 426 irrtümlich imperf.; im Kommentar S. 387 richtig.

45. Akkad. *padû*, hebr. *pdh*, ugarit. *pdy* (WUS 2194), arab. *fadā*, äthiop. *fadaya*.

46. Zum Problem der Summenangabe vgl. R. Yaron, Minutiae Aramaicae I. *JSS* 13 (1968): 202f.

47. Vgl. Milik, a.a.O., S. 551.

48. Anders Milik, a.a.O., S. 551: "la laine au (poids) trop bas, de qualité inférieure, en mauvais état."

Zahlung der ersten Rate verständigt werden; sie ist durch TŠY in Syene abzurufen. Im Verzugsfalle droht MKBNT mit Klage gegen TBY. Der Adverbialausdruck *tnh* (Z. 10) scheint anzudeuten, daß Memphis Gerichtsstand ist. Es ist freilich ebensogut denkbar, daß der Geschäftsgang von Z. 6–10 nichts mit dem vorausgehenden Satze Z. 4–6 zu tun hat. Volle Sicherheit wird sich in der Sache kaum erreichen lassen.

[KORREKTURZUSATZ: Der vorliegende Aufsatz war im Frühjahr 1969 abgeschlossen. J. P. Hayes and J. Hoftijzer, Notae Hermopolitanae, VT 20 (1970): 98–106 konnte ich angesichts der Verzögerung des Druckes zwar zur Kenntnis nehmen, aber nicht mehr verwerten. Die Verfasser erörtern S. 101f. das Problem Hermopolis 1,9f. und kommen in Einzelheiten zu denselben Resultaten wie sie hier vorgetragen werden. Von der Richtigkeit des Vorschlages, *ʾt ʿrb ʿlyky* mit "you have something that may serve as pledge" zu übersetzen, kann ich mich freilich nicht überzeugen. Hayes und Hoftijzer rekonstruieren den Zusammenhang wie folgt: "*Ḥrwṣ* has to pay *Tpmt*, but is presumably unable to do so; the payment must come from Syene. Against this background it seems to be very reasonable that the addressee *Rʿyh* who is (or feels herself) responsible for him (see letter 1) is asked to send for the moment a pledge to *Tpmt*." Wenn es sich so verhält, warum dann eine Pfandgabe von seiten der RʿYH? Warum nicht die Zahlung der Schuldsumme aus Syene an TPMT? Wenn aber die Familie, hier vertreten durch RʿYH, zahlungsunfähig ist, warum fragt dann MKBNT an, ob ein Pfandgegenstand vorhanden ist? Er müßte doch in jedem Falle aufgetrieben werden können; der Konditionalsatz bleibt unverständlich.]

# Isaiah 6:1 "his train filled the temple"

G. R. DRIVER

WHATEVER the Hebrew noun here used may mean, the Revised Version's "train" cannot stand; for, so far as Accadian sculptures and Egyptian paintings show, men never and women rarely, if ever, had trains to their robes.[1] Indeed, a train, which is an elongated part of a robe or skirt trailing on the ground behind the wearer, must have been barely possible in the ancient world, where ground and floor can often have been unsuitable for such appendages.

The meaning of *šûlîm* (Levy) or *šûlayim* (Jastrow),[2] "flowing robes, skirt, train, hem; buttocks, extremities," and of *ṣammāh* "veil; tresses," as each is variously translated, is shrouded in ambiguity, as these renderings show; but the meaning of each word can be considerably narrowed down when they are examined in the light of the context in which they occur, of the translations offered in the ancient versions and by Jewish lexicographers, and of the cognate languages.

The relevant passages in which *šûlîm* occurs are the following:

(A) ושוליו מלאים את ההיכל (Is. 6:1);
(B) גלי צמתך חפשׂי שבל תלי שׂוק (Is. 47:2);

1. Cp. Jastrow, *Bildermappe zur Religion Babyloniens und Assyriens* [1912]: *Taf.* 48/172 (male), Gunkel, *ABAT* [1927]: 28/66 (female), and Pritchard, *ANEP* [1954]: 38/125 (female), 39/132 (male), 200/611 (male deity). In these pictures the skirts of the females only just reach the ground, those of the males scarcely touch it.

2. No evidence is given for the du. form, which perhaps rests on the supposition that "buttocks" may have been the original sense of the word.

(C) גלו שוליך ונהמסו עקביך (Jer. 13:22);
(D) חשפתי שוליך על פניך (Jer. 13:26);
(E) וגליתי שוליך על פניך (Nah. 3:5);
(F) טמאתה בשוליה (Lam. 1:9).

The meaning of *šûlîm* is clear in one connection, apart from these passages: that is where the writer, describing the High Priest's vestments, says that "thou shalt make pomegranates of blue and of purple and of scarlet round about the skirts thereof (*šûlāyw*)" and "a golden bell and a pomegranate upon the skirts of the robe (*šûlê hamm*$^{ec}$*îl*) round about" (Exod. 28:33–34; cp. 39:24–26). The LXX have λῶμα "fringe" and Aquila has ἀπόληγμα "hem," Symmachus and Theodotion have τὰ πρὸς ποδῶν, while Jerome has *pedes*; the Peshitto and the Targums have equivocal terms. Jewish lexicographers vary slightly amongst themselves, having "trailing skirt" (Ibn Janâh) and "fringe" or "hem" (D. Qimḥî, Solomon b. Parchon, alFâsî). Clearly, "hem" is right in this connection, for it is a part of the robe to which the pomegranates and bells are attached or of which they are an element. The Mishnaic Hebrew *šûlîm* "rim at the bottom of a vessel, the saucer under a vessel" as well as "hem, skirt" and "lower part of the body, abdomen, belly" (Jastrow) seems also to be in favor of "hem" rather than "skirt."

At the same time, this meaning appears impossible in any of the passages set out at the head of this article; and not only the Mishnaic use of the word but also the cognate Arabic *sawila* "was flaccid, lax, pendulous" and especially "(the belly below the navel) hung loosely down" and *sawlatu(n)* "flaccidity of the belly or other members of the body" (Freytag, Lane) [3] suggest that the word may also denote the "buttocks, lower parts, extremities" of the body. Further, the ancient translators have this meaning in several of the passages under discussion; for the LXX has "hind-parts" (C) and τὰ ὀπίσω "the parts behind" (D, E). Jerome has *femora* (D), *pudenda* (E), and *verecundiora* (C). From these translations and from the Mishnaic usage Geiger [4] has rightly argued that its meaning must have been in all these cases the *nates* of a man and *der herabhangende Mutterschoss* of a woman.

The Hebrew *gālāh, gillāh* "uncovered" takes as its object that which is uncovered or revealed,[5] not the object which is removed so that something else may be uncovered, revealed or laid bare. The probability therefore is that in two of the passages under discussion (C, E) it has just the same force

3. Also Arabic *sahâbu ᵓaswalu* "clouds loosely formed and having ragged edges hanging down" (Lane).
4. In *Urschrift und Uebersetzungen der Bibel* [1857], pp. 390–93.
5. Cp. Pesh. at I Cor. 11:5, 13 for the corresponding Syriac usage.

when the object will be the part of the body uncovered or laid bare, namely *šûlîm* "buttocks, extremities" or the like and not the clothing, e.g., "skirt," that is removed. Similarly *ḥāśaf* "stripped" may once be used as removing a woman's flowing train (Is. 47:2, where however the sense is by no means clear) and somewhat similarly twice as drawing off water or wine (Is. 30:14, Hagg. 2:16); elsewhere the object is the arm that is laid bare (Is. 52:10 Ezek. 4:7) or the rump that is exposed (Is. 20:4), as also in "I have stripped bare/exposed thy buttocks" (D). In two of these passages (D, E) God's action is said to be *ᶜal pānāyik* "against thy face," i.e., the face of the woman who is the object of His action. The English "I will discover thy skirts upon thy face" (R.V.) or "before they face" (R.V., margin), even if paraphrased as "I have stripped off thy skirts before thy face"[6] is virtually meaningless; what must be meant is "in thy despite," i.e., "to thy shame" or the like, as in "thou shalt have no other gods in my despite (*ᶜal pānay*)," i.e., so as to dishonor me (Exod. 20:3; Deut. 5:6; cp. Deut. 21:16).

The interpretation here proposed for *šûlîm* "extremities" (or the like) rather than "skirts" has also the advantage that it agrees strictly with "thy heels" or perhaps rather "back-parts" which are exposed (C), as the Pesh.'s "are uncovered" and Targ.'s "are seen" suggest. No certainly cognate verb is known; and the LXX's "was made an example," Aquila's "were defiled" and Vulg.'s *pollutae sunt*, suggest that the ancient translators were uncertain of its meaning.[7] The important point is that, if parallelism of thought is a true criterion, both nouns must denote parts of the body. This conclusion is confirmed by the biblical "her impurity is in her lower regions (*bᵉšûlêāh*)," i.e., "her belly" or the neighboring parts of her body (F); and the Mishnaic "the impurity" (*sc.*, that collected in the bowels of a dead dog which has eaten filthy food) comes out by way of its buttocks (*derek šûlāyw*)ᵓ[8] here puts any kind of clothing out of the question.

Only the famous "His train" or "skirts filled the temple" (A), as the clause is usually translated (R.V.), remains to be discussed.

Clearly the "hem" of God's robes cannot be right; for the hem cannot possibly have filled the temple, and "skirt" seems nowhere to be the meaning of the noun. The only possible rendering, then, as Geiger has seen,[9] is "his

6. S. R. Driver *Book of the Prophet Jeremiah* [1906], p. 81.

7. May the Acc. *ḫamāṣu* I "to strip off (clothing)" II "to strip (a person)" be cited in illustration of the Hebrew *ḥāmas* "stripped" in spite of the incorrect sibilant equation, which the alternative Bab. *ḫimṣātu* = Ass. *ḫimsātu* "illgotten gains" seems to illustrate (s. Buhl, *Hebr. u. Aram. Hwb.* [1921], pp. 532–33)?

8. Mishnah, *Oholoth*, xi, 7.

9. Op. cit., p. 391.

lower limbs" or "extremities filled the temple." God is depicted in ultra-anthropomorphic imagery as having lower limbs or extremities exactly as He is said elsewhere to have arms (Exod. 15:16, Deut. 4:24 *plus*), and hands (Is. 10:32, 49:23 *plus*) and feet (Exod. 24:10 *plus*), and so on. This interpretation alone explains the renderings of three of the ancient versions: the LXX's "glory" and the Targum's "the splendor of His glory" as well as the Vulgate's *ea quae sub ipso erant*. These are obviously euphemisms to avoid the somewhat coarse (as these translators will have thought) anthropomorphism of the ancient prophet. The Rabbis similarly sought to avoid the anthropomorphism; so Saᶜadyāh and Ibn Janâḥ have "his rays," while Ibn Ezra thinks of the "hanging draperies" covering God's throne. None of these interpreters can have objected to the notion of God being clothed in flowing robes[10] and have attempted to conceal them under a euphemism, if only because such an idea is found elsewhere in the Old Testament (e.g., Is. 63:2, Dan. 7:9). Only the notion of His lower limbs can have seemed to require a euphemism to avoid it.

The picture of God sitting on a throne with His extremities filling the body of the temple can be illustrated by Assyrian sculptures depicting this or that god seated on a throne within a shrine which his "extremities," i.e., skirt and feet, completely fill.[11] These pictures show that the Hebrew prophet may have meant either the skirt or the extremities, but Hebrew usage seems to show that the extremities, i.e., all the limbs below the trunk, are meant. Let no one suppose, however, that the prophet will have imagined God's extremities or lower limbs as exposed to view; the pictures suggest that he will have regarded Him as clothed in a long robe reaching to the ankles and leaving only the feet uncovered.

The translation of "uncover thy *ṣammāh*" (B) depends on the sense of the noun, whether it means "veil" (Michaelis with alFâsî and Ibn Parchon)[12] or "plait, tresses of hair" (Ewald with D. Qimḥî).[13] In three other passages in which it occurs it clearly denotes "veil" (Ct. 4:1, 3:6, 7); and the Mishnaic Hebrew *hēṣēm* "tied up (the hair)"[14] and the Judaic Aramaic *ṣamṣēm*

10. Gray, *Book of Isaiah* [1912], p. 103.

11. Pritchard, op. cit. [1954], pp. 178/529 (Shamash) and 221/693 (Ea).

12. Guidi, *Note Ebraiche* [1927] 13 *ap.* Koehler *Lexicon* [1953], p. 806; cp. Lagarde, *Proverbien* [1863], pp. 84–85.

13. Wetzstein *ap.* Delitzsch, *Hoheslied u. Koheleth* [1875], pp. 437–38.

14. All respectable girls were veiled in the ancient East (s. Driver & Miles, *Assyrian Laws* [1935], pp. 127–29) even before marriage (Gen. 24:65; cp. Ruth 3:15, Ct. 5:7); but this does not mean that they necessarily refused a chance to glance at a man by momentarily uncovering "one eye" (Ct. 4:9). The text of this last passage has been condemned as *grammatisch und sachlich unmöglich* (Rudolph, *Hohes Lied* [1962], p. 149); it is in fact sound both in grammar and in content. For *ᵓaḥad* "unit" is here a noun, as commonly elsewhere before *min* "of," in the

"veiled (the head or the face)" as well as the Arab *ṣammatu* "veil" support this rendering of the word, with which the LXX, Symm. and Pesh., agree. If however "veil" is meant, the verb can hardly be *gillāh* "uncovered," of which the object elsewhere is that which is uncovered; but, if *gallî* "uncover" is read as *gōllî* "roll up," this objection is met. No Vss. support such a revocalization of the verb here; but in one passage (C) the Pesh. has "the ends of thy robe have been rolled up," reading *nagōllû* "they have been rolled up," which is there impossible, for *niglû* "they have been uncovered";[15] and this misrendering of the Pesh. proves that the idea is not impossible.

At the same time a Hebrew *ṣammāh* "tress of hair" has been plausibly restored in

רבו משׂערות ראשי  שׂנאי חנם
עצמו מצמיתי  איבי שׁקר

they that hate me without cause are more
than the hairs of my head;
they that would cut me off are numerous,
(even) my treacherous enemies

(Ps. 59:5), where *maṣmîtay* "they that would cut me off" is commonly taken to be an error for *miṣṣammātî* (Hare) or[16] *miṣṣamôtay* (Peters) "than my lock(s)." The Arabic *ḍamma* "drew together, threaded (a needle)," from which *ḍimâmu* "thread, cord" is derived, as well as the Hebrew *ṣammîm* "trap with cords/strings," may be held to justify the assumption of a Hebrew *ṣammāh* "lock(s)" or the like, although it provides no absolute proof in default of other evidence, when the line may be rendered: "my treacherous enemies / are more numerous than the tresses of my hair," which certainly has the advantage of suiting

---

constr. st. (s. Bauer & Leander, *Hist. Gramm. d. Hebr. Spr.* I [1922]: 622 §79[b]), used like the corresponding Arabic word in *ʾaḥadu-ʾlnâsi* "one of the people" and *lam yubqû . . . ʾaḥadu-ʾlnâsi* "one of the people" and *lam yubqû . . . ʾaḥada banî Hilâli*[n] "they did not leave . . . one of the sons of Hilâl" (Wright, *Gramm. of the Arab. Lang.* II [1933], p. 236, and Reckendorff, *Arab. Synt.* [1921], pp. 204–5). Other Hebrew instances are easy to find (Gen. 21:15, 22:2, II Sam. 2:18, 13:13), even though only before plural nouns; but the gender is immaterial in the present explanation of the idiom. The idea, too, of an oriental girl veiling only one eye or glancing out of one momentarily while keeping the other veiled is attested by ancient writers (e.g., Tertullian, *de Virg. Vel.*, pp. xvii, 6–7 and Finkel, *Risâlat alQiyân of Jâḥiẓ*, p. 72) as well as by modern observers (e.g., Niebuhr, *Reisebeschreibung nach Arabien* I [1744], p. 304 and Lane, *Manners and Custom of the Modern Egyptians* [1860], pp. 47, 52); the custom is also depicted in various illustrated works (e.g., Kitto, *Cyclop. of Bibl. Lit.* [1862], p. 773 fig. 324 and Mackie, in Hastings, *Dictionary of the Bible* I [1910], p. 628 fig. 3). I have myself seen three veiled girls walking side by side in a street in Beirut turn round and uncover one eye to glance at a passing man; but few commentators on the Old Testament appear ever to have visited the Middle East.

15. The confusion of *gālāh* "uncovered" and *gālal* "rolled up" occurs elsewhere (e.g., Is. 38:12, Jer. 11:20, 20:12 Ps. 119:22).

16. Cp. *JBL*, 77 [1954]: 133–34.

the parallelism in sense of the two verses and yields a sense that is obviously preferable. If accepted, two roots (the one with *ṣ* and the other with *ḍ*) must be postulated; and no objection can be brought against such an assumption.

What then is *šōbel* "lock(s) of hair" or "train, skirt of a robe" (B)? The LXX's and Pesh.'s "white hairs" suggest the former, and the cognate Arabic *sabalu(n)*, *sabalatu(n)* "hairs hanging down over a camel's nose; moustache, beard" seem to support it, while the Arabic *sabalu(n)* "long garments hanging down" and *musbilu(n)* "trailing one's skirt" support the latter. The Vulgate's *humerus* and Saᶜad.'s *ᶜaḍdu(n)* "upper arm" are guesses based on the context and devoid of philological proof; Ibn Parchon has "hair," Ibn Janâḥ has "veil," and Qimḥî has "leg, foot." The word occurs nowhere else in Hebrew literature, so far as the dictionaries show, and its meaning must have been long forgotten. Further, the verb throws no light on its meaning; for *ḥāśaf* "stripped" can take as its object either the covering stripped off or, as most often, that which is stripped of its covering. What seems to settle the problem is that Scroll A has *šûlayik* "thy buttocks, lower limbs, extremities," which is the earliest evidence, apart from that of the Vss., for the meaning of the word, while Scroll B agrees with the Massoretic text. Scroll A, however, being otherwise unsupported, may be at fault, while Scroll B may, and perhaps even probably, has preserved the original reading. If so, the verse may be translated: "take mill-stones, grind corn, roll up [sic] thy veil, | strip off the skirt, reveal the thigh, pass through rivers," with rolling up the veil in the first clause; for the veil must have been more of an inconvenience grinding corn than wading through rivers. So women in the East commonly uncover their faces when grinding corn, as shown in many illustrations.[17]

Alternatively the verse may be rendered: "take mill-stones, grind corn, | roll up [sic] thy veil, uncover the long locks, | reveal the thigh, pass through rivers," if the translations of the LXX and Pesh. and one of the meanings of the cognate Arabic words is preferred.

Possibly the best conclusion is that the Hebrew *šōbel* "flowing locks, skirt" is equivocal, like the Mishnaic Hebrew and Judaic–Aramaic *šippûl(â)* "border (of a tent-curtain or skirt), foot (of a mountain), lower limbs, sexual organs (of a woman)" and Syriac *šfôlâ* "extreme end (of a wood or hill), base (of an altar), border (of a garment)," and that the evidence is insufficient to decide which meaning is intended with absolute certainty, even if the balance is slightly in favor of "skirt" in the present context.

17. E.g., Frohmeyer & Benzinger, *Bilderatlas zur Bibelkunde* [1905], pp. 143/291 and 144/297 and Gressmann, op. cit., pp. 81/186.

If then *gillāh* "uncovered" normally takes as its object what is uncovered and not that which is removed so as to uncover something else, what is the correct translation of גלה כנף אביו "he hath uncovered his father's skirt" (Deut. 27:20, R.V.; cp. 23:1, R.V.)? It clearly cannot mean that the offender has removed his father's "skirt" so as to reveal what is under it; further, the Hebrew *kānāf* "fold, corner, wing" nowhere denotes the "skirt" of a garment.

Fundamentally this word describes something curved or bent, which the Judaic–Aramaic *kᵉnaf* (intr.) "crowded together"; *kannòf* "assembled, folded, creased"; *ʾitkᵉnif* "was compressed, met together"; and the Arabic *kanafa* "hedged in, protected"; *kannafa* "surrounded," though probably only denominative verbs, reflect.[18] Accordingly the Hebrew noun means primarily "fold, wing, corner, boundary" like the Syriac *kenfâ* "fold, wing, arm, flank, boundary" and the Arabic *kanfu(n)*, *kanafu(n)* "fold, wing, side, tract (of country)." The *kānāf* of a garment is the corner of a rectangular piece of cloth folded over (like the Latin *sinus* "fold") to form a pocket (Hagg. 2:11; cp. Ezek. 5:3) and the four corners to which tassels may be attached (Deut. 22:12; cp. Num. 15:38); so Saul caught hold not of the "skirt" (R.V.) but of the "corner" of Samuel's mantle (I Sam. 15:27) and similarly David snipped off the "corner" of Saul's mantle (I Sam. 24:5,6,12). Elsewhere, *kānāf* may be used loosely of the "extremity, edge, end," i.e., "corner" (and nowhere the "skirt") of a garment (Jer. 2:34; Ezek. 5:3; Hagg. 2:12; Zech. 8:23).[19] Even when Ruth says to Boaz "spread thy skirt over me" (Ruth 3:9, R.V.; cp. Ezek. 16:8, R.V.), the whole skirt is not necessarily meant; for the action is symbolical and the corner or edge of the skirt may well stand for the whole skirt.[20]

In the passages here discussed *kānāf* "corner, fold, extremity" is variously interpreted by the ancient translators,

now as a garment, e.g., "veil" συγκάλυμμα (LXX at Deut. 23:1, 27:30), ἀναβολή (LXX at Ezek. 5:3); *operimentum* (Jer. ibid.), *amictus* (Jer. at Ezek. 16:8), *pallium* (Jerl at Ruth 3:9);

18. Cp. Hebrew *kāfan* "was twisted" (Ezek. 17:1, where *kānaf* "turned to one side" as a variant reading in some Hebrew MSS. is noticeable) and "was hungry," Syrian *kfen* "was hungry" and Arabic *kafana* "spun (wool), wrapped in a shroud" (s. Brockelmann *GVGSS* I §98, 2δ).

19. Cp. Aramaic אחדון . . . , בכנפי לבשך (Cowley, *Aram. Pap. Aḥ.*, p. 171) with מ[ר]אה אחז כנף (Cooke, *N.-Sem. Inscr.*, 62, 11).

20. The Bab. *sissiktu* "fringe, hem (of a garment)" is similarly used as representing the personality of the wearer (s. Lewy in *RHR*, CX [1934]: 31–3, Malamat, in *VTS*, XV [1966], pp. 225–26; cp. Driver & Miles, *Bab. Laws*, I, pp. 291–92). A similar symbolical act is found also amongst Arabs (Jacob, in *Stud. in Arab. Dicht.* IV [1897]: 22–3 and W. R. Smith, *Kinship and Marriage in Early Arabia* [1907], pp. 104–5).

now as the "border" or "edge" or "fringe" of a garment, e.g., κράσπεδον (LXX at Zech. 8:23; Symm. at Ezek. 5:3); *ora* (Jer. at I Sam. 24:5,6), *fimbria* (Jer. at Zech. 8:23);

now as the "corner" of a garment, e.g., τὸ ἀκρὸν τοῦ ἱματίου (Symm. at I Sam. 15:27, Ezek. 5:3); *angulus* (Jer. at Num. 15:38), *summitas* (Jer. at I Sam. 15:7, Ezek. 5:3);

and now as the "flap" or "fold" of a garment, e.g., πτέρυγες (LXX at Ezek. 16:8); πτερύγιον (LXX at Num. 15:38, I Sam. 24:5, 6, Ruth 3:9; Aq. at Ezek. 5:3 and Ἑβρ. at Ezek. 16:8).

Briefly, while occasionally taking the word to mean a garment (possibly a skirt), these ancient translators generally regard it as describing the border or corner of a garment; but, while allowing that it can denote something like the "extremity" of a garment, they nowhere take it as standing for the extremities of the body.

Whatever the value of these translations may be, the notion that the word in גלה כנף אביו "he uncovered the *kānāf* of his father" denotes a part of the body is supported not only by the general use of the verb but also by the parallel ערות אביו גלה "he uncovered/laid bare the nakedness of his father" (Lev. 20:11 *alq.*), and the corresponding ראה ערותו "he saw his nakedness" (Lev. 20:17) confirms that in all these expressions the *kānāf* is not the covering which is removed for such a purpose but what is uncovered so as to be seen.

Accordingly, in גלה כנף אביו "he uncovered his father's extremities," these are not the borders or corners of the garment which he is wearing but the "curved end" of the trunk of the body where the sexual organs are situated; it is then here a euphemism for the actual "privies." The Arabic *mâ kasaftu laʾimratin kanfan* "I have not uncovered the flank/bosom/womb of a woman,"[21] i.e., "I have not had intercourse with her," illustrates the Hebrew expression as here interpreted. In other words, both the Hebrew and the Arabic words mean "extremities," including the sexual organs of both sexes as depending from the trunk.

The Targ.'s mistranslation of this word by *sitrâ* "privies" where it means the "corners" of a robe (Jer. 2:34; cp. Ezek. 5:3) confirms its use as a euphemism for the sexual organs, or remotely, the "extremities" of the trunk. In this passage the sense is clear; for blood on the hands and feet (cp., LXX's and Pesh.'s "hands") can easily be washed off, whereas it is to all intents and

21. De Goeje, *Fragm. Hist. Arab.*, I. p. 248 (s. II, pp. 78–79).

purposes indelible on any part, e.g., the "corners," of a robe. That is why murderers commonly take steps to dispose of any garment which may betray them by blood-stains; so here the blood-stains on the corners of their robes are the indelible proof of their crimes.

This sense assigned to the word under discussion is found also in other connections, as in *ʾarbaʿ(at) kanfôt hāʾāreṣ* "the four corners of the earth" (Is. 11:12, Ezek. 7:12), i.e., the four "points" of the compass, and loosely also in *kanfôt hāʾāreṣ* "the flanks of the earth" (Job. 37:3, 38, 13), i.e., the "boundaries" of the known world; while *kᵉnaf hāʾāreṣ* "the corner of the earth" (Is. 24:16) means "the farthest point(s) of the known world."[22] Finally, it is used in a somewhat different sense in ערוך בכנפי הוניך "valued at the extremities of thy wealth," i.e.. costing anything to thy last farthing (J.b.Sir. 38:11), where emendation is certainly needless, even though the ancient translators have obviously misunderstood it.

Only two passages remain where *gillāh* "uncovered" seems superficially to denote "removed" the covering itself from that which it covers, namely ויגל את מסך יהודה (Is. 22:8) and מי גלה פני לבושו (Job 41:5). If the present arguments are sound, the former will mean not "and he took away the covering of Judah" (R.V.) but "he uncovered the defences of Judah," i.e. exposed or unmasked them in some way to attack e.g., by removing their screen of protecting troops; and the second must be translated not "who can strip off his outer garment?" (R.V.) but "who has laid bare his outer garment?", i.e., who has exposed his "soft under-belly" to attack, e.g., by luring the beast from the water or mud where he has been lurking so as to come under his guard and be able to penetrate "his doublet of hide."[23]

Finally, the Q. *gālāh* "uncovered, disclosed" is used with the ellipse of the object to mean "uncovered the land; i.e., went into exile, departed" with human beings as the subject (*passim*) and (superficially intrans.) "removed" i.e., "departed, vanished" with things as the subject (Is. 24:11, Job. 20:28, Prov. 27:25); and the Ni. *niglāh* "was removed" serves as the passive form with a neuter subject in דורי נסע ונגלה מני "my habitation is pulled up (like

22. The singular form does not call for alteration to (*kanf'* as an abbreviation for) *kanfôt* (Cheyne, *Isaiah* [1899], p. 172) or for *kanfê* (Joüon, in *Biblica* XVI [1935]: 201–4) *hāʾāreṣ* in spite of some Vss. (LXX, Vulg., Pesh., Saʿad.).

23. Acc. *rasānu* "to pour out; to soak, irrigate; to tan" explains the Hebr. *resen* "tanned hide, leather," whether the leathery hide of the beast's under-belly (as here) or "strap, thong; reins" (Is. 30:28 Ps. 32:9 Jb. 30:11). Clearly in the first clause *pᵉnê lᵉbûšô* "the surface of his clothing" is the outer covering of scales, which are easily penetrated, while in the second clause "the doublet of his leather/his doublet of leather" is the inner hide on to which the scales are fixed (s. Dhorme *Livre de Job* 378). The alteration of *risnô* "his (doublet of) leather" to *siryōnô* "his breastplate" (Wright "*Book of Job*" 193 w. LXX and Coptic Vs.) is unnecessary.

a tent) and removed/taken away from me" (Is. 38:12). Thus both subject and object of the verb are always in the O.T. that which is uncovered or disclosed, never that which is removed so that something else may be uncovered or disclosed, even when the basic sense of the verb is obscured by an ellipse of the object with the active form or by the use of the passive form derived directly from it. This is so even in such expressions as לא גלו על עונך "they have not disclosed (anything) about thine iniquity" (Lam. 2:14) and גלה על חטאתיך "he discloses (everything) about thy sins" (Lam. 4:22).

Accordingly, the meanings of the three words here discussed may be differentiated and summarized in the following manner:

*šûl:* what is lax or loosely pendent, such as "buttocks, lower limbs; fringe, hem" and as resembling these last two objects "rim; saucer (under a bowl)";

*šōbel:* what is flowing, hanging down, whether "long hair" or "skirt";

*kānāf:* what is bent or curved, such as "wing (of a bird, an arm, and so on); fold; corner, edge; boundary, extremity; sexual organs."

The meaning of the second term unfortunately still eludes definition; but the cognate *šibbōlet* "flowing stream" and "ear of grain, spike of an olive-branch" in a metaphorical sense (Zech. 4:12) and *š*$^e$*bûl*/*š*$^e$*bîl* "path" as flowing onward agree with the basic sense assumed for the root.

I greatly appreciate the opportunity of offering this slight contribution to the complimentary volume being prepared for presentation to a colleague whose work in our common field of study is as remarkable as is his achievement in inspiring a school of successors to carry it on in the same spirit.

אפילו שיחת תלמידי חכמים צריכה לימוד

# Die Psalmen als Geschichtsquelle

OTTO EISSFELDT

VIELE Psalmen des Alten Testaments enthalten Hinweise auf Israels Geschichte, und wenigstens drei von ihnen, die Psalmen 78,[1] 105, und 106 sind geradezu metrisch gegliederte Übersichten über diese Geschichte, die mit den Patriarchen oder mit Israels Aufenthalt in Ägypten beginnen und mit Israels Landnahme oder einem späteren Ereignis schließen. Diese historischen Erinnerungen sind größtenteils den alttestamentlichen Büchern Genesis bis II Könige entnommen, aber einige Angaben stammen doch aus sonst uns unbekannten Überlieferungen. Diesen Angaben sollen die folgenden Untersuchungen zugewandt sein.

## DIE IN DEN ÜBERSCHRIFTEN ÜBER 14 DAVIDS-PSALMEN GENANNTEN DATEN AUS DAVIDS LEBEN

Wie in der jüdisch-christlichen Überlieferung Mose zum Verfasser oder doch Empfänger der israelitischen Gesetze und Salomo zum Autor der biblischen Weisheitsschriften, wie "Sprüche Salomos," "Prediger Salomo," und "Weisheit Salomos" geworden ist, so gilt ihr David als Dichter der israelitischen Lieder, in erster Linie unserer Psalmen. 73 von ihnen, also fast die

1. O. Eißfeldt, Das Lied Moses Deuteronomium 32:1–43 und das Lehrgedicht Asaphs Psalm 78 samt einer Analyse der Umgebung des Mose-Liedes (*SAL*, Philol.-hist. Kl. Band 104, Heft 5) 1958, S. 26–43 und W. F. Albright, *Yahweh and the Gods of Canaan* (1968), S. 15, 40, 79, 134, 184, 220f., wie Albrights Buch auch für andere Psalmen neue und beachtenswerte Ansetzungs- und Erklärungsvorschläge enthält.

Hälfte, enthalten in ihrer Überschrift *l^e dāvîd*, was doch wohl "Von David (herrührend)" und nicht etwa "Von David (handelnd)" bedeutet, und bei 14 von ihnen—bei Pss. 3, 7, 18, 30, 34, 51, 52, 54, 56, 57, 59, 60, 63, und 142 —wird der Anlaß, aus dem David diese Lieder gedichtet hat, genannt. Im Falle von Ps. 30 läge die Erwähnung einer Gelegenheit, bei der David diesen Psalm gedichtet hat, freilich nur dann vor, wenn das in seiner Überschrift "Ein Psalm, Lied zur Einweihung des Hauses, von David" genannte Haus (*bajit*) auf den Palast Davids, von dessen Erbauung II Sam. 5:11 berichtet, oder auf die II Sam. 6:17 erzählte Errichtung eines für die Lade bestimmten Zeltes und nicht, wie es meistens geschieht, auf das 8 Jahrhunderte jüngere, nämlich 165 v.Chr. gefeierte Tempelweihfest von I Makk. 4:52–59; II Makk. 10:1–8; John-Ev. 10:22 zu beziehen ist. Anderseits kann zu den Psalmen, die in ihren Überschriften außer dem Autor den Anlaß nennen, mit einem gewissen Recht auch Ps. 127 gerechnet werden, dessen Überschrift so lautet: "Ein Wallfahrtslied, von Salomo." Denn die Herleitung dieses Liedes von Salomo ist sicher durch den Anfang des eigentlichen Psalms veranlaßt, der diesen Wortlaut hat: "Wenn nicht Jahwe das Haus (*bajit*) baut, mühen sich die umsonst, die daran bauen." "Das Haus" hat man als den Tempel verstanden, und damit lag die Zuschreibung dieses vom Bauen eines Hauses handelnden Liedes an den Erbauer des Jerusalemischen Tempels, an Salomo, sehr nahe.

Im folgenden werden—unter Weglassung der wohl die Vortragsart angehenden, trotz sehr vieler auf ihr Verständnis gerichteten Bemühungen noch vieldeutig gebliebenen Termini technici—die Überschriften der eben genannten 14 Davids-Psalmen mitgeteilt. Dabei sind die Stellen aus den Samuelisbüchern, die von den in den Psalmen-Überschriften angedeuteten Geschehnissen mehr oder weniger ausführlich erzählen, in Klammern hinzugefügt: Ps. 3:1 "Von David, als er floh vor seinem Sohn Absalom" (II Sam. 15:1–18); Ps. 7:1 "Von David, wegen der Worte des Benjaminiten Kusch" (Diese Anspielung an—wohl David fluchende—Worte eines Benjaminiten Kusch hat keine Entsprechung in den Samuelisbüchern); Ps. 18:1 "Von David, als ihn errettet hatte Jahwe aus der Faust aller seiner Feinde und aus der Hand Sauls" (I Sam. 17—II Sam. 21; Ps. 18:1 ≅ II Sam. 22:1); Ps. 30:1 "Psalm, Lied zur Einweihung des Hauses, von David" (II Sam. 5:11; 6:17); Ps. 34:1 "Von David, als er sich geisteskrank stellte vor Abimelech und dieser ihn fortjagte" (I Sam. 21:11–16, wo der Philisterkönig von Gath Achis und nicht, wie Ps. 34:1, Abimelech heißt); Ps. 51:1–2 "Von David, als zu ihm kam der Prophet Nathan, weil er eingegangen war zu der Bathseba" (II Sam. 11:1–12,25); Ps. 52:1–2 "Von David, als der Edomiter

Doeg Saul Meldung machte und ihm sagte: Gekommen ist David in das Haus Achimelechs" (I Sam. 22:6–23); Ps. 54:1–2 "Von David, als die Siphiter kamen und Saul sagten: Hält sich nicht David bei uns versteckt?" (I Sam. 26); Ps. 56:1 "Von David, als ihn die Philister in Gath festnahmen" (I Sam. 21:11–16); Ps. 57:1 "Von David, als er auf der Flucht vor Saul war in der Höhle (I Sam. 22:1; 24:4); Ps. 59:1 "Von David, als Saul Leute beauftragte, das Haus zu bewachen, ihn zu töten" (I Sam. 19:10–17); Ps. 60:1–2 "Von David, als er angriff Aram-Naharaim und Aram-Zoba und Joab umkehrte und Edom im Salztale schlug, 12000" (II Sam. 8:3–13; [I Kön. 11:15–16] mit einigen Abweichungen von Ps. 60:1–2); Ps. 63:1 "Von David, als er sich aufhielt in der Wüste Juda" (I Sam. 22–26); Ps. 142:1 "Von David, als er sich aufhielt in der Höhle" (I Sam. 22:1; 24:4).

Die in den Überschriften von 14 Davids-Psalmen genannten Entstehungsanlässe bedeuten eine Enttäuschung. Mit zwei Ausnahmen, die sogleich vorgeführt werden sollen, stützen sich diese Angaben nicht auf zuverlässige Überlieferung, sondern auf bloße Kombination. Die hier in Betracht kommenden Psalmen stellen größtenteils Klagelieder eines von Feinden verfolgten Frommen dar, die mit einem Gebet des Frommen um Errettung aus dieser Not verbunden sind. Nun ist der von seiner Flucht vor Saul bis in sein hohes Alter, ja bis zu seinem Tod reichende Abschnitt des Lebens Davids ständig mit Anfeindungen von Gegnern ausgefüllt gewesen. So konnten die Psalmen, in denen sich ein Beter über seine Feinde beklagt und Jahwe um Bestrafung dieser Feinde und um seine eigene Rettung bittet, eigentlich alle auf kritische Situationen im Leben Davids zurückgeführt werden. Dennoch darf man diese Versuche, bestimmte Ereignisse in Davids Laufbahn als Anlässe der soeben genannten 14 Psalmen auszugeben, nicht geringschätzen; vielmehr verdienen sie als Anfänge literarkritischer Datierung sonst unbekannter Literaturdenkmäler alle Achtung, und wir haben um so weniger Grund, sie gering zu schätzen, als die Psalmen-Forschung unserer Tage in der zeitlichen Ansetzung einiger Psalmen häufig um mehrere Jahrhunderte, gelegentlich um fast ein Jahrtausend schwankt. So wurden im 19. Jahrhundert Psalmen wie 2 und 110 der Zeit der Makkabäer zugeschrieben, während sie heute vielfach in der Zeit Davids oder doch seiner ganz Israel beherrschenden Dynastie angesetzt werden.

## PSALM 51 UND PSALM 18

Die beiden Psalmen-Überschriften, die historisch zuverlässig zu sein scheinen, sind die der Psalmen 51 und 18, von denen die erste in Ps. 51:1–2 die Schuld nennt, die David dadurch auf sich geladen hatte, daß er mit der Bathseba, der Frau des hethitischen Hauptmanns Uria, Ehebruch getrieben hatte. Denn die Angabe von II Sam. 12, 13 daß David dem Propheten Nathan auf seine eindrucksvolle Bußpredigt das Bekenntnis abgelegt habe: "Ich habe gegen Jahwe gesündigt," kann historisch sein. David war ja einerseits stark sinnlich veranlagt und scheute auch vor der gewaltsamen Beseitigung eines Mannes nicht zurück, der ihm bei der Ausführung seines Begehrens im Wege stand, anderseits aber ein Mann von tiefer und echter Frömmigkeit. Selbst die Verse 18–19 von Ps. 51, in denen David die Gewißheit ausspricht, daß Jahwe keine Mahl-und Brandopfer von Tieren wünsche, sondern ein zerbrochenes und zerschlagenes Herz, ist David zuzutrauen. Hingegen ist der V. 20–21 umfassende Schluß unseres Psalms, der die Bitte um den Wiederaufbau der Mauern Jerusalems ausspricht und dem die Erwartung hinzufügt, daß dann Jahwe auch an Tieropfern wieder Gefallen finden werde, unecht. Diese beiden Verse setzen vielmehr die 587 v.Chr. geschehene Zerstörung Jerusalems voraus. Dafür, daß durch Hinzufügung einer Schlußstrophe an ein älteres Lied dieses der Gegenwart angepaßt wird, ließen sich ja unschwer manche Parallelen aus unseren Gesangbüchern an die Seite Stellen.

Psalm 18, der samt seiner Überschrift zweimal im Alten Testament steht, einmal im Psalter und das andere mal II Sam. 22 vor den "Letzten Worten Davids" (II Sam. 23:1–7), will nach seiner Überschrift (V. 1) von David gedichtet oder rezitiert sein, als Jahwe ihn aus der Gewalt aller seiner Feinde und aus der Gewalt Sauls gerettet hatte. Nach dem Ausdruck des Vertrauens des Beters auf Jahwe (V. 2–4), der Klage über schlimme Gefahren, die zur Anrufung Gottes führten (V. 5–7a), und der Erhörung durch Gott, der in majestätischer Theophanie dem Frommen zur Hilfe kommt (V. 7b–20), der Gewißheit, daß Jahwe dem Beter sein Wohlverhalten auch weiter lohnen wird (V. 21–43), dem Gebet um Fortsetzung der Hilfe gegen die Feinde und um deren Vernichtung (V. 44–49) schließt der Psalm in V. 50–51:

> 50 Darum preise ich dich unter den Völkern, Jahwe,
> und singe deinem Namen,
> 51 der groß macht die Hilfen seines Königs
> und Huld erweist seinem Gesalbten,
> dem David und seinen Nachkommen in Ewigkeit.

So könnte David schon im Rückblick auf die mannigfachen Hilfen seines Gottes, die er erfahren hat, und im Vorausblick auf die ihm von Gott zugesagte Dauer seiner Dynastie gedichtet haben. Die Erwähnung der Nachkommenschaft Davids in V. 51 ist kein hinreichender Anlaß zur Ansetzung unseres Psalms in einer Zeit, in der nicht mehr David selbst, sondern einer seiner Nachkommen auf dem Thron saß.

So läßt sich von den 14 Psalmen, deren Überschriften ihre Entstehungszeit nennen, doch von zwei wenigstens die Möglichkeit ernsthaft erwägen, daß ihre Überschriften zutreffen und zuverlässige Geschichtsquellen darstellen.

## RELIGIÖS-POLITISCHE IDEOLOGIE DES VOREXILISCHEN ISRAEL

Bei der engen Verbundenheit von Nationalgefühl und Religion, wie sie der Antike überhaupt und dem alten Israel insbesondere eigentümlich ist, versteht es sich von selbst, daß sich die Wechselfälle in Israels politischer Geschichte auch in Israels kultisch-religiösen Liedern spiegeln. Dem gilt es nachzugehen, und zwar in der Weise, daß in aller Kürze die Psalmen vorgeführt werden, die eine derartige national-religiöse Haltung einnehmen. Dabei versteht es sich von selbst, daß in der Mehrzahl der hierher gehörenden Psalmen David und seine Dynastie eine große Rolle spielen. Zunächst wäre da Ps. 2 zu nennen, der trotz aller Text-und Erklärungs-Schwierigkeiten doch das klar erkennen läßt, daß die Ehrfurcht vor Jahwe und dem Vertreter der Davidischen Dynastie zusammengehören; seine Verse 1–8:

1 Warum toben Völker,
und Nationen sinnen Eitles?
2 Die Könige der Erde stellen sich hin,
und die Mächtigen schließen sich zusammen
gegen Jahwe und seinen Gesalbten.
3 'Wir wollen zerreißen ihre Fesseln
und von uns werfen ihre Stricke'.
4 Der im Himmel thront, lacht,
Adonaj spottet ihrer.
5 Einst redet er zu ihnen in seinem Zorn,
und in seinem Grimm schreckt er sie:
6 'Ich habe aber eingesetzt meinen König
auf dem Zion, meinem heiligen Berge'.
7 Kundtun will ich Jahwes Satzung,
er sprach zu mir: "Mein Sohn bist du,
ich habe dich heute gezeugt.
8 Fordere von mir,
und ich gebe dir Völker zu deinem Erbe
und zu deinem Besitz die Enden der Erde"

zeigen das deutlich. Dasselbe gilt von Ps. 20, in dem es heißt:

2 Es erhöre dich Jahwe am Tage der Not,
es erhöre dich der Gott Jakobs!
3 Er sende dir Hilfe vom Heiligtum
und aus Zion stütze er dich!
4 Er gedenke all deiner Gaben,
und dein Brandopfer erkläre er für fett!
5 Er gebe dir nach deinem Herzen,
und all dein Vorhaben erfülle er!
6 Wir wollen jubeln über dein Heil,
und im Namen unseres Gottes frohlocken.
7 Jetzt weiß ich, daß Jahwe seinem Gesalbten hilft,
daß er ihn erhört von seinem heiligen Himmel
durch hilfreiche Taten seiner Rechten,

und von Ps. 21, der anfängt:

2 Jahwe, über deine Kraft freut sich der König
und über deine Hilfe, wie freut er sich sehr

und weiterhin das gute Verhältnis Jahwes zu dem König betont. Bei Ps. 45, der nach V. 2 dem König gilt—in diesem Falle freilich wohl nicht dem judäischen, sondern dem des Nordreichs Israel—können wir sogar mit einiger Wahrscheinlichkeit den genauen Anlaß dieses Liedes angeben, nämlich die Hochzeit des israelitischen Kronprinzen oder Königs Ahab mit Isebel, der Tochter des Ethba$^{c}$al, Königs von Tyrus. Ps. 46,[2] der in V. 6 Jerusalem als die "heiligste der Wohnungen" des in Jerusalem heimischen $^{c}$Eljon bezeichnet, hat dagegen wieder David oder einen Angehörigen seiner Dynastie im Auge und identifiziert dessen Sieg mit dem Siege Jahwes. Denn wenn es in V. 10 von Jahwe heißt:

10 Der Kriegen ein Ende macht bis ans Ende der Welt,
Bogen zerbricht und Spieße zerschlägt,
Wagen mit Feuer verbrennt,

so sind hier die Jahwe zugeschriebenen Taten des Königs gemeint, und die an die Völker gerichteten Worte Jahwes in V. 11:

11 Laßt ab und erkennt, daß ich Gott bin,
erhaben über die Völker, erhaben auf der Erde!

schließen die Allmacht des davidischen Königs mit ein. Ähnliches gilt von Ps. 48, der in V. 6–8 von dem Heranzug der vereinigten Könige der Welt gegen Jerusalem, dem Scheitern dieser Unternehmung spricht und es mit der Zerschmetterung von Tarsis-Schiffen durch einen Ostwind vergleicht.

2. O. Eißfeldt, Psalm 46 (Kleine Schriften IV [1968], S. 8–11).

Betrübte Rückblicke auf—leider vergangene—Zeiten, in denen Jahwe seinem Volke gnädig war und ihm die Herrschaft über andere Völker nicht nur zugesagt, sondern auch erwirkt hat, stellen Ps. 80[3] und Ps. 89[4] dar, von denen der erste, wohl aus dem Jahre 727 v.Chr., der zweite vermutlich aus der Zeit nach 587 v.Chr. stammt. Die beiden Lieder unterscheiden sich aber dadurch, daß das erste wohl des von Jahwe gewirkten früheren Glücks Israels dankbar gedenkt, dabei indes David und seine Dynastie mit keinem Wort erwähnt, während Ps. 89 Israels Macht über die anderen Völker an David und seine Dynastie geknüpft sein läßt und trotz der wenig ermutigenden gegenwärtigen Lage Israels doch mit der Erinnerung an die früheren David gegebenen Verheißungen sowie mit dem Hinweis auf die jetzigen Verhöhnungen seines Gesalbten und damit mittelbar mit dem Gebet um Errettung Israels und seines Königs schließt.

Das Ineinandergehen der israelitischen nationalen Politik und der Jahwe-Religion wird besonders deutlich durch Ps. 82[5] veranschaulicht, der Jahwe in der Ratsversammlung Els, des obersten Gottes, gegen die anderen Götter auftreten und sie als ihre oberste Pflicht, die Rechtspflege und die Fürsorge für die Schwachen, vernachlässigend und als dem Tode geweiht hinstellt, während Jahwe die Herrschaft über alle anderen Völker verheißen wird.

Ps. 83, der an Jahwe die dringende Bitte richtet, Israel aus der ihm von einer großen Koalition feindlicher Völker drohenden Gefahr zu erretten, die Feinde so gründlich zu vernichten, wie er es mit den Midianitern und mit Sisera und Jabin getan hat, und sie auf diese Weise erkennen zu lassen, daß Jahwe der Höchste in aller Welt ist, hat sich sehr verschiedene Ansetzungen gefallen lassen müssen. Beliebt war um die Wende des letzten Jahrhunderts seine mit Hinweis auf I Makk. 5 verbundene Herleitung aus der Makkabäerzeit, also etwa 170–63 v.Chr., während H. Gunkel[6] ihn "in der uns fast gänzlich unbekannten Zeit von Esra bis Alexander d.Gr." ansetzen möchte, Ed. König[7] ihn "die Situation von 2 Ch. 20," also das zweite Viertel des 9. Jahrhunderts v. Chr., widerspiegeln läßt, und Gressmann[8] unter Auffassung des in 83, 9 genannten Assur nicht als "das große Weltreich

3. O. Eißfeldt, Psalm 80 (Alt-Festschrift [1953], S. 65–78; Kleine Schriften III, [1966], S. 221–32).

4. O. Eißfeldt, Psalm 80 und Psalm 89 (*WdO* 3 [1964–66], S. 27–31; Kleine Schriften IV [1968], S. 132–36).

5. O. Eißfeldt, El und Jahwe (*JSS* 1 [1956], S. 25–37 [englisch], Kleine Schriften III [1966], S. 386–97 [deutsch]).

6. *Die Psalmen* (1926), S. 365.

7. *Die Psalmen* (1927), S. 359.

8. Die Schriften des Alten Testaments in Auswahl, Zweite Abteilung, Erster Band [1910], S. 68.

der Assyrer," sondern als der "Nomadenstamm der Assuriter, der im Alten Testament mehrfach genannt wird (Gen. 25:3,18; Ps. 83)," ihn aus der Zeit Sauls herleitet. Diese Verschiedenheit der Meinungen über das Alter von Ps. 83 erklärt sich auch daraus, daß bei der Aufzählung der Feinde Israels in V. 7–9, wo Edom, die Ismaeliter, Moab, die Hagriter, Gebal, Ammon, Amalek, Philistäa, Tyrus, Assur, Söhne Lots genannt werden, vielleicht ein Schema benutzt worden ist und daher nicht nach einer historischen Situation gesucht werden darf, in der alle hier vorkommenden Völker gleichzeitig Israel bekriegt hätten. So gefährlich die von unserem Psalm beschriebene Bedrohung Israels oder vielmehr Judas gewesen sein mag, so gewinnt man doch nicht den Eindruck, daß Juda für die Dauer aus dem Kreis der politisch maßgebenden Völker ausgeschieden wäre. Vielmehr kann der Psalm mit dem Ausdruck der Erwartung schließen, daß die anderen Völker Jahwe als den Höchsten anerkennen und damit auch Juda respektieren werden. An Situationen, in denen Juda feindlichen Koalitionen gegenüber gestanden hat, ist kein Mangel. Nun gibt V. 9 mit seiner Aussage: "Auch Assur hat sich mit ihnen verbündet" einen deutlichen Hinweis auf die Zeit unseres Psalms: er muß aus einer Zeit stammen, in der sich Assur um Syrien und Palästina kümmerte, den Nordstaat zur Hälfte annektierte und Judas Nachbarvölker sich bei der Bedrohung des ihnen verhaßten Juda der Hilfe Assures erfreuen konnten. Auch Ps. 84, im übrigen Ausdruck eines frommen Judäers, der den Tempel zu Jerusalem und die ganze Stadt von Herzen liebt, setzt mit der an Jahwe gerichteten Bitte, seinem Gesalbten gnädig zu sein, offenbar voraus, daß ein Angehöriger der Davidischen Dynastie auf dem judäischen Thron sitzt: Zum Glück des frommen Dichters unseres Psalms gehört außer der Möglichkeit, ständig im Tempel weilen und sich der Bauten der Hauptstadt freuen zu können, auch die Gewißheit, daß ein Nachkomme Davids auf dem judäischen Thron sitzt und nicht nur für die Aufrechterhaltung von Ruhe und Ordnung sorgt, sondern auch die erhebende Erinnerung an die Regierung des Begründers der noch auf dem Thron sitzenden Dynastie Davids wach hält und pflegt. Dem Beter unseres Psalms gleich werden viele, viele Judäer ihre Verbundenheit mit Jahwe und seinem Tempel und ihre Anhänglichkeit an ihr Volk und seine trotz allem stolze Geschichte zu vereinigen gewußt haben. Die Polemik vieler Propheten gegen falsche Einschätzung des Tempelkultus darf uns gegen diese Tatsache nicht blind machen. Ps. 108 ist ein Gebet um Errettung aus großer Not, in der sich—das wohl vorexilische—Israel befindet, und gibt der Zuversicht, daß Jahwe diese Not wenden und die Feinde Israels zertreten werde, Ausdruck. Dabei enthalten die Verse 8–11:

[8] Jahwe sprach in seinem Heiligtum: "Ich werde frohlocken, aufteilen Sichem,
das Tal Sukkot vermessen.
[9] Mir gehört Gilead, mir Manasse, und Ephraim ist der Helm meines Hauptes,
Juda mein Scepter,
[10] Moab meine Waschschüssel, auf Edom werfe ich meinen Schuh,
über Philistäa juble ich.
[11] Wer geleitet mich zu einer festen Stadt,
wer führt mich nach Edom?"

offenbar Hinweise auf ganz bestimmte Geschehnisse, aber da diese mehrdeutig sind, hilft uns das in der Ansetzung unseres Psalms nicht weiter. Nur das läßt sich sagen, daß auch Ps. 108 von der Verbundenheit nationaler Haltung und religiöser Gesinnung zeugt und darum in der vorexilischen Zeit anzusetzen sein wird. An dem—im übrigen nach vielen Richtungen mehrdeutigen—Psalm 110 ist das eine über jeden Zweifel erhaben daß er von engster Verbundenheit des Jahwe-Kultes mit der Davidischen Dynastie zeugt. Das zeigt schon sein Anfang:

[1] Spruch Jahwes an meinen Herrn:
"Setz dich zu meiner Rechten,
bis ich mache deine Feinde zum Schemel für deine Füße."
[2] Dein mächtiges Scepter sendet Jahwe aus Zion:
"Herrsche über deine Feinde."

Das stärkste, auch uns Heutige noch ergreifende Zeugnis engster Verbundenheit exilierter Judäer mit ihrer Religion und deren Symbol, dem Jerusalemischen Tempel, und der ihn beherbergenden Stadt Jerusalem stellt Ps. 137 dar:

[1] An den Kanälen von Babel, dort saßen wir weinend,
wenn wir an Zion dachten.
[2] An die Mitte ihrer Weiden
hängten wir unsere Harfen.
[3] Denn dort baten uns unsere Fänger um Lieder
und unsere Peiniger um Freudelaut:
"Singt uns ein Zionslied!"
[4] Wie könnten wir singen ein Jahwe-Lied
im fremden Lande?
[5] Wenn ich dein vergäße, Jerusalem,
so schrumpfe meine Rechte,
[6] es klebe meine Zunge an meine Kehle,
wenn ich deiner nicht gedächte,
wenn ich nicht erhöbe Jerusalem
zu meiner größten Freude!

7 Gedenke, Jahwe, den Edomitern,
den Tag von Jerusalem,
die sagten: "legt bloß, legt bloß
bis in ihren Grund!"
8 Tochter Babel, du Verwüsterin,
wohl dem, der dir vergilt, das, was du an uns getan!
9 Wohl dem, der packt und zerschmeißt
deine Kinder an einem Felsen!

## DIE LADE JAHWES IN DEN PSALMEN

Fünf Psalmen, nämlich 24,[9] 47, 78, 106, und 132[10] kommen auf die Lade Jahwes zu sprechen und enthalten einige Angaben,[11] die geeignet sind, auf die Geschichte dieses angesehenen Führungs-und Kriegssymbols Israels neues Licht zu werfen. So sollen diese Angaben hier vorgeführt werden, und zwar nicht nach der Ordnung unseres Psalters, sondern in der Folge der Geschichte der Lade, die diese erfahren hat.[12] Da wären dann zunächst zwei Verse aus dem Psalm 106 zu nennen, der eine Rückschau auf die eine ununterbrochene, mit seinem Aufenthalt in Ägypten beginnende Kette der Abfälle Israels von Jahwe darstellt und in V. 19–20 so lautet:

19 Sie machten sich einen Jungstier am Horeb
und beteten dieses Bild an,
20 und sie vertauschten ihre Ehre
mit der Gestalt eines Rindes, das Gras frißt.

Denn "ihre Ehre" (*k^e^bôdām*) bezeichnet offenbar hier ebenso die Lade, wie es I Sam. 4:21–22 der Fall ist, wo die schwangere Frau des Eli-Sohnes Phinehas ihren infolge des Verlustes der Lade an die Philister zu früh geborenen Sohn "Fort die Ehre" (*ʾî kābôd*) nennt und ausdrücklich sagt, daß diese Namengebung durch den Verlust der Lade veranlaßt ist, und wie in V. 61 des noch zu behandelnden Psalms 78[13] die Lade "Jahwes Kraft" (*ʿuzzô*) und "Jahwes Zier" (*tipʾartô*) genannt wird. Ps. 78, ein historischer, mit

9. O. Eißfeldt, Jahwe Zebaoth (Miscellanea Academica Berolinensia II, 2 [1950], S. 128–50. 1 Taf.mit 4 Abb., Kleine Schriften III [1966], S. 103–23. Taf.V mit 4. Abb.)

10. O. Eißfeldt, Psalm 132 (*WdO* 2 [1954–59], S. 480–83; Kleine Schriften III [1966], S. 481–85).

11. O. Eißfeldt, Psalm 76 (*ThLZ* 82 [1957], Sp. 801–8; Kleine Schriften III [1966], S. 448–57) hält es im Anschluß an Ed.König und A. Weiser für möglich, daß Ps. 76:3, "Und es ward in Salem seine Hütte und seine Wohnung in Zion" die Einholung der Lade nach Jerusalem durch David im Auge hat. Dann wäre die Reihe der Psalmen, die auf die Lade zu sprechen kommen, durch Ps. 76 zu ergänzen.

12. Vgl. O. Eißfeldt, Die Lade Jahwes in Geschichtserzählung, Sage und Lied (Das Alterum 14 [1968], S. 131–45).

13. Vgl. Anm. 1. und weiter unten.

Israels Aufenthalt in Ägypten beginnender und mit der Erwählung Davids zum König über Gesamtisrael schließender Rückblick auf Israels Geschichte, der vor allem bei dem Übergang der politischen und kultischen Macht von den Nordstämmen auf den Südstamm Juda verweilt, kommt in V. 60–61, wie schon angedeutet, auf den Verlust der Lade zu sprechen und sagt da von Jahwe:

60 Er verwarf die Stätte von Silo,
das Zelt, das er aufgeschlagen hatte unter den Menschen,
61 und er gab seine Macht in die Gefangenschaft
und seine Zier in die Hand eines Feindes.

Erzählen Ps. 106 und Ps. 78 von der Anfertigung der Lade am Horeb oder genauer von ihrer Bedrohung durch das Jungstierbild und von ihrem Verlust an die Philister, so haben es Ps. 132, Ps. 24, und Ps. 27 mit der mühereichen und strapazenvollen Auffindung der Lade durch David, von ihrer Einholung in die von ihm eroberte Stadt Jerusalem und von ihrer Überführung in den von ihm erbauten Jahwe-Tempel durch Salomo zu tun. Ps. 132, dessen Verfasser offenbar noch uns unbekannt bleibende Traditionen über die Auffindung der Lade durch David zur Verfügung gestanden haben, bringt in seiner zweiten Hälfte, in V. 11–18, die Mitteilung des Schwures Jahwes, daß die Dynastie Davids ewig in Jerusalem auf dem Thron sitzen solle und schließt so:

17 Dort lasse ich sprießen ein Horn dem David,
richte her eine Leuchte für meinen Gesalbten.
18 Seine Feinde kleide ich in Schande,
aber auf ihm blüht sein Diadem.

Die erste Hälfte unseres Psalms, V. 1–10, die in V. 1–2 den Dichter, in V. 3–5 David, in V. 6–9 David und seine Begleitung am Wort sein läßt, und zwar so, daß mit der in V. 6 genannten Wohnung Jahwes und mit dem ebenda erwähnten Fußschemel Jahwes die vorläufige Stätte der Lade in Kirjat Je<sup>c</sup>arim gemeint ist, und V. 8–9 die Aufforderung an Jahwe zu dem von festlich gekleideten Priestern und von jubelnden Frommen begleiteten Aufbruch nach seiner ständigen Wohnung in Davids Palast enthalten, und in V. 10 wieder der Dichter das Wort ergreift:

1 Gedenke, Jahwe, David
alle seine Mühen,
2 der Jahwe geschworen,
dem Starken Jakobs ein Gelübde dargebracht:

3 "Nicht gehe ich in mein gastliches Zelt,
nicht besteige ich mein Ruhebett.
4 Nicht gönne ich Schlaf meinen Augen,
meinen Wimpern Schlummer,
5 bis ich finde die Stätte für Jahwe,
eine Wohnung für den Starken Jakobs.
6 Seht, wir haben von der Lade gehört in Ephratah,
haben sie gefunden im Felde von Jaᶜar.
7 Laßt uns eingehen in seine Wohnung,
uns niederwerfen vor dem Schemel seiner Füße!
8 Auf, Jahwe, zu deiner Ruhe,
du und deine mächtige Lade!
9 Deine Priester sollen sich würdig kleiden,
und deine Frommen jubeln.
10 Um Davids, deines Knechtes, willen
weis das Antlitz deines Gesalbten nicht ab!"

Ps. 24[14] gleicht in seiner jetzigen Gestalt unserem Adventsliede "Macht hoch die Tür, die Tor macht weit," das, wie dieser Anfang zeigt, von der zweiten Hälfte des Psalms, V. 7–10, abhängig ist und nach Ausweis der 5. Strophe mit ihrem "Komm, o mein Heiland Jesu Christ, meins Herzens Tür dir offen ist" die alttestamentliche Vorlage verchristlicht hat, weist nämlich neben der Aufforderung an die Tore Jerusalems, sich für den starken Kriegsgott Jahwe, den Jahwe der Heerscharen, zu öffnen in V. 1–6 zwei ganz andere literarische Stücke auf, nämlich einen Hymnus auf Jahwe (V. 1–2) und eine Einlaßliturgie, die von den für das Betreten des Tempels gültigen Bedingungen handelt (V. 3–6). Die eine bedeutsame kultische Feier, die Einholung der altehrwürdigen Lade in seine eben gewonnene Hauptstadt Jerusalem durch David, begleitende zweite Hälfte unseres Psalms ist also ebenso auf eine höhere religiöse und sittliche Ebene erhoben worden, wie das bei unserem Adventslied mit seinem dem alten Psalm entnommenen Abschnitt der Fall ist. Ihrer ursprünglichen Bestimmung nach aber stellt, wie an anderer Stelle gezeigt worden ist, die zweite Hälfte von Ps. 24 den bei der als Staatsakt ausgestalteten feierlichen Einholung der Lade und des sich auf oder an ihr offenbarenden Jahwe Zebaoth gesungenen Festkantus dar:

7 Erhebt, ihr Tore, eure Häupter,
und erhebt euch, ihr uralten Pforten,
daß der König der Ehre einziehe!
8 "Wer ist denn der König der Ehre?"
Jahwe, stark und ein Held,
Jahwe, ein Kriegsheld.

14. Vgl. Anm. 9.

9 Erhebt, ihr Tore, eure Häupter,
und erhebt euch, ihr uralten Pforten,
daß der König der Ehre einziehe!
10 "Wer ist denn der König der Ehre?"
Jahwe Zebaoth,
er ist der König der Ehre.

Berichtet II Sam. 6 von der Einholung der Lade nach Jerusalem durch David und stellt Ps. 24:7–10 den bei dieser Feier vorgetragenen Kantus dar, so scheint Ps. 47 das Lied zu sein, das bei der I Kön. 8:1–11 ausführlich und anschaulich erzählten Überführung der Lade aus Davids Palast in den von Salomo errichteten Tempel gesungen worden ist. Jedenfalls paßt Ps. 47 gut in diese Feier hinein, wie denn in diesem Psalm für das Hinaufziehen der Lade oder Jahwes aus dem Palast Davids in den Jahwe-Tempel das Wort *ᶜālāh* gebraucht wird, dessen Kausativform (*häᶜᵃlāh*) "hinaufbringen" in I Kön. 8:1, 4 das Hinauftragen der Lade bezeichnet:

2 Alle Völker schlagt in die Hand,
jubelt Jahwe zu mit Jauchzen!
3 Denn Jahwe ist der Höchste,
furchtbar, ein großer König über die ganze Erde.
4 Er tritt Völker unter uns
und Nationen unter unsere Füße.
5 Er erwählt für uns unsere Erbe,
die Zier Jakobs, den er liebt.
6 Hinaufzieht Jahwe mit Jubel,
Jahwe mit Posaunenschall.
7 Besingt Jahwe, singt,
singt unserem König zu, singt!
8 Denn König der gazen Erde ist Jahwe,
singt ein Kunstlied!
9 Jahwe herrscht über die Völker,
Jahwe sitzt auf seinem heiligen Thron.
10 Die Fürsten der Völker sind versammelt,
das Volk des Gottes Abrahams.
Denn Jahwe gehören die Schilder der Erde,
er ist hocherhaben.

## DIE VORSTELLUNG DER LADE ALS BEHÄLTNIS DER GESETZESTAFELN UND IHRE ÜBERWINDUNG

Die eben betrachteten Psalmen erwähnen also Geschehnisse mit der Lade, die von ihrer Anfertigung am Horeb bis zu ihrer Unterbringung im Allerheiligsten des Jerusalemischen Tempels reichen. Dabei erscheint die Lade überall als Führungs-und Kriegsemblem, während ihre Rolle als Behältnis der Dekalog-Tafeln, die ihr von Ex. 25:10–22; 40, 20; Deut. 10:1–5 und anderen Stellen zugeschrieben wird und infolgedessen das Feld beherrscht, überhaupt nicht erwähnt und noch nicht einmal angedeutet wird. Dabei hätte—sollte man meinen—es sehr vielen Psalmendichtern doch nahe gelegen, die Aufgabe der Lade, den Dekalog zu bergen, zu erwähnen. Ausdrücke für "Gesetz," "Gebot," "Satzung," und dergleichen kommen im Psalter recht häufig vor, nicht nur in Psalm 119, der unter dem Zwang, 22 achtzeilige Strophen zu bilden und diese acht Zeilen mit demselben Alphabet-Buchstaben beginnen zu lassen, für das "Gesetz," dessen Preis er sich vorgenommen hat, immer neue Ausdrücke finden muß, sondern auch in vielen anderen Psalmen. Alphabetisch aufgezählt sind diese—meistens im Plural vorkommende—Benennungen des "Gesetzes" die folgenden *ʾimrāh* "Rede," *dābār* "Wort," *ḥōq* und *ḥuqqāh* "Satzung," *miṣwāh* "Gebot," *mišpāṭ* 'Recht," *ʿēdût* "Zeugnis," *piqqûd* "Befehl," und *tôrāh* "Gesetz." Wenn trotzdem die Lade als Behältnis für die Dekalog-Tafeln niemals im Psalter erwähnt wird, so ist das höchst merkwürdig und doch wohl nur daraus zu erklären, daß die ältere und historisch zutreffende Vorstellung von der Lade als Führungs-und Kriegsemblem sich neben der jüngeren, die sie als Behältnis für die Gesetzestafeln verstanden wissen wollte, behauptet hat. Das mag damit zusammenhängen, daß die Psalmen oder doch die meisten von ihnen älter sind, als vielfach angenommen wird, nämlich aus einer Zeit herrühren, in der sich die neue Auffassung von der Art und der Zweckbestimmung der Lade noch nicht durchgesetzt und die ältere überflügelt hatte, d.h. spätestens aus der ersten Hälfte des 6. Jahrhunderts v.Chr. Das älteste Zeugnis für die jüngere Auffassung der Lade ist Deut. 10:1–5, wo Mose am Wort ist und sagt:

> [1]Zu dieser Zeit sprach Jahwe zu mir: "Haue dir zwei Steintafeln wie die ersten und steig zu mir auf den Berg und mache dir eine Lade aus Holz, [2]und ich werde schreiben auf die Tafeln die Worte, die auf den ersten Tafeln gestanden haben, die du zerschmettert hast, und lege sie in die Lade." [3]Und ich machte eine Lade aus Akazienholz und haute zwei Steintafeln wie die ersten und stieg auf den Berg mit den beiden Tafeln in meiner Hand. [4]Und der schrieb auf die Tafeln wie die erste Schrift die zehn Worte, die Jahwe zu euch gesagt hatte auf dem Berg aus dem Feuer am Tage der Versammlung, und Jahwe gab sie mir. [5]Und ich wandte mich und stieg von dem Berge herab und legte die Tafeln in die Lade, die ich gemacht hatte, und sie blieben dort, wie Jahwe befohlen hatte.

Wenn die eben gemachten Ausführungen zutreffen und die Psalmen darum nur von der Rolle der Lade als Führungs- und Kriegsemblem zu sagen wissen, weil die Auffassung der Lade als Gesetzesbehältnis noch nicht bekannt war, so wirft das nicht nur auf die Art der Lade, sondern auch auf die Frage, was eigentlich ursprünglich im Mittelpunkt des Sinai- oder

Horeb-Geschehens gestanden habe, neues Licht. Daß das nicht der ethische Dekalog von Ex. 20 und Deut. 5 gewesen sein kann, wird dann vollends klar. Denn Deut. 10, 1–5 stellt offensichtlich eine Weiterentwicklung der Maßnahmen dar, mit denen ein Redaktor durch seine Zusätze in Ex. 34:1, 4 "wie die ersten, und ich will auf die Tafeln die Worte schreiben, die auf den ersten Tafeln gestanden haben, welche du zerschmettert hast" und "wie die ersten" den in Ex. 34 steckenden kultischen J-Dekalog zur Wiederholung des ethischen Dekalogs in Ex. 20 gemacht hat. Die Rolle der Lade, die L, J und E als Führungs-und Kriegsemblem aufgefaßt haben, hat dieser Redaktor bestehen lassen, was im einzelnen schwer zu erkennen ist, weil später ein Redaktor der verhältnismäßig umfangreichen Anweisung über die Lade (Ex. 25:10–22) und deren knapperer Ausführung (Ex. 37:1–9), wie sie P bietet, zuliebe die älteren Berichte über die Lade gekürzt hat. Aber das gilt jedenfalls, daß die älteren Erzählungsfäden von einem Zusammenhang zwischen den Gesetzestafeln und der Lade nichts gewußt und die Vorstellung von der Lade als Behältnis dieser Tafeln nicht gekannt haben. Daß die nach der Zerschmetterung der ersten Tafeln durch Mose auf Jahwes Befehl angefertigten zweiten Tafeln von Gott mit demselben Dekalog beschrieben seien, geht auf einen deuteronomistischen Redaktor zurück, und ebenso ist es diesem zuzuschreiben, daß die Lade, die früher bei L, J und E ein hochverehrtes Symbol war und daher nach Ex. 33:1–6 unter Verwendung von kostbarem Material angefertigt worden ist, an Würde verloren hat, wie sie nach Deut. 10:1–5 aus bloßem Akazienholz hergestellt wird.

So gewinnen die uns über das Sinai- oder Horeb-Geschehen vorliegenden Berichte perspektivische Tiefe, die sich nach oben und nach unten noch über das allgemein angenommene Maß hinaus verlängern läßt. Was die Verlängerung nach oben angeht, so habe ich in meinen Aufsätzen "Die älteste Erzählung vom Sinaibund"[15] und "Das Gesetz ist zwischeneingekommen. Ein Beitrag zur Analyse der Sinai-Erzählung"[16] (*ThLZ* 91 [1966], Sp. 1–6 = Kleine Schriften IV [1968], S. 209–14) zu zeigen versucht, daß sich in Ex. 24:13a, 14, 15a; 34:10–13, 15–16; 32:17–18, 25–29 deutliche Spuren von einer Erzählung erhalten haben, die sich die Bundschließung als allein in mündlichen Abmachungen Jahwes und der Vertreter Israels, Moses und Josuas, bestehend vorstellt, wobei der Schwerpunkt auf der Israel von Jahwe verheißenen Austreibung der Kanaaniter aus ihrem Lande liegt und Israels Verpflichtung, seinerseits jede Verbindung mit den Kanaanitern zu unterlassen und die durch sie ermöglichte Gefährdung der Allein-

15. *ZAW* 73 (1961), S. 137–46; Kleine Schriften IV [1968], S. 12–20.
16. *ThLZ* 91 (1966), Sp. 1–6; Kleine Schriften IV [1968], S. 209–16.

verehrung Jahwes in Israel zu vermeiden, nur eine Art Echo auf die göttliche Zusage darstellt. Die Verlängerung nach unten hin, die ebenfalls möglich ist, mag hier nur an zwei Äußerungen veranschaulicht werden, an Jeremias Wort vom Neuen Bunde in Jer. 31:31–34 und an Jesu Vertiefung alttestamentlicher Gebote, wie er sie Matthäus 5:21–48 vornimmt. Das von Jeremia vernommene Wort Jahwes lautet:

31 Tage werden kommen, Ausspruch Jahwes, da schließe ich mit dem Hause Israel und mit dem Hause Juda einen neuen Bund, 32 nicht wie der Bund, den ich mit ihren Vätern schloß, als ich sie bei der Hand nahm, sie herauszuführen aus dem Lande Ägypten, welchen Bund mit mir sie gebrochen haben und ich sie zwingen mußte, Ausspruch Jahwes. 33 Vielmehr dies ist der Bund, den ich mit dem Haus Israel schließe nach diesen Tagen, Ausspruch Jahwes: Ich lege mein Gesetz in ihr Inneres und schreibe es in ihr Herz, und ich will ihnen zum Gott sein und sie sollen mir zum Volk sein, 34 und nicht braucht einer seinen Freund oder einer seinen Bruder mehr zu lehren: "Lern Jahwe kennen." Denn sie werden mich alle kennen, Kleine und Große, Ausspruch Jahwes. Denn ich vergebe ihre Schuld und gedenke ihrer Sünde nicht mehr.

Die vertiefte Auslegung alttestamentlicher Gebote, wie sie Jesus in der Bergpredigt vornimmt, beginnt aber so: 21 "Ihr habt gehört, daß zu den Alten gesagt ist: Du sollst nicht töten! Wer aber tötet, ist des Gerichts schuldig. 22 Ich aber sage euch, daß jeder, der seinem Bruder zürnt, des Gerichts schuldig ist." Diese von Jeremia und von Jesus vorgenommene Vertiefung der älteren Vorstellung vom Gesetz hat die Lade überflüssig gemacht, wie Jeremia es in 3, 16 auch ausdrücklich feststellt, daß in der von ihm verkündigten Heilszeit die Lade mit dem Bundesgesetz Jahwes keine Rolle mehr spielen werde.

# Textkritisches zu Deuterojesaja

KARL ELLIGER

Dem verehrten Jubilar, dem er nicht nur manche wissenschaftliche Anregung verdankt, sondern auch dessen menschliche und wirtschaftliche Hilfe durch CARE-Pakete zur Überwindung der Nachkriegssituation er in lebhafter Erinnerung behält, erlaubt sich der Verfasser, zwei aus seiner Arbeit an einem Kommentar entstandene neue Textvorschläge zu Deuterojesaja als bescheidenes Zeichen seines Dankes auf den Geburtstagstisch zu legen.

Der eine Vorschlag betrifft den Anfang von Jes. 44:12. 𝔐[1] lautet folgendermassen:

*ḥārāš barzæl maᶜᵃṣād | u-pāᶜal bap-pæḥām.*

𝔊 setzt *hoti* voran und übersetzt weiter: *ṓxyene téktōn sídēron*, was nach Delitzsch u. a. einem *hēḥēd ḥārāš brzl* oder nach Gesenius u. a. einem *jāḥēd ḥārāš brzl*—so neuerdings wieder *BHS*, auch Westermann, der allerdings *jāḥēd* erst hinter *mᶜṣd* einfügen will—entsprechen soll. Aber schwerlich ist *jḥd* durch Haplographie (vgl. v. 11 Ende) ausgefallen. Das ist natürlich nicht unmöglich. Aber nach 𝔊s ganzer Übersetzungsart ist es wahrscheinlicher, dass 𝔊 das Verbum frei ergänzt hat. An 𝔊 hat sich 𝔖 angeschlossen: *dlṭš przlʾ ngrʾ*, denkt also, wie wohl schon 𝔊 an den "Zimmermann," der das Eisen schärft, was gewiss nicht richtig ist. 𝔗 denkt an den Schmied: "Der Schmied (*npḥʾ*) macht aus Eisen (eine Axt)," fügt aber ebenfalls das Verbum frei ein

1. Die Sigla sind die der Biblia Hebraica Stuttgartensia.

(doch s. auch unten) und trennt *brzl* von *ḥrš*, was angesichts v. 13aα schwerlich richtig ist. 𝔙 faber ferrarius = 𝔐.

Braucht man also bis hierher 𝔐 nicht zu beanstanden und jedenfalls auf Grund der Versionen keine Korrektur vorzunehmen, so ändert sich das beim dritten Wort. *maᶜᵃṣād* ist offenbar verderbt. Der so bezeichnete Gegenstand erscheint als Werkzeug zur Holzbearbeitung Jer. 10:3 und ist als solcher bei der Metallbearbeitung natürlich fehl am Platze. Als Partizipium von der Wurzel *ᶜṣd* "schneiden" aufgefasst—so Muilenburg—fällt das Wort völlig aus dem Stil der Umgebung, die durchgehend Perfektum oder Imperfektum gebraucht. Aus dem gleichen Grunde ist auch Torreys Vorschlag *mᵊᶜaṣṣēb* (vgl. Hi. 10:8) abzulehnen. An sich wäre das Verbum *ᶜṣd* "schneiden, abschneiden, ausschneiden" (vgl. Köhler, Wörterbuch s. u. *mᶜṣd*) durchaus brauchbar, sei es als ḳal *ᶜāṣad* oder als pi. *ᶜiṣṣēd*. Denn die Schilderung der Arbeit des Metallarbeiters könnte gut damit begonnen haben, dass er sich das nötige Werkstück von dem Eisenbarren ab- oder grob aus ihm herausschneidet. Dann müsste ein Wort für dieses Anfangsstück als Objekt zu jenem Prädikat ausgefallen sein. Und sollte nicht wenigstens ein Konsonant dieses Wortes in dem *m* vor *ᶜṣd* erhalten sein? Natürlich sind dann viele Lösungen denkbar. Aber nimmt man das *m* als Schlusskonsonanten, geht von da zurück und nimmt Ausfall durch Haplographie an, so ergibt sich ein *l* als mittlerer Radikal. Sollte es Zufall sein, dass die einzige ernsthaft in Frage kommende Wurzel dann *glm* ist? Auf diese Weise stellt sich ungesucht das Wort *golæm* ein, das "etwas Ungestaltetes," "formlose Masse," Ps. 139:16 speziell "Embryo" bedeutet (vgl. Baumgartner, Wörterbuch) und dem Sinne nach zweifellos gut passt. Ich schlage daher vor *golæm ᶜāṣad* (*ᶜiṣṣēd*). Das Auge des Schreibers irrte von dem *l* von *brzl* auf das *l* von *glm* ab, so dass ein *l* und dazu *g* unter den Tisch fielen.

Schon die alten Übersetzungen haben an dem *mᶜṣd* herumgeraten. 𝔊 übersetzt den Rest von v aα und v aβ *skepárnō(i) eirgásato autó*, fügt also frei die Präposition *b-* ein und lässt die folgende Kopula beiseite, dazu die "Kohlen," mit denen sie bei ihrem Verständnis des Satzes nichts zu beginnen wusste (erst in 𝔊ᴠᴸ/ᵓ\ᵘ·ᵃ· ist *en ánthraxi(n)* nachgetragen). 𝔖 hat sich wieder in das Gefolge von 𝔊 begeben: *wbᶜšpᵓ spjh* "und mit der Zimmeraxt glättet er ihn (oder: haut er ihn ab)"; auch hier fehlt *bpḥm*. 𝔗 interpretiert den Satz *u-pāᶜal bap-pæḥām* als "und er bläst ein Feuer an in den Kohlen"; nicht ausgeschlossen ist, dass diese Interpretation einzig aus dem Wort *bpḥm* herausgesponnen ist und dass *wpᶜl* in dem "er macht" (*ᶜbjd*) des vorangehenden Satzes steckt, wo dann auch 𝔗 sich über die Kopula hinweggesetzt haben würde. 𝔙 (faber ferrarius) lima operatus est: in prunis (et in malleis formavit illud) "hat mit der Feile gearbeitet; in Kohlen . . ."; auch hier ist die Kopula unterdrückt, nur ist *bpḥm* beibehalten, aber gegen 𝔐 zum Folgenden gezogen. Die modernen Verbesserungsversuche streichen entweder das *mᶜṣd* kurzerhand—so nach Duhm u. a. zuletzt wieder Steinmann, Penna, North, Fohrer—oder sie gehen von der Annahme aus, dass der Überlieferungsfehler erst hinter dem *m*, ja erst beim letzten Buchstaben von *mᶜṣd* beginne: Klostermann, Budde, Fischer *mǣ ᶜāṣēb* "wie müht er sich!" oder Torrey, Kissane, Ziegler *məᶜaṣṣēb*, was dann bei Kissane noch zur Einfügung von *hap-pæsæl* fuhrt. Auch die Kopula vor *pāᶜal* wird teils gestrichen (Penna), teils in das Impf-präfix verwandelt (*jipᶜal* nach Duhm u. a. zuletzt wieder North, Westermann) und danach *pŏᵒlō* eingesetzt (Budde, Westermann, BHS). Dass alle diese Versuche nicht befriedigen, liegt daran, dass man den Fehler an der falschen Stelle sucht und z. T. sich auf die Versionen verlässt, die selbst schon mit dem Text experimentierten.

Der oben gemachte neue Lösungsvorschlag dürfte wenigstens grundsätzlich in die richtige Richtung weisen und hat auch das für sich, dass er den überlieferten Konsonantenbestand mit Einschluss des v aβ unangetastet lässt.

Er lautet also

*ḥārāš barzæl | golæm ᶜāṣad | u-pāᶜal bap-pæḥām*

Der Handwerker in Eisen
schmiedet die Urform aus
und bearbeitet sie in der Kohlenglut.

Trifft der Vorschlag zu, dann liefert Jes. 44:12 neben dem unsicheren Ps. 139:16 einen weiteren Beleg für das im AT sonst nicht bezeugte Wort *golæm*.

Bei dem anderen Vorschlag geht es um Jes. 53:6b/7. Nach 𝔐 lautet der Text:

6b *w-jhwh hipgīaᶜ bō ᵓet ᶜᵃwōn kullānū*
7 *niggaś wə-hūᵓ naᶜᵃnæ | wə-lōᵓ jiptaḥ-pīw*
*kaś-śǣ laṭ-ṭæbaḥ jūbāl | ū-kə-rāḥēl li-pnē gōzəzǣhā næᵓᵆlāmā*
*wə-lōᵓ jiptaḥ pīw*

An der ersten Zeile nimmt man gewöhnlich keinen Anstoss. Aber sie ist schwerlich in ihrem ursprünglichen Zustande überliefert. Weder stilistisch noch metrisch passt sie zu ihrer Umgebung; so, wie sie jetzt dasteht, ist sie Prosa. Ein Parallelismus ist nicht mehr vorhanden; zu dem üblichen Doppeldreier fehlen mindestens eine, eher zwei Hebungen. Zwar der Anfang bα scheint intakt zu sein; aber in v b$\beta$ wird alles fraglich: die prosaische nota accusativi sucht in der ganzen Perikope ihresgleichen -ʾ*t* ist v 8 *a$\beta$*. 9a$\alpha$.$\beta$. 12a$\beta$.$\varepsilon$ stets die Präposition "mit" -; ferner fällt der Singular *ᶜāwōn* auf, wo bisher (5 a$\alpha$. $\beta$ bzw. 4a$\alpha$.$\beta$) stets von den Sünden und Krankheiten im Plural die Rede war und das auch nachher so bleibt (11 b sicher, 8 b$\beta$ und 12 b, wo in 𝔐 der Text verderbt ist, so gut wie sicher); schliesslich bezeugt 𝔊 (*taĩs hamartíais hēmõn*) das *kl* nicht, sondern scheint *ᶜᵃwōnōtēnū* gelesen zu haben. 𝔔ᵃ geht mit 𝔐, auch 𝔔ᵇ, wo hinter ʾt ᶜwn der Text weggebrochen ist, ebenso 𝔙, wahrend 𝔖 𝔗 zwar das "(unser) aller," aber wie 𝔊 auch den Plural "Sünden" übersetzen.

Wie der Text von v 6 b ursprünglich einmal gelautet hat, ist kaum mehr zu sagen. Zwar könnte man zu seiner Wiederherstellung noch das jetzige Anfangswort von v 7 heranziehen, das ja sicher vor dem eigentlichen Anfang des Verses steht (s. unten). So sieht Torrey es in der Form *nᵉgāśō* als das ursprüngliche Prädikat des v 6 b$\beta$ an :"unser aller Schuld liess er ihn zahlen," während er in v 6 b$\alpha$ das *hpgjᶜ* elliptisch versteht: "(aber Jahwe) liess (ihn) die Strafe treffen." Gewiss ergibt sich auf diese Weise ein annehmbarer Doppeldreier. Aber ist schon der elliptische Gebrauch von *hpgjᶜ* schwierig, so erst recht der Gebrauch von *ngś* "beitreiben, drängen" mit dem doppelten Akkusativ, der 2 Kö. 23:25 nur scheinbar belegt ist (cf. BHK). Auch Mowinckel beanstandet v 6b, sucht aber den Fehler in der Mitte, wo er aus ʾ*t* ein dem *hpgjᶜ* paralleles Prädikat *hæʾᵆtāhū* "er brachte über ihn" gewinnt und damit ebenfalls einen annehmbaren Doppeldreier. Aber auch hier ist der Akkusativ des Pronomens prekär (vgl. die einzige Parallele Jes. 21:14), und obendrein ist der Ausdruck ausserordentlich matt. Immerhin dürfte Mowinckel mit seiner Annahme einer Verderbnis gerade in der Mitte der Zeile auf der rechten Spur sein, weil es kaum Zufall ist, dass auch in der darunter stehenden Zeile 7 a$\alpha$ die Mitte Schaden gelitten hat (s. unten). Darf man das ʾ*t* als Rest eines ehemaligen *ḥaṭṭāʾēnū* oder *ḥaṭṭōʾtēnū* in Anspruch nehmen und dieses Wort als Objekt des v b$\alpha$, der in seiner jetzigen Form schwerlich mehr als zwei Hebungen ausmacht? Die Parallele dazu wäre in dem einfachen *ᶜᵃwōnōtēnū* der 𝔊-Vorlage noch erhalten. Und wenn das *kl* nicht blosses Füllsel sein sollte, dann ist es vermutlich aus den Resten des dem *hpgjᶜ* parallelen Prädikats zusammengeklaubt. Die Verderbnis des Textes ist alt, aber mehr als die ursprüngliche Struktur ist nicht mehr zu erkennen; einem Rekonstruktionsversuch sind deutlich Grenzen gesetzt.

Anders ist es bei der folgenden Zeile 7 a$\alpha$, die ebenso wie 6b nicht mehr in ihrer ursprünglichen Form erhalten ist. Wieder hat das Unglück die Mitte betroffen. Der Text war hier offenbar in beiden Zeilen verschmiert oder sonstwie beschädigt; was man aus ihm noch entziffert hatte, war anscheinend zunächst auf den Rändern notiert und wurde hernach von verschiedenen Abschreibern verschieden verarbeitet, jedenfalls in der 𝔊-Vorlage anders als in 𝔐. 𝔐 hat in 7 a$\alpha$ wie in 6b mehr aufgenommen als die 𝔊-Vorlage, hat aber dabei in 7 keine glücklichere Hand entwickelt als in 6. Wie man sich das Zustandekommen des jetzigen Textes auch denken mag, so dürfte nicht zu bestreiten sein, dass das betonte *wᵊ-hūʾ* nicht nur aus grammatisch-stilistischen Gründen genauso an den Satzanfang gehört wie in 5.12, sondern auch weil es sachlich offenbar dem ebenso betont vorangestellten *w-jhwh* 6b entspricht. Wenn 𝔊 mit *kaì autós* den v 7 beginnt, so trifft sie gewiss das Ursprüngliche. *ngś* fehlt bei ihr (wie in 7 *kl*), es sei denn, dass sie es in ihrer Fortsetzung *dià tò kekakōsthai* mit *nʿnh* zusammengezogen hätte, was freilich gegen die sonst in c 53 bei ihr zu beobachtende Art ginge. Es war grundsätzlich nicht zu beanstanden, dass Torrey *ngś* im vorhergehenden Verse unterbringen wollte (s. oben), weil er richtig sah, dass erst mit *w-hwʾ* der neue Vers beginnt. Die Kopula zu *nʿnh* zu versetzen (Grätz, Cheyne; cf. BHS), ergibt zwar einen grammatisch nicht mehr anstössigen Satz, hat aber 𝔔$^{a.b}$ und die Versionen gegen sich; 𝔖 lasst *hwʾ* freilich ganz fort, während sie es 4. 5. 11. 12 regelmässig übersetzt, aber schwerlich, weil es in ihrer Vorlage fehlte, sondern doch wohl in der richtigen Erkenntnis, dass es im gegenwärtigen Zusammenhang sinnlos ist. 𝔙 hilft sich, indem sie *w-hwʾ nʿnh* als Zustandssatz zu begreifen sucht: oblatus est quia ipse voluit. (NB. Wie Volz, Steinmann, Penna übersetzt Westermann: "Gepeinigt duldete er demütig"; sie helfen sich also ähnlich wie 𝔙, nur dass die Umkehrung von Haupt- und Zustandssatz grammatisch äusserst fragwürdig ist.) 𝔙 leitet dabei *ngś* von der Wurzel *ngš* "sich nähern (bes. in kultischem Sinne)" ab, wie das auch *σ' ϑ' prosḗchthē* und 𝔖 *qrb* "er trat herzu" tun sowie 𝔗 *bʿj* "er betete," dem dann *mjtwtb* "er wurde erhört" = *nʿnh* von *ʿnh* I "antworten" entspricht, während 𝔖 (*wʾtmkk* "er wurde niedergestreckt"), *σ'(ϑ') ḗkousen* an *ʿnh* II "sich ducken" usw. denken und ebenso 𝔙, auch 𝔊 (*dià tò kekakōsthai*). Zu dem im Sinne von 𝔊 𝔖 𝔙 verstandenen *nʿnh* passt zweifellos das *ngs* nur—und zwar gut—als Niphal von *ngś* "treiben, drängen," wie 𝔐 es will. Man muss nur konsequent sein und es nicht nur dem Sinne nach, sondern auch in seiner Stellung mit *nʿnh* wieder verbinden und es aus seiner auch in 𝔐 im Grunde immer noch vorhandenen Stellung am rechten Rande endlich befreien. Auch seine ursprüngliche Stelle ist mit einiger Sicherheit auszumachen. Schiebt man es sofort hinter *w-hwʾ* ein, hätte man Ausfall der Kopula vor *nʿnh* anzunehmen. Besser ist es, diesen Text zu lassen, wie er ist, und mit dem Ausfall von *w-ngś*—die Kopula wurde am Rande nicht mitnotiert—hinter *nʿnh* zu rechnen.

Dass hier in der Mitte des Stichus die alte Textverderbnis anzusetzen ist, zeigt auch die Fortsetzung. Denn es besteht kein Grund für die Annahme, dass der zweite Halbstichus von vornherein als Zweier beabsichtigt war. Die fehlende Hebung ist auch noch vorhanden, nur an ganz anderer Stelle, nämlich am Ende des v 7. Das im zweiten Halbstichus zu ergänzende Wort war mitsamt seinem Stichwort(satz) *w-lʾ (j)ptḥ (pjw)* am Rande notiert. Die Notiz wurde in ihrer Funktion nicht mehr erkannt und das Ganze am Ende eingefügt. Erst bei dieser Gelegenheit, wenn nicht noch später, erhielt das *nʾlm* die Femininendung, weil man es auf das Mutterschaf bezog. Aber es fügt sich weder allein noch zusammen mit seiner jetzigen Fortsetzung in das Metrum. Setzt man es an seiner ursprünglichen Stelle ein, ergibt sich in v 7aα ein tadelloser Doppeldreier, gleichlang mit den übrigen Stichen in c 53; überdies tritt dann der auch stilistisch ebenmässige Bau der Zeile wieder ans Licht. Zu lesen ist also

*wᵊ-hūʾ naᶜᵃnǣ wᵊ-niggaś | næʾᵆlam wᵊ-lōʾ (j)ptḥ pīw*

In dieser Zeile fällt das Imperfektum *jptḥ* auf. 𝔔ᵃ bezeugt es in v a, in v b dagegen das Perfektum. In 𝔔ᵇ ist an der zweiten Stelle der ganze Text weggebrochen; an der ersten klafft gerade am Wortanfang eine Lücke, in der ebensogut *jpt* wie *pt* gestanden haben könnte. 𝔊 übersetzt beidemal mit Präsens, 𝔖 beidemal mit Perfektum, 𝔗 das erste Mal mit Perfektum, das zweite Mal mit Partizipium—der Konsonantentext lautet beidemal *ptḥ*—, 𝔙 das erste Mal mit Perfektum, das zweite Mal mit Futurum; auch α′σ′ϑ′ übersetzen das erste Mal mit Aorist, das zweite Mal fehlt. Das Impf. ist nicht unmöglich (sog. Impf. iterativum s. Gesenius-Bergsträsser, Hebr. Gramm. II §7b); aber vielleicht ist doch das Perfektum ursprünglich.

Noch ein Wort zum Ende des Verses! An 7aαβγ wird man bis auf das *nʾlmh* kaum etwas beanstanden müssen. Freilich bieten sowohl 𝔔ᵃ als auch 𝔔ᵇ *l-ṭbwḥ*, also inf. ḳal statt des Substantivs *ṭæbaḥ*. Ferner bleibt in 𝔔ᵃ *k-rḥl* ohne Kopula; aber 𝔔ᵇ stimmt mit 𝔐 überein, ebenso 𝔊 𝔖 𝔗 𝔙. Bei *gzzjh* geht 𝔔ᵃ (𝔔ᵇ fehlt) mit 𝔐; so auch 𝔗. Aber 𝔊 𝔖 𝔙 übersetzen im Singular; und das dürfte ursprünglich sein, weil ein Schaf nicht mehrere Scherer hat. In v 7b mit Einschluss des letzten Wortes von 7 aγ geht 𝔔ᵃ bis auf *ptḥ* (s. oben) mit 𝔐; 𝔔ᵇ ist leider bis auf die beiden letzten Buchstaben zerstört. 𝔊 *áphōnos* fasst die Form *nʾlmh* als Partizipium und Attribut zu *rḥl* auf und setzt v b durch Hinzuziehung von *hoútōs* ausdrücklich ab. 𝔖 trennt schon *nʾlm* (sic!) von dem Vorhergehenden und bezieht den Satz *štjq hwʾ* "stumm war er" deutlich nicht auf *rḥl*, das sie mit dem ebenfalls feminen *nqjʾ* "Opferlamm" wiedergibt. 𝔙 geht mit 𝔐, ebenso 𝔗 abgesehen davon, dass es wie 𝔊, auch einige Mss𝔊 *nʾlmh* als Partizipium aufgefasst hat. Mit 𝔐 𝔊 𝔗 𝔙 *nʾlmh* bei v aγ zu belassen, schafft einen Vierer, der das Doppeldreiermetrum stört und wo dann auch die Streichung des alleinstehenden v b als versehentliche Wiederholung (nach Lagarde, Klostermann, Duhm, Budde, Volz und vielen anderen neuerdings Ziegler, Steinmann, BHS) nichts hilft. Mit 𝔖 das *næʾælam* zu v b zu ziehen (so Torrey, Fischer und wieder Westermann)—vielleicht hat das Wort erst zu diesem Zwecke zufällig seine ursprüngliche Form (s.ob.) wiedererhalten—schafft einen alleinstehenden Dreier, der ebenfalls aus dem Metrum fallt. *nʾlmh* zu streichen (Köhler), macht nur aus dem Dreier einen Zweier. Aber auch es mitsamt dem v b zu streichen (Haller und wieder Fohrer), ist ein Gewaltakt, dem die oben vorgeschlagene Lösung doch wohl vorzuziehen ist.

Das Ergebnis der Untersuchung sind Verse, die sich ohne Schwierigkeit in das Doppeldreiermetrum des Mittelstücks der Komposition 52, 13–53, 12 einfügen und, soweit ihr Text mit einiger Sicherheit zu rekonstruieren ist, folgendermassen lauten:

6b *w-jhwh hipgīʿ bō. . . . .     . . . . . ʿawōnōtēnū.*
7 *wə-hūʾ naʿanǣ wə-niggaś | nǣʾælam wə-lōʾ pātah pīw*
*kaś-śǣ laṭ-ṭǣbaḥ jūbāl | ū-kə-rāḥēl li-pnē gōzəzāh*

6b "Aber Jahwe liess ihn treffen. . . . . . . . .
. . . . . . . . . . . . . . . ʿunsere Vergehenʾ
7 ʿʾUnd er, gebeugt ʿund bedrängtʾ.
ʿer blieb stummʾ und ʿtatʾ den Mund nicht auf
Wie das Lamm, das zur Schlachtung geführt wird.
und wie das Mutterschaft von seinem ʿSchererʾʿʾ."

# Father and Son as Terminology for Treaty and Covenant

F. CHARLES FENSHAM

PROFESSOR W. F. Albright has referred occasionally in his writings to the antiquity of the Old Testament covenant idea. His various references are original insights into the complex problems of treaty and covenant and have advanced our knowledge considerably.[1] It seems thus fitting to make a few observations on this subject in this *Festschrift* in honor of a great scholar and friend.

The comparability of Old Testament covenant forms with ancient Near Eastern treaties is an established fact as a result of research by recent scholars.[2] In any kind of comparison terminology should play an important role. Much has been done already by scholars on this subject, e.g., W. L. Moran, H. B. Huffmon, D. J. McCarthy, and others.[3] Of all the terminology used for treaty and covenant those concepts which give expression to relationship between the partners, are to be regarded as the most important. One of our

1. Cf. the discussion in one of his latest works *Yahweh and the Gods of Canaan* (1968), pp. 92–93.

2. Literature on this subject has increased tremendously. For an almost exhaustive list of books and papers cf. D. J. McCarthy, *Der Gottesbund im Alten Testament* (1966) and F. Vattioni, Recenti Studi sull' alleanza nella Bibbia e nell'antico Oriente *AION* 77 (1967): 181–226.

3. Cf. W. L. Moran, A Note on the Treaty Terminology of the Sefîre Stelas, *JNES* 22 (1963): 173–76; idem, The Ancient Near Eastern Background of the Love of God in Deuteronomy, *CBQ* 25 (1963): 77–87; H. B. Huffmon, The Treaty Background of Hebrew *Yada*ᶜ, *BASOR* 181 (1966): 31–37; H. B. Huffmon and S. B. Parker, A Further Note on the Treaty Background of Hebrew *Yada*ᶜ, *BASOR* 184 (1966): 36–38; D. J. McCarthy, Hosea 12:2 Covenant by Oil, *VT* 14 (1964): 215–21; *idem*, Notes on the Love of God in Deuteronomy and the Father–Son Relationship between Yahweh and Israel, *CBQ* 72 (1965): 144–47.

problems with a comparison of these concepts is to determine whether the meaning of a given concept has changed during many centuries of its usage. We have, furthermore, to determine whether a concept, which is borrowed from international politics into religious terminology, of the relationship of Yahweh and his people is somehow changed in its nuances of meaning.

With these problems in mind we want to investigate the Father–Son terminology in treaty and covenant. The importance of this relationship has been noted by Dennis J. McCarthy, but the wide range of its usage in ancient Near Eastern treaty material is not discussed,[4] and it seems necessary to study this material to get a clear picture of its usage in the Old Testament. It is true that concepts like father and son or the two combined are used in many ways in ancient Near Eastern and Old Testament texts, e.g., in the family sphere, in the educational or wisdom sphere, etc. It is not surprising that Father–Son was also applied to the international political field or even to the relationship of officials. An example of the latter usage occurs probably in a Mari letter between Ḫabdu-Mâlik and Indiniatum in which Ḫabdu-Mâlik calls himself "the son" (*mâru*) of Indiniatum.[5] Another example occurs in a letter from Ugarit, where a certain king from Birutu calls the *šakin*-official of Ugarit "my son."[6] This application of "son" in the Mari letters complicates the interpretation of this concept, especially when there is uncertainty about the position which the correspondents held. Furthermore, it is observed that in certain letters between Šamši-Addu and, e.g., his son Iasmaḫ-Addu, who acted as viceroy, the terms Father–Son give expression not only to a legal relationship but also to a family relationship. This should caution against attributing to this concept the same meaning. In our research on the Father–Son relationship in treaties of the ancient Near East we have discovered traces of it in the Mari letters and the Amarna letters. There are probably many other examples, especially in the vast correspondence in cuneiform. This paper is, however, only a test check from certain literature at our disposal.

## I

The Mari letters have already proved to be a rich field of study in international relations and diplomacy.[7] In connection with the Father–Son con-

4. Cf. McCarthy, *CBQ* 27 (1965): 144–47.

5. Cf. M. L. Burke in Textes diverses, *ARM* XIII (1964), p. 100 and J.-R. Kupper, Correspondence de Kibri-Dagan, *ARM* III (1950), pp. 88–89.

6. Cf. Jean Nougayrol, *PRU* III (1955), p. 12.

7. Cf., e.g., J. M. Munn-Rankin, Diplomacy in Western Asia in the Early Second Millennium B.C., *Iraq* 18 (1956): 68–110. For a history of this time cf. Horst Klengel, *Geschichte*

cept we draw attention to a letter from king Abi-Samar to king Iaḫdulim of Mari in which the former king reminds Iaḫdulim of his promise, according to the principles of international treaty relationships, to protect the treaty partner against the hostility of Šamši-Addu (letter 1).[8] It is interesting to note that Abi-Samar calls Iaḫdulim "my father" (*a-bi-ia*) in this clear treaty background.[9] Unfortunately, the text is broken from line 16 onward. This is an obstacle to the correct interpretation of the letter. It is, however, noteworthy that the letter is concluded with these two sentences: "Abi-Samar is not my son and my house has nothing to do with his house. (My) house is your house and Abi-Samar is your son." The first sentence obviously describes a broken relationship and might be a quotation. The last sentence, however, describes the treaty solidarity between the two partners. In both sentences the word "son" is used as a treaty term probably denoting vassalage. If we compare the situation reflected in this letter with the clauses of protection in Hittite vassal treaties in which the overlord promises protection for the vassal when attacked by an enemy, the whole position becomes clear.[10] Abi-Samar the vassal (son) of Iaḫdulim the overlord (father) demands protection against enemies according to the legal rights incorporated in the international agreement.

An interesting parallel to the situation described in this Mari text occurs in the Accadian correspondence of Ugarit in which Suppiluliuma, on account of the protection clause of the vassal treaty, praises Niqmadu of Ugarit for his fidelity during a rebellion of kinglets in Northern Syria. It is then stated that Niqmadu, when attacked because of his fidelity to Suppiluliuma, requested military aid from his overlord in the very words of the protection clause.[11] The treaty background of Father–Son in the Mari text under discussion is obvious from this example.[12]

In a group of letters published in *ARM*, II, 57–64 certain persons call themselves "sons" of Zimri-Lim and call Zimri-Lim "father." In one of these letters (60) Zimri-Lim calls himself "father" of Kabia.[13] These designations seem to be used for the relationship between higher officials and king,

---

*Syriens im 2 Jahrtausend v.u.Z.* (1965) and J.-R. Kupper, Northern Mesopotamia and Syria, *Cambridge Ancient History*, II (1963).

8. Cf. for the historical situation Klengel, *Geschichte*, pp. 15, 19, 112–15, 275.

9. Cf. Georges Dossin, Correspondence de Šamši-Addu, *ARM* I (1950), pp. 24–25.

10. Cf. F. Charles Fensham, Clauses of Protection in the Hittite Vassal-Treaties and the Old Testament, *VT* 13 (1963): 133–43.

11. Jean Nougayrol, *PRU* IV (1956): 49, lines 11ff.

12. Cf. for an Old Testament example Jos. 9–10 and F. Charles Fensham, The Treaty between Israel and the Gibeonites, *BA* 27 (1964): 96–100.

13. C.-F. Jean, Lettres diverses, *ARM* II (1950), pp. 116–27.

with one important exception—Ḫalisûmu, king of Ilânṣûrâ, who complains about the activities of Ḫammurapi of Kurda.[14] From these letters we may deduce that the relationship of trust between a king and a higher official may be expressed by the terms Father–Son.

Another piece of evidence comes from a letter from Aplaḫanda, king of Carcemish, to Iasmaḫ-Addu.[15] In the introductory formula Aplaḫanda designates himself as "the brother" (a-ḫu-ka) of Iasmaḫ-Addu. In line 17 in a broken text he refers to Šamši-Addu as "my father."[16] It is clear that Aplaḫanda regarded himself as the brother or equal of Iasmaḫ-Addu, son of Šamši-Addu and viceroy of Mari, but the older king and overlord is called "father." This can be augmented by the letter of Iatar-Ami son of Aplaḫanda to Zimri-Lim, king of Mari. Iatar-Ami calls himself "son" of Zimri-Lim.[17] In line 29 he refers to Zimri-Lim as "my father." In the discussion of these texts, Dossin is of the opinion that the designations father and son can be ascribed to the fact that a young king on his accession to the throne will naturally call his older colleague and neighbor "father" and refer to himself as "son."[18] This is one of the possible approaches to the study of this relationship. On the other hand, especially in light of all the comparable material, it is more acceptable to regard the designations Father–Son as treaty terminology. In a treaty relationship of a more friendly type the minor regards himself as the son of the overlord.

To these references we can add two other examples. A certain Ili-Ištar writes to Zimri-Lim to show his fidelity as follows: "I am like your servant and never shall my mayor (*sukaku*) let go the hem of the garment of my father. I am a faithful son of this country."[19] Ili-Ištar promises to Zimri-Lim that his mayors (officials or sheikhs) will not be unfaithful to the treaty. To let go the hem of the garment[20] means to break the treaty. It is thus obvious that Father–Son is used in this text as treaty terminology in a treaty background. The second example is from a letter from Ibâl-Adad to Zimri-Lim

14. Cf. Klengel, *Geschichte*, III and also F. M. Tocci, *La Siria nell'età' di Mari* (1960), p. 64. Kabiia was certainly governor of the district Kaḫat, cf. J. Bottéro and A. Finet, *ARM* XV (1954), p. 150.

15. Georges Dossin, Correspondence de Iasmaḫ-Addu, *ARM* V (1952), pp. 20–21.

16. For the historical situation in which Aplaḫanda lived cf. Klengel, *Geschichte*, pp. 20ff., Tocci, *La Siria*, pp. 25ff.

17. Cf. Georges Dossin, Un cas d'ordalie par le dieu fleuve, *Symbolae ad iura orientis antiqui pertenentes Paulo Koschaker dedicatae* (1939), pp. 112–18.

18. Cf. Dossin, *Symbolae*, p. 116, and *ARM* V, p. 124.

19. Cf. Georges Dossin, Une mention de Hattuša dans une lettre de Mari, *RHA* 5 (1939): 72 and J. M. Munn-Rankin, *Iraq* 18 (1956): 80.

20. On the hem of the garment cf. P. Koschaker in *Actes du xx^e congrès international de orientalistes* (1940), pp. 117–19, and Munn-Rankin, p. 80.

concerning a certain kinglet Arišen.[21] It says that "since the day when he (Arišen) seized the hem of the garment of Zimri-Lim . . . the town of Burundu (has become) the town of Zimri-Lim and Arišen, his son."[22] Again in a definite treaty background "son" is used. It is also noteworthy from the letter published by Dossin in *RHA* that "slave" or "vassalage" (*wardu-ka*) can be used with "son" interchangeably. The designations of overlord (*bêlu*) and slave (*wardu*) are superfluously used in the Mari texts to denote vassalage, although they are also used to illustrate humility and submissiveness. They became clichés in the chancellory language of those days and also in later times.[23] We may suppose that the terms "son" and "slave" can be synonymous, but that in certain cases a "slave" in vassalage of a more relentless type, would not have called himself the "son" of the overlord.

To summarize, first, these designations are used in a definite family setting in the case of the correspondence between Šamši-Addu and his sons. It is, however, noticeable that the family ties of the correspondents incidentally incorporate the meaning of the treaty relationship. Second, these designations are used between a higher and lower official. Third, they indicate a relationship between a king and his official. Evidence from the Hittite texts shows that a kind of treaty or agreement was made between the king and his officials or even his soldiers.[24] It is not farfetched to suppose that the same practice was also known in Mari and the vicinity. In the fourth place, the Father–Son relationship is also employed in an international treaty background. The Mari letters show that this kind of relationship was popular when special friendship was cultivated between overlord and vassal, but apparently these designations refer to vassalage and not to a parity treaty.

## II

The Hittite treaties form one of the most complete collections of treaty material in the ancient Near East. It may only be chance that nowhere else were such a complete set of treaties excavated. The fact that so many Hittite treaties are known accounts for the superfluous application by modern scholars of the Hittite types to other treaty forms. It is indeed true that the various types of Hittite treaties and their terminology have clarified many

21. Cf. C.-F. Jean, Arišen dans lettres de Mari, *Sem* I (1948): 19–21.

22. Cf. Munn-Rankin, p. 80. Jean translates *maru-šu* as "son vassal," cf. Jean, p. 21.

23. Cf. J. C. Greenfield, Treaty Terminology in the Bible, *Fourth World Congress of Jewish Studies, Papers* (1967), pp. 117–19.

24. Cf. Einar von Schuler, *Hethitische Dienstanweisungen für höhere Hof und Staatsbeamte* (1957), and Johannes Fredrich, Der hethitische Soldateneid, *ZA* 35 (1924): 161ff.

problems with treaties and covenants from other areas. There is an interesting phenomenon in Hittite vassal treaties, where sometimes an agreement is not only made with the vassal but also with the people. The designations which are applied, are in Accadian *mârê*, "sons" of the land and in Sumerian logogram *LU*$^{meš}$ "people" of the land. The designation "sons of the land" is also a fixed expression for the citizens or people of a given country.[25] "Sons of the land" need not be interpreted as referring to sons of the treaty. We discuss this point because the double reference to vassal and people bears somehow on the Old Testament covenant, as we shall see. In the treaty of Manapa-Dattas "the sons" are included in the curse formula.[26] In the Mitanni treaty a separate curse and blessing formula for "the sons of the land" are incorporated.[27] In the Ḫajasa treaty they are even mentioned, apart from the vassal, as treaty receivers.[28] Important for our discussion is the employment of both vassal and people as receivers of the treaty. This may explain why "son" as a covenant term is employed for both king and Israel in the Old Testament.

## III

The Amarna correspondence presents a field for further intensive study of treaty relations, in light of the latest research.[29] Traces of Father–Son relationship are clearly visible in certain letters between the kinglets and their Egyptian overlords. The occurrence of this designation in a correspondence predominantly from Southern Syria and Palestine is a very important clue to a possible background for Old Testament developments.[30] If we take into account that the Israelites arrived not long after the Amarna correspondence was concluded, its importance for a better understanding of Old Testament concepts is clear.

In a letter from Rib-Adda to the Pharaoh (*EA* 73) a more familiar expression is used as a form of address, in contrast to certain other letters.[31] The

25. Cf. W. von Sonden, *AHW*, p. 616.

26. Cf. J. Friedrich, Die Staatsverträge des Hatti-Reiches in hethitischer Sprache, *MVAeG*, 31 (1926): 4 §19, 29ff.

27. Cf. E. F. Weidner, *Politische Dokumente aus Kleinasien* (1923) 1 lines 59ff., 70ff.; 2 lines 25ff., 35ff., 44ff., and 53ff.

28. Cf. Friedrich, 6 IV, §35ff., and also V. Korošec, *Hethitische Staatsverträge* (1931), pp. 57–58.

29. Cf. L. M. Muntingh, *Die Sosiale Struktuur binne die Woongebied van die Kanaäniete gedurende die Laat-Bronstydperk* (1963), 1ff. Dissertation of the University of Stellenbosch.

30. For a discussion of these letters cf., e.g., Ed. F. Campbell, *The Chronology of the Amarna Letters* (1964) and W. F. Albright, The Amarna Letters from Palestine, *Cambridge Ancient History* II (1966).

31. Cf. J. A. Knudtzon, *Die El-Amarna Tafeln*, I (1915), pp. 370–73.

historical situation is clear. Byblos was continually pestered by enemies of all kinds and Rib-Adda was requesting aid in the form of archers (*ṣâbê pitati*).[32] This request was quite probably made on account of the treaty which existed between the Pharaoh and Rib-Adda and it may have been based on the protection clauses. It is thus noteworthy that in this letter Rib-Adda calls the Pharaoh "my father" and himself "the son" of the Egyptian king. Note, e.g., the following expression: "While you are a father and overlord to me, I have directed my face to you."[33] Further on he says: "I am your faithful servant" (*ar(a)d (k)i-it-ti-ka a-na-ku*). For our study it is important that here, as in the Mari texts, the designations "Father–Son" and "Overlord–slave" are used without contradiction. A letter comparable to EA 73 is EA 82, where again the Pharaoh is addressed as "my father" and Rib-Adda calls himself "your son."[34] The historical situation in this letter is about the same as in EA 73. Rib-Adda complains about the hostility of ᶜAbdi-Ashirta and his allies the Ḫapiru. He even mentions that if he should be injured by his enemies, the Pharaoh would be held responsible for it on account of negligence. In my opinion this negligence only makes sense in light of the clause of protection, the one obligation laid on the overlord in vassal treaties. In EA 96 we have an interesting situation in which the designation "father" is used by a high official (*râb ṣâbe*) of Egypt for himself in relation to his "son" Rib-Adda.[35] Also EA 73 gives the impression that Rib-Adda had somebody else in mind while writing—not always the Pharaoh. The Egyptian high official, as a substitute for the Pharaoh, regards himself as the treaty partner of the king of Byblos.

In the same category with EA 96 may be classified various letters of Aziri to Dûdu, a high official of Egypt (especially EA 164).[36] We can discern that this official also takes the place of the Pharaoh from the terminology used in connection with him. Aziri calls him "my overlord, my father" and designates himself as "your son." Most illuminating is the following expression from EA 158:14ff.: "Lo, you are my father and my overlord and I am your son. The lands of the Amurri are your lands and my house is your house."[37] This can be compared with the words of the Mesopotamian kinglet Abi-Samar to Iaḫdulim of Mari discussed above: "(My) house is your house and

32. Cf. W. F. Albright and W. L. Moran, A re-interpretation of an Amarna Letter from Byblos (Ea 82), *JCS* 2 (1948): 246.

33. Cf. lines 35–37.

34. Cf. Albright and Moran, p. 241.

35. Cf. Knudtzon, pp. 442–45.

36. Ibid., pp. 660–63.

37. Ibid., pp. 642–43.

Abi-Samar is your son." It is significant how conservatively certain international legal expressions were preserved. The treaty background of Father–Son in Aziri's correspondence is undeniable, even if we consider the fact that both the Pharoah and his high official are addressed as "father."

In EA 44 a "son of a king" Zikar addresses the Pharaoh as "my father" and refers to himself as "your son."[38] The designation "son of the king" is problematic. Weber–Ebeling are of the opinion that it refers to an official in a border district.[39] It is perhaps also possible to take *mâr šarri mâru-ka* as a tautological expression. This should not be strange in light of the fact that in this letter a few unusual expressions occur, e.g., the greeting formula is only directed to the overlord and not to the writer of the letter. On the other hand the most natural explanation is to take it as "prince." It is thus better to surmise that a "prince" has written this letter.[40]

From our investigation on the usage of Father–Son it is clear that in the Amarna letters the treaty background predominates. It is noteworthy that both Pharaoh and his high officials could be addressed as "father." The continuous requests for military aid can be explained from the protection clauses of vassal treaties. It is, furthermore, interesting to note that the conceptions father and overlord, as well as son and servant, are interchanged.

## IV

In our discussion of Father–Son in the Old Testament we want to draw attention to traces of these designations in the treaty between two partners. An important example occurs in 2 Kings 16. The historical situation is as follows: In 738 B.C. Tiglath-pileser, king of Assyria, succeeded in subduing a confederation of Syrian and Palestinian kings. Among these kings were the king of Israel and also a mysterious Azriau of Yaudi. Various scholars have proposed to identify Azriau with Azariah (Uzziah) of Judah, which seems acceptable.[41] This probably means that already in 738 Israel, Aram, and Judah were made vassals of Assyria, probably confirmed by a treaty contract as the discovered vassal treaties of Esarhaddon show.[42] This is borne out by the description in 2 Kings 16. In the meantime the Israelites, under Pekah

38. Ibid., pp. 306ff.

39. O. Weber and E. Ebeling, *Die El-Amarna Tafeln*, II (1915), p. 1096.

40. For *mâr šarri* cf. W. von Soden, *AHW*, p. 615.

41. Cf. E. R. Thiele, *The Mysterious Numbers of the Hebrew Kings* (1965), pp. 125ff, and John Bright, *A History of Israel* (1959), pp. 252–53, and against this identification, Martin Noth, *Geschichte Israels*[2] (1954), p. 233, note 3.

42. Cf. D. J. Wiseman, *The Vassal-Treaties of Esarhaddon* (1958) and R. Borger, Zu den Asarhaddon Verträge aus Nimrud, *ZA* 54 (1961): 173–96.

and the Aramaeans, decided to revolt against the Assyrians and tried to get Judah involved in their rebellion. They were turned down by Uzziah and the same policy of fidelity to Assyria was continued by Ahaz, his son. The result was that the rebels turned against their Assyrian ally in the south. Consequently Ahaz, as a faithful servant of Assyria, sent an embassy to his overlord to request military aid, a common custom, as we have seen in the Mari, Amarna, and Ugaritic material. The language in which the request is couched, is noteworthy: "I am your servant and your son, come and save me from the king of Aram and from the king of Israel who took action against me." The fact that Ahaz calls himself the servant and son of Tiglath-pileser shows that a treaty relationship already existed. It is erroneous to surmise that in these words Ahaz proposed the forming of a treaty. For our study, however, the combination of servant and son is very important because it shows that, as in the Mari and Amarna material, these concepts can be interchanged. It is thus remarkable that from the time of Mari in the eighteenth century B.C. up to the eighth century B.C., roughly a thousand years, exactly the same terminology is used in the same situation. It, furthermore, shows that the Hebrews were well aware of the employment of a concept such as "son" in a treaty sphere. The fact that Tiglath-pileser took action to protect his vassal from the hostility of his neighbors is an indication that the ancient principle of the protection of an overlord was carried out.

In the second place we want to discuss the usage of Father–Son in a covenant context. The concept "father" (*ʾāb*) used for God, is scarce in the Old Testament. A close scrutiny of its use shows that different concepts are used for God as father.[43] E.g., in the family sphere God is designated as the Father of Israel and Israel is his first-born (Jer. 31:9). The same may be true of expressions which designate God as a man who carries his son (Deut. 1:31) or a man who educates his son (Deut. 8:5). In the sphere of God's activity as Creator of Israel can be placed an expression like: "Is He not your Father who created you?" (*qnh* Deut. 32:6) and in Is. 64:7 (*MT*) the Lord is called "our Father" and Israel the clay which He modelled into man (*yṣr*). This usage can be paralleled by the Ugaritic appellation for El., viz., "father of mankind" (*ʾabʾadm*).[44] Another meaning is the juridical, where God is regarded as the protector and father of the orphan and widow (Ps. 68:6).[45]

43. Cf. G. Quell, *ThWNT*, V (1954): 959–74.

44. Cf. C. H. Gordon *Ugaritic Textbook* (1965), p. 250.

45. Cf. F. Charles Fensham, Widow, Orphan and the Poor in Ancient Near Eastern Legal and Wisdom Literature, *JNES* 21 (1962): 129ff. A very good parallel to Ps. 68:6, but where "father" is applied to a ruler, occurs in the Eloquent Peasant, viz., "Because you are the father of the orphan, the husband of the widow . . . " Cf. E. Suys, *Étude sur le conte du fellah plaideur* (1933), pp. 24–25.

Finally, in a few instances the concept "father" is used for the Lord in a covenant meaning. It is especially employed in 2 Sam. 7:14, where Nathan brings the message of the future of the Davidic covenant. It is stated about the son of David: "I shall be a father to him and he will be a son to me." The covenant context in which these words are used is beyond cavil.[46] Usually the idea of Father–Son in this verse is held as an adoption formula.[47] It is, however, noteworthy that in light of parallel occurrences in ancient Near Eastern treaty material these words can better be understood as expressing a convenant relationship.[48] It is also possible that in this kind of text a fusion of the adoption and covenant connotations takes place (cf. also Ps. 2:7). The king of Israel is in the act of covenant forming as son of the Lord. Another noteworthy phenomenon in 2 Sam. 7 is the usage of servant (*ᶜebed*) for the king as covenant partner (e.g., verse 5). This can be paralleled by the same occurrence in the Mari and Amarna literature as in the example from 2 Kings 16. We can thus establish without doubt that in 2 Sam. 7:14 "father" (*ᵓāb*) is used as a covenant term.

In Ps. 89:27 the poet states: "Thou art my Father, my God and the rock of my salvation." The relationship between David and God is expressed by the word "my Father" (*ᵓābî*). Various scholars have regarded the expression "my Father" as an adoption formula.[49] For others it denotes a moral relationship.[50] Lipiński, however, considering parallel material from the ancient Near East as well as the covenant character of Ps. 89, feels that the expression is used here in a covenant sense.[51] It is quite obvious that this verse is employed in close relationship to 2 Sam. 7:14. The style of both the expressions of Ps. 89:27 and 2 Sam. 7:14 is strongly reminiscent of such expressions as "I am a faithful son of this country" in the Mari letters and "Lo, you are my father and my overlord and I am your son" in the Amarna letters. Especially the latter example is as close as one might expect to come to the expression in Ps. 89:27 and 2 Sam. 7:14. It is thus clear that the biblical reference in Ps. 89 is used to illustrate the fidelity of the Israelite king and his willingness to stay in the covenant relationship with the Lord. These examples seem to

46. Cf. e.g., James Muilenberg, The Form and Structure of the Covenantal Formulations, *VT* 9 (1959): 347ff., and Klaus Seybold, *Das Davidische Königtum im Zeugnis der Propheten* (1967), pp. 79ff. Dissertation of the Christian-Albrechts University of Kiel.

47. Cf., e.g., Hugo Gressman, *Der Messias* (1929), 9ff.

48. K. Seybold, pp. 89–90.

49. E.g., S. Mowinckel, *He that cometh* (1956), p. 78, G. Von Rad, *Theologie des Alten Testaments,* I (1957), pp. 49ff; H.-J. Kraus, *Psalmen,* II (1960), p. 623.

50. Cf., e.g., R. Kittel, *Die Psalmen* (1922), p. 11; cf. also the discussion of G. W. Ahlström, *Psalm* 89 (1959), pp. 111ff.

51. E. Lipiński, *Le poème royal du Psaume LXXXIX 1–5, 20–38* (1967), pp. 58ff.

eliminate the view that divine kingship existed in ancient Israel.[52] The idea of an overlord as father was borrowed from international legal terminology and incorporated into religious writing to give expression to a covenant relationship.

Another interesting piece of evidence comes from Jeremiah (3:19). The prophet uses sarcasm to show how the Lord would have liked to regard the unfaithful Judaeans as "sons" (*bānîm*) and how they would have called Him "my Father" and would not have become apostate. The apostasy of the people of God is described in terms of an unfaithful wife, as in the case of Hosea.[53] Volz proposes that "my father" is used here by the bride (the Judaeans) for her bridegroom.[54] It has thus a family concept. In light of our investigation it seems quite possible to place this verse in the covenant sphere of meaning. The ideal relationship between the Lord and his people is sketched. They will be his sons and He will be their father. The fact that the covenant relationship is here described as a relationship between the Lord and the Judaeans[55] and not between the Lord and the king, as in 2 Sam. 7:14 and Ps. 89:27, is important.

The last example in which "father" is employed and which we want to discuss is in Mal. 1:6. This verse begins with a general metaphor borrowed from the sphere of authority. "A son honors his father and a servant his lord." Then the question is asked: "If I am a Father, where is my honor?" This question is asked as a result of the defiling of sacrifices by presenting cultic unacceptable animals.[56] It is thus a transgression of cultic legal principles as laid down in Lev. 22:22–25.[57] It is probable that with the combination of son and servant in the first part of the verse and then with the rhetorical question asked to accuse the unfaithful people that the word "father" denotes here a covenant term. If God is the Overlord of the people why do they dishonor him by transgressing his commandments?

The above examples of the usage of "father" in a covenant meaning can be augmented by examples of the employment of "son" with the same meaning. We will make no attempt to discuss the wide variety of usages of "son"

52. Cf. Jean de Fraine; *L'Aspect réligieux de la royauté Israélite* (1954), pp. 271–72; Ahlström, op. cit., and for a critical discussion K.-H. Bernhardt, *Das Problem der altorientalischen Königsideologie im Alten Testament* (1961), pp. 222ff. and 263.

53. Cf. John Bright, *Jeremiah* (1965), pp. 23, 25.

54. Paul Volz, *Der Prophet Jeremia* (1922), p. 38.

55. Cf. W. Rudolph, *Jeremia* (1947), p. 25 where "house of Israel," "Sons of Israel," and "Israel" are regarded as referring to the Judaeans.

56. Cf. F. Horst, *Die Zwölf kleinen Propheten*[3] (1964), p. 266.

57. Cf. E. Sellin, *Das Zwölfprophetenbuch* (1922), p. 543.

(*bēn*) in the Old Testament,[58] but will only draw attention to the employment of this concept in a covenant context, beginning with the oldest reference to Israel as "sons" in the Old Testament, viz., Deut. 32.[59] In verse 5 it is stated that those who acted treacherously against Him are not to be regarded as his sons, but it is difficult to build any arguments on this verse because of its bad state of preservation.[60] In verse 19 we have another reference to sons, stating that the Lord was vexed on account of the insults of his sons and his daughters.[61] In this case the combination of sons and daughters testifies against the possibility of a covenant meaning because nowhere in the Old Testament or the ancient Near East is "daughters" used as a covenant term. In verse 43 MT there is the following expression: "Truly the blood of his servants (*ᶜăbādāw*) he will requite." It is interesting to note that in a Qumrân manuscript 4Q "hissons" (*bānāw*) is read instead of "his servants."[62] This variant reading is noteworthy in light of the fact that in the ancient Near East as well as in the Old Testament "son" and "servant" are used interchangeably, as we have seen. There is, if we take both words as covenant concepts, no difference whatsoever in meaning. The context in which this expression is used has strong covenantal overtones. It is obvious that the Lord in the last part of Deut. 32 (from verse 41 on) describes his action against his adversaries and those of Israel. Here we have a longer exposition of the protection clause of treaty and covenant. The covenantal character of Deut. 32 stands beyond cavil since the studies of G. E. Wright and Julien Harvey.[63] It is thus understandable that the Lord as major partner in the covenant will promise protection against mutual enemies.

According to the latest studies Hosea is shot through with the covenant idea.[64] Two important occurrences of "son" in Hosea have direct bearing on

58. Cf. especially Georg Fohrer, *ThWNT*, VIII (1967), pp. 340–54, for an outstanding discussion of the meanings of "son" in the Old Testament.

59. For a date roughly at the end of the first millennium B.C. for this chapter cf., Otto Eissfeldt, *Das Lied Moses Deut. 32:1–43 und das Lehrgedicht Asaphs Psalm 78 samt einer Analyse der Umgebung des Mose-Lierdes* (1958); W. F. Albright, Some Remarks on the Song of Moses in Deuteronomy XXXII, *VT* 9 (1959): 339–46, espec. 339, and P. W. Skehan, The Structure of the Song of Moses in Deuteronomy, *CBQ* 13 (1951): 153–63. Skehan only says it is early. Cf. also G. E. Wright, The Lawsuit of God: A Form-Critical Study of Deuteronomy 32, *Israel's Prophetic Heritage* (1962), pp. 26–67.

60. Cf. Wright, p. 28.

61. For the translation "vexed" cf. Wright, p. 30.

62. Cf. W. F. Albright, *VT* 9, p. 341.

63. Cf. also Julien Harvey, *Le plaiyoder prophétique contre Israël après la rupture de l'alliance* (1967), pp. 32–36.

64. Cf., e.g., H. W. Wolff, "Wissen um Gott" bei Hosea als Urform von Theologie, *EvTh* 12 (1952–53): 533–54; A. Feuillet, L'universalisme et l'alliance dans la religion d'Osée, *Bible et Vie Chrêtienne* 18 (1957): 27–35; F. C. Fensham, The Covenant-Idea in the Book of Hosea, *OTWSA* (1964–65): 35–49.

the covenant. In Hos. 2:1 (MT) it is said in a "Heils" pronouncement that the Israelites will no longer be called "not my nation," but will be designated by "sons of the living God." The phrase "not my people," best illustrated by Hos. 1:9, refers to a break of covenant.[65] It is thus obvious that the expression "sons of the living God" refers to a restored covenant. It is worth noticing that here again the covenant partner of the Lord is visualized as Israel and not the king as representative of the people. The same is also true of the second relevant text in Hosea, viz., Hos. 11:1. Here in a historical setting it is said that the Lord loved (*ʾāhab*) Israel while he was a child[66] and that He called his son (my son) from Egypt. The expression "my son" is differently interpreted by modern scholars, e.g., H. W. Wolff has connected it with ancient Near Eastern texts, but has decided that Canaanite myth and cult have played a vital role to force Hosea to take a radical view, contrary to the closely connected Canaanite idea of father and mother gods.[67] It does not seem necessary to search for such a complicated explanation but to accept that we have here a covenant term. Wolff is close to a satisfactory explanation in referring to a passage in the Karatepe inscription, which is slightly later, as Hosea (Hosea ca. 750 B.C.—Karatepe ca. 720 B.C.). King ᶜZTWD says that he is made a father (or placed in fatherhood) by every king on account of his righteousness and wisdom as well as the goodness of his heart.[68] It is clear that ᶜZTWD refers here to his position as overlord of other kings. When the Lord says, according to Hosea, that Israel is his son and connects this to the exodus, he is obviously referring to the covenant relationship. It is also noteworthy that in Ex. 4:23 the Lord requests the Pharaoh to send his son (my son) to serve him or else the first-born son of the Egyptian king will be killed. We may have in this text a contrast between "my son" and "your son," but in the light of our investigation it may as well be interpreted as referring to the close relationship between Yahweh and his people, although the Sinai covenant was not as yet contracted, according to biblical tradition.

In Deut. 14:1 it is said: "You are the sons of the Lord" and then they are

65. For the covenant application of an expression like "I shall be your God," and the like, cf. Alfred Jepsen, Berith, *Verbannung und Heimkehr* (1961), pp. 161ff., and cf., especially for the covenant meaning of this part, H. W. Wolff, *Hosea* (1961), pp. 30–31; cf. also C. van Leeuwen, *Hosea* (1968), pp. 42–43.

66. Love is also a covenant term, cf. W. L. Moran, The Ancient Near Eastern Background of the Love of God in Deuteronomy, *CBQ* 25 (1963): 77–87 and also the already cited paper of D. J. McCarthy, *CBQ* 27 (1965): 144–47.

67. H. W. Wolff, *Hosea*, p. 256.

68. H. Donner-W. Röllig, *Kananäische und aramäische Inschriften*, I (1962), p. 5 for the text, and II (1964), p. 36 for a translation.

forbidden to act according to heathen customs.[69] What is the exact meaning of "sons of the Lord" in this text? E. König has proposed that the "Rangstellung" of Israel to God is indicated by "son,"[70] but does not explain the real purpose of its usage. König, like other scholars, is perplexed by this problem. To me an explanation from a covenantal background is the most satisfactory. The Israelites are the covenant partners of the Lord, therefore they are not allowed to partake in cultic practices of a foreign god. If they should partake, it would mean that the covenant is broken. Various other references to Israel as rebellious children (*bānîm sôrĕrîm*) in Is. 30:1; lying children (*bānîm keḥāšîm*) in Is. 30:9; and faithless children (*bānîm šôbābîm*) in Jer. 3:14 may also be interpreted as referring to covenant partners who are unfaithful to the covenant and its stipulations.

We conclude with the discussion of two important points. In the first place, we want to draw attention to the fact that "son" is used in the Old Testament for both king and people. In the light of our discussion of the same phenomenon in certain Hittite treaties, we may surmise that the receivers of the covenant are both the king and the people. In certain traditions the king, as representative of the people, is called "son." In other traditions Israel or Judah is designated as "sons" or "son." In Hosea, e.g., Israel is described as son. This might be due to the fact that the northern prophet was unwilling to recognize the northern Israelite king with his synchretistic religion as a covenant partner of Yawheh. Jeremiah was unwilling to regard the Judaean kings as covenant partners because of their weaknesses and failures. On the other hand, the tradition of the king as "son" developed into the Messianic expectations of later Judaism, and, on the other hand, the tradition of Israel as "son" foreshadowed the special role of Israel among the nations of the world.

In the second place, the interchanging of covenant concepts such as "father and lord," "son and servant," gives us a fresh approach to terminology in connection with the relationship between the Lord and his people. If a minor covenant partner could be called either "son" or "servant," a new dimension in the meaning of servant (*ᶜebed*) is opened. In the past we have made a distinction between these two concepts by placing "son" in a more favorable and "servant" in a more unfavorable position. In light of our investigation these concepts were apparently synonymous for more than a thousand years. Viz., the vassal of treaty or covenant, we may conclude that, e.g., "the servant of the Lord" (*ᶜebed Yahweh*) in the second part of

69. Cf. G. E. Wright, *Deuteronomy*, IB, II (1953), p. 421.
70. E. König, *Das Deuteronomium* (1917), p. 125.

Isaiah refers to a covenant partner. It is also surprising that the word "servant" is used not only for an individual but also for Israel (Is. 49:3). The seeming contradiction may be explained by the fact that the king and Israel were regarded as "sons" or "servants" of the Lord. And so when we approach the New Testament, where "Father–Son," "God–Christ" often appear, a whole new world of interpretation becomes possible.

# A Re-Study of an Elephantine Aramaic Marriage Contract (*AP* 15)

JOSEPH A. FITZMYER, S.J.

It was to be expected that E. G. Kraeling's publication of the *Brooklyn Museum Aramaic Papyri* would shed light on some of the problems of older, well-known Elephantine texts. This article is a reconsideration of an Elephantine marriage contract which is often quoted in A. E. Cowley's version, but which needs a new, comprehensive presentation, because data from Kraeling's publication support certain interpretations of details in it that others have proposed, but which were strangely neglected by Cowley and others who treated the text. The foreword of Kraeling's volume acknowledges its indebtedness to Professor William F. Albright, in whose honor the present volume is being published. His interest in things Aramaic has been manifested in many ways during his scholarly career, and it is a privilege to include here a study of this Elephantine text as a tribute to a revered teacher. In it I hope to bring together items from many of the studies and discussions of the text to improve the understanding of the text as a whole. Recent studies of the legal aspects of the Elephantine contracts have also added to our understanding of this document.

The text of the marriage contract was first published by A. H. Sayce and A. E. Cowley in 1906 as papyrus G in the collection, *Aramaic Papyri Discovered at Assuan.*[1] This contract has been difficult to understand, partly because the papyrus is fragmentary and partly because its terminology and phraseology were often ambiguous. When it is studied today against the

1. (London: A. Moring, 1906), pp. 43–44 (with plates); Cairo Museum No. 37110.

background of other marriage contracts from Elephantine, especially two in the Kraeling collection, some of the ambiguity can be resolved. In Cowley's publication at least three other texts belong to this genre, although they are rather fragmentary.[2] Among the Brooklyn Museum papyri there are three further contracts that can be used for comparative purposes.[3]

The papyrus in which we are interested contains the contract of a marriage, apparently the third one, of Miphṭaḥiah, the daughter of Maḥsiah, with Esḥor, the son of Ṣeḥo. It sets forth the terms of the marriage agreement: the date (line 1), the identification of the contracting parties (lines 2–3), the formal agreement of marriage (4), the record of the payment of the bride-price (4–6), of the dowry money brought by the bride (6–7), and of the valuable possessions brought with her (7–13). There follows the sum total of the amounts involved in the contract (13–15) and a record of the husband's acknowledgment of all this (15). Then a further list catalogues objects brought by the bride, the value of which is not determined (15–16). Certain stipulations begin in line 17: the bride's right to her husband's property should he die childless (17–20); his inheritance of his wife's property should she die childless (20–22). In case the bride divorces her husband she must pay the divorce fee, but she will be free and have the right to take what is hers (22–26). In case the husband divorces his wife he forfeits the bride-price, and she will be free and have the right to take what she brought to the marriage (26–29). The wife is further protected against a third party who might seek to drive her away from her husband's house and possessions (29–31). The husband is to be fined if he claims that he has another wife or other children (31–34); he is also to be fined if he tries to withdraw his property from his wife (35–36). Witnesses to the contract (37–39).

The Aramaic text of the marriage contract should be read as follows:[4]

1 ב[5]2 [ל]תשרי [הו יום] 6 לירח אפף [שנת . . . ארתחשס]ש מלכ[א]
2 אמר אסחור בר [צחא] ארדכל זי מלכא למח[סיה א]רמי זי סון לדגל
3 וריזת לאמר אנה [א]תית ביתך למנתן לי [ל]ברתך מפט⟨ח⟩יה לאנתו
4 הי אנתתי ואנה בעלה מן יומא זנה ועד עלם יהבת לך מהר
5 ברתך מפטחיה [כסף] שקלן 5 באבני מלכ[א] על עליך וטב לבבך
6 בגו הנעלת לב[יתי] מפטחיה בידה כס[ף] תכונה כרש 1 שקלן 2 באבני
7 מלכא כסף ר 2 ל10 הנעלת לי בידה לבש 1 זי עמר חדת חטב

2. See *AP* 18, 36, 48 (pp. 54–56, 131–32, 153).

3. See *BMAP* 2, 7, 14 (pp. 139–50, 199–222, 291–96).

4. In the transcription of the text, square brackets [ ] denote words or letters that have been editorially restored in a lacuna, angular brackets ⟨ ⟩ my editorial additions, and braces { } my editorial deletions. In the translation that follows parentheses ( ) are used to spell out an abbreviated word, or to indicate English words added for the sake of style, or (in line 36) to indicate an erasure that can still be read.

8 צבע ידין הוה ארך אמן 8 ב5 [ש]וה כסף כרשן 2 שקלן 8
9 באבני מלכא שביט 1 חדת הוה ארך אמן 8 ב5 שוה
10 כסף שקלן 8 באבני מלכא לבש אחרן זי עמר נשחט הוה
11 ארך אמן 6 ב4 שוה כסף שקלן 7 מחזי 1 זי נחש שוה
12 כסף שקל 1 ר 2 תמ[סא] 1 זי נחש שויה כסף שקל 1 ר 2 כסן זי נחש 2
13 שוין כסף שקלן [2] זלוע 1 זי נחש שוה כסף ר 2 כל כספא
14 ודמי נכסיא כסף כרשן 6 שקל⟨ן⟩ 5 חלר[ן] 20 כסף ר 2 ל10 באבני
15 מלכא על עלי [וט]יב לבבי בגו שוי 1 זי גמא בה נעבצן
16 זי אבן 4 פק 1 זי סלק כפן 2 פרכס 1 זי חצן חדת תקם חפנן 5 שנן משאן 1
17 מחר או יום א[חר]ן ימות אסחור ובר דכר ונקבה לא
18 איתי לה מן מפ[טח]יה אנתתה מפטחיה הי שליטה בביתה
19 זי אסחזר ונכס[והי] וקנינה וכל זי איתי [ל]ה על אנפי ארעא
20 כלה מחר או יום ⟨אחרן⟩ תמות מפטחיה ובר דכר ונקבה לא
21 איתי לה מן אסחור בעלה אסחור הו ירתנה בנכסיה
22 וקנינה מחר [או י]ום אחרן תקום [מפ]טחיה בעדה
23 ותאמר שנאת לאסחור בעלי כסף שנאה בראשה תתב על
24 מוזנא ותתקל ל[אס]חור כסף שקלן 7 ר 2 וכל זי הנעלת
25 בידה תהנפק מן חם עד חוט ותהך [ל]האן זי צבית ולא
26 {י}דין ולא דבב מחר או יום אחרן יקום אסחור בעדה
27 ויאמר שנאת [לאנ]תתי מפטחיה מהרה [י]אבד וכל זי הנעלת
28 בידה תהנפק מן חם עד חוט ביום חד בכף חדה ותהך
29 לה אן זי צבית ולא דין ולא דבב ו[זי] יקום על מפטחיה
30 לתרכותה מן ביתה זי אסחור ונכסוהי וקנינה ינתן לה
31 כסף כרשן 20 ויע[בד] לה דין ספרא זנה ולא אכל אמר
32 איתי לי אנתה אחרה להן מפט⟨ח⟩יה ובנן אחרנן להן בנן זי
33 תלד לי מפטחיה הן אמר איתי לי ב[נן] ואנתה אחר⟨נ⟩ן להן
34 מפטחיה ובניה אנתן למפטחיה כס[ף] כרשן 20 באבני
35 מלכא ולא אכל [אהנ]תר נכסי וקניני מן מפ[טח]יה והן העדת המו
36 מנה {{קבל ס[פר אחר]ן}} אנתן למפטחיה [כסף] כרשן 20 באבני מל[כא]
37 כתב נתן בר ענניה [ספרא זנה כפם אסחור] ושהדיא בגו
38 פנוליה בר יזניה [...]יה בר אוריה מנחם בר [ז]כור
39 שהד רעיבל ב[ר ]

## TRANSLATION

[1]On the 2[5th of] Tishri, [that is, the] 6th [day] of the month of Epiph, [the 25th year of Artaxerx]es, [the] king, [2]Esḥor bar [Ṣeḥo], a royal architect, said to Maḥ[siah], an [A]ramean of Syene, of the [3]Warizath garrison: I have [co]me (to) your house (to ask you) to give me your daughter Miphṭa⟨ḥ⟩iah in marriage. [4]She is my wife and I am her husband from this day forward. I have given you the bride-price for [5]your daughter Miphṭaḥiah, 5 [silver] shekels by roya[l] weight; you have received it and you are satisfied [6]with it. Miphṭaḥiah has brought into [my] hou[se] with her a dowry su[m] of

1 karsh, 2 shekels by royal [7]weight, (in) silver (of) 2 qu(arters) to the ten-piece. She has (also) brought with her to me: 1 new garment of wool, striped [8]with dye on both edges, measuring 8 cubits by 5, worth (in) cash 2 karshin and 8 shekels [9]by royal weight; 1 new shawl, measuring 8 cubits by 5, [wo]rth [10](in) cash 8 shekels by royal weight; another garment of wool, finely woven, [11]measuring 6 cubits by 4, worth (in) cash 7 shekels; 1 bronze mirror, worth [12](in) cash 1 shekel, 2 qu(arters); 1 bronze bo[wl], worth (in) cash 1 shekel, 2 qu(arters); 2 bronze cups, [13]worth (in) cash [2] shekels; 1 bronze pitcher, worth (in) cash 2 qu(arters). All the money and [14]the value of the possessions are 6 silver karshin, 5 shekel⟨s⟩, 20 hallur[in], (in) silver (of) 2 qu(arters) to the ten-piece by royal [15]weight. I have received it [and] I am [sa]tisfied with it. (Also) 1 reed couch, on which there are [16]4 stone inlays; 1 *pq* of *slq*; 2 ladles; 1 new *prks* of palm-leaves; 5 handfuls of castor oil; 1 (pair of) leather (?) sandals. [17]Should Esḥor die tomorrow or some o[the]r day, having no child, (either) male or female, [18]by his wife Miph[ṭaḥ]iah, Miphṭaḥiah is entitled to the house [19]of Esḥor, [his] possessions and property, and all that he has on the face of the earth, [20]all of it. Should Miphṭaḥiah die tomorrow or ⟨some other⟩ day, having no child, (either) male or female, [21]by her husband Esḥor, Esḥor shall inherit her possessions [22]and her property. Should Miphṭaḥiah rise up in an assembly tomorrow [or] some other [da]y [23]and say, "I divorce my husband Esḥor," the divorce fee is on her head; she shall sit by the [24]scale and weigh out to Esḥor 7 silver shekels, 2 qu(arters); and all that she brought [25]with her, she shall take out, from straw to string, and go [wh]erever she pleases, without [26]suit or process. Should Esḥor rise up in an assembly tomorrow or some other day [27]and say, "I divorce my [wife] Miphṭaḥiah," his bride-price shall go forfeit; and all that she brought [28]with her, she will take out, from straw to string, on one day (and) at one time, and she may go [29]wherever she pleases, without suit or process. [Whoever] rises up against Miphṭaḥiah [30]to drive her out of Esḥor's house or his possessions or his property, shall pay her [31]20 silver karshin and shall carry out in her regard the stipulation of this document. I shall not be able to say, [32]"I have another wife, other than Miphṭa⟨ḥ⟩iah, and other children, other than those that [33]Miphṭaḥiah will bear to me." If I do say, "I have other chi[ldren] and a wife, other than [34]Miphṭaḥiah and her children," I shall pay Miphṭaḥiah 20 sil[ver] karshin by royal [35]weight. Nor shall I be able to [with]draw my possessions and my property from Miph[ṭaḥ]iah. If I do remove them [36]from her (according to [some ot]her doc[ument]), I shall pay Miphṭaḥiah 20 silver karshin by royal weight. [37]Nathan bar ᶜAnaniah wrote [this document at the behest of

Esḥor]. The witnesses to it are [38]Penuliah bar Yezaniah, [ ]iah bar Uriah, Menaḥem bar [Z]akkur. [39]Witness: Reᶜibel ba[r ].

## GENERAL REMARKS

The text is an example of what the Arameans and Jews at Elephantine in the fifth century B.C. called *s<sup>e</sup>par ᵓintū*, "a document of marriage" (or, more strictly, "of wifehood"); see *AP* 14:4; 35:4–5; *BMAP* 10:7,9; 12:18. The difference between it and the later *k<sup>e</sup>tûbāh* among the Jews has often been noted. How old the custom is that is represented by this text is hard to say. The reference to a written contract in Tob. 7:14 seems to be the oldest. In any case, the marriage contracts from Elephantine have a set form that enables one to compare them and use them for interpretation.[5]

When Sayce and Cowley originally published this text they did not correctly understand the verb *hnᶜlt* in line 6 and their attempt to explain the total of the objects mentioned in lines 6–13 did not succeed. Though other suggestions were made for the interpretation of these lines,[6] Cowley's subsequent smaller edition repeated the original understanding of the text found in the *editio princeps*, at least on this point.[7] A more recent translation of the text was provided by H. L. Ginsberg, in two slightly differing forms,[8] but he made no attempt to render lines 6–16. Since the identification of some of the objects in the list was problematic—and still is, in fact—he prudently did not try to translate them in such a collection of texts as that for which his version was prepared. However, a notation he gives in the first edition highlights the problem; he writes: "Lines 6–16, Ashor's [or Mahseiah's] gifts to Miphtahiah and—perhaps—hers to him."[9] For the problem was, first, to determine whether the verb *hnᶜlt* was a first singular form (referring to Esḥor, who had the contract written), or a second singular masculine form (referring to

5. For the historical questions involved in this matter see J. J. Rabinowitz, *Jewish Law: Its Influence on the Development of Legal Institutions* (New York: Bloch, 1956), pp. 39–100; R. Yaron, *Introduction to the Law of the Aramaic Papyri* (Oxford: Clarendon, 1961), pp. 44–53; A. Verger, *Ricerche giuridiche sui papiri aramaici di Elefantina* (Studi semitici, 16; Rome: Centro di studi semitici, 1965), pp. 105–30; S. Greengus, "The Aramaic Marriage Contracts in the Light of the Ancient Near East and the Later Jewish Materials" (Master's thesis, University of Chicago, 1959). For the stereotyped character of the text, see R. Yaron, "The Schema of Aramaic Legal Documents," *JSS* 2 (1957): 33–61.

6. For instance, L. Freund, "Bemerkungen zu Papyrus G. des Fundes von Assuan.," *WZKM* 21 (1907): 169–77; S. Jampel, "Der Papyrusfund von Assuan," *MGWJ* 51 (1907): 617–34, esp. pp. 621–22; M. Lidzbarski, *Ephemeris*, 3. 129–31.

7. See *AP*, pp. 46–47. In this he was followed by C. Clermont-Ganneau, Review of *APA*, *RCHL* 62 (1906): 341–54, esp. p. 349; W. Staerk, *Die jüdisch-aramaeischen Papyri von Assuan* (KlT, 22/23; 1907), p. 28; P. Leander, *LFAA*, #41g.

8. See *ANET*, pp. 222–23; compare the first and second editions (1950, 1955).

9. *Ibid.*, p. 223.

Maḥsiah, the father of the bride), or a third singular feminine form (referring to Miphṭaḥiah, the bride). Cowley noted the lack of distinction between such forms in the bare consonantal text.

Several writers had seen clearly that *hnʿlt* must be understood as the third singular feminine wherever it occurs in this papyrus,[10] and Kraeling confirmed this, noting that the Brooklyn Museum contracts had the same expression.[11] In *BMAP* 7:5 we read, *hnʿlt ly yhwyšmʿ ʾḥtk lbyty tkwnh zy ksp kršn š[ql]n 2 ḥlrn 5* . . ., "Yahuyishmaʿ, your sister, has brought to me, into my house, the dowry of 2 silver karshin, 2 shekels, 5 ḥallurin. . . ." Similarly in *BMAP* 2:4, *hnʿlt ly tmt bydh lbš 1 zy ʿmr šwh ksp šqln 7*, "Tamut has brought with her to me 1 garment of wool, worth in cash 7 shekels." These texts make it clear that the bride's dowry and possessions are indicated in the contract by the phrase *hnʿlt ly X lbyty* or *hnʿlt ly X bydh*, in which *X* stands for the proper name of the woman. Lidzbarski wanted to restore *hnʿlt ly* [*brtk*] in line 6 and *hnʿlt ly* in line 7. Kraeling suggested the restoration of *ly* twice in lines 6 and 7. The restoration is correct for line 7, but a glance at the photo of the papyrus reveals that *ly* alone is not sufficient in line 6, since the lacuna is too long. Moreover, the head of the letter that follows *lamedh* is not clearly that of a *yodh*, but is possibly that of a *beth*, since this letter is written with different stances in the papyrus. If *yodh* is correct, then one should read *ly* [*lbyty*], as in *BMAP* 7:5. But if it is a *beth* that follows *lamedh*, then perhaps one should read simply *lb*[*yty*], "to my house." This would be less crowded. Note too that Cowley read *lb*[.

The same understanding of *hnʿlt* is to be given to the word in lines 24 and 27, "all that she brought with her," as Lidzbarski suggested earlier, but which Cowley did not accept. This suggestion is now confirmed by *BMAP* 7:22, *kl zy hnʿlt bbyth yntn lh tkwnth wlbšyh*, "all that she brought into his house he shall give to her, her dowry and her garments." Cf. *BMAP* 2:10.

One reason why Cowley did not accept the suggestion of Freund and Jampel, who wanted to understand *hnʿlt* as the second singular masculine, referring to Miphṭaḥiah's father, Maḥsiah, was that for him "the sum total in l. 14 shows that the presents were given by the same person who paid the 5 shekels."[12] But since he did not correctly understand several other ex-

10. For example, W. Staerk, *Alte und neue aramäische Papyri übersetzt und erklärt* (KlT, 94; 1912), p. 44; M. Lidzbarski, *Ephemeris*, 3. 129; B. Cohen, "Dowry in Jewish and Roman Law," *AIPHOS* 13 (1953): 57–85, esp. p. 61.

11. See *BMAP*, p. 146. In this he was followed by S. Greengus, "Aramaic Marriage Contracts," p. 59; R. Yaron, "Aramaic Marriage Contracts from Elephantine," *JSS* 3 (1958): 1–39, esp. p. 6.

12. See *AP*, p. 47; also Cowley's note on line 14, p. 48.

pressions in the text, he insisted that Esḥor, not Miphṭaḥiah, was the subject of the verb *hnᶜlt*. The five shekels in line 5 represent the *mhr*, "the bride-price," paid by the groom to the bride's father, Maḥsiah. This is not the "dowry," and though Cowley obviously used this English term for *mhr* in a loose sense, it is indicative of his basic misunderstanding of the contract as a whole. He understood the difference between "bride-price" and "dowry," as is obvious from his reference to Gen. 34:12. However, he misunderstood the term *ksp tkwnh* in line 6, translating it as "the cost of furniture." It is now clear that this is "dowry money," whatever may be the etymological explanation of the phrase. In any case, Cowley was right in saying that the *mhr* of 5 shekels was included in the sum given in lines 13–14.

To arrive at the sum of 6 karshin, 5 shekels, and 20 ḥallurin, one must total up the dowry (*ksp tkwnh*), the value of the objects brought by Miphṭaḥiah, and the bride-price (*mhr*) that Esḥor paid. Thus:

| LINE | OBJECT | | VALUE | | |
|---|---|---|---|---|---|
| 5 | Esḥor's *mhr* | | | 5 shekels | |
| 6 | Miphṭaḥiah's *ksp tkwnh* | | 1 karsh | 2 shekels | |
| 7–8 | ,, | *lbš 1 zy ᶜmr* | 2 karshin | 8 shekels | |
| 9–10 | ,, | *šbyṭ 1* | | 8 shekels | |
| 10–11 | ,, | *lbš ᵓḥrn zy ᶜmr* | | 7 shekels | |
| 11–12 | ,, | *mḥzy 1 zy nḥš* | | 1 shekel | 2 R |
| 12 | ,, | *tmsᵓ 1* | | 1 shekel | 2 R |
| 12–13 | ,, | *ksn 2* | | 2 shekels[13] | |
| 13 | ,, | *zlwᶜ 1* | | | 2 R |
| | | | 3 karshin | 34 shekels | 6 R |

Cowley had shown that a *krš* equalled a ten-shekel piece and that *R*, probably standing for *rbᶜᵓ*, "quarter," i.e., a quarter of a shekel, equalled ten ḥallurin.[14] Hence the above total is easily converted to 6 karshin,

13. There is a lacuna at this point in the papyrus and one stroke of the number following the plural *šqln* remains. In the *editio princeps*, Sayce and Cowley restored the number as [3], without justifying it. But Cowley later restored it more accurately as [2], while still admitting the possibility of [3]. Lidzbarski (*Ephemeris*, 3. 130) also read the number 3. His interpretation of the sum in lines 13–14, however, was erroneous. It was based on his insistence that *šql*, a singular, in line 14 was originally followed only by one stroke, i.e., 6 karshin, 1 shekel, 20 ḥallurin. This represented only Miphṭaḥiah's money and possessions. It did not include the 5 shekels of the *mhr* but did include the extra shekel restored in line 13. Then he suggested that four extra strokes were later added in line 14 to represent the value of the objects listed (without prices) in lines 15–16. It is, however, now clear that the latter objects were not included in the sum and there is no evidence of a later addition of four strokes.

14. Kraeling (*BMAP*, pp. 39,146) maintains that the *ḥallūr* represents a tenth of the silver shekel. This may be right for the Babylonian scale but it cannot be correct in these Elephantine texts. See S. Greengus, "Aramaic Marriage Contracts," pp. 44–51; his discussion strangely hesitates in this matter.

5 shekels, and 20 ḥallurin, the sum formulated in lines 13–14. Cowley was, then, right in maintaining that the bride-price was included in the sum so formulated.

But does it mean that all that is included in the total came from one and the same person? This was Cowley's conclusion and the reason why he insisted that *hnʿlt* was the first singular form, referring to Esḥor's presents. It is, however, clear from *BMAP* 7 that this conclusion is erroneous. Though *BMAP* 7:15 is fragmentary at one point, enough is preserved to show that the dowry and the bride-price were both included in the total, even though these sums come from different persons: *[k]l [m]ʾn[y . . . . . . n]ḥš wtk[w]ntʾ wmhrʾ ksp kršn šbʿh h[w 7 š]q[l]n tmnyh hw 8 ḥlrn 5 bʾbny mlkʾ ksp 2 r lʿśrtʾ*, "all the vessels of [ and] bronze, and the dowry, and the bride-price (equal) seven, that is 7, silver karshin, eight, that is 8, shekels, 5 ḥallurin by royal weight, (in) silver of 2 qu(arters) to the ten-piece."[15]

The reason for the inclusion of the *mhr* in the sum total has been explained in various ways. What seems to be clear is that the *mhr* was no longer a "bride-price" in the strict sense, i.e., a price paid to the father (or guardian) of the bride. Evidence from Alalakh, Babylonia, and Egypt indicates that the father at least turned it over to the daughter.[16] S. Greengus thinks that it was not paid at all, but represents merely "a penalty which would be forfeited by the divorcing party."[17] H. L. Ginsberg thinks rather that the *mhr* becomes

15. A similar detailed list can be constructed for *BMAP* 7 to total up to this sum. However, the text is broken in places and the following list represents only my own way of restoring the individual values:

| LINE | OBJECT | VALUE | | |
|---|---|---|---|---|
| 5 | *mhr* | 1 karsh | | |
| 5–6 | *tkwnh zy ksp* | 2 karshin | 2 shekels | 5 ḥallurin |
| 6–7 | *lbš 1 zy qmr* | 1 karsh | 2 shekels | |
| 7 | *gmydh 1 zy qmr* | 1 karsh | | |
| 8–9 | *lbš 1 mʿdr* | | 7 shekels | |
| 9–10 | *šbyṭ 1* | | 8 shekels | |
| 10 | *lbš 1* | | [1 shekel | 20 ḥallurin] |
| 11 | *šnṭʾ 1* | | [1 shekel | 10 ḥallurin] |
| 11–12 | *?* | | [1 shekel] | |
| 12 | *? 1 ktn blyh* | | 1 shekel | |
| 13 | *mḥzy 1* | | 1 shekel | |
| 13–14 | *tmsʾ 1* | | 1 shekel | 10 ḥallurin |
| 14 | *ks 1* | | [1] shekel | |
| 14 | *ks 1* | | | 20 ḥallurin |
| 15 | *zlwʿ 1* | | | 20 ḥallurin |
| | | 5 karshin | 26 shekels | 85 ḥallurin |
| | *or* | 7 karshin | 8 shekels | 5 ḥallurin |

16. See R. Yaron, *Introduction*, p. 48; "Aramaic Marriage Contracts," p. 6.

17. "Aramaic Marriage Contracts," p. 57; see also R. Yaron, *Introduction*, p. 48; A. Verger, *Ricerche*, p. 112.

the divorce fee.[18] The reason for the dispute in the last instance involves *BMAP* 2, where no *mhr* is mentioned and the sum written on the outside of the papyrus differs considerably from that written inside. I shall leave this question aside, since it does not concern the contract now under study. The important thing to realize is that the *mhr* is included in the sum total and is regarded as something that belongs to the bride.[19]

After these general remarks we can proceed to the analysis of the text of the contract itself.

## COMMENTARY

1. *b2*[*5 l*]*tšry*: "On the 25th of Tishri." This is the first part of the dating of the contract, which is also done according to the Egyptian calendar in the following phrase. The correspondence of Tishri and Epiph is also found in *BMAP* 4:1 and 7:1. See S. H. Horn and L. H. Wood, "The Fifth Century Jewish Calendar at Elephantine," *JNES* 13 (1954): 1–20. The preposition *b* is common in such dates and probably is an abbreviation for *bywm*; it is usually followed by the cardinal number written in a cipher. In *AP* 26:16 one can find the number written out (and preceded by four hundred). The preposition *l* has been restored on the basis of its frequent usage (see *BMAP* 1:1; 3:1; 4:1; 8:1; 9:1; 10:1; 12:1,10), when the name of the month is not preceded by *byrḥ* or *lyrḥ*. Kraeling omitted it in *BMAP* 6:1, but see plate VI; it is to be restored also in *BMAP* 2:1 (before [*tmwz*]). It is omitted, however, in *BMAP* 5:1.

[*hw ywm*] *6 lyrḥ ʾpp*: "That is, the 6th day of the month of Epiph." This double dating is found in all the marriage contracts from Elephantine, but not in all other documents. See R. Yaron, "The Schema," p. 34; E. G. Kraeling, *BMAP*, pp. 51–52. The restored form *hw*, without a final *aleph*, is normal in the Elephantine texts; see I. N. Vinnikov, *Slovar*, p. 194. Judging from the commonly used *šnt*, which is the construct state, the word *ywm* should also be so regarded. Since the name of the Egyptian month is always written in these texts simply as *ʾpp*, I vocalize it as Epiph, not Epiphi. The latter is derived from Greek transcriptions of the name in papyri, but it is not universal in Greek by any means. Alongside of it one finds rather frequently *Epip*, *Epeip*, *Epeiph*, and in Coptic also *Epēp* or *Epep*. See F. Preisigke *Wörterbuch der griechischen Papyrusurkunden*, 3/1 (1929), p. 86. There is no

18. "The Brooklyn Museum Aramaic Papyri," *JAOS* 74 (1954): 153–62, esp. pp. 156, 159.

19. The issue is further complicated by the occurrence of the forfeiture phrase as a penalty for the bride in *BMAP* 7:24.

evidence that the Aramaic form would have been pronounced with a final *i*-vowel. Cf. J. Černý, *ASAE* 43 (1943): 173–81; *BIFAO* 57 (1958): 207.

[*šnt*] *25 ʾrtḥšs*]*ś mlk*[ʾ]: "The 25th year of Artaxerxes, the king." The restoration of the year depends on the usually admitted relation of this contract to *AP* 14, which is clearly dated to this year of Artaxerxes. The latter document is the settlement of a claim connected with the divorce of Miphṭaḥiah from her second husband in 440 B.C. The new third marriage, of which the present text is a record, probably took place a short time afterward. In any case, if it is wrong the date is off only by a year or so. But Horn and Wood (*JNES* 13 [1954]: 13) prefer to date this text in 435 B.C. (?), with some hesitation.

The king is almost certainly Artaxerxes I Longimanus (464–24). The name is written in the official Aramaic transcription used in many of these texts, *ʾrtḥšsś* (*AP* 6:2; 7:1; 10:1; 13:1; *BMAP* 1:1; 3:1; 4:1; etc.). In *BMAP* 2:1 it is written simply as *ʾrtḥš*, which Kraeling rightly considers to be "a scribal error." In *KAI* 274:1; 275:1 we find the name *ʾrtḥšsy mlkʾ br zy Zrytr*; but is it the same? According to H. H. Schaeder (*Iranische Beiträge I* [Schriften der Königsberger Gelehrten Gesellschaft, Geisteswissenschaftliche Kl., 6/5; Halle: M. Niemeyer, 1930], p. 268) the Aramaic form found in the Elephantine texts represents the Persian *Artaxšasśa* (< Old Persian *Artaxšathra*), whereas the forms in biblical Aramaic (*ʾArtaḥšaśtʾ* [Ezr. 4:7], *ʾArtaḥšaśtāʾ* [Ezr. 4:7], or *ʾArtaḥšastāʾ* [Ezr. 7:1]) are attempts to come even closer to the Persian form with the final *-a*.

2. *ʾsḥwr br* [*ṣḥʾ*]: "Esḥor bar Ṣeḥo." The groom's father's name is supplied from *AP* 20:3,20. The groom's name here is Egyptian, equalling *nś-Ḥr*, "Belonging to (the god) Horus," a form of name that is often transcribed into Greek with initial *Es-* or simply *s-* (see H. Ranke, *Die ägyptischen Personennamen* [Glückstadt: Augustin], I [1935], p. 178, 7). But in three other Elephantine documents the children born of the marriage recorded in this contract are listed thus: "Yedaniah and Maḥsiah, 2 in all, sons of Esḥor bar Ṣeḥo by Miphṭaḥiah, daughter of Maḥsiah" (*AP* 20:3); "Yedaniah bar Nathan and Maḥsiah bar Nathan, his brother, their mother being Mibṭaḥiah, daughter of Maḥsiah bar Yedaniah" (*AP* 25:3); "Maḥsiah bar Nathan 1, Yedaniah bar Nathan 1, in all 2, . . . we have divided between us the slaves of Mibṭaḥiah, our mother" (*AP* 28:2–3). There is little doubt that the same children and parents are meant, though this has been contested (see E. Volterra, "'*Yhwdy*' e '*ʾrmy*' nei papiri aramaici del V secolo provenienti dall'Egitto," *ANL*, Rendiconti, Sc. mor. 8/18 [1963]: 131–73; cf.

R. Yaron, "Who is Who at Elephantine," *Iura* 15 [1964]: 167–72; and Volterra's reply, ibid., pp. 173–80). And yet Esḥor's name subsequently appears as Nathan in *AP* 25 and 28. Cowley speculated: Did Esḥor become a proselyte and take a Jewish name, Nathan (*AP*, p. 47)?

The patronymic *bar Ṣeḥo* is given here in its conventional vocalization. The father's name *Ṣḥʾ* is Egyptian and represents *Ḏd-ḥr*, "Horus has spoken," or possibly "The face of X (a god) has spoken," because of the disappearance of final *r*. The name is apparently transcribed into Akkadian as *Ṣi-ḫa-a* and into Greek as *Teōs* or *Tachōs* (see H. Ranke, *Ägyptische Personennamen*, I. 411,12; G. Fecht, *Wortakzent und Silbenstruktur: Untersuchungen zur Geschichte der ägyptischen Sprache* [ÄF 21; Glückstadt: Augustin, 1960], p. 84, #151, n. 254).

*ʾrdkl zy mlkʾ*: "A royal architect," or "a builder to the king" (Ginsberg), i.e., some sort of government-hired builder. The name of the profession is found in AP 14:2, spelled *ʾrdykl*; it occurs in later Aramaic as *ʾardīkᵉlā* or *ʾardēkᵉlā*. This is basically an Akkadian word, reflecting the Babylonian (*w*)*arad ekalli*, "palace slave." The meaning of the word, however, developed within the Mesopotamian area and came to denote not a social class but a profession, specifically a workman in the building trade. See further, A. L. Oppenheim, "AKK. arad ekalli = 'Builder,'" *ArOr* 17/2 (1949): 227–35. In this sense it is used in these texts.

*lmḥ*[*syh*]: "To Maḥsiah," the father of Miphṭaḥiah. He is the son of Yedaniah (*AP* 25:3) and appears again in *AP* 5:2,9,12,20; 6:3,22; 8:1,18, 28,35; 9:1,5,16; 11:14; 13:1,17bis,21; 14:2; 25:3,7; *BMAP* 1:13. The name is undoubtedly Hebrew, *Maḥsi-yāh*, "Yahu is my refuge." It occurs also in Jer. 32:12; 51:59; but its Masoretic vocalization is questionable. The root of it is *ḥsy*, and one can understand how the Masoretic pointing *Maḥsēyāh* developed (as a *maqtal*-type); but one may ask whether it is accurate for the fifth century B.C. In any case, the vocalization *Meḥasiah* (S. Greengus, *Aramaic Marriage Contracts*, p. 122) is wrong.

[ʾ]*rmy zy ṣwn*: "An Aramean of Syene." This same identification is given to Maḥsiah in *AP* 5:2; 13:2; 14:3. But in *AP* 6:3 he is called *Yhwdy bbyrt Yb*, "a Jew in the fortress of Yeb," and identified in *AP* 8:2 as *Yhwd*[*y*] *mhḥsn byb byrtʾ*, "a Jew owning property in Yeb, the fortress." Again in *AP* 9:2 he seems to be called a *y*[*hwdy zy b*]*ʾb*, but the text is very fragmentary here. On the problem of one and the same person being called a "Jew" and an "Aramean" in the Elephantine papyri, see E. Volterra, *ANL*, Rendiconti, Sc. mor. 8/18 (1963): 131–73. He seeks to distinguish such persons. But R. Yaron (*Iura* 15 [1964]: 167–72) suggests that the terms *yhwdy* and *ʾrmy* were used to designate the same persons, but from different points of view. He thinks that *yhwdy* was used "especially in documents in which some non-Jewish factor is involved," and thus serves to identify the persons as such. But the Jews of Elephantine used the term *ʾrmy* "amongst themselves." This issue is far from settled, and there seems to be little at present in the text to allow of a solution.

The word *ʾrmy* is an appositive to a proper name, and yet occurs in the absolute state (see T. Nöldeke, *ZA* 20 [1907]: 142; P. Joüon, "Notes grammaticales, lexicographiques et philologiques sur les papyrus araméens d'Egypte," *MUSJ* 18 [1934]: 1–90, esp. pp. 10–11). This is true when the absolute is followed by some determination, as here.

The name *swn*, Syene, is usually vocalized after the Greek *Syēnē* or the Hebrew *Sᵉwēnēh* (Ezek. 29:10). Cf. the Coptic *Souan* and Arabic *ʾAswân*.

*ldgl Wryzat*: "Of the Warizath garrison." The same identification is given to Maḥsiah in *AP* 5:3; 6:4; 13:2; 14:3; but in *AP* 8:2; 9:2 he is said to belong to the *dgl Hwmdt*, "the Hawmadat garrison." The exact meaning of *dgl* is obscure. It is often said that it means basically a "standard" or "banner," but this is far from clear (see Y. Yadin, *The Scroll of the War of the Sons of Light against the Sons of Darkness* [New York; Oxford, 1962], p. 39). In these texts it seems to denote a military unit or detachment of undetermined size; cf. Num. 1:52; 2:2–3,10,17–18,25,31,34. To identify it as a military unit is not to deny a social organization that may also be involved in it. The shift from the Warizath garrison to the Hawmadat may represent a real transfer. The proper name of the garrison is not easily explained; it is almost certainly Persian. In *BMAP* 8:11 it occurs as a personal name. Was the name of the garrison derived from the name of some chief or official in it? In any case it is interesting to note that the majority of names of such garrisons at Yeb or Syene are either Persian or Akkadian (e.g., *Hawmadat*, *AP* 8:2; 9:2; *Bagapat*, *TA* 5:7,9; *ʾAtroparan*, *AP* 6:9; *ʾArtabanu*, *AP* 6:3; *ʾIddinnabū*, *AP* 20:2; *BMAP* 14:2; *Nabūkudurr*[*i*], *AP* 7:3; *ʾArpaḥu*, *BMAP* 5:2; *Nmsw*, *BMAP* 3:2). B. Porten (*Archives from Elephantine*, p. 30) takes this as evidence that the *dgln* were named after their "respective non-Jewish commanders."

3. *lʾmr*: "Saying," a stereotyped, fossilized Peal infinitive of *ʾmr*, which has persisted in such syntactical contexts, introducing direct statements. It is obviously akin to the Hebrew *lēʾmōr*, and yet it cannot be written off as a Hebraism, *pace* T. Nöldeke, *ZA* 20 (1907): 137. Peal infinitives without the initial *mem* are found in early Aramaic texts; see Sf I B 32 (*lśgb*); Hadad 13, 14 (*lbnʾ*). On the other hand, the real Aramaic form, *mʾmr*, is found in *AP* 32:2 and *A* 115. It may be due to the Canaanite influence on early Aramaic and is therefore a stereotyped form that has persisted.

*ʾnh* [*ʾ*]*tyt bytk*: "I have come to your house." This seems like a useless detail in the otherwise closely worded contract, and it may represent an historical phrase that is here preserved. It is peculiar in Aramaic. Though there are many instances of verbs expressing motion toward a place with an object and no preposition (see Sf III 5, *yhkn Ḥlb*; Padua I v 5, *tʾtwn Mṣryn*; I r 3, *ʾytyt hmw Mnpy*; *BMAP* 13:3, ([*yhy*]*twn Mnpy*); *AP* 42:7 (*ḥt Mnpy*); *AP* 83:2 (*mṭʾ Ṣḥʾ Mnpy*); *AD* 6:2,4,5; contrast *AP* 37:11; 42:11. This is apparently a lone instance of such an expression with a common noun as the object; compare *BMAP* 14:3 (*ʾnh ʾtyt ʿlyk bbyt*[*k*]) and *BMAP* 7:3 (*ʾnh ʾtyt ʿl* [*by*]*tk*); *BMAP* 2:3 (*ʾnh ʾtyt ʿlyk*). These examples make one suspect that the phrase in this text is simply a scribal error.

*lmntn ly* [*l*]*brtk*: "(To ask you) to give me your daughter." The cumbersome infinitival construction (where the infinitive's subject is different from that of the main verb on which it depends) is perhaps explained by *BMAP* 7:3, *ʾnh ʾtyt ʿl* [*by*]*tk wšʾlt mnk lnšn Yhwyšmʿ*, "I have come to your house and asked of you the woman Yahuyishmaʿ." But the expression found in this text had apparently become stereotyped, since it is also found in *BMAP* 2:3.

*Mpṭ⟨ḥ⟩yh*: "Miphṭaḥiah." The same scribal omission of *ḥ* occurs in line 32. The name is a dissimilated form of the more original *Mibṭaḥiah*, "Yahu is my security," *Mibṭaḥī-yāh*, found in *AP* 8:2; 9:3,7,10,12; 14:2,14; 20:3; 25:3,7; 28:3,5,6. The dissimilation of the voiced bilabials occurs also in *AP* 13:2,4. The shift from *p* > *b* is found in earlier Aramaic texts: *nbš*, Sf I A 37; *btn* Sf I A 32; *ʾlb*, Panammu I.34. But the opposite shift is more rarely attested.

This is apparently Miphṭaḥiah's third marriage. From *AP* 14 (dated ca. 440 B.C.) it seems that her second marriage ended in divorce from an Egyptian named Piʾ. From *AP* 8:6 it is clear that Miphṭaḥiah was earlier married to Yezan bar Uriah (ca. 460 B.C.). Miphṭaḥiah thus appears to be an adult divorcee, but she is still given in marriage to Esḥor by her father.

*lʾntw*: "In marriage," or more strictly "for wifehood." This expression occurs again in *AP* 48:3; *BMAP* 2:3; 7:3. It states the purpose of the agreement that is recorded in this contract. Lidzbarski (*Ephemeris*, 3.80) called attention to the use of this phrase in official Jewish marriage contracts of a later date and compared the Mishnah, *Ketuboth*, 4:7ff. He also noted that Targum Onqelos on Gen. 16:3 translated the Hebrew phrase *leʾiššāh* by *leʾintū*. Kraeling (*BMAP*, 146) further compared the expression to the Assyrian *nadānu ana aššūti*.

4. *hy ʾntty wʾnh bʿlh mn ywmʾ znh wʿd ʿlm*: "She is my wife and I am her husband from this day forward," literally "from this day and forever." The

same formula is found in *BMAP* 2:3–4; 7:4 (but with the omission of *w-* before *ᶜd* in the latter text). These words actually record the formal agreement that constitutes the marriage; Esḥor acknowledges his relationship to Miphṭaḥiah. The acknowledgment is formulated solely from the standpoint of the groom. The bride's consent is undoubtedly presupposed, but not recorded, if expressed at all. The omission of this undoubtedly reflects the attitude toward women in the ancient Near East. A few isolated texts record the bride's consent, but they are so isolated as to preclude any generalizations (see Gen. 24:8,58; C. H. Gordon, "The Status of Women in Nuzi Texts," *ZA* 43 [1936]: 149). Even in the case of an adult marriage, such as Miphṭaḥiah's third, the consent is not recorded. This raises the question whether *bᶜlh* is too weakly translated merely as "her husband."

The last part of the agreement, *mn ywmʾ wᶜd ᶜlm*, is also found in documents other than marriage contracts (e.g., *AP* 8:9; 14:6–7; 20:9–10; *BMAP* 4:4–5; 10:8). It in no way guarantees the indissolubility of the marriage, because a provision is made in the contract itself for divorce. Contrast the formula in Mur. 20 i 3–4. Cf. S. Loewenstamm, "From This Time and Forevermore," *Tarbiẕ* 32 (1963): 313–16.

In Hos. 2:4 one finds the Hebrew counterpart of this agreement negatively expressed, *hîʾ lôʾ ʾištî weʾānōkî lôʾ ʾîšāh*. Though this is scarcely a formal divorce formula, it undoubtedly reflects the ancient marriage formula that we find in this Aramaic text.

*yhbt lk mhr brtk Mpṭḥyh*: "I have given you the bride-price for your daughter Miphṭaḥiah." The noun *mhr* is related to the Hebrew *mōhar* (Gen. 34:12; Ex. 22:16; 1 Sam. 18:25). The construct is to be vocalized *mehar*, and the emphatic is either *muhrāʾ* or *mohᵒrāʾ*; *pace* R. Yaron, *Introduction*, p. 45, n. 1, the Aramaic vocalization is not uncertain. No *mhr* is mentioned in the contract *BMAP* 2, and this has been variously interpreted (see H. L. Ginsberg, *JAOS* 74 [1954]: 156; R. Yaron, *Introduction*, p. 57; S. Greengus, "Aramaic Marriage Contracts," pp. 41–64). The *mhr* is in reality the same as the Akkad. *terḫatu*; the bride-price was an institution at Ugarit(see *UT* 77:19–20 *watn mhrh labh*) and also in ancient Egypt. But by Saite and Persian times it had lost the implication of a purchase of the bride; though nominally paid to the father or guardian, it apparently became the property of the bride. This usage is reflected in the Elephantine texts too.

5. [*ksp*] *šqln 5*: "5 silver shekels," or possibly "a sum of 5 shekels." At times—even in this text—*ksp* seems to be used generically in the sense of "money" or "cash," and it is not easy to tell to what extent it retains the nuance of "silver." My translation shifts back and forth between these two

senses, depending on which seems more appropriate. Note the expression in *BMAP* 2:6 *wdmy nksy*ʾ *ksp ksp šqln* 7, etc., where the double *ksp* may be dittographical; but it may also be an attempt to formulate the two nuances mentioned. The form *šqln* is vocalized with the ending *-īn* by T. Nöldeke (*ZA* 20 [1907]: 139) and P. Leander (*LFAA*, #45a). This vocalization of the masculine plural absolute has been questioned by H. L. Ginsberg, "Aramaic Dialect Problems," *AJSL* 52 (1936): 99–101, who prefers to vocalize it as *-ān* because of the defective spelling.

*b*ʾ*bny mlk*[ʾ]: "By royal weight," literally, "by (*or* according to) the stones of the king." This expression occurs again in lines 6–7, 9, 10, 14–15, 34–35, 36, and frequently in other Elephantine texts. The reference is to a standard of silver conforming to governmental stone-weights, which were apparently carried in small pouches and officially used. A similar expression is found in 2 Sam. 14:26. Another standard was apparently also used at Elephantine, for in *AP* 11:2 we learn of "stones of Ptaḥ," [*b*ʾ]*bny Ptḥ*; cf. *AP* 26:21, *tqlt prs*, "the Persian weight." See further B. Porten, *Archives from Elephantine: The Life of an Ancient Jewish Military Colony* (Berkeley: University of California Press, 1968), pp. 63–64.

*ᶜl ᶜlyk wṭb lbbk bgw*: "You have received it and you are satisfied with it," literally, "it has entered into you and your heart is content therewith." The expression occurs again in line 15. The verb *ᶜl* is the 3rd sg. masc. pf. Peal of *ᶜll*, "enter," and *ṭb*, which is sometimes written as *ṭyb* (see *AP* 2:9; 15:15; 20:9; *BMAP* 3:6; 12:6,14,26; etc.), is to be understood as a stative 3rd sg. masc. pf. Peal of *ṭyb* (a form like *myt* in *AP* 5:8 or *rim* in Dan. 5:20). The adverb *bgw* is in reality a prepositional phrase, *b* + *gaww* ("interior"), simplified and contracted to *b*ᵉ*gô*; for similar uses of it, see *AP* 2:9; 8:28; 9:6; *BMAP* 1:4,10; etc. The implications of this formula in Aramaic business law and its relation to the long recognized analogues in Old Babylonian (*libbašu ṭāb*, "his [the seller's] heart is satisfied") and in Demotic (*dj.k-mtj hꜣtj(.i)*, "you [the buyer] have satisfied my heart") have been extensively investigated in the recent book of Y. Muffs, *Studies in the Aramaic Legal Papyri from Elephantine* (Studia et documenta ad iura orientis antiqui pertinentia, 8; Leiden: Brill, 1969). On pages 53–56 he discusses the implications of the phrase in the clause regarding the *mhr*.

6. *hnᶜlt lb*[*yty*] *Mpṭḥyh bydh*: "Miphṭaḥiah has brought into my house with her," literally, "has caused to enter my house in her (own) hand." See the general remarks above (p. 142) for the reasons for understanding *hnᶜlt* as the 3rd sg. fem. and for the reading *lb*[*yty*] or *ly* [*lbyty*]. The *n* in the form represents the resolution of the secondary doubling of the first radical of the

Double ʿAyin root *ʿll*. It is not simply a substitution of nasalization for gemination (which is true in this case); but sometimes other liquids are used (e.g., *Dammeśeq* > *Darmeśeq*; *kuss*$^{eʾ}$*āʾ* > *kurs*$^{eʾ}$*āʾ*). The phrase used here should be compared with *BMAP* 7:5; 2:4.

*ks*[*p*] *tkwnh krš 1 šqln 2*: "A dowry sum of 1 karsh, 2 shekels." The meaning of *ksp tkwnh* has not always been correctly understood; indeed, R. Yaron (*Introduction*, p. 50) seems to think that its "exact meaning . . . is not clear" at all. Sayce and Cowley translated it hesitatingly, "money for an outfit," and Cowley subsequently used "the cost of furniture." W. Staerk rendered it "als (bar-)wert ihrer Ausstattung" (*Alte und neue aramäische Papyri*, p. 44). Kraeling (*BMAP*, p. 209) related it to Nah. 2:10 and translated it "substance of silver." The amount designated by *ksp tkwnh* certainly does not include the value of the items subsequently listed, as the list of them and its total reveal (see above, p. 143). It almost certainly represents a sum of money or an amount of silver distinct from the other items and from the *mhr*; it was the dowry sum in the strict sense. The only thing that may be uncertain about it is the etymology, since *tkwnh* seems to be derived from the root *kwn* with a preformative *t*. See P. Leander (*LFAA* #43 j''''), who also translated it "Ausstattung." It is the money which has been put up by the bride for the marriage.

The *krš* is equal in these texts to ten (heavy) silver shekels, or to the *ʿśrtʾ*, "ten-piece," which is often written in a cipher, as in the following line. The name *krš* that is being used in these Aramaic texts from Egypt is undoubtedly derived from the Persian monetary system, but the weight is not exactly the same in Egypt as in Persia. Ten Elephantine shekels weigh 87.6 grams, whereas the karsh-weights found at Persepolis and outside of Egypt weigh between 83.33–83.36 grams. This is roughly 4.3 grams less than the Egyptian ten shekels, or a half shekel less. See further below, on line 7.

The *šql* used at Elephantine seems to have weighed 87.6 grams. This calculation is based mainly on *AP* 35:3, *ksp š 2 hw* [*ks*]*p sttry 1*, "the sum of 2 shekels, that is the sum of one stater," and *BMAP* 12:5, *ksp krš ḥd hw 1 šqln tlth hw 3 ksp ywn sttry 6 šql 1 ḥd*, "the sum of one karsh, that is 1, three shekels, that is 3, (in) the money of Greece, 6 staters, one, ⟨that is⟩ 1, shekel." See also *BMAP* 12:14. This shows that the Elephantine shekel was equivalent to a half of a stater, or the Athenian tetradrachm, which weighed at this time 17.52 grams. See B. Porten, *Archives*, pp. 64–65.

*bʾbny mlkʾ*: See comment on line 5.

7. *ksp r 2 l10*: "(In) silver (of) 2 qu(arters) to the 10-piece." This expression occurs again in line 14, and in other texts (*BMAP* 7:32). Often the word

is written out, *ᶜśrtᵓ* (*AP* 6:15; 8:14,21; 9:15; *BMAP* 3:16), but the abbreviation *r* is widespread. Its meaning as *rbᶜᵓ* (*ribᶜāᵓ* or *rubᶜāᵓ*), "quarter," is widely admitted today, and almost certainly has nothing to do with the word *rᶜy*, found in *AP* 73:6,13,15,17, *pace* S. Greengus, *Aramaic Marriage Contracts*, p. 51. Other phrases that are similar to this one in these texts make the identification of *r* as a quarter shekel almost certain, for one also finds *ksp r 2 lkrš 1* (*AP* 20:15; 25:15–16; *BMAP* 4:15) and *ksp zwz lᶜśrtᵓ* or *l10* (*BMAP* 3:15,18; 7:17; 8:8), and *ksp zwz lkrš 1* (*BMAP* 3:6). In these phrases the *r 2* is equivalent to the *zûz*, or half shekel, indicating that *r 2* is to be understood as *ribᶜīn 2* or *rubᶜīn 2*. The "quarter" is the equivalent also of 10 ḥallurin. See R. Yaron, "*Ksp zwz*," *Lešonénu* 31 (1966–67): 287–88, B. Porten, *Archives*, pp. 62–67, 305–7. The phrase probably does not indicate an alloyed kind of silver, but rather an adjustment of the lighter Persian weight to the standard used in Egypt. This is the plausible explanation well worked out by B. Porten. There is only one slight difficulty in it, and that is to explain the constant appearance of *ksp* at the beginning of this phrase; perhaps one should rather translate "(with) 2 silver qu(arters) to the tenpiece (*or* karsh)."

*hnᶜlt ly bydh*: See comment above on line 6.

*lbš 1 zy ᶜmr ḥdt ḥṭb ṣbᶜ ydyn*: "1 new garment of wool, striped with dye on both edges." This phrase begins the list of the items other than money that Miphṭaḥiah brought with her to the marriage; the first is an expensive woolen garment. The word for "wool," *ᶜmr*, occurs in this text, written ca. 440 B.C., with an initial *ᶜayin*. But in a text dated ca. 420 B.C. we find the word written with an initial *qoph* (*BMAP* 7:6,7,13). The form *ᶜmr* also appears in the still earlier text of *BMAP* 2:4 (dated ca. 449 B.C.). The shift from *q* > ᶜ is also attested in Jer. 10:11 (both *ᵓarqāᵓ* and *ᵓarᶜāᵓ*). The *qoph* is certainly older, and its persistence in *BMAP* 7, after the shift to *ᶜayin* has taken place, is noteworthy. Cf. *AP* 20:5 (*qmr*, ca. 420 B.C.); 36:3 (*qmr*, undated); 42:9 (*qmr*, undated).

The word *ḥṭb* is found with the full spelling *ḥṭyb* in *BMAP* 7:7, confirming the participial explanation proposed by Cowley, who compared it to *ḥṭbwt* in Prov. 7:16, "striped cloths."

The form *ṣbᶜ*, which also occurs in *BMAP* 7:8; 14a; *AP* 42:9, has been understood by Cowley, Leander (*LFAA* #34a), and Kraeling (*BMAP*, p. 317), as a participle, "dyed." The latter, however, gives a more plausible explanation in his commentary (*BMAP*, p. 210), where he takes it as a noun (*ṣbᶜᵓ*), related to Akkad. *ṣību, ṣīpu*. Hence, "striped with dye." The form *ṣbᶜ* has not yet turned up with the full spelling which might support the participial interpretation.

Both Cowley and Kraeling understood *ydyn* to mean "on both sides." G. R. Driver (*PEQ* 87 [1955]: 93) sensed the difficulty in this interpretation, maintaining that "no material can be dyed only on one side." He preferred to understand the word to mean "twice dyed," to make the color fast. He compared the biblical phrase *ʿśr ydwt* (Dan. 1:20; Gen. 43:34), and called attention to the twice-dyed Tyrian purple garments called *dibapha* (Pliny, *NH* 9.63,137). This is certainly a preferable interpretation, but is there not another possibility? Cannot *ydyn* mean on "two edges"? Cowley had compared the Babylonian use of *idu* for his interpretation, but this would just as well support the idea of "edges" (*CAD* 7.12). Moreover *BMAP* 7:8,10 seems to express this idea in a more specific fashion in giving the measurements of the stripes, *pšk 1 lpm 1*, "1 handbreadth on each border" and "2 fingerbreadths to each border." *Ydyn* would in this interpretation be taken adverbially.

8. *hwh ʾrk ʾmn 8 b5*: "Measuring 8 cubits by 5," literally, "being (in) length 8 cubits by 5." The same expression occurs again in lines 9, 10–11. The word *ʾrk* has the same adverbial function that *ydyn* has in the preceding expression.

*[š]wh ksp kršn 2 šqln 8*: "Worth (in) cash 2 karshin and 8 shekels," or "worth 2 silver karshin, 8 shekels." It is this sort of phrase that suggests that *ksp* may no longer have the strict meaning of "silver," and that it is an attempt merely to record the monetary value of the goods. The form *šwh* is either the Peal active participle (*šāwêh*), "equalling," or (less likely) the passive participle (*šᵉwêh*) with active force, "being worth." Cf. the examples of the latter in biblical Aramaic: *dḥyl* (Dan. 2:31); *mhymn* (Dan. 2:45). Expressions similar to this phrase occur again in lines 9–10, 11, 11–12, 12, 13(bis). The value of this expensive woolen garment can be realized by comparing it to the price of a piece of property sold in *BMAP* 3:4–6, which is just half of the value given here.

9. *šbyṭ 1 ḥdt*: "1 new shawl." The meaning of *šbyṭ* is not certain. Cowley explained it as "closely-woven" stuff, adding that from its size it could only have been some kind of shawl. Kraeling (*BMAP* 7:9) accepted this meaning too; Staerk used simply "Gewebe" (*Alte und neue aramäische Papyri*, p. 45). Kutscher (*JAOS* 74 [1954]: 236) related the word to Syriac *šbṭʾ*, "a smooth cloth."

10. *lbš ʾḥrn zy ʿmr nšḥṭ*: "Another garment of wool, finely woven." The only enigmatic word here is *nšḥṭ*, which Cowley related to the Hebrew *šāḥûṭ* in Jer. 9:7, which is explained by commentators as the equivalent of *nmšk*, "drawn out," and in 2 Chr. 9:15, of "gold drawn out," i.e., beaten thin.

Lidzbarski (*Ephemeris*, 3. 80) followed him in this and noted that the form may be a Niphal, a technical trade-term, possibly borrowed from the Phoenician. Cf. P. Leander, *LFAA* #21b. A related word is said to have been found in a Punic text (see J. Solá-Solé, *Sefarad* 20 [1960]: 277–79); but even if it is correctly read there it does not seem to have any pertinence to this text. Another form with the initial *n-* is found in line 15, *nᶜbṣn*; but its meaning is not fully understood either.

11. *mḥzy 1 zy nḥš*: "1 bronze mirror." The word *mḥzy* is normally considered fem. (see P. Leander, *LFAA* #43s''''), but it is treated here, perhaps erroneously, as masc., being modified by the masc. ptc. *šwh*. Cf. the later Aramaic *miḥzītaʾ*, and *BMAP* 2:5, *mḥzy 1 šwyh ksp ḥlrn 7 plg*, in which *šwyh* is fem.

12. *ksp šql 1 r 2*: "(In) cash 1 shekel, 2 qu(arters)." The abbreviation *r 2* means "2 quarters" of a shekel, or 20 ḥallurin. See the comment above on line 7.

*tm[sʾ] 1 zy nḥš*: "1 bronze bowl." Cowley had restored the lacuna as *tm[hy]*, "tray"; Lidzbarski (*Ephemeris*, 3. 131) preferred to read *tm[ny]*, but he did not attempt to translate it. The word *tmsʾ* is now clearly read in *BMAP* 7:13 in a very similar context of dowry items, and Kraeling rightly suggested that it be read here too. The meaning of it, however, is not clear; Kraeling compared it to an Assyr. noun, *namsītu*, "bowl." This is, of course, possible, but it does not explain all the problems in the word. It is apparently feminine, since *šwyh* follows as a modifier. This would suggest that the final -ʾ here stands for the fem. sg. abs.; in the rest of the list the item usually stands before the cardinal in the absolute state.

*ksn zy nḥš 2*: "2 bronze cups." A similar expression occurs in *BMAP* 7:14; cf. *AP* 61:1,3,4,13,14. Kraeling (*BMAP*, p. 212) quotes Herodotus (2:37), who records that Egyptians drank from bronze cups (*ek chalkeōn potēriōn pinousi*).

13. *zlwᶜ 1 zy nḥš*: "1 bronze pitcher." The same expression occurs in *BMAP* 7:15; *AP* 36:4; cf. *BMAP* 7:18. The item mentioned here is undoubtedly not a "bowl" (so Cowley and Kraeling understood it), but a spouted jug or pitcher.

*kl kspʾ wdmy nksyʾ ksp kršn 6 šql⟨n⟩ 5 ḥlr[n] 20*: "All the money and the value of the possessions are 6 silver karshin, 5 shekels, 20 ḥallurin." Cowley was certainly correct in regarding *šql* as a scribal error for *šqln*. Lidzbarski's explanation (see *Ephemeris*, 3. 80, 130), which seeks to retain the singular *šql*, is too ingenious and strained to be convincing; see the general remarks above, p. 143, n. 13. The sum total given here represents not only the dowry money and the value of the items just enumerated but also includes the bride-price (see above p. 143). Cf. *BMAP* 7:15 for the justification of this view. It is now clear that this total does not merely represent Esḥor's "own gifts," the value of which is stated because the deed is written in his name and he wants "to make the most of them" (so Cowley). Nor is the lack of a price in the list of items that follows this total due to Esḥor's judgment that it was unnecessary "to state the value of what he receives." All the objects belong to Miphṭaḥiah's dowry. What is not valued must have been considered of little value; but a couch with stone inlays (?) is hard to understand in this category. In any case, the *mhr* has been included in the sum total, probably for the reason already given above (see p. 143).

*ḥlr[n] 20*: "20 ḥallurin," or a half shekel. The word *halluru* meant in Akkadian a "chickpea," and became the name of a small weight. In the Babylonian scale, it represents one tenth of a shekel. See *CAD* 6.47–48; A. Ungnad, "Aus den neubabylonischen Privaturkunden," *OLZ* 11 (1908), Beiheft, pp. 26–28. However, according to the scale used in these papyri 40 ḥallurin = 1 shekel, as Cowley rightly established (*AP*, p. xxxi). Though *plg* is used to indicate a half of a ḥallur, it apparently was not used after *šql*. On the other hand, *zwz* could have been used, or else the phrase we have here, 20 ḥallurin. However, Kraeling (*BMAP*, p. 146) sought to regard the *ḥallur* as a tenth of the shekel, as in the Babylonian system. But this cannot be right. In totals the lower figures are always converted to the next higher weight, when they equal a unit or units of it. There would be no reason to write "20 ḥallurin," if ten of them equalled a shekel; this would have appeared as two shekels more. Moreover, the phrase in *BMAP* 7:14 would be meaningless, *šql 1 ḥ 10*, "one shekel, 10 ḥ(allurin)."

*ksp r 2 l10 bʾbny mlkʾ*: See the comments on lines 6–7 above.

15. *ʿl ʿly [wṭ]yb lbby bgw*: See the comment on line 5 above.

*šwy 1 zy gmʾ*: "1 reed couch." The form *šwy* is probably the same as the later Aramaic word *šiwwāy*, "couch" (see G. H. Dalman, *ANHW*, p. 417).

*gmʾ*: This word must be understood as the Aramaic equivalent of the Hebrew *gōmeʾ*, "papyrus (nilotica)." It is known in Coptic as *kam* and in later Aramaic as *gamyāʾ*. For its Egyptian origin, see T. O. Lambdin, "Egyptian Loanwords in the Old Testament," *JAOS* 73 (1953): 145–55, esp. p. 149.

*bh nʿbṣn zy ʾbn 4*: "On which there are 4 stone inlays," literally, "on it (there are) 4 inlays (?) of stone." No relative pronoun occurs in the similar phrase in *BMAP* 7:17. The expression should be compared with the relative clause in Dan. 3:1, without a conjunction (see H. Bauer and P. Leander, *Grammatik des Biblisch-Aramäischen*, #108a). The meaning of *nʿbṣn* is unknown.

The following number 4 suggests that the ending *-n* is plural. Sayce and Cowley wondered whether it might denote the stone feet of the reed couch; F. Peiser (*OLZ* 11 [1908]: 28) sought an Assyrian cognate in *ḫabāṣu* "swell up." Kraeling (*BMAP*, p. 213) related it to the Jewish Aramaic root, *ᶜbṣ*, "grow pale," and to the noun *ᶜbṣʾ*, "tin," suggesting that it might mean "inlays." Possibly it is another technical trade-expression, a borrowed Niphal form; see comment on *nšḥṭ* (line 10 above). The *ʾbn* is specified as *šš*, "alabaster," in *BMAP* 7:18 (see E. Y. Kutscher, *JAOS* 74 [1954]: 236; H. L. Ginsberg, ibid., p. 159). Cf. Amos 6:4, *miṭṭôt šēn*.

16. *pq 1 zy slq*: "*1 pq* of *slq*." The meaning of this phrase is still unknown. J. N. Epstein (*JJLG* 6 [1908]: 366, n. 3 suggested that *pq* might be another form of *bq*, related to *baqbūq*, "Krüglein." G. R. Driver compared it with the Akkad. *paqqu*, "bowl," and Scheftelowitz with Old Persian *pāka*, "cooking pot." But all these attempts seem to be difficult because the word has turned up as *pyq* (*BMAP* 2:6). In the latter passage one might be tempted to think that it is a measure smaller than *ḥpn*; but this meaning suits neither this passage nor *BMAP* 7:18. J. Reider (*JQR* 44 [1953–54]: 340) translates *pyq zy slq* as "a bottle of herbs," maintaining that both words occur in the Talmud, though with slightly different meanings; *slqʾ* is a "beet" or "well-boiled vegetable." Is it possible that *pyq* is related to the Hebrew *pīqāh*, "spindle whorl"? Note that a different phrase using *slq* occurs in *BMAP* 7:18, *dmn zy slq 1*, which Kraeling translates as "value of 1 *slq*," concluding that *slq* must refer to some metal or coin (p. 147).

*kpn 2*: "Two ladles," or "2 bowls." In *BMAP* 7:19 the *kpn* are specified for "the carrying of ointment."

*prks 1 zy ḥṣn ḥdt*: "1 new *prks* of palm-leaves." The meaning of *hsn* is now clear, "palm leaves," written *ḥwṣn* in *AP* 20:6; *BMAP* 7:17. In the former passage the phrase *mʾny ᶜq wḥwṣn*, "vessels of wood and palm-leaves," would suggest that *prks* is a receptacle of some sort. Jean-Hoftijzer (*DISO*, p. 235) think that it is a "boite à cosmétiques," and T. Nöldeke (*ZA* 20 [1907]: 148) suggested that it might be a tray or a small basket.

*tqm ḥpnn 5*: "5 handfuls of castor oil." This phrase and the following one are written above line 16, and it is not certain where one should insert them in the line. It makes little difference in the long run. The meaning of *tqm* was not understood for a long time. Cowley (*AP*, pp. 49, 308) regarded it as a form of *qwm*, and suggested the meaning "containing," without explaining its morphology. M. Kamil and E. G. Kraeling used the meaning, "jar." But it is now certain that it means "castor oil" (see P. Grelot, "L'huile de ricin à Eléphantine," *Semitica* 14 [1964]: 63–70; see further H. Farzat, "Encore sur le mot *tqm* dans les documents araméens d'Eléphantine," *Semitica* 17 [1967]: 77–80; A. Dupont-Sommer, "Note sur le mot *tqm* dans les ostraca araméens d'Eléphantine," *Semitica* 14 [1964]: 71–72). The word also occurs in *AP* 37:10; *BMAP* 2:6; 7:20; *HermWPap* 2:13; 3:12; 4:7; 5:5. The context of the two *BMAP* passages relates *tqm* to other oils or ointments: *mšḥ bśm plg ḥpnʾ tqm ḥpnn 6*, and *mš[ḥ ḥpnn] 2 mšḥ zyt ḥpnn 4 mšḥ m[b]śym ḥpn 1 tqm ḥpnn 5*. Grelot related the word to Demotic *tgm* (sometimes spelled *tkm*), and to older Egyptian *dgm*, "castor (oil)." He cited its use in lamps, and B. Porten (*Archives*, pp. 92–93) has pointed out its use in anointing.

Cowley read the phrase as *tqm ḥ 8*, taking *ḥ* as an abbreviation for a measure, as in *AP* 24:38 (and 41). This may be correct in the latter place, but it is to be noted that *ḥ* otherwise occurs as an abbreviation for *ḥlr* (*BMAP* 7:14,15,27). Lidzbarski (*Ephemeris*, 3.131) hesitatingly suggested the reading *ḥpnn 5*, which is now almost certain, given its clear full writing in *BMAP* 2:6; 7:20,21; *HermWPap* 2:13; 3:12; *AD* 6:3,4,5. The difficulty is that the head of *p* is not clearly made, though the shaft is slightly curved; the two following strokes (for *nn*) are barely distinguishable from the unit strokes in the number that follows.

Aramaic *ḥpnʾ* is the cognate of Hebrew *ḥōpen* and Akkad. *upnu*, "hollow of the hand, handful." Used as a measure of oil it presents a difficult image, but the word was used to designate a commonly used amount, and its original meaning was undoubtedly forgotten. Its amount for this period is unknown. G. R. Driver (*AD*, p. 60) gives an approximation of 500 gr. and cites a third century A.D. inscription of Shapur I where *ḥwpn 5* is given as half a Greek *modios* (see M. Sprengling, "Shahpuhr I, the Great on the Kaabah of Zoroaster (KZ)," *AJSL* 57 [1940]: 387, 390).

*šnn mśʾn 1*: "1 (pair of) leather sandals." This same expression, the meaning of which is really unknown, occurs in *BMAP* 2:5. *mśʾn* probably is the same as the later Aramaic word, "shoe, sandal," see 1QapGn 22:21 (*ʿrqʾ dmsʾn*); cf. J. N. Epstein, *ZAW* 33 [1913]: 225. The real difficulty is the meaning of *šnn*, which seems to be a construct state with *mśʾn*. In *BMAP* 7:20 it occurs before *zy ṣl*, which almost certainly means "of leather" (compare Jewish Aramaic *ṣallā*; and *AP* 37:10). This again relates the word to an item like sandals. Kutscher (*JAOS* 74 [1954]: 234, n. 6) queried whether *šnn* could reflect the Old Assyrian *šēnān*, "two shoes." J. Reider (*JQR* 44 [1953–54]: 339) understands the phrase to refer to a "leather bag." Whatever the meaning of it is, it is almost certain that *šnn* is not a measure continuing the preceding phrase, as T. Nöldeke once thought (*ZA* 20 [1907]: 147).

This brings us to the end of the dowry items in the contract. From this point on, various stipulations regarding the marriage agreement are recorded.

17. *mḥr ʾw ywm ʾ[ḥr]n*: "Tomorrow or some other day," a stereotyped phrase that denotes some vague time in the future. It occurs again in lines 20,22,26; and in other Elephantine papyrus texts (e.g., *AP* 5:6,8; 9:8,13; *BMAP* 2:7,9,10,12,13; 7:21). J. J. Rabinowitz ("Meaning of the Phrase *mḥr ʾw ywm ʾḥrn* in the Aramaic Papyri," *JNES* 14 [1955]: 59–60); *Jewish Law*, pp. 159–63) has compared the phrase to the Hebrew *tmwl šlšwm*, "yesterday and the day before yesterday," i.e., "in the past." He would accordingly translate the Aramaic phrase, "tomorrow or the day after (tomorrow)." He further cites kindred expressions from an Akkadian text of Ras Shamra (*urram šēram*, "demain, après-demain" [Thureau-Dangin's translation]), of Boghazkoi, and a Demotic text of the seventh century B.C. Y. Muffs (*Studies*, p. 206) notes that the Aramaic phrase is merely the last in a long line of idioms which express the idea of "(if), some time in the future," and that no idiom is a literal translation of any other. He cites also Ugar. *śḥr ʿlmt* and Neo-Assyrian *ina šērtu ina lidiš*. In this he is almost certainly correct, for although Rabinowitz' parallels, especially the one to Hebrew, might suggest that *ʾḥrn* implies "after" (like *ʾḥr*), it is to be noted that in all other cases where *ʾḥrn* occurs, it means "other" (= *ʾoḥ°rān*). Kraeling (*BMAP*, p. 147) asked whether *ywm ʾḥrn* means "another day" or "the next day," and compared *Baba Mezia* 17a, *lmḥr wlywmʾ ʾḥrʾ*. This is a later expression, and may possibly mean "the next day." But it should be noted that it is in the emphatic state, and it is not quite the same thing. For this reason I prefer to remain with the translation given above, basically the same as that used by Cowley. The omission of *ʾw* in *AP* 1:4 is undoubtedly a scribal error.

*ymwt ʾsḥwr*: "Should Esḥor die." The same form of the conditional sentence, with the protasis in the imperfect and without the conjunction *hn*, is also found in lines 20,22,26, and in *BMAP* 2:7,9,11,12; 7:21,34. It is to be contrasted with *BMAP* 7:24 (*whn yh[wy]š[mʿ] tśnʾ* . . .) and also with *AP* 15:35 (*whn hʿdt hmw*, "If I do remove them") or *BMAP* 2:14 (*whn hnṣlth mnk*, "and if I take him away from you"). They are all future conditions. E. Y. Kutscher (*JAOS* 74 [1954]: 234) explains the differences between them, by pointing out that *hn* usually takes the perfect (as in Arabic with *ʾin*), but only if the verb follows immediately after *hn*; the further it is removed from the conjunction the more it tends to occur in the imperfect. Sometimes the imperfect is used when the verb follows immediately, but the converse is not true. It never appears in the perfect if it is removed from *hn*. Hence in a clause without *hn* the verb will be in the imperfect. Kutscher's explanation is generally valid; one case, however, may be problematical: in *BMAP* 3:22a one finds *wlʾ khln pṣln lh yth*, "and (if) we are not able to recover it for him." It seems to be a conditional use of the perfect without *hn*. In the preceding sentence *hn* was used with the perfect, and possibly the *w*- before the verb is to be understood as resuming it.

*wbr dkr wnqbh lʾ ʾyty lh*: "Having no child, male or female," literally, "and there is not to him, a child, male or female." The same expression occurs again in lines 20–21.

18. *Mpṭḥyh hy šlyṭh bbyth zy ʾsḥwr*: "Miphṭaḥiah is entitled to the house of Esḥor," literally, "has power (*or* authority) over Esḥor's house." The problem in this clause is to determine the sense of *šlyṭ b*, since it undoubtedly expresses a legal situation different from that of Esḥor in the event of Miphṭaḥiah's death. According to line 21 he will inherit her property (*yrtnh*). The same inheritance is expressed in *BMAP* 7:35. Unfortunately, the papyrus is broken in *BMAP* 7:29 and the phrase that is used of the bride there is not clear (see *BMAP*, p. 206; cf. J. T. Milik, *RB* 61 [1954]: 250; R. Yaron, *JSS* 3 [1958]: 8–9 [Yaron is convinced that *yrt* was not used of the woman]). L. Freund (*WZKM* 21 [1907]: 177) has pointed out the different legal terms used here, and suggests that whereas the husband would inherit his wife's property in the case of her death without children, the wife would be entitled only to the usufruct (*Nutzniessungsrecht*) of Esḥor's house and property, which would revert to her husband's family at her death. Yaron (*JSS* 3 [1958]: 9–10), while not rejecting Freund's interpretation, has an alternate explanation. The husband's right was laid down by law and is thus referred to as inheritance (*yrt*); the provision in the contract concerning him is merely declarative, not constitutive. But Miphṭaḥiah's right is created by the contract. There is really no evidence to support one or other of these interpretations, and so either is plausible. In *BMAP* 2:11,12 *šlyṭ* is used of both the husband and the wife; but since this document records the marriage of a slave, there is probably a different legal situation here.

19. *wkl zy ʾyty [l]h ʿl ʾnpy ʾrʿʾ klh*: "And all that he has on the face of the earth, all of it." The last word *klh* is either suffixal or an alternate form of the emphatic state of *kl* (with a final *he* instead of final *aleph*). If it be suffixal, its vocalization would differ depending on the noun that it resumes: *kulleh*, resuming *kl zy*, or *kullah*, resuming *ʾrʿʾ*. For one could also translate, "and all that he has on the face of the whole earth." On the other hand, if it be emphatic, it could still be resumptive to either of these expressions. A full

discussion of *kl* in such expressions can be found in my article, "The Syntax of *kl*, *klʾ* in the Aramaic Texts from Egypt and in Biblical Aramaic," *Biblica* 38 (1957): 170–84, esp. pp. 183–84. The resumptive use of *klh* after *kl zy* is also paralleled in 1QapGn 10:13; 12:10; 16:11; see my commentary, p. 198, #4.

21. *ʾsḥwr hw yrtnh bnksyh wqnynh*: "Esḥor shall inherit her possessions and her property." For the significance of this clause, see the comment on line 18 above. The use of *hw* may be emphatic; but it may also be merely influenced by the corresponding feminine in line 18, even though the expression differs. Instances of the emphatic use can be found in *AP* 6:4,12–13; 10:15; 13:10; 20:9; *A* 24,84; *BMAP* 3:10; 5:14; 7:35.

22. *tqwm Mpṭḥyh bʿdh wtʾmr*: "Should Miphṭaḥiah rise up in an assembly and say." The phrase is clear except for the problematic word *bʿdh*. Sayce and Cowley rendered it, "in the congregation," as did Cowley later in his small edition; he was followed by S. Greengus, *Aramaic Marriage Contracts*, pp. 72–73; R. Yaron, *JSS* 3 (1958): 14–16; Y. Muffs, *Studies*, p. 59. Kraeling (*BMAP*, p. 147), believing that the preposition *bʿd* occurred in *BMAP* 11:10, sought to translate the word as a preposition here: "on account of her/him," or "on his own (or her) behalf." G. R. Driver (*PEQ* 87 [1955]: 92) sought rather to understand *bʿdh* as "behind her," an expression meaning "to find fault with." But neither Kraeling's interpretation nor Driver's have proved acceptable. H. L. Ginsberg (*JNES* 18 [1959]: 148–49) disposes of the alleged preposition in *BMAP* 11:10, by showing that the text really reads *bʿbrny* "over my security (or pledge)." In his translation of this text he returned to the meaning "congregation," but correctly interpreted it as indefinite, "in a congregation." P. Leander (*LFAA* #55b) and E. Y. Kutscher (*JAOS* 74 [1954]: 234) also supported the absolute sense of "congregation," and the latter regarded the noun as a Hebraism, found also in Syriac. He compared Job 30:28, *qamtî baqqāhāl* (an interesting material parallel which has nothing to do formally with marriage or divorce).

The importance of the phrase lies in the need of a public declaration in the case of divorce. The further question about whether this was a court that would examine the reasons for the divorce, or whether *ʿēdāh* refers to a specific number of persons before whom the declaration had to be made before it was considered valid is one that cannot be resolved on the basis of the data now available. See S. Funk, "Die Papyri von Assuan als älteste Quelle einer Halacha," *JJLG* 7 (1909): 378–79; R. Yaron, *Introduction*, pp. 53–56; B. Porten, *Archives*, p. 210.

Another more basic consideration that this document manifests is the possibility that a Jewish woman at Elephantine could divorce her husband.

In this matter she was the equal of her husband, her *bʿl*. For the implications of this, see R. Yaron, *Introduction*, p. 53.

23. *śnʾt lʾsḥwr bʿly*: "I divorce Esḥor my husband," literally, "I have come to hate (*or* simply) I hate Esḥor." This formula for the declaration of divorce is found again in line 27, and in *BMAP* 2:7,9; 7:21; for a slightly different formulation, see *BMAP* 7:25. It had already become stereotyped, whereas it undoubtedly expressed originally the motive for the divorce. On the problem of the origin of this term for "divorce," see J. J. Rabinowitz, *Jewish Law*, p. 40; R. Yaron, *JSS* 3 (1958): 32–34.

*ksp śnʾh brʾšh*: "The divorce fee is on her head," i.e., she will be held responsible for the payment of the divorce fee, the amount of which is set forth in the next phrase in the contract. For the idiom *brʾšh*, denoting responsibility, see my note in *TS* 26 (1965): 669, n. 10, apropos of Mt. 27:25. J. J. Rabinowitz ("Demotic Papyri of the Ptolemaic Period and Jewish Sources," *VT* 7 [1957]: 398–400) compares a phrase in P. Dem. Leiden 376, lines 28–29, to the Aramaic and New Testament phrase; but it is not parallel at all, since it lacks the phrase "on the head of."

*ttb ʿl mwznʾ wttql l*[*ʾs*]*ḥwr ksp šqln 7 r 2*: "She shall sit by the scale and weigh out to Esḥor 7 silver shekels, 2 qu(arters)." This clause is clear, except for the meaning of *ttb*, which also occurs in *BMAP* 7:26 but is omitted in *BMAP* 2:9–10. Sayce and Cowley understood it as a form of *twb*, "she shall return," and in this they were followed by Cowley (*AP*, p. 46), Leander (*LFAA* #39b), Verger (*Ricerche*, pp. 117, 119). However, T. Nöldeke (*ZA* 20 [1907]: 148) interpreted it rather as the impf. Peal of *ytb*, and was followed in this by L. Freund (*WZKM* 21 [1907]: 174), E. G. Kraeling (*BMAP*, pp. 207, 215), H. L. Ginsberg (*ANET*², p. 223). Still another possibility was suggested by S. Jampel (*MGWJ* 51 [1907]: 622), seeking to interpret it transitively, as if it were *tytb*, "Sie soll als Hauptsumme das Scheidungsgeld auf die Wage legen." Similarly, R. Yaron, *JSS* 3 (1958): 13; *Introduction*, p. 54 ("she shall put on the scales"); J. J. Rabinowitz (*VT* 7 [1957]: 398–400) understood it rather as the Aphel of *twb*, "she shall pay according to the scales." However, Cowley's Peal impf. of *twb* would be defectively written and the only other example of such defective spelling in Leander's *LFAA* (#39b) is *tqm*, a form that is now seen to have nothing to do with *qwm* (see comment above on line 16). The defective spelling of the Aphel of *twb* (Rabinowitz' suggestion) is likewise unparalleled; and the same must be said about Jampel's *tytb*. In the long run, then, the best solution is that of Nöldeke, *ttb* as the 3rd sg. fem. Peal impf. of *ytb*, "she shall sit." There are other figurative expressions in this text which would parallel this interpretation.

The *ksp śnʾh* is given here as seven and one-half shekels. While it is one and one-half times the bride-price paid in line 5, as Ginsberg has pointed out (*ANET*², p. 223), it is to be noted that the divorce fee is always seven and one-half shekels in these texts, when it is explicitly mentioned. See *BMAP* 2:8,10; 7:26. The penalties, however, for divorce are not always the same; sometimes it involves the payment of the divorce fee, which may have been this fixed sum; sometimes it involves the loss of the bride-price. In this case, the woman divorcing her husband must pay the divorce fee. In *BMAP* 2 the *mhr* was of the same sum as the divorce fee; but that was probably coincidental.

24. *wkl zy hnʿlt bydh thnpq*: "And all that she brought with her, she shall take out," literally, "all that she brought in her hand." See the general remarks above, p. 142.

25. *mn ḥm ʿd ḥwṭ*: "From straw to string." This is Y. Muff's happy translation of an alliterative phrase, expressing figuratively a totality by the use of extremely small samples. It occurs again in line 28, and in *BMAP* 2:8,10. The second element in it was always clear, *ḥwṭ*, "a thread." The first was long a problem. Cowley (*AP*, p. 46) took it as "both shred (?) and thread." G. R. Driver (*JRAS* [1932]: 78) suggested, "both broom and thread," as the humblest symbols of a woman's work in the house. But E. A. Speiser ("A Figurative Equivalent for Totality in Akkadian and West-Semitic," *JAOS* [1934]: 200–3; see also p. 299) pointed out a convincing Akkadian parallel and suggested the translation "straw" for *ḥam*. In the treaty between Suppiluliumma and Mattiwaza one finds *ḫāma u ḫuṣāba . . . ul ilqi*, "he did not take away (even) a straw or a splinter" (see *CAD* 6:259). Though the expression is not the same, several commentators have called attention to Gen. 14:23, *miḥūt weʿad śᵉrōk-naʿal*, "from a thread to a sandal-strap," rendered in Aramaic in 1QapGn 22:21 as *mn ḥwṭ ʿd ʿrqʾ dmsʾn*.

*wthk [l]hʾn zy ṣbyt*: "And she shall go wherever she pleases," literally, "wherever she has pleased." The phrase occurs again in line 28. The form *thk* is probably the impf. of *hwk*; cf. Sf III 5,6; Sf I A 24; T. Nöldeke, *ZA* 20 (1907): 142. This clause stands in contrast to *BMAP* 7:28, *wthk lbyt ʾbwh*, "and she shall go to her father's house." The difference is that Miphṭaḥiah has been married before. See Y. Muffs, *Studies*, p. 55, n. 5.

*wlʾ {y}dyn wlʾ dbb*: "Without suit or process." The expression occurs again in line 29, and often in the Elephantine texts (e.g., *AP* 6:12; *BMAP* 3:12,13,14; 9:18,19—note the defective spelling of *dn* in *BMAP* 1:5 and the hypercorrection of *zyn wzbb* in *BMAP* 3:17). An Akkadian expression underlies it: *tuāru dīni ū dabābi laššu*, "a re-opening of the case and the litigation is not to be" (see *CAD* 3.153); compare the Greek formula in later papyrus texts: *aneu dikēs kai kriseōs.* E. Y. Kutscher (*JAOS* 74 [1954]: 239–40) notes that the Aramaic formula is undoubtedly the link between the Akkadian and the Greek examples.

27. *mhrh [y]ʾbd*: "His bride-price goes forfeit," literally, "he shall lose his bride-price (*muhreh*)," or possibly "he shall lose her bride-price (*muhrah*)," i.e., the bride-price he paid for her. This is one of the most contested phrases in the Elephantine marriage contracts. Whose is it and who loses it? Part of the problem is the determination of the meaning of the suffix (*-eh* or *-ah*?); part of it is the meaning of the verb *yʾbd.* It was also complicated for a long time by the misunderstanding I have already mentioned several times about the inclusion of the *mhr* in the sum total of lines 13–15. It is, however, realized today that the penalties for divorce in these Elephantine contracts, are not always the same. The verbal form *yʾbd* could also be intransitive, "his bride-price is lost." No *mhr* is mentioned in *BMAP* 2, and hence none is lost. In *BMAP* 7:25 the loss of the *mhr* is included in the woman's penalty for divorce (in addition to the payment of the divorce fee). H. L. Ginsberg (*JAOS* 74 [1954]: 159) has discussed the problems of *BMAP* 7 and thinks that the phrase is misplaced there. Whatever the solution to the problem of *BMAP* 7 is—and it is hotly debated—the understanding of *AP* 15 is less problematic. The loss of the *mhr* is clearly the penalty imposed on Esḥor; hence, either "he shall lose his bride-price" or "his bride-price is lost."

*wkl zy hnʿlt bydh*: See above, p. 163.

28. *bywm ḥd bkp ḥdh*: "On one day (and) at one time." The phrase seems to mean that there cannot be any partial or temporary withholding of her property. The same expression occurs in *BMAP* 7:28.

29. *w[zy] yqwm ʿl Mpṭḥyh*: "Whoever rises up against Miphṭaḥiah." Cowley had restored the lacuna with *w[hn]*, translating, "But if he should rise up." Many commentators followed him; and the clause, thus interpreted of an act of the husband, led to the theory of divorce by illegal expulsion in these texts. There was always a difficulty in this understanding, in that Esḥor was made to speak of himself in the third person (*mn byth zy ʾsḥwr*, line 30). In *BMAP* 7:30–32, part of the formula occurs again, but the context is unfortunately broken. The formula, however, is found in *BMAP* 6:16, which is not a marriage contract but a deed recording a gift of a house to a daughter by her father. He makes sure by the formula that she will not be driven out of it by some outsider without legal consequences: *zy yqwm ʿlyky ltrktky mn btyʾ*, "Who rises up against you to drive you out of the houses. . . ." This sense must be introduced into the marriage contracts. Esḥor is thus

making sure that Miphṭaḥiah will have the right to his house and property. The phrase is undoubtedly aimed at relatives of his. See also *AP* 46:8. This interpretation has been confirmed by a similar clause in a Demotic marriage contract from Elephantine, which begins with "Anyone in the world who . . ." (P. Dem. Berlin 13593, dated 198 B.C.; W. Erichsen, *AbhPAW*, Philos.-hist. Kl., 1939, Nr. 8, p. 10). See R. Yaron, "Aramaic Marriage Contracts: Corrigenda and Addenda," *JSS* 5 (1960): 66–70, esp. pp. 66–69. As a result of this interpretation, this clause is not concerned with a form of divorce at all. But compare A. Verger, *Ricerche*, pp. 125–30.

30. *ltrkwth mn byth zy ʾsḥwr wnkswhy wqnynh*: "To drive her out of Esḥor's house and his possessions and his property." Cowley was embarrassed by the phrase *byth zy ʾsḥwr*, which contains nothing more than the prospective suffix and means only "Esḥor's house," or "the house of Esḥor." There is no need of the cumbersome translation, "from his, Esḥor's, house." Once this is seen, it is possible also to restore *BMAP* 7:30 differently. Instead of simply [*y*]*qwm* ᶜ[*nnyh* . . .], one should read, [. . . *wmn y*]*qwm* ᶜ[*l Yhwyšm*ᶜ] *ltrkwth* . . ., "And whoever rises up against Yahuyishmaᶜ to drive her away . . ." Instead of *mn*, one could also restore *zy*. The expression *qwm* ᶜ*l*, in the sense of violent or illegal activity against a person, is also found in the Bible; see Deut. 28:7; Jdgs. 9:18; 20:5. On the nature of this *clausula salvatoria*, see J. J. Rabinowitz, *Jewish Law*, pp. 48–64.

*yntn lh ksp kršn 20 wy*ᶜ[*bd*] *lh dyn sprʾ znh*: "He shall pay her 20 silver karshin and shall carry out in her regard the stipulation of this document." The stipulation is the prescription set forth in lines 29–31, *w*[*zy*] *yqwm* . . . *znh*. The stipulation thus sets a stiff penalty, since the sum of 20 karshin is very high, as can be seen by comparing it with the total dowry sum in lines 13–15; see also the comment on the woolen garment in line 8 (p. 154 above). Sayce and Cowley had restored *wy*ᶜ[*md*], translating it, "and (the terms of) this deed shall hold good for her." Cowley later changed the restoration to *wy*ᶜ[*dy*] and translated, "and the provisions of this deed shall be an*nulled*, as far as he is concerned." H. L. Ginsberg (*ANET*², p. 223) left the lacuna blank: "and the law of this deed shall [ ] for her." The phrase, however, has turned up in *BMAP* 7:32: *wy*ᶜ*bd* [*lh*] *dyn sprʾ znh*, whence the reading adopted here. See also *AP* 14:3; *BMAP* 7:40; Ezr. 7:26 for related expressions. The penalty *ksp kršn 20*, is imposed again in lines 34, 36, and seems to be a fixed penalty in marital offenses.

31. *wlʾ ʾkl ʾmr ʾyty ly ʾnth ʾḥrh lhn Mpṭ⟨ḥ⟩yh*: "I shall not be able to say, 'I have another wife, other than Miphṭaḥiah.'" The clause insures the unicity of the marital agreement. The formula used here is slightly different from that

in *BMAP* 7:36, where it is stated that "[Anani shall no]t [be able to ta]ke [another] wife," i.e., another wife in the future. It is a protection against future polygamy. Here the formula assures Miphṭaḥiah that Esḥor has no other wife or children who can lay claim to his house or property. For the children born of Miphṭaḥiah and Esḥor, see *AP* 20:3; 25:3. Cf. B. Porten, *Archives*, p. 254.

33. *hn ᵓmr*: "If I do say." See the comments on the syntax of the conditional sentence above, on line 17.

*ᵓyty ly b[nn] wᵓnth ᵓḥr⟨n⟩n lhn Mpṭḥyh wbnyh*: "I have other children and a wife, other than Miphṭaḥiah and her children." The clause is not smoothly constructed here, and the form *ᵓḥrn* is undoubtedly a scribal error, as T. Nöldeke suggests (*ZA* 20 [1907]: 136).

34. *ᵓntn lmpṭḥyh ks[p] kršn 20*: "I shall pay Miphṭaḥiah 20 silver karshin." The penalty is the same as in line 31.

35. *wlᵓ ᵓkl [ᵓhn]tr nksy wqnyny*: "Nor shall I be able to withdraw my possessions and my property." Sayce and Cowley restored [*ᵓhn*]*tr*, the Haphel impf., "take away," admitting that the *resh* was doubtful. The root is otherwise unattested in early Aramaic, occurring possibly in an uncertain Nabatean text, *CIS* 2. 224. When it does occur later, the causative stem has the nuance of "loose, throw off." But, as far as I can see, no one has suggested a better restoration. The clause prohibits the withdrawal of Esḥor's property from Miphṭaḥiah as long as the marriage persists. As R. Yaron puts it, "the wife had to concur in the alienation of property by her husband. Her dissent could not indeed invalidate the transaction, but the penalty-clause would be a sufficient safeguard" (*JSS* 3 [1958]: 25).

*whn hᶜdt hmw mnh*: "And if I do remove them from her." See the comments on line 17 above.

36. *qbl s[pr ᵓḥr]n*: "According to some other document." The whole phrase is set in double braces to indicate the scribal erasure of this clause. It is impossible to say what was behind the attempt to erase; it certainly leads one to suspect that de facto there existed some other document to which Esḥor may have been in some way still obligated.

37. *ktb ntn br ᶜnnyh [sprᵓ znh kpm ᵓsḥwr]*: "Nathan bar ᶜAnaniah wrote [this document at the behest of Esḥor]." The scribe, Nathan bar ᶜAnaniah, appears also in *AP* 10:20; 13:17; *BMAP* 2:14 in the same capacity. He signs his name as a witness in *AP* 8:32; 9:20, and he was apparently the father of several sons (*AP* 18:3; 22:128; *BMAP* 7:42). The lacuna which occurs here is restored as in *AP* 5:15; 6:17; *BMAP* 7:43. The phrase *kpm* means literally "according to the mouth of," i.e., at the dictation of (someone). Cf. *AP* 2:18; 11:16 (*ᶜl pm*). The scribe's name is recorded before that

of the witnesses to the document, as in many other of these Elephantine texts. This seems to conform to contemporary Egyptian practice; see E. Seidl, *Ägyptische Rechtsgeschichte der Saiten- und Perserzeit* (Ägyptische Forschungen. 20; Glückstadt: Augustin, 1956), p. 71.

*wšhdyʾ bgw*: "The witnesses to it," literally, "thereto," or possibly "within," since *bgw* clearly functions here as an adverb. Cowley and Kraeling understood *bgw* in the first sense, "thereto." R. Yaron (*JSS* 2 [1957]: 45–46) thinks that the word has a more technical sense, explained in part by a Mishnaic prescription (*Baba Bathra* 10:1: "A plain document has its witnesses within [on the recto]; a tied up document has its witnesses on its back [the verso]"), and in part by a phrase in a Judean deed of sale: *k[t]bh dnh pšyṭ wḥtmw bgwh* (line 14), "this document is simple and they have signed (it) on the inside" (see J. T. Milik, *RB* 61 [1954]: 182–90). Yaron is correct in pointing out the striking similarity in phrasing in the last instance. He also notes that the Elephantine practice of signing the contract on the inside differed from the contemporary Egyptian practice. He does not think that the Elephantine practice differed from the Jewish custom, disagreeing with J. J. Rabinowitz (see *BASOR* 136 [1954]: 16), who cited Jer. 32:10. If the Elephantine expression *bgw* has the technical meaning that Yaron suggests, then it is very cryptic and stereotyped. On the other hand, the equally stereotyped adverb *bgw* occurs many times in these texts (see comment on line 5 above). The full formula for the introduction of the names of the witnesses who signed the contract can also be found in many texts (e.g., *AP* 1:8; 2:19; 3:22; 5:15; 8:28; *BMAP* 2:14; 7:43; 8:10; etc.).

38. *Pnwlyh br Yznyh*: "Penuliah bar Yezaniah." This witness appears only here in the Elephantine texts, but he may be the father of several children (see *AP* 13:13; 18:5; 22:110; 25:19). The first name, *pnwlyh*, means "Turn to Yahu," as T. Nöldeke (*ZA* 20 [1907]: 134) points out, comparing the plural element in it to a name like *Hwdwyh* (*AP* 20:18; Ezr. 2:40; 1 Chr. 5:24; 9:7). For the sense of it, see Isa. 45:22. The other name, *Yznyh*, is not easy to explain. It occurs several times in these texts from Elephantine (*AP* 6:9; 9:2; 19:8; 25:4; 66:10) and is undoubtedly related to *Ydnyh*. In the comment on *dyn wdbb* (in line 26) I called attention to the hypercorrection in *zyn wzbb*, found in *BMAP* 3:17. Though one might be tempted to think in terms of this root *dyn* in these names, the form is unlikely as an impf. of *dīn*. It is probable that *yznyh* represents the older spelling of *ydnyh* and that we have to do with a root *ʾzn*/*ʾdn* with the initial aleph completely quiesced. The vocalization would then be *Yēzanyāh* (< *yiʾzan-yāh*), "May Yahu listen." Cf. 2 Kgs. 25:23 (*Yaʾazanyāhû*). Similarly M. Noth, *IPN*, p. 198.

[ ]*yh br ᵓwrhy*: "[ ]iah bar Uriah," and there are several possible restorations for the first name: *Reᶜūyāh* (*AP* 22:118), *Hôšaᶜyāh* (*AP* 25:2), *Yĕzanyāh* (*AP* 6:9; 9:2, etc.).

*mnḥm br* [*z*]*kwr*: "Menaḥem bar Zakkur," who also appears in *BMAP* 2:15 as a witness.

39. *śhd Rᶜybl b*[*r* ]: "Witness: Reᶜibel ba[r ]." One might at first hesitate about the function of *śhd* in such a line-up of witnesses, especially after the introductory formula in line 37. Does it follow the preceding name or precede the following? In some instances elsewhere it is also difficult to tell (*BMAP* 3:23b,24; 5:17; 8:10), but in others it clearly precedes the name (*AP* 18:4; *BMAP* 10:18–20; 11:13–14; 12:33–34; cf. *BMAP* 2:15; 9:23,25, 26). This should be taken, then, as the norm and applied even to the cases about which one might hesitate at first. Moreover, it is sometimes clear even from the handwriting. The form *śhd* is a participle, and may actually have so functioned originally (i.e., So-and-so is witnessing). But it is clearly a stereotyped formula in these texts and has been so understood in my translation.

With the name *Reᵉᶜībel* ("Bel is my friend"), compare *Bytᵓlrᶜy* (*BMAP* 8:11), "Bethel is my friend," and *Rᶜyh* (HermWPap 1:1; 2:16; 3:3), "Yahu is my friend."[20]

20. My thanks are due to Professor Klaus Baer, of the University of Chicago, for help in analyzing some Egyptian terms in this paper. The formulation is, however, my own, as well as any misuse of his generous time and concern.

# Zur Einwirkung der gesellschaftlichen Struktur Israels auf seine Religion

GEORG FOHRER

## I

Im Verlauf seiner Geschichte hat Israel tiefgreifende Wandlungen seiner gesellschaftlichen Struktur erfahren. Am Anfang dieser Geschichte standen weder ein Volk noch eine ethnisch einheitliche und in sich geschlossene Gruppe von Stämmen. Vielmehr handelte es sich um Sippen, Gruppen und Stämme von sehr unterschiedlicher Herkunft, deren gemeinsames Merkmal darin bestand, daß sie Nomaden oder Halbnomaden mit dem Bestreben nach Seßhaftwerden im Kulturlande waren. Ihre religiösen Vorstellungen waren weitgehend dadurch geprägt. Nach der Landnahme in Palästina bildete sich unter Einbeziehung weiterer Volkselemente, die nicht zuletzt kanaanäischen Ursprungs waren, allmählich das israelitische Volk. Der Übergang zur Seßhaftigkeit und zum Ackerbau, den der größere Teil der Israeliten vollzog, führte zu einer weitreichenden Umbildung der gesellschaftlichen Organisation, die die Religion und ihren Kultus einschloß. Aus der notvollen Lage der vorstaatlichen Zeit in Palästina—gekennzeichnet durch die kriegerische Auseinandersetzung mit den Kanaanäern, die Abwehr neuer Eindringlinge aus Steppe und Wüste und die Kämpfe mit den meist überlegenen Philistern—erwuchs nach zeitlich und örtlich beschränkten Anfängen das Königtum. Es zeitigte durch die Organisation des Staates weitere gesellschaftliche Wandlungen. Vor allem wirkten die politisch-gesellschaftlichen Erfordernisse, die sich insbesondere aus dem gleichberechtigten Zusammenleben von Israeliten und Kanaanäern im Staat ergaben, auf die religiösen Verhältnisse ein und hatten einen staatlich geförderten Synkretismus zur Folge, der schließlich das Wesen des Jahweglaubens gefährdete. Auch in der Folgezeit ergaben sich soziale und wirtschaftliche Wandlungen infolge des Hineinwachsens in die Stadtkultur und des Übergangs von der Natural- und Tauschwirtschaft zur Geldwirtschaft. Sie riefen—wie schon das Problem einer dem Bauerndasein angemessenen Form des Jahweglaubens und das Ringen mit der synkretistischen Tendenz des Königtums—neue religiöse Reaktionen hervor, die der Religion Israels wesentliche Züge verliehen haben.

Zweifellos haben auch die religiösen Vorstellungen und Verhältnisse von Anfang an in geringerem oder größerem Maße die gesellschaftliche Struktur beeinflußt. Dies gilt in erster Linie vom Jahweglauben, der beispielsweise auf das Rechtsleben und die Form des Königtums in Israel eingewirkt hat und der in der deuteronomischen Reform des Königs Josia für die Gestaltung des gesamten Volkslebens und Staatswesens richtungweisend sein sollte. Doch diese Fragen sind bereits des öfteren erörtert worden, während der umgekehrte Vorgang—die Einwirkung der gesellschaftlichen Situation und der gesellschaftlichen Kräfte auf die Religion—bisher wenig Beachtung gefunden hat. Daher sollen im Folgenden unter Beschränkung auf die vorexilische Zeit einige Beobachtungen und Feststellungen zusammengetragen werden.

## II

Weithin nimmt man an, daß die Frühisraeliten Kleinvieh- bzw. Eselnomaden waren, die von der Steppe regelmäßig ins Kulturland wechselten und in reger Beziehung zu ihm standen, bis sie sich unter dem Einfluß des Kulturlandes zu Halbnomaden auf dem Wege zum Seßhaftwerden entwickelten und schließlich den letzten Schritt zur festen Niederlassung taten. So werden auch die Patriarchen als hin- und herziehende Kleinviehbesitzer geschildert, die am Recht auf die für ihr Vieh lebenswichtigen Brunnen interessiert sind, sich gelegentlich schon Besitztum an Grund und Boden sichern und mit der Viehzucht eine gewisse Ackerkultur verbinden.

Solches Nomadendasein führt zu bestimmten gesellschaftlichen Formen und weist charakteristische Verhaltensweisen und religiöse Eigenarten auf. Zwei grundlegende Lebensgesetze, die für lange Zeit die Wandlung der gesellschaftlichen Struktur nach der Seßhaftwerdung überdauert haben, waren die weitgehende Gastfreundschaft mit der Schutzpflicht des Gastgebers für den Gast und die Verfolgung des zustehenden Rechts auf dem Wege der privaten Vollstreckung, vor allem durch die Blutrache. Auch andere urtümliche Handlungen und Haltungen sind nach dem Übergang zum seßhaften Leben erhalten geblieben, weil sie entweder in Glauben und Kultus der späteren Zeit integriert wurden oder neben der anerkannten Religion als von ihr bekämpfter Aberglaube fortbestanden. Dazu gehören die Beschneidung, ein Teil der Trauerbräuche und eine Reihe von Tabus.[1]

Durch die gesellschaftliche Struktur bedingt und geformt sind die frühisraelitischen Sippenreligionen (bzw. Stammesreligionen). Da jede Sippe (und wohl auch jeder Stamm) einen jeweils eigenen Gott verehrt hat, gab es eine Vielzahl solcher Religionen;[2] daher hat die alttestamentliche Überlieferung mit der Feststellung recht, daß die Väter andere Götter verehrt haben (Gen. 35:1–7; Jos. 24:2.14f.). Solche Götter waren der *păḥăd jiṣḥaq*, der *ʾᵃbîr jăʿᵃqob*, der *ʾăbän jiśraʾel* und vielleicht der *magen ʾăbraham.* Zumindest in diesen Fällen spielte die persönliche Beziehung zwischen der Gottheit und dem Sippengründer und Kultstifter eine wesentliche Rolle.

Der Sippengott war weder ein Himmelsgott noch an ein lokales Heiligtum gebunden, sondern ein Wege- und Schutzgott der wandernden Nomaden. Das Gottesbild ist ganz und gar durch die Eigenart der nomadischen Gesellschaft geformt. W. Eichrodt hat es folgendermaßen beschrieben: Die Nomaden "wissen sich auf göttliche Leitung besonders angewiesen, da sie zwischen eifersüchtigen und oft feindlichen Mächten sich hin- und herbewegen und mit ihrem schwerfälligen Troß nur kleinere Märsche machen, ohne, wie der leicht bewegliche Beduine, jedem Schlag ausweichen zu können. Wo aber die Wüste bereits durch ihre Unwirtlichkeit schreckt und die Nähe des Kulturlandes mit seinen oft wenig günstigen Bewohnern Lebensbedürfnis ist, da flüchtet sich der Mensch in die Obhut des Gottes, der die Wege und ihre Gefahren kennt und sicher hindurchleitet, der aber auch die Herzen der Anwohner günstig stimmt und die Verträge mit ihnen unter seinen Schutz nimmt (Gen. 21:22ff.; 23:3ff.; 26:26ff.; 31:44ff.; 33:19f.; 34:8ff.; 35:5; 38:1). Von ihm kommt das Gedeihen der Herden, auf dem der Reichtum der Wandernden beruht, von ihm auch die schlaue List, die dem Schwachen gegen den Starken hilft und ihn in verzweifelten Lagen einen rettenden Ausweg finden läßt (Gen. 20:2ff.; 26:7ff.; 30:31ff.; 31:7ff.; 32:7ff.)." Die Redewendung, daß die Gottheit "mit" dem Menschen ist oder sein will, drückt dies alles am besten aus.[3] So tritt deutlich "die Besonderheit des soziologischen Verbandes zutage, der . . . das religiöse Verhältnis trägt."[4]

Ein weiterer Zug, der bei den schon nach Landbesitz strebenden Früh-

1. Vgl. G. Fohrer, *Geschichte der israelitischen Religion* (1969), §2,3.
2. W. Eichrodt, Religionsgeschichte Israels, in *Historia Mundi*, II (1953), S. 378.
3. Vgl. dazu H. D. Preuß, ". . . ich will mit dir sein!," *ZAW* 80 (1968), S. 139–73.
4. W. Eichrodt, a.a.O. S. 378.

israeliten hinzutritt, ist die göttliche Zusage solchen Besitzes, die neben der Verheißung zahlreicher Nachkommenschaft steht. So erzählt der Jahwist in Gen. 15:1bβ–2, 7–12, 17–18, wie Abraham nach seiner Klage über seine Kinderlosigkeit auf Geheiß Jahwes aus getöteten und teilweise zerteilten Tieren eine Gasse bildet, durch die nach Einbruch der Dunkelheit ein rauchender Ofen und eine Feuerfackel hindurchfahren:

An jenem Tage gab Jahwe dem Abram eine Zusicherung und sprach: "Deinen Nachkommen will ich dieses Land geben, vom Strom Ägyptens bis zum großen Strom, dem Euphratstrom."

Dem liegt, wenn es sich auch nicht um den ursprünglichen Wortlaut handelt, eine alte Überlieferung zugrunde. Nach ihr hat die Gottheit eine Verheißung von Landbesitz und Nachkommenschaft gegeben und ist zwecks ihrer Verwirklichung eine dauernde Verpflichtung eingegangen. Derartige Überlieferungen gehören zum Urgestein der Patriarchen- und Moseerzählungen.[5] In ihnen kehren die Darstellungen von Gotteserscheinungen mit Segen, Kulturlandbesitz- und Nachkommenverheißung häufig wieder. Formal und inhaltlich bilden sie als Landanspruchserzählungen oder sogar als Landnahmeerzählungen verschiedener israelitischer Gruppen, die sich auf die Verheißungen ihrer Sippengötter beriefen, den alten Kern der Pentateuchüberlieferung. Damit zeigt sich erneut, daß die Erfordernisse und Bedürfnisse der nomadischen Gesellschaft die frühisraelitischen Sippenreligionen, aber auch den mosaischen Jahweglauben bestimmt haben.

Dies gilt ebenso für den Kultus. So dürfte das Passa-Opfer ursprünglich zu Beginn der im Frühjahr erfolgenden Wanderung aus der Steppe in das Kulturland stattgefunden haben.[6] Das von der Moseschar mitgeführte Zelt kann als eine Art Wanderheiligtum gelten, wie es den Notwendigkeiten des nomadischen Lebens entspricht; nach arabischen Parallelen ist anzunehmen, daß es klein und leer war und in erster Linie als Offenbarungsstätte gedient hat, an der man das Losorakel oder den göttlichen Rechtsentscheid einholte. Ein anderes Wanderheiligtum der Nomaden war die tragbare Lade. Entgegen anderslautenden Ansichten war sie weder für das Zelt der Moseschar bestimmt, noch kann sie überhaupt als ein Palladium dieser Gruppe gelten, da erst die priesterschriftliche Darstellung Zelt und Lade zusammengefaßt hat und da die älteste Bezeichnung der Lade den Namen "Jahwe" nicht enthält, sondern "Elohimlade" lautete (I Sam. 3:3; 4:11).[7]

5. Vgl. G. Fohrer, *Introduction to the Old Testament* (1968), §19.

6. Vgl. L. Rost, Weidewechsel und altisraelitischer Festkalender, *ZDPV* 66 (1943): 205–16 (= *Das kleine Credo und andere Studien zum Alten Testament* [1965], S. 101–12).

7. Vgl. J. Maier, *Das altisraelitische Ladeheiligtum* (1965).

Vielmehr war die Lade ein vorpalästinischer und vorjahwistischer Kultgegenstand einer israelitischen Gruppe und wurde von dieser bei ihrer Einwanderung nach Palästina mitgebracht. Am ehesten dürfte es sich um die mittelpalästinische Stämmegruppe handeln, die die Überlieferung über die Einwanderung durch den Jordangraben bewahrt hat, in deren Zusammenhang die Lade erwähnt wird, und in deren Bereich die Lade ihren Standort zeitweilig in Gilgal und sodann in Silo erhalten hat. In allen genannten Fällen sind die kultischen Einrichtungen und Gegenstände durch die gesellschaftliche Struktur des Nomadentums bestimmt.

Ähnliches zeigt sich schließlich für den ethischen Bereich. Der aus Lev. 18:7–12,14–16 zu erhebende ursprüngliche Dekalog (mit einem jetzt ausgefallenen Satz nach 18:9) weist mit dem Kreis der Personen, mit denen eine geschlechtliche Vereinigung nicht stattfinden soll, auf die Lebensverhältnisse der nomadischen Sippe hin. Diese sollte durch Lebens- und Verhaltensregeln über die sexuelle Betätigung geschützt und umhegt werden. So stellt die Urform von Lev. 18 das Zeugnis für ein Sippenethos dar, das der Erhaltung der nomadischen Lebensform diente.[8]

Mit alledem sollen die frühisraelitische Religion und der mosaische Jahweglaube keineswegs aus der bestehenden gesellschaftlichen Struktur hergeleitet und aus ihr erklärt werden. Durch letztere wurden nur einzelne Strukturelemente, Einrichtungen und Kultgegenstände bedingt. Unberührt davon sind die grundlegenden Züge des personalen Elements und der Wechselbeziehung zwischen Gottheit und Mensch. Sie stellen unmittelbare und unableitbare Wesensmerkmale des Glaubens dar.

## III

Nach dem Seßhaftwerden der Israeliten in Palästina war die nomadische Sippen- und Stammesorganisation überholt.[9] In den neuen Verhältnissen wandelten Sippe und Stamm sich in den Orts- und Gauverband um. Da nicht mehr die personelle Zugehörigkeit zu Sippe oder Stamm, sondern die Niederlassung in einer Ortschaft oder einem Territorium maßgeblich wurde, war die Aufnahme von Angehörigen anderer Stämme und von Kanaanäern möglich, wie umgekehrt Israeliten sich in kanaanäischen Städten niederließen. Ferner ergab sich eine neue wirtschaftlich bedingte Gliederung. Der

8. K. Elliger, Das Gesetz Leviticus 18, *ZAW* 67 (1955): 1–25 (= *Kleine Schriften zum Alten Testament* (1966), S. 232–59); *Leviticus* (1966), S. 229ff.

9. Vgl. G. Fohrer, Altes Testament—"Amphiktyonie" und "Bund"?, *ThLZ* 91 (1966): Sp. 801–16, 893–904 (= *Studien zur alttestamentlichen Theologie und Geschichte* [1949–66], [1969], S. 84–119).

Einfluß der Sippenältesten schwand und ging auf diejenigen über, die über den meisten Grundbesitz verfügten, die Ortsbewohner mit geringerem Besitz in Abhängigkeit von sich brachten, die Ämter bekleideten und oft zu einer Art Adel erwuchsen. Sind die meisten Israeliten zunächst Bauern geworden, die in geschlossenen Ortschaften wohnten, so führte schließlich für einen Teil von ihnen der Weg weiter zu einer Stadtwirtschaft im eigentlichen Sinn. Die daraus folgende Weiterbildung der gesellschaftlichen Struktur war ein Grund für die entstehende Entfremdung und den späteren Gegensatz zwischen Stadt und Land—sofern letzterer nicht wie die Abneigung der judäischen Landbevölkerung gegen Jerusalem darin wurzelte, daß die Stadt eine vorwiegend kanaanäische Einwohnerschaft besaß.

Von der veränderten Situation waren die frühisraelitischen Sippenreligionen am stärksten betroffen. Bald wurden die Sippengötter mit lokalen Heiligtümern und nicht mehr mit den seßhaft gewordenen Sippen verbunden; aus Wegegottheiten wurden Ortsgottheiten. Da ferner nur dasjenige von Bestand war, was in dem veränderten Dasein in Palästina fortwirkte, blieben aus der nomadischen Zeit in erster Linie die Sippenkulte selbst und die Namen der Kultstifter lebendig, während die Kultsagen in Vergessenheit gerieten, weil sie keine Beziehung zum Lande hatten. Allmählich starb sogar ein Teil der Kulte ab, weil er dem Dasein im Kulturlande nicht gemäß war. Nur diejenigen, die mit wichtigen Heiligtümern verbunden waren, blieben in der israelitischen Gesamtüberlieferung erhalten. Doch an die Stelle ihrer Kultsagen traten die Heiligtums- und Kultlegenden der jeweiligen, bereits kanaanäisch gewesenen Heiligtümer. Außerdem wurden wenigstens dort, wo es sich um heilige Stätten Els handelte, die Sippengötter mit diesem gleichgesetzt.

Auch der mosaische Jahweglaube wurde nach seiner Einwurzelung in den israelitischen Stämmen von der geänderten gesellschaftlichen Struktur berührt. Zwar ist es aus vielen Gründen unwahrscheinlich, daß die Israeliten nach seiner Übernahme einen sakralen Stämmebund gebildet hätten, der hauptsächlich in der vorstaatlichen Zeit geblüht und mit seinen Institutionen noch lange nachgewirkt haben soll. Aber der Jahweglaube wurde infolge der palästinischen Situation durch die Umweltbedingungen und die kanaanäische Religion betroffen. Denn da sich die Lebensweise der Israeliten im Übergang zum Ackerbau und danach auch zum Stadtleben der Lebensweise der kanaanäischen Bevölkerung angenähert hatte, ergaben sich notwendig engere Beziehungen zu deren Welt, auch wenn sie ihrem Wesen nach als fremd empfunden wurde. Die Israeliten konnten die Errungenschaften des Kulturlandes nicht ohne die Gedanken und Erfahrungen erlangen, aus denen sie gespeist wurden. Mit der neuen Lebensweise und ihrer gesellschaftlichen Organisation waren die Vorstellungs- und Verhaltensweise aufs engste verquickt, die die Israeliten bei den Landesbewohnern vorgefunden hatten. Unausweichlich näherten sie sich mehr oder weniger stark der kanaanäischen Lebensweise, Kultpraxis und den religiösen Vorstellungen an oder sahen sich genötigt, sich damit kritisch auseinanderzusetzen.

1. Ein erstes Beispiel für die aus der palästinischen Situation sich ergebenden Folgen hängt mit der Ackerkultur zusammen. Nicht nur bei den Kanaanäern, sondern auch bei den Israeliten scheint die Anschauung geherrscht zu haben, daß über den Regen und damit über Fruchtbarkeit und Gedeihen der Vegetationsgott Baal verfüge, während Jahwe in den Geschicken der Völker und Menschen am Werke sei, seinem Volke Israel Hilfe und Schutz gegenüber anderen Völkern gewähre und in Kampf und Schlacht über ihm walte. Dies mußte den israelitischen Bauern dazu führen, den kanaanäischen Gott Baal als bedeutsame Macht anzuerkennen und zu verehren. So haben es wenigstens die Israeliten des Karmelgebietes gehalten, wie die Erzählung von Dürre und Regenspenden in der Eliaüberlieferung zeigt (I Reg. 17:1; 18:1aβ–2,16–17,41–46),[10] aber gewiß nicht sie allein. Die Stierbilder, die im israelitischen Reich aus dem Baalkultus übernommen worden waren und als Symbole Jahwes dienten, besagen genug über die unter den Erfordernissen der gesellschaftlichen Struktur des israelitischen Bauerntums beginnende Umwandlung Jahwes in eine Erscheinungsform Baals.

Natürlich gab es Kräfte, die sich dagegen wandten und auf den herkömmlichen Elementen des alten Jahweglaubens beharrten. Doch sie waren meist konservativer oder sogar restaurativer Art und verknüpften den Jahweglauben mit einer andersartigen gesellschaftlichen Struktur, die im Kulturlande überlebt war. Besonders die Rechabiten, die einigermaßen deutlich in Erscheinung treten, lebten in Palästina wie Nomaden in der Steppe. Sie lehnten mit der kanaanäischen Religion zugleich die Kultur Palästinas und ihre Folgen für die gesellschaftliche Organisation ab, tranken keinen Wein, bauten kein Haus, bearbeiteten keine Äcker und Weingärten, sondern wohnten in Zelten. So legten sie selbst es dem Jeremia dar, der ihre Treue gegenüber den Anordnungen ihres Gründers mit der mangelnden Treue der Israeliten gegenüber dem göttlichen Willen verglich:

Sie sagten: Wir trinken keinen Wein, denn Jonadab ben-Rechab, unser Ahnherr, hat uns geboten: "Weder ihr noch eure Söhne dürft jemals Wein trinken. Ihr dürft

---

10. Vgl. G. Fohrer, *Elia*, (1968²).

kein Haus bauen, keinen Samen aussäen und keinen Weingarten anpflanzen oder besitzen, sondern ihr sollt euer Leben lang in Zelten wohnen, damit ihr viele Tage auf dem Boden lebt, auf dem ihr hin und her wandert." (Jer. 35:6–7)

So waren die Rechabiten in Palästina wandernde Nomaden geblieben. In ihrer restaurativen Art verbanden sie den Jahweglauben in seiner nomadischen Form mit der nomadischen Lebenshaltung und Gesellschaftsordnung zu einer unauflöslichen Einheit und hielten deren Annahme für vom göttlichen Willen gefordert und für die Existenz Israels unerläßlich. Doch hätte die allgemeine Befolgung dieser überholten Grundsätze ebenso zum Untergang Israels und des Jahweglaubens geführt wie das schrankenlose Sicheinfügen in die kanaanäische Welt. Von der alten wie von der neuen gesellschaftlichen Struktur her war der Jahweglaube gefährdet.

Demgegenüber hat Elia die dem Jahweglauben gemäßen Folgerungen aus der neuen Situation gezogen oder sie zumindest für berechtigt erklärt, falls er sie schon vorgefunden haben sollte: Angesichts einer übermäßig langen Dürre, die die kanaanäische Religion nicht erklären konnte, verkündete er, daß Jahwe diese Unterbrechung des jahreszeitlichen Zyklus bewirkt und daß er—nicht jedoch Baal—den Regen zurückgehalten habe und allein wiederbringen könne. Damit erschien Jahwe erstmalig als Spender des Regens. In der veränderten Situation des israelitischen Bauerntums hat Elia auf diese Weise das Gottesbild des Jahweglaubens ausgeweitet und der gesellschaftlichen Struktur angepaßt: Israel verdankt die Kulturgüter des Landes allein seinem Gott, der nicht nur Hilfe und Schutz vor den Feinden gewähren, sondern zudem ständig seinen Segen walten lassen kann. Damit wurde die Verehrung Jahwes zu einem dringlichen Anliegen des israelitischen Bauern erhoben; sie entsprach der gesellschaftlichen Struktur seines Lebens.

2. Ein zweites Beispiel ergibt sich aus der Struktur der gebildeten Schicht Israels, die vor allem im Zusammenhang mit dem Königtum und der Organisation des Staates entstanden ist. Seitdem Salomo sich bemüht hatte, sein Reich auch an der internationalen Kultur seiner Zeit und Umwelt teilhaben zu lassen, war mit der Weisheitslehre ein wichtiges Bildungs- und Erziehungsmittel in Israel eingeführt worden.[11] Gewiß war sie zunächst auf den Königshof und die der Ausbildung der führenden Schicht dienenden Schulen beschränkt. Doch war gerade dadurch ihr Einfluß beachtlich und in steter Ausdehnung auf weitere Kreise des Volkes begriffen.

11. Vgl. G. Fohrer, Die Weisheit im Alten Testament, *ThWNT* VII S. 476–96 (= *Studien zur alttestamentlichen Theologie und Geschichte* [1949–66], [1969], S. 242–74).

Vor allem der Form der Lebensweisheit lag ein Ideal der Bildung und Formung des ganzen Menschen zugrunde, das die führende Schicht der Gesellschaft prägte und von dieser aus wieder das gesamte Leben einschließlich der Religion zu beeinflussen imstande war. Mittels der Weisheitslehre sollte der Mensch bewußt erzogen werden—als der "Kaltblütige" (Prov. 17:27) im Gegensatz zum "Jähzornigen" (Prov. 14:29), als der Mensch mit "gelassenem Sinn" (Prov. 14:30), der seine Affekte und Triebe beherrscht. Die dadurch bestimmte Lebensauffassung der führenden Schicht wies zweifellos einen gewissen utilitaristischen und eudämonistischen Zug auf, der nicht ohne Einwirkung auf den Jahweglauben geblieben ist. Jedes wie immer geartete Verhalten entspricht danach nicht nur einer bestimmten Grundhaltung, sondern erstrebt auch einen bestimmten Zweck und Erfolg. Ja, Verhalten und Ergehen des Menschen entsprechen einander. Eine gute Tat muß stets einen guten Erfolg nach sich ziehen, eine Missetat dagegen Unheil. Dieser Vergeltungsglaube ergriff auch den Jahweglauben und führte zu heftigen Auseinandersetzungen, wie vor allem das Buch Hiob für die Spätzeit zeigt.

So ergab sich einerseits die Notwendigkeit der Kritik und Abwehr gegenüber der Weisheitslehre, wie schon Jesaja sich gegen die sich klug dünkenden Politiker Jerusalems gewandt (Jes. 5:21; 29:14; 31:1–3) und ihnen die überlegene Weisheit Jahwes entgegengesetzt hat. Andererseits konnte die Weisheitslehre, die nun einmal der gesellschaftlichen Struktur der Oberschicht ebenso entsprach wie der Glaube an die Fruchtbarkeit gewährende Macht Baals der Struktur des frühen israelitischen Bauerntums, in ihren wesentlichen Zügen unter Abwandlungen und Änderungen ebenso in den Jahweglauben eingefügt werden wie der Glaube an die Segensmacht Jahwes in der Natur. Auf diesem Wege hat die gesellschaftliche Struktur durch die Aufnahme des Bildungsgutes auf den Glauben eingewirkt.

Wie die interreligiöse Weisheitslehre wurden andere Überlieferungen und Vorstellungen, die primär der Struktur der führenden Schicht gemäß waren, dem Jahweglauben angepaßt und zugeordnet, so die Vorstellung vom Schöpfergott und die im Atrachasis-Epos dargelegte Urgeschichte. Beide fanden im Werk des Jahwisten, der sicherlich aus der gebildeten Schicht Judas stammte, ihren ersten Niederschlag.

3. Ein drittes Beispiel sind die Maßnahmen und Reaktionen, die sich aus dem Entstehen eines durchgebildeten israelitischen Staates ergeben haben. Seit den politischen und militärischen Erfolgen Davids, dem auch die kanaanäischen Stadtstaaten Palästinas zugefallen waren, lebten Israeliten und Kanaanäer in einem Staat unter einer gemeinsamen Regierung neben und

miteinander und besaßen grundsätzlich gleiche Rechte und Pflichten. Auch die Einteilung des Staatsgebietes von Nordisrael in zwölf Distrikte durch Salomo, die sich möglichst eng an die Territorien der israelitischen Stammesgebiete und kanaanäischen Stadtstaatengebiete anschloß, konnte keine völlige Trennung herbeiführen, weil in manchen Gegenden Stammesbesitz und Stadtbesitz ineinander übergingen. In solchen Fällen lebten Israeliten und Kanaanäer in einem Distrikt unter einem königlichen Beamten miteinander. Aus politischen Gründen war es unerläßlich, daß sie einander rechtlich gleichgestellt waren und daß die Regierung darüber hinaus versuchen mußte, eine allen gemeinsame ideologische Grundlage zu schaffen. Letzteres konnte praktisch nur mittels einer allen gemeinsamen Staatsreligion geschehen; ihre Bildung wurde durch den in Jerusalem von phönizischen Handwerkern und nach kanaanäischem Vorbild errichteten Jahwetempel eingeleitet. Damit begann—bedingt durch die gesellschaftliche Struktur der Bevölkerung des Staates—ein staatlich geförderter Synkretismus, der auf eine Verschmelzung von Jahweglaube und kanaanäischer Religion hinauslief.[12]

Dieser Prozeß ging von Jerusalem aus und wirkte sich in einem nicht näher bestimmbaren Maße im Staatsgebiet von Juda aus. Er wurde zwar durch die sog. Reformen einiger judäischer Könige unterbrochen oder zurückgedrängt, aber bis zu den umfassenden Maßnahmen Josias nicht zum Stillstand gebracht oder rückgängig gemacht. In Nordisrael blieb der Prozeß anscheinend auf die staatlichen Heiligtümer in Betel und Dan beschränkt, die ein Stierbild erhielten, wie Hosea es später auch für Samaria voraussetzt (Hos. 8:5–6; 10:5–6). Sonst wurde das kanaanäische Element zurückgedrängt. Nur die Dynastie Omri suchte Israeliten und Kanaanäer gleichmäßig zu behandeln, führte durch ihr Vorgehen jedoch ihre eigene Ausrottung durch Jehu herbei, nachdem sich die religiöse Opposition in Elia, Elisa und der Quellenschicht des Elohisten zu Wort gemeldet hatte.

Denn in weiten israelitischen Kreisen mußte die politisch bedingte tolerante Haltung gegenüber den Kanaanäern bedenklich erscheinen, weil sich aus der Rücksicht auf die gesellschaftliche Struktur des Staates gefährliche religiöse Folgen—eben die synkretistischen Bestrebungen—ergaben.[13] Aus deren Ablehnung folgte eine völlig andere Grundhaltung, die ihrerseits die politischen und gesellschaftlichen Verhältnisse zu beeinflussen suchte.

12. Vgl. J. A. Soggin, Der offiziell geförderte Synkretismus in Israel während des 10. Jahrhunderts, *ZAW* 78 (1966): 179–204.

13. Vgl. G. Fohrer, Israels Haltung gegenüber den Kanaanäern und anderen Völkern, *JSS* 13 (1968): 64–75.

Sie findet sich in den Quellenschichten des Jahwisten (Ex. 34:11–12) und des Elohisten (Ex. 23:28,32–33):

> Siehe, ich will vor dir die Amoriter, die Kanaanäer, die Hetiter, die Peresiter, die Hiwwiter und die Jebusiter vertreiben. Hüte dich wohl davor, der Bevölkerung des Landes, in das du kommst, Zusicherungen zu geben. Sie könnte sonst, wenn sie unter dir wohnen bleibt, zu einem Fallstrick werden.
>
> Ich will Entmutigung vor dir hersenden, daß sie die Hiwwiter, die Kanaanäer und die Hetiter vor dir vertreibt. Gib ihnen und ihren Göttern keine Zusicherungen! Sie sollen in deinem Land nicht wohnen bleiben, damit sie dich nicht zur Sünde gegen mich verleiten. Wenn du ihre Götter verehrtest, würde es dir zu einem Fallstrick werden.

Formal und inhaltlich bilden diese Aussagen jeweils einen geschlossenen Zusammenhang mit drei Gliedern: (a) Vertreibung der Kanaanäer, um die Zusage des Landbesitzes an Israel zu verwirklichen; (b) Warnung an Israel, durch vertragliche Zusicherungen Ausnahmen von der Vertreibung zu machen; (c) mit der Begründung, daß dies religiöse Gefahren—die Verführung zum Abfall von Jahwe—nach sich ziehen müsse.

Vom formalen Gesichtspunkt aus ist das erste der drei Glieder das primäre: das Motiv der Vertreibung. Denn die vom Jahwisten und Elohisten vertretene Haltung geht von der Auffassung aus, daß Palästina das Land Jahwes sei, aus dem er infolgedessen die eingeborene Bevölkerung vertreiben könne, um seine Zusage an Israel zu verwirklichen. Die Warnung vor Zusicherungen an die zu vertreibende Bevölkerung mit der Begründung—also das zweite und dritte Glied—bilden eine Erweiterung. Sie soll den religiösen Einfluß der Kanaanäer auf Israel mit dem daraus folgenden Abfall von Jahwe als Wirkung dessen erklären, daß die Kanaanäer nicht vollständig vertrieben worden sind, weil die Israeliten sie aufgrund von Zusicherungen und Verträgen im Lande geduldet und in die Staatsbevölkerung einbezogen haben. Dies zeigt, daß der wirkliche Ausgangspunkt der den Kanaanäern feindlichen Haltung jener Synkretismus war, der durch die tolerante politische Haltung gefordert schien oder begünstigt wurde. Sachlich ist daher das dritte Motiv maßgeblich: die religiöse Gefährdung infolge der Umbildung der gesellschaftlichen Struktur der Staatsbevölkerung infolge der Einbeziehung der Kanaanäer. Diese Gefährdung wäre vermieden worden, wenn Israel mit den Kanaanäern nicht Verträge geschlossen hätte, die sie zum Bleiben berechtigten, sondern sie bis zum letzten Mann vertrieben hätte.

Darin spricht sich eine echte religiöse Opposition gegen die politische und gesellschaftliche Struktur des israelitischen Staates gerade wegen ihrer religiösen Folgen aus. Noch schroffer ist sie im Deuteronomium formuliert, das weniger vom Vertreiben als vielmehr vom Erschlagen, Ausrotten und Vertilgen der Kanaanäer redet. Die Einwirkung der gesellschaftlichen Struktur auf die Religion Israels durch den staatlich geförderten Synkretismus und durch die auf diese Weise geweckte Opposition liegt auf der Hand.

## IV

Schon die wirtschaftlichen Unternehmungen Salomos hatten zur Folge, daß in Israel eine soziale Umschichtung begann. Auch wenn der Handel königliches Monopol war, gelangte doch ein für das arme Palästina verhältnismäßig großer Reichtum ins Land. Allmählich bildete sich eine Schicht von reichen Städtern, vor allem in Jerusalem. Neben dieser kleinen Schicht entstand eine Schicht von Besitzlosen, die in der Folgezeit immer mehr anwuchs.

Diese Situation verschärfte sich durch den Übergang von der Natural- und Tauschwirtschaft zur Geldwirtschaft, der sich im Verlauf der Königszeit vollzog. Zugleich stellte das in Israel weithin durchgesetzte absolute Königtum altorientalischer Prägung das eigene und staatliche Wohl über dasjenige der "Untertanen" und legte diesen Steuerlasten und Frondienste auf. Dagegen wurde jene Minderheit begünstigt, die zur Geldwirtschaft überging und sich am Handel beteiligte, so daß sie zu Reichtum und Macht gelangte. In Auswirkung dessen dehnte sie ihren Besitz auf Kosten der breiten Volksschichten in zunehmendem Maße aus. Die darauf bezüglichen Prophetensprüche lassen vermuten, daß dieser Prozeß im 8. Jahrh. in großem Umfang im Gange war.

Insbesondere der Übergang von der Natural- zur Geldwirtschaft, den das Königtum eingeleitet und gefördert hat, zumal er nach der Eingliederung Israels in das altorientalische Staatensystem und infolge der Entfaltung seiner Kultur unvermeidlich war, hat zu einer tiefreichenden gesellschaftlichen Umschichtung geführt. Zwar wurde zugunsten der Mehrheit der Bevölkerung, die weiterhin Bauern oder Viehzüchter blieb oder bleiben wollte, die Bestimmung getroffen, daß bei Darlehen kein Zins verlangt werden dürfe (Ex. 22:24; Lev. 25:36–37; Dtn. 23:20), tatsächlich aber setzte sich die allgemeine altorientalische Entwicklung durch.

Eine kleine Schicht bereicherte sich, während breite Volksschichten entrechtet und enteignet wurden. Immer mehr freie Bauern verloren ihren Besitz, der in den Händen verhältnismäßig weniger Großgrundbesitzer vereinigt wurde. Die von ihren Äckern Verdrängten zogen zum kleineren Teil in die Städte oder großen Ortschaften, in denen sie eine Art Proletariat bildeten. Zum größeren Teil wurden sie Pächter und Hörige der neuen Besitzer. In jedem Falle büßten sie mit dem Landbesitz ihre staatsbürgerlichen Rechte und Pflichten ein, so daß die aus den freien Vollbürgern bestehende örtliche Rechtsgemeinde in Frage gestellt und das Staatsgefüge in Mitleidenschaft gezogen wurde. Als Hörige traten sie ferner aus ihrer bisherigen Sakral- und Kultgemeinschaft aus und in diejenige ihrer neuen Herren über. Sie wurden also politisch, rechtlich und religiös entmündigt.

Am Ende standen sich einerseits der König mit seinem Hofe und die Masse der Untertanen gegenüber, andererseits die reichen und machtbewußten Patrizier, Großgrundbesitzer, Großkaufleute oder sogar Handwerker und die durch die Leistungen an den Staat mitgenommenen, durch die Besitzer von Geld und Sachgütern übervorteilten breiten Volksschichten einschließlich der verarmten oder zu Hörigen herabgedrückten Bauern und Viehzüchter.

Auf die Religion Israels wirkte diese Änderung der gesellschaftlichen Struktur Israels unmittelbar nur insofern ein, als die hörig gewordenen Bauern und Viehzüchter in eine andere als ihre angestammte Sakral- und Kultgemeinschaft überführt wurden und dort gegen ihren Willen zur Teilnahme an fremden Kulten genötigt werden konnten. Eine stärkere Einwirkung auf die Religion Israels war mittelbarer Art und ist vornehmlich an der Reaktion auf die veränderte gesellschaftliche Struktur und ihre Folgen erkennbar.

1. Die Reaktion zeigte sich einmal in den Forderungen, die an den König erhoben wurden.[14] Er sollte Sozialherrscher sein und die göttliche Gerechtigkeit verkörpern. So sagt Ps. 45:7–8 von einem nordisraelitischen König:

> Du führst ein gerechtes Zepter,
> du liebst das Recht, hassest den Feind,
> darum hat dich "Jahwe," dein Gott, gesalbt.

Dem judäischen König wird in Ps. 101 bei der Thronbesteigung eine Proklamation in den Mund gelegt, in der es in v. 2a,5,7 heißt:

> Ich will auf makellosen Wandel achten,
> "die Treue hat bei mir ihr Heim."
> Wer heimlich einen anderen verleumdet,
> den bringe ich zum Schweigen.
> Wer stolze Augen und ein hochmütiges Herz hat,
> den kann ich nicht ertragen.
> In meinem Hause darf nicht weilen,
> wer Trug verübt.

14. Vgl. A. Alt, Der Anteil des Königtums an der sozialen Entwicklung in den Reichen Israel und Juda, in: *Kleine Schriften zur Geschichte des Volkes Israel*, III (1959), S. 348–72.

Selbst wenn der Dichter wie in Ps. 72 vom Weltherrscher redet, unterbricht er sich doch zweimal, um die königliche Hilfe für die Armen und Elenden zu erwähnen (v. 4,12). Daher lautet die elementare Forderung an den König stets, daß er gerecht herrscht und Recht schafft. Neben der Warnung vor Ungerechtigkeit findet sich diejenige vor Anhäufung großen Reichtums aus den Abgaben der ausgeplünderten Untertanen (Prov. 29:4).

2. Die Reaktion zeigte sich ferner und noch eindeutiger in den Worten der Propheten.[15] Sie wandten sich gegen diejenigen, die der Besitzgier und dem Machthunger die Zügel schießen ließen. So verurteilte Amos den Kornwucher der Kaufleute:

Hört dies, die ihr den Armen nachstellt,
um die Elenden aus dem Weg zu schaffen,
und sagt: "Wann geht der Neumond vorüber, daß wir[c] verkaufen können,
und der Sabbat, daß wir Korn anbieten?
Daß wir das Maß verkleinern und die Preise steigern,
betrügerisch die Waage fälschen?"
Jahwe hat beim Stolze Jakobs geschworen:
"Ich will eure Taten niemals vergessen!" (Am. 8:4–7)

Jesaja und Micha wandten sich gegen das "Bauernlegen" durch die Mächtigen im Lande:

Wehe denen, die Haus an Haus reihen
und Feld an Feld fügen,
bis sonst kein Raum mehr ist
und ihr allein ansässig seid
im Lande! (Jes. 5:8)

Wehe denen, die Böses planen[c]
auf ihrem Lager
und es im Morgenlicht ausführen,
weil sie die Macht dazu besitzen!
Begehren sie Felder, so rauben sie sie,
Häuser, so nehmen sie sie.
Sie üben Gewalt gegen Herr und Haus,
gegen Mann und Eigentum. (Mi. 2:1–2)

Es sind die führenden Schichten, die das eigene Volk schlimmer als eine fremde Soldateska ausplündern. Daher läßt Jesaja Jahwe die Anklage erheben:

Und ihr, ihr habt den Weingarten abgebrannt;
was ihr den Armen raubtet, ist in euren Häusern.
Was fällt euch ein?! Ihr zerschlagt mein Volk
und zermalmt das Antlitz der Armen! (Jes. 3:14b–15)

15. Vgl. auch H. Donner, Die soziale Botschaft der Propheten im Lichte der Gesellschaftsordnung in Israel, *OrAn* 2 (1963): 229–45.

In noch krasseren Worten spricht Micha von den Führern Israels:

> Sie fressen das Fleisch meines Volkes
> und ziehen ihm das Fell über die Ohren⊂⊃,
> zerstückeln es wie Fleisch im Topf,
> wie Fleisch im Kessel. (Mi. 3:3)

In alledem sind die Propheten für das Recht der wirtschaftlich Schwachen eingetreten und haben auf den besonderen Schutz hingewiesen, dessen die Witwen, Waisen und Fremden bedürfen. Sie haben die Lebensrechte derjenigen verteidigt, die bei einer Wandlung der gesellschaftlichen Struktur benachteiligt zu werden pflegen. Damit haben sie nicht die neue Wirtschaftsentwicklung als ganze abgelehnt, wohl aber den unerhörten Bruch des Rechts angeprangert, unter dem sie sich vollzog. Der Übergang zur Geldwirtschaft rechtfertigte für sie nicht, daß man die Bauern durch Kornwucher und hohe Zinsen zu Schuldnern machte, ihnen dann das Land zu niedrigem Preise nahm und es sie als Pächter und Hörige bearbeiten ließ. Zweckmäßigkeit und Erfolg in wirtschaftlichen Fragen, auf denen sich letztlich die gesellschaftliche Ordnung aufbaut, erlauben für das prophetische Urteil keineswegs die Entrechtung und Enteignung breiter Volksschichten. Über allen Wünschen und Notwendigkeiten des wirtschaftlichen Lebens und der damit zusammenhängenden gesellschaftlichen Struktur stehen die grundlegenden Rechte des Menschen. Seine Existenz gilt mehr als Sachwerte, ihre Gefährdung bedroht den Bestand der Gesellschaft.

Insbesondere ging es den Propheten darum, daß nicht nur einige wenige den Grund und Boden allein besaßen. Denn sie verfügten damit nicht nur über das Grundelement des wirtschaftlichen und sozialen Lebens, sondern auch über die Wohnmöglichkeiten des Menschen—ganz abgesehen von den politischen und religiösen Folgen. Freilich kannte die Prophetie kein absolutes menschliches Eigentum, für das sie eingetreten wäre, sondern nur menschlichen Pachtbesitz aus der Hand Jahwes. Von da aus galt die Anhäufung solchen Besitzes in einer Hand als Versündigung gegen Jahwe, wie auch die Jagd nach Geld und die Gier nach Lebensgütern als gottwidrig verurteilt wurden.

Der Versuch Nietzsches, die Stellungnahme der Propheten wie die gesamte Auffassung des Alten Testaments als Sklavenaufstand zu deuten, geht fehl. Die Propheten waren keine Vertreter der Sklaven, sondern vertraten das Recht der Schwachen von Gott aus und aufgrund des Glaubens. Sie behaupteten das unverlierbare göttliche Recht der Entrechteten. Daher bedurften sie keiner politisch oder gefühlsmäßig gefärbten Ableitung ihrer Kritik und ihrer Forderungen, sondern nur des Hinweises auf den göttlichen Willen.

Ebensowenig lassen sie sich soziologisch in der Weise deuten, daß die Ursachen ihrer geschichtlichen Erscheinung in wirtschaftlichen und sozialen Zuständen, in der gesellschaftlichen Struktur oder sogar in einem damit verbundenen Klassenkampf beschlossen lägen. Die Propheten haben zwar zu den Zuständen ihrer Zeit Stellung genommen, aber darin liegen nicht der Grund und das Motiv ihres Auftretens. Sie sind nicht aus einem Proletariat hervorgegangen, sondern aus den Kreisen der Besitzenden oder aus der Oberschicht. Sie haben ebensowenig in einem Zwiespalt mit ihrer "Klasse" gelebt, der sie zum "Proletariat" getrieben hätte. Jesaja erwartete bezeichnenderweise nicht eine Diktatur des Proletariats, sondern eine Regeneration der im Staate führenden Schicht (Jes. 1:21–26), durch deren einfache Beseitigung kein Idealstaat, sondern lediglich eine Anarchie als eine zum vollen Tode führende Form des göttlichen Gerichts entsteht (Jes. 3:1–9).

Die Äußerungen der Propheten folgten aus ihrem Glauben und waren religiös-ethisch bedingt: Soziales Handeln ist zugleich religiöses Tun und Heiligung Gottes; der glaubende Fromme ist zugleich ein sozial denkender und handelnder Mensch:

> Wenn nun jemand gerecht ist,
> Recht und Gerechtigkeit übt,
> "auf" den Bergen nicht ißt
> und seine Augen nicht erhebt
> zu den Götzen des Hauses Israel;
>
> wenn er die Frau des Nächsten nicht verunreinigt
> und sich einer unreinen Frau nicht nähert,
> niemanden bedrückt,
> sein Pfand ⊂⊃ zurückgibt,
> keinen Raub verübt;
>
> wenn er sein Brot dem Hungrigen gibt
> und den Nackten mit einem Kleid bedeckt,
> nicht auf Wucher leiht,
> keinen Zins nimmt
> und seine Hand vom Frevel zurückhält⊂⊃;
>
> wenn er in meinen Satzungen "wandelt"
> und meine Rechte beachtet,
> "sie" zu tun—
> der ist gerecht;
> er soll bestimmt am Leben bleiben, spricht ⊂⊃ Jahwe.
>
> (Ez. 18:5–9)

Die Grundlagen eines solchen Handelns sind Gerechtigkeit und Liebe, die für das gesamte Leben als grundlegend betrachtet werden. Die örtliche Rechtsgemeinde in Israel hatte eine Ordnung des menschlichen Zusammenlebens in dem Sinne versucht, daß jedem das Seine zuteil werde und also Gerechtigkeit herrsche. Als sie an dem Übergang zur Geldwirtschaft zerbrochen war, haben die Propheten das Ganze des Lebens durch das Mit- und Ineinander von Gerechtigkeit und Liebe erneut unter den göttlichen Willen stellen wollen. Darin liegt ihre Antwort auf die Wandlung der gesellschaftlichen Struktur ihrer Zeit; es ging ihnen nicht nur um das Heil, sondern auch um das Wohl des Menschen. Daher zeigte sich ihnen die Entscheidung für Gott gerade am rechten Verhalten zum Mitmenschen. Nicht Gottesdienst rettet den schuldigen Menschen vor dem Gericht, sondern rechtes soziales Handeln im täglichen Leben (Jes. 1:10–17). Insgesamt hat die durch die veränderte gesellschaftliche Struktur herausgeforderte prophetische Stellungnahme zu neuen und tiefen Einsichten geführt.

## V

In der exilischen und nachexilischen Zeit hat sich die Wandlung der gesellschaftlichen Struktur Israels fortgesetzt, vor allem durch die im Exil begonnene Umbildung der Deportierten in eine Schicht von Kaufleuten und Händlern. Man kann fragen, ob von da aus nicht weitere Einwirkungen auf die Religion Israels erfolgt sind und ob nicht die Ausbreitung der Vergeltungslehre damit zusammenhängt. Doch wird sich dies nur schwer beantworten lassen. Wohl aber läßt sich umgekehrt sagen, daß in der exilischen und nachexilischen Zeit der Jahweglaube in wachsendem Maße die gesellschaftliche Struktur beeinflußt und sich damit endgültig als stärker denn diese erwiesen hat.

# The Structure of Psalm 137

DAVID NOEL FREEDMAN

PSALM 137 is one of the few poems in the Bible concerning the date and provenience of which there is general scholarly agreement. It is reasonably certain that it was composed in Babylon during the first half of the sixth century B.C.E. It echoes vividly the experience and emotions of those who were taken captive, and may, therefore, be assigned to the first generation of the Exiles. It is roughly contemporary with the bulk, if not the whole, of Lamentations, with which it shares both contents and mood. Likewise, it belongs to the time of Ezekiel, bridging the period from Jeremiah to Second Isaiah. From these and other biblical literature it is clear that there was a major revival of Hebrew poetry during this period. The national catastrophe imposed a burden on Judah's prophets and poets no less than on its political and ecclesiastical leaders. The mingled despair and hope of the people evoked an appropriate literary response.

A study of the Psalm, with particular regard for its stylistic devices and metrical structure, should provide us with some insight into the state of the art in the sixth century, during the last great period of classic Hebrew poetry. So far as the text is concerned, there is little choice but to follow *MT*. Regrettably, almost nothing of Ps. 137 has survived in the Psalm Scroll from Cave 11 of Qumran;[1] nevertheless, one variant has been preserved in

1. The official edition is by J. A. Sanders, *The Psalms Scroll of Qumran Cave 11*, vol. IV in *Discoveries in the Judaean Desert of Jordan* (Oxford, 1965). Only parts of vss. 1 and 9 have been preserved: Columns XX and XXI (Plate XIII), pp. 41, 42.

vs. 1 which we regard as more original than, and superior to, *MT*.[2] In general *LXX* and the other versions follow *MT*, and where they diverge, the readings do not inspire confidence or materially improve the picture. Furthermore, in view of its impressive metrical symmetry we believe that the poem is complete as it stands, and that we have it as it was composed without significant subsequent alteration. If in fact the end product is the work of a later editor, we can only marvel at his skill in erasing all the usual signs of such activity.

The principal observation about the poem is that it has a unified structure, in spite of abrupt shifts in content and tone (e.g., at vs. 7 and again at vs. 8). The over-all pattern is at once chiastic and symmetrical or balanced. Thus the Introduction (vss. 1–2) is linked with and balanced by the Conclusion (vss. 8–9). An effective stylistic device (*inclusio*) is used to bring out both points: Babylon is explicitly mentioned at the beginning and end of the Psalm (vss. 1 and 8). The impression of symmetry is strengthened by a more detailed strophic analysis which shows that both sections consist of five units of approximately equal length. The body of the poem (vss. 3–7) consists of three parts: an opening (vs. 3) and a closing (vs. 7) forming a frame around the central section (vss. 4–6). Once again detailed analysis confirms the initial impression of structural symmetry: the opening and closing comprise four units each of equal total length, and these together exactly match in length the central section (vss. 4–6). The central part has a similar envelope structure, with the outer elements (vss. 4 and 6b) enclosing the nucleus (vss. 5–6a), which is a perfect chiasm, and the heart of the whole poem.

Before proceeding to a verse-by-verse analysis of the Psalm, some discussion of Hebrew meter is in order. After using several stress or accent systems in the investigation of Hebrew metrics, I am satisfied that such systems are too vague in principle and too flexible in application to produce adequate results. The widespread variation among scholars illustrates both points and exposes a substantial degree of subjectivity on the part of those working on these materials. On the other hand, weighted quantitative systems, concerned with syllable length as well as number, have proved too complicated to apply effectively; there is no reason to suppose that such methods were employed by the poets themselves. In place of either type we have chosen a relatively objective and simple syllable-counting system, designed to describe accurately the metrical structure of the poem under consideration. The purpose is to provide a widely applicable and acceptable, as well as a neutral, procedure for describing the phenomena and, thus, establish a

2. The reading is in vs. 1: *bbbl* for MT *bbl*. See discussion ad loc.

framework within which scholars can test their theories of poetic composition and debate the relevant issues. Without insisting that the Hebrew poets consciously or deliberately counted syllables in composing their works, we observe that their poems exhibit patterns with a degree of regularity and repetition which is best captured by a syllable-counting process.

Admittedly there is some difference of opinion among scholars as to the exact number of syllables in a given line, or even word. At one extreme are those who follow Massoretic vocalization slavishly, and count secondary vowels of late origin, as in segolate nouns and words containing laryngeals, or even *pataḥ* furtive, which can hardly be justified. At the other extreme are those who attempt to reconstitute the full vocalization as they imagine it to have been at the time of composition. Such an effort is certainly laudable and, to the extent that the objective can be achieved, very worthwhile. But it must be recognized that there are significant gaps in our knowledge of the historical morphology and phonology of Hebrew, and as yet a reliable reconstruction is beyond us.

In the analysis of Psalm 137 we have adopted a compromise position, following Massoretic vocalization generally. However, where there is compelling evidence for a vocalization involving a different number of syllables for a given word, we accept that against *MT*. The only significant departures from *MT* in the Psalm have to do with secondary vowels: e.g., *ʾeʿleh* (vs. 6) instead of *MT ʾaʿ$^{a}$leh* (on the change from Hiphil to Qal, see comments on the verse); segolates, which were monosyllabic in the classical period and are so treated here: e.g., *hassālʿ* for *MT hassālaʿ*; the name Jerusalem which was pronounced *y$^{e}$rūšālēm*, or the like, in the biblical period, with four syllables in accordance with the Kethib, as against the Qere *perpetuum*, *y$^{e}$rūšālayim*, which is clearly secondary and not attested until the Dead Sea scrolls of the second and first centuries B.C.E. The correctness of the four-syllable pronunciation in the sixth century B.C.E. is confirmed by the inscription in a burial cave, not far from Lachish, containing the name Jerusalem, spelled *yršlm*.[3] The inscription, which is the oldest preserving the name Jerusalem, can be dated paleographically to the sixth century or, roughly, the same time as the poem.[4] The same spelling occurs in the pentagram stamps of the late fourth century B.C.E., to which the Greek transcription *Ιερουσαλημ* in the LXX corresponds.

3. J. Naveh, "Old Hebrew Inscriptions in a Burial Cave," *IEJ*, XIII (1963): 74-92, especially 84–85.

4. In the article, Naveh expressed a preference for a date in the late eighth century (pp. 87–92); he has since shifted to the early sixth century, in agreement with other leading paleographers. This information is based on a private conversation.

We accept Massoretic contractions, e.g., *dibrē* (vs. 3), and *libnē* (vs. 7), and ignore so-called half-open syllables on the grounds that such syllables were never pronounced, but serve as a grammarian's device to explain certain linguistic phenomena. On the other hand, syllables with vocal shewa are counted, unless of secondary origin. No formal notice is taken of vowel length in syllable counting because of the acknowledged difficulty in distinguishing between tone-long and pure-long, and short and very short. Even the distinction between short and long is not always clear because of pre-tonic lengthening and shortening. It is quite likely that the poet recognized and made use of the different vowel lengths, but we do not find the evidence adequate to make decisions in borderline cases. As with accents or stresses, there are too many variables, though the matter is worthy of further investigation. We suppose, perhaps optimistically, that the differences tend to cancel out, and that it is a sufficient indication of metrical symmetry and balance to count the syllables without regard to their length.

We assume that the poet, while bound by the usual conventions of his craft, also had considerable freedom in the choice of archaic and exotic words and forms and could adjust the pronunciation of words to suit his purposes. We believe that he exercised such options to achieve metrical objectives. For the most part, we will refrain from exercising the same options in recreating a hypothetical original text and will limit ourselves to those features which have been preserved in the text, having survived all the natural efforts to eliminate oddities in the course of transmission. It is reasonable to suppose that the original was even more symmetrical and structured, but our purpose will be to show those aspects in what has survived in the existing text. We do this in order to avoid charges of manipulation or circular reasoning, i.e., to create what we wish to demonstrate, and because we believe that, in spite of editorial and scribal changes in the course of transmission, the metrical patterns used by the poet have been sufficiently preserved to make a convincing case.

Metrical and stylistic details are examined in the following stanza-by-stanza analysis of the Psalm.[5]

I

| | | |
|---|---|---|
| *ᶜal n$^{e}$hārōt [b$^{e}$]Bābel* | (1a) | By the rivers in Babylon |
| *šām yāšabnū / gam bākīnū* | (1b) | there we sat down / loudly we wept |

5. In the translation, for which we make no other claim, we have attempted to preserve the rhythm, or at least the syllable count, of the original. This inevitably creates a certain awkwardness, since English on the whole tends to run longer than Hebrew. By exercising some of the privileges assumed by English language poets, however, we have generally succeeded in matching the number of syllables.

| | | |
|---|---|---|
| *b$^{e}$zokrēnū $^{\circ}$et-Ṣiyyōn* | (1c) | —when we remembered Zion— |
| *$^{c}$al $^{ca}$rābīm b$^{e}$tōkāh* | (2a) | By the laurels in its midst |
| *tālīnū kinnōrōtēnū* | (2b) | we hung up our many-stringed lyres. |

1a) We read *bbbl* with 11QPs$^{a}$ against *MT bbl*, and vocalize *$^{c}$al n$^{e}$hārōt b$^{e}$bābēl.*[6] The preference is based upon the following considerations: (a) Accidental haplography in copying an original sequence of three successive *b*'s is more likely than the deliberate addition of a *bēt*, or the accidental dittography which would produce at the same time an acceptable result: (b) The parallelism with vs. 2a *$^{c}$al $^{ca}$rābīm b$^{e}$tōkāh* is more precise, and such precision is characteristic of this poet's work. Compare, e.g., the exact repetition of *'ašrē še-* in vss. 8,9, which complement and correspond to vss. 1,2. (c) The resultant meter (7 syllables instead of 6) is more in keeping with the rest of the stanza. The pattern 7:8 for vs. 1ab matches exactly the parallel vs. 2ab (also 7:8).

1b) We read *gm* as the cognate of Ugaritic *g* = voice, plus the adverbial *m*, with the meaning "loudly," following M. Dahood; see most recently his article, "The Independent Personal Pronoun in the Oblique Case in Hebrew," *CBQ*, XXXII:1 (January, 1970): 86–90, specifically p. 86, fn. 4 with references cited there.

As already indicated, the Introduction (vss. 1–2) consists of five units of 7 or 8 syllables each, or more exactly of two double-units (1ab and 2ab) connected by a single element (1c) with the following pattern: 7–8:7:7–8. While 1c is clearly linked with the preceding unit it is also connected with the following one; it specifies the occasion or reason for the related actions in 1ab and 2.

To be noted as well is the extensive use of alliteration, assonance, and similar sound effects to produce a mournful tone in keeping with the content of the Psalm. The effect is achieved by the repeated occurrence of the labials *b* and *m*: e.g., the sequence *bbbl šm yšbnw gm bkynw bzkrnw*, and *$^{c}$rbym btwkh*, simulates the sound of the wind in the willows, resonating over the waters; while the keening note of the pronominal ending *-nū* is sounded again and again in these verses: *yšbnw*, *bkynw*, *bzkrnw*, *tlynw*, *knrwtynw*.

## II

| | | |
|---|---|---|
| *kī šām š$^{e\circ}$ēlūnū* | (3a) | For there they asked of us— |
| *šōbēnū dibrē-šīr* | (3b) | our captors words of a song |
| *w$^{e}$tōlālēnū śimḥā* | (3c) | those who mocked us rejoicing— |
| *šīrū lānū miššīr Ṣiyyōn* | (3d) | "Sing to us from Zion's songbook." |

6. Sanders, *The Psalms Scroll of Qumran Cave 11*, p. 41, and *The Dead Sea Psalms Scroll* (Ithaca, New York, 1967), p. 73.

The second unit (vs. 3) continues the content and maintains the tone of the Introduction; it serves as a transition to the central statement of the lament (vs. 4, beginning with *ʾēk*). There is an added note of poignancy in the reference to the mockery (if our interpretation of the unique term *tōlālēnū* is correct) of their captors. The sadness and despair of the exiles articulated in vss. 1–2 are aggravated by the derisive demand that they sing one of the joyous songs of Zion (the Songs of Ascents would be particularly appropriate in view of vs. 6; see the comments below). This demand leads in turn to the agonizing protest of vs. 4, and an entirely different kind of song about Jerusalem: the terrible oath of remembrance and return, as well as the prayer for divine vindication against the enemies of his people.

Verse 3 has a number of points of lexical and syntactic interest. The main clause, 3a, *kī šām šeʾēlūnū,* is modified by two phrases in paratactic construction, each supplying a subject (or nominative appositive) and a second object for the verb. Thus *šōbēnū* and *tōlālēnū* have the same function in the sentence and should be interpreted as parallel or complementary terms. Since *šwbynw* is the Qal active participle m. pl. with a 1st person pl. suffix, we might expect *twllynw* to have the same form and derive it from the root *tll* = to mock, taunt. The slightly anomalous vocalization (i.e., the second syllable *lā* instead of the expected *le*) may be explained in a variety of ways, including uncertainty about the form on the part of the Massoretes. Behind the secondary root *tll* lies the primary root *hll*, which means "to boast" both in the Qal and the Hithpael conjugations. In fact, the latter may provide the connecting link to the root *tll*. Attention may also be drawn to the root *htl*, with a similar meaning, "to mock." Whatever the precise derivation and form of the term in this Psalm, we can hardly be wrong in placing it in the semantic and morphological field represented by the several related roots; we can therefore translate: "boastful ones, mockers." In the light of this analysis we should interpret the terms *šwbynw* and *twllynw* in complementary or combinatory fashion, i.e., "our boastful captors" or more likely "those who captured us—those who mocked us"; "our captors, who mocked us."

In similar fashion, the expressions *dibrē-šīr* and *śimḥā* serve as objects of the main verb *šeʾēlūnū*. The terms may be regarded as parallel in meaning, since *šīr* often denotes a happy song suitable for festive occasions, as indicated by the Psalms and other hymns to which the title *šīr* is attached. Note as well the contrast between *šīr* and *qīnā* in Amos 8:10. At the same time, the terms are complementary and should be combined as their association in other contexts suggests: cf. Gen. 31:27, Isa. 30:29. Reading them together, we arrive at the following sense: "words of a song of joy, i.e., joyous lyrics."

Our contention is that the poet has constructed a sophisticated, stylized quatrain by skilfully rearranging the elements of a straightforward declarative sentence, which ran approximately as follows: "For there our mocking captors demanded of us the lyrics of a happy song."

The last clause of vs. 3 is also dependent on the main verb *šᵓlwnw*; it further specifies the demand voiced in vs. 3a, and described in general terms in 3b and 3c. Here, in the form of a direct quotation, the joyous lyrics are identified with "Zion's song." If the preceding preposition is to be understood partitively or selectively, then the construct form *šīr* must be interpreted as a collective: i.e., the song-book or hymnal of Zion. We may render the request as follows: "Sing for us out of Zion's hymnal," i.e., one or more of the songs of Zion.

As previously observed, vs. 3 continues both the theme and tone of vss. 1–2. The plaintive personal note is stressed in the repeated occurrence of the 1st person plural pronominal suffix (*-nū*), four times in vs. 3, making a total of nine for the first three verses. There is only one other occurrence of this suffix in the poem (vs. 8), making a sum of ten for the Psalm as a whole. The grammatical distribution of these forms is as follows: three occurrences as pronoun subject of a perfect form of the verb: *yšbnw*, *bkynw*, *tlynw*; three as pronoun object of the verb: *šᵓlwnw*, *šyrw lnw*, *šgmlt lnw*; three as pronoun suffix attached to nominal forms: *knrwtynw*, *šwbynw*, *twllynw*; the remaining form is as pronoun subject of an infinitive in a prepositional phrase: *bzkrnw*. The pronominal prefix (*nā-*) occurs in vs. 4, but the morphologic and phonemic differences separate this use from the others.

To balance the repeated use of voiced labials (*b* and *m*) in vss. 1–2, we have persistent repetition of sibilants in vs. 3, especially *šin*, perhaps to reflect the stubborn silence of the exiles in the presence of their masters. Note the sequence: *šm šᵓlwnw šwbynw . . . šyr . . . šyrw . . . mšyr*; cf. *śmḥh* and *ṣywn*.

## III

| | | |
|---|---|---|
| *ᵓēk nāšīr ᵓet-šīr-Yahwē* | (4a) | How can we sing Yahweh's song |
| *ᶜal ᵓadmat nēkār* | (4b) | on alien soil? |
| *ᵓim ᵓeškᵉḥēk(ī) Yᵉrūšālēm* | (5a) | If I forget thee, Jerusalem, |
| *tiškaḥ yᵉmīnī* | (5b) | may my right arm wither |
| *tidbaq lᵉšōnī* | (6a) | may my tongue stick |
| *lᵉḥikkī ᵓim lōᵓ ᵓezkᵉrēkī* | (6b) | to my palate, if I remember thee not! |
| *ᵓim lōᵓ ᵓeᶜlē ᵓet-Yᵉrūšālēm* | (6c) | Surely, I will ascend Jerusalem |
| *ᶜal rōᵓš śimḥātī* | (6d) | with joy on my head. |

Verses 4–6 constitute the core of the Psalm. Out of the despair of their present situation and in response to the taunts and demands of their captors

the exiles make their response. It is impossible to sing Yahweh's song on foreign ground. At the same time, it is not only possible but necessary to swear, in a dreadful oath, undying devotion to Jerusalem and to affirm in the face of geo-political reality the certainty of a return in joy to the Holy City. In place of the collective lament: "How can we sing Yahweh's song on alien soil?" the psalmist shifts to the intensely individual oath which each exile must invoke upon himself with all its terrible consequences.

Vs. 4a. The use of the construct chain (*šîr-Yhwh* = Yahweh's song) reinforced by *ʾet*, the sign of the definite direct object, indicates that a specific composition is meant. We would normally think of the anthology of sacred songs, the Hymnal of the Temple, more explicitly perhaps the Songs of Ascents (Pss. 120–134) or the Songs of Zion (e.g., Pss. 48, 74, 87, 125, 126, 149). If a particular hymn was intended, however, we may speculate that it was the Song of the Sea (Exod. 15:1–18), which, as we have argued elsewhere, has a reasonable claim to be regarded as Israel's national anthem.[7] It also serves as the model for the "new song" (cf. Isa. 42:10, Pss. 33:3, 40:4, 96:1, 98:1, 144:9, 149:1) which will celebrate the "new Exodus" from exile in Babylonia.

The use of *ʾet*, while rare and perhaps questionable in the earliest Hebrew poetry (e.g., it does not occur at all in the Song of Deborah, Judg. 5:1–31, or in the Song of the Sea), can hardly be denied as deliberate on the part of the poet in later compositions. It occurs six times in Ps. 137, twice with proper nouns (*ʾet-Ṣiyyôn* vs. 1, and *ʾet-Yᵉrûšālēm* vs. 6), twice in construct chains, also involving proper nouns (*ʾet-šîr-Yhwh* vs. 4, and *ʾēt yôm Yᵉrûšālēm* vs. 7), and twice with nouns defined by possessive pronominal suffixes (*ʾet-gᵉmûlēk* vs. 8, and *ʾet-ʿôlālayk* vs. 9). The pairing of parallel constructions suggests a deliberate pattern, with *ʾet* performing a double function: for emphasis and to fill out the meter. Dahood's proposal that *ʾt* in vss. 1 and 6 (our first pair) is to be read as *ʾatt*, the independent pronoun 2nd person feminine singular, is attractive,[8] but in view of the other unquestioned occurrences of *ʾet* as the sign of the definite direct object it is preferable to interpret these instances as well in accordance with the tradition.

The closing phrase of vs. 4, *ʿal ʾadmat nēkār*, evokes the similar *ʿal* phrases of the opening unit (vss. 1,2) and summarizes them. For the exiles, Babylon is the alien territory referred to, where no song of Yahweh can be sung or even attempted. At the same time, vs. 4 is structurally parallel to vs. 6cd.

7. F. M. Cross, Jr., and D. N. Freedman, "The Song of Miriam," *JNES*, XIV (1955): 237–55, esp. 237, fn. f.

8. Dahood, *CBQ*, XXXII (1970): 86–87.

The sentence structure and sequence of parts of speech are almost identical: introductory particle (*ʾyk* and *ʾm lʾ*), verb in the 1st person imperfect (*nšyr* and *ʾʿlh*), *ʾt* plus the direct object (*ʾt-šyr-Yhwh* and *ʾt-Yrwšlm*, and closing phrase with *ʿl* followed by two nouns, one of which is feminine singular the other masculine singular.

Vss. 5–6ab also exhibit structural balance, but it is chiastic in nature. Thus we have *ʾm ʾškḥk* paralleled by *ʾm-lʾ ʾzkrky* (5a and 6b), while *tškḥ ymyny* is matched exactly by *tdbq lšwny* (5b and 6a): the compact interlocking pattern is accentuated by the use of alliteration, assonance, and even internal rhyme. The striking double chiasm at the very center of the poem is the major clue to its basic structure: a series of concentric shells with an *X* at the center.

In view of the exact parallelism between the members of the chiastic pair: *tiškaḥ yᵉmînî* and *tidbaq lᵉšōnî* (in addition to the initial alliteration and closing rhyme, we have precise matching of vowels both as to quality and length, with the single exception of *ō* for *ī* in the second syllable of the second word of each element), we suggest that there was a similar precision in the balance between the members of the other chiastic pair: hence read *ʾeškᵉḥēkī* (5a) for *ʾeškāḥēk* (MT) to match *ʾezkᵉrēkī* (6b). The use of the archaic form of the pronominal suffix in 6b is apparently deliberate, and it is reasonable to suppose that the poet intended to use the same suffix in the parallel expression. It may be added that no revision of the written text (i.e., the Kethib: consonants and vowel letters) is necessary if we accept the proposal that the *yōd* at the beginning of the following word, *Yᵉrūšālēm*, could also serve to mark the end of the preceding word, *ʾeškᵉḥēkī*. In a number of cases where sense and other considerations require the same letter both at the end of one word and at the beginning of the next word, the letter is actually written only once.[9] Whether such a practice originated in and perpetuates simple scribal haplography, or was deliberately adopted at some point in the transmission of texts, the result is much the same. Applied with due caution, it is a useful device for resolving certain difficulties in the text and in this case for discovering a refinement in style which might otherwise have escaped detection.

The interpretation of the word *tiškaḥ* (5b) "wither" as a homonym of the common root "to forget" was first proposed by W. F. Albright in 1941, and has been widely adopted.[10] Other examples in the Bible, derived from the

9. Dahood, ibid., p. 88, fn. 7.

10. W. F. Albright, "Anath and the Dragon," *BASOR*, No. 84 (1941): 14–17, esp. p. 15, fn. 3. Cf. also J. H. Patton, *Canaanite Parallels in the Book of Psalms* (Baltimore, 1944), pp. 26–27.

same root (which has a cognate in Ugaritic) have been identified.[11] In spite of certain reservations, this seems the best solution to an otherwise difficult problem. It is in the nature of such oaths to refer to a physical calamity of major proportions (cf. Job 31:22, with reference to the "shoulder" and "arm"), and the common root *škḥ* can hardly sustain such a meaning. On the other hand, there is no evidence of any textual corruption; word-play or paronomasia is a common device in such contexts and particularly appropriate here (i.e., to match the consequence with the dereliction, at least by sound and form).[12] It may be added that *yāmīn*, like *yād*, designates the forearm including the hand.

Looking now at the metrical pattern of vss. 5–6ab, we observe that vs. 5 has 14 syllables according to our revised interpretation (i.e., reading *ʾeškeḥēkī* and *Yerûšālēm* in place of *ʾeškāḥēk* and *Yerûšālayim* [Qere]; these changes balance out so the total remains the same). The natural break in vs. 5 comes after *Yrwšlm*, giving the syllabic division as 9:5. Vs. 6ab also has 14 syllables. The sense break comes after *leḥikkī*, which produces the following pattern: 8:6. This division is sufficiently close to the prevailing structure in the section under consideration (vss. 4–6) to merit acceptance as it stands. Nevertheless, closer inspection suggests a different arrangement which more clearly reflects the evident chiasm of the couplet. The rigorously balanced pair: *tiškaḥ yemīnī* // *tidbaq lešōnī* are matching parts in this symmetrical structure. The implication is that the term *leḥikkī*, while belonging with *tidbaq lešōnī* so far as sense is concerned, should be taken with the following *ʾim lōʾ ʾezkerēkī* so far as the meter is concerned. Such a procedure would produce the following stanza form:

| | |
|---|---|
| *ʾim ʾeškeḥēkī Yerûšālēm* | 9 |
| *tiškaḥ yemīnī* | 5 |
| *tidbaq lešōnī* | 5 |
| *leḥikkī ʾim lōʾ ʾezkerēkī* | 9 |

The metrical pattern 9:5 // 5:9 sharply defines the chiastic structure. The opening and closing clauses neatly balance, as do the two central units. The unmatched terms (*Yrwšlm* and *lḥky*), which break the monotony of repetition, fill out the meter in both instances.

This passage is important in the continuing discussion of the nature of Hebrew prosody and, in particular, the widely asserted claim that sense and

11. Dahood, *Psalms I*, vol. 16 in *The Anchor Bible* (New York, 1966), p. 190; *Psalms II*, vol. 17 in *The Anchor Bible* (1968), pp. 72, 78, 228–29.
12. For comparable usage, cf. Isa. 5:7.

structure are congruent, i.e., that all lines are end-stopped. While we are concerned here with a minor division within a line, there is a strong implication that form and sense do not always coincide and that content and meter are not necessarily commensurate.

With regard to the chiastic pattern proposed here, there is an excellent parallel in Ps. 101:7. In that verse we have a clear case of double chiasm which may be diagrammed as follows:

| | | |
|---|---|---|
| *lōʾ-yēšēb b$^{e}$qereb bētī* | (7a) | Shall not dwell within my house |
| *ʿōśē r$^{e}$miyyā* | (7b) | the doer of deceit, |
| *dōbēr š$^{e}$qārīm* | (7c) | the speaker of lies |
| *lōʾ-yikkōn b$^{e}$neged ʿēnāy* | (7d) | shall not abide before my eyes. |

The parallelism is precise throughout, including the order of the words and the parts of speech employed. The longer clause in each case begins with the same negative particle (*lōʾ*) and continues with a verb in the imperfect 3rd m. s. form (*yēšēb* // *yikkōn*); there follow compound prepositions of identical form (*b$^{e}$qereb* // *l$^{e}$neged*), and nouns with the 1st person singular suffix (*bētī* // *ʿēnāy*). The shorter phrase in each case consists of a Qal active participle, m. s., followed by a noun (*ʿōśē r$^{e}$miyyā* // *dōbēr š$^{e}$qārīm*). The syllable count for each pair of parallel terms is exactly the same, as inevitably are the total numbers (8:5 / 5:8; or 7 instead of 8 if we count the segolate forms as monosyllabic). The quatrain in Ps. 137:5–6ab is slightly less rigorous in structure, but derives from essentially the same metrical pattern.

Vs. 6cd is remarkable in a number of ways, not least because the traditional translation and interpretation have rarely if ever been challenged. The RSV reflects the common view: "if I do not set Jerusalem above my highest joy." However, the proposed interpretation of the verb *ʿlh* in the Hiphil is otherwise unattested in the Bible, and it is never used, figuratively or literally, with a city or other demographic entity. The Qal form of *ʿlh* is often used with geographic locations, on the other hand, and we suggest that it should be substituted for the Hiphil in this verse. No change in the written text is involved and only a very slight one in the vocalization of the first syllable, according to Massoretic rules (i.e., *ʾe-* for *ʾa-*; in classical times the forms were probably indistinguishable, as is true of most imperfect forms in *lamed he* verbs). While *ʿlh* is generally followed by a preposition before the place or place-name, there are many examples where no preposition is used. A close parallel to the reading we propose is to be found in II Sam. 19:35, . . . *kī ʾe$^{ʿe}$lē* . . . *Y$^{e}$rūšālayim*, "that I should go up . . . to Jerusalem." There is one example in which the verb is followed by the sign of the definite direct object, as we suppose the case to be here: Num. 13:17, . . . *waᶜᵃlītem ᵓet-hāhār*, "and you shall ascend the mountain."[13]

While vs. 6cd continues the 1st person singular affirmations of vss. 5–6ab, there is a shift away from the direct address to Jerusalem, unless we accept Dahood's proposal that *ᵓt* is to be read *ᵓatt*, the 2nd f. s. pronoun, and construed as the object of the verb.[14] In view of the structural parallels with vs. 4, however, including specifically the occurrence of *ᵓet* as the sign of the definite direct object after the verb, it is preferable to interpret *ᵓt* in vs. 6 in the same fashion. We must acknowledge the shift in person as a deliberate device of the poet. The use of *ᵓim lōᵓ* at the beginning of the line shows that the force of the oath is still felt, but the clause is less tightly bound to the preceding couplet (5–6ab). The rendering as a strong asseverative: "Surely I will ascend Jerusalem . . ." is therefore justified.

The final phrase of the verse (6d) *ᶜal rōᵓš śimḥātī*, usually understood as a construct chain and rendered "above my highest joy," is also without attestation in the Hebrew Bible, or convincing parallel. A better rendering would be "upon my festive head," following Dahood.[15] But the meaning of such a phrase is not at all clear, and the sentence as a whole is less than convincing. Fortunately, there is a striking parallel to the expression in the Psalm, the syntactic structure and meaning of which are not in doubt. In Isaiah 35:10 = 51:11,[16] the composition of which must be dated within a generation of that of the Psalm, we read:

| | |
|---|---|
| *ūpᵉdūyē Yhwh yᵉšūbūn* | And Yahweh's redeemed shall return |
| *ūbāᵓū Ṣiyyōn bᵉrinnā* | and they shall enter Zion with a shout, |
| *wᵉśimḥat ᶜōlām ᶜal-rōᵓšām* | with eternal joy upon their heads. |

Our immediate concern is with the third unit of the passage, which provides the decisive clue to the correct interpretation of the enigmatic phrase in Ps. 137:6. Except for the changes in word order, the position and person of the pronominal suffix, and the addition of the term *ᶜōlām*, the expressions are the same. It becomes clear, then, that the Psalm passage is not to be analyzed as a single construct chain, but rather as a prepositional phrase plus another noun. It may then be rendered: "upon (my) head (is) my joy" or "with my joy upon (my) head." It should be noted that the pronominal suffix is often omitted with parts of the body, especially when there is no doubt about the

13. Cf. also II Kings 16:5 (Jerusalem); Jer. 31:6 (Zion); II Kings 19:14; 20:5,8; 23:2; Jer. 26:10 (the house of Yahweh).

14. Dahood, *CBQ*, XXXII (1970): 87.

15. Ibid.

16. Cf. Isa. 61:7.

reference. Alternatively, the suffix attached to *śimḥā* may serve in a dual capacity and also define *rōʾš*.

There are other affinities between the two passages which deserve consideration. According to Isa. 35:10, it is when the redeemed of Yahweh return to Zion that everlasting joy will be upon their heads. According to our interpretation of Ps. 137:6cd, the setting would be the same: when the Psalmist (also an exile) ascends Jerusalem, his joy will be upon his head. Exactly what the expression *śimḥā ʿal rōʾš* denotes is not explained, but it is reasonable to suppose that some visible object or physical action was originally involved, though the use here may be figurative. Hence, we may have here an allusion to the well-known practice of anointing the head on festive occasions, and *śimḥā* may be the semantic equivalent of *šemen śāśōn* (cf. Isa. 61:3, Ps. 45:8, Prov. 27:9, and not least Ps. 23:6).

## IV

| | | |
|---|---|---|
| *zᵉkōr Yahwē libnē ʾEdōm* | (7a) | Yahweh, recall to Edom's sons |
| *ʾēt yōm Yᵉrūšālēm* | (7b) | the day of Jerusalem! |
| *hāʾōmᵉrīm ʿārū* | (7c) | Who were saying, "Strip bare! |
| *ʿārū ʿad hayᵉsōd bāh* | (7d) | Strip bare to its foundation." |

Vs. 7 introduces the final section of the poem (vss. 7–9), which corresponds to the opening unit (vss. 1–3). There is a logical connection between this verse and the preceding block of material, as the poet proceeds from his oath of loyalty to Yahweh to the demand that Yahweh vindicate his justice by dealing in the same measure with those who had invaded Judah and destroyed Jerusalem. There is, nevertheless, a sharp grammatical break as Yahweh is addressed directly for the first time. With respect to content as well, a new element is introduced by the reference to the sons of Edom. Dahood's proposal to take "Yahweh" as the direct object of the verb "remember," and "the sons of Edom" as the subject (with the *lamed* construed as a vocative particle) is novel and ingenious, but the evidence, grammatical and syntactic, in this verse and elsewhere in the Bible is against his interpretation.[17] The use of *zkr* in the imperative, with God as subject, is frequent in the Psalter; it also occurs with the preposition *lᵉ* attached to the personal object (cf. Exod. 32:13; Deut. 9:27). Furthermore, *ʾēt yōm Yᵉrūšālēm* is the direct object of the verb. The traditional analysis and interpretation are therefore inevitable and correct: "Yahweh, remember Jerusalem's day (of catastrophe) in respect of the Edomites. . . ."

17. Dahood, *CBQ*, XXXII (1970): 87, fn. 6.

The second clause of vs. 7 (cd) yields a satisfactory sense as it stands. We may render literally: "Who were saying: 'Lay bare! lay bare as far as the foundation in it (Jerusalem).'" The implied object of the verbs may be secured from the 3rd f. s. suffix attached to the preposition $b^e$: "lay it bare." It is also possible to take the prepositional phrase as the object of the verb, even though the use of the verb with $b^e$ is otherwise unattested in the Bible; i.e., "Strip it to the foundation." There is no substantial difference in meaning, however.

The nearest parallel to the clause is to be found in Hab. 3:13, in its present form a product of the same age.[18] The latter passage, which is difficult and possibly corrupt, may be rendered as follows:

| | | |
|---|---|---|
| *māḥaṣtā rō'š mibbayit rāšā*ᶜ | (13c) | You crushed inward the head of the Evil One |
| ᶜ*ārōt y*ᵉ*sōd* ᶜ*ad-ṣawwā'r* | (13d) | Laying him open backside to neck. |

We take *mbyt* as the adverb *mibbayit* meaning "within, on the inside, inwards," and modifying the construct chain *rō'š rāšā*ᶜ, into which it has been inserted.[19] In the second clause, we take ᶜ*ārōt* as an unusual form of the infinitive absolute, which is parallel to the perfect form *māḥaṣtā* in the first clause.[20] The movement described, from fundament to neck, is the reverse of that in Ps. 137, in which the walls are demolished from top to bottom, laying bare the foundations.

With respect to the meter, vs. 7 consists of two lines with 14 and 13 syllables each, making a total of 27. This is the same total as vs. 3, with which vs. 7 corresponds in the structure of the poem. While there is no parallelism in vs. 7 and both lines are continuous, it is nevertheless possible to find a natural pause or break in each line. In the first line there is a caesura after *libnē 'Edōm*, producing the following division: 8 + 6 = 14. In the second line

18. The best treatment of Hab. 3 remains that of W. F. Albright, "The Psalm of Habakkuk," *Studies in Old Testament Prophecy*, ed. by H. H. Rowley (Edinburgh, 1950), pp. 1–18. For his view of vs. 13, see pp. 11, 13, 16–17, fns. nn through qq.

19. For a possible parallel to this use of *mibbayit* in relation to the body, cf. II Kings 6:30, ᶜ*al b*ᵉ*śārō mibbayit*. There is increasing evidence for the deliberate insertion of particles and words between the construct and absolute in construct chains. A paper on the subject is in preparation, but consider, in addition to the familiar occurrence of prepositions in construct chains (e.g., *hry bGlb*ᶜ, II Sam. 1:21), and enclitic *mem* (e.g., Deut. 33:11 *mtny-m qmyw*; Ps. 18:16 *'pyqy-m ym* // *'pyqy ym* II Sam. 22:16), the following cases: Ezek. 39:11 *mqwm-šm qbr* (I owe this example to Prof. Nahum Sarna), and these instances from Hosea 14:3 *kl-tś'* ᶜ*wn*; 8:2 *'lhy yd*ᶜ*nwk Yśr'l*, which must be read, "O God of Israel, we know you"; and 6:9 *drk yrṣḥw-škmh*.

20. Cf. G-K, #75n. Albright's comment is pertinent, "The Psalm of Habakkuk," p. 17 fn. pp.

there are various possibilities. From the point of view of sense, the break should come after *hāʾōm$^{e}$rīm*, but this produces a strongly unbalanced division: 4 + 9 = 13. Also plausible is a pause after the second verb (*ʿārū*), which was favored by the Massoretes. The resulting division is 8 + 5 = 13. Comparison with vs. 3, however, suggests a third possibility. Vs. 3 consists of four units with the following syllable count: 6, 6, 7, 8 making a total of 27. As we have already pointed out, 3b and c naturally belong together, while 3a and d form an envelope around them. Metrically, then, 3a and d can be counted as 6 + 8 = 14, which corresponds to vs. 7a, 8 + 6 = 14. Likewise 3b and c may be counted as 6 + 7 = 13, to match 7b, which is also 13. If the correlation is to be pursued further, then the break in vs. 7b should come before the second *ʿārū*, giving a count of 6 + 7 = 13, the same as 3bc. The rendering would be: "Lay it bare! Lay it bare to its foundation!"

It may be added that the reference to the Edomites, while unexpected in a poem about Babylon, is entirely appropriate in the immediate context, corresponding closely to other sixth century oracles about the Edomites and their role in the destruction of Jerusalem: cf. Obadiah, Ezekiel 35, etc.

| | | |
|---|---|---|
| *bat-Bābel hašš$^{e}$dūdā* | (8a) | Daughter Babylon the doomed |
| *ʾašrē šey$^{e}$šallem-lāk* | (8b) | Happy he who renders you |
| *ʾet-g$^{e}$mūlēk šeggāmalt lānū* | (8c) | the payment which you paid out to us. |
| *ʾašrē šeyyōʾḥēz w$^{e}$nippēṣ* | (9a) | Happy he who grasps and shatters |
| *ʾet-ʿōlālayk ʾel-hassālʿ* | (9b) | your children upon the cliff. |

The poem closes as it opens, with an explicit reference to Babylon (cf. *Bābel* in vs. 1 and *bat-Bābel* in vs. 8), thus forming a characteristic *inclusio*. But the correlations between the two sections (vss. 1–2 and 8–9) extend beyond this rather simple device to other considerations of structure and style. Thus the Introduction and Conclusion are materially longer than the standard units making up the body of the poem (vss. 3–7). The latter are characteristically in couplet (vss. 3 and 7) or quatrain (i.e., double-couplet, vss. 4–6) form, with syllable counts of 27 and 54, comprising a symmetrical whole. The opening and closing sections fall into a different pattern, each consisting of a pair of matching lines modifying a pivotal phrase or clause. The result in each case is a longer section of 37 or 38 syllables in contrast with the pattern in the body of the poem. In vss. 1–2, the parallel clauses are introduced by the preposition *ʿal*, whereas in vss. 8–9 the common introductory expression is *ʾašrē še-*. In the opening section, the additional unit comes in the middle, between the balancing couplets:

Beside the rivers in Babylon
there we sat down, loudly we wept—
when we remembered Zion—
Beside the poplars in its midst
we hanged up our lyres.

The pivotal clause, "when we remembered Zion," which gives point and cohesion to the section and links it with the body of the poem, goes naturally with the preceding line, but it can also be taken with what follows, since both actions were occasioned by the remembrance of Zion.

In the closing section, the additional unit comes at the beginning, but it is structurally linked with both of the following clauses:

O daughter Babylon, destined for destruction—
Happy shall he be who renders to you
your payment which you paid to us—
Happy shall he be who seizes and smashes
your children against the cliffs.

The metrical count is as follows:

| | | | | |
|---|---|---|---|---|
| Vs. 1) | 7 + 8 | | 7 | (Vs. 8 |
| | 7 | = 37 // 38 = | 7 + 9 | |
| Vs. 2) | 7 + 8 | | 8 + 7 | (Vs. 9 |

The patterns are remarkably similar. Each of the couplets has 15 syllables, except for one which has 16 (vs. 8c), while the added unit has 7. The longer lines break down into subdivisions of 7 and 8 syllables, again with a single exception where we have 7 and 9.

In vs. 8a, *MT hašš*$^{e}$*dūdā*, literally, "the destroyed," is often emended to *haššōdēdā* or *haššādōdā* on the basis of limited versional evidence, with the meaning, "the destroyer." While the proposed emendation is superficially more plausible, especially when associated with world-conquering Babylon, the more difficult reading in *MT*, the passive participle, can be defended, both on the basis of the immediate context (i.e., the poet's intention) and a series of remarkable parallels in contemporary or nearly contemporary biblical literature, specifically Jer. 51:47–57. In the Jeremiah passage, as in the Psalm, emphasis is placed on the doctrine of divine retribution in relation to the impending destruction of Babylon. In Jeremiah there is repeated reference to the destroyer(s) whom Yahweh will bring against Babylon. While it is clear that Babylon will be destroyed because it has destroyed others, the words derived from the root *šdd* are used exclusively of the action to be taken against Babylon, never by Babylon. In other words, Babylon is destined for and doomed to destruction.[21] Since the literary and verbal similarities between the two passages are considerable, it is better to accept *MT* here and interpret the reference as a proleptic statement of the irreversible fate already determined and soon to be accomplished. It is precisely the imminent destruction of Babylon that is described picturesquely in the following clauses in vss. 8–9 of the Psalm. The destruction of Babylon will conform to the standard of divine retribution: payment will be in kind and in equal measure. As Babylon did to others, so it shall be done to her.[22] A vivid example of such retribution, which at the same time illustrates prevailing practice all over the ancient world, including the Babylonians themselves, suffices to complete the case. The appalling procedure is fully attested.[23]

## STRUCTURAL ANALYSIS

Psalm 137 is characterized by an envelope construction in which the outer sections fold around the inner ones producing a cohesive and integrated whole. Thus the opening and closing sections (vss. 1–2 and 8–9) form an *inclusio* which is keyed on the word *Bābel.* The body of the poem, likewise, consists of an outer shell, vss. 3 and 7, and an inner core, vss. 4–6. Even this core follows the same pattern, with vss. 4 and 6cd forming a frame around the nucleus at the very center of the poem. This nucleus is an artfully designed chiastic couplet which is at once the dramatic high point or apex of the poem and the axis linking the parts and exhibiting the essential structure of the whole (vss. 5–6ab).

It may be noted that vs. 3 in itself is an example of a complicated form of the envelope construction. The center section (3bc), while dependent on the main verb *šeʾēlūnū*, is a tightly knit unit in which the parallel components interlock: e.g., "our captors" // "our mockers"; "words of a song (lyrics)" // "joy." In our view, the sense or intention of the poet can be expressed as follows: "Our mocking captors (demanded of us) happy songs." The last unit (3d) expresses directly the demand mentioned at the beginning. Thus

21. Typical are vss. 55–56 (cf. also vss. 48, 53), which may be rendered as follows: For Yahweh will destroy (*šōdēd*) Babylon. . . . For a destroyer has come against her, against Babylon. Her warriors have been captured, and their bows broken. For Yahweh is a God of retribution (*gemūlōt*); he will pay back in full (*šallēm yešallēm*).

22. Cf. Jer. 51:49.

23. Cf. II Kings 8:12; Isa. 13:16; Hosea 14:1; Nahum 3:10.

we are justified in grouping 3a with 3d and 3b with 3c, producing a metrical pattern 6 + 8 = 14 and 6 + 7 = 13, making a total of 27, matching the structurally comparable verse 7, which breaks down as follows: 7ab, 8 + 6 = 14; and 7cd, 6 + 7 = 13, making the same total of 27. A schematic representation of the Psalm follows:[24]

| | | | | | | | |
|---|---|---|---|---|---|---|---|
| | I | | | | | V | |
| Vs. 1a) | 7 | | | | | 7 | (8a |
| 1b) | 8 | | | | | 7 | (8b |
| 1c) | 7 | | 37 | | 38 | 9 | (8c |
| 2a) | 7 | | | | | 8 | (9a |
| 2b) | 8 | | | | | 7 | (9b |
| | II | | | | | IV | |
| Vs. 3a) | 6 | | | | | 8 | (7a |
| 3b) | 6 | | | | | 6 | (7b |
| 3c) | 7 | | 27 | | 27 | 6 | (7c |
| 3d) | 8 | | | | | 7 | (7d |
| | | | | III | | | |
| Vs. 4a) | 7 | 12 | | 54 | 14 | 9 | (6c |
| 4b) | 5 | | | | | 5 | (6d |
| | | | 5a) | 9 | | | |
| | | | 5b) | 5 | 28 | | |
| | | | 6a) | 5 | | | |
| | | | 6b) | 9 | | | |

In order to make the case for an intentional and fairly precise metrical structure we have dealt with the text of the poem as it has come down to us. No changes have been made in the consonantal text and only a few minor

24. For the sake of comparison, we offer an analysis of the Psalm according to the common stress/accent system:

| | | | | |
|---|---|---|---|---|
| Vs. 1) | 2:2:2 | | 2:2:3 | (8 |
| 2) | 2:2 | | 3:2 | (9 |
| Vs. 3) | 2:2:2 | | 3:2 | (7 |
| | 4 | | 3:2 | |
| Vs. 4) | 2:2 | | 3:2 | (6cd |
| | 5) | 2:2 | | |
| | 6ab) | 3:2 | | |

The pattern is roughly the same as that exhibited by the syllable-counting method. Variations are possible, and a somewhat more rigorous pattern can be reconstructed. But, given both the vagueness and flexibility of the system, it is hard to see what is gained by such an approach.

ones in the vocalization. Even if we were to follow *MT* slavishly, the general pattern would still be quite visible. However, by attempting to recover earlier forms of pronunciation and to recognize special stylistic features, we hope to reproduce more exactly the original structure as created by the poet. The Massoretes can hardly have been aware of such details.

# Tafel, Buch und Blatt

KURT GALLING

Seit langem war aus assyrischen Kolophonen bekannt,[1] daß der zur Zeit Sargons und Sanheribs tätige Nabu-zuqup-kēnu aus Kalaḫ die astrologische Omenserie *Enuma Anu Enlil*[2] aus ihm vorliegenden Holztafeln auf Tontafeln übertragen hat. Solche innen gewachsten Tafeln konnten aus Tamarisken-oder Zypressenholz bestehen (*ZA* 42 [1934]: 207). Überraschenderweise wurde 1953 in einem Brunnenschacht in Nimrud eine für Sargon bestimmte Luxusausgabe dieser Omenserie mit noch 23 Tafeln, teils aus Elfenbein, teils aus Walnußholz gefunden (Maße der Tafeln: 33,8 × 15,6 cm). Auf einer Tafel waren noch Reste in Wachs lesbar.[3] Der Nimrudfund und früher veröffentlichte, teilweise mißdeutete Darstellungen aus dem assyrischen und nordsyrischen Raum geben Veranlassung, einige Probleme des altisraelitischen Schreibwesens erneut[4] zu behandeln.

1. Cf. neuestens H. Hunger, *Babylonisch-assyrische Kolophone* (1968), Nr. 297ff.

2. E. Weidner in *AfO* 14 (1941–44): 172ff; 308ff., und 17 (1954–56): 71ff.—W. G. Lambert in *JCS* 16 (1963): 64ff.

3. D. J. Wiseman in *Iraq* 17 (1955): 1–13—M. Howard, ibidem, S. 14–20. Nach der Inschrift auf dem elfenbeinernen Buchdeckel war das Faltbuch für den Palast Sargons in Dur-Scharrukin bestimmt. Der König starb vor der Übergabe des Buches, sodaß es in Nimrud verblieb, wo es der goldenen (?) Scharniere beraubt von den Soldaten Sanheribs in den Brunnenschacht geworfen wurde und auf diese Weise der Nachwelt erhalten blieb. *Habent sua fata libelli!*

4. Cf. O. Eissfeldt, *Einleitung in das AT*[3] (1964): 909ff. Zur Klapptafel speziell: O. Procksch, Der hebräische Schreiber und sein Buch, in *Festschrift E. Kuhnert* (1928): 1–15. Zu Leder und Papyrus bei den Griechen: C. Wendel, *Die griechisch-römische Buchbeschreibung verglichen mit der des Vorderen Orients* (1949).

1. *Die Holztafel.* Die vorgenannten Holzarten: Tamariske, Zypresse und Walnuß sind in Palästina gleichfalls heimisch. Wie sich aus Grabfunden in Jericho (K. M. Kenyon, *Jericho I* [1960]: 267) ergibt, hat man auch andere Hölzer für die Herstellung von Möbeln und Geräten gewählt, sodaß sich über die Hölzer der im AT genannten Schreibtafeln nichts Näheres aussagen läßt. Werden, wie für den Dekalog, Tafeln aus anderem Material vorausgesetzt, so ist eine Apposition erforderlich, beim Dekalog *ʾeben* (sg oder pl). Entgegen der landläufigen Vorstellung ist übrigens nur in Ex. 31:16 gesagt, daß die Worte des Dekalogs in die steinernen Tafeln eingemeißelt wurden (Reminiszenz an den Terminus in Sir. 45:11c). Veranschaulichen könnte man sich das an dem sog. Bauernkalender von Geser (*ANEP*, 272), dessen Datierung W. F. Albright verdankt wird (*ANET*, 320). Sonst heißt es immer, die Dekalogworte seien auf die Steine geschrieben. Das hieße einen Kalküberzug substituieren, wovon bei den im Freien (!) aufgestellten Tafeln des Gesetzes in Dtn. 27:2f, 8 die Rede ist. Eine solche Vorstellung ist am ehesten denkbar, wenn es auch in Palästina Holztafeln gegeben hat, die innen geweißt waren.[5] *lūᵃḥ/lūḥōt* braucht man für Holzbretter auch ohne Zusammenhang mit dem Schreiben. So begegnet das Wort bei den Seitenbrettern des transportablen Brandopferaltars (Ex. 27:8) oder beim Verrammeln einer Tür durch ein Zedern-Brett (Ct. 8:9; nach 𝔖 𝔏 𝔙 besser pl statt sg). Wenn bei den Kesselwagen des Tempels (1 Reg. 7:27,36) von *lūḥōt* gesprochen wird, so wohl wegen der eingravierten Bilder.[6] Für Schiffsplanken findet sich im MT von Ez. 27:5 der Dual *lūḥōtāyim.* Man hat gemeint, der Dual solle andeuten, daß sich die Planken auf beiden Seiten des Schiffsrumpfes befänden-das ist jedoch von der Sache her selbstverständlich! Eher wäre an ein Überlappen von jeweils zwei Planken zu denken, die das Eindringen von Meerwasser verhindern sollen. V löst mit *tabulas maris* (= *lūhōt* + *yām*?) den angeblichen Dual auf. Mit H. P. Rüger, Das Tyrusorakel Ez. 27 (Diss. theol. Tübingen, 1961) empfiehlt es sich jedoch, 𝔗 (*gšrk*) folgend, pl c suff 2ps sg (*lūḥōtāyik*) zu lesen, da in den umgebenden Versen die Anrede an Tyrus obwaltet. Kehren wir zu *lūᵃḥ* = Schreibtafel zurück! In dem um 625 anzusetzenden Text in Hab. 2 heißt es (Hab. 2:2): "Und Jahwe hob an und sprach: Schreibe die Vision auf und verdeutliche

5. Die Schreibtafeln der Aegypter des NR hatten vielfach innen eine Gipsschicht, auf die man mit der Binse schrieb. Auch die Griechen kannten so geweißte Tafeln (leukoma).

6. Von *deltoi chalkai* ist in 1 Macc. 8:22; 14:18 die Rede, Man kann auch auf die Kupferrolle von Qumran verweisen (*DJD* III [1962]: 199ff), die die Kopie einer Schatzliste (auf Leder oder Papyrus) darstellt, und zu deren Inhalt es 2 erheblich jüngere Parallelen gibt (Spätjüdischer Traktat über die Kultgeräte des Tempels und ein arabisches "Buch der Perlen" aus Ägypten [J. T. Milik, a.a.O., S. 279]).

(sie) auf Tafeln, damit sie jeder geläufig lesen kann." Unter "Vision" ist ein nachfolgendes Gotteswort gemeint (zum Sprachgebrauch cf. Nah. 1:1; Jes. 1:1). *ūbāʾ ēr* ist imp, 𝔊 faßt es nach Dtn. 27:8 als eine Art adverbiellen Infinitiv (*ū baʾēr*) auf: *kai saphōs*. Beide Imperative zielen auf die Lesbarkeit. W. H. Ward (*ICC*, 1911) und E. Sellin (*KAT*, 1930) statuieren ein *bʾr* II (cf. *KBL*², jedoch nicht mehr *KBL*³) und übersetzen: "und grabe es ein auf Tafeln" (Stein- bzw. Tontafeln). Im Hintergrund dieser Sachexegese steht letztlich die abwegige These von H. Winckler, man habe im vorexilischen Israel die offiziellen Dokumente auf Tontafeln in Keilschrift abgefaßt.[7] Ein *bʾr* II ist auch aus dem Grunde abzuweisen, weil es im AT für "eingraben/einzeichnen" andere Termini (*ḥāraš* /*pātaḥ*) gibt. Die Tafeln in Hab. 2:2 sind vielmehr die eines hölzernen Diptychons, in dessen Innenseiten die Vision notiert werden soll. Das zur Aufzeichnung bestimmte Wort ist in 2:4 (+ 5?) oder—nach K. Elliger (*ATD*)—zugleich noch in Hab. 3 zu sehen.

In die letzten Jahre vor 701 wird man Jes. 30:8 zu datieren haben. Hier stehen *lūᵃḥ* und *sēper* nebeneinander: "Nun geh, schreibe es *ʿal lūᵃh*—in ihrer Gegenwart—und *ʿal sēper* ritze es ein, damit es erhalten bleibe für späteren Tag, für immer und ewig!" Einige MSS 𝔊 𝔙 sagen eingangs: "Und nun," eine für einen Neuansatz charakteristische Wendung. *luᵃḥ* ist coll sg, also mit "Tafeln" zu übersetzen. *ʾittām* (in ihrer Gegenwart) hat auch 𝔖 vorgefunden; 𝔊 (1QIsᵃ) las *ʾōtām*, was sich mit: "Schreibe es" stößt, und läßt das "ritze ein" unübersetzt. Die Praesenz zweier Verben und die von zwei Schreibmaterialien (?) legt eine aufgliedernde Exegese nahe. Ein Text soll auf einem öffentlich ausgestellten Diptychon (𝔊 *epi pyxiou*. 𝔙 *super buxum*) stehen, ein zweiter Text (Duplikat ?) auf einem Schriftblatt aus Leder. B. Duhm (*HAT* 1892) und andere, zuletzt H. Schunk, *ZAW* 78 (1966): 48ff, streichen nicht nur das Interpretament "in ihrer Gegenwart," sondern auch *ʿal lūᵃḥ*. Zur Begründung führt Duhm an, daß Holztafeln leicht verwittern[8] und gewiß nicht erneuert wurden, wohingegen die Aufzeichnung auf eine Lederrolle bzw. durch wortgetreue Abschriften (sic!) die Ewigkeit des Gotteswortes garantiere. Wäre *sēper* eine Lederrolle, so paßt

7. H. Winckler in *Altoriental. Forschungen III* (1902): 165ff. Ihm folgen A. Cowley, *Aramaic Papyri in the Fifth Cent. B.C.* (1923): XXVf, J. Benzinger, *Hebr. Archaeologie*³ (1927): 176 und noch E. Sellin Einl. in das AT⁶ (1933): 8. Die einzigen für den Gebrauch der Keilschrift in vorexilischer Zeit angeführten Texte sind die Kontrakte von 651 und 549 aus Geser (cf. K. Galling in *PJ* 31 [1935]: 81ff.), aber diese stammen von der assyrischen Besatzungsmacht!

8. Daß sich Holztafeln lange erhalten können, und zwar nicht nur in Ägypten, beweist die aus dem 7. Jh vChr stammende etruskische Schreibtafel, die in *Iraq* 17 (1955), Taf. III abgebildet ist.

das Einritzen nicht dazu.[9] Wohl aus dieser Erkenntnis hat 𝔊 (ob sie an Leder oder Papyrus denkt, kann hier gleich sein) den Befehl des Einritzens übergangen. U.E. verlangt der kunstvoll chiastische Aufbau einen anderen, einheitlichen Aspekt. Es korrespondieren *lūaḥ* und *sēper* miteinander und *sēper* meint die Schreibfläche des Diptychons, das eine Wachsschicht zum Einritzen besitzt. Der aufzuschreibende Text ist, wie die Parallele von Hab. 2:2 und das "(und) nun" nahelegen, nicht in etwas Vorausgegangenem, sondern im Nachfolgenden zu sehen (30,9–14[17]). Was das in *BHSt* (W. Thomas) *metri causa c*𝔙 zur Streichung empfohlene *ʾittām* angeht, so wird diese Einfügung nicht auf Zeitgenossen Jesajas zielen, die den Text später lesen (so u.a. Delitzsch), sondern denkt vermutlich an praesente Zeugen (die Jünger Jesajas [8:16]? Einfluß von 8:2 ?).

Fragen wir nach weiteren und jüngeren Belegen für *lūaḥ* (und *delet*), so ist auch der griechische Sprachbereich hinzuzunehmen. Im Traktat Schab XII, 4 wird verboten, mehr als 2 Buchstaben auf zwei Winkelbretter oder zwei Buchtafeln (*lwḥy pnqs*) zu schreiben, weil sie zusammengehören (2 x zwei Buchstaben wären möglich, wenn sie nicht zusammengehören: XII, 5). *Pnqs* = *pinax* ist ein Diptychon mit innen gewachsten Tafeln (Raschi b. Schab 104b). Von einem Schreiben in gefalteter Tafel (*en pinaki ptyktō*) ist in Ilias VI, 168f die Rede. Häufiger ist der Terminus *deltos*, wobei vornehmlich an Klapptafel(n) gedacht ist (Her. VII, 239; Aristophanes, Thesm. 776). Euripides (Iph Taur, 727) spricht von vieltürigen Falten einer Schreibtafel. Daß *deltos* ein Lehnwort aus dem Semitischen ist, hat man seit langem vermutet. Maria L. Mayer (Istituto Lombardo, Rendic. Lett 94 [1960] S.344f) hat für den Weg der Übernahme auf die im 5. Jh in Zypern belegte Dialektvariante *daltos* hingewiesen. Das hebr. *delet* bezeichnet primär die Tür (Türflügel). Man konnte den Ausdruck für ein Diptychon übernehmen, da sich die Tafeln eines Faltbuches in den Scharnieren wie eine Tür drehen. Wenn in Jer. 36:23 von *dᵉlātōt* (= Spalten, Kolumnen[10]) einer *mᵉgillat sēper* die Rede ist, die der König Jojakim mit dem Schreibermesser abtrennt, so ist offensichtlich der Terminus "Türen" vom Diptychon für die Kolumnen der Papyrusrolle[11] übernommen. *delet* als Abbreviatur für ein hölzernes

9. *ḥāqaq*/*ḥāqā* bedeutet "einritzen" im Vollsinn des Wortes! Cf. Ez. 4:1; 8:10; 23:14; 1 Reg. 6:35.

10. Kolumne bedeutet ursprünglich wie Stele eine beschriftete Säule. Die Verkleinerungsform *columella* im übertragenen Sinne für Buchseite bzw. Spalte begegnet zuerst bei Rufinus, apol. adv. Hier. 2:36. Den Hinweis verdanke ich Prof. Widmann, Mainz.

11. Die in Ägypten entstandene LXX spricht in Jer. 43:2 (= *MT* 36,2) von *chartion bibliou*, d.h. einer Schriftrolle aus Papyrus. Das ist in diesem Fall auch für die originale Situation in Palästina zutreffend. *Mᵉgillā* (aram. *mᵉgillᵉtā*) findet sich im Spätbabylonischen der Perserzeit als *magallatu* (*AHW*, S. 584) und meint dort eine Leder-Rolle.

Diptychon findet sich auch im Ostrakon Nr. 4 von Lachis (*KAI*, 194; *TGI*², S. 76). Hier beteuert der Absender: "Und nun, entsprechend allem, was mein Herr mir anbefahl, hat dein Knecht getan. Ich habe notiert auf die Tafel (*ᶜl hdlt*) alles genau so, wie es mein Herr mir anbefahl." Da danach erst mit "und nun" ein Neues beginnt, gehören beide Akte zusammen: die Ausführung des Befohlenen und die zur Kontrolle bestimmte Notiz auf einer Klapptafel.[12]

Dem in Nimrud gefundenen Original eines Faltbuches (s.o., Anm. 3) kann man assyrische Darstellungen beiordnen. Auf ihnen begegnet außer der Tontafel[13] auch die Kombination von Tontafel und Papyrus, sowie die von Leder und Klapptafel in den Händen jeweils eines von 2 Schreibern. Daß immer 2 Schreiber nebeneinander auftreten, erklärt sich von ihrem Einsatz beim Aufzeichnen von Kriegsbeute o.ä., deren Zahlen auf diese Weise kontrolliert werden konnten. Keilschrift wird sowohl auf der Tontafel wie auf der innen gewachsten Holztafel geschrieben. Leder[14] und Papyrus bilden die Schreibfläche für das Aramäische. Das Nebeneinander von Tontafel- und Papyrusschreiber ist nachweisbar auf einem Relief aus Nimrud und einem Fresko aus Til Barsib, zu datieren mit Tiglatpileser III

12. So richtig bei J. Reider, *JQR* 29 (1939): 236. In Ugarit ist einmal auf einem Tontäfelchen (Rückseite) als einziges Wort *dlt* geschrieben (*Syria* 28 [1951]: 24), wohl im Sinne von "Übungstafel."

13. Die bislang älteste Darstellung (um 850) eines Tontafel-Schreibers findet sich u.E. auf dem Tigrisquellen—(Bronze-) Relief von Balawat (R. D. Barnett, *Assyrische Palastreliefs*, Prag oJ, Taf. 145), und zwar im oberen Bild. Dem Meißelnden gegenüber steht in langem Gewand der Schreiber, dessen Rechte den Griffel hält. In Ugarit (cf. C. H. Gordon, *Ugaritic Textbook*, [1965]) begegnet *lḥ* (117, 10) und mehrfach *lḥt* als feminine Variante (kein Plural!). Da man damls keine Holztafeln mit Wachsflächen benutzt hat, handelt es sich um Tontafeln (wie in Amarna Nr. 143:23; 358:9) und der Sache nach um Briefe. Der auf *lḥt* folgende epexegetische Genetiv zielt auf das Thema der Mitteilung. So in 2064, 21 (Pflugrinder) und in 2060, 17; 2061, 9f (Essensrationen). Das in 2009, 5 apostrophierte Schreiben der Mutter heißt *lḥt šlm*, d.h. eine Mitteilung (oder Wunsch?) über das Wohlbefinden. Daraus ergibt sich, daß man *lḥt spr* (in 138, 6f) nicht mit "Brieftafel" übersetzen darf, sondern mit "Tafel enthaltend ein *spr*." Dieses *spr* wird nach der Liste Gordon 64 als Aufzählung von Personen (oder Sachen) zu denken sein. Ich verdanke die Hinweise Dr. H. P. Rüger—Tübingen.

14. Aus einem von M. Dietrich in *WdO* 4 (1967): 87f behandelten Brief Sargons an einen Kommandanten in Ur, wohl aramäischer Abkunft, erfährt man des Kommandanten Bitte: "Wenn es dem König recht ist, möchte ich gern *ina libbi sipri* (auf Leder in Aramäisch) schreiben," wogegen der König lieber einen Brief in Akkadisch sähe! Im Brief ABL 633 r 14 wird durch die Formulierung *ina nibzi ar-ma-a-a* das benutzte Schreibmaterial nicht mitbestimmt (*CAD* A/2 sagt ohne Begründung: Papyrus). *nibzu*, auch aramäisch belegt (cf. Cowley [Anm. 7] zu Nr. 11:6), ist jedes Dokument, vergleichbar dem hinsichtlich des Schreibmaterials offenen Terminus *sēper* im *AT*. Das Gleiche gilt von *egirtu* (*ʾiggeret*). In den aram. Texten aus Elephantine—außer Cowley cf. auch E. G. Kraeling, *The Brooklyn Aramaic Papyry* (1953)—ist das Schreibmaterial der Papyrus, dagegen sind die Briefe des Satrapen Aršam (von Babylonien nach Aegypten gesandt) aus Leder (G. R. Driver, *Aramaic Documents of the Fifth Century B.C.*² [1957]).

Plate 1. Nimrud.

(745–725),[15] sowie auf einem Relief vom Musasirfeldzug Sargons (721–705).[16] Die in den bisherigen Bildbeschreibungen offene Entscheidung: "Papyrus *oder* Leder?," kann definitiv geklärt werden: Wo das Schreibblatt gerade herunterhängt, handelt es sich um Papyrus, wo es sich unten rollt, handelt es sich um Leder (s.u.) Im Nimrudrelief (*Abb. 1*) steht hinter dem bartlosen Tontafelschreiber ein Bartloser, der auf *Papyrus* schreibt. Auf dem Fresko von Til Barsib (*Abb. 2*) folgt dem bärtigen Tontafelschreiber ein Bartloser (mit aramäisch frisiertem Haupthaar) und in dem Muṣaṣir-Relief sind beide Schreiber bartlos (Eunuchen). Auf diesen drei Darstellungen schreibt jeweils der zweite Schreiber in aramäischer Sprache auf Papyrus.

15. S. Smith, *Assyrian Sculptures in the British Museum* (1938), Taf XI (Nimrud-Relief)—F. Thureau-Dangin & M. Dunand, *Til Barsib* (1936), Taf L. Für eine Datierung unter Tiglatpileser III oder kurz davor: A. Moortgat, *Alt-Vorderasiatische Malerei* (1959), 14ff—kurz nach Tiglatpileser III: B. Hrouda, *Die Kulturgeschichte des assyrischen Flachbildes* (1965): 114.

16. J. Nougayrol, Un fragment méconnu du "Pillage de Musasir," *RA* 54 (1960): 203ff (Im Louvre wiederentdeckt und eingeordnet).

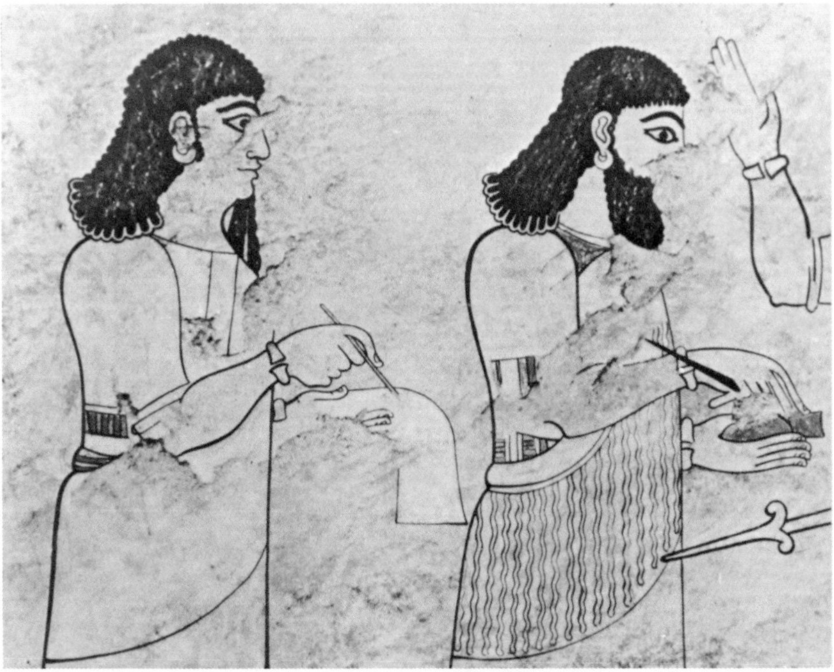

Plate 2. Til Barsib.

Von den sich bei A. Paterson, *Palace of Sennacherib* (1915) findenden Schreiberdarstellungen sind, wie E. Unger, *RLV* II, S. 430 herausstellt, nur 2 (Taf. 60/1; 70/73) mit Sanherib (705–681) zu verbinden. Das erstgenannte Relief ist unvollständig erhalten. Im Lachisrelief (Taf. 70–73) ist die Wiedergabe der den Gefangenen (mittlere Reihe) Entgegentretenden undeutlich, doch sind es auch hier 2 Schreiber. Die übrigen Darstellungen aus Niniveh (Paterson, Taf. 40/1; 52; 53/4; 94/5), sowie das Fragment in *APO* 20 (1963): 198, gehören in die Zeit Assurbanipals (668–633). Aramäisch schreibt man jetzt immer auf Leder (Zur unteren Aufrollung cf. auch den Lederstrick für die Gefangenen in Layard, Mon. II, Taf. 50) und assyrisch nicht auf einer Tontafel, sondern auf einem Diptychon. Im Fragment der Glasgow Art Gallery (*AfO* 15 [1945/51]: 137, Abb. 1) halten der bärtige und der bartlose Schreiber—entgegen der Erklärung E. Weidners—in ihrer Linken eindeutig ein Diptychon, erkennbar an der Scharnierreihe in der Mitte (*Abb. 3*). Es wäre abwegig aus den genannten jüngeren Reliefs zu schließen, daß man in der Zeit Sanheribs und Assurbanipals generell den importierten

Plate 3. Niniveh.

Papyrus durch das einheimische Leder ersetzt hat. Es ist vielmehr anzunehmen, daß den ins Feld mitgenommenen Schreibern die weniger empfindliche Lederrolle für die Weitergabe ins Hauptquartier oder in Archive als geeigneter erschien.

Es empfiehlt sich, den assyrischen Bildern noch 4 aus dem nordsyrischen Raum anzufügen. Der bekannte Orthostat aus Cinǧirli (um 730 vChr) mit dem Bild des Königs Barrakib zeigt vor diesem stehend seinen (bartlosen)

Plate 4. Maraš I.

Schreiber im Grußgestus und in der Bereitschaft, ein Diktat aufzunehmen (*ANEP*, 460). Er hält in der linken Hand einen "aegyptischen" Schreibkasten (cf. Ez. 9:2f, 11 *geset*). Dieser Schreibkasten veranlaßt C. Wendel a.a.O. (Anm. 4, S. 86) zu der These, der Schreiber des Königs Barrakib habe eine schon etwas geöffnete Lederrolle unter den linken Arm geklemmt. Aber das ist nicht richtig. Das Diptychon, dessen Scharniere markiert sind, kann auch aus glatten Holztafeln bestanden haben, deren jeweilige Texte man abwischen konnte (cf. Num. 5:23; Ps. 69:20). Sie konnten auch innen geweißt sein. In beiden Fällen war es möglich, sich der Binse und der Tusche zu bedienen. Außer diesem gut bekannten Schreiberbild sind noch 3

Plate 5. Maraš II.

Reliefs (Basaltorthostaten) heranzuziehen, die aus dem c. 50 km ndl. von Cinğirli gelegenen Maraš stammen und etwa um 700 zu datieren sind. Das am besten erhaltene Relief (M. Riemschneider, *Die Welt der Hethiter* [1954], Taf. 75) zeigt auf den Knien der Mutter (Amme?) den kleinen Prinzen Tarhumpias (*Abb. 4*). Er hat in der Rechten den Griffel und hält mit der vorgestreckten Linken an einem Band seinen Jagdfalken. Unter der geschlossenen Hand ist das Tuschgerät zu sehen. Rechts oben—sozusagen freischwebend—dann das Diptychon mit Verschlußknopf. Auch auf dem 2. Relief aus Maraš ist—entgegen kultischer Interpretation—eine Familienszene dargestellt. Vor der thronenden Fürstin und einem Esstisch steht ein größerer Junge, wohl der Sohn, dessen Bildung durch die Schreibgeräte dokumentiert wird (*Abb. 5*). Mit der Linken drückt er eine Tafel an sich. E. Akurgal (*Kunst der Hethiter* [1961]: 102) deutet diese als Tontafel, M. Riemschneider (a.a.O., zu Taf. 77) denkt an ein innen gewachstes Diptychon. Dies scheint mir zutreffender, auch wenn bei der groben Arbeit des Reliefs nichts von Scharnieren zu erkennen ist. Merkwürdig ist die Haltung der linken Hand. Man würde erwarten, daß die eingewinkelten Finger den Rand der Tafel hielten. Eine solche Handhaltung zeigt das 3. Relief von Maraš (E. Akurgal, *Späthethitische Bildkunst* [1949], Taf. 42B). Der jugend-

Plate 6. Maraš III.

liche Schreiber (*Abb. 6*), dessen Rechte den Griffel umfaßt, hält die Tafel vor seiner Brust. Die Tafel ist unten links ausgeschwungen, was sich bei Tontafeln belegen läßt, doch ist es auch hier nicht auszuschließen, daß der Bildhauer eine Klapptafel wiedergeben wollte.

2. *Das Buch.* Diese in der Überschrift der Studie verwendete Übersetzung von *sēper* ist Vereinfachung eines komplexeren Tatbestandes. Das hebr. *sēper* ist vieldeutig, vom Verbum *sāpar* = zählen, erzählen gebildet, ist es einerseits Terminus für die Mitteilung (Dokumente verschiedenster Art), unter anderem auch für einen Brief (*kātab sēper*), andererseits aber auch für die zur Beschriftung gewählte Schreibfläche (*kātab ᶜal sēper*).[17] Das Material

17. Dan. 1:4 spricht von Jünglingen, die man lehren solle *sēper* und *lāšōn* der Chaldäer. *Sēper* ist also hier: Schrift-Schreibweise! In gleichem Sinne spricht Est. 1:22; 3:12; 8:9 von *kᵉtāb*.

der Schreibfläche ist durch das Wort *sēper* nicht festgelegt. Es kann Papyrus, es kann Leder sein, aber auch die Tonscherbe (Ostrakon), auf die man mit Tinte schrieb und für die wir zahlreiche Beispiele des 8.–5. Jhs aus Palästina kennen,[18] ist ein *sēper*, wie sich dem Lachisbrief Nr. 3 entnehmen läßt.

Für Papyrus als Schreibmaterial gibt es im *AT* nur vereinzelte Zeugnisse. Da ist einmal die Schriftrolle des Baruch mit dem von Jeremia diktierten Text,[19] die der König Jojakim auf einem offenen Kohlenbecken verbrannte,[20] und außerdem die beidseitig beschriebene Schriftrolle, die der Prophet Ezechiel verzehren soll (Ez. 2:8–3:3). Auch die fliegende Schriftrolle, Nachtgesicht Sacharjas (5:1) mit den Riesenmaßen von 5 × 10 m, auf der der Fluch über die Meineidigen und Diebe verzeichnet ist,[21] mag man sich eher aus Papyrus als aus Leder vorstellen. Wegen des palästinensischen Klimas haben sich nur wenige Papyri erhalten, so in dem 17 km sdl. von Qumran gelegenen Murabba *ᶜāt* (8. Jh) und in der Höhle abu sinjeh östl. von Samaria (4. Jh).[22] Der letzten judäischen Königszeit gehören Tonbullen aus Lachis an, deren Rückseite Papyrusfasern aufweisen und so den Gebrauch von Papyrus für Urkunden bezeugen.[23] Die Griechen bezeichneten ein besonders festes aus dem Bast der Papyrusstaude hergestelltes Schiffstau als *hoplon byblinon* (Od. XXI, 391),[24] daneben kannte man (Her. V, 58) das aus dem Papyrusmark gewonnene Schreibmaterial (*chartēs*) als *byblos/biblos*.[25] Importierter Papyrus zum Schreiben war zweifellos kostbar, und die kleinasiatischen Jonier scheinen diesen Luxusartikel erst gegen Ende des 7.

18. Cf. die Liste der palästinischen Ostraka (bis 1966) von M. Weippert in H. Haag, *Bibel-Lexikon*² (1968), Sp. 1277ff. In Ägypten gibt es neben Ostraka aus Ton auch solche aus abgesplittertem Kalkstein. Von dieser Art ist auf dem *tell ed-duwēr* als (bisher) einziger Beleg ein Ostrakon des 7. Jhs mit hebr. Namen und Zahlzeichen aufgetaucht (*Biblia e Oriente* 9 [1967]: 117).

19. Nach W. Rudolph, Jeremia³ (1968): 231 hat Jeremia für das Diktat der Urrolle Niederschriften benutzt. Dies lehnt A. Baumann, Urrolle und Fasttag, *ZAW* 80 (1969): 350ff ab. Baumann nimmt unter dem Aspekt eines bevorstehenden Fasttages eine durchdachte, nicht rein chronologische Anordnung der Jeremia-Worte an. Dies macht u.E. die Gedächtnisakrobatik des Propheten vollends unwahrscheinlich.

20. Geschah das Abtrennen mit dem Federmesser jedesmal, wenn 3 bis 4 Kolumnen vorgelesen waren, oder nur einmal? Das letztere statuiert A. Baumann, a.a.O., S. 371, Anm. 66.

21. K. Galling, *Studien zur Geschichte Israels im persischen Zeitalter* (1966), S. 118ff.

22. *DJD* II (1961): 93–194: Palimpsests: Lettre, Liste des personnes (VIII. Jh); *BA* 26 (1963): 110ff.

23. Cf. die Gedalja-Siegel aus Lachis (Lachis III, S. 348 und G. Ernest Wright, *Biblical Archaeology* [1957], Abb. 128) und zahlreiche in einem Krug in Lachis (1966) gefundene Tonbullen der späten vorexilischen Zeit (Y. Aharoni in *IEJ* 8 [1968]: 165ff).

24. Für die Hellespontbrücke des Xerxes halfen die Phöniker mit Tauen einer Hanfart, die Ägypter mit solchen aus Papyrusbast (Her. VII 34).

25. Nach Her V, 58 nannten die kleinasiatischen Jonier seit alters, d.h. seit der Einfuhr aus Ägypten die Papyrusrollen (biblioi) *diphterai*, sie verwendeten mithin die Bezeichnung ihrer einheimischen Lederrollen auch für das neue Schreibmaterial.

Jhs in größerem Umfange übernommen zu haben. Dabei ist keineswegs sicher, daß der Terminus *byblos* auf die phönikische Stadt Byblos als Umschlaghafen hinweist. Man hat dies zumeist der um 1076 spielenden Geschichte des Wenamon entnommen, wo zur Bezahlung von Zedernholz unter den aus Aegypten mitgebrachten Waren neben 500 Rinderhäuten und 500 Seilen auch 500 Papyrus-Rollen genannt werden. Es kann sich um Rollen des Schreibpapyrus gehandelt haben, aber denkbar ist bei dieser Reihe auch, daß es gerollte Matten waren.[26]

Hatte man in Palästina keinen Papyrus zur Verfügung, so brauchte man keineswegs auf schriftliche Mitteilungen zu verzichten, besaß man doch in den von Schafen und Ziegen stammenden Tierhäuten ein einheimisches und gut zu verwendendes Schreibmaterial. Den Beweis für eine schon im ausgehenden 2. Jt bestehende Lederindustrie liefert der kanaanäische Name der sdl von Hebron zu suchenden Stadt *qiryat sēper* (Jud. 1:12; Jos. 15:15), was Gr einmal mit Kariathsophar transkribiert, aber immer mit *polis grammaton*—Stadt der Buchstaben, übersetzt. Für die Lage dieses Ortes hat W. F. Albright den unter seiner Leitung ausgegrabenen *tell beit mirsim* vorgeschlagen.[27] M. Noth nannte im Blick auf die im *sēl ed -dilbe* gelegenen Wasserbecken und Quellen den *tell ṭarrāme*,[28] und ich meinerseits die *chirbet rabūd*, die nach Oberflächenuntersuchungen in der Spätbronzezeit bestanden hat.[29] Die "Buch-Stadt" war jedenfalls kein Handelsplatz für den aus Ägypten importierten Papyrus, sondern lieferte in der Eisenzeit die präparierten Tierhäute nach Juda und Jerusalem. Nach Esr. 2:55 gab es unter den Nachkommen der Sklaven Salomos eine Gruppe *b^e^nē hassōperet*. Das ist zu interpretieren: "Nachkommen des mit der Leder-Bereitung Betrauten." Man darf auch nicht bezweifeln, daß die zum Schreiben präparierten Tierhäute im vorexilischen Juda und Israel den Vorrang gegenüber dem importierten Papyrus besaßen. Bei der konkreten Nennung von *sēper* bleibt gleichwohl die Materialbestimmung offen. In zwei Situationen dürfte man das Leder wegen seiner geringeren Empfindlichkeit bevorzugt haben. Einmal, wenn es um die Deponierung von Dokumenten ging, zum anderen, wenn Briefe einen weiten Weg zu durchlaufen hatten. Zu dem erstgenannten

26. Im Unterschied zu der Übersetzung und Erklärung in *AOT*, S. 75 und *ANET*, S. 28 spricht E. Edel in TGI² (1968): 46 von "großen Matten." Daß man aus Papyrus Matten (Matratzen) hergestellt hat, sagt Theophrast, Hist. plant. IV, 8, 3 (*psiathoi*).

27. W. F. Albright, *The Archaeology of Palestine and the Bible* (1932): 77ff. Der Verfasser dieser Studie denkt mit Dankbarkeit an die Sommerwochen des Jahres 1930 zurück, in denen er der Grabung beiwohnen durfte!

28. M. Noth in *JPOS* 15 (1935): 44.

29. K. Galling in *ZDPV* 71 (1954): 135ff. H. Donner, ibidem 81 (1965): 24f; A. Kuschke, ibidem 84 (1968): 86 (Brief von Y. Aharoni).

Fall kann man auf das unter Josia im Tempel gefundene, dort zuvor deponierte Gesetzbuch verweisen (2 Reg. 22:8ff; cf. Dtn. 31:24f), für den zweiten Fall wären zu nennen: der Brief des Aramäerkönigs von Damaskus nach Samaria (2 Reg. 5:5), der Brief Jeremias an die Exilierten in Babylon und der von dort kommende Protestbrief (Jer. 29:1ff, 25ff). Auch das Dokument mit den Heilsworten für die Exilierten des Nordreiches (Jer. 30–31) dürfte auf Leder geschrieben sein. Bei den Briefen[30] des Assyrerkönigs Sanherib und des Babyloniers Merodach-Baladan an Hiskia, die—entgegen Procksch—sicher nicht auf Tontafeln in akkadisch, sondern aramäisch verfaßt waren (cf. 2 Reg. 18:26ff!), wird es sich um Schreiben auf Leder gehandelt haben. Solche Briefe konnte man nach 2 Reg. 19:14; Jes. 37:15 aufrollen und ausbreiten. Dies ist sowohl bei Papyrus wie bei Leder möglich, aber paßt nicht zu einer Tontafel. Galt ein Brief mehreren Empfängern (1 Reg. 21:8f, 11; 2 Reg. 10:1f, 6) so wird von Briefen gesprochen, obwohl es nicht mehrere gleichlautende Schreiben waren. Instruktiv ist in dieser Hinsicht Jer. 25:25,29, wo das an die Priester von Jerusalem gerichtete Schreiben im Plural, beim Vorlesen vor einer Person im Singular (*sēper*) bezeichnet wird. Bei der doppelten Urkunde wechseln in Jer. 32:10,14 die Numeri. Das ist durchaus einleuchtend, da es sich um zwei gleichlautende Texte auf einem (teils versiegelten, teils offenen) Blatt handelt. Wenn wir analog gestaltete, zT auch in Krügen aufbewahrte Verträge im ptolemäisch-römischen Ägypten auf Papyrus kennen,[31] so beweist das für die Jerusalemer Urkunde bzw. deren Schreibmaterial nichts. Da aber die Buchrolle des Baruch (Jer. 36) aus Papyrus bestand, ist es sehr wohl möglich, daß auch der Ackerbauvertrag Jeremias auf Papyrus geschrieben war. Was die dem Deuteronomisten zugänglichen (auf Grund offizieller Annalen verfaßten) "Notizen der Tage" der Könige von Israel und Juda (cf. auch 1 Reg. 11:41 für Salomo) angeht, so lesen wir, daß sie *ᶜal sēper* geschrieben vorlagen. Da synchronistisch geordnete Klapptafeln—so Procksch—sicher nicht in Frage kommen, wird man an Lederrollen zu denken haben, denen der Deuteronomist die ihm wichtigen Notizen entnahm. Sie hatten archivalischen Wert, ähnlich wie die Lederrollen am persischen Hof (cf. Esr. 4:15; 6:1f)[32] und

30. In 2 Reg. 19:14 bzw. Jes. 37:14 ist statt pl der Singular zu lesen (so auch *BHS*). Nach 𝔊 Jes. 39:1 (2 Reg. 20:12) kommen Briefe "und Gesandte" und Geschenke nach Jerusalem. Hier sind *sᵉpārīm* und (?) *sarīsīm* vermutlich zwei Wahllesarten der 𝔊 *sᵉpārīm* meint jedenfalls an dieser Stelle ein einziges Schreiben.

31. Cf. L. Fischer, *ZAW* 30 (1910): 137f; E. Hammershaimb, *VT* 7 (1957): 24f.

32. Im Abschluß seines Rechenschaftsberichtes über seinem Grabe in Behistun berichtet Darius I (Col. IV, 88: R. Kent, *Old Persian* [1953]: 132), daß von seiner arisch abgefaßten Inschrift Abschriften, d.h. Übersetzungen auf Tontafeln (in Neubabylonisch) und auf Pergament/Leder (in Aramäisch) angefertigt und in die Provinzen seines Reiches geschickt

die in Jerusalem deponierte Urkunde über die zurückgegebenen Tempelgeräte (Esr. 1:7–11).[33] In Jer. 50:61 wird akzentuiert von einem *sēper* gesprochen. Das meint ein einzelnes Blatt, auf dem die aus verschiedenen Zeiten stammenden Orakel Jeremias gegen Babylon zusammengefaßt waren. Das anbefohlene Versenken des Blattes im Eufrat läßt eher an Leder als an Papyrus denken.

3. *Das Blatt.* Das dritte Stichwort unserer Studie zielt auf den nur einmal im AT (Jes. 8:1) vorkommenden Terminus *gillāyōn.* In den spannenden Monaten des syrisch-ephraimitischen Krieges soll der Prophet Jesaja auf ein großes *gillāyōn* mit einem Menschen-Griffel den geheimnisvollen Namen seines Sohnes ("Eilebeute-Raschraub") schreiben und sich dazu zwei zuverlässige, namentlich genannte Zeugen nehmen. *gillāyōn* gehört mit *gālā* zusammen, was: glätten, polieren bedeutet.[34] Unabdinglich ist bei Papyrus das Glätten,[35] begegnet aber auch bei der Präparierung von Tierhäuten.[36] Auszuscheiden hat eine—von *gālal* abgeleitete?—Übersetzung von gillāyōn mit "Siegel,"[37] zumal dann nicht von "schreiben," sondern von "gravieren" (*pātaḥ*) gesprochen sein müßte. Wie von mir in *ZDPV* 56 (1933): 209ff des Näheren dargelegt ist, bestand der Zweck der Urkunde darin, das Kind für ein Jerusalemer Geburtsregister anzumelden. Ein derartiges Register setzt auch Jer. 22:30 voraus. Bei den wenigen Worten des Textes—außer dem Kindesnamen nur die Zeugenunterschriften (und das Datum?), fragt man sich, warum der *gillāyōn* groß sein soll. Mein Vorschlag war und ist *gilyōn gōrāl* = Los- (Allmende-) Blatt zu lesen. P. Katz hat in *JThSt* 37 (1946): 130f aufgezeigt, daß 𝔊$^{A}$ mit *chartou tomon kainou megalou* sowohl *gādōl* = *megalou* als auch *gōrāl* = kainou (verschrieben aus *klērou*) gekannt hat (Cf. jetzt auch *BHSt*). In dem "Blatt" sehen 𝔙 (tabula) und 𝔖 (*lu*$^{a}$*ḥ*)

---

wurden. Daß der aramäische Text der Behistunschrift tatsächlich in die fernen Provinzen gelangt ist, beweist die freilich jüngere Nachschrift auf Papyrus, die die Juden in Elephantine besaßen (Cowley, S. 248ff). Nach Diodor 2,32,4 waren die Annalen am persischen Hof auf Lederrollen geschrieben, die man auch für die *siprayya* in den Schatzhäusern in Ekbatana (Esr. 6:1ff) voraussetzen muß.

33. K. Galling, *Studien zur Geschichte Israels* (1966), S. 78ff.

34. Im Boutique-Katalog Jes. 3:18ff werden nach diversen Schmucksachen der Jerusalemer Frauen in Vers 22f Textilien genannt, darunter auch gilyonim (𝔊: *diaphanē Lakōnika* = durchsichtige Gewänder). Bestanden sie aus Baumwolle (cf. Her. III, 47.106) oder aus Papyrus (cf. *Plin. Hist. nat.*, XIII, 22)? In einem assyrischen Vertragstext (*AfO* VIII [1932]: 20) wird gesagt, daß man bei Vertragsbruch würde Papyruskleider schandenhalber tragen müssen! Da *gālā* = glätten/polieren auch von Bronzeplatten gesagt werden kann (Sir 12,11c), erklären—sachlich zu Unrecht sowohl 𝔙 als 𝔗 in Jes. 3:22 die *gilyōnīm* als Spiegel.

35. A. Lucas, *Ancient Egyptian Materials and Industries* 4 (1962): 139.

36. S. Krauss, *Talmudiche Archäologie II* (1911): 262f.

37. So R. P. P. Auvray in *La sainte Bible* (1957)—in der Anmerkung allerdings in Frage gestellt.

eine Holztafel. Aquila (*diphtherōma*), Th (*kephalis*) und wahrscheinlich auch Sym (*teuchos*) zielen auf Leder. Aber diese Jahrhunderte jüngeren Vorstellungen sind ebenso wenig beweisend wie die der Mischna (Jad. III, 4) die unter *gilyōnīm* die unbeschriebenen Randstücke einer unbrauchbar gewordenen Schriftrolle (aus Leder/Pergament) verstanden wissen wollen.[38] Da für Juda und Jerusalem durch die Palimpseste von Murabba ᶜāt (s. Anm. 22) der Gebrauch von Papyrus im 8. Jh. nachweisbar ist, dürfte es sich auch bei dem in Jes. 8:1 genannten *gillāyōn* um ein Papyrusblatt gehandelt haben. Dies ist nach D. Jones, *ZAW* 67 (1955): 230f auch die Meinung von D. Diringer, während G. R. Driver nur allgemein von einem Plakat spricht. In Jes. 8:1 heißt es weiter, daß der Prophet die Aufzeichnung *bᵉḥereṭ ᵃᵉnōš* durchführen soll, das hieße wörtlich übersetzt: mit einem Jedermanns-Griffel. Aber dies ist ja sowohl für den schreibenden Jesaja als die unterzeichnenden Zeugen doch sachlich das Naheliegende, und auch die Kontrastierung mit der "Gottesschrift" (Ex. 32:16) hilft nicht weiter. Nach H. Gressmann, *Der Messias* (1929): 329 soll man vokalisieren *bᵉḥereṭ ʾanūš*, was freilich nicht "mit hartem Griffel," sondern im Gegenteil: "mit schwachem = weichem Griffel" zu übersetzen ist (cf. *KBL*³, *ānaš* I). "Schwacher Griffel" ist eine (metri causa gewählte?) poetische Formulierung für die zur Tintenschrift benutzte Binse, hebr. *ᶜēṭ* (Jer. 8:8 𝔊: *schoinos*; Ps. 45:2). Der für einen Stein (Jer. 17: 1f ist im Zusammenhang mit dem Bildwort vom "steinernen Herzen" in Ez. 11:19; 36:26 zu sehen) oder für eine Felswand benutzte Griffel (Hi 19:23f)[39] ist ein *ᶜēṭ barzel*.

Abschließend noch ein Wort zu dem Substantivum *sōpēr*. Der ungenannte Schreiber von *meṣad hashavyahu*, der auf einem Ostrakon die Klage eines erregten Arbeiters wortwörtlich aufzeichnete (*KAI*, 200; *TGT*², S. 70f) mag außer privaten auch amtliche Schreiben erledigt haben, wie die für die Offiziere tätigen Schreiber der Lachis-Ostraka. An Berufsschreiber wird man auch bei der Aufzeichnung der Tora Jahwes (Jer. 8:8) zu denken haben, da der Vorwurf Jeremias den verantwortlichen Priestern gilt, wenn er von einem Lügengriffel der Schreiber spricht. *Sōpēr* konnte aber auch der Titel eines hohen Beamten sein, der neben dem "Sprecher" (*mazkīr*)—nach ägyptischem Vorbild[40]—seit den Tagen Davids und Salomos in Jerusalem

38. K. G. Kuhn, Giljonim und Sifre ninim, *BZAW* 26 (1960): 24ff.

39. Der Wunsch Hiobs: "Geschähe es doch nur, daß meine Worte geschrieben würden in einer Inschrift, daß sie eingemeißelt würden mit eisernen Griffel und mit Blei, als Zeugen ausgehauen im Felsen"! wird von den nachfolgenden Versen her als Hinweis auf eine der Rechtfertigung dienenden Grabschrift zu verstehen sein. Cf. K. Galling, in *WO* II (1954): 1ff.

40. R. de Vaux, Titres et fonctionaires égyptiens à la cour de David et Salomon, *RB* 48 (1939): 394ff; J. Begrich, Sopher und Mazkir, *ZAW* 58 (1940/41): 1ff.

amtierte. Dieser *sōpēr* unterstand unmittelbar dem König, führte den Ministervorsitz in einer speziellen "Halle des Schreibers" (Jer. 36; cf. *PJ* 27 [1931]: 51ff) kontrollierte die Tempelkasse und überbrachte Anfragen des Königs an Prophet und Prophetin (2 Reg. 12:11; 19:2; 22:3,8,12).[41] In der persischen Periode waren dem Statthalter in Samaria und Jerusalem Schreiber beigeordnet, die in analoger Weise ein führendes Amt besaßen (Esr. 4:8f,17,23; Neh. 13:13). Ihnen vergleichbar sind die Provinz- und Finanzschreiber in den Elephantinetexten (A. Cowley, Nr. 2:12,14; 17:1,6) und wohl auch die Schreiber im Dienst des Satrapen Aršam (Anm. 14). Mag die Bezeichnung *sōpēr māhīr* zunächst den Ausbildungsgrad bezeichnen (= der geschickte Schreiber),[42] wie in Ps. 45:2, so begegnet sie allgemeiner gefaßt titelartig bei dem weisen Minister Achikar.[43] In dem aramäisch verfaßten Edikt Artaxerxes' II. wird Esra ein "Schreiber des Gesetzes des Himmelsgottes genannt" (Esr. 7:12), womit ein vom Großkönig legitimiertes Amt innerhalb der babylonischen Diaspora gemeint sein dürfte.[44] Einen anderen Akzent gibt der Chronist (Esr. 7:6) diesem Titel mit der Übersetzung: "ein geschickter Schreiber im Gesetz des Mose," denn er versteht darunter im Sinn seiner Zeit einen im Gesetz bewanderten Schrift-Gelehrten. Ein derartiger Aspekt ist dann zugleich die Voraussetzung dafür, daß man nach IV. Esra. 14:18ff in Esra den Autor (Kompilator) des hebräischen Kanons sehen konnte.

41. Der "Briefschreiber" des Fürsten von Byblos, der in der Geschichte des Wenamon zweimal erwähnt wird (cf. *TGI*² [1968]: 47f) ist dessen Minister im Amt eines *sōpēr*.

42. E. Ullendorf, The Contribution of South Semitics to Hebrew Lexicography, *VT*, VI [1956]: 195, betont zu recht, daß *māhīr* nicht auf die Schnelligkeit des Schreibens zielt. *Māhīr* bedeutet: erfahren-geschickt. Zwischen dem *sōpēr māhīr* und dem *sš m-h-r* im Papyrus Anastasi I besteht kein Zusammenhang, letzterer gehört in einen militärischen Bereich. Auch kennt der Verfasser den *t-p-r y-d-ʾ* (= den sōpēr *yōdeʿ*). Cf. A. F. Rainey, The Soldier-Scribe in Papyrus Anastasi I, *JNES* 26 (1967): 58–60.

43. Text bei A. Cowley, S. 212 (Col. 1, 1ff), deutsche Übersetzung von H. Gressmann in *AOT* (1926): 454.

44. K. Galling, *Studien zur Geschichte Israels* (1966): 166f.

# Tell el-Kheleifeh Inscriptions

NELSON GLUECK

THE central importance of Tell el-Kheleifeh, located approximately in the center of the north shore of the Gulf of Aqabah, the eastern arm of the Red Sea, is illustrated, among other things, by various inscriptions found there. Some are penned in ink or incised on ostraca of sherds of kiln baked pottery. Others stem from seal impressions stamped on the pottery before firing. In one instance, the stone of a seal signet ring bore a clear retrograde inscription reading, *lytm*, "belonging to Jotham"[1] (Pl. 1). They are invaluable for establishing periods of occupation.

Few in number, limited in scope sometimes to a single personal name or to fragmentary lists of names, or broken receipts for wine imports, the inked, incised, or impressed ostraca inscriptions give important information about some of the local, national, and international conditions and influences affecting the economic, cultural, and religious life of Tell el-Kheleifeh in different periods.

Minaean, Judaean, Edomite, Phoenician, and Aramaic inscriptions were found. Some of them belonged to the late seventh, or first half of the sixth, and others to the fifth–fourth centuries B.C. They deal with peoples and scripts extending from Phoenicia to northern Arabia. Their approximate dates can be established by the excavation levels in which they were found,

1. Reg. no. 7022; Avigad, *BASOR* 163 (Oct. 1961): 18–22; Glueck, *BA* XXVIII:3 (1965): 86; *BASOR* 79 (Oct. 1940): 13–15.

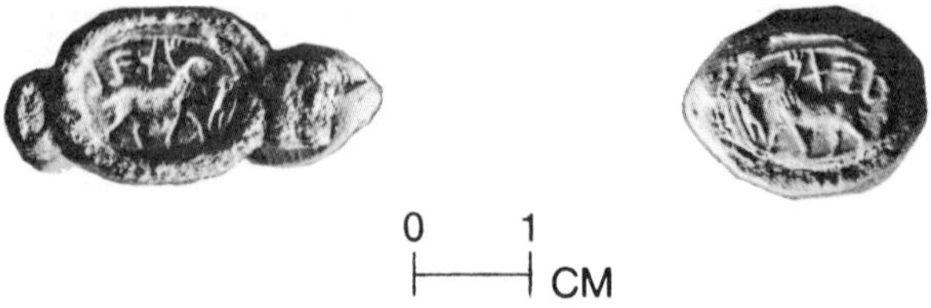


Plate 1. Jotham seal and impression, reading *l y t m*.

the kinds of pottery on which they were penned or incised or stamped, the character of the scripts employed, and the types of names listed.

## CURSIVE EDOMITE SCRIPT

One of the most interesting ostraca, reg. no. 6043, was excavated near the top of the downward sloping southeast side of Tell el-Kheleifeh[2] (Pl. 4), close to the surface in Level IV, dating to the seventh–sixth centuries B.C. The entire Period IV level of occupation, with its several subdivisions, is Edomite. Taking advantage of the disturbed political situation attendant upon the Syro–Ephraimitic war, the Edomites regained control of Elath in

Plate 2. Edomite lapidary graffito on small jar.

2. Room 70, P:16, Neg. 22,689A-C.

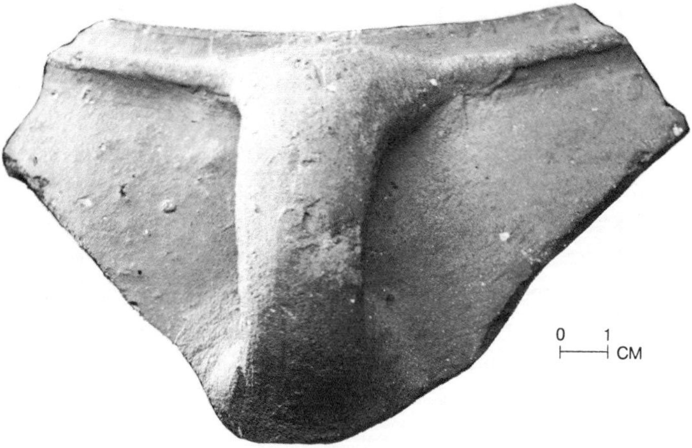


Plate 3. Obverse of cooking pot fragment with profiled rim.

733 B.C. (II Kings 16:6), with Judah never again strong enough to dispute it.[3] Elath remained Edomite until near the end of the sixth century B.C. For some time after their recapture of Elath, the Edomites apparently did not undertake the construction of the completely new city of Period IV. Its history extends from about the end of the eighth or more probably from some time in the early seventh century B.C., to about the end of the sixth century B.C.

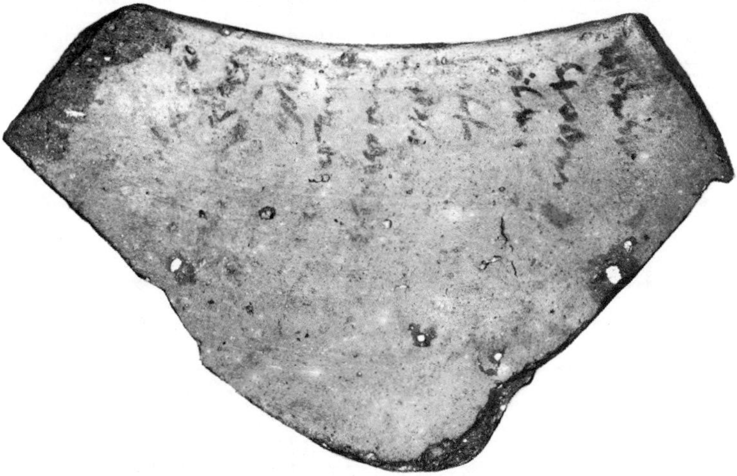

Plate 4. Reverse of cooking pot fragment with Edomite inscription.

3. Glueck, *BASOR* 72 (Dec. 1938): 9–11; *BA* XXVIII:3 (1965): 86–87; Albright, *BASOR* 82 (April 1941): 14–15.

Ostracon, reg. no. 6043 (Pl. 3), was part of a wheelmade, wet-smoothed, hard-baked cooking pot with elaborately profiled or ribbed or collared rim, to which originally were attached two loop-handles, one on each side, with oval section. We had previously found numerous examples of this type of cooking pot at many places in Edom and Moab, and elsewhere in Transjordan, and had assigned them to the latter part of Iron II between the eighth and sixth centuries B.C.,[4] when it went out of existence.[5] In view of the level in which it occurred and the generality of other potsherds found with it, it is impossible to date this particular sherd, with its profiled rim and attached loop-handle, any earlier than the end of the seventh century B.C., and any later than the end of the sixth century B.C., with the likelihood that it may belong to the first half of the sixth century B.C.[6]

The fragment of pottery used for ostracon, reg. no. 6043, made a very convenient piece of writing material. The scribe could grasp the loop-handle on the outer surface while he dipped his brush into the ink and painted the words on the inner surface in rows at right angles to the top of the inside of the rim. The inner surface is brownish-buff and the outer is grayish-buff in color, with numerous small and comparatively large white grits and small shallow holes or depressions appearing on both surfaces.

The ostracon contains an Edomite name list[7] written in the cursive Edomite script.[8] As will be seen, the Qosᶜanal seal impressions and the room 49 graffito on a jar (reg. no. 374), which we now read *lᶜAmiru(n)*,[9] found also in Level IV, are inscribed in the lapidary Edomite script.[10] To judge from the script alone, the date of the Edomite ostracon, reg. no. 6043, belongs to the seventh–sixth centuries B.C.,[11] corresponding thus both to the level in which it was found and to the kind of Iron II cooking pot fragment on which it was written.

The faint writing on ostracon, reg. no. 10,007, seems also to belong to the Edomite cursive script.[12]

Visible on ostracon, reg. no. 6043, are parts of ten lines of Edomite

4. Glueck, *BASOR* 82, p. 3; *AASOR* XV, p. 136; Albright, Tell Beit Mirsim, *AASOR* XII, p. 81, Pls. 35, 56; p. 88, Pl. 40:2.
5. Albright, *BASOR* 82, p. 15; cf. Harding, *QDAP* XI (1945): 71:27.
6. Albright, *BASOR* 82, pp. 11, 14–15; Naveh, *BASOR* 183 (Oct. 1966): 30; *Yediot* XXX:1–2 (1966): 41.
7. Albright, *BASOR* 82, p. 13; *BASOR* 71 (Oct. 1938): 17; Glueck, *OSJ*, pp. 110–11.
8. Naveh, *Yediot* (Hebrew) XXX:1–2 (1966): 41; *BASOR* 183, p. 30, n. 25, characterizes the script of ostracon, reg. no. 6043, as being Edomite; cf. Albright, *BASOR* 82, p. 14.
9. Glueck, Albright, *BASOR* 71, pp. 17–18; Glueck, *BASOR* 72, pp. 9–13; see below, p. 235.
10. Albright, *BASOR* 82, p. 14; Naveh, *BASOR* 183, p. 30, n. 25.
11. Cf. Albright, *BASOR* 82, p. 11.
12. Cf. below, pp. 237 f.

cursive script containing a list of Edomite names. There were certainly originally two more lines above the top one, another below the bottom one, and clear traces of previous writing of a palimpsest between lines 1 and 2, 2 and 3, 9 and 10. Originally, the horizontal lines of the ostracon, beginning at the right side, stretched across most of the widest expanse of the ostracon in its present form. Only the first parts of the lines were legible when the ostracon was discovered. I have corrected my original transliteration in light of suggestions by others:[13]

| | | | |
|---|---|---|---|
| Line 1: | *rʿʾl*[14] | | |
| 2: | *bdqw(s)*[15] | *bdʾ*[16] | *bd--*[17] |
| 3: | *šlm*[18] | | |
| 4: | *qwsb (nh)*[19] | | |
| 5: | *pgʿqws*[20] | | |
| 6: | *nʿm (n)*[21] | | |
| 7: | *škk*[22] | | |
| 8: | *rpʾ*[23] | *rph*[24] | |
| 9: | *pgʿq (w) s*[25] | | |
| 10: | *qwsny*[26] | | |

## CURSIVE PHOENICIAN

Ostracon, reg. no. 2070 (Pl. 6), written in cursive Phoenician[27] was found near the bottom of Level V. The ostracon sherd belonged originally to a rather coarse jar, wheelmade, wet-smoothed, hard-baked, grayish-brown, with medium and tiny white grits. The obverse side and, to an even

13. Cf. Albright, *BASOR* 82, pp. 13–14; Naveh, *Yediot* XXX:1–2, pp. 39–44; *BASOR* 183, pp. 27–30.
14. Albright, *BASOR* 82, p. 13; Naveh, *Yediot* XXX:1–2, p. 41; *BASOR* 183, p. 28; Cross, verbally. The reading, *rgʿʾl* also seems possible to me; cf. *rgʿʾ* in Lidzbarski, *Handbuch der Nordsemitischen Epigraphik* (*Handbuch*), p. 368.
15. Suggested to me by F. M. Cross.
16. Albright, *BASOR* 82, pp. 13–14.
17. Naveh, *BASOR* 183, pp. 27–28.
18. Albright, *BASOR* 82, p. 13.
19. Albright, *BASOR* 82, pp. 13–14; cf. Naveh, *BASOR* 183, p. 28; *Yediot* XXX:1–2, p. 41.
20. Albright, *BASOR* 82, p. 13; cf. Naveh, *BASOR* 183, p. 28; *Yediot* XXX:1–2, p. 41.
21. I now suggest *nʿm (n)*. Cf. *BASOR* 82, p. 13.
22. Albright, *BASOR* 82, p. 13; Naveh, *BASOR* 183, p. 28; Cross, orally.
23. Naveh, *BASOR* 183, p. 28; *Yediot* XXX:1–2, p. 41; Cross, orally.
24. Albright, *BASOR* 82, p. 13.
25. Albright, *BASOR* 82, p. 13; Naveh, *Yediot* XXX:1–2, p. 41; *BASOR* 183, p. 28; Cross, orally.
26. Albright, *BASOR* 82, p. 13.
27. Naveh, *BASOR* 183, p. 27; *Yediot* XXX:1–2, p. 39.

greater degree, the reverse side are pitted with small indentations that occurred during the baking of the jar, the clay of which was not well levigated. The inscriptions on both sides of this ostracon seem to come from different writers[28] and are considerably different from the writing on ostraca, reg. nos. 2071 and 2069,[29] with the exception of the last line of reg. 2071.[30]

The obverse side of the ostracon has five lines of inscription (Pl. 5) some of the letters of which are blurred or faded. The difficulty I originally found with the form of the *lamedh* in lines 3 and 4, if the script were to be considered Aramaic, has been removed by Naveh's study showing that this ostracon is written in a Phoenician cursive script of the Persian period[31] and belongs to the late fifth or early fourth century B.C.[32] The dating of the script fits in excellently with the Level V it was found in, which on purely archaeological criteria is to be dated to the fifth–fourth centuries B.C. This is the date we had previously given to the three ostraca found in Level V of Room 50.[33] The transliteration is:

| Reg. 2070 obverse | | 2070 reverse | |
|---|---|---|---|
| 1. | ᶜ*(bd)---m*[34] | 1. | *plg*ᵓ[39] |
| 2. | ᶜ*bd*ᵓ *š(m)n*[35] | 2. | *knšy*[40] |
| 3. | ᵓ*bšlm*[36] | 3. | *(bdrmn)*[41] |
| 4. | *šlmlḥy*[37] | | |
| 5. | *š*ᶜ*db*ᵓ*l*[38] | | |

28. Albright, *BASOR* 82, p. 11; Naveh, *BASOR* 183, p. 27; *Yediot* XXX:1–2, p. 39.

29. Glueck, *BASOR* 80 (Dec. 1940): 4–8; Naveh, *Yediot* XXX:1–2, p. 39; *BASOR* 183, p. 27; see below, pp. 232 f.

30. Glueck, *BASOR* 80, pp. 4, 5, 7.

31. Naveh, *BASOR* 183, pp. 27–28; *Yediot* XXX:1–2, p. 39.

32. Naveh, *BASOR* 183, p. 27; *Yediot* XXX:1–2, p. 39.

33. Glueck, *BASOR* 80, pp. 4–10; ostraca, reg. nos. 2071, 2069, 7094.

34. The first word may read ᶜ*bd*; we read the last consonant of the second word as a *mem*; cf. Glueck, *BASOR* 82, p. 7; Cooke, *A Text-Book of North-Semitic Inscriptions*, p. 26, under Sidon, line 2.

35. Cf. Glueck, *BASOR* 82, p. 7; Naveh, *BASOR* 183, p. 27; *Yediot* XXX:1–2, p. 40; Lidzbarski, *Handbuch*, p. 417, Pl. IV:1, line 2; IV:2, line 2.

36. Glueck, *BASOR* 82, pp. 7, 9; Naveh, *BASOR* 183, p. 27.

37. Naveh, *Yediot* XXX:1–2, p. 40; *BASOR* 183, p. 28, n. 9; Glueck, *BASOR* 80, p. 4 for mention of "*lḥy*."

38. Glueck, *BASOR* 82, p. 7; Cross has orally suggested the possibility of reading "*šmr*" instead of "*š*ᶜ*d*"; cf. Naveh, *Yediot* XXX:1–2, p. 40; *BASOR* 183, pp. 27, 28.

39. Glueck, *BASOR* 82, p. 9; Cross has suggested to me the possibility of a *samekh* instead of a *gimel*; Naveh, *BASOR* 183, p. 27 reads "*p*-ᵓ."

40. Naveh, *Yediot* XXX:1–2, p. 40; *BASOR* 183, p. 28, n. 12; Glueck, *BASOR* 82, p. 9. For "*knšy(tn)*" cf. Lidzbarski, *Handbuch*, p. 298.

41. Cross has suggested to me the possibility of reading the first two letters of the last line as "*bd*." I believe that in the blob of the second last letter of the bottom line I can make out a "*mem*" and would read the final letter as a "*nun*" and the third last letter as a "*resh*," thus

Plate 5. Obverse of ostracon 2070.

Two of the three ostraca found in Level V at Tell el-Kheleifeh, together with the Phoenician ostracon, reg. 2070, were written in the cursive Aramaic script of the late fifth, early fourth, centuries B.C.[42] They are ostraca, reg. nos. 2071 and 2069. Belonging to this cursive Aramaic script group of the fifth–fourth centuries is also ostracon, reg. no. 7094, found just below the top surface and undoubtedly belonging originally to Level V. We shall return to it later on.

Plate 6. Reverse of ostracon 2070.

getting "*rmn.*" This entire word would read then *Bod-rumman*; cf. Lidzbarski, *Ephemeris für semitische Epigraphik III*, p. 316; *Handbuch*, p. 369; Ryckmans, *RB* 48 (1939): 247–49. The *Bod* element occurs also in the first part of the second line of ostracon, reg. no. 6043, as Albright originally recognized; cf. Albright, *BASOR* 82, p. 13; Lidzbarski, *Ephemeris III*, p. 304.

42. Naveh, *BASOR* 183, p. 27; *Yediot* XXX:1–2, p. 41; Albright, *BASOR* 82, pp. 11, 14; Glueck, *BASOR* 80, pp. 3–5.

## CURSIVE ARAMAIC

The cursive Aramaic, fifth–fourth century inscription of ostracon, reg. no. 2071 (Pl. 7), consists of four lines, now broken at the left, brushed onto a sherd of a thin-walled, hard-baked, wheelmade jug of brownish-buff ware with numerous tiny white grits. The inscription is almost at right angles to the direction of the wheel marks visible on the inner surface of the sherd. Under the four visible lines may be seen clear traces of an older erased text or palimpsest. The transliteration of reg. 2071 reads:

1. *šlmn ʿbd*
2. *lḥy ʿbd*[43]
3. *bʿlyt (n)*[44]
4. *ʾšbʿ (l)*[45]

Plate 7. Ostracon 2071.

## OSTRACON REG. NO. 2069

The finest and clearest of all the Tell el-Kheleifeh ostraca was another in cursive Aramaic script of the fifth–fourth centuries B.C. found together with ostraca 2070 and 2071. This ostracon, reg. no. 2069 (Pl. 8), is on a fragment of a wheelmade jug of hard-baked, reddish-buff ware with numerous

43. The *ḥeth* is somewhat different from the one in the Phoenician ostracon, reg. no. 2070, where the same name of *luḥai* occurs. (For the diminutive vocalization, *luḥai*, see Albright in *BASOR* 80, p. 6, n. 6); in fact the Phoenician *ḥeth* in line 4 of reg. no. 2070 may furnish the explanation for the second character of the fourth line of reg. no. 2071, which then might possibly be read as *ʾḥbʿ(m)*, tentatively suggested to me by Cross, instead of the suggested *ʾšbʿ(l)*; cf. I Chron. 8:33; Albright in *BASOR* 80, p. 7, n. 8a.

44. Glueck, *BASOR* 80, p. 7.

45. Glueck, *BASOR* 80, pp. 4, 7; Albright, *BASOR* 80, p. 7, n. 8a had originally suggested the possibility of reading *ʾšbʿ(l)*, Eshbaal (I Chron. 8:33). This fourth line would seem to have been written by a different hand than the one that penned the first three lines and to be related less to the Aramaic cursive script of the lines above it than to the Phoenician script of reg. no. 2070; cf. Naveh, *BASOR* 183, p. 27.

Plate 8. Ostracon 2069.

tiny grits. The remaining part of the ostracon is almost as clear as when it was first written.[46] It is strikingly similar to one found by Aharoni at Tell Arad, dated to the same fifth–fourth centuries B.C. period of Aramaic ostraca.[47] Its transliteration is as follows:

| | | |
|---|---|---|
| *qrplgs*[48] | *ṭpyʾn*[49] | (?)[50] |
| *ḥmr* | *ṭpyʾn* | II |
| *ḥmr* | (?) | |

## OSTRACON 7094

As Albright[51] first pointed out, ostracon fragment, reg. no. 7094 (Pl. 12), belongs to the same type of late fifth–fourth centuries B.C. cursive Aramaic script as ostraca, reg. nos. 2071 and 2069. Ostracon 7094, found just below the surface, must be assigned to the almost completely worn away Level V.

46. Glueck, *BASOR* 80, pp. 6–10; Albright, *BASOR* 82, p. 11.

47. Aharoni and Amiran, *Yediot* XXVII:4 (1963): 225–26, Fig. 3 and Pl. 7:2; cf. Dothan, *IEJ* 15:3 (1965): 141, 151, Fig. 7:13.

48. Albright in *BASOR* 80, p. 9, n. 12, has suggested that the word *qrplgs*, if correct may be the Greek καρπολόγος, occurring in fourth century B.C. inscriptions and denoting a collector of taxes in kind.

49. Prof. H. C. Youtie, in a letter of Nov. 15, 1940, to W. F. Albright, *BASOR* 80, p. 8, n. 11, identifies *ṭpyʾn* with Jewish–Aramaic *ṭpyʾ*, Mishnaic *ṭāfî* "jug with narrow neck" used for wine and oil. Albright points out that: "The Aramaic word must be vocalized *ṭᶜ fîʾah*, plur. *ṭᶜfîʾân*, as in our ostracon (reg. no. 2069); it is derived from the Aramaic stem *ṭpʾ*, 'to close, seal tight,' and means 'closed, sealed'." Thus the second line of ostracon, reg. no. 2069, *ḥᶜmar ṭᶜfîʾân II*, may be translated as "wine, jars, 2."

50. The enigmatic, partly blurred sign at the end of the first line seems to represent a numeral, even as the two diagonal strokes at the end of the second line seem to signify the number 2.

51. Albright, *BASOR* 82, p. 11.

It bears a single name, Barshallum, appearing in transliteration as *brslm*.[52] The clarity of the script compares favorably with that of ostracon 2069. It is written on a hard-baked, wheelmade, wet-smoothed jar fragment of grayish-brown ware. The likelihood is that the extant final letter should be the first long stroke of a *mem* rather than of a *waw*, such as I had originally read it.[53] Such a *mem*, however, would be different from the one in ostracon 2069 and indeed closer to the Edomite cursive *mem* on ostracon 6043 (which mentions a *slm* [*shallum*] in the third line) and to that of the lapidary Edomite *mem* of the graffito 374, both of which belong, probably, as we have seen above, to the first half of the sixth century B.C.[54]

## LAPIDARY EDOMITE

A lapidary Edomite graffito was found on one of four small, round-bottomed jars[55] (Pl. 2), in one of the Level IV Tell el-Kheleifeh rooms, together with a broken bowl with a *qwsᶜnl* seal impression above its ring base.[56] The jar is wheelmade, wet-smoothed, of light creamy gray ware with numerous small grits, medium-baked, with a friable surface with numerous surface holes and breaks. The surface of the vessel is so soft that it is difficult to make out exactly whether or not some of the lines of the graffito, incised after baking, were original. Like the related lapidary Qausᶜanal seal impressions and the cursive Edomite ostracon, reg. no. 6043, this graffito is to be dated to about the first half of the sixth century B.C.[57] Naveh dates them to the seventh–sixth centuries B.C.[58]

My copy of the graffito is somewhat different from that of Harding.[59] The first three letters are clear, namely the *lamedh*, the open *ᶜayin* (which appears in the lapidary Qausᶜanal seal impressions and the cursive Edomite ostracon, reg. no. 6043) and the *mem*. The fifth and sixth letters are more difficult to read. The fifth letter may be a *resh*, related to the *resh* at the beginning of the eighth line of ostracon 6043, and the sixth letter may be a *waw* related to the

52. Glueck, *BASOR* 80, p. 9, Fig. 5 and p. 10; Sachau, *Aramäische Papyrus und Ostraka aus . . . Elephantine*, Papyrus 18, col. 1:20; 3:1; 5:3.

53. Glueck, *BASOR* 80, p. 8.

54. Naveh, *Yediot* XXX:1–2, p. 43, n. 26; *BASOR* 183, p. 30.

55. Reg. no. 374.

56. Reg. no. 381.

57. Albright, in a letter to me of Aug. 13, 1938, had shown then that the letters of the graffito could not precede the seventh century B.C. nor be later than the fifth, and in all probability belonged to the sixth century B.C.

58. Naveh, *BASOR* 183, pp. 29–30; *Yediot* XXX:1–2, pp. 42, 43; Albright in *BASOR* 71, pp. 17–18; Glueck, *BASOR* 72, pp. 9–13; *OSJ*, p. 110; Albright, *BASOR* 82, cf. reg. no. 6043, pp. 12–13.

59. Glueck, *BASOR* 71, p. 17, Fig. 7; Harding, *BASOR* 72, p. 9, Fig. 2.

*waw* of the *qws* words in ostracon 6043, particularly to the *waw* in line 4 there. The sixth letter could also possibly be a *nun*, although the *waw* seems more likely.

The fourth letter is particularly difficult to read because of a large surface break in the right center. The short diagonal line at the outer lower left of the fourth letter seems to be superfluous and accidental and therefore the rest of the letter could possibly be read as *yodh*. I had originally attempted the transliteration as *lᶜmṣrn* (belonging to *ᶜAm(ṣrn)*.[60] My present suggestion is that the Edomite graffito 374 be transliterated as follows: *lᶜmyrw(n)*, that is, "belonging to *ᶜAmīrû* (or *ᶜAmirân*)."[61]

## OSTRACON REG. NO. 8058

Ostracon, reg. no. 8058[62] (Pl. 9), belongs to finds near the surface that can be assigned to Period V of the fifth–fourth centuries B.C. at Tell el-Kheleifeh. Incised on a small, hard-baked, well-levigated, creamy buff sherd with tiny grits are remains of three lines of inscriptions. Only the bottom tips of the top line are visible, if indeed they belong at all to letters. The second line is composed of somewhat crudely incised letters, with faint illegible traces of a fourth one. The transliteration is *ᵓrš*. Underneath the *š* is the remnant of a clear, single letter, a *resh*. If one turns the ostracon upside down and looks at it from the bottom point of the broad right side, another *aleph* is visible. If the *aleph* is to be added to the first three characters, the word would read in transliteration *ᵓršᵓ*. One is reminded of the "Arad bowl," where the word "Arad" is written forward and backward.[63]

Plate 9. Ostracon 8058.

60. Glueck, *OSJ*, p. 111, Fig. 60; for Albright's original suggestions, cf. *BASOR* 71, p. 18.
61. For *ᶜmy*, cf. Ryckmans, *RB* 48 (1939): 247–49; for *ᶜmyru*, cf. Lidzbarski, *Handbuch*, p. 343; Cook, *A Glossary of the Aramaic Inscriptions*, p. 93.
62. Reg. no. 8058.
63. Aharoni and Amiran, *Yediot* XXVII:4 (1964): pp. 225–26.

Professor F. M. Cross, in a letter to me of Jan. 13, 1966, agreed with my reading, although when I first sent him a photograph I had not noticed that by turning it upside down another *aleph* could be seen. He writes: "Is it possible that an *aleph* follows *shin*. . . . At all events, *ʾrš* or *ʾršʾ* makes perfect sense. The script is Phoenician without doubt. The form emerges in late seventh century and is characteristic of sixth and early fifth centuries formal hands. The *shin* is equally significant. This rounded, simplified form characterizes Phoenician in the period ca. 600–400. . . . The personal name is well known in its several forms: *ʾrš*, *ʾršʾ*. . . ."

We believe, from the level in which it was found, that this ostracon should be assigned a fifth-century date.

## OSTRACON 9027

The parts of the two letters or signs incised on ostracon, reg. no. 9027 (Pl. 10), found in surface debris, are apparently too incomplete to be read. Professor F. M. Cross, who examined it, pointed out in a letter to me of Jan. 13, 1966, that the letters do not conform to any of the other scripts on ostraca from Tell el-Kheleifeh. They could possibly be parts of Minaean letters related to those on the large sixth century Minaean jar from Tell el-Kheleifeh.[64] Professor Ryckmans, who had originally dated these north Minaean inscriptions to no later than the eighth century B.C.,[65] informed me orally in the summer of 1965 that he had changed his mind and dated them now to the sixth century B.C. This is in harmony with the position of this

Plate 10. Ostracon 9027.

64. Reg. no. 469; Glueck, *BASOR* 71, pp. 15–17.

65. Ryckmans, *RB* 48 (1939): 247–49; Boneschi, P., "Les monogrammes sud-arabes de la grande jarre de *Tell el-Ḫeleyfeh* (Ezion-geber)," in *RSO* XXXVI (1961): 213–23.

incised Minaean jar in Level IV at Tell el-Kheleifeh, belonging to the seventh–sixth centuries B.C.

## OSTRACON 10,007

Several almost completely illegible or hopelessly blurred ostraca were found. One of them seemed to be in a late, cursive Edomite script with two letters of a word in a middle line being visible, reading *ḥm*, to which an *r* may have been attached, reading *hmr* (*ḥᶜmar*), wine. This ostracon, reg. no. 10,007 (Pl. 12), came from the debris of Level V, which is to be dated to the fifth–fourth centuries B.C.[66]

Belonging to the lapidary Edomite script of the seventh–sixth centuries B.C. are the numerous *Qwsᶜnl* (*Qausᶜanal*) seal impressions from Period IV

Plate 11. Two *qws'nl* seal impressions.

66. Cf. above, p. 230.

Plate 12. Ostraca 7094, 10,007 and illegible 8096.

occupation of Tell el-Kheleifeh.[67] The entire seal impression reads in transliteration *lqwsᶜnl ᶜbd hmlk*, meaning "belonging to Qausᶜanal, the servant of the king."[68] Albright pointed out when the seal impressions were first published that the script containing the open *ᶜayin*, the *dalet* with unusual stance and the particular *hê* could not be dated before the seventh century B.C.[69] There is no question but that the Qausᶜanal seal impressions and the lapidary Edomite graffito[70] on the small, round-bottomed jar, reg. no. 374, are to be dated approximately no later than to the first half of the sixth century B.C. This is borne out, too, by the seventh–sixth centuries B.C. date of the Period IV archaeological level at Tell el-Kheleifeh in which all the Qausᶜanal seal impressions were found.

After the Edomites recaptured Elath from the Judaeans in the time of Uzziah's grandson, Ahaz, the Judaeans were never again able to regain possession of this important site. The two-hundred-year struggle between the Judaeans and the Edomites for the control of Ezion-geber: Elath thus came to an end. There ensued a period of efflorescence for Edom, including Elath. The settlement that the Edomites erected on the ruins of the previous city, sometime after they had conquered it, was one of the largest and most prosperous ever constructed there. The new city of Period IV was completely

67. Naveh, *BASOR* 183, p. 30; *Yediot* XXX:1–2, p. 43.
68. Glueck, *BASOR* 72, pp. 11–12; 79, p. 15.
69. Albright, *BASOR* 72, p. 13, n. 45.
70. Glueck, *OSJ*, p. 110.

Plate 13. Mudbrick house at Tell el-Kheleifeh. East wall in foreground shows the thieves' hole, patched.

Edomite and endured apparently in these distinctive sub-phases until about the end of the sixth or the beginning of the fifth century B.C. Stamped on jars and bowls of the Period IV Edomite city was the seal impression, which in translation reads: "Belonging to Qausᶜanal, the Servant of the King."[71]

One of the finest houses of the Period IV Edomite city of Elath, composed of two large rooms, contained numerous pieces of pottery bearing, usually on the top or on the bottom of the rather broad and flattish loop-handle attached to each jar, one or sometimes two of the Qausᶜanal seal impressions. Apparently all of them were stamped with the same seal[72] (Pl. 11) or with seals so alike that the impressions were indistinguishable one from another. The same type of Qausᶜanal stamped pottery was also found in the other rooms of the Edomite Period IV city and sometimes on the back of a bowl.[73]

The Edomite house in which the Qausᶜanal pottery was found must have been some sort of a storehouse for particularly valuable late Iron II pottery. There is clear evidence that a hole had once been breached in the east wall of Room 28 and then patched up[74] (Pl. 13). It can be conjectured that thieves had broken into the storehouse to get at the pottery stamped with the

71. For discussion of the first part of the name of *Qwsᶜnl*, cf. Glueck, *BASOR* 72, pp. 11–13.
72. Cf. reg. no. 463.
73. Reg. no. 381.
74. Glueck, *OSJ*, p. 106, Fig. 54.

seal of the Edomite governor[75] of the city, or at their contents, as well as at the other especially marked pottery stored there.

Some of the stamped jars were found almost intact in Rooms 27 and 28. They were of a fairly uniform size, wheelmade, wet-smoothed, pear-shaped, with rounded base, neck in the form of a truncated cone, profiled rim, and broad flattish loop-handle. The ware was generally creamy buff with a light grayish core, well levigated and with tiny grits.

The type of profiled rim characteristic of these Qausᶜanal jars is closely related to the profiled rim of the coarse cooking pot sherd on which ostracon, reg. no. 6043, is written. This type of rim, as we have seen above, could not be dated before the eighth century B.C., and not at all after the sixth century B.C. when it went out of existence.[76]

Closely associated with this type of seventh–sixth century B.C. profiled rim pottery, and, indeed, both in Rooms 27 and 28, found together with Qausᶜanal stamped jars, is a practically uniform type cup of carinated form, with rounded body and rounded or somewhat flattened base, high everted rim and single, generally rounded or slightly flattened loop-handle at the bottom of which there is frequently a potter's mark[77] (Pl. 14).

Found also in Rooms 27 and 28 in the same context, together with Qausᶜanal jars and small single-handled carinated cups, are closely related small carinated handleless cups or bowls of a finer quality,[78] made of hard-baked, dark grayish ware, well levigated, with fine gray and white grits, wheelmade, wet-smoothed, and usually with several parallel horizontal bands of dark brown paint near the base of the high outturned rim. In the case of reg. no. 758, there is also a thin band of paint of similar color on the lip of the rim (Pl. 14). Sometimes, as in the case of reg. no. 663, the bands of paint are superimposed over more or less horizontal, somewhat irregular, almost contiguous fine lines of burnishing. These three types of vessels seem to occur throughout the entire length of Period IV.

The most striking similarities exist between the handleless carinated and sometimes burnished cups from Tell el-Kheleifeh from Room 42 and "Assyrian" cups, as Petrie called them from his excavations at Tell Jemmeh.[79]

75. Glueck, *BASOR* 79, p. 13; 72, pp. 11–12; Albright, *BASOR* 71, p. 18; 72, p. 13, n. 45.

76. Albright, *BASOR* 82, p. 15; see above, notes 4, 5.

77. Reg. nos. 456, 458, 462, 435, 925, 36, 461, 922, 923, 926, 457, 459; Glueck, in *Eretz Israel Vol. 9, W. F. Albright Volume*, Pl. VII:1,2.

78. From Room 27, Dr. 82, reg. no. 758; Dr. 113, reg. no. 757; from Room 28, Dr. 114 reg. no. 217.

79. Petrie, *Gerar* (London), pp. 7, 20, and 23, Pls. XLVII, XLVIII, LXV:1; *Beth Pelet* I, Pl. XXVIII and XLVII; Amiran, *The Ancient Pottery of Eretz Yisrael*, pp. 350, 356, 361.

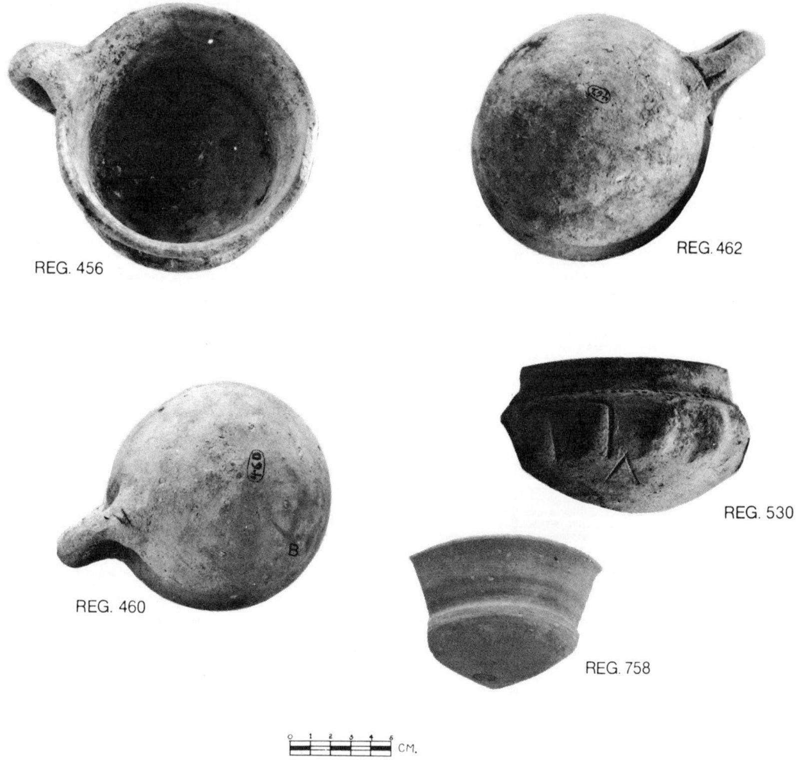


Plate 14. Carinated cups.

Such vessels have been found at Tell el-Far$^{c}$ah,[80] Samaria,[81] and Hazor,[82] where they appear in seventh century levels.[83] A broken, small, carinated "Assyrian" type bowl or cup was found at Ain Qudeirat (Kadeshbarnea) by Dothan,[84] who assigned it to the eighth–seventh centuries B.C. He shows also

80. DeVaux, *RB* LVIII:3 (1951): 419, Fig. 12:3, Pl. XV; Amiran, *The Ancient Pottery of Eretz Yisrael*, p. 350, Fig. 306; p. 351, Fig. 99:1–4; $^{c}$*Atiqot* II (1959): 129–32.

81. Crowfoot et al., *Samaria-Sebaste* III, p. 126, Fig. 11:15, 17, 18, 22, 23 (Pd. VII); p. 122, Fig. 10:8 (Pd. VI); p. 153, Fig. 18:9, 10; Reisner, Fisher, Lyon, *Harvard Excavations at Samaria* I, p. 288, Fig. 163.

82. Yadin, *Hazor* II, Pl. XCVIII:44.

83. For connections between Assyrian and Israelite–Judaean pottery from end of eighth century on, cf. Mallowan, "The Excavations at Nimrud," *Iraq* XII (1950), Pl. XXXII:1–2 and p. 183; Amiran, *The Ancient Pottery of Eretz Yisrael*, p. 350; p. 351, Pl. 99: 1–4; $^{c}$*Atiqot* II (1959): 129–32; Oates, Joan, "Late Assyrian Pottery from Fort Shalmaneser," *Iraq* XXI (1959): 130–46; Lines, Joan, "Late Assyrian Pottery from Nimrud," *Iraq* XVI (1954): 164–67; Glueck, in *Eretz Israel Vol. 9, W. F. Albright Volume*, Pl. VII:1, 2.

84. Dothan, *IEJ* 15:3 (1965): 140, 147, fig. 5:4; cf. the Iron II carinated bowls with flat or slight disc bases from Ashdod published by Dothan, *IEJ* 14:1–2 (1964): 93, fig. 3:1, 2;

from there a fine, broken, carinated spaced ring burnished bowl, which apparently is to be dated to the same time.[85] Parallels occur in or near Amman[86] and at ᶜAroᶜēr.[87]

To judge thus from the seventh century B.C. "Assyrian" parallels, the carinated cups and small bowls from Period IV of Tell el-Kheleifeh would have to be dated to the seventh–sixth centuries B.C., as also the Qausᶜanal jars.

---

*Yediot* XXVIII:3–4 (1964): Pl. XVI:6; cf. also Harding, *ADAJ* I (1951): 39, fig. 1:9 for Iron II carinated, flat-based bowl from Amman.

85. Dothan, *IEJ* 15:3 (1965): Pl. 31A.

86. Harding, "An Iron-Age Tomb at Sahab," *QDAP* XIII (1948): Pl. XXXV:66, and p. 94; p. 101, fig. 7:66; p. 97, fig. 3:13–15; p. 98, fig. 4:16–19; XI (1945): 70:7, 8; *ADAJ* I (1951): 39, fig. 1:9, for Iron II carinated flat-based bowl from Amman.

87. Olávarri, "Sondages à ᶜArôᶜer sur l'Arnon," *RB* 72:1 (1965): 85, fig. 1:3; p. 87, fig. 2:7.

# The Redaction of the Plague Narrative in Exodus

MOSHE GREENBERG

No general conception has greater importance for understanding the formation of the Pentateuch than that put forward by W. F. Albright some three decades ago[1] that the present text shows the maximal variations among the traditions of Israel's earliest history. Inquiry into the pentateuchal redaction, a specimen of which is presented here, is the best validation of that seminal insight, whose author has liberally sown and harvested so many fields.

Biblical scholarship evinces a growing interest in the design of composite creations. Without denying compositeness, scholars of late are focusing more attention on the final product of redactional work than has been the case heretofore; principles or patterns of order are being sought out. Two widely diverging but representative investigations of the organization of the book of Exodus are E. Galbiati's *La Struttura Letteraria dell'Esodo* (1956) and U. Cassuto's *Commentary on the Book of Exodus* (Hebrew, 1952; English, 1967). Both contrast with such continuations of analytical criticism as M. Noth's

1. "The tendency of ancient Oriental scribes and compilers to add rather than to subtract . . . means that the divergences between narratives in the parallel documents *J* and *E* should not be considered as average variation, i.e., as typical of the differences between the documents, but rather as *maximum* variation; the real difference between the narratives . . . was thus materially smaller than is commonly supposed" *From the Stone Age to Christianity* (1940), p. 46 (1957 ed., p. 80).

*Exodus Commentary* (German, 1959; English, 1962) and G. Fohrer's *Überlieferung und Geschichte des Exodus* (1964). Analytical criticism has tended to depreciate the work of the redactor as derivative and second-rate.[2] The seekers after design have joined hands with them in obscuring the art of the redactor by their one-sided focus. Concentrating on the literary merits of the present text, they have shied from accounting for its roughnesses and flaws, and thus give no indication of what the redactor accomplished when he fashioned it out of its pre-existing parts. But unless the redactor's contribution is distinguished from what he received, no proper estimate of his art can be made. The perfunctory treatment of the redactor's work by Noth and Fohrer is hardly a greater obstacle in the way of such an estimate than the exclusive interest in the final product shown by the seekers after design.[3]

The plague narrative of Exodus is a good example of redactional activity. It contains all that is needful for gauging the skill and observing the method of the redactor; both the building blocks of the narrative and the design of the completed structure are clearly discernible. Detailed accounts of the design of the narrative are available elsewhere;[4] the following observations are necessary for the analysis of the redaction to be made in the sequel.

The plague narrative unfolds in three gradually (but not consistently) escalating triplets of plagues, capped by a tenth plague outside the framework of triplets. Thus:

| | | |
|---|---|---|
| 1. Blood | 4. Insect swarms | 7. Hail |
| 2. Frogs | 5. Pestilence | 8. Locusts |
| 3. Lice | 6. Fever boils | 9. Darkness |
| | 10. Firstborn death | |

The arrangement is determined by an invariable pattern of introductory formulas. In the first plague of each triplet, God charges Moses to present himself to Pharaoh in the morning (by the Nile) to warn him of the coming blow (7:15; 8:16; 9:13); in the second plague, God sends Moses into Pharaoh's palace to warn him (7:26; 9:1; 10:1); in the third, God commands Moses (and Aaron) to start the plague without giving warning (8:12; 9:8; 10:21). Each triplet has a distinctive motif, alluded to in the charge made

2. Fohrer speaks of the redaction as "jene Arbeit untergeordneter und zweitklassiger Geister" (p. 5); F. V. Winnett (*The Mosaic Tradition* [1949]) expresses himself similarly (p. 13).

3. I have discussed the problem a bit more fully in "The Thematic Unity of Exodus III–XI," *Fourth World Congress of Jewish Studies, Papers*, vol. I (1967), pp. 151, 154.

4. See Cassuto's commentary; Winnett, pp. 3–15; S. Loewenstamm, *Masoret Yeṣiʾat Miṣrayim Behištalšelutah* (The Tradition of the Exodus in its Development) (1965); pp. 34f. Good observations are to be found in D. J. McCarthy's study, "Moses' Dealings with Pharaoh," *CBQ* 27 (1965): 336ff., but I cannot perceive the design he describes.

in its initial plague. In the first triplet the motif is the superiority of God (and his agents) to Egypt's magicians ("that you may know that I am YHWH" [7:16; cf. 8:6]); in the second triplet it is God's presence "in the midst of the land" (8:18), signalized by his directly bringing on plagues that made a separation between Israel and the Egyptians (8:18f.; 9:4,6); in the third triplet, it is God's incomparability ("there is none like me in all the earth" [9:14]), shown by plagues "whose like had never been before or after" (9:18,24; 10:6,14). An accumulation of motifs is visible as the narrative reaches its climax (9:26; 10:23b; 11:6,7,8). These elements of design suffice as a background for our inquiry into the work of redaction.

That inquiry must start with a determination of the shape in which the traditional material reached the redactor; only then can we try to define his role in the formation of the present narrative. We have to work backward from the text that is before us. A blatant contradiction, a break in progress, a marked change of style and tone—these are, as a rule, most plausibly accounted for by the assumption that heterogenous elements, originally independent of one another, have been combined. The less integrated the disturbance is into its context, the later it may be assumed to have been combined. For plasticity and integrative capability are characteristic of early stages of transmission; rigidity and unassimilability, characteristic of the quasi-canonical status of the material in the time of the redaction. The grossest disturbances are thus to be ascribed to the last redactional stage of combination, while lesser disturbances belong to earlier development of the tradition complexes.

A word on rubrics: This is part of a larger study of the book of Exodus in which (so far) it has been found necessary to posit two main tradition-complexes as pre-existent to the redaction. Their rubrics are simply *A* and *B*, corresponding roughly to *JE* and *P* respectively.

a. Notwithstanding the design of the plague narrative, there is considerable evidence that the present text is not of one piece.

1) In the first two plagues inconsistencies regarding the identity of the brother who is to signal the blood plague (7:17 and 19), the nature of the signal, and the scope of the waters affected in both plagues (7:17, 21 and 19; 7:28; and 8:1), suggest that elements of two versions of the story of these plagues have been combined.

2) The last plague of each triplet (lice [3], boils [6], darkness [9]) differs from the rest in having no forewarning to Pharaoh. This formal divergence, in itself quite tolerable and innocuous, becomes suspicious when it is combined with further evidence of heterogeneity.

In the story of the boils:

a) the sudden unmotivated reappearance of Aaron and the magicians after their absence since the plague of lice;

b) the backward glance in the introduction of the hail plague to the pestilence (9:15), skipping over the intervening plague of boils;

c) the absence of the direct action of God, thematic for the second triplet.

In the story of the darkness:

d) the incongruity of darkness intervening between the destruction of food and livestock (hail, locust) and the death of the firstborn—aggravated by the implication of 10:17 that the series of plagues had reached its climax;

e) the absence of the thematic clause of the third triplet ("never the like before or after").

To this must be added the appearance of doublets now given by the pairs, lice–swarms of insects, pestilence–fever boils, and—because of the darkness motif in locusts (10:5, but especially verse 15)—locust–darkness. Were these three plagues always part of the same series as the other six? The suspicion that they were not is strengthened by the omission of just these three in the poetic evocation of the plague story in Ps. 78:44–51.[5]

b. When the elements making for inconsistency in the first two plagues are isolated, they turn out to be homogeneous with the narrative of the lice plague (cf. 7:19, 8:1 with 8:12; then 7:20,22, 8:2 with 8:13). The agency of Aaron, a leading motif in these passages harks back, in turn, to the accreditation sign (7:9ff.), which is obviously cast in the same mold. That clue leads to the further realization that the notice of the magicians' success (or lack of it) (7:11f.,22, 8:3,14) and the obduracy formula of 7:13 also belong to this narrative strand (7:22; 8:15; cf. the fragment in 8:11). Inasmuch as the accreditation sign is part of *B*'s narrative, we may assign these elements of the plague story to *B* as well.

The selfsame elements—Aaron, the magicians, and the obduracy formula—are present in the tale of the boils (9:8–12) and indicate that it too belongs to *B*.

The association of the darkness plague (10:21–23,27[6]) with this narrative strand is more problematic. It lacks forewarning like lice and boils; like boils, it lacks the thematic motif of its triplet; it is substantially unlike the environing plagues. These features argue for heterogeneity with the preceding narra-

5. In the other poetic echo, Ps. 105:28–36, boils goes unmentioned. Of all the plagues, boils is thus the most poorly attested: Loewenstamm, 39f.

6. The rest of the text (vss. 24–26, 28ff.) contains no allusion to the darkness plague but links up with the locust plague's negotiations; see below.

tive. Against a connection with *B*, however, is the absence of Aaron and the magicians. Critics have noted that the onset of darkness by a signal from Moses is like that of hail and locusts (9:22ff.; 10:12f.) and unlike that of the other plagues (blood, frogs, lice—by a signal from Aaron; boils a variant thereof; swarms, pestilence—by direct action of God). Moreover, the obduracy formula in the episodes of hail, locusts and darkness differs from all the rest in the clause, "so he did not let the Israelites go / so he would not let them go" (9:35; 10:20; 10:27). Hence some critics postulate three distinct narrative traditions in the plague story, *P* (contained in our *B*), *J* (contained in our *A*), and *E*—the longest stretch of which comprises the darkness plague.

However, the elements assigned to *E* are so fragmentary[7] that its reality is very dubious. As concerns darkness, *E*'s supposed hallmark—Moses' staff—is wanting: Moses outstretches his hand, not his staff, toward the sky (10:22; contrast 9:23 and 10:13).

As for the obduracy formula, the phrase "let the Israelites go" is, in fact, part of *B*'s formula in 6:11 and 7:2 (*šillaḥ ʾet B. Y. meʾarso*). As early as 8:11 the predominance of *B*'s formulas is felt, so that in the present form of the story its elements occur in all but two episode endings.

| | |
|---|---|
| Accreditation sign: | *ḥazaq leb, lo šamaʿ, kaʾ $^{a}$šer dibber Y.* (*B*) |
| Blood: | ditto (*B*) |
| Frogs: | *hakbed leb* (*A*, cf. 7:14; 10:1), *lo šamaʿ, kaʾ$^{a}$šer dibber Y.* (*B*) |
| Lice: | *ḥazaq leb, lo šamaʿ, kaʾ$^{a}$šer dibber Y.* (*B*) |
| Swarms: | *hakbed leb, lo šillah ʾet haʿam* (*A*) |
| Pestilence: | *kabed leb, lo šillah ʾet haʿam* (*A*) |
| Boils: | *ḥizzeq leb, lo šama, kaʾ$^{a}$šer dibber Y. ʾel Moše* (*B*) |
| Hail: | *hakbed leb* (*A*), *ḥazaq leb, lo šillaḥ ʾet B. Y. kaʾ$^{a}$šer dibber Y. b$^{e}$yad Moše* (*B*) |
| Locust: | *ḥizzeq leb, lo šillah ʾet B. Y.* (*B*) |
| Darkness: | *ḥizzeq leb* (*B*), *loʾ aba l$^{e}$šall$^{e}$ḥam* (free variant) |
| Summation (11:10): | *ḥizzeq leb, lo šillaḥ ʾet B. Y. meʾarso* (*B*)[8] |

7. References to Moses' staff are supposed to be a sign of *E.*: 7:15, 17; 9:22f.; sporadic "redundancies" such as 9:24a, 25a, are assigned to *E*. Such redundancies may, in fact, reflect an epic-poetic substratum of the language of the narrative in which parallelism was the norm. (As evidence of such a substratum Cassuto ["*Rešit Hahistoriografia Beyisraʾel,*" *Eretz Israel* I (1951): 85ff.] cites the non-prosaic *natan qolot* and *tih$^{a}$lak* in 9:23.)

8. The minor variations are typical of the style of repetitious passages in biblical narrative.

As a detachable stereotype, the obduracy formula is by itself a poor index of ascription for the entire episode to which it is attached.[9]

All in all, then, the supposed components of *E* may be left in one or the other major tradition-complex whose postulation has until now been adequate to account for the present text. To which shall we assign the darkness episode? The divergences between it and its environment (*A*) have already been listed: these stand in the way of an ascription to *A*. But does not the absence of Aaron and the magicians rule out ascribing it to *B*?[10] Not necessarily. For if it be so ascribed, the following pattern in *B*'s narrative may be discerned:

1) The accreditation sign having been imitated by the magicians,

2) Moses has Aaron produce blood, which is imitated by the magicians;

3) Moses has Aaron produce frogs, which is imitated by the magicians;

4) Moses has Aaron produce lice, which the magicians could not do;

5) Moses, helped by Aaron, produces boils; "the magicians could not stand before Moses because of the boils";

6) Moses produces darkness, and "for three days no one could get up from where he was";

7) God puts Egypt's firstborn to death, finally moving Pharaoh.[11]

The climax in the order of agents of the plagues—Aaron, Moses and God—is matched by the plagues' increasing severity: the first three are imitable by the magicians, the second three overwhelm them and then all Egypt. This climax accounts for the disappearance of the correlatives, Aaron and the magicians, in the darkness plague. All told, *B*'s plagues number seven, six (3 plus 3) capped by one, a classic pattern found as well in the creation story (Gen. 1:1—2:3). Not one of these plagues is destructive or lethal before the very last. Demonstration of God's might through prodigies that humble men is their primary object, rather than punishment.

In identifying the narrative tradition of this series with *B*, a certain difficulty arises. The episodes narrated purely and entirely in *B*'s style—lice and

9. How free-floating the elements of the formula were is suggested by 4:21's combination of *ḥizzeq leb* (*B*) and *lo šillaḥ ʾet haʿam* (*A*) in a passage whose contents precludes ascription either to *B* or the main narrative of *A*.

10. W. Rudolph (*Der "Elohist" von Exodus bis Josua* [*BZAW* 68 (1938)], p. 21), at a loss to connect darkness with any major tradition-strand, declares it a "supplement of unknown origin."

11. That Pharaoh was unmoved until the last plague of *B*'s series is inferable from lice and boils, whose formulation is pure *B*. The pleas and concessions that now appear in frogs and darkness are to be assigned to *A*, in which they regularly appear (see ahead). That *B* told of the firstborn plague and made God its direct agent may be inferred from the anticipatory notice in 12:12, a *B* passage.

boils—contain no address of Moses and Aaron to Pharaoh, and the lack of such an address in the darkness episode argues for identifying it too with *B*'s narrative. Yet 7:2—*B*'s commission narrative—expressly prepares the ground for Moses and Aaron to address Pharaoh with the demand to let Israel go. Where does *B* relate those demands? In the present residue of *B*, nowhere; but in the tale of blood and frogs where the *B* element is supplementary to *A*'s narrative, demands occur in the *A* narrative. It must be surmised that *B*'s narrative of blood and frogs told of a demand made of Pharaoh in the style of 7:2, but that it was replaced in the final redaction by the richer equivalent found in the other narrative strand.

c. What remains after *B* has been isolated is the *A* strand. It contains the following episodes:

1) After warning Pharaoh by the river, Moses strikes the Nile and turns it to blood—Pharaoh is unmoved.

2) After warning Pharaoh in his palace, frogs from the Nile cover Egypt;[12] Pharaoh begs Moses to pray for relief and promises to release Israel.

3) After Moses warns Pharaoh by the river, God brings on swarms of insects, separating Goshen from the rest of Egypt; Pharaoh promises a conditioned release and begs Moses to pray for relief.

4) After Moses warns Pharaoh in his palace, God strikes down Egypt's livestock with a pestilence, sparing Israel's herds; Pharaoh is unmoved.

5) After Moses warns Pharaoh (by the river), he signals the onset of unprecedently severe hail, destroying vegetation and exposed men and animals; Pharaoh begs Moses to pray for relief and promises to release Israel.

6) After warning Pharaoh in his palace and rejecting a conditioned release of Israel, Moses signals the onset of an unprecedented plague of locusts, wiping out the rest of Egypt's vegetation; Pharaoh begs just one more pardon which, when granted, does not result in his allowing Israel's departure.

The final firstborn plague (7) is announced.

The river-palace pattern of introductory formulas orders *A*'s series into three pairs (blood–frogs, swarms–pestilence, hail–locusts). The last two pairs are, in addition, internally bound by express themes (separation, unprecedentedness). (In the present text the theme of the first pair is governed by *B*'s interest in demonstrating God's superiority to the magicians.) But the substance of the plagues suggests rather two sets of three plagues each: the first set consisting of nuisances, the second, of destroyers of non-human life.

12. By whose agency is unknown since *B* has been given exclusive right to speak on the matter.

Accordingly, the entire series has the character of graduated punitive blows, capped by the death of the firstborn. Once again the pattern of seven (3 + 3 + 1) appears.[13]

*A*'s plague series, unlike *B*'s, gives the impression of being itself the product of a development. One wonders whether the incongruity between substance (3 + 3) and form (2 + 2 + 2) was there from the first. The wider implications of the plagues referred to in 9:15–16 and 10:1–2 give the appearance of later reflections. The inconsequence that has arisen from the extension of certain plagues beyond their expected limits also points to evolution in the tradition. Thus the problematic reappearance of cattle as victims of the hail (9:19) after their "total" destruction by the pestilence (9:6) can be resolved on the verbal level (Ibn Ezra); but what underlies the problem is more than a verbal nuance: it is the extension of what is properly a vegetation plague (n.b. 10:5b) to human and animal victims. Similarly with the swarms: they are described as ubiquitous nuisances, just like the frogs (cf. 8:17 with 7:28), yet the "whole land of Egypt was ruined" by them. The phrase, while vague, is yet enough to constitute an unwanted anticipation of the later vegetation destroyers, the hail and locusts. The tendency to expand the scope of the plagues endured; it is responsible for the final sum of ten, synthesized by the redactor, as well as for the continued elaboration of the plagues found in the midrash.

The elaborations that in the course of time gave *A*'s narrative its complex character do not amount to or hang together as a third narrative strand. They were natural extensions of the material in *A*. Their integration into *A*'s text is so smooth as to justify the assumption that it was already accomplished by the time *A* reached the final redactor.[14]

d. The redactor thus had at his disposal two seven-membered versions of

13. R. Smend (*Ezrählung des Hexateuch* [1912] 126f.; cited by Fohrer, p. 71 fn. 29) has further noted that plagues 1 and 4, 2 and 5, 3 and 6 have similar effects on Pharaoh [cf. the correspondence between days 1–4, 2–5, and 3–6 in the creation story of Gen. 1] and that the effects intensify (a) within each series from 1 to 3 and from 4 to 6; (b) in the second series in relation to the first. Pharaoh's responses, then, vacillated in an ascending spiral according to *A*. This regularity of vacillation was destroyed by the combination of *A* and *B*, but neither depicted Pharaoh's responses in an ascending line, as Gressman tried to do (*Mose und seine Zeit* [1913], p. 70, fn. 3).

14. Evidence that this is the case is the reference in the reflective expansion 9:15f. to the pestilence, ignoring the intervening boils; evidently the expansion antedates the final fusion of the narratives of *A* and *B*, at which time boils came in between.

That the plague tradition was fluid during biblical times may be inferred from the variants in Ps. 78:45ff. Both frogs and swarms are there called consumers and destroyers of the land; they are directly conjoined to the locusts. Plants and animals, but not men, are victims of the hail. Men and not animals are struck by the pestilence. The divergences have been perceptively treated by Loewenstamm, 26ff.

the plagues, overlapping at the beginning and end, each with its own inner rationale and climax. He proceeded to mesh them as follows:

Since *B*'s first item, the accreditation sign, differed from all the rest in not inflicting discomfort or harm, it was excluded from the patterned block of plagues. These began, accordingly, with blood and frogs which stood at the head of the plagues proper in both versions. The theme of these plagues was determined by the narrative of *B*, which made them continuations of the Aaron-magicians contest started in the immediately preceding accreditation episode. Hence just so much of *B*'s narrative as was needed to bring this to the fore was introduced into *A*'s version (viz. 7:19–2a[a], 21b–22; 8:1–3). The third plague had to be *B*'s lice, in which the contest was decided.

A sequence of three formally distinct episodes was now constituted that decided the disposition of the rest of the episodes: two plagues preceded by warnings (the first in the morning by the river, the second in the palace), followed by a third without warning.

A traditional number sequence of six (3 + 3) items augmented by one more was elaborated upon by the redactor to make room for the total of ten different plagues related by the two versions. Three sets of three, with the capper at the end, would accommodate the material nicely. With formal criteria governing the arrangement the intermeshing of the remaining items was reasonably smooth. The second series was made up of *A*'s swarms and pestilence (warnings), followed by *B*'s boils (no warning), which associated well with pestilence. Next came *A*'s hail and locusts (warnings), then *B*'s darkness (no warning) which was linked through the darkness motif to the locusts. Since both series were in a climactic order, their interweaving did not produce an inept result. The presence of the key motif "coming to know YHWH" in both *A* (7:16, etc.) and *B* (cf. 7:5) helped too. But strict ascending order, pattern in Pharaoh's responses, and consistency of theme throughout all parts had to be sacrificed (perhaps happily, from an artistic viewpoint).

With the interweaving of traditions, adjustments had to be made. *B*'s theme now prevails in the first two plagues, perhaps displacing a different one of *A*. The formulation of the penultimate plague, prior to the death of the firstborn posed a special problem. In *B*'s version the death of the first-born followed the plague of darkness—a symbolic premonition of it; in the other version, it followed the locust plague (note the premonition of it in 10:17, "this death"). Arranging darkness and locust in series resulted in some awkwardness. The locust plague, which Pharaoh states is the last he'll undergo (10:17) is now followed, when he reneges, not by the last plague but by the last-but-one. The negotiations of 10:24ff., now following the darkness, in fact make no reference to the darkness but link up well with the preceding locust plague (10:19). It may therefore be assumed that in *A*'s account the locust plague was followed by another round of sterile negotiations ending in the announcement by Moses of the final plague (Fohrer, 65 fn. 17). With the interposition of *B*'s darkness episode the last round of negotiations had necessarily to be attached to this last-but-one plague.

*B*'s narrative of the plagues was contained within the *inclusio* formed by 7:2–6 and 11:9–10. This framework having been retained, its formulas of obduracy came to dominate the episode endings, in which a formula of obduracy regularly occurred. *A*'s formula still appears at the endings of swarms and pestilence (8:28; 9:7; cf. 9:34; 10:1); but in 8:12b (frogs) and everywhere else the richer variety of clauses found in *B*'s formulation has prevailed. It is reasonable to attribute this prevalence to the effect of *B*'s *inclusio*.

The strange placement of 11:1–3 is unlikely to be original, though it is hard to find a smoother context without radically rewriting the present text of the ninth plague. The displacement of these verses together with the removal of the warning of the last plague to 4:22f. seem to be results of the redactorial reshaping of the beginning and end of the entire plague series.

To sum up: The plague narrative is the product of an elaborate growth of traditions, which reached the redactor in two crystallizations—partly overlapping, partly divergent. The present shape of the material was arrived at by intermeshing the two in as unforced a manner as possible. While the prefinal components influenced the final form, the latter, with its original structure, is one of the most striking evidences of the redactor's art. Moreover, through him *A*'s conception of the plagues as punishment has been fused with *B*'s conception of them as demonstrations of God's power. The result is an added dimension: a sense of the multivalence of events. Such enrichment of the values of the narrative is characteristic of the redactorial work throughout the Pentateuch.[15]

15. Contrary to Noth's opinion in his otherwise illuminating summary of the redactional work in *Überlieferungsgeschichte des Pentateuch* (1948), p. 271.

# Scripture and Inscription: The Literary and Rhetorical Element in Some Early Phoenician Inscriptions

JONAS C. GREENFIELD

W. F. ALBRIGHT's interest in early Hebrew poetry is well known. From an early article dealing with the Song of Deborah[1] until his recent *Yahweh and the Gods of Canaan*, problems of style and rhetoric, of verse and prose have been one of his major preoccupations.[2] Together with H. L. Ginsberg and M. D. Cassuto he was a pioneer in relating the poetic and stylistic features of Ugaritic with those of Hebrew poetry. This concentration on Ugaritic and its relationship to Hebrew has become a major preoccupation of both biblical and North West Semitic studies and the number of scholars interested in this subject has increased. This is rightly so, despite possible excesses, since the texts from Ras Shamra continue to shed light on the biblical text and continue to be understood in light of the Hebrew text. The reason for this is obvious—the Hebrew Bible and the Ugaritic Corpus are the two great bodies of literature in a "Canaanite" language that have come down to us. The literature of the vital center is lacking. For Canaan proper during the Amarna Age we can only hear faint echoes and phrases in the Amarna letters from Palestine and Phoenicia;[3] for Phoenicia during the biblical period we do not have even one

1. "The Earliest Forms of Hebrew Verse," *JPOS* 2 (1922): 69–86.

2. *Yahweh and the Gods of Canaan*, (London, 1968), pp. 1–46.

3. A. Jirku, "Kanaanäische Psalmenfragmente in der vorisraelitischen Zeit Palästinas und Syriens," *JBL* 52 (1933): 108–20. This article, already antiquated when it was written, remains the only survey of the problem published to date. Albright in "The Egyptian Correspondence of Abimilki, Prince of Tyre," (*JEA* 23 [1937]: 190–203) has shown Egyptian influence in the phraseology of these letters.

literary document. Nevertheless, the work of some scholars has shown important contacts between the literary traditions of the ancient Near East and the phraseology of the surviving Canaanite (Phoenician) and Aramaic inscriptions.[4]

I believe, however, that further analysis of the Phoenician inscriptions can give us a clue as to what might have been typical of Phoenician literary style by way of parallelism, word pairs, clichés, ideational patterns, and other rhetorical means. I have attempted to show in my article on the "Stylistic Aspects of the Sefire Inscriptions" that elements of idiom and style for early Aramaic could be extracted by patient analysis of that inscription.[5] In forthcoming studies the Zakir inscription will be shown to contain elements of the "Danklied," and both the Kilamuwa inscription and the Arslan Tash amulet will be examined in light of their poetic structure.[6]

In this paper some of the early Phoenician inscriptions will be analyzed with this purpose in mind. It would be proper to emphasize that the purpose is not the accumulation of parallels with the Hebrew Bible, which have often long since been noticed, but rather to indicate the continuity of a set phrase, idiom or idea as part of the common poetic and rhetorical heritage.

## 1. AHIRAM (*KAI* 1)

Stylistic features are apparent in the oldest known Phoenician inscription, that on the Ahiram sarcophagus.[7] The way of listing potential malefactors *wʾl mlk bmlkm wskn bsknm wtmʾ mḥnt* . . . (1.2) is an example. This can be compared with *wʾm mlk bmlkm wrzn brznm ʾm ʾdm ʾš ʾdm šm* . . . (Karatepe III 12–13) and also with similar formulations in Mesopotamian materials.[8] An instance of a formula worthy of study in the Ahiram inscription is found in the first two lines of the curse against any highly placed person who would desecrate the sarcophagus:

4. I refer in particular to the following three articles: H. L. Ginsberg, "Psalms and Inscriptions of Petition and Acknowledgement," *Louis Ginsberg Jubilee Volume I* (New York, 1945), pp. 159–71; S. Gevirtz, "West Semitic Curses and the problem of the origins of Hebrew Law," *VT* 11 (1961): 137–58; D. H. Hillers, "Ritual Procession of the Ark and Ps. 132," *CBQ* 30 (1968): 48–55. Gevirtz's article, in particular, is of importance for my study; I have not noted in detail where I agree or disagree with his interpretations or comparisons.

5. "Stylistic Aspects of the Sefire Treaty Inscriptions," *Acta Orientalia* 29 (1965): 1–18.

6. The Mesha inscription (*KAI* 181), although frequently studied in the one hundred years since its discovery, may also be re-studied from this point of view.

7. For this inscription cf. Gevirtz, loc. cit., pp. 146–47; Albright, *JAOS* 67 (1947): 155–56. Cross and Freedman *Early Hebrew Orthography*, pp. 13–14.

8. For the Mesopotamian tradition, which lists potential malefactors simply with *lu*, cf. *CH* xxvib 40–44 *lu šarrum lu bēlum lu iššakkum u lu awīlūtum ša šūmam nabiat* or the lists in Neo-Assyrian contracts, e.g., *ARU* 123, 11. 14–16.

| | |
|---|---|
| *tḥtsp ḥṭr mšpṭh* | "may his staff of judgment be broken"[9] |
| *thtpk ksʾ mlkh* | "may his seat of kingship be overturned" |

(The relationship with earlier Ugaritic material has been noted by all who have dealt with these lines and will be discussed briefly below.)

For the purpose of this study we note that the line contains a number of clichés. The first is the scepter, *ḥṭr*, and the chair, *ksʾ*, as signs of kingship. In the Mesopotamian area these are well attested. Suffice it to refer to the epilogue of the Codex Hammurapi where the breaking of the scepter by Anu and the removal of the throne by Sīn are used to threaten anyone who might alter the inscription (CH xxvib 50–51; xxviib 45–46).[10] The scepter and chair are found together in a blessing in some neo-Assyrian letters where the gods are asked to give the king, besides longevity (*ūmū arkūti*) and eternity (*šanāti darâti*), *ḫaṭṭu išartu* and *kussû darû*, "a just scepter and an everlasting throne."[11] From the Hebrew Bible we first note this cliché in the royal Psalm (45:7) *kisʾekā ʾelohim ʿōlām wāʿed* // *šebeṭ mīšōr šebeṭ malkūtekā*, "your mighty throne last forever, a just scepter is your royal scepter."[12] The cliché is so well understood that its elements can be used for the rulers themselves. Amos 1:5 is a good example:

| | |
|---|---|
| *wešābartī bĕrīaḥ Dammeśeq* | "I will break the bolt of Damascus[13] |
| *wĕhikrattī yōšēb mi-Biqʿat ʾAwen* | and cut off the ruler from Biqʿ at Awen |
| *wĕtōmēk šebet mi-Bet ʿEden* | and him that holds the scepter from Beth-Eden" |

Here the *yōšeb*, "occupant of the throne," and *tōmek šebeṭ*, "holder of the scepter," are used for the Aramean rulers. These symbols of royalty are part of the enthronement reference in the Hadad inscription from Zincirli: *gm yšbt ʿl mšb ʾby wntn hdd bydy ḥṭr ḥl[bbh]*, "I also sat on my father's throne and Hadad placed the scepter of *ḥlbbh* in my hand" (*KAI* 214, 8–9).[14]

9. Gevirtz, loc. cit., p. 147 translates *tḥtsp* as "peeled off," but the proof for *ḥsp* "to peel" is not as positive as he states in n. 2 of that page; context and parallels favor "be broken."

10. Threatened removal (*eṭēru* or *ekēmu*) of scepter and throne are found in the annals of Sargon (ed. Lie, 1. 269): *eṭēr ḫaṭṭi u kussī šarrūtišu*, and in the annals of Senecherib (p. 130, col. vi, 82–83): *ḫaṭṭa u kussâ līkimšuma*.

11. Cf. *HABL* 260, 3–6; 262, 3–5; 350, 3–6; 811, 3–5; 1117, 3–4. These letters are in the Neo-Babylonian rather than the Neo-Assyrian dialect. [See Addenda.]

12. The writer is well aware of the difficulties in this and other biblical texts which he will be rendering in this study in a traditional manner. The point made in the study is not affected by these translations and there is no need to enter into the particular problems of these texts.

13. The term *bariaḥ* "bolt" remains difficult and in all likelihood *bariaḥ* is a "ram," as in Aramaic (*barḥā*). For this verse cf. most recently G. Buccellati *Cities and Nations of Ancient Syria* (Rome, 1964), pp. 52–53.

14. For the role of the "throne" among the Hittites cf. A. Archi "Trono regale e trono divinizzato nell'Anatolia ittita," *Studi micenei ed egeo-anatolici* I (1966): 76–120. The scepter does not play a similar role.

The second cliché is the reference to the royal scepter in the Ahiram inscription as the *ḥṭr mšpṭ*, "the scepter of justice." This is paralleled by the *ḫaṭṭu išartu* in Akkadian and the *šebeṭ mīšōr* in biblical Hebrew (cf. examples above). The durability of the throne and the justness of the royal scepter go together. The third cliché is the "breaking of the scepter" and the "overturning of the throne." The two terms are not found together, to my knowledge, in Akkadian. An example of "breaking the scepter" is found, as just noted, in Codex Hammurapi xxvib 50–51. "Overturning the throne" is also rare—the verb used being *šubulkatu*. Of the two examples usually noted I will quote the later one (a curse from an inscription of Assurbanipal): *kussā šarrūtīšu liš(a)balkitma*, "may they overturn his royal throne." (Streck, *Assurbanipal* 248 11. 93–94).[15]

The best parallel to the phrase in Aḥiram is its well known forerunner in Ugaritic:

a) *lysᶜ alt ṭbtk*
b) *lyhpk ksa mlkk*
c) *lyṯbr ḫṭ mṯpṭk* (*UT* 49.VI 27–29)

The Ugaritic version is fuller, but the true import of clause (a) escapes us, since it contains the word *alt* which has not been satisfactorily interpreted to date. All the elements are found in it: throne and scepter; scepter of justice; "breaking" and "overturning." There was good reason for H. L. Ginsberg, in 1935, to consider the Ahiram passage a quotation from a Canaanite epic.[16]

The Hebrew parallels have gone, on the whole, unnoticed. In some the staff alone is broken, but the throne does not seem to be mentioned. One example is Isa. 14:5: *šābar YHWH maṭṭe rĕšāᶜīm šebeṭ mōšĕlīm*. However, an examination of later verses shows that Helel ben Shachar is condemned for setting his throne too high and he falls to earth, hewn down (*nigdaᶜta*). The same is true of Jeremiah 48:17b: *ʾēkā nišbar maṭṭe-ᶜoz maqqel tifʾārā*, where in the following verse the occupant of the throne of Moab is told to descend. Yet it must be admitted that in both these verses nothing happens to the throne. The clearest parallel (Ps. 89:45) was first noted by H. L. Ginsberg.[17] The Massoretic text, *hišbattā miṭṭĕhorō wĕkisʾō lāʾāreṣ miggartā*, hides one of the

15. Cf. too *KBoI*, rev. 64 *kussâka lišbalkittu* "may they overthrow your throne" (Weidner, *Bo.St.* 8 [Leipzig, 1923]: 34). Both passages quoted by Heidel, *AS* 13, 58.

16. *Orientalia* 5 (1936): 179, n. 3.

17. H. L. Ginsberg, who first drew the parallel with the Ugaritic text (*JAOS* 65 [1945]: 65 n. 2) proposed reading *maṭṭeh yādō* by comparing Ugar. *mṭ yd*. For a recent rendering of the unchanged consonantal text cf. G. Ahlstrom, *Psalm 89* (Lund 1959), p. 137. He is followed by M. Dahood, *The Psalms II* (N.Y., 1968), p. 319. But Dahood's rendering of *miṭhārō* as "his splendor" is not acceptable for the putative Ugaritic *ṯhr* "gem" does not exist. This vocable occurs as an adjective meaning "pure" and describing *iqni* in *UT* 51, V. 81. 96.

terms. There has been agreement among most scholars that this verse calls for some emendation. The one that is often proposed and which does least violence to the Massoretic text is *hišbattā maṭṭeh hōdō wĕkisʾō lāʾāres miggartā*, "you brought to nought his glorious scepter and hurled his throne to the ground."

Although neither *šbr* nor *hpk* is used, the verbs found in the text have their own validity. We find the root *šbt* with *šbr* in Ezek. 6:6; 30:18; Ps. 46:10. The root *mgr* is a late root, otherwise known only from post-exilic material. It occurs, for example, in *CAP* 30,14: *ʾgwrʾ zk bnh hskḥ wʾgwry ʾlhy mṣryn kl mgrw*, "they found this temple built but all the temples of the Egyptian gods they threw down." So too in one of the recently published Qumrān Psalms: *bĕnē nafši wĕʾal tĕmaggĕrāh* literally: "build my soul and do not throw her down."[18]

An interesting variant on this theme is to be found in Haggai 2:22:

a) *wĕhāpaktī kisseʾ mamlākōt*
b) *wĕhišmadtī ḥozeq* ⟨*mamlakot*⟩ *gōyīm*[19]
c) *wĕhāpaktī merkābā wĕrōkbēhā*
d) *wĕyārdū sūsīm wĕrōkbēhem*
e) *ʾiš bĕḥereb ʾaḥīw*

Clause (a) uses the standard image, but *mamlākōt* "kingdoms" replaces Ugaritic/Phoenician *mlk* "kingship" (unless we assume a Phoenician *mamlākōt* "king"); in clause (b) the might of the nations is destroyed rather than the staff broken; clauses (c–d) replace the standard image of clause (a) with the might of the Persian period—horses, chariots, and riders.

The overturned chair remained a feared imprecation in later times. The Talmud (BT Gittin 35a) preserves the story of a woman who in her deep anger at Rabba bar Rab Huna cursed him *lyhpkwh lkwrsyh* "may they overturn his chair."[20] His students, to avert possible trouble, turned the chair over.

## ADDENDUM

Z. Falk in "Two Symbols of Justice," *VT* 10 (1960): 72–74, has emphasized the use of the throne and scepter as symbols of justice. A. Demsky in *Leshonenu* 34 (1970): 185–86 has noted some of the parallels to "overturning the throne" in the second line of this inscription. Demsky's paper appeared in

18. *The Psalm Scrolls of Qumran Cave II* (*DJD* IV, [Oxford, 1965] ed. J. A. Sanders), Col. XXIV, 1. 5. This verb is also found in the early Jewish liturgy.

19. I assume that *mamlākōt* is an instrusion from the previous clause.

20. I follow here the reading of the MSS recorded by M. S. Feldblum, *Diqduqe Sopherim, Tractate Gittin* (New York, 1966), *a.l.*

spring 1970 while the material in this part of my article was presented in April 1969 at a public lecture in Jerusalem and at a Hebrew University seminar.

An excellent early example of throne and staff together as symbols of Kingship may be found in a recently published Mari letter *ARM* X, 1–18: *šarrūtum* [*ḫa*]*ṭṭum*⌜*u*⌝ ^iṣ⌜*ku*⌝*ssum* . . . *ana Zimrilim nadnat* "kingship, [sce]pter and throne, . . . has been given to Zimrī-Lim." These words, shouted by a crowd, in a vision, are reported to Zimrī-Lim (cf. W. Moran, *Biblica* 50 [1969]: 46).

## 2. TABNIT (*KAI* 13)

*a*) 1.4: *wʾl trgzn*   1.6: *wʾl trgzn*   1.7: *wrgz trgzn*

The biblical parallels to these lines have long been noted: (a) *lāmā hirgaztani lĕhaʿalōt ʾōtī* (I Sam. 28:15) and (b) *šĕʾōl mittaḥat rāgzā lĕkā liqrat boʾĕkā* (Isa. 14:9).[21] The action of rousing the dead from their "rest" is expressed by the verb *rgz*, whose basic meaning is "to shake, disturb." The punishment for disturbing the dead is two-fold: the denial of *zrʿ*⟨*wtʾr*⟩ *bḥym tḥt šmš* and *wmškb ʾt rpʾm*. The commentators on this curse have noted the biblical passages about the *rephaim* and have usually been content with that. We would add that the words chosen for the inscription come from a set literary and ideational pattern and these can be clarified by analysis of the biblical parallels. In the "Witch of Endor" story (I Sam. 28) it is clear that one of the results of Saul's disturbing (*rgz*) Samuel was a curse that Saul and his children would die on the morrow (v. 19). Although there is no explicit curse the bodies of Saul and his children were desecrated (II Sam. 21). Saul's death was typical of "one who fell upon the field," and he didn't find *mškb ʾt rpʾm*.[22] The same framework fits the Helel ben Shachar narrative in Isa. 14. The *rephaim* are disturbed by the intruder (v. 9), Sargon of Assyria, in the guise of the King of Babylon.[23] His punishment is clear—improper burial and death for all the King's children (vv. 18–20). The King's earlier actions and his overweaning pride earned him this fate, but the literary framework

21. Surprisingly, neither Cooke, *NSI*, nor Donner–Röllig, *KAI*, refer to any biblical verses. S. R. Driver in *Notes . . . Book of Samuel* (Oxford 1913) in commenting on I Sam. 28:15 (p. 216) refers to these passages, as does Slouschz, *Thesaurus*, p. 16. I would add that the use of *rgz* in Job. 3:17, 26 is also pertinent.

22. In Gilgamesh XII, 151–52 we are told of a person *ša šalamtašu ina ṣēri nadāt* "whose corpse had been cast upon the steppe," that *eṭemmašu ina erṣetim ul ṣalil* "his ghost does not rest in the netherworld."

23. For this identification cf., most recently, H. L. Ginsberg, *JAOS* 88 (1968): 49–52. I find that Ginsberg (p. 51, n. 27) makes the relevant comparisons with the Tabnit inscription and the Gilgamesh passage. He also compares Ezek. 32:22. I would add that in Ezek. 32 *škb ʾt* is used for lying in the netherworld alongside someone (cf. Slouschz, *Thesaurus*, p. 17).

requires, as in the Saul tale, the *rgz* of the dead. I have restored above the reading of Tabnit *wtʾr bḥym tḥt šmš* on the basis of Eshmunazor (1.12) and would add that the phrase *wʾl yqbr bqbr* found in that inscription (1. 8) must surely have been understood in Tabnit. Certainly the full formula fits well with the premises outlined above concerning the literary framing of the fate of Saul and his children and that of the "King of Babylon."

b) *k tʿbt ʿštrt hdbr hʾ* (1.6)

This is the only occurrence of the word *tʿbt* in Phoenician. The formula matches the biblical *kî toʿăbat YHWH ʾelōhekā hūʾ* (e.g., Deut. 25; 17:1). This phrase is used particularly in Deuteronomy for the strongest warning in cases of possible ethical or cultic transgressions. This is also true of Jeremiah and Ezekiel while in Proverbs its use is more general. All these books are relatively close in date to Tabnit and Eshmunazor.

## 3. ESHMUNAZOR (*KAI* 14)

The Eshmunazor inscription merits serious attention from the stylistic point of view.[24] It contains elements of vocabulary and idiom that set it apart from the other known Phoenician inscriptions (except the Tabnit inscription).

A. Vocabulary:
- a) *ʾrṣ dgn* "land rich with grain" in *ʾrṣt dgn hʾdrt* (1.19) cf. Heb. *ʾereṣ dāgān wĕtīrōš* (Deut. 33:28; 2 Kings 18:32).
- b) *bqš* (1.5) "to seek" known from Ugaritic (*bqṯ*) and Hebrew.
- c) *gzl* (1.3, 12) *nifʿal* "to be snatched away," see below.
- d) *sgr* (1.9,21) *yifʿil* "to hand over," see below.
- e) *tʾr* (1.12), see below.

B. Idiomatic and Stylistic Elements:
- a) *dbr . . . . lʾmr : dbr mlk ʾšmnʿzr mlk ṣdnm lʾmr*
  "spoke King Eshmunazor, King of Sidon, saying" (1.2)

This phrase, so well known from biblical Hebrew, is found only here in Phoenician. We may assume that it was a standard formula in Phoenician and surely part of the formulary of royal pronouncements.

b) *ngzlt bl ʿty* "snatched away before my time"

1) *gzl* with this meaning is rare in biblical Hebrew (perhaps Micah 3:2; Prov. 4:16). In Mandaic *gzl* is both "to steal" and "to separate" (cf. Drower-Macuch, *Mandaic Dictionary* [Oxford, 1963], pp. 86–87). Syraic *glz* comes close to Phoenician *gzl*. I note particularly the use of *gulzānā* "orbatio"

24. The most recent discussion of the dating of this inscription from the epigraphic point of view, giving a full treatment of other considerations, is that of J. B. Peckham, S.J., in *The Development of the Late Phoenician Scripts* (Cambridge, 1968), pp. 76–101.

(Brockelmann, *Lex. Syr*² 117–18). Both Hebrew *grz* in *nigraztī* (Ps. 31:23 a *hapax*) and *gzr* in *nigzāru* (Ps. 88:6 and cf. Isa. 53:8) are used in the context of a person who thinks himself almost "snatched off" by death.

2) *bl ᶜty*: this is the same as Hebrew *bĕlōᵓ ᶜittekā*, "before your time" (Qoh. 7:17) and *wĕlōᵓ ᶜet*, "before (their) time" (Job 22:16). In both verses used in association with premature death. In the Qoheleth passage the verb is simply *mūt* "to die," but in Job it is *qummĕṭū*, the *puᶜal* of *qmṭ*. The context of this verse favors "snatched away" and indeed this is the translation preferred by most ancients and moderns.[25] Etymology is more difficult, since *qmṭ* in Mishnaic Hebrew, Aramaic, Syriac, and Arabic is usually "to bind, fold." Syriac does know a *qmaṭ* "prehendit."[26] Premature death is often noted in the epitaphs on tombs. Early death in relation to royal figures is also a *topos* in the Bible, e.g., *hiqṣarta yemē ᶜalūmāw* (Ps. 89:46 and cf. too Isa. 38:10–12 and Ps. 102:24–25).

c) *ytm/bn ᵓlmt*

The parallelism *ytm//ᵓlmnt* is well known from Ugaritic and Hebrew. But the term *ben ᵓalmānā* is rare in Hebrew, found only in relation to the Tyrean artisan of 1 Kings 7,14. The same phrase *mar almatti* is found in Akkadian but this is not the normal word for "orphan."[27] Although this may be a realistic biographical statement concerning Eshmunazor, mentioning it here adds to the pathos of the situation.

d) *bn msk ymm ᵓzrm*

This phrase has caused the commentators no end of trouble. Hoftijzer has assembled most of the interpretations.[28] This writer tends to favor *msk ymm* = Heb. *yĕmē mispār* "few years."[29] One should add that Tur-Sinai has proposed to equate the root *ᵓzr* with Akkadian *ezēru* "to curse."[30] The meaning would then be "of few, cursed days," continuing the theme of *ngzlt bl ᶜty*.

e) *nśᵓ//ᶜms*
*wᵓl yśᵓ ᵓyt ḥlt mškby*
*wᵓl yᶜmsny bmškb z ᶜlt mškb šny*
"and let him not take away the casket in which I am resting and let him not carry me off from this resting place to another resting place" (ll. 5–6)

25. Cf. Vulgate: *sublati*; Targum *ᵓitbeṭīlu*, *Pešitta ᵓetkliw*; Saᶜadya: *ᵓuḥṣū* (ed. Derenbourg, p. 72; cf. R. Ecker *Die Arabische Job-Übersetzung des Gaon Saadja ben Josef al-Fajjumi* [München, 1962], p. 177). In *JPS* and *RSV* "snatched away." The meaning of *watiqmeṭeni* in Job 16:8 remains obscure because of the unclear context.

26. Cf. Brockelmann, *Lex. Syr.*², p. 672. An ancient suggestion is that *qmṭ* in biblical Hebrew should be considered the metatheses of *qṭm* "to cut off," but this is not plausible.

27. *CAD* A, part I, 353b.

28. Cf. Hoftijzer, *DISO*, p. 7 s.v. *ᵓzr* I.

29. Cf. Cooke, *NSI*, a.l. p. 33.

30. Quoted by N. S. Slouschz, *Thesaurus of Phoenician Inscriptions* (in Hebrew; Tel Aviv, 1942), p. 19. For *ezēru* cf. *CAD* "E" p. 427.

The parallelism of *nś*ʾ//ᶜ*ms* in this phrase has long since been noted and has been compared with biblical Hebrew ᶜ*ms*//*nś*ʾ in Isa. 46:3:

*ha-*ᶜ*ămūsīm minni-beṭen*
*ha-nĕśūʾim minni-rāḥam.*[31]

The same pair is found in the difficult *nĕśūʾōtēkem* ᶜ*ămūsōt* of verse 1 of that chapter. In all likelihood it is also to be sought in Neh. 4:11: *wĕha-nōśĕʾīm ba-sebel* ᶜ*ōmĕśīm*, a phrase which has its share of textual difficulties. The first part *nś*ʾ *bsbl* has been plausibly explained by M. Held as "to carry the basket."[32] One has the feeling that ᶜ*ōmĕśīm* (a hyper correct form of ᶜ*ōmĕsīm*) lacks a word like *bĕkātēf* "those that carry on the shoulder" or the name of an instrument or container.

The same pair is also known from Ugaritic. The occasion is after the death of Baᶜal when Anat commands Shapash to help her carry off and bury Baᶜal:

| | |
|---|---|
| *gm tṣḥ lnrt ilm špš* | She calls out aloud to Shapash torch of the gods |
| ᶜ*ms m*ᶜ *ly aliyn b*ᶜ*l* | lift, please, Aliyn Baᶜal on to me |
| *tšm*ᶜ *nrt ilm špš* | the torch of the gods Shapash does obey |
| *tšu aliyn b*ᶜ*l* | she lifts up Aliyan Baᶜal |
| *lktp* ᶜ*nt ktšth* | sets him on the shoulders of Anat |

(*UT* 62, 10–15; *Corpus* 6, I, 10–15.)

Anat's command is phrased as ᶜ*ms*, while Shapash's action is described as *nś*ʾ. A skillful use of the pair *nś*ʾ//ᶜ*ms* emerges in these verses. The pair *nś*ʾ//ᶜ*ms* then can be traced in Ugaritic, biblical Hebrew, and Phoenician. Biblical Hebrew knows another pair which has very much the same function: *nś*ʾ//*sbl* (Isa. 46:7; 53:4).[33]

Two proverbs in Aḥiqar that bring together various "carrying" verbs are worth quoting at this point:

1) *nšʾyt ḥlʾ wṭ*ᶜ*nt mlḥ wlʾ ʾyty zy yqyr mn* [*k*ᶜ*s*ʾ] (Aḥiqar 1.111)
"I have lifted sand and I have carried salt but there is naught which is heavier than [rage]" (H.L.G., *ANET*² 429a).[34]

31. The Hebrew parallels noted already in Cooke, *NSI*, a.l.

32. Cf. M. Held, *JAOS* 88 (1968): 94–95. A study of this sort of broken parallelism is needed. For Hebrew cf. E. Z. Melammed, "Breakup of Stereotype Phrases as an Artistic Device in Biblical Poetry," in *Studies in the Bible*, ed. Chaim Rabin, (*Scripta Hieros* 8 [1961], pp. 113–53).

33. Cf. most recently for this pair M. Held, loc. cit., p. 92.

34. Our restoration (*k*ᶜ*s*) follows H. L. Ginsberg's interpretation and his reference to Job 6:2–3 and Prov. 27:3. The word *k*ᶜ*s* occurs in Aḥiqar 189; the restoration *zpt*ʾ preferred by Cowley (*CAP*, p. 216) is supported by the Syriac (no. 45, ed. Rendel Harris, p. 45 [Syr.]).

2) [. . . .] *šbq ḥmr wlʾ ysblnhy ynšʾ bwt mn knth [wyn]šʾ m[wb]lʾ zy lʾ zy [lh ʿm zylh] wṭʿwn gmlʾ yṭʿnnhy* (Aḥiqar 1.90–91)
"An ass which leaves (*its load*) and *does not carry it* shall take a *load* from its companion and take the b(urde)n which is not (its own with its own) and shall be made to bear a camel's load" (H.L.G., *ANET*² 428b).[35]

In Aḥiqar 1.111 we find *nśʾ//ṭʿn*. In analyzing the use of these verbs it is worth noting the following facts concerning *ṭʿn*: (a) in biblical Hebrew it is a *hapax* (Gen. 45:17) but serves the same function as *ʿms* and *nśʾ*, all three verbs are to be found in Gen. 44–45; (b) that in Mishnaic Hebrew *ṭʿn* is used frequently for "to load, bear" (Jastrow 544; Ben Yehuda 1897); (c) that in the Aramaic Targumim *ṭʿn* translates both *nśʾ* and *ʿms*, while in Syriac it translates *nśʾ*.[36] We have then in Aramaic *nśʾ//ṭʿn*, a parallel pair to *nśʾ//ʿms*.

In Aḥiqar (11. 90–91) we find that the pairs *sbl//nśʾ* and *nśʾ//ṭʿn* have been combined to a complex of three verbs *sbl//nśʾ//ṭʿn* used together.

It was noted above that Hebrew *ʿms//nśʾ* is found in Isa. 46:3 and *nśʾ//sbl* in 46:7. It is however proper now to look again at vv. 3b–4 of Isa. 46:

| | |
|---|---|
| *ha-ʿămūsīm minni-beṭen* | "carried from the belly" |
| *ha-nĕśūʾīm minni-raḥam* | "borne from the womb" |
| *wĕʿad-ziqnā ʾanī hūʾ* | "and until (your) old age I am the one |
| *wĕʿad-śēbā ʾănī ʾesbol* | and until (your) hoary age I will carry (you) |
| *ʾănī ʿāśītī wĕʾănī ʾeśśāʾ* | I have created and I will bear (you) |
| *waʾănīʾesbol wĕʾamalleṭ* | and I will bear (you) and keep (you) alive." |

Although I have translated the verbs *ʿms, nśʾ sbl* literally, the writer assumes for these verbs, in the passages under discussion, also their secondary meaning "to provide for, take care of, support."[37] In vv. 3 and 4, taking these verbs solely in their literal meaning "carries" makes no sense. The point of these verses is that God can provide for his people from birth to old age. In this verse, as elsewhere in Second Isaiah, the verb *ʿāsā* means "to create." I understand *malleṭ*, here as well as often elsewhere, as being the cognate of Akk. *bulluṭu* "to keep alive."[38] This adds to the poetic impact of the use of *nśʾ//sbl*

35. We have followed H. L. Ginsberg in his intepretation of this proverb. He follows the restorations proposed by D. H. Baneth (*OLZ* [1914]: 296–97) but diverges from him in interpretation. This proverb lends itself to still other interpretations, but they do not affect the basic point made here.

36. Cf. J. Levy, *Chaldaisches Woerterbuch über die Targumum* I (Leipzig, 1867), pp. 313–14, for Targumic references and Brockelmann, *Lex. Syr.*², pp. 283–84 for Syriac.

37. For a different view of *nśʾ//sbl* in Isa. 46:4, cf. Y. Muffs, *Studies in the Aramaic Legal Papyri from Elephantine* (Leiden, 1969), pp. 39, n. 4 and 198, and for a different understanding of these verses cf. John L. McKenzie, *Second Isaiah* (N.Y., 1968), pp. 85–87. I hope to return to the problem of *sbl* in the near future.

38. Cf. *CAD* "B" 59–62. Note that Akk. *bulluṭu* can mean "to provide with food."

in v. 7. Vs. 3–4 contain then *ʿms*, *nśʾ* and *sbl*, and although the context of the verses are dissimilar and the nuances of the verbs different there can be no doubt that in both Isa. 46:3–4 and Aḥiqar 90–91 the same functional group of verbs is being used.

| | |
|---|---|
| f) *wʾl ykn lm mškb ʾt rpʾm* | "may they not have rest with the Rephaim |
| *wʾl yqbr bqbr* | may they not be buried in a grave |
| *wʾl ykn lm bn wzrʿ tḥtnm* | may they not have son or seed in their place" |

Our limited comments on the Rephaim and these lines in general may be found above in the discussion of the Tabnit Inscription. The two late inscriptions quoted here will indicate the continuity of the tradition. The first is a Palmyrene inscription.

| | |
|---|---|
| (*wʾnš lʾ yptḥ ʿlwhy gwmḥʾ dnh ʿd ʿlmʾ*) | ("and may no man ever open up this niche;) |
| *lʾ yhwʾ lh zrʿ wgd ʿd ʿlmʾ* | may he never have seed or fortune |
| *wlʾ yqšṭ lmn zy yptḥyhy ʿd ʿlmʾ* | and may it never go well for him who opens it |
| *wlḥm wmn lmʾ yśbʿ* | and may he not be sated with bread or water" |

(Cooke *NSI* 145; *CIS* ii *4218*)

The first line of this curse matches the third of Eshmunazor, while the last line would seem to be a reference to the clean food and water that those who are at rest in Hades receive.[39]

The second instance is from the Maʿnū inscription in Early Syriac from Sherrin, first published by Pognon and most recently restudied by the late A. Maricq.[40] In that part of the curse formula that has survived we find the last two elements of the Eshmunazor curse:

> *wkprʾ lʾ yhwʾ lh wbnyʾ dyrmwn ʿprʾ ʿl ʿynwhy lʾ yštkḥwn lh*
> "may he not have a grave nor may there exist children who will throw dust on his eyes" (11. 7–9).
>
> g) *ysgr*
> *wysgrnm hʾlnm hqdšm ʾt mmlk⟨t⟩ ʾdr ʾš mšl bnm lqṣtnm* . . . . (9–10)
> "may the holy gods deliver them to a mighty king who will rule over them to 'destroy' them . . . ."

39. The one who receives a proper burial and who has someone to tend his ghost with the proper rituals of water libation and food (*kispu*) will drink pure water and proper food in the netherworld while the others have to rely upon scraps thrown in the streets: *kusīpāt akāli ša ina sūqi nadā ikkal* (Gilg. XII, 154).

40. H. Pognon, *Inscriptions sémitiques de la Syrie, de la Mésopotamie et de la region de Mossoul* (Paris, 1907), p. 17; A. Maricq, *Classica et Orientalia* (Paris, 1965), pp. 135–36.

It has scarcely been noticed that this verse has a parallel in Isa. 19:4:

> *wĕsikkartī ʾet-miṣrayim bĕyad ʾădonīm qāše umelek ʿaz yimšol-bām*
> "and I will hand Egypt over to a mighty lord and a powerful king will rule over them."[41]

The parallels between Eshmunazor and Isaiah are clear:

| *Eshmunazor* | *Isaiah* |
|---|---|
| *wysgrnm* | *wskrty* |
| *ʾt mmlk⟨t⟩ ʾdr* | *byd ʾdnym qšh* |
| *ʾš ymšl bnm* | *wmlk ʿz ymšl-bm* |
| *lqṣtnm* | vs. 5f. |

The verb *sgr*, here in the yifil imperfect, is the technical term for "handing over" slaves, prisoners, escapees, and for forced deportation. A translation such as "abandon" proposed by Rosenthal does not bring out the desired nuance.[42] In Eshmunazor the verb is in the *yifʿil*, which matches the frequent use of *sgr* in the *hifʿil* in Hebrew. Early Aramaic also has *hskr* in the Sefire inscriptions. The following verb *mšl*, optative in mood, is also part of the technical language, for besides the usual meaning "to rule" it has the technical meaning of "to have power over, possess."[43] The verb *lqṣtnm* is not easy to translate.[44] There can be no doubt in my mind that it must be associated with biblical Hebrew *lĕqaṣṣōt* used in II Kings 10:32:

> *bĕyāmīm hāhēm hēḥēl YHWH lĕqaṣṣōt beyiśrāʾel*
> "in those days Y. began to cut off part of Israel" (RSV).

In the biblical passage the referrent is clearly the loss of territory, while in Eshmunazor it is probably loss of life.

It has been proposed to emend *skrty* of Isa. 19:4 to *mkrty*.[45] I think that the comparison with Eshmunazor *cannot* be used against this proposal. The root *skr* is not used in Hebrew with this meaning and it is hard to find a reason for its use here; in the Herodian book hand *mem* and *samekh* are similar enough to lead to mistakes. In addition *mkr* has this meaning frequently[46] and is so used in Ezek. 30:12 where the subject once again is Egypt. Finally *mkr* is

41. G. B. Gray, *Isaiah*, vol. I (I.C.C.), to Isa. 19:4 (p. 325) calls attention to Eshmunazor, but neither Cooke, Slouschz, nor Donner–Röllig refer to Isaiah in their works.

42. Cf. *ANET*², p. 505.

43. E.g., Exod. 21:8.

44. This verb occurs also in *CIS* I 3784, 1. 7.

45. Although Gray, *Isaiah*, loc. cit., proposed the reading *mkrty* he attempted to defend the reading *sikkartī*, but his semantic arguments are not valid. Neither is recourse to Aramaic *skr* satisfactory, since there is no other trace of it in Hebrew. On the other hand *sgr* in the *Genesis Apocryphon* (22, 17) is in all likelihood a Hebraism.

46. E.g. Jud. 2:14; 10:7.

used in parallelism with *hsgr* in Deut. 32:30 and its presence in Isa. 19:4 would in no way detract from that verse's common heritage with Eshmunazor 9–10.

h) *ʾl ykn lm šrš lmṭ wpr lmʿl wtʾr bḥym tḥt šmš* (11–12)

The essay by H. L. Ginsberg, "Roots Below and Fruit Above," has assembled the biblical material pertinent to this verse,[47] but the phrase *tʾr bḥym* remains difficult. The context of *tʾr* is best established by such verses as I Sam. 16:18; Isa. 52:14; 53:2 (//*hadar*) where *toʾar* is really not only "good looks" but a special transcendent quality. It is possible that this word is to be added in the Tabnit inscription 1.7: *ʾl y⟨k⟩n l⟨k⟩ zrʿ ⟨wtʿr⟩ bḥym.*

## KARATEPE (*KAI* 26)

The Karatepe inscription, which was widely discussed in the years after it was discovered, is now taken for granted.[48] But it deserves fuller discussion from the stylistic point of view. In an earlier study I dealt with I 7, *wpʿl ʾnk ss ʿl ss wmgn ʿl mgn wmḥnt ʿl mḥnt*, noting parallels in Akkadian, Hebrew, and Aramaic.[49] Two of the blessings of this inscription use rhetorical devices worthy of attention. The first is:

> *wbrk bʿl k[r]ntryš ʾyt ʾztwd ḥym wšlm wʿz ʾdr ʿl kl mlk*
> "May Baʿal Krntrys bless Azitawada with life and health and great power over every king." (III 2–4)

Of particular interest in this blessing is the phrase *ḥym wšlm*, which may be translated simply as "life and health." It goes without saying that this formula is an ancient one and it calls to mind the typical blessing for life and health that one finds in Old Babylonian letter greeting formulas:

> *ᵈšamaš liballiṭka lū šalmāta lū balṭāta*
> "May Shamash grant you life; may you be well, may you live"
> (*YOS* 2, 66, 4–5)

There is no need to trace the development, combinations, and permutations of these formulae, since this has been done in a recent work on *Die Gruss-und Höflichkeitsformeln* by Erkii Salonen.[50] Suffice it to say that in Neo-Babylonian

47. In *Hebrew and Semitic Studies Presented to G. R. Driver* (Oxford, 1963), pp. 72–76.
48. Although the comparative aspect was noted in many articles *KAI* is deficient on this score.
49. *JSS* 11 (1966): 103–5.
50. *Studia Orientalia Fennica* XXXVIII (Helsinki, 1967). For the Neo-Babylonian formulae see pp. 99–103. Frequent occurrences of *šalāmu u balāṭu* / *šulmu u balāṭu* can be found s.v. *balāṭu* in *CAD* "B" 46ff. Cf. too Hirsch, *AfO* 22 (1968/69): 44.

letters the greeting is frequently stated simply $DN_1$ & $DN_2$ *šulum u balāṭu ša PN liqbû*, "May $DN_1$ & $DN_2$ command the life and health of PN."

The same formula, "life and health," is found in a series of Aramaic letters.[51] We read in Hermopolis III, 1.5:

> *ʾl ʾḥy wḥprᶜ mn ʾḥk mkbnt šlm wḥyn šlḥt lk*
> "to my brother Wḥprᶜ from your brother Makkibanit (greetings) of health and life I send you."

The same formula may be restored without hesitation in Letter VII, 1.1.: [*šlm wḥ*]*yn šlḥt lky*. This formula, as Mme. E. Bresciani the editor of these letters states, is also found in an Aramaic Ostracon document from Egypt:

*ʾl mry mykyh ᶜbdk gdl šlm wḥyn šlḥt lk*
"to my lord Micaiah (from) your servant Gadol (greetings) of health and life I send to you" (Cler.-Gan. 70, 1–3, [*RHR* 130 (1945):20]).

I do not believe that it has been noticed that this same phrase occurs in Mal. 2:5:

> *bĕrītī haytā ʾittō haḥayyīm wĕhašālōm*
> "my covenant was with him for life and health."[52]

The phrase "life and health" in the Karatepe inscription then is not an independent phrase devoid of all connections; it belongs rather to an old blessing formula which was undoubtedly well known and meaningful.

The final blessing in this inscription is:

*ʾps šm ʾztwd ykn lᶜlm km šm šmš wyrḥ*
"but the name of Azitawada will endure forever, as does the name of the sun and the moon." (IV, 1–3).

The eternal quality of the sun and the moon are combined with the blessing for "life and health" in the blessing formula from the end of an earlier royal inscription—this one an inscribed cylinder of Samsu-Ilūna of Babylon:

*šulmam u balāṭam ša kima Sîn u Šamaš darium ana qištim liqīšūšum ana širiktim lišrukūšum*
"may they (the gods) grant him as a gift and bestow upon him as a present health and life eternal as the moon and sun." (*YOS* 9, 35, pl. XIII:148–54).

51. E. Bresciani and M. Kamil (editors), *Le lettre aramaiche di Hermopolis* (Roma, 1966). Letter III is on p. 392; Letter VII on p. 412. For these letters cf. this writer and B. Porten, "The Aramaic Papyri from Hermopolis," *ZAW* 80 (1968): 216–31.

52. One is tempted, were it not for the clear context that militates against it, to amend *bryty* to *brkty*.

A reference to this same idea surely lies behind the phrase which comes at the end of a recently published fragmentary Ugaritic text: *btk ugrt lymt špš wyrḫ wnᶜmt šnt il* (*Ugaritica V*, 2, rev. 10–12).[53] It may best be translated "in the midst of Ugarit for the days of the sun and the moon and the pleasant years of El." Comparison with the Old Babylonian and with Karatepe makes it clear that eternity is meant.

This phrase was part of the normal stock of similes throughout the Canaanite language group, for we find it used also in a variety of forms in the Hebrew Bible.[54] The Davidic house is promised eternity in Ps. 89:

37. *zarᶜō lĕᶜōlām yihye* *wĕkisʾō kašemeš negdī*
38. *kayāreaḥ yikkōn ᶜōlām* *weᶜēd ba-šaḥaq neʾĕmān selā*
"His seed will endure forever and his throne is as the sun before me;
As the moon it will endure forever and the 'witness' on high is faithful."

The sun and the moon, *šmš* and *yrḥ*, endure forever, *ykn ᶜlm* (//*lᶜlm yhyh*) and serve as signs of the durability of the Davidic dynasty. In Ps. 72, a royal Psalm, we read:

v. 5 *yīrāʾūkā ᶜim-šemeš welifnē yāreaḥ dōr-dōrīm*
"They will 'fear' You as long as the Sun (exists) and with the Moon for eternity."[55]

The durability of the King's name (and fame) is celebrated in:

v. 17 *yĕhī šĕmō lĕᶜōlām lifnē šemeš yikkōn šĕmō*
"may his name endure forever and with the sun may his name endure," etc.

We have emended the *MT* which had the meaningless *yinnōn* (Ketib *ynyn*) to accord with Karatepe and Ps. 89.[56] It may be ventured that reference to the moon has dropped out here (*wĕyitbārĕkū bō ᶜim yāreaḥ*). Be that as it may there can be no doubt that we have here the same formula as that found in Karatepe and lying behind the phrase now known from Ugarit.

53. The Ugaritic text is on p. 554, and Virolleaud's translation, which is wide of the mark, is on p. 557. C. H. Gordon in the Supplement of his *Ugaritic Textbook*, p. 555, under no. 19. 2447, supplies the correct translation.

54. R. T. O'Callaghan compared the following verses with the Karatepe inscription in passing in *VT* 4 (1954): 165.

55. Cf. n. 12 above. The use of *ᶜm* and *lpny* in this verse is problematic. For *ᶜm* cf. Daniel 3: 33; 4: 31.

56. This emendation was previously adduced from the context; it now has strong epigraphic support. The *nun* and *kaf* were similar in the early Hebrew alphabet.

### ADDENDUM

The Samsu-Ilūna inscription previously known from *YOS* 9, 35 has now been reedited and translated by E. Sollberger as "Samsu-Ilūna's Bilingual Inscription C" in *RA* 6 (1969): 29–40. It is noteworthy that both this passage and the Old Babylonian passage quoted in the first addendum refer to Amurrite rulers. Are these the earliest examples of a North West Semitic tradition?

# History and Cult in the Old Testament

E. HAMMERSHAIMB

A THOROUGH discussion of the topic which I have chosen cannot be accomplished in a single article. Instead of giving a short survey of all the problems combined with the topic I have concentrated on some essential points.

As a general and principal basis for the following treatment, it is to be understood in advance that, in my opinion, the Old Testament does not form a unity in terms of a religion. There are numerous reflections in the Old Testament, and it is often impossible to place them in chronological relationship because of the complicated circumstances which apply to the tradition of the texts. These remarks concern the Old Testament as a whole, and therefore apply to the problems which will be investigated in the following discussion.

For the sake of clarity I must define my interpretation of some of the terms which will be used, because they are often used in rather a different sense by those who have dealt with them. First and foremost, the term *history*. I need not go into a discussion concerning the fact that the Old Testament historiography is something different from historical research in the modern sense of the word. I must, however, make it clear that by history and historical events I am referring to activities or phenomena which directly affect people or are placed in relationship to them, and by historical accounts I am referring to accounts which deal with such events. As an example: a war between two peoples is an historical event, and an account of this war is historical—

regardless of its value. An occurrence in nature such as an earthquake, or a long-lasting drought is historical when it affects mankind. On the other hand, faults in the strata of the earth which took place in the far distance geological past are not historical events. It is something else again when peculiar formations in nature cause people to speculate about their origin. The tales of such events are not history, but legend (in German: Sage). Thus the word "legend" is different from the word "history," because it is used to convey an imaginary happening, whether it involves something in the environment or in the life of man.

Likewise, it would be well to define the relationship between history and *myth*, since this question has caused much dissension, which to a great extent —but not entirely—is due to disagreement concerning the definition of the word "myth." On the basis of the Greek meaning of myth, in earlier literature it was agreed to a wide extent that a myth was a story about gods and divine beings and their deeds.[1] In more recent times the most important contribution to the discussion of this question is from the English "myth-and-ritual school," represented by scholars like A. M. Hocart, S. Hooke, and E. O. James, who connect myth with cult, where myth complements rite. Thus Hooke emphasizes that a common feature for the early ritual patterns in the Ancient East is the circumstance that they consisted not only of things done but of things said, and as a closer definition of his interpretation of myth the following thesis is typical: "In general the spoken part of the ritual consists of a description of what is being done, it is the story which the ritual enacts. This is the sense in which the term "myth" is used in our discussion. The original myth, inseparable in the first instance from its ritual, embodies in more or less symbolic fashion the original situation which is seasonally re-enacted in the ritual."[2]

Hooke's formulation is attractive in several respects, not only because of the view which he takes of myth but because of the brief and precise manner in which he expresses this interpretation. However, this formulation does not solve the question of the further development of myth, when Hooke speaks about "the original myth, inseparable in the first instance from its ritual." In the formulation it is implicit that myth can be separated from ritual, and, furthermore, the formulation presents no opinion concerning the source of the narrative elements of myth. Here we are faced with the constantly

1. See H. Gunkel, *Genesis* 5 (1922), p. XIV: "Mythen" . . . sind Göttergeschichten, im Unterschiede von den Sagen, deren handlende Personen Menschen sind.

2. See S. H. Hooke, *Myth and Ritual* (London, 1933), p. 3, cf. Hooke, *In the Beginning* (Oxford, 1948), p. 18, and G. Widengren in his article "Myth and History in Israelite–Jewish Thought," *Culture in History, Essays in Honor of Paul Radin* (New York, 1960), pp. 467f.

recurring problem concerning the primary relationship between myth and history, where the two extreme points of view—to express it briefly—are represented by the euhemeristic interpretation which stems from Euhemeros, the Stoic who thought that the Greek gods originally were historical figures who after their death were made the object of a divine cult. According to this, myth would be secondary to the primary importance of history. Or, in other words, one could speak of history becoming myth. The other extreme would be to make history of myth, where the motive of the rituals is detached from myth and becomes history. The problem is obscured by the fact that plausible examples can be used to support both views, and therefore many scholars have abandoned this approach to the problem and declared that "history and myth are almost inextricably mixed."[3]

Nevertheless, I believe that it is wise to separate myth from history in principle because by nature they are so very different. It is characteristic of myth that the situations it contains are performed again and again in the ritual drama, because it lies in the nature of the cult myth that it re-enacts that which is contained in its words. When myth belongs to the annually recurrent rituals, those who participate repeat the exact words and acts, and thus the meaning of the cult lies in the fact that those who participate always experience the power created by the words and acts of the ritual. In history, however, the same event never recurs in exactly the same way. The persons, the place, the period, and the social and political conditions, etc., are never identical, even though there may be striking similarities. Therefore, in contrast to myth, "Einmaligkeit" is a characteristic of history. Naturally this does not exclude the possibility that an historical event may have been recounted on numerous occasions, and it may have been handed down orally from one generation to the next, but that does not make it become myth. It only becomes myth if in one form or another it is adopted into the cult and is thus re-experienced in a manner entirely different from that in which one experiences a tale. It could happen merely by a brief reference to one of the stories known to all the members of the cult. Conversely, those members of the cult who are familiar with a certain motif can feel that it is occurring in an historical event, and it is then interpreted as a realization of something well known from the cult.

Before going on to a closer investigation of how the considerations taken into account here stand in relationship to the material contained in the Old Testament, it is necessary to explain how the idea of time was understood

3. Quotation from Pieter Geyl, which Widengren adduces as a motto for his above mentioned article.

by the ancients—especially in ancient Israel. It has often been emphasized that today we consider history as something in constant progression from one or another period in a far distant past to a period lying infinitely in the future. Thus history can be outlined graphically as intervals of time indicated on a straight line. Today our calendar is, among other things, an expression of this understanding. Such an abstract notion of time was foreign to ancient Orientals, even though in some places they also had a calendar system which in reality was not different from ours. However, this applies only to the highly developed urban societies. During the Old Testament period there was also an urban culture in Israel—primarily in the two capitals Jerusalem and Samaria, during the period of the Kings, but before that time the predominant culture was agricultural, having survivals from a nomadic culture, and both continued to exist side by side with the emergence of urban civilization.

We are treading on uncertain ground when we speak about Israel before the migration into Canaan, and only with the greatest caution can we base our theories on traditions concerning the connection between early Israel with both Babylon and Egypt. The presentation of the patriarchs as nomads having herds of sheep and goats and the beginnings of agriculture are common to these traditions. Even up to the present time, we know of nomadic tribes who during their wanderings stay at any one place only long enough to sow and harvest a small amount of grain. The narratives in Genesis seem to indicate that before the patriarchs finally settled in Canaan they belonged to just this type of semi-nomadic tribes. During their stay in Egypt, the Israelites also differed from the Egyptians by being shepherds (cp. Gen. 46:34).

Although many scholars have taken a very sceptical view of the Old Testament accounts about the Israelite's sojourn in Egypt and their subsequent departure and have rejected the idea that they can be used to establish a realistic portrayal of this period; to me, it seems impossible to understand the later development of the history of the Israelites without taking their stay in Egypt and the desert into account.[4] For the period which followed, we have a far greater number of sources consisting of texts as well as archaeological material. The books of Joshua, Judges, Samuel, and Kings describe the struggle which took place between Israel and the people of Canaan. The clear evidence from the Old Testament must be regarded as proof that regardless of the fact that there were periods when these two peoples lived side

4. Thus, W. F. Albright on several occasions, e.g., *From the Stone Age to Christianity* (Baltimore, 1946), pp. 183f.

by side peacefully, and could make treaties with one another, the conflict between them was often so great that it resulted in open combat.

The Old Testament leaves us in no doubt about the final victory of Israel. However, we may confidently assert that conflicts in the sphere of culture and religion were even more significant. Here, the prophetical texts of the Old Testament, with their evidence of the spiritual struggle between the two peoples, play an important role.

During the period of their adjustment to a life in a sedentary country; the Israelite tribes had to learn how to survive in this society by following the example of the Canaanites. In a settled country, one could not survive with having herds of sheep and goats only, because it was necessary to have oxen for agriculture. Man and beast were both dependent upon the natural change of the seasons, when, after the dry season, the rains came in autumn and the grasses grew again, giving nourishment for the cattle and making the soil suitable for ploughing and sowing seeds. When the rains stopped, in the spring, the warmth of summer came to ripen the grain and fruit. This recurrent rhythm of the year is attested in several cult patterns in the ancient Orient (cp. p. 270), and of special significance for the understanding of the Old Testament is the cult of the Canaanites. In this cult, the change between the season of rain and the season of drought is described as a struggle between the God Baʾl and his opponent Mot (Death). Baʾl is the god of the cattle, and his female partner Anat is a goddess in the shape of a heifer. Baʾl reigns during the season of the rains, but dies when the drought comes and vegetation withers; then he is buried and Mot reigns during the hot season. The renewal of Baʾl's power when the season of rain begins is described as a revival and his resurrection and reinstatement as king. The god El presides over these two gods and takes care that the balance between them is observed. All are aware of the necessity of the seasons of rain and of warmth. If one season is prolonged—or fails to come—it affects the crops and thereby the prosperity of the people.

Obviously, people who have culture of this nature would regard time in a manner which differs greatly from that of modern man. These people conceived of time as a cycle finding its expression in the changing acts of the cultic drama. Year after year the cycle is repeated in the same manner—and so it is meant to be.

From this succinct account of the Canaanite cult drama it will be evident that it is based on the texts found at Ras Shamra and a specific understanding of these texts. Concerning the Canaanites, who lived in Palestine when Israel invaded the country, and their religion we have very little direct evidence.

Before the archaeological discoveries were made at Ras Shamra one had to rely primarily on the Old Testament. The historical books in the Old Testament and the prophetical texts contain numerous sources which directly or indirectly form a reaction against the Baʾl cult. The argument that we have only a very one-sided knowledge of the Baʾl religion because we know it only through a reaction against it has lost some of its significance since the discoveries at Ras Shamra. These discoveries involve finds which are roughly contemporary with the period of the early migration of the Israelite tribes into Palestine. Admittedly, these discoveries were not made in Palestine but in Northern Syria and in an urban, heterogeneous society. However, they can assist us in understanding the cultural and religious conflicts between the invading Israelites and the settled Canaanites, since they confirm the picture of the Baʾl religion of the Canaanites in the Old Testament texts.

Immediately after the first publications of these discoveries, the interpretation of the nature of the texts provoked great disagreement among scholars, and even after a generation of intensive study we still find divergent opinions with regard to their correct interpretation.

Some scholars have accepted them as literary documents. For example, one referred to them as (cult) legends composed in literary style which could be understood and enjoyed for their own sake.[5]

On the other hand there were those who supported the myth-and-ritual school and maintained that these texts were a confirmation of the ideas which, as early as the 1930's, had been applied to the Ancient Near East as a whole and that the Ras Shamra texts were closely related to the temple cults of ancient Ugarit.[6] This interpretation was supported by the fact that the texts belonged to the Temple archives. In spite of the fact that the texts were found in the great temple of Baʾl and Dagon, and even though one of the texts (IIAB) is specifically concerned with the temple of Baʾl, it was asserted by others that this did not constitute conclusive evidence that they had been recited at cult festivals, nor that they had been used as a "libretto" in the performance of cult dramas.

In the third volume of "Myth, Ritual, and Kingship," which S. H. Hooke published in 1958, de Langhe in his contribution[7] rejects the cultic interpretation. He does not question the existence of a Baʾl temple, nor that sacrifices were made to Baʾl, nor that Baʾl occupied a prominent position in the

5. See W. Baumgartner, Ugaritische Probleme und ihre Tragweite für des Alte Testament, *ThZ* 3 (1947): 81–100 (esp. pp. 89f.).

6. This group of scholars is represented by names such as T. H. Gaster, F. Hvidberg, I. Engnell, G. Widengren, and A. Kapelrud.

7. *Myth, Ritual and Kingship in the Ras Shamra Tablets*, pp. 122–48.

pantheon of Ugarit. Neither does he dispute his "decisive role in maintaining and renewing the fertility and well-being of persons and things." He even goes so far as to say that *a priori* he is willing to admit the possibility of "dramatic performances at regular intervals." But when, at last, he raises the question: "What role did the cycle of the texts AB play in it?", he replies: "The only answer yielded by examination and analysis of the texts under discussion is: a myth with epic aspects. All the rest dissolves into hypothesis."[8]

Hooke's article in the same volume[9] is a strong defense of the entire "school" and its fundamental points of view, to which G. Widengren's contribution subscribes with a wealth of important observations to support the cultic interpretation of the texts.[10]

Previously, I have supported the cult-mythical interpretation of the AB texts without reservation, and I am still of the opinion that those who support this interpretation have presented such strong arguments for their basic views that one cannot justly question the existence of cult festivals of the nature which they postulate. But I believe that some doubt can be raised as to whether the AB cycle in its *present* form represents the cult texts themselves. After renewed study of the texts, I feel inclined to call them a literary adaptation of the actual cult texts. If so, it is difficult to say how far this adaptation differs from the original cult texts. For my part, I consider this irrelevant. The fact which I believe to be most important is that under all circumstances the texts are based on a cult drama of the type, and having the significance which, in my opinion, the myth-and-ritual school have made probable by their research.

Therefore, according to my definition of the word "myth," it is doubtful whether the AB texts can be so classified; it is more likely that they are examples of what I would call a dissociation of myth from cult, of which we have several instances in the Old Testament.

Before leaving the subject of the Ras Shamra texts, I must briefly refer to yet another group of texts, the correct interpretation of which affects our subject. I am referring to the so-called Keret texts, also possibly including the Danel texts, or Aqhat texts as they are usually called now. Virolleaud viewed the first Keret text (I K) essentially as an historical text, or at least as a text containing many historical references.[11] Although some obvious errors had to be corrected in his initial interpretation, there are still some who

8. Loc. cit., p. 141.
9. *Myth and Ritual: Past and Present*, op. cit., pp. 1–21.
10. *Early Hebrew Myths and Their Interpretation*, pp. 149–203.
11. See Charles Virolleaud, *La légende de Keret, roi des Sidoniens* (Paris, 1936).

maintain the historical view.[12] Against this view, is the purely cultic interpretation, having nothing to do with the historical approach, as defined by I. Engnell, among others, who calls the Krt-cycle "simply another parallel of the AB-cycle."[13]

In my opinion, neither of these two interpretations is feasible without modification. Keret (or Karit) is a primeval King of Ugarit, but whether, or when, a ruling king by that name ever existed is not known. He belongs to a mythical age and does not occur among the other royal names of Ugarit.[14]

The likelihood of the cultic interpretation of the Keret texts is supported by the observation that the king in Ugarit wanted to strengthen his power by the cult, and in this cult there are motifs similar to those well-known in the dynasty of David (cp. in particular, 2 Sam. 7). There are also features which could be interpreted as a reflection of a state of conflict between the ruling King and one of his sons (cp. 2 K 6:25ff.); but here again, it does not necessarily reflect an historical event but could be a recurrent motif having similarities to the deposition of the Babylonian King and his reinstatement, as we know about it from the New Year's festival.[15]

In the text 2 K, the illness of the king as something which projects beyond history and is related to the general pattern of the cult seems to be clearly indicated by the coincidence of the illness with phenomena in nature (cp. 2 K 2:81ff.). Therefore, it is likely that the Keret texts are a poetic, literary adaptation of the cult texts or a further development of motifs which occur in the cult—just as has been suggested with reference to the AB cycle. If so, there are probably also associated features which touch upon some historical material—both in names of persons as well as places.

The purpose of this review of the cult of the Canaanites with regard to opinions concerning the relationship between the aspects of mythology and history in the cult is intended to outline the background necessary for the understanding of the same phenomena in the Old Testament.

We have extensive information about the cult in ancient Israel in the legal material contained in the Pentateuch. This applies to both the various kinds of sacrifices, their aims, and to whom and for whom they are offered, and to the particular and periodically recurrent cult festivals. The

12. Cf. de Langhe, op. cit., pp. 144–48.

13. See I. Engnell, *Studies in Divine Kingship in the Ancient Near East* (Uppsala, 1943), pp. 143–73.

14. Nor has the royal seal from Ugarit the name Keret, see Claude Schaeffer, *Mission de Ras Shamra, Tome VI, Le palais royal d'Ugarit III* (Paris, 1955), planche XI and XVII and p. XLIII.

15. On this feast in Babylon see Johannes Pedersen, *Israel, Its Life and Culture,* III–IV, (London & Copenhagen, 1940), pp. 747ff., with his references.

advances made in research during the predominance of literary critical approach are due to the discussion which it provoked concerning the relative age of the various laws and their placement in relationship to the doctrines of the prophets by which many of the hitherto accepted views were reversed. During the next period of research, the investigations of religious history awakened a growing understanding of the importance which the comparative material had in the study of the Old Testament. During this period, Gunkel was the great name among the scholars. His research on the psalms formed the basis for regarding the Old Testament Psalms as sources for the cult in the temple of Jerusalem in the time before the exile. The Scandinavian scholars, led by Sigmund Mowinckel,[16] would not treat the psalms of the Old Testament merely as psalms to be recited or sung in the temple during the post-exilic period or to be used merely for personal edification.

On the basis of the so-called royal psalms (especially Pss. 47; 93; 95–100), Mowinckel developed his particular theory about a festival which he called Yahweh's coronation festival and which was to take place annually in Ancient Israel.[17] This festival celebrated Yahweh's reinstatement to royal power (יהוה מלך), this being similar to Baʾl's accession to power during the Canaanite autumn festival which we have discussed earlier in this article. Some scholars went even further and thought that Yahweh was also celebrated as a dying and resurrected God and that the one who assumed the role of Yahweh in the cult drama was the King.

There were protests against Mowinckel's theory. Its great weakness was that such a festival is not mentioned in the Old Testament—neither in the laws, nor by the oldest prophets, nor in the earliest historical writings. These objections do not, however, exclude the possibility nor the likelihood that Yahweh's assumption of the royal power has existed as a motif in the Israelite cult, merely that we know nothing about whether it comprised a special festival. It is far more likely that it became part of the ancient New Year's festival. Yahweh had appeared as king of all the world for the first time when he created the world, and it is this particular idea of creation which is a prominent feature in the royal psalms (see 95:4f.; 96:10; 100:3). As a parallel to this, one can refer to the fact that the creation epic "Enūma elish" in Babylon was part of the ritual of the New Year festival's fourth day.[18] Therefore it is natural that in Israel at the New Year's festival, Yahweh's

16. See S. Mowinckel, *Psalmenstudien I–VI, Kristiania* (Oslo, 1921–24).
17. See *Psalmenstudien*, vol. II (1922).
18. See *ANET*, p. 332.

renewal of the covenant between him and his people, Israel, was celebrated. It was part of the covenant that Yahweh had adopted Israel as his favored people and would protect them against their enemies. It is worthy of note that the psalms often contain brief references to events in the history of Israel. Apart from the story of creation, which we regard as a cosmic event not affecting a single people, Ps. 95, after speaking of Yahweh as creator (vv. 3–5), mentions events from the desert wanderings (vv. 8–10: Meriba and Massa). In this instance it is in the form of a warning, but in other psalms a list of Yahweh's merciful deeds toward the people occurs; for example, in Ps. 136, which first praises Yahweh as the creator (vv. 3–9) and thereafter enumerates deeds of salvation in the history of the people: the deliverance from Egypt, the crossing of the Red Sea, their wanderings and battles in the desert, and finally the bestowal of the land of Canaan (vv. 10–22).

What has been said here with regard to the psalms of the Old Testament will have to suffice to indicate the obvious difference between cult among the Canaanites and that of Ancient Israel, because phenomena in the cycle of nature, among the Canaanites, are almost completely dominant, whereas, among the Israelites such phenomena are combined with the acceptance of events which have occurred in the history of the people as being of specific importance in the cult.

This is brought out even more clearly by other instances in the Old Testament. When the Deuteronomist refers to the procedure which is applied to the presentation of the first crop in the new country, after Israel had taken possession of it, he includes a reference to the past history of the people almost in the nature of a confession of faith (Deut. 26:1ff.).[19] There it is prescribed that the priest should take the basket containing "some of the first of all the fruit of the ground" from the hand of him who presents the offering, place himself before the altar and say: "A Syrian ready to perish was my father, and he went down to Egypt, and sojourned there, few in number; and he became there a nation, great, mighty, and populous; and the Egyptians evil entreated us, and afflicted us, and laid upon us hard bondage: and we cried unto the Lord, the God of our fathers, and the Lord heard our voice, and saw our affliction, and our toil, and our oppression: and the Lord brought us forth out of Egypt with a mighty hand . . . and has given us this land" (vv. 5–9).

The situation which this law seems to foresee would occur regularly at the

19. Cf. Gerhard von Rad, *Das formgeschichtliche Problem des Hexateuchs* (1938), reprinted in *Gesammelte Studien zum Alten Testament* (1958), pp. 11–16 (Das kleine geschichtliche Credo), and Leonhard Rost, *Das kleine Credo und andere Studien zum Alten Testament* (1965), pp. 11–25.

time for the harvest to ripen in the new country; and it is worthy of note that a concentrated resumé of historical events relating to the people should be read or recited in connection with the offering of the first fruits of the harvest. We find ourselves far removed from the actual cult drama.

In the great festivals, also—and above all in the feast of Passover—historical motifs play a prominent role. From the Jewish Passover traditions it is well known that the youngest person present at a certain time asks the father of the household what this meal means, whereupon the father of the house recounts the entire Old Testament narrative of Israel's release from Egyptian bondage, her sojourn in Egypt, Moses being called upon to lead his people, the plagues, and the deliverance from Egypt. The accounts are found in Ex. 1–15, in which we also find the account of the founding of the Passover in chapter 12. The law of Passover and the unleavened bread is taken up in several places in the Old Testament: Ex. 23:14f.; 34:18,25; Lev. 23:5–8; Num. 28:16–25; Deut. 16:1–8,16f.; Ez. 45:21–25. In their brevity none of the sources have anything to say about the reading of an account of the institution of Passover. Nor does one find any reference to this custom in the detailed accounts of the Passover during the time of Hezekiah and Josiah in 2 Chr. 30 and 35, respectively. Nor is there any reference in the much briefer account of Josiah's Passover festival in 2 Kings 23:21–23.

Nevertheless, it is very unlikely that Passover, the most important of all of the festivals in the history of Israel, should not have contained references to the historical events which the Old Testament associates with Passover. This is not merely a supposition. It finds support in several references which actually state that what happens at Passover, is a commemoration of Israel's conditions in Egypt (cp. Ex. 12:14; 13:2; Deut. 16:3,12). A meaning far more active than our word "commemoration" lies in the Hebrew root *zkr*.[20] It is a re-enactment of what once happened (Ex. 12:25–27), and this means that it is re-experienced in the cult festival. Johannes Pedersen is, therefore, probably right in saying that Ex. 1–15 was part of the Passover legend.[21] The nature of the legend is such that one cannot find exact historical accounts in it, nor can one establish its date of origin. With the passing of time, it may have been altered by additions and omissions.

On the evening of Passover, the participants in the feast relive the exodus from Egypt by consuming the Passover meal in great haste. The meal

20. Cf. P. A. H. de Boer, *Gedenken und Gedächtnis in der Welt des Alten Testaments* (Stuttgart, 1962).

21. See Johannes Pedersen, *Israel, Its Life and Culture*, III–IV, pp. 384–415 and 728–37.

consists of unleavened bread and bitter herbs in reminiscence of the Land of Bondage, and this happens with one's staff in one's hand, with sandals on one's feet, and with one's loins girded (Ex. 12:11). The events in connection with the exodus from Egypt are relived in the course of the festival night (on the fourteenth day of the first month): at the beginning of the evening the Passover lamb is slaughtered (Ex. 12:6), by midnight Yahweh smites the firstborn in the land of Egypt (12:29), and at day-break Yahweh's victory over the enemies of Israel has been accomplished when the Egyptian army has perished in the waves of the sea (14:24ff.).[22]

As I have previously mentioned, one cannot utilize Ex. 1–15 in an attempt to reconstruct the historical course of events in detail. Nevertheless, it must be taken for granted that behind this account there are realities which, by those who experienced them, were looked upon as proof that in a singular fashion and with superior power Yahweh had freed his people from serfdom in Egypt. The distinction between the natural and the supernatural was not nearly as obvious among peoples of antiquity as it is today. Therefore, anything which happened could be interpreted as something which Yahweh himself enacted and arranged for his chosen people.

Consequently, the core of the matter is not to ask how much we may acknowledge as being true in this account, but to state that at that time, as well as afterward, Israel looked upon events as having taken place at the command of Yahweh as part of his plans for his own people, and that this belief in Yahweh and his concern for Israel is reflected in the fact that the account of the Passover was included in the ritual festival itself.

If we were to more closely examine the original nature of the Passover, we should see how significant the historical element was in connection with this festival. Here I must refrain from an investigation of this question and merely give my point of view, that the Passover and the feast of the Unleavened Bread are two different festivals, the former being originally a nomadic festival in connection with which the firstborn lambs were sacrificed in the spring;[23] the latter an agricultural festival connected with the harvesting of the barley. Chronologically, the two festivals generally coincided and could, therefore, be combined after the invasion of Israel into Palestine. Originally, both festivals were connected exclusively with life in a natural environment in the annual cycle, without historical reference.

22. Cf. Johannes Pedersen, loc. cit., p. 411. He considers it a matter of course that the texts were recited and "that it took place by parts of it being assigned to different people, who dramatised the stories not only by reciting the words."

23. Johannes Pedersen, op. cit., p. 398, refers as a parallel to the Arabian *ʿatīra* festival which was celebrated in the spring when the young of the flocks had been born.

The change in the nature of the festival of Passover which occurs in Israel also occurs in connection with the other two great feasts of ingathering: the festival of Weeks and the feast of Tabernacles, but most clearly with regard to the feast of Tabernacles. Originally it was undoubtedly a feast celebrated upon the completion of the harvesting of the fruit, similar to the Canaanite autumn festival (see Jud. 9:27; 21:20f.). During this festival, it was an ancient custom to live in tabernacles. The nature of the festival was changed when the Israelites adopted it, and the tabernacles were constructed artificially in remembrance of the sojourn in the desert (Lev. 23:33–43). Also, the feast of Weeks, which was originally connected with the harvesting of the wheat, assumes an historical aspect, albeit less pronounced than that which applies to the Passover and the feast of Tabernacles. The participants were to remember the serfdom in Egypt (Deut. 16:9–12), and in later Judaic literature this festival turns into a memorial of the Commandments given on Mount Sinai.[24]

I have emphasized that for Ancient Israel no great gap existed between history and myth. We have numerous examples indicating that myth merges into history, or that historical motifs are adopted into the cult. Conversely, it was also quite natural for them to view their experiences as an actual realization of myth. In several places Egypt is referred to as Rahab, by which the victory of Pharaoh and his army drowned in the waves, becomes one and the same as the victory which Yahweh won over the prehistoric monster in primeval times (cp. Is. 30:7; 51:10). Peculiarly enough, Rahab can even be used as a geographical name for Egypt in line with Babel and other names in Ps. 87:4.[25]

Thus, although we do find examples of the movement from history to myth, there is no doubt, in my opinion, that the tendency to think in terms of history is predominant in the Old Testament. The ancient conception of time which was prevalent among the Canaanites, and which was originally expressed by the annually recurrent festivals connected with the cycle of nature, was gradually replaced by another concept marked by historical events.[26] As long as the ancient cult festivals and their cult dramas existed, it was much easier to recreate historical events by using dramatic performances accompanied by recitations in several different voices; but when the

24. Cf. J. Bonsirven, *Le Judaïsme palestinien au temps de Jésus-Christ*, II (Paris, 1935), p. 123, with his references in note 9.

25. On this "mythization" of history, see Widengren, *Myth and History*, p. 479. The historification of myth is explicitly treated by J. Hempel in his article "Glaube, Mythos und Geschichte im Alten Testament," *ZAW* (1953), pp. 109–67.

26. I must here desist from dealing with the idea of time in Ecclesiastes and in the Book of Jubilees.

temple cult gradually changed and finally ceased to exist altogether, the ancient festivals could only survive as actual "commemoration" festivals, to a very limited extent. Most of the ancient rites still survive in the orthodox Jewish feast of Passover.

In works dealing with the religion of Israel one often meets with the assertion that the idea of the holy revelation in history—in contrast to nature—is something unique to Israel. In Israel, Yahweh is conceived of as being the god of history, who took care of his chosen people in particular. Accordingly, there would be a distinction between the concept of history held by Israel and that held by other peoples. However, this contention is not correct. We have numerous examples among other peoples indicating a belief that events have been an expression of the will of the Gods. It is sufficient to refer to the comprehensive material which Bertil Albrektson has collected and analyzed in a very convincing manner.[27]

However, it is impossible to reject the view of history as being an expression of divine guidance as having far more prominent acceptance in ancient Israel than among neighboring peoples. The difference becomes even more conspicuous when one compares the cult texts. Even though a few historical features also appear in the cult texts of other peoples, these incidents are sporadic in comparison with the dominant role which the historical element plays in the cult of Israel. If one must insist upon a significant difference, it has to be found within these limits.

I have tried to elucidate some of the problems connected with the understanding of the cult in ancient Israel—especially the role which history has played as a part of the cult, but I have not dealt with a number of problems of a more systematic nature. For instance, I have only taken into consideration *that* historical events in ancient Israel were construed as a revelation of the will of Yahweh, but I have not indicated by *whom* they were interpreted as such, nor by *what means*. Neither have I attempted to discuss the problems of religious philosophy, which are the true problems of history. That which incites the greatest contradiction and disagreement is, to use the words of Karl Barth: "that vertical line which comes from above and intersects the horizontal line of history."

27. See B. Albrektson, *History and the Gods. An Essay on the Idea of Historical Events as Divine Manifestations in the Ancient Near East and in Israel* (Lund, 1967).

# Yahweh and Mari

HERBERT B. HUFFMON

The interpretation of the divine name Yahweh has been a longstanding interest of the scholar honored by this volume. It therefore seems appropriate to offer here some observations, drawn from the Mari texts, that suggest further support for the interpretation of the name Yahweh, advocated by the honoree, and that illustrate a process through which such a divine name might arise. This paper will not otherwise enter into the voluminous debate on the etymology and origin of Yahweh.

Since the time of Friedrich Delitzsch's famous lecture before the Kaiser in January, 1902, scholars have been discussing the possibility that the divine name Yahweh is attested among the elements in Amorite personal names. Delitzsch cited three names from the Old Babylonian period, viz., *Ya-aḫ-wi-AN*, *Ya-wi-AN*, *Ya-ú-um-AN*, as variant spellings of a name meaning "Yahweh is God."[1] Delitzsch soon encountered considerable opposition to his interpretation of the names. Indeed, it is quite clear that his third example, *Ya-ú-um-AN* (and subsequent variants), does not come into consideration since it is an Akkadian name meaning "Mine is the God."[2] The remaining two names do not seem to belong together either. In spite of assertions to the

1. F. Delitzsch, *Babel und Bibel, Erster Vortrag* (5th ed.; Leipzig, 1905), pp. 49–50, 78–80. The first edition appeared in 1902, without notes. [For the abbreviations used in the references see W. von Soden, *Akkadisches Handwörterbuch* (Wiesbaden, 1959–).]

2. This was first pointed out by Benno Landsberger. See now W. von Soden, "Jahwe 'Er ist, Er erweist sich'," *WO*, III/3 (1966); 178, and the lexicons.

contrary, the two spellings do not occur for the name of any one person.[3] Even when the same person appears a number of times, most notably—over fifteen occurrences—in the case of *Ya-wi-AN* (once, *Ya-wi-i-la*), king of Talhayum, the initial element is always spelled the same way.[4] And although it has been suggested that the two names both reflect **ḥwy*, "live,"[5] it is clear that if the two belong together they reflect **hwy*, "be, become (to)."[6] Accordingly, we must recognize the existence of a verbal element in Amorite names that parallels the traditional interpretation of Yahweh as an imperfect verb.

Against Fritz Hommel and Heinrich Zimmern (later followed by many others), who explained *Ya-wi-AN* as "God exists," Delitzsch argued that since no personal names compounded from *hwy/hyh* were known in North Semitic, the name must be understood as meaning "Yahweh is God."[7] Delitzsch's analysis of this name has recently gained the support of André Finet in connection with the name of the Mari personage *Ya-wi-AN* (once, *Ya-wi-i-la*).[8] For Finet, a name meaning "Ilâ—or the God—Is," would be blasphemous, so the name actually means "Ilâ is Yawi," Ilâ being an Amorite form of El, head of the Canaanite pantheon. That is, the name equates two divinities, and—for Finet—the name *Ya-wi-ᵈIM* means "Adad is Yawi" and the name *Ya-wi-ᵈDa-gan* presumably means "Dagan is Yawi."[9] Finet comments, "the god Yawi is a newcomer, a syncretistic deity to whom his devotees claim to assimilate the local gods such as Ilâ/El or Adad [or Dagan]."[10] Yawi, of course, is the same as Yahweh.

3. *Contra* M. Schorr, *VAB* 5, p. 294 ("sicher") and von Soden, *WO*, III/3, p. 181 ("wahrscheinlich"), who refers to Schorr. The two texts in question—one of unknown date (but perhaps from the reign of Apil-Sin to judge from one paternity) and the other from the time of Sin-muballit—have but one personal name in common (*XXX-ri-me-ni*: *CT* VIII.34/Bu. 91–5–9, 544, line 5; *CT* VIII.20/Bu. 91–5–9, 314, line 34'; different daughters are mentioned) and at that a frequently recurring name.

4. To the references in Huffmon, *Amorite Personal Names in the Mari Texts . . .* (Baltimore 1965), p. 39, add *ARMT* XIII.139–150 (13 times) and Jean, "Arišen," p. 23, line 41 (!).

5. So J. Barth, *Babel und israelitisches Religionswesen* (Berlin, 1902), p. 19, as cited by Delitzsch, p. 79.

6. See the discussions by F. M. Cross, Jr., "Yahweh and the God of the Patriarchs," *HThR*, 55 (1962): 252, and Huffmon, pp. 72–73. The old suggestion (see H. V. Hilprecht, in *EBPN*, p. 114a) that *ya-wi* means "he speaks/has spoken," recently reaffirmed by G. Buccellati, *The Amorites of the Ur III Period* (Naples, 1966), p. 151, is not very convincing if only because related verbal forms are unattested in Northwest Semitic or Arabic. Akkadian *awûm*, "speak," is probably denominative from *awātum*, "word" (*cf.* Ug. *hwt*, "word"), and further cognates are unknown.

7. See Delitzsch, p. 79.

8. See above (and n. 4). See also Finet, "Iawi-Ilâ, roi de Talḫayûm," *Syria*, 41 (1964): 118–22.

9. Finet, pp. 118–21. For the names see Huffmon, pp. 159–60. On the name *Ya-aw/wi-ši-bu* see Huffmon, pp. 68, 185; von Soden, p. 187 (note).

10. Finet, p. 121.

In response to Delitzsch's argument the point has often been made that semantic parallels can be cited from Akkadian names with elements from *bašû*, "be, exist, be in evidence," and from Ugaritic and Phoenician names with elements from *k(w)n*, "be, become."[11] Finet seeks to reverse the argument by asserting that the old Babylonian (and later) name *Ibašši-ilum* is not to be explained as "The God Is," which would be blasphemy, but rather as "The God—or Ilum/El—is Ibašši (= Yawi)."[12] By positing an otherwise unknown god, Ibašši, one may deny the apparent semantic parallel. But, as noted by W. von Soden in reply, there is no need to posit such a deity and the name *Ibašši-ilum* is not an assertion of existence but an expression of thanks, viz., "The God Continually Shows Himself (as a powerful helper)."[13] A more pertinent onomastic parallel would be Ugaritic (and Phoenician) names such as *Ya-ku-un-AN*, "May El/God be Constant,"[14] since the linguistic relationship of Amorite *ya-wi* to Ugaritic *ya-ku-un* is closer than it is to Akkadian *ibašši*, "a present,"[15]

Although a similar explanation is quite possible for *Ya-wi-AN*, viz., "May God/El be Constant," the balance of probability favors a more common type of name, a name that refers to divine aid in childbearing. Keeping to Amorite names with a comparable structure, we find examples with the following verbal elements: *yabni*, "(the deity) has built (the line, with a child)" / "may (the deity) build . . ."; *yawṣi*, "(the deity) brought out (a child)" / "may (the deity) bring out . . ."; *yaḥwi* / **yaḥwi*, "(the deity) has given life (to a child)" / "may (the deity) give life . . ."; *yakin*, "(the deity) has created (a child)" / "may (the deity) create . . ."; *yantin*, "(the deity) has given (a child)" / "may (the deity) give . . .."[16] *Ya-wi-AN* (and *Ya-wi-$^{d}$IM*, etc.) would fit nicely into this class of names and mean "God/El Has Brought (a child) into

11. See Huffmon, p. 72; Frauke Gröndahl, *Die Personennamen der Texte aus Ugarit* (Rome, 1967), p. 153.

12. Finet, p. 122. Finet's point about *Ibašši-ilāni* as grammatically incorrect is equally mistaken, as it is well known that *ilāni* is sometimes construed as a singular ("pantheon"); see Delitzsch, pp. 75–76; W. G. Lambert, *BWL*, p. 67.

13. Von Soden, p. 179.

14. See Gröndahl, pp. 42, 153, 336. Von Soden's conclusion for Yahweh, "Er ist, Er erweist sich," is not too different.

15. This is not the occasion to discuss at length the Amorite verbal system, concerning which the present writer differs from von Soden. The analogies seem closer to Ugaritic and the Early Canaanite of the Amarna correspondence and lead to the working hypothesis that *lqtl* and *yqtl* elements, which parallel each other, should both be taken as asseverative or jussive.

16. For the names see Huffmon, pp. 177, 184, 191–92 (where a *G* should probably be ruled out), 221–22, and 244, respectively. For semantic discussion and parallels see M. Noth, *Die israelitischen Personennamen* . . . (Stuttgart, 1928), pp. 169–75, 212–13; J. J. Stamm, *MVA(e)G* 44, pp. 136–46, 148–51.

Being" / "May God/El Bring (a child) into Being." But whichever interpretation of the Amorite element one follows—simple or causative—it is clear that we have a verbal form comparable to Yahweh, a name that itself is not necessarily clear even though a causative sense seems more likely for the divine name also.

Apart from comparable verbal forms, the Mari texts also furnish some clues as to how a divine name such as Yahweh might have arisen. Divine names, as is well known, often derive from epithets that are commonly or particularly associated with a deity. In reference to Mesopotamia, whence we have thousands of divine names, W. G. Lambert has remarked that "the epithets more commonly addressed to a deity were often in the course of time transformed into names, and these show the attributes ascribed to the god."[17] Lambert also notes, apropos of the importance of Sumerian litanies for the god lists, that "in some cases the epithets applied to one deity in these litanies appear in god lists as the subsidiary names of that deity."[18] As for Canaanite religion, Baal and associated Baal names such as Baal-Shamem, "Lord of the Heavens," and Baal-Hammon, "Lord of the Altar," are obvious illustrations of such epithets. But it must be borne in mind that personal names which thank, implore, or describe the deity are also basic evidence for divine epithets.

Divine names comparable to Yahweh, i.e., with similar verbal elements (in Akkadian, the preterit), are rather rare in the Mesopotamian god lists. Three, however, are known from the Mari texts of the Old Babylonian periods.[19] These names may help to illustrate the process of formation of divine names.

Itur-Mer, "Mer Has Returned," is a god known almost exclusively from the Mari and Terqa (Hana) texts.[20] This god first appears in a recently published "pantheon" list from Mari and dating to the Ur III-Early Isin period.[21] The deity is also now known to have had the title LUGAL *Ma-ri*$^{ki}$, "King of Mari."[22] The divine name Itur-Mer is a variation on the god Mer, who also is attested in Mari texts of the Ur III-Early Isin and Old Babylonian

17. Lambert, "Götterlisten," *RLA* III/7 (Berlin, 1969): 479a.
18. Lambert, p. 478b.
19. For a possible additional example of such a name for the Ur III-Early Isin period, see G. Dossin, "Un 'panthéon' d'Ur III à Mari," *RA*, 61 (1967): 99, line 19': $^{d}$*Ik-ru-ta-an*. The name remains unexplained (see below, n. 41).
20. See Huffmon, pp. 271–72, with references (and see below); add *ARM* X.4.32; 10.6; 51.5; 63.16. Itur-Mer also occurs in *CT* XLIII, No. 29 (*AbB* 1, No. 29), which probably comes from the Middle Euphrates area; note the reference to Šubat-Enlil.
21. Dossin, p. 100, line 31.
22. *ARM* X.63.16.

periods.[23] That is, the name Itur-Mer refers to a quality of the god Mer, specifically that he "returned" or "again showed favor." The name may even specifically refer to the resettlement or resurgence of Mari, since Mer is also an old variant form of the place name, Mari.[24] In this connection we may note the Old Babylonian personal name involving the city of Tupliaš, viz., *Itur-Tupliaš*.[25] It is also important to emphasize that although *itur* or related simple forms are not listed among the divine epithets,[26] there is abundant evidence from personal names for this kind of reference to a deity, the sense in personal names being that "(the god) has returned (with an additional child)."[27] The background of the divine name Itur-Mer is accordingly most apparent in an epithet found in personal names.

A similar divine name is that of the special Terqa deity, spelled both Ikrub-El (34 times) and Yakrub-El (15 times)[28] and known only from the Mari texts. Due to the frequency of the Amorite form, *yakrub*, the coupling with El, and the use of the Amorite form in an Akkadian personal name,[29] it seems preferable to interpret the divine name as Amorite. Semantically the name is probably to be explained by reference to Akkadian *karābu*, "pray, bless, dedicate," rather than to Old South Arabic *krb*, "dedicate." Accordingly, the probable sense of the name is "El Has Blessed" or "May El Bless." References in texts as well as in personal names—the latter not especially frequent—amply attest the propriety and frequency of such requests or descriptions of a deity. Even a glance at the Akkadian and Hebrew lexicons, for example, offers sufficient evidence. Yakrub-El is a divine name that emphasizes El's connection with blessing. It could easily have derived from a phrase such as "may El bless (the king / the people, etc.)," the former being easily paralleled in later Akkadian sources.

Itur-Mer and Ikrub/Yakrub-El may be classified as extended divine names combining a separate divine name with a preterit or "imperfect" verbal element. As such they are not easily paralleled among divine names from Mesopotamia, as a perusal of the god lists shows,[30] although analogies are

23. See Huffmon, p. 272, with references. Add, from a Hana text, *I-din-$^{d}$Me-er* (Th. Bauer, "Neues Material zur 'Amoriter'-Frage," *MAOG* 5 [1929]: 2, line 2).

24. See Dossin, "Inscriptions de fondation provenant de Mari," *Syria*, 21 (1940): 157–59.

25. See Stamm, pp. 84–85.

26. K. Tallqvist, *StOr* 7, p. 241, cites only *mutir*.

27. Stamm, p. 146.

28. See Huffmon, p. 76 (n. 88); add the occurrences in the Kibri-Dagan correspondence, *ARMT* XIII.108–135.

29. Huffmon, p. 76, n. 88.

30. See, *inter alia*, A. Deimel, *Pantheon Babylonicum* (Rome, 1914), Nos. 1482 (*I-túr-ma-ti-su*), 1553 (*Il-te-bu*; see below), 1585 (*Iq-bi-da-mi-iq*), 1611 (*Iš-me-ka-ra-ab*), and 2009 (*Li-bur-dan-nu*).

less rare in Canaanite and other sources.[31] However, the Mari texts also provide an example of a divine name in which the name consists of only a verbal element with a hypocoristic ending. This god, *ᵈIk-šu-du-um*, appears but once.[32] Together with the god Lagamal he is going in procession from Mari to Terqa, the home of Ikrub/Yakrub-El. The association with Lagamal, "Merciless," a deity connected with Nergal and at one time having the title "King of Mari,"[33] fits together with the later appearance of the god Ikšuda/u, who, in the list AN = *Anum*, is one of the four dogs of Marduk.[34] Ikšuda, "He Overwhelmed," would be a suitable description for a companion of Lagamal. As Marduk's dog, Ikšudu, like his associate Iltebu, "He Growled (?)," may well have been an amulet against demons, as is suggested by at least one text.[35] However, it is rather hard to imagine what Marduk's dog would have been doing in a procession from Mari to Terqa. Whether the Mari occurrence involves a separate Ikšudum or, as seems more likely, a deity originally not associated with Marduk—but perhaps with Enlil—who was later taken over by Marduk, cannot be determined. What is clear is that we find a divine name consisting merely of a verbal element. As such, the process of formation is illustrated by the personal name found at Mari, *Ik-šu-u[d]-a-ya-bi-šu*,[36] "He (the god) Conquered His Enemies," and may be filled out with such later names as *Šamaš-kāšid-ayyābī*,[37] "Šamaš, Conqueror of the Enemies," using a phrase well known as a divine and royal epithet.[38] In addition, a title of Nergal is *kāšid ilāni li[mnūti]*,[39] "conqueror of the evil gods." Accordingly, the divine name Ikšudum makes excellent sense as a descriptive title or as an abbreviated form of a divine title.

It is striking that the divine names Itur-Mer, Ikrub/Yakrub-El, and Ikšudum are known from Mari, since these are uncommon forms of divine names. It suggests a possibility within the mixed Amorite–Mesopotamian

31. See Cross, pp. 254–55.

32. *ARMT* XIII.111.5–9.

33. *See CAD*, G, pp. 23–24.

34. *CT* XXIV, 16.21; 28.75 (Deimel, No. 1545). This other occurrence of Ikšudum was apparently overlooked by D. O. Edzard in his comments on *ARMT* XIII.111: "Pantheon und Kult in Mari," in J.-R. Kupper, ed., *La civilisation de Mari* (XVᵉ Rencontre assyriologique internationale) (Paris, 1967), pp. 62–63.

35. A. Falkenstein and W. von Soden, *Sumerische und akkadische Hymnen und Gebete* (Zürich, 1953), pp. 306–10, 396–97, esp. 309 (*KAR* 26).

36. *ARM* IX.9.9. The name does not seem to occur elsewhere in Old Babylonian texts.

37. See Tallqvist, *APN*, pp. 210–11.

38. See Tallqvist, *StOr* 7, pp. 113–14; M.-J. Seux, *Épithètes Royales akkadiennes et sumériennes* (Paris, 1967), pp. 137–38. Note that Yahdun-lim, king of Mari, is to receive from Šamaš a "mighty weapon which conquers the enemies" (*kāšid ayyābī*): Dossin, "L'inscription de fondation de Iaḫdun-Lim roi de Mari," *Syria*, 32 (1955): 9, 16 (iv.18).

39. Tallqvist, *StOr* 7, pp. 113–14.

culture of the area. These names are paralleled by personal names to some extent, and especially in the case of Itur-Mer, but no personal names with *ikrub* or *yakrub* are known from Mari and there are only two names with *ikšud*.[40] The more important parallels are found in divine epithets, although it must be remembered that personal names also provide divine epithets. In other words, these divine names seem to derive from epithets rather than from names of persons which are subsequently transformed into divine names.[41] One may, accordingly, see in these divine names illustrations of a process of formation of new divine names, a process of which Yahweh may be the end product. That is to say, the use of *ya-wi* in Amorite personal names indicates an association that might have led to a divine name such as *ᵈYa-wi-AN*/ Yahweh-El or, like Iksudum, to Yahweh itself.

There is no denying that the name Yahweh might have arisen otherwise, but it is worth while to bear in mind that so far as names are concerned, an element such as *yahweh* is best known in Amorite personal names and, in so far as early Canaanite is concerned, examples are restricted to a place name in Egyptian topographical lists[42] and to a learned lexicographical text from Ugarit.[43]

40. In addition to the name cited above, note *Ik-šu-ud-ap-pa-šu* (*ARM* I.118, 120; VII.10. [10]; VIII.1.36; 62.[16]); see Stamm, pp. 127–28.

41. Note in this connection Dossin's interpretation of the enigmatic *ᵈIk-ru-ta-an* (above, n. 19) as perhaps reflecting the name of an important person, a landowner, which later became a place name and ultimately the name of the deity of that place (p. 102). For Ikšudum, Edzard (see above, n. 34) suggests that it was either a name abbreviated from **ikšud-X* or a nominalization of *ikšud*, "he is at hand."

42. See Huffmon, p. 72.

43. See J. Nougayrol, et al., *Ugaritica V* (Paris, 1968), pp. 244–45, 421 (RS 20.123 . . . ii.28').

# Elia und das Gottesurteil

A. JEPSEN

DIE Gestalt Elias hat im Judentum, im Christentum und im Islam eine starke Nachwirkung gehabt.[1] Schon im Neuen Testament wird Elia nächst Abraham, Mose und David am häufigsten genannt. Was war es um diesen Mann, daß ihm eine solche Wirkung beschieden war? Worin besteht seine geschichtliche Größe? Wie ist diese zu erkennen? Es soll im folgenden vor allem um diese letzte Frage gehen, wie es möglich ist, eine geschichtliche Größe wie Elia zu erfassen.

Das Problem stellt sich uns dadurch, daß wir weder eine Sammlung von Eliasprüchen haben, wie bei Amos und Hosea, noch überhaupt so etwas wie urkundliche Nachrichten oder chronistische Mitteilungen. Was wir haben, sind Erzählungen über Elia, die der deuteronomistische Bearbeiter[2] des Königsbuchs in seinen Geschichtsbericht eingefügt hat. Wir sehen also Elia zunächst durch die Brille des Dtr., in der Funktion, die dieser ihm im Zusammenhang seines Werks gegeben hat. Dieses Eliabild des Dtr. gilt es zunächst zu erfassen.

Was hat den Dtr. eigentlich veranlasst, die Eliageschichten aufzunehmen? Er wollte doch eine Geschichte schreiben, die das Handeln Jahwes an Israel und Juda darstellte. In diese Geschichte aber gehörten für ihn die Propheten mit hinein, als die Sprecher Jahwes, die vor allem die Dynastien Israels mit

1. Vergleiche die Literatur bei J. Jeremias im *ThWNT*, Art. *Ηλιας* und in der Encyklpädie des Islam, Art. Ilyas, von G. A. Wensinck.

2. Es braucht hier nicht entschieden zu werden, ob es ein oder zwei deuteronomistische Bearbeiter gegeben hat.

dem Gotteswort begleiteten. So beruft und verwirft Ahia von Silo den Jerobeam, so verwirft Jehu ben Chanani den Baesa und sein Haus, so endlich auch Elia das Haus Ahabs. Die fast gleich lautenden deuteronomistischen Einfügungen in 1 Kg. 14; 16; 21 lassen erkennen, wie der dtr. Verfasser die drei Gestalten in Parallele zueinander gesehen hat. Gottes Wort begleitet die Geschichte, und was er spricht, das hält er gewiß, wie es zuletzt in den Worten an Jehu deutlich wird, 2 Kg. 10:30f.; 15:12.

Aber zu dieser Funktion Elias hätte schließlich ein kurzer Abschnitt genügt, so wie er jetzt dem Jehu ben Chanani gewidmet ist, oder allenfalls die Naboterzählung, auf die der Bericht in 2 Kg. 9f. zurückgreift. Wenn der Dtr. von Elia mehr erzählt, so muß eine Überlieferung vorhanden gewesen sein, die auf der einen Seite seinem Anliegen entgegenkam, aber auch mehr enthielt, das er nicht übergehen konnte oder wollte. Wie es scheint, wollte der Dtr. das aufnehmen, was etwas über das Verhältnis Elias zum Ahabhause enthielt, und damit den Untergang der Dynastie Omris begründete. So beginnen die Kapitel 17—19 mit einem Wort an Ahab und enden mit dem Auftrag, die Gegner des Ahabhauses, Hasael, Jehu und Elisa für ihre Aufgabe zu berufen. Kap. 21 begründet das Urteil über Ahab und 2 Kg. 1 das über den Ahabsohn Ahasja. Wenn der Dtr. aber darüber hinaus noch etwas mehr bringt, was nicht umbedingt dazu gehört, so doch wohl, weil er die ihn angehenden Aussagen schon in einem festgefügten Zusammenhang vorfand. Was er aber aus der ihm vorliegenden Eliaüberlieferung aufnimmt, hat das Eliabild der Folgezeit bestimmt.

Welches nun sind die charakteristischen Züge der vom Dtr. aufgenommenen Eliatradition? Elias Gestalt wird in ihr als einmalig oder erstmalig empfunden; jedenfalls genügt die Schilderung der Boten, er sei ein "Ba$^{c}$al se$^{c}$ar" und nur mit einem Gürtel aus Fell bekleidet, um Ahasja erkennen zu lassen, daß es Elia der Thisbiter gewesen sei, der ihnen begegnete, 2 Kg. 1. Auch sonst tritt er meist allein, ohne Anhang auf.[3] Der Tradition scheint es nicht leicht gewesen zu sein, Elia in seiner Funktion richtig zu bezeichnen; er heißt entweder "Elia" oder "Elia der Thisbiter"; an zwei Stellen spricht er es selbst aus, er sei allein als "Nabi für Jahwe" übrig geblieben, 18:22; 19:14; an zwei weiteren wird er "Gottesmann" genannt, 17:18, 24; 2 Kg. 1:9ff. Diese letzten Bezeichnungen zeigen jedenfalls, in welcher Weise die Tradition die Gestalt des Elia einzuordnen suchte. Entscheidend ist jedenfalls für ihn sein Verhältnis zu Jahwe. Dieses wird als besonders eng und persönlich dargestellt: Elia steht vor dem Angesicht Jahwes wie ein Diener vor seinem

3. Nur zweimal 18:42f.; 19:5 wir ihm ein נער zugeschrieben, dessen Funktion aber unklar bleibt.

Herrn 17:1; 18:15. Jahwe wird "dein Gott" genannt, 17:12; 18:10. Elia betet zu ihm: "Mein Gott," 17:20, 21. Es ist, als wolle die Tradition den Namen "Elia" = "Mein Gott ist Jahwe" in seinem vollen Sinn ausdeuten.

So redet Jahwe mit ihm und sendet ihn, wie ein Herr seinen Knecht: 17:2, 8; 18:1; 19:15; 21:17; dazu auch 19:9b. (In 19:5, 7 sowie 2 Kg. 1:3 tritt an die Stelle Jahwes der "Engel Jahwes"). Jahwe sendet ihn, wohin er soll: Zum Bache Krith und zur Witwe in Zarpath, zu Ahab oder zu Hasael, Jehu und Elisa; zum Gottesberg oder zu Ahasja; Elia hört immer das Wort Jahwes und gehorcht seinem Auftrag.

Aber Jahwes Verhältnis zu seinem Boten geht noch weiter: Er erhält ihn auch und schützt ihn vor Gefahr; am Bache Krith läßt er ihn von den Raben ernähren und in Zarpath von einer Witwe, die immer genug Mehl und Öl auch für ihn hat. Für den Weg durch die Wüste sättigt er ihn mit Brot und Wasser, die 40 Tage vorhalten; und wenn Verfolgung droht, kann Gott ihn verbergen oder geradezu durch einen Sturmwind entführen lassen, 17:3ff., 8ff.; 19:4ff.; 18:9ff.; 2 Kg. 2. Weiter: Gott erhört ihn auch: Auf sein Gebet zu Jahwe seinem Gott, läßt Gott den Sohn der Witwe wieder lebendig werden; auf sein Gebet hin läßt Jahwe Feuer vom Himmel fallen und entzündet das Opfer, ja verzehrt sogar die Menschen, die den Mann Gottes unehrerbietig behandeln. So ist es kein Wunder, wenn zuletzt Gott den Elia im feurigen Wagen entrückt.

Steht Elia so ganz bei Jahwe in seinem Auftrag und in seiner Nähe, so ist er den Menschen gegenüber der einsame Bote, der ihnen unversehens, ja rätselhaft entgegentritt. Am anschaulichsten macht das wohl die lange Rede Obadjas, 18:9ff., die keinen anderen Sinn haben dürfte, als den, deutlich zu machen, was es um Elia ist. Wo kommt er nur so plötzlich her? Und dabei hat Ahab ihn in aller Welt suchen lassen! Gewiß, er steht jetzt vor Obadja; aber wer weiß, ob er nicht alsbald von einem Sturmwind hinweggerissen wird. Unheimlich, nicht zu fassen, so tritt er den Menschen ent gegen.

Unheimlich und beunruhigend ist auch das Wort, das er verkündigt: Wenn er es sagt, dann bleibt der Regen aus, und wenn er es sagt, dann gibt es Regen! Wenn er es sagt, ist immer Mehl im Kad und Öl im Krug; wenn er es sagt, muß auch der König sterben! Sein Wort ist wirkendes Wort in einer besonderen Weise, weil es in Auftrag und Vollmacht Jahwes gesprochen ist. So ist auch sein Wort an Ahab und Isebel vollmächtiges Wort, das sich erfüllt.[4] Wie Jahwe sein Gebet erhört, so bekennt er sich auch zu dem von Elia gesprochenen Wort.

4. Zur Gestalt Isebels in der Eliageschichte vergleiche jetzt vor allen Steck, Überlieferung und Zeitgeschichte in den Eliaerzählungen.

Es ist schon ein eigenartiges Bild, das die Tradition von Elia überliefert: Dieser Elia unterscheidet sich sowohl von Vorläufern, wie Nathan und Ahia, wie von den Schriftpropheten nach ihm. Sie alle verkünden auch Gericht, die späteren sogar den Untergang Israels und Judas; aber von keinem wird berichtet, daß Jahwe sich so zu seinem Wort bekannt habe.[5] Der einzige, von dem ähnliches berichtet wird, ist Elisa; aber gerade bei ihm weiß die Tradition, daß er nur zweidrittel des Geistes Elias empfangen habe. Elia bleibt für die Tradition ein Einsamer, der kraft seiner Verbindung mit Jahwe über das mächtige Wort verfügt, zum Heil und zum Unheil. Und selbst, wenn dieser Elia zu Tode verzweifelt ist, Gott hat für ihn immer noch einen Auftrag.

Was stellt dieses von der Tradition gestaltete Eliabild eigentlich dar? Über den Sitz der Tradition lassen sich nur allgemeine Aussagen machen. Es müssen jedenfalls jahwetreue Kreise gewesen sein, in denen die Erinnerung an Elia, den Bekenner Jahwes, wach erhalten wurde. Ob es einen Kreis von "Schülern" Elias gegeben hat, ist jedenfalls mit Sicherheit nicht auszumachen; zu sehr wird er als der große Einsame geschildert. Möglich ist, daß die Kreise um Elisa auch die Eliatradition gepflegt haben; völlig sicher aber ist auch das wohl nicht. So bleibt man besser bei der allgemeinen Bezeichnung "jahwetreue Kreise."

Das genügt aber, um die Form der Tradition als "Legende" zu bestimmen, in dem Sinn von "Tradition einer Glaubensgemeinschaft." Damit ist über Geschichtlichkeit oder Ungeschichtlichkeit noch gar nichts gesagt; es genügt die Feststellung, daß bestimmte Kreise mit dieser Überlieferung ihrem Glauben Ausdruck verleihen wollten.

Damit aber ist auch der Sinn der Tradition erfaßt: Es geht um das Bekenntnis zu Jahwe, der duch Elia, seinen Boten, in Israel geredet und gehandelt hat, in unerhörter, einmaliger Weise, und Israel zu sich zurückgeführt. So allein werden die Elialegenden historisch richtig verstanden, als Bekenntnis des Glaubens an Jahwe und Elia, seinen Gesandten.

Ist damit auch schon "Elia" historisch erfaßt? Ja und nein. Auf der einen Seite gilt, daß Elia nur in der überkommenen Tradition erfaßbar ist; so wie die Tradenten ihn gesehen haben, so hat er in der weiteren Geschichte gewirkt. In seiner Einmaligkeit, ist er mit Mose verglichen bezw. zu ihm in Parallele gestellt worden. An diesen Elia der Tradition haben sich die weiteren Überlieferungen angeschlossen; dieser ist insofern der geschichtlich wirksame Elia. Daher könnte man sich mit diesem Traditionsbild begnügen, denn nur dieses ist uns eindeutig erkennbar. Ja, man könnte noch einen Schritt

5. Ausnahmen wie etwa das Heilungswunder Jesajas sind selten.

weitergehen: Wie immer der historische Elia gewesen sein mag, die Legende ist die Deutung seiner historischen Gestalt. Diese haben wir nur in der Legende, als der einzig faßbaren Auswirkung seiner geschichtlichen Wirksamkeit.

Aber auf der anderen Seite fragt der Historiker grade bei einer solchen Quellenlage weiter: Läßt sich aus dem Bild der Tradition ein "historischer Kern" herausarbeiten? Wir sind hier nicht in der verhältnismäßig günstigen Lage, in der sich etwa der Geschichtsschreiber gegenüber der Franziskuslegende befindet; denn er hat immerhin einige echte Dokumente, die auf den heiligen Franz zurückgehen, von denen aus er die Legendentradition interpretieren kann. Welche Möglichkeiten stehen uns zur Verfügung, wenn wir versuchen wollen, aus dem tradierten Eliabild einen "historischen Elia" zu gewinnen?

Was suchen wir aber eigentlich, wenn wir vom historischen Elia reden? Doch wohl einen Bericht, über die Worte, die Elia "wirklich" gesprochen, die Taten, die er "wirklich" vollführt hat. Schon diese Frage setzt voraus, daß er das eine oder andere nicht getan oder gesprochen hat. Was gibt uns Anlaß zu dieser Voraussetzung?

Ein ernsthafter Anlaß ist gegeben, wenn der Nachweis geführt werden kan, daß eine Erzählung in der tradierten Form noch nicht zur Zeit Elias formuliert worden sein kann. Um solche Nachweise hat sich H. O. Steck m.E. mit Erfolg bemüht. Da ist einmal die Isebeltradition, wie sie vor allem in 1 Kg. 21 vorliegt. Sowohl in 2 Kg. 9 wie in 1 Kg. 21:17–20 ist Ahab der eigentlich schuldige an dem Tod Naboths. Dem Ahab gilt daher auch das Drohwort Elias. Wenn in 21:1–16 Isebel als die böse Anstifterin gilt, der in V. 23 das Urteil gesprochen wird, so muß hier doch wohl eine historische Verschiebung vorliegen, entstanden in einer Situation, in dem sie einen stärkeren Einfluß hatte, d.h. in der sie als Königin-Mutter die Politik der beiden Söhne bestimmt hat. Es ist in diesem Fall nicht entscheidend, ob Elia diese Zeit noch erlebt hat; historisch kann nur eine Variante sein: Entweder trägt Ahab die Verantwortung oder Isebel. Da spricht aber die Version in 2 Kg. 9 wohl eindeutig für die Schuld Ahabs. Damit wird freilich auch die Nachricht von der Verfolgung der Jahwenabis durch Isebel für die Zeit Ahabs, für die sie jetzt berichtet wird, zweifelhaft. Möglich ist natürlich, daß sie später erfolgt ist. So ist in diesem Fall sehr wahrscheinlich zu machen, daß die Eliatradition aus einer anderen Situation heraus neu formuliert worden ist.

In einem zweiten Fall läßt sich nicht die gleiche Sicherheit, wenn auch große Wahrscheinlichkeit erreichen, nämlich bei dem Auftrag an Elia,

Hasael, Jehu und Elisa zu salben. Hier kommen verschiedene Überlegungen zusammen. Einmal chronologische: Die Tradition versetzt Elia in die Zeit Ahabs und Ahasjas; Ahab ist frühestens 853, Ahasja also frühestens 852 gestorben, beide kaum viel später. Die Salbung Hasaels und damit auch Jehus kann frühestens nach Sommer 845 erfolgt sein; denn damals war Hadadeser noch König in Damaskus. Die Tradition verbindet den Auftrag an Elia mit Ereignissen aus der Zeit Ahabs; sollte Elia wirklich sieben Jahre oder mehr mit der Ausführung des Auftrags gewartet haben? Zum anderen wird die Salbung Hasaels und Jehus auch Elisa zugeschrieben; was die Salbung Jehus angeht, wahrscheinlich mit größerem Recht, da der Bericht darüber eng mit der Darstellung der Revolution Jehus verbunden ist. Das führt zum dritten darauf, daß der Sinn dieses Auftrags in 19:15 wohl darin zu suchen ist, daß das ganze verderbliche Wirken Hasels, Jehus und Elias damit gerechtfertigt werden soll, daß Jahwe schon Elia aufgefordert hat, diese drei zu ihrem Amt zu berufen.[6] Wir wissen aus der Zeit Jehus nur einiges über seine Anfänge, über die Vernichtung des Ahabhauses und des Baaldienstes; was sonst alles in dieser Anfangszeit geschehen ist, auch durch Elisa, ist uns nicht überliefert. Wir können es nur der Tatsache entnehmen, daß eine solche Rechtfertigung, wie sie in 19:15–18 vorleigt, als nötig erschien. Wenn aber dieser Auftrag Jahwes frühestens erst in die Anfangszeit Jehus hineingehört, so liegt auch hier kein historisches Ereignis vor. Damit ergibt sich die Möglichkeit, daß die ganze Horebscene, deren Abschluß die Verse 15–18 bilden, in denselben Zusammenhang gehört.[7]

Damit sind zwei Erzählungskomplexe auf Grund historischer Überlegungen als nicht zur alten Eliaüberlieferung gehörig erkannt. Den übrigen Traditionen gegenüber versagen solche Argumente; sie lassen sich nicht ohne weiters als historisch später entstanden und damit als unhistorisch nachweisen. Sind sie damit aber nun schon historisch? Schwerlich. Welchen Maßstab haben wir nun, um das Historische vom Unhistorischen zu trennen? Die Wunder? Doch die ganze Überlieferung ist vom Wunder geprägt, die Geschichten von Kap. 17 nicht weniger als die vom Himmelsfeuer in Kap. 18 und 2 Kg. 1. Ist das Versagen und Herbeiführen des Regens nicht

6. Vergl. Steck S. 78ff.

7. Die Analyse von Kap. 19 ist sehr umstritten; ich sehe den alten Bestand in: V. 3a β.b, 4, 5, 6 (ohne: er aß und trank) 7, 8, 9a. bα, 11aα (bis: עֹבֵר), 13a, bα, 15–18. D.h. am Gottesberg erhält Elia gewissermaßen einen letzten Auftrag. Es wäre natürlich denkbar, daß der gegenwärtige Schluß einen älteren verdrängt hätte, der aber jedenfalls auch ein Gotteswort enthalten haben müßte; denn die Gotteserscheinung als solche kann ebensowenig den Schluß gebildet haben wie jetzt die Klage Elias, selbst wenn, oder gerade wenn diese zum alten Text gehört, was mir nicht mehr unbedingt sicher ist.

ebenso wunderhaft? Es blieben allenfalls die Sendung an Ahab durch das Wort Jahwes, 21:17 und die an die Boten Ahasjas durch den Engel Jahwes, wenn nicht auch gerade hier das Wunderhafte im Auftreten Elias betont werden soll: Hast du mich wirklich gefunden? Wir müßten schon einen sehr rationalen Maßstab anlegen, wenn wir innerhalb dieser, ganz durch das Wunder geprägten Überlieferung mehr oder weniger Wunderhaftes unterscheiden wollten.[8]

So ist es wohl richtiger zu fragen, ob innerhalb der Tradition Schichten festzustellen sind, die eine Geschichte der Eliaüberlieferung erkennen lassen. Die Bezeichnung Elias gibt dafür wohl die besten Anhaltspunkte.[9]

Eine Schicht nennt Elia den "Thisbiter": 17:1; 21:17 (Vers 28 ist späte Wiederholung von Vers 17); 1:3, 8. D.h.es gehören hierher zunächst: Die Ankündigung der Dürre; das Gerichtswort an Ahab und das an Ahasja. Eine andere Erzählungsgruppe bezeichnet Elia als Gottesmann: 17:17–24; 1:9–16. Beide Abschnitte lassen sich leicht aus dem Zusammenhang lösen, die erste hat keine innere Verbindung mit der Geschichte von der Dürre, wie sie in 17:3–16 immerhin gegeben ist. Die zweite ist eine Erweiterung zu 1:2–8, 17, die das Anliegen der Erzählung verschiebt.

Was nun noch übrig bleibt, sind, außer der Entrückung Elias, die Abschnitte 17:2–6, 7–16; 18. Hier wird Elia nicht direkt benannt, sondern nur einige Male in Verbindung mit den Nabis gebracht.

Daß die zweite Gruppe, die aus zwei Einsätzen in einen vorgegebenen Zusammenhang besteht, eine jüngere Schicht darstellt, ist wahrscheinlich. Die erste Gruppe dagegen, dürfte den erzählten Ereignissen zeitlich am nächsten stehen. Das gilt zunächst für das Bruchstück 21:17–20, das sich mit 2 Kg. 9 berührt. Von da aus dürfte ein Schluß auf die beiden anderen Erzählungen immerhin erlaubt sein. Fraglich bleibt die richtige Beurteilung der dritten Gruppe, vor allem des Kap. 18, dem sich die Überlegungen nun vor allem zuwenden sollen.

Seit wohl zuerst A. Alt die Erzählung von dem Gottesurteil als ein besonderes Traditionsstück herausgehoben hat,[10] hat sich mehr und mehr gezeigt, daß die literarische Einheit, die jetzt in Kap. 17–19 vorliegt, nicht ursprünglich ist, sondern daß hier verschiedene Überlieferungen verbunden sind. Im

8. Worin hat der Erzähler das Wunder bei der Witwe zu Zarpath gesehen? Wie verstand er es, daß das Mehl im Kad und das Öl im Krug nicht ausging? Nach Kriegsende haben viele in Deutschland es als echtes Wunder erfahren, daß ihnen das Brot und die Kartoffeln nicht ausgingen, obgleich es oft so aussah, als sei das letzte verbraucht.

9. Ich nehme damit Gedanken wieder auf, die ich schon früher vertreten habe, jetzt aber praecisieren möchte; vergl. Nabi, S. 58ff.

10. Vergl. Albrecht Alt, Das Gottesurteil auf dem Karmel, Kleine Schriften zur Geschichte des Volkes Israel II, S. 135ff.

ersten Teil bildet die Obadjaerzählung mit der Rede in V. 9–14 eine Sonderüberlieferung. Voraussetzung der Rede sind zunächst V. 7, 8; aber auch die Verse 5, 6, die erkläten, warum Elia den Obadja allein trifft, sowie V. 2b + 3a lassen sich von der Obadjascene nicht trennen. Den Abschluß aber muß immer V. 15 gebildet haben, die Zusicherung, Obadja könne unbesorgt Elia bei Ahab anmelden. V. 16 ist Überleitung zu der Begegnung mit Ahab. V. 17 aber kann die alte Fortsetzung zu V. 2a sien: Elia macht sich auf den Weg zu Ahab, und als Ahab ihn sieht, . . . V. 1, 2a, 17, 18a bilden also den Eingang zu einer eigenen Überlieferung, welches ist die Fortsetzung? Im gegenwärtigen Zusammenhang die Karmelscene, ob aber auch im ursprünglichen? Würthwein[11] hat, m.E. mit Recht darauf hingewiesen, daß der König in dieser Geschichte keine Rolle spielt; in V. 21–39 treten nur Elia und die Baalspropheten auf, zwischen ihnen steht das Volk, das zu einer Entscheidung aufgerufen wird.

Dann aber gliedert sich dieses Kapitel:

| | | |
|---|---|---|
| 1, 2a | | |
| | 2b, 3a, 5–15 | |
| | | 16 |
| 17, 18a (b) | | |
| | | 19, 20 |
| | 21–39 | |
| | | 40 |
| 41–46 | | |

D.h. es liegen drei Überlieferungskreise vor:

1) Elia und Ahab: 1, 2a, 17, 18a, 41–46.
2) Elia und Obadja: 2b, 3a, 5–15.
3) Elia und das Volk: 21–39.

Der erste Kreis gehört sachlich als Fortsetzung zu 17:1,d.h.aber doch, auch wenn die Bezeichnung Thisbiter nicht auftaucht, zur Thisbiterschicht. Der zweite Kreis hat seinen Sinn in der Darstellung Elias: Welch ein unheimlicher Mensch, der nirgends zu finden ist und den jeden Augenblick ein Jahwegeist entführen kann. Sachlich ist er also den Gottesmannerzählungen verwandt.

Und der dritte? Wohin gehört er? Diese Erzählung hat verschiedene Deutungen gefunden, bei Alt und Fohrer mehr eine staatspolitische, bei

11. Vergl. E. Würthwein, Die Erzählung vom Gottesurteil auf dem Karmel, *ZThK* 59 (1962): 131–44.

Würthwein mehr eine kultpolitische. Welches ist ihr Sinn und wie ist sie in die Eliaüberlieferung einzuordnen?

Der Ablauf der Erzählung ist in sich klar. V. 21 bringt die Einführung: Elia tritt an das Volk heran; die Forderung, die er stellt: "Wenn Jahwe Gott ist, folget ihm, wenn aber Baal, folget ihm," zeigt die Situation dieses Volkes. Es sind Menschen die es für möglich halten, mit dem angestammten Jahwedienst den Baalsdienst zu verbinden, für die der Baalsdienst also eine ständige Möglichkeit, ja Notwendigkeit bedeutet. Denn das Wesen einer Gottheit fordert ihre Verehrung. Ein solches Volk stellt Elia in die Entscheidung eines Entweder-Oder. Es ergibt sich für ihn diese Alternative an der Wesenheit Gottes. Gott kann nur einer sein; daher gebührt nur einem die Nachfolge. Man kann nicht zugleich zwei Göttern nachgehen wollen, das ist sinnlos. (Die Bedeutung des hier gebrauchten Bildes ist nicht ganz deutlich; aber die Redensart muß etwas umschreiben wie: "Auf zwei Bällen tanzen" oder ähnliches; jedenfalls etwas, das die Unvereinbarkeit dessen ausdrückt, was das Volk für vereinbar hält.)

Das Unverständnis des Volkes dieser Forderung gegenüber ist verständlich; es schweigt. Denn das ist doch der Sinn der Gottheiten, daß sie alle zusammen verehrt werden.

So macht Elia ein Angebot: Er geht aus von seiner Situation: Er steht als einziger Prophet Jahwes den 450 Propheten Baals gegenüber; was kann er allein gegen so viele ausrichten? Wie es zu dieser Situation gekommen ist, wird hier nicht angedeutet; es genügt die zahlenmäßige Übermacht der Baalspropheten herauszustellen. Trotzdem stellt Elia als einzelner sich dieser Menge. Sein Vorschlag ist: Man schaffe zwei Stiere herbei; jede Partei soll einen zum Opfer zurichten und auf das Holz des Altars legen, aber kein Feuer anzünden. Beide sollen dann ihren Gott anrufen; der Gott, der das Gebet erhört und mit Feuer antwortet, der hat sich als Gott erwiesen. Dieser Vorschlag gibt beiden Seiten die gleichen Chancen und so stimmt jetzt das ganze Volk zu. Die Ausführung des Vorschlags gliedert sich in zwei Abschnitte: V. 25–29 das vergebliche Bemühen der Baalspropheten V. 30–38 der erfolgreiche Anruf Elias. Das Bekenntnis des Volkes, V. 39, schließt ab.

Die Heranschaffung der Stiere wird, wie üblich, nicht erwähnt; als sie da sind, überläßt Elia den Baalspropheten den Vortritt. Sie sollen sich den ihnen passenden Stier aussuchen (damit es hinterher nicht heißen könnte, es habe am Stier gelegen); sie sollen überhaupt mit ihrem Opfer und Gebet beginnen; er will ihnen viel Zeit lassen.

So beginnen die Propheten Baals ihr Tun: Sie nehmen sich einen Stier, legen ihn auf den Altar und rufen ihren Gott an: Baal erhöre uns! Aber, es erfolgt keine Antwort. So versuchen sie es mit verschiedenen Riten, durch die sie in immer größere Erregung kommen: Sie hinken um den Altar herum, sie ritzen sich mit Schwerter und Spießen, bis das Blut fließt, ja, sie geraten in wilde Raserei. Trotzdem: Keine Stimme, keiner, der Antwort gibt, kein Zeichen eines Aufmerkens. Es ist nicht verwunderlich, daß Elia sie zwischendurch anstachelt: Ihr müßt lauter rufen; "er" ist ja doch ein Gott; aber vielleicht ist er gerade beschäftigt, oder macht gerade eine Reise zu einem fernen Tempel, oder er schläft gar! Wohl selten ist in so wenigen Worten Götterglaube so verhöhnt worden.

Bis über Mittag läßt Elia den Propheten Baals Zeit; dann verschwinden sie von der Bildfläche. Nun, nachdem Baal seine Machtlosigkeit erwiesen hat, versammelt Elia alles Volk bei sich. Er errichtet (wieder?) einen Altar, mit einem Graben ringsherum, schichtet Holz darauf, zerteilt den Stier, legt ihn aufs Holz, und läßt dann das Ganze dreimal mit vier Eimern Wasser übergießen, sodaß auch der Graben sich noch mit Wasser füllt; offensichtlich, um das Wunder noch größer erscheinen zu lassen. Dann tritt Elia an den Altar heran und spricht sein Gebet. Dabei scheint zunächst V. 37 dem Zusammenhang besser zu entsprechen; denn das Gebet: Jahwe, erhöre mich, entspricht dem Gebet in V. 26; zum anderen geht es darum, daß dieses Volk erkennt, daß Jahwe wirklich Gott, und d.h. allein Gott ist. (V. 36 scheint das Anliegen etwas zu verschieben und könnte zu einer späteren Überarbeitung gehören.) Nur auf dieses Gebet hin, fällt Feuer vom Himmel und entzündet das Opfer und das Holz und brennt so stark, daß auch das Wasser im Graben verdampft. Damit hat Jahwe sich als Gott erwiesen und alles Volk stimmt in das Bekenntnis ein: Jahwe, er ist wirklich Gott. So bilden die Verse 21–39 einen in sich geschlossenen Zusammenhang; ob sie und inwieweit sie ursprünglich mit dem vorher und nachher Erzählten zusammengehören, ist damit nicht entschieden. Der Aufbau ist klar:

V. 21: Die Forderung Elias an das Volk; das Volk schweigt.
V. 22–24: Der Vorschlag Elias; das Volk nimmt ihn an.
V. 25–38: Das Gottesurteil.
- V. 25–29: Der vergebliche Anruf der Baalspropheten
- V. 30–38: Der erfolgreiche Anruf Elias

V. 39: Das Bekenntnis des Volkes.

Die Hauptpartner sind daher Elia und das Volk; es geht darum, das Volk zum Bekenntnis für Jahwe hinzuführen. Die Propheten Baals sind nur insofern in das Geschehen einbezogen, als die Machtlosigkeit Baals dargetan werden soll, der weder durch Anruf noch durch mannigfaltige Riten zum

Eingreifen veranlaßt werden kann und damit sich als Nicht-Gott erweist. Ein Gott müßte hören, wenn es doch um den Erweis seiner Gottheit geht! Jahwe bekennt sich zu dem schlichten Gebet Elias und zeigt eben damit seine Gottheit.

Das bedeutet aber doch, daß hier die Frage nach dem wirklichen Gott d.h. dem wirkend eingreifenden Gott gestellt ist. Es geht nicht allein darum, daß für Israel nur Jahwe Gott ist; sondern es ist dem Baal die Qualität "Gott" überhaupt abgesprochen, wie es ja auch in der herausfordernden Rede Elias V. 27. zum Ausdruck kommt. Das heißt aber, daß nur Jahwe das Attribut "Gott" für sich in Anspruch nehmen kann, oder daß der wirkliche Gott nur der ist, der als Jahwe Israel zu seinem Volk gemacht hat. Eben darum wird dieses Volk in die Entscheidung gestellt, ob es weiterhin sich zu diesem Gott bekennen oder einem machtlosen "Nicht-Gott" folgen wolle, mögen dessen Anhänger auch noch so viel versprechen und "Hokuspokus" machen.

Mit diesem respektlosen Wort ist sicher umschrieben, was der Erzähler meint, wenn er das Auftreten der Propheten Baals darstellt. Aber kann auch ein überzeugter Monotheist so respektlos von den Anhängern anderer Götter, bezw. von diesen Göttern selbst reden, wie es hier geschicht? Voraussetzung ist doch wohl eine Entscheidungssituation wie sie hier dargestellt wird, nämlich die Entscheidung, ob Israel weiterhin in seinem Gott Jahwe den einen Gott sehen will, neben dem es keinen anderen gibt, oder ob man zwei Gottmächte anerkennen kann. Eine Situation, die dadurch gekennzeichnet ist, daß den 450 Propheten des Baal nur einer entgegentritt, der sich auf die Seite Jahwes stellt. Menschlich gesehen, eine aussichtslose Lage; aber der eine ist dessen gewiß, daß er den Einen auf seiner Seite hat, der allein Gott ist. So kann er das Volk, Israel, zu diesem seinem Gott zurückführen.

Wie ist diese Erzählung historisch zu beurteilen?

1) Der Erzähler läßt Elia eine Entscheidung von ungeheurer Tragweite treffen. Unabhängig von der Frage, ob und in wieweit es einen Monotheismus in Israel schon in älterer Zeit gegeben hat, ist hier mit eindeutiger Schärfe von dem Gott Israels als einzigem die Aussage: "Er ist Gott" gemacht. Wenn Baal kein Gott ist, dann ist es auch kein anderer, unter welchem Namen er auch auftritt. Auch im Alten Testament gibt es vor Deuterojesaja wenig stellen, die mit so überlegener Klarheit den anderen Mächten jeden Anspruch auf göttliche Verehrung absprechen.

2) Hat der Erzähler selbst erst diesen Glauben ausgesprochen, oder hat er ihn mit historischem Recht dem Elia zugeschrieben? Hier könnte historische Skepsis der ersten Alternative zuneigen; aber mit welchem Recht?

Bei wem liegt die Beweislast? Doch wohl bei dem, der ein als geschehen berichtetes Ereignis als nicht geschehen ansehen möchte. Er müßte dann die Erzählung etwa als "Beispielerzählung" verstehen; aber eine solche literarische Einordnung setzt eine Entscheidung in der historischen Frage schon voraus, die ja noch zur Diskussion steht. Im Zusammenhang der Elialegenden kann und darf nach dem etwa vorliegenden geschichtlichen Kern gefragt werden. Beschränkt dieser sich auf den Namen Elia, an den der Erzähler seine Darstellung angeknüpft hätte, oder gehört noch mehr dazu?

3) Wenn Elia in die Zeit Ahabs und Ahasjas gehört (danach wird er nicht mehr genannt), so ist das die Zeit, in der ein Baalkult auch im Staat Israel anerkannt war. Ganz abgesehen von den Nachrichten über Ahab in 1 Kg. 16, die Baalmassebe, die schon Joram entfernt und der Baaltempel in Samaria, den erst Jehu zerstört, sprechen eine eindeutige Sprache. Diese Aussagen würden erheblich verstärkt, wenn A.Alts These stimmt, daß die Gründung Samarias durch Omri den Zweck gehabt habe, auch der kanaanäischen Bevölkerung zu einer Art Gleichberechtigung im Gesamtverband Israel zu verhelfen. Damit bekam auch der von den Kanaanäern verehrte Baal eine Stellung, die einer Nebenordnung neben Jahwe praktisch gleich kam, wenn nicht sogar in Samaria Baal der vorzüglich verehrte Gott war. Das bedeutete aber, daß im Staate Israel nicht mehr nur Jahwe, sondern ebenso Baal Anspruch auf göttliche Verehrung erhob. Die Situation zwischen Jahwe und Baal, wie sie in 1 Kg. 18:21–39 vorausgesetzt wird, entspricht unserer geschichtlichen Kenntnis.

4) Auch das ist dann nicht verwunderlich, daß es in Israel 450 Baalspropheten gegeben haben soll; denn solches Nabitum gehörte zum Baalsdienst. Ihnen steht Elia als einziger gegenüber.

5) Wenn also die Situation der Erzählung der uns erkennbaren geschichtlichen Wirklichkeit entspricht, so ist damit noch nicht das Geschehen selbst gesichert. Welches Geschehen? Solange man V. 40 als integrierenden Bestandteil der Erzählung ansah, stand man vor der Schwierigkeit, daß doch erst Jehu die Propheten und Priester Baals beseitigt habe, daß also diese Ausrottung nicht gut auf Elia zurückgeführt werden konnte. Damit aber wurde die ganze Erzählung zu einer Rückprojektion des Handelns Jehus. Wenn aber Würthwein im Recht ist, und der ganze Aufbau der Erzählung scheint dafür zu sprechen, daß sie mit V. 39 schließt, d.h. mit dem Bekenntnis des Volkes, dann stellt sich die Frage nach dem Geschehen anders. Dann geht es zunächst nicht um die Ausrottung des Baalsdienstes, sonden um ein Bekenntnis des Volkes, um die Rückführung des israelitischen Volksteils zu Jahwe. Das würde bedeuten, daß hier durch Elia Menschen in

Israel erneut auf ihre Bindung an Jahwe, den alleinigen Gott, hingewiesen wurden. Ist das wahrscheinlich zu machen? Einen Hinweis könnte es vielleicht geben. Wie kommt es, daß Joram, trotz seiner Mutter, die Baalmassebe[12] in Samaria beseitigen läßt? Es muß doch schon eine jahwegläubige Reaktion auf den Baaldienst gegeben haben, der Joram nachgab oder nachgeben mußte. Wie ist diese Reaktion entstanden? Haben wir einen Anlaß, bei dieser doch sicherlich berechtigten Frage nach dem Grund des Handelns Jorams an dem Bericht in 1 Kg. 18:21–39 vorbei zu gehen? Das würde bedeuten, daß Elia einen Teil, vielleicht einen führenden, des Volkes Israel dazu gebracht habe, wieder allein Jahwe zu verehren und damit auf den Baaldienst zu verzichten, ja, seine Zurückdrängung zu fordern. Der Bericht ist zeitlich nicht fixiert; es steht nichts im Wege, ihn in die letzte Zeit Ahabs zu verlegen. In die wahrscheinlich sehr kurze Regierungszeit Ahasjas fällt eine ähnliche Forderung Elias dem König gegenüber. Die Auswirkung fiele dann in die Anfangszeit Jorams, ohne freilich schon ans Ziel zu gelangen (etwa, weil nun ein Gegenschlag Isebels erfolgte).

Gewiß ist das eine historische Kombination; aber ist sie unwahrscheinlicher als das, was etwa A.Alt über die Geschichte des Karmels zusammengetragen hat, oder gar das, was Fohrer über die Hintergründe dieser Geschichte glaubt sagen zu können? Mir scheint das "weniger" sei im Grunde ein "mehr," weil es stärker in der wirklich erkennbaren Geschichte verankert ist.

6) Nun noch einmal zum Geschehen selbst. Daß diese Erzählung stilisiert ist, zeigt der Aufbau deutlich genug; das Ganze ist auf den Schluß, das Bekenntnis des Volkes, ausgerichtet. Damit aber braucht die Frage nach dem wirklichen Geschehen nicht ausgeschaltet zu sein. Wenn die Wirkung eines solchen Bekenntnisses zu spüren ist, darf man auch fragen, was dazu geführt hat, auch wenn jede Antwort unsicher bleibt. Das Bekenntnis ist dadurch hervorgerufen, daß Elia bei einer Auseinandersetzung mit den Propheten Baals Sieger blieb. Darf man noch hinzufügen, daß bei dem Sieg ein himmlisches Feuer, das heißt doch wohl ein Blitz, eine besondere Rolle spielte.[13] Gewiß sind wir damit an der Grenze des historisch Faßbaren; aber zweierlei bleibt m.E.: Wahrscheinlich die Erinnerung an ein Geschehen, das in dem Handeln Jorams zur Wirkung kam; sicherlich die Darstellung dieses Vorgangs als eines Rufes zur Entscheidung für den einen Gott, neben dem keiner Anspruch auf diesen Namen hat.

12. Ob man besser an den Baalaltar denken sollte, vergl. 16:32, ist nicht ganz sicher, spielt aber in unserem Zusammenhang keine entscheidende Rolle.

13. Wenn die Erzählung aus dem Zusammenhang der Dürregeschichte herausgelöst ist, braucht das Erscheinen eines Blitzes nicht zu verwundern.

7) Noch eine letzte Frage: Wo ist dieses Ereignis zu lokalisieren? Nach dem gegenwärtigen Zusammenhang eindeutig auf dem Karmel. Wenn aber die Erzählung so abzugrenzen ist, wie es hier im Anschluß an Würthwein geschehen ist, sind dann die Worte in V. 19, 20 auch maßgebend für den ursprünglichen Sitz von V. 21–39? Festzustellen ist, daß im gegenwärtigen Text dieser Verse der Karmel nicht genannt wird. Muß man trotzdem an der Lokalisierung des Sammlers festhalten? Es sei an die mancherlei Schwierigkeiten erinnert, die sich aus ihr ergeben: (a) Wo auf dem Karmel ist das Geschehen anzusetzen? Daß die Tradition seit alters verschiedene Stellen angibt, ist unbestritten, aber bei dem alt überlieferten Zusammenhang verständlich. Aber jede der angenommenen Stellen hat ihre besondere Schwierigkeit. (b) Wer soll der auf dem Karmel verehrte Baal sein? Melqart? Baalschamaim? Oder der Baal des Karmel? (c) Wenn, wie heute auf Grund der bekannten Inschrift[14] angenommen wird, der Baal des Karmel gemeint ist, hat dieser Ortsgott wirklich 450 Propheten? Oder, wenn sie woanders herkommen, woher dann? Liegt hier wirklich eine Haupt- und Staatsaktion vor?[15] Würden alle diese Fragen nicht hinfallen, wenn man die Verse 21–39 wirklich als Eigenüberlieferung hinnähme?

Ja, aber wo soll man dann die Erzählung ansetzen? Der Bericht selbst gibt keinen Ort an. Welchen könnte man dann vermuten? Die Akteure sind Elia, der an keinen Ort gebunden erscheint; ferner das Volk, d.h. Israeliten, die dem Baalkult zu verfallen drohen; das bedeutet, daß sie mit Kanaanäern in vielfache Berührung kommen. Endlich ist da eine große Schar von Propheten Baals. Wo sind diese in der letzten Zeit Ahabs am ehesten zu suchen? Mir scheint: in Samaria. Hier, in der Umgebung der neuen Stadt ist sicherlich auch die Versuchung zum Abfall von Jahwe am größten. So könnte sich aus der Erzählung selbst am ehesten die *Vermutung* ergeben, daß sie ursprünglich in der Gegend von Samaria spielte. Dann braucht man nicht mehr auf dem Karmel zu suchen, braucht auch nicht zu erklären, wie soviele Baalspropheten dorthin kommen. Wohl aber darf man die Frage wieder stellen, mit welchem Baal sich Elia auseinanderzusetzen hatte, und die Antwort Eißfeldts gewinnt dann neue Wahrscheinlichkeit.

Aber verbindet die Tradition nicht eben doch Elia nur mit dem Karmel? Ganz so einhellig, wie es früher schien, doch wohl nicht. Es ist das Verdienst von A.Alt, eine Eliatradition bei Samaria wieder entdeckt zu haben und

14. Vergl. dazu Otto Eißfeldt, Der Gott Karmel, SAB, Klasse für Sprachen, Literatur und Kunst, Jhg. 1953, Nr. 1 (Berlin, 1954). K. Galling, Der Gott Karmel und die Ächtung der fremden Götter, in: Geschichte und Altes Testament, Festschrift A.Alt, *BHTh* 16 (Tübingen, 1953): 105–25.

15. Wie solche A.Alt a.a.O. und G. Fohrer, Elia, annehmen.

zwar in doppelter Hinsicht. Einmal dadurch, daß er eine frühchristliche Eliakirche auf dem Schech schaᶜale entdeckte, südöstlich von Samaria, und zum anderen dadurch, daß er auf Traditionen stieß, die 1925 in Sebastije erzählt wurden. Ich zitiere: "Ein Bauer von Sebastie wusste mir denn auch etwas Wunderbares von der Stätte zu erzählen: Vor Zeiten sei hier ein langer Krieg zwischen Muslimen, Christen und Juden gewesen; da habe schließlich Gott vom Himmel Feuer fallen lassen gleich einem Stern und habe so für immer die Gegner auseinander gejagt."

In diesem kurzen *ιερος λογος* haben wir offenbar die Erklärung für den Namen des Schech schaᶜale; er ist der Heilige des göttlichen Feuers, das hier zur Erde fiel. Meinem Erzähler war dieser Zusammenhang kaum bewußt; die Person des Schech spielt in seinem Bericht überhaupt keine Rolle, und das Wort schaᶜale kam darin nicht vor. Aber die Form der Erzählung, die ihm allein geläufig war, braucht ja nicht die ursprüngliche zu sein. Ist vielleicht ihr Stoff nur so völlig "zersagt," daß die Elemente auseinander getreten sind und daß nun im Bewußtsein der Leute die Person und die Sache, der Heilige und das Wunder getrennt für sich fortleben?

Die Antwort gab mir der Wächter auf dem tell von Sebastie. Er erklärte auf meine Frage sofort, der Schech schaᶜale sei in Wirklichkeit Elias; der habe von dort oben das himmlische Feuer auf die Boten fallen lassen, die ihn an den Hof des Königs von Israel holen sollten. Man sieht: In dieser Form des *ιερος λογος* ist die Verbindung der Elemente, die in dem Bericht des Bauern ganz zerfallen waren, noch durchaus lebendig."[16]

So weit A.Alt. Die Verbindung des Elia mit dem Hügel des Schech schaᶜle ist um so merkwürdiger, als sie ja durch die biblische Überlieferung nicht unmittelbar an die Hand gegeben war. Sollte aber die erste der beiden von Alt berichteten Traditionen nur eine "Zersagung" der zweiten sein, sollte sich in ihr nicht eine selbständige Überlieferung erhalten haben, die eben letztlich auf die Geschichte von dem Gottesurteil zurückgeht? Gewiß ist das alles kein Beweis für die oben vermutete Lokalisierung des Gottesurteils in der Gegend von Samaria, aber jedenfalls ist die frühe Verbindung des Elia mit dieser Gegend schon in altchristlicher Zeit ein Hinweis darauf, daß man das Wirken Elias hierher verlegt hat. Und die Geschichte vom Gottesurteil ist sicherlich älter und bedeutsamer als die von der Bestrafung der Königsboten.

Eine Frage bleibt dann allerdings, warum schon ein früher Sammler diese Erzählung an den Karmel verlegte. Die Antwort kann m.E.nur sein, daß

16. Vergl. A.Alt, Ein vergessenes Heiligtum des Propheten Elias, *ZDPV* 48 (1925): 393ff. Zitat S. 394.

die Dürreerzählung schon bald mit dem Karmel verbunden war, und daß die Einordnung des Gottesurteils in sie zwangsläufig zu der Lokalisierung am Karmel führte. Die Verbindung der Eliatradition mit dem Karmel kann durchaus historische Gründe haben; nur das Gottesurteil gehört wahrscheinlich nicht dort hin.

Was ergibt sich aus dem allem? Alle vorgetragenen Überlegungen sprechen dafür, daß die Tradition ein "echtes" Bild des historischen Elia erkennen läßt. "Echt" in dem Sinn, wie ein guter Maler eine Landschaft besser erfaßt als eine Fotografie. Elia ist nicht nur, wie Nathan und Gad, im Namen Jahwes aufgetreten, sondern ist für ihn eingetreten, in einer Situation, in der das nicht selbstverständlich war. Und zwar nicht nur so, daß Jahwe für Israel der alleinige Gott sein sollte, sondern so, daß Jahwe allein das Attribut "Gott" zukommt. Oder: der eine Gott ist es, der als "Jahwe" Israel geführt hat und dem Israel daher verpflichtet ist. Es geht also um mehr als darum, den Baalsdienst in Israel abzuwehren; vielmehr war das Anliegen Elias, in dem Gott Israels den alleinigen Gott zu erfassen.

Von da aus wird Elias geschichtliche Stellung verständlich. Er ist wirklich der Einsame gewesen, von König und Volk unverstanden, und doch in seinem Auftreten und Reden vom Geheimnis umwittert, im Dienste seines Gottes, dem allein er Gottheit zuerkannte. Darf man noch eine historische Kombination wagen? Diese könnte so aussehen: Gegen Ende der Regierung Ahabs (oder auch etwa zu Anfang der Regierung Jorams) gelingt es ihm, einen größeren Kreis in Israel zur Ablehnung des Baaldienstes zu bewegen, mit dem Ergebnis, daß Joram eine Baalmassebe in Samaria entfernen läßt. Aber weitere Schritte in dieser Richtung wußte Isebel zu verhindern, sodaß erst Jehu die Ausrottung des Baaldienstes gelang. Die Tradition hat noch eine Erinnerung an dieses Eingreifen Isebels bewahrt; aber sie läßt Elia eben deshalb am Horeb den Auftrag seines Gottes empfangen, die Gegner des Ahabhauses zu ihrem Amt zu berufen.

Mag diese Tradition auch unsicher bleiden, die geschichtliche Grösse und Wirkung Elias, wie die Tradition ihn dargestellt hat, bleibt davon unberührt. Ist er doch in seiner Bezeugung der alleinigen Gottheit Jahwes der Vorläufer der Schriftpropheten von Amos (9:7) an.

# The Identity of the Suffering Servant

ARVID S. KAPELRUD

Few questions have aroused so much interest among scholars as that of the identity of the Suffering Servant in the Book of Second Isaiah. Who was this mysterious figure? Many answers have been suggested and no attempt to give a full review of them will be made here.[1] Only few of the hypotheses will be mentioned, so far as they throw any light on my attempt at a solution.

As already indicated in my book on Second Isaiah,[2] it is most likely that the Servant Songs, like the rest of the book, Ch. 40–55, go back to Second Isaiah himself. There are, however, some problems which will have to be considered, even though they cannot all be discussed here. This latter necessity carries with it consequences which again create new problems. There is no solution to the ʿEbed Yahweh question without problems.

James Muilenburg, who concurs in the above observation, has suggested that the Servant of Yahweh be interpreted as Israel.[3] This is not a new interpretation, but one which has been often in the foreground in the discussion. It has its difficulties, as Mowinckel rather briefly has remarked: "The Servant is a concrete person, no collective nation."[4] This sounds logical, but it is not practical when we consider the ancient Hebrew ways of thinking. The

1. A full discussion in C. R. North, *The Suffering Servant in Deutero-Isaiah* (London, 1948. 2nd ed. 1956).

2. *Et folk på hjemferd* (Oslo, 1964), pp. 49ff.

3. The Book of Isaiah, chapters 40–66, *IB*, vol. V (1956): 408.

4. *Det Gamle Testamente*, vol. III (Oslo, 1944), pp. 194ff.

modern, sharp distinction between the individual and the group was not made by the ancient Hebrew. We shall return to this.

First let us consider the objections to the Servant in the ʿEbed Yahweh songs being actually "the servant Israel" in the other text passages. As Muilenburg has already pointed out,[5] they are summarized clearly by the German Old Testament scholar Johann Fischer.[6] In his opinion ʿEbed Yahweh and the servant Israel are fundamentally different in their characters. Israel is doubtful and disheartened and must constantly be admonished to rely on God (40:27; 41:8ff.; 44:1f.), while ʿEbed Yahweh conquers his desperation through an unshakable faith in God (49:4; 50:7–9). The servant Israel is a sinner from birth (48:4), while ʿEbed is without sin and guilt (50:5; 53:4–6). The servant Israel suffers in deportation for his own sins (42:18–25; 43:22–28; 47:7; 50:1; 54:7), while ʿEbed suffers for the sin of others (53:4–6,9,11f.). The servant Israel seems to lose his courage under his trials (40:27; 49:14; 50:1f.), while ʿEbed suffers patiently (53:7), and voluntarily, for the good of others (53:4ff.). The servant Israel suffered unwillingly, and sought revenge over his enemies (41:11–16; 42:13–15). Finally, ʿEbed Yahweh had a special task: to suffer for Israel, and he could thus, in Fischer's and other scholars' opinions, not be identical with Israel (52:13–53:12).

Also the passage in 49:5f. where Yahweh gives ʿEbed Yahweh the task of bringing Jacob back and gathering together Israel, seems to indicate that the Servant cannot be identical with Israel.

It is on this basis, which Fischer has summarized, that scholars have tended to identify a single person as the Servant of Yahweh. Bernhard Duhm, the first scholar to separate the songs from the rest of the context, thought that they were composed by a prophet and Torah teacher who had contracted leprosy.[7] This theory was taken up by other scholars, e.g., H. S. Nyberg in an article "The Man of Pain" (Smärtornas man), in 1942.[8] Duhm dated the songs at approximately the middle of the fifth century B.C., about 100 years later than Second Isaiah.

Sigmund Mowinckel was the next scholar to enliven the discussion with his book "Der Knecht Jahwäs" (Kristiania, 1921). As indicated in Acts 8:34, the Norwegian scholar tried to show that it was the prophet himself, Second Isaiah, to whom the Songs referred—not a future figure, but a

5. Muilenburg, p. 408.
6. Das Buch Isaias, *HS* (Bonn, 1939), Teil II, pp. 10–11.
7. *Das Buch Jesaja übersetzt und erklärt* (Göttingen, 1892, 4th ed. 1922).
8. *Smärtornas man, Svensk Exeġetisk Årsbok VII* (1942), pp. 5–82.

contemporary. In Mowinckel's opinion this is obvious in the description in the passages 42:6f.; 49:1–6.

Mowinckel's hypothesis was favorably received and was accepted by many scholars, e.g., Hermann Gunkel, Max Haller, Emil Balla, and Hans Schmidt. It was accepted also by Ernst Sellin in a somewhat modified form. He reckoned the Servant in the three first Songs to be the prophet, but considered the fourth Song to be a lamentation composed by the disciple of the prophet, the Third Isaiah, whose work is found in Isaiah 56–66. This view was accepted by Karl Elliger[9] and Paul Volz,[10] who separated the fourth Song from the others, as a composition from a much later period. Someone had written about the prophet and interpreted his work long after his time.

Mowinckel himself came to accept this point of view, since obviously the prophet had not been able to write about his own death. As late as in 1944, Mowinckel, like Sellin, had changed his opinion to a third one: the Servant was a prophet, a real historical person, who lived shortly before the time of the author of the Songs.[11]

As early as 1791 C. F. Stäudlin suggested that the phrase referred to the prophet Isaiah.[12] Since that time biblical scholars have held many other opinions: Moses, the kings Uzziah (who was smitten by leprosy, II Chron. 26:19ff.), Hiskiah, Josiah, Jehojachin; Zerubbabel and his oldest son Meshullam, Eleazar, and the prophet Jeremiah; illustrating the difficulty in identifying ᶜEbed Yahweh as a specific historical person. One or several points may accord with the ᶜEbed figure, but nowhere do all the pieces of the puzzle present a clear picture. What is said of ᶜEbed Yahweh is of such dimensions and scope that none of the suggested figures fits the frame, not even such remarkable personalities as Moses and Jeremiah. Here are world historical perspectives and traces of an ideology outside the sphere of history and inside a cultic world, where individuals and collectives have combined in a kind of osmosis.

It may be objected that exaggerated descriptions are by no means unknown in the Old Testament. It was part of Oriental style to use strong colors and to underline through exaggeration, and the ᶜEbed Yahweh Songs use strong colors, but more importantly they speak of events which already were part of the past and which had far reaching effects into their world. The lives

9. Deuterojesaja in seinem Verhältnis zu Tritojesaja, *BWANT*, 4. Folge, Heft 11, 1933.

10. Jesaja 53, in Budde Festschrift, *BZAW* 34, pp. 180–90, and *Jesaja II übersetzt und erklärt* (Leipzig, 1932).

11. See note 4, cf. p. 196.

12. *Neue Beiträge zur Erläuterung der biblischen Propheten* (Göttingen, 1791).

and work of the prophets, kings, and leaders mentioned above did not have such dimensions. Even the task of Moses was restricted to his own people, as was the work of Jeremiah, cfr. Jer. 1:5,10ff. Their missions can hardly be interpreted as so world-encompassing as that of the Servant in the Songs. In any case, the Songs seem not to be directly historically or personally oriented, but have reference to the cultic ritual.

From a modern viewpoint this is not always clear, because we are used to thinking in other categories. But we do have some viewpoints of value, in our consideration of personality above the cultic or the ritual. If we take the words in the Servant Songs objectively, it is clear that a personal address, a "you," could be used also as a collective address. Such a group could be represented by a person, preferably the king, the high priest, or a prominent prophet acting as its spokesman.

But this was not necessarily true, as may be seen in the Book of Second Isaiah, where Israel again and again is addressed as an individual, with "you." Also within the Servant Songs such an interpretation is natural in light of the intense, emotional address and appeal to a "you." This is carried throughout the whole book so we cannot attribute it only to the Servant Songs. The means of expression thus gives no basis for interpretation of the Songs as speaking of an individual.

On the other hand, there is no doubt that the verses in Is. 49:5f. cause some difficulties for an interpretation of the Servant as Israel. This is true in spite of the fact that in verse 3 in the same chapter the Servant and Israel are directly identified—an identification unacceptable to those scholars adhering to the "individual" interpretation, who declare the word "Israel" to be a later addition. Since the old versions have the word, this seems a too convenient way of getting rid of a problem word in the text.

If the Servant in the Songs is to be understood as Israel, it seems clear that these strongly emotional songs, with their peculiar tone, sprang forth from special experiences which made it natural to emphasize a certain aspect of this Israel. This characteristic seems to separate the Songs, to some extent, from their surroundings, and has caused scholars to isolate them as foreign elements in the context. The British Old Testament scholar Skinner,[13] and others, believe that "the ideal Israel" is referred to, but this seems a very abstract interpretation. Muilenburg is of the opinion that it refers to "a strong minority of faithful men."[14] In all probability, Muilenburg considered the prophet as living and working in Babylon and that prevented him

13. *The Book of the Prophet Isaiah Chapters XL–LXVI* (Cambridge, 1898, 2nd ed. 1917).
14. P. 410.

from defining this minority more exactly. As I have tried to show elsewhere,[15] it is probable that Second Isaiah lived in Judah and viewed the events in Babylon from some distance. This makes it easier to define the "minority" of which Muilenburg speaks. All the features which are delineated in the description of the Servant of Yahweh in the Songs may be applied to *the exiles, as this group was seen by those who were not exiles themselves.*[16] This interpretation is fundamental for a correct understanding. As already mentioned, the cult terminology plays a great role, and here there are probably also remnants of ancient king ideology.

There are features in the ᶜEbed Yahweh Songs which may have had parallels in the great year festival in Babylonia–Assyria, the Akitu. Features from this feast may then have passed into the autumn and New Year feasts in Israel. The Akitu feast was closely connected with the year cycle, growth, and crop. The king played a central role, and in the dramatic scenes he acted on behalf of the god. As the fertility god had to go down into the earth in the dry period, to stand forth later in all his glamour and take his seat on the throne of the gods, so also was the king humiliated in the New Year feast, deprived of his royal regalia and "deposed," until he again was enthroned. All this was experienced in the cult and played dramatically in order to bring about fertility and victory in the new year.

It was not the person of the king that predominated. The king played the role of the god, and in this drama he was the god. In a few days he lived through the same cycle of fate through which the god—either Baal, Marduk, or Assur—lived in the course of the year. The king could do it because he was the chosen of the god, the anointed one, God's servant. On him special duties and a special responsibility were placed. He mediated between god and man. He represented his people and his country. They were included as part of his world. If all went well with him, it also went well with the people. He was not only an individual, he was at the same time representative of a people, a community. The picture may be even more clear if we say that he *was* a people. In the king the division between individual and group was neutralized in a particular way. When the king was exalted, took his seat on the throne, and homage was paid to him it brought good for the whole people, and they could look forward to happiness and peaceful days. When the king

15. Levde Deuterojesaja i Judea?, *NTT* 61 (1960): 23–27, and *Et folk på hjemferd* (Oslo, 1964), pp. 27–34.

16. This definition is close to that of Otto Kaiser, to whom the Servant is Israel of the Gola, who succeeds to the role of the king, and embodies a prophetic function also. See O. Kaiser: Der königliche Knecht: Eine traditionsgeschichtlich-exegetische Studie über die Ebed-Jahwe-Lieder bei Deuterojesaja. *FRLANT*, N.F. 52 (Göttingen, 1959): 65.

was humiliated and scorned he did not suffer for himself alone, he bore the indignities also for the people he represented.

We cannot and shall not connect the Akitu feast directly to the ʿEbed Yahweh Songs. There has been no actual historical reference, even if there is a connection. But considering this possibility helps us to better understand the Songs.

Here we may see that the sharp distinction between individual and collective interpretation did not exist in ancient time. That is an important point to take into account, which may determine our interpretation.

Both Ivan Engnell[17] and Otto Kaiser[18] have emphasized the role of the king as mediator between God and his people. He represented God to the people and was thus the special servant of Yahweh. At the same time he represented the people before God and was then one with his people, so when he said "I" this "I" meant the whole people. The individual, the king, and the people could not be separated in such circumstances. We are reminded of the situation in the Servant Songs, where the individual and the collective become one. When the Servant is addressed with a "you" or is speaking himself as "I," it is the exiled people who stand forth, represented in an individual. Kaiser suggests that it was the prophet who represented the people and that the kingship, also ideological, had played out its role. The prophet concerned here, Second Isaiah, was himself one of the exiled and, in Kaiser's opinion, he carried the burden and identified himself completely with the people. In Kaiser's view it is thus one and the same thing to say that the Servant was Israel or that it was the prophet himself.[19]

Here Kaiser is on very unsafe ground. There is actually not the least shadow of proof that Second Isaiah rejected kingship and considered its role finished. That the prophet speaks of the kingship of Yahweh is neither proof nor indication. Also in the time of the kings, even notably then, Yahweh was paid homage as king. Second Isaiah preached the restoration of Israel, and part of the restoration was that the people again have a king from the dynasty of David. In no passage does the prophet repudiate such an idea, for him this was obvious. When he speaks about the restoration of Jacob's tribes in the passage 49:6, this solemn means of expression does not mean that he wanted to go back to the situation before the monarchy was introduced, as Kaiser has suggested. Through David the monarchy was woven into the life

17. The Ebed Yahweh Songs and the Suffering Messiah in Deutero-Isaiah, *BJRL* 31 (1948).

18. See note 16 above. Cfr. p. 64.

19. P. 132.

of the people in such a way that it could not easily be cut out. Also the Messiah expectations speak about that.

Kaiser himself says: "Immer wieder fanden wir Anklänge an die Königsideologie."[20] But we must ask: Is it accidental that king-ideological ideas may be traced in the background of several of the Songs? The answer is close at hand in the Old Testament. It is not accidental, because the king still, in spite of all disasters and exiles, is the real representative of the people —he *is* the people. It is therefore reasonable to conclude that he personified the exiled people in the Servant Songs.

The king was no abstract figure to Second Isaiah, a point which is worth emphasizing. We are apt to forget that the legitimate king of Judah in 598 B.C., the eighteen-year-old Jehojachin, who had just received the royal dignity after his deceased father, King Jehoiachim, had been deported to Babylon in the same year after Nebuchadrezzar's second attack on Jerusalem. He was kept there as a prisoner while his uncle "reigned" in Judah under Babylonian control. He was a prisoner also after the fall of Jerusalem, until 562. Then King Nebuchadrezzar died, and his successor, Amel-Marduk (in the Old Testament called Evil-Merodach) released King Jehojachin from prison, but did not let him leave Babylon. Jehojachin, who was then fifty-four years old, was installed in a wing of the royal palace, where he was treated as a royal guest. He had his family with him and a series of servants. It is not known when he died, but we may reckon that he lived during the childhood of Second Isaiah.

What role the pathetic figure of King Jehojachin played for those still living in Judah may be indicated by the fact that they reckoned the time from his deportation, shortly after his ascension to the throne, not from the ascension of Zedekiah (cfr. Ezek. 1:2, 8:1). Jehojachin was their real king, their real representative.

The tragic life story of King Jehojachin shows how close at hand the idea of the suffering king as a representative of the people was for a prophet like Second Isaiah (cfr. also Jer. 22:24–30). Few, if anyone, could symbolize the people in this time like Jehojachin. Therefore we may re-write the words of Kaiser, mentioned above, thus: it is one and the same thing to say that the Servant of Yahweh was the suffering and exiled people or that he was the suffering and exiled king.

Finally, let us consider the differences of opinion among scholars. In the Servant Songs the prophet seems to involve himself more with the problems than is the case in the other passages and he seems less optimistic. Just as

20. P. 64.

with the prophets, whose spiritual lines were so divergent, we must expect to find sudden turns, unexpected changes, oscillations between great heights and depths. There is nothing strange in the suggestion that Second Isaiah may have seen fundamental problems with changing points of view. Our post-Aristotelian demand for logical consistency in words and acts was unknown to the prophet and his contemporaries.

If we compare the Servant Songs carefully with the rest of chs. 40–55, we may see, as Muilenburg has pointed out, that many of the contrasts mentioned by Fischer have their background in somewhat different points in the passages.[21] They must therefore not be judged with the strict measure of consistent logic. That is true, e.g., about Israel's expiation of sin, which according to 40:2 was double payment for the sin. This may have a special meaning when Israel is compared with other peoples, a comparison which was quite natural for a prophet who saw his people as specially chosen by Yahweh. But with all its sin Israel was nevertheless a people set apart.

The other contrasts are not always so sharp in the texts as in Fischer's and other scholars' descriptions.[22] Also the Servant in the ᶜEbed Yahweh Songs was on the verge of losing his courage, like the servant Israel, the contrast on that point is actually very small. Both triumphed over their desperation and their despondency. The descriptions are different, but so are their objects. The strong and impulsive reactions of the prophet made him see Israel's situation and task from a different point of view which was nonetheless congruent.

In this prophet, where universalism and nationalism are almost synonymous, many components were bound together that logically should not be so bound.[23] So we must have very strong reasons for isolating the Servant Songs from the rest of the context. They have a special place in the text and a peculiar tone, but in their own way they are part of the whole. The tone overlies a deeper undertone through the preaching of Second Isaiah. Style and form in the Servant Songs are well in line with the rest of the text, they are not more incongruous with the context than many other oracles in Second Isaiah, and the context will be no better if we take them out. In the end the message of Second Isaiah and of the Servant Songs was one and the same: a message of salvation and deliverance for a people that needed comfort more than prophecies of doom.

21. P. 410.
22. So also Muilenburg, p. 410.
23. See D. E. Hallenberg, Nationalism and "the Nations" in Isaiah XL–LV, *VT* 19 (1969): 23–36.

# The Junctural Origin of the West Semitic Definite Article

THOMAS O. LAMBDIN

All of the West Semitic languages attested from the first millennium B.C. onward possess a morpheme which functions more or less as a definite article. In Aramaic it is suffixed to nouns and adjectives as the so-called emphatic state; in the remaining languages it is prefixed. The generally prevailing view of Semitists would derive these article morphemes, not identical in the various languages, from a number of demonstrative particles which by one process or another have taken on a determining function. This type of derivation is unsatisfactory for several reasons: (1) the independent existence of such particles in the earlier stages of the languages in question cannot be demonstrated; (2) the position of these particles appears to violate syntactic requirements of earlier Semitic in general and of the individual languages in particular; (3) the development of the definite article would appear to be unrelated in each of the major subgroups: Canaanite, Aramaic and Arabic.[1] I wish, therefore, to propose in this paper a hypothesis which accounts for the development of the article morphemes from a single phonological feature present in the earlier common language and thus posits a single origin for the definite article in all

1. A first step toward a more general solution of the problem was made by E. Ullendorff, "The Form of the Definite Article in Arabic and Other Semitic Languages," in *Arabic and Islamic Studies in Honor of Hamilton A. R. Gibb*, ed. by George Makdisi (Leiden, 1965), pp. 631–37, where he proposes that the Arabic article resulted from a dissimilation of consonant gemination, the latter being, as in Hebrew and Phoenician, the more original form. He does not pursue the matter further, attributing a vague expressive function to the gemination in the earlier language. His (implicit) rejection of the particle theories is noteworthy, however.

the West Semitic languages. The hypothesis cannot be proved in the strict sense of the word, since that would require data which we lack at present. Its value, I believe, rests in the explanation it provides for certain residual features in the attested languages, the economy of reconstruction it affords, and in the syntactically consistent framework it presupposes.

A detailed discussion of determination in early Semitic would take us too far afield. Suffice it to say that the explicitly marked categories definite-indefinite did not occur; the basic distinctions were rather bound-unbound, and for the adjective at least, predicate-attributive. Our problem, then, is comparable to that of Indo-European, namely the transition from a period of the language without a definite article to one with one. Latin (to Romance), Greek, and Germanic have in common the exploitation of a demonstrative adjective for this purpose, the demonstrative force gradually weakening to that of mere determination. The indefinite article similarly derives from the numerical adjective "one."[2] Because the West Semitic article cannot be traced back morphologically to an earlier demonstrative adjective or pronoun, such a simple solution is not available to our problem.

The problem is not without theoretical interest. The emergence of both a new semantic contrast (definite/indefinite) and a new morpheme (the article itself) virtually requires a development along the following lines:

1) The emergent category ($A'$) was originally implicit ($<$) in some other category ($A$) which was marked ($=$) by an element ($M$) of the language. This may have been, e.g., a morpheme or a construction.

2) In the course of time $M$ became ($\rightarrow$) formally composite ($M + M'$). This could happen in a variety of ways; for example, by the rise of allomorphisms through independent phonological development, or by reanalysis of $M$ through analogy.

3) Presumably unrelated development on the semantic side led to the possibility of decomposing $A$ into $A + A'$, probably because the new category $A'$ had support for its independent existence elsewhere in the structure of the language.

4) As a result of steps (2) and (3), it became possible for a speaker of the language to associate $A'$ with $M'$, as long as $M$ was still explicitly associated with $A$. These stages may be summarized as

| | | |
|---|---|---|
| 1) | $M = (A > A')$ | |
| 2) | $M \rightarrow (M + M')$ | $(M + M') = (A > A')$ |
| 3) | $(A > A') \rightarrow (A + A')$ | $(M + M') = (A + A')$ |
| 4) | Since $M = A$, | $M' = A'$ |

2. Egyptian offers an exact parallel in its development of definite and indefinite articles after the period of Middle Egyptian.

If we examine the problem of the West Semitic article in this light, we should expect to find some clue to its origin in the earliest attested stages of the various languages, provided of course that the genesis of the form does not lie so far in the past as to have been completely obscured by later generalizations. Prior to the isolation of $M' = A'$ in step (4), what later became the definite article ($M'$) would only occur together with $M$. If any of our language data come from the period when $M'$ was isolable but not yet generally extended as an expression of $A'$, we should expect $M'$ to appear as a feature of at least some constructions involving $M$, redundant when viewed anteriorly, but essential when viewed posteriorly. Before giving substance to the hypothesis, it is necessary to review certain features of definite article usage in Early Aramaic and Biblical Hebrew.

## ARAMAIC

In Imperial Aramaic and to a lesser extent in the later literary dialects the absolute and emphatic states of a noun correspond roughly to the categories indefinite and definite respectively. It is evident from the following table (using Biblical Aramaic as an example) that the emphatic suffix *-ā* (< Early Aramaic **-aʾ*)[3] is suffixed to the construct form and not to the absolute, at least from a *synchronic* point of view.

| | MASCULINE | | FEMININE | |
|---|---|---|---|---|
| | *Singular* | *Plural* | *Singular* | *Plural* |
| Absolute | (zero) | *în* | *ā* | *ān* |
| Construct | (zero) | *ê* < **ay* | *at* | *āt* |
| Emphatic | *ā* | *ayyā* | (*ə*)*tā* | *ātā* |

Whatever origin is postulated for the emphatic state must account for this rather unusual feature. Certainly the suggestion of a postfixed demonstrative particle does not come to grips with this and other basic syntactic problems involved.[4]

Equally perplexing is the use, in various dialects and periods, of the absolute and emphatic states in relation to the categories definite and indefinite.

3. I follow J. A. Fitzmyer, *The Aramaic Inscriptions of Sefîre* (Rome, 1967), pp. 147–48, and F. M. Cross and D. N. Freedman, *Early Hebrew Orthography* (New Haven, 1952), p. 24, in regarding the final *aleph* in Early Aramaic as consonantal. There is no clear evidence to the contrary.

4. For a survey of particle theories see, most recently, Kjell Aartun, "Zur Frage des bestimmten Artikels im Aramäischen," *Acta Orientalia* 24 (1959): 5–14.

The following table presents, I believe, a more accurate picture of the situation than do the simple equations absolute = indefinite and emphatic = definite:

| | *Early Aramaic* | *Later Aramaic* |
|---|---|---|
| Construction-bound | emphatic = definite | absolute = indefinite |
| Construction-free | absolute = definite or indefinite | emphatic = definite or indefinite |

The meanings of the terms construction-bound and construction-free will be made clear in the following discussion.

Since we are interested in origins, let us examine the use of the "articled" or emphatic form in the earliest Aramaic texts of a length adequate for our purposes, namely the treaties from Sefîre (eighth century), following the exemplary edition of J. Fitzmyer.[5] Here we find the emphatic suffix used:

| | | |
|---|---|---|
| 1) | on a noun before a demonstrative adjective (*gbrʾ znh*)[6] | 27 instances |
| 2) | on a noun before a relative pronoun (*gbrʾ zy*) | 15 instances |
| 3) | on an otherwise unqualified noun (*gbrʾ*) | 10 instances |
| 4) | on a noun in a mixed construction, | 2 instances |

namely

| | | |
|---|---|---|
| I A 38 | *qštʾ wḥṣyʾ ʾln* | the bow and these arrows |
| II B 2 | *ʿdyʾ wṭbtʾ z[y]* | the treaty and the amity which . . . |

Because there is no semantic ambiguity in the demonstrative adjective, we may characterize (anteriorly) the use of the emphatic state in group (1) as 100 per cent redundant or construction-predictable, since absolute + demonstrative adjective is not a permitted construction. The same is undoubtedly true of the instances in group (2), since absolute + relative pronoun is apparently permitted only when the absolute noun is preceded by some qualifier such as *kl* (e.g., III 1/2 *kl gbr zy*, any man who . . .).[7] This

5. Reference in note 3 above.

6. I use the designation "adjective" for the demonstrative pronoun in attributive position, in which it shows gender and number concord with its antecedent.

7. The phrase *bywm zy* (I B 31) is a possible exception to this statement if *ywm* is taken as an absolute form (so Fitzmyer, *op. cit.*, p. 69). It could, however, be taken as a construct (cf. Hebrew *bəyôm* before *ʾăšer* or a finite verb). In a proper relative clause after either an emphatic or absolute noun we should expect a resumptive pronoun in a nonaccusative oblique relationship; *bywm zy* belongs rather to the class of relative conjunctions like *ʾn zy* (where) and *ʾyk zy* (just as). The restoration in III 19 *w[m]lkn [zy sḥr]ty* (and the kings of my neighborhood), even if correct, is not a counter-example, since *zy* is not functioning here as a relative pronoun (that would require a preposition before *sḥrty*), but as the marker of a determinative phrase.

distribution is very striking since it means that slightly over 80 per cent of all the emphatic forms in these inscriptions are construction-bound and not determined by an a priori choice of definite versus indefinite meaning. The implications of this will be taken up below. An extrapolation from the table suggests that at its origin the emphatic state was 100 per cent predictable by construction and that the Sefîre inscriptions represent a stage of linguistic development not too far removed from that original situation.[8] While most of the Imperial Aramaic texts from the fifth century exhibit a later stage of development in their more extended use of the emphatic form, the Hermopolis letters are surprisingly close to the Sefîre inscriptions in this regard.[9]

The preceding observations will appear gratuitous unless it is borne in mind that we are dealing with an emergent element in the language. Before the contrast definite/indefinite became generalized, there must have been a stage in which the rudimentary article still co-occurred predominantly with the construction in which it originated. This would be true even if we were to accept a particle origin for the article: in the period prior to generalization, usage should reflect in some way the original meaning of such a particle (e.g., demonstrative, vocative) more clearly than would the later stages of the language. In these terms, our texts do not support a particle origin.

## BIBLICAL HEBREW

*The form of the article: synchronic versus diachronic reconstruction.* If one were to write a synchronic rule-grammar for Hebrew, the definite article could quite legitimately be given a base form **han-*, from which appropriate phonetic rules would lead to the actually attested forms. These rules would include (1) the assimilation of *n* to a following consonant; (2) the gradual loss of gemination with certain guttural consonants, accompanied by the compensatory lengthening of *a* to *ā*; (3) the dissimilation of *a* to *e* in certain environments; and (4) the syncope of *h* after the prepositions *bə*, *lə*, and *kə*.[10] Without the support of comparative data, it would be naive to assume that such a base-form as **han-* has any diachronic reality, i.e., that it represents a real

8. At the other end of the continuum, then, are the late dialects such as Syriac, Mandaean, and Modern Aramaic, where the absolute form becomes the restricted form, syntactically and functionally. The definite/indefinite contrast between emphatic and absolute is lost almost completely, and the demonstrative adjectives come into play when such distinctions are required.

9. See the excellent publication by E. Bresciani and M. Kamil, *Le lettere aramaiche di Hermopoli* (Atti della Accademia Nazionale dei Lincei, Memorie [Classe di Scienze morali, storiche, e filologiche], Serie VII, Vol. XII, Fasc. 5 [1966]).

10. This is only an approximate statement of what such rules would contain. The real rules would be more complicated, both in content and ordering.

historical antecedent. Such an assumption presupposes that all instances of a given linguistic phenomenon result from the same historical process. That this is incorrect is illustrated by consonant gemination in Hebrew. Historically this has at least three sources: (1) morphological, as in *D* (Piel) verbs, where it is an inherited feature; (2) phonological: (a) from an assimilated *n*, as in I-*Nun* verbs, the Niphal imperfect, etc.; or (b) from a junctural relationship, which will form part of our discussion in the following section of this paper; or (c) from unknown causes, perhaps dialectal or merely optional, as in the plural *gəmallîm*. Equally ambiguous is an initial *h*- which is subject to syncope when placed intervocalically. The synchronic rule in Hebrew probably originated in the developing Hiphil verbal system: **yuhaqtil* > **yaqtil* > *yaqtēl*, which then contrasted with the inherited imperative *haqtēl* < **haqtil*. Systematic pressure from elsewhere, e.g., Piel imperative: imperfect:: *qattēl*: *yəqattēl*, led to the synchronic interpretation of Hiphil *yaqtēl* as **yəhaqtēl* and thus an *h*-syncope rule was established. To illustrate a subsequent application of the rule, the Niphal imperfect *yiqqātēl* < **yanqatil* was then interpretable as **yəhiqqātēl*, which led to the formation of a new imperative form *hiqqātēl*. Other examples are frequent and need not be cited here.

*The category "definite."* In Biblical Hebrew a noun is classified as definite if:

1) it is a proper name,
2) it has a possessive pronomial suffix,
3) it has the definite article prefixed,
4) it is in construct with one of the preceding.

The category is established formally on the basis of two syntactic features: (a) the presence of the definite article on an attributive modifier, and (b) the preposing of the particle *ʾet* when the noun is the direct object of a transitive verb. We thus have the following contrasting constructions:

| | | |
|---|---|---|
| a) | *báyit qāṭōn* | a small house |
| | *habbáyit haqqāṭōn* | the small house |
| | *habbáyit hazzeh* | this house |
| b) | *rāʾîtî báyit* | I saw a house. |
| | *rāʾîtî ʾet-habbáyit* | I saw the house. |

Note that in (a) one of the two articles in each of the definite constructions is redundant, while in (b) either the *ʾet* or the article in the definite construction is redundant.

The noun with a pronominal suffix occupies a special status in both of these constructions. In (a) there is a noteworthy tendency to deviate from the normal pattern and to omit the article on the attributive when it is a demonstrative, e.g.,

| | | |
|---|---|---|
| Joshua 2:14 | *ᵓet-dəbārēnû zeh* | this matter of ours |
| Gen. 24:8 | *miššəbūᶜātî zōt* | from this oath of mine |
| Deut. 11:18 | *ᵓet-dəbāray ᵓēlleh* | these words of mine |

In construction (b) such nouns tend not to have a prefixed *ᵓet* when they designate parts of the body of the subject, e.g., *wayyišlaḥ yādô*, and he put forth his hand.

A second type of deviation involves constructions of type (a) in which the article occurs on the attribute but not on the noun. This is most frequent when an ordinal number stands in attributive position, e.g.,

Gen. 1:31 *yôm haššiššî* the sixth day

but it also occurs elsewhere, as in

II Sam. 12:4 *ləᵓîš heᶜāšîr* to the rich man.

Finally, it should be noted that in archaic poetic material the general absence of the definite article is paralleled by the absence of the *nota accusativi*. Also characteristic of this material is the use of *zeh* or *zû* as a relative pronoun, e.g.,

Ex. 15:16 *ᶜam-zû qānîtā* the people whom you have created.

Having no article, the noun in such constructions appears to be in the construct state, but in all the examples I have examined the consonantal text would also permit their interpretation as absolutes (e.g., *mqwm*, *hr*, *ᶜm*, *šrt*, *drk*, *ᵓrḥ*). Compare the *ywm zy* of the Sefîre texts discussed in the preceding section.

## THE HYPOTHESIS

1) The germinal category "definite" was originally implicit in at least two major constructions in early Northwest Semitic: (a) a noun followed by an appositionally placed demonstrative pronoun; (b) a noun followed by a relative clause introduced by a relative pronoun, which originally had the same form as the demonstrative but which gradually diverged from it in ceasing to

undergo modifications for number and gender. The definiteness of the second construction contrasted with the indefiniteness of a noun modified by an asyndetic relative clause.

| | | |
|---|---|---|
| a) | **malku ð-*[11] | this king |
| b) | **malku ð- baḥarū(hŭ)* | the king whom they chose |
| | **malku baḥarūhŭ* | a king whom they chose. |

2) A special close juncture existed between a noun and certain preposed and postposed words, among them, at least, the demonstrative pronouns *ð-*, *ðāt-*, *ʾill-*, *huʾa(t)*, *hiʾa(t)*, *hum(m)a(t)*, *hin(n)a(t)*.[12] This juncture was (or came to be) realized phonetically by the gemination of the first consonant following the word boundary. Thus, sing. **malku* + *ð-* > **malkuðð-*, plural **malakūm/na* + *ʾill-* > **malakūm/naʾʾill-*.

3) With the phonological loss of final short vowels before open juncture, and the concomitant loss of case distinctions, the short vowels trapped in these constructions, like those in a similar situation before the pronominal suffixes, achieved a neutral state in *-a-*: **malkaðð-*, pl. *malakīm/naʾʾill-*.

4) At this point Pre-Hebrew and Pre-Aramaic went separate ways. Let us follow through the Aramaic first. The singular forms **malkaððin(āh)*, fem. **malkataððā*, contrasted with the free (unbound) forms **malk*, fem. *malkā(h)*. Thus, with the development of the fem. sing. absolute in *-ā(h)*, the noun stems in the demonstrative construction came to be identified not with the free (absolute) form, but with the bound (construct) form. At the same time, at least in some of the dialects, the fem. absolute ending *-ān* replaced the older *-āt*.[13]

| | Singular | | Plural | |
|---|---|---|---|---|
| | masc. | fem. | masc. | fem. |
| absolute | *malk* | *malkā* | *malakīn* | *malakān* |
| construct | *malk* | *malkat* | *malakay* | *malakāt* |
| with demonstrative | *malkaððin(āh)* | *malkataððā* | *malakīnaʾʾill-* | *malakātaʾʾill-* |

11. Because this family of demonstrative pronouns was inflected in the earlier language and we cannot be sure about the vocalization, I have often represented them schematically in this paper.

12. I employ the terms "open" and "close" to describe two types of word-juncture. The characteristics of the latter, which is the marked member of the pair, will become apparent during our discussion.

13. There is evidence for the sporadic retention of *-t* in both the singular and plural feminine absolute after the normal Aramaic forms in *-h* and *-n* had developed. The conditioning factors for this are not clear and require some study.

The stage is obviously set for the masc. plural *malakīnaʾʾill-* to be replaced by *malakay* + *aʾʾill-*. The *-yy-* resulting from this analogical formation remains problematic: **malakayyaʾʾill-*.

5) The mixed constructions cited above on p. 318 now become relevant. I suggest that the emphatic state owed its independent existence to this type of construction, in which it first emerged as an interrupted or hyphenated form, i.e., when "this-x and this-y" came to be expressed as "this-x and -y":

*malkaððin(āh) wagabraððin(āh)* → *malkaʾ wagabraððin(āh)*

or, with the plural demonstrative, *malkaʾ wagabraʾʾill-*. The final *ʾaleph* is probably purely phonological in origin, since the language at this period does not tolerate final short vowels.[14] Once the emphatic form became isolable as the first member of a compound noun phrase before the demonstratives and relatives, its full extension belonged to the recorded period of the language.

The development presented above is obviously schematic and oversimplified. Not only did similar constructions emerge in connection with the relative pronoun **ð-* (*zy* in Aramaic), but the real language situation must have included a fairly large number of mixed constructions that enhanced the isolability of the emphatic form. This could have been true especially of noun-adjective nuclei before relatives and demonstratives, as in:

| | |
|---|---|
| **malk ṭāba* + *ðin(āh)* | this good king |
| **malk rabba* + *ðī* | the great king who . . ., |

which would lead logically to absolute noun plus emphatic adjective, had the emphatic ending not been subsequently generalized to both members. Counterparts of these intermediate forms survive in Hebrew and Arabic and are noted in the appropriate sections. Let us return to the sequence of probable development in Hebrew.

4′) In Hebrew the contrast between free and prejunctural form led to a different fracture: *malk* : *malakīm* :: *malk hazzi* : *malakīm haʾʾillay*, where *h* results simply from the reverse application of the *h*-syncope rule that had

14. Another possible instance of *aleph* is open juncture as the realization of a final short *a* is the normally proclitic conjunction *p-* (and), written separated as *pʾ* (Zinjirli, 8th century; *KAI* 214:17,13; *KAI* 215:22). It is also conceivable that the prepositive quantifier **kull-*, which may likewise have been followed by junctural gemination in the manner of Hebrew *še-* and *ma-* (see below) was separated out as **kullaʾ* before open juncture as a result of sequence interruption. For the syntactic and formal problems of **kullaʾ*, see J. A. Fitzmyer, "The Syntax of *kl, klʾ* in the Aramaic Texts from Egypt and in Biblical Aramaic," *Biblica* 38 (1957): 170–84.

developed by this time. The first extension of the article as such was probably to the attributive adjective, on the analogy:

predicate : attribute :: *zeh* : *hazzeh* :: *ṭob* : *haṭṭob*;

constructions with ordinal numbers (*yôm haššiššî*) and others, like *ʾîš heᶜᶜāšîr*, belong to this stage of development.

Two special points should be made at this time. First, the junctural origin of the article would account for the frequent omission of the article on a demonstrative attribute after a noun with a possessive suffix. The presence of the suffix, as a terminal morpheme, precluded, in our opinion, a close juncture with the following word. Thus such phrases as *dəbārēnû zeh*, cited above, clearly represent the retention of the original construction, which (perhaps dialectically or stylistically) resisted the generalization of the article found in *dəbārēnû hazzeh*.

Thus far we have concentrated on the formal mechanisms whereby the article came into being. Our hypothesis would be enhanced if we could point to some place in the language, independent of the relative and demonstrative constructions, where the category "definite" was emerging in a rudimentary way. This occurred, I believe, with the *nota accusativi*, whose original meaning must have been comparable to that of, say, the Japanese postpositive particle *wa*, in repeating something already mentioned (an "echo" function) or singling out the logical subject of the sentence (an isolating function); both uses tend naturally toward definite rather than indefinite in languages where these latter distinctions are made. Indeed, it is very likely that this particle *ʾ*iyăt*- ended in -*a*[15] and by virtue of proclitic juncture (see below) contributed formally as well as semantically to the birth of the article: *ʾ*iyata* + *malk* > *ʾ*iyatammalk* > ʾ*et-hammálk*. It is not accidental, then, that in the archaic language the absence of the article coincides with the absence of ʾ*et*.

## JUNCTURAL DOUBLING

Our main evidence for junctural doubling comes from Biblical Hebrew. I would single out the following relevant instances:

1) After the conjunction **wa*- in its converting function on the jussive or apocopated imperfect, as in *wayyiktōb* (and he wrote), *wayyḗšeb* (and he sat).[16]

15. Hebrew ʾ*ōtāk* and ʾ*ōtānû* would support this, as well as the ubiquitous final -*a* of the Arabic prepositions and particles, presumably a reflection of the adverbial function (hence accusative case form) of prepositional phrases in general. Ethiopic has the same final -*a*, but this is also the mark of a construct form (any case), and therefore ambiguous.

16. This must be understood in the context of the developing verbal system. The original contrast between the preterite/jussive stem **yaktub* (pl. **yaktubū*) and the imperfective **yaktubu* (pl. **yaktubūna*) was apparently also marked by a difference in stress: **yáktub*, **yaktúbu*.

2) After the relative pronoun *še* (< **ša*) and the interrogative pronoun *māh*. Examples of these are common.[17]

3) Closely parallel to the junctural doubling posited in our hypothesis is that marked by the *daghesh conjunctivum*, which is used (optionally) to mark close juncture (otherwise defined by the suppression or shifting of the stress in the first member).[18] This occurs only after the vowels *-ā(h)* and *-e(h)*, e.g.,

| | |
|---|---|
| Ex. 21:31 | *yēᶜāśé(h) + lô' → yēᶜắśe(h) llô'* |
| Ps. 91:11 | *yəṣawwé(h) + lāk → yəṣawwe(h)-llāk,* |

and is common only before monosyllabic words (most forms of *bə* and *lə*) or dissyllabic words with penultimate stress. The parallel to our discussion is clear, since this is precisely characteristic of the relative/demonstrative forms **ðí*, **ðát-*, etc.

4) A special subgroup of (3) supports our contention that after the loss of the short-vowelled case endings before open juncture, those found medially in the constructions under study were neutralized to *-a-*. These are the periphrastic genitives of the type:

| | | |
|---|---|---|
| Ps. 3:3 | *yəšūᶜātā(h)-llô' = yəšūᶜấ(h) + lô'* | his salvation [lit., (the) salvation to him] |

Although the two forms coalesced in many root types, the original stress difference led to the preservation of the contrast in verbs *3ae infirmae* (Heb. *yíben* vs. *yibnéh*), while a reflex of the original closed/open syllable distinction survived in verbs *mediae w/y:* **yáqum/yaqū́mu* > Heb. *yāqṓm/yāqûm* and in the analogical Hiphil forms, **yaqtil/*yaqtīlu* > Heb. *yaqtēl/yaqtîl*. The most striking evidence for the accentual contrast survives in the sequence form *wayyiktṓb* (< **wa* + *yáktub*, the old preterite form, replaced in non-sequential usage by the perfect), as opposed to *wəyiktōb* (< **wayaktúbu*, the imperfective form). The junctural gemination of *wayyiktōb* is thus a stress conditioned phenomenon. Note that the stress contrast survives intact in a number of root types, e.g., *wayyḗšeb/wəyēšḗb*.

17. These words and others suggest that gemination between a proclitic and words with initial stress may have been the rule rather than the exception. It may have occurred even with the prepositions *bə, lə, kə*, as in *la* + *málk* = *lammalk*; the doubling would have been retained when it corresponded to the newly developed article, but dropped elsewhere. Thus, there may never have been a stage of the language when such combinations as**lahammálk* actually occurred. The forms *bammā́h, kammā́h, lā́mmah, bazzeh* (I Sam. 21:10) are relevant here. On the other hand, *bā, lā* and *kā* are the realization of these prepositions according to the normal rules of *syllable* juncture, namely, simple pretonic lengthening.

18. I am espousing what is probably a minority opinion among Hebraists concerning the phonetic significance of *daghesh conjunctivum*. For relevant literature see G. Bersträsser, *Hebräische Grammatik* (Hildesheim, 1962), pp. 65–66. I find the arguments against interpreting it as marking gemination completely unconvincing, but readily admit that there is no positive proof to support me, other than the *daghesh* itself. In Semitic the phenomenon is found elsewhere, e.g., in certain forms of the postverbal dative in Syrian Arabic and in all immediately postverbal forms of *b-* and *l-* in Amharic.

where the linking vowel *-ā-* < **a* is preserved in juncture, as is the old absolute form of the feminine ending **-at*. Thus, from **yašūᶜata* + *láhu* at an earlier stage, we have **yašūᶜatalláhu*, subsequently divided as *yəšūᶜātā(h)-llô*, since there was no pressure for interpreting the doubling as a definite article. On the other hand, the related, but rarely attested, demonstrative *hallāzeh/hallāz* shows the article-conditioned division:

| | | | |
|---|---|---|---|
| Gen. 24:65 | *hāʾîš hallāzeh* | * . . . *a* + *la-zi* | this man |
| I Sam. 14:1 | *mēᶜéber hallāz* | | from this side |

The second example is especially interesting in that the article does not occur on the determined noun; cf. *ʾîš heᶜāšîr* above.

5) A kind of inverse corroboration is afforded, I believe, by the (usually) postverbal particle *nāʾ*, which occurs frequently with *daghesh conjunctivum* after the cohortative, e.g., *niktəbā(h)-nnāʾ*. While W. L. Moran[19] is certainly correct in seeing a close relationship between the Hebrew cohortative and the *yaqtula* form of Amarna Canaanite, certain formal problems are left unresolved. Unless the final vowel of *yaqtula* was long or anceps, how did it survive the general loss of short vowels in Pre-Hebrew? The merging in Hebrew of several disparate forms into a single injunctive paradigm, i.e., first person cohortative, second person imperative or jussive, third person jussive, and the subsequent analogical use of one of these forms (improperly) in the function of another strongly suggest that *yaqtula* did in part merge with *yaqtul* and *yaqtulu*.[20] The cohortative ending, as well as the so-called emphatic imperative in *-āh*, owes its survival, I believe, to the concurrent use of the energic form in *-anna*, as *yaqtulánna*, which, by virtue of the existence of junctural doubling, is reinterpretable as **yaqtula* + *nā*. By assuming a constant interplay between the two forms, we can understand the partial preservation of the *yaqtula* form as well as its association with the injunctive paradigm. This also provides us with the etymology of the particle *naʾ*.

## PHOENICIAN

The persistent absence of a written article on an attributive demonstrative in Phoenician would pose a serious problem for our hypothesis, were it not a fact that internal evidence provides us with a reasonable alternative to the interpretation of this construction. Because this alternative is based on ortho-

19. W. L. Moran, "Early Canaanite *yaqtula*," *Or* 29 (1960): 1–19.
20. E.g., the use of the cohortative as the converted (preterite) sequence form.

graphic considerations, it is necessary to survey in some detail the evidence of the earlier inscriptions, down to the middle of the first millennium B.C.

It is generally assumed that the definite article in Phoenician has the same basic form as that of Hebrew, namely *ha* plus the doubling of the following consonant; nothing is known of its allomorphisms other than the recognized syncope of the initial *h* after the prepositions *b-*, *l-*, and *k-*. Concerning the use of the article in constructions involving the demonstrative adjective, Friedrich states:[21]

> Im Phönizischen scheint keine Regel über Setzung oder Nichtsetzung des Artikels beim Substantiv erkennbar. In *ʾrn* [*z*]*n* "dieses Kästchen" kann das Fehlen des Artikels altertümlich oder dialektisch sein, aber bei Ešmunazar wechselt Setzung und Nichtsetzung in derselben Wendung unterschiedslos.

That there is inconsistency in the use of the article, and that this is due in part to the chronological and dialectal heterogeneity of the inscriptions, is undeniable. The actual situation in the Eshmunazar inscription and elsewhere, however, is not quite so chaotic as this quotation would suggest. Let us begin by constructing a paradigm of article usage in the Yeḥawmilk inscription (Byblos, fifth/fourth century B.C.):[22]

| | Simple Noun | | | Construct Chain | |
|---|---|---|---|---|---|
| a) | *mlk* | a king | e) | *bn mlk* | a king's son |
| b) | *hmlk* | the king | f) | *bn mlk* | the son of the king |
| c) | *hmlk zn* | this king | g) | *hbn mlk zn* | this son of the king (?) |
| d) | *hmlk hʾ* | that king | h) | **hbn mlk hʾ* | that son of the king (?) |

Examples:

a), (b), (e) passim.
c) *whʿprt zʾ* and this colonnade (?) (line 6)
d) *hʾdm hʾ* that man (line 15)
f) Only with a proper name as nomen rectum: *mlk Gbl* the king of Byblos (line 1), plus many others. On *whʿpt ḥrṣ* (line 5), see below.
g) *hmzbḥ nḥšt zn* this copper altar (line 4)
*whptḥ ḥrṣ zn* and this gold engraving (?) (line 4)

When, however, a preposition precedes, the *h* of the article is syncoped. This applies to ALL prepositions, not only to the usual *b-*, *k-*, *l-*. This includes *ʿl*/*ʿlt*, on, in, upon, and the compound prepositions *btkt*, in the midst of, *lʿn*,

21. J. Friedrich, *Phönizisch-punische Grammatik* (Rome, 1951), pp. 139–40.

22. Texts are cited from *KAI* = H. Donner and W. Röllig, *Kanaanäische und Aramäisch Inschriften*² (Wiesbaden, 1968–). Yeḥawmilk = *KAI* No. 10; Eshmunazar = *KAI* No. 14; Azitawadda (Karatepe) = *KAI* No. 26.

in the sight of. If we do not assume *h*-syncope, we must assume that the use of a preposition deletes the definite article, which I find completely untenable. Examples:

| | | |
|---|---|---|
| b) | *btkt ᵓbn* | in the middle of the stone (line 5) |
| | *lᶜn ᵓlnm* | in the sight of the gods (line 10) |
| c) | *ᶜlt mzbḥ zn* | on this altar (line 11/12) |
| | *ᶜlt ᶜprt zᵓ* | on this colonnade (line 12) |
| | *ᶜlt mqm z* | (from) on this place (line 14) |
| d) | *ᶜl mlᵓkt hᵓ* | on that work (line 13) |
| f) | *btkt ᵓbn* and *lᶜn ᵓlnm,* | if analyzed as prep. plus noun plus noun |
| g) | *ᶜl ptḥ ḥrṣ zn* | on this gold engraving (?) (line 5) |
| | *lᶜn ᶜm ᵓrṣ z* | before this citizenry (line 10) |

The article appears with *h* after the object marker *ᵓyt*; e.g., *ᵓyt hᵓdm hᵓ*, that man (line 15). Returning to the Eshmunazar inscription (Sidon, fifth century B.C.), we find that of the twelve occurrences of a noun modified only by a demonstrative adjective, eight are preceded by a preposition (e.g., *bqrb z* in this grave); two by the object marker *ᵓyt*:

| | |
|---|---|
| *ᵓyt mškb z* | this resting-place (line 4) |
| *ᵓyt ḥln z* | this coffin (line 10), |

and two occur free:

| | |
|---|---|
| *hmmlkt hᵓ* | that king (line 22) |
| *whᵓdmm hmt* | and those men (line 22). |

With the exception of the application of the *h*-syncope rule after the object marker the use of the article in this inscription is remarkably consistent with that of the paradigm we established above.

Moving to the long Azitawadda inscription (Karatepe, eighth century B.C.), we note only deviations from our paradigm:

a) The article appears unsyncoped after *ᵓyt*, with one exception: *wᵓyt ᵓdm hᵓ* and that man (line IV, 1).

b) In the multiple occurrences of *wᵓlm* and the gods (e.g., I, 8) and *wᶜm z* and this people (e.g., IV, 7), and in *wzbḥ* and the sacrifice (IV, 2) the expected article does not appear. It is hardly a coincidence that all of these examples have a prefixed conjunction, which obviously allowed *h*-syncope in the dialect of this text.

c) The article appears regularly on nouns after *kl* (all) when a definite sense is required, as in *kl hmlkm* (I, 19), and likewise on the *nomen rectum* in *wᵓyt sml hᵓlm* and the image of the gods (IV, 18/19). Against these examples we have *kl ʾln qrt*, all the gods of the city (III, 5), *bsml ʾlm z*, in this image of the gods (IV, 15/16).[23]

d) The article appears on an apparent *nomen regens*: *hbrk bʿl* (line 1).[24]

In the light of the foregoing evidence I would make the following deductions about the zero allographs of the definite article in Phoenician.

1) *h*-syncope seems absolutely certain post-prepositionally, as the Yehawmilk and Eshmunazar inscriptions demonstrate. Granting this,

2) since *btkt* and *lʿn* are analyzable as preposition plus construct noun, as well as preposition alone, the article is likewise present on all *nomina recta* where the sense requires it.

3) Since *ʿn* and *ʾln* are undoubtedly plural constructs (i.e., **ʿênê*, **ʾilānê*), the allomorphism of the Phoenician article was closer to that of Arabic than that of Hebrew, in that the vowel after the initial *h* was also syncoped: **laʿênê ʾʾilānîm*, **kul ʾilānê qqart.*

4) *h*-syncope after *ʾyt* and *w*- varies from dialect to dialect, but is reasonably consistent within a given inscription. There is no reason not to read the article after either of these words, as required.

23. With the exception of the Karatepe examples just noted, the appearance of the article on a *nomen rectum* is extremely rare in the early language, the well-known example of the Yeḥimilk inscription (*KAI* No. 4) notwithstanding: *kl mplt hbtm ʾl* all the ruins of these temples.

24. The question of the article on the *nomen regens* in Phoenician has been raised recently, once in connection with the phrase *hkkbm ʾl* in the Pyrgi inscription (see J. Fitzmyer, "The Phoenician Inscription from Pyrgi," *JAOS* 86 [1966]: 295–96), which I would interpret as simply "these stars" (*pace* M. Dahood, *Or* 34 [1965]: 170–72), and once in the discussions about the Paraíba forgery (cf. F. M. Cross, "The Phoenician Inscription from Brazil, A Ninteenth-Century Forgery," *Or* 37 [1968]: 445). Adduced in support of such a construction are the above mentioned *hbrk bʿl* and a late Tyrian example (c. third century B.C.) from a badly broken context, where we have on consecutive lines *ʾyt ḥsy hsp z* and *ʾyt hḥsy hsp z* (cf. G. A. Cooke, *A Textbook of North-Semitic Inscriptions* [Oxford, 1903], No. 8), presumably meaning "this half of the *sp*." The two examples cited in our examples under (g) from the Yeḥawmilk inscription are problematic. If one insists that the article cannot appear on a *nomen regens*, then *nḥšt* and *ḥrṣ* must be construed as appositives, an uncomfortable interpretation because of the following demonstrative. On the other hand, to accept the presence of the article on the *nomen regens* goes against the overwhelming testimony of Hebrew and Phoenician. I suspect that the answer lies between the two extremes: it is certainly not irrelevant that the first noun in all but one of these examples is modified by the following demonstrative. I propose that Phoenician may distinguish (where Hebrew does not) between:

| | |
|---|---|
| this house of the king | *hbt mlk z*(*n*), and |
| the house of this king | *bt mlk z*(*n*). |

Thus, the *h* of *hbt* really marks the construction as *h*(*bt-mlk*) *zn* and is only superficially an article on a *nomen regens*. The phrase *hbrk bʿl* is complicated by the presence of a passive participle as *nomen regens*. Whether we view it as an epithetic compound or as an example of improper annexation, akin to Hebrew *hallābûš habbaddîm* (the one clothed in linen), this sole possible exception hardly justifies scrapping the rule. The only other example I have noted is the phrase *whʿpt ḥrṣ* in line 5 of Yeḥawmilk. Since this stands fifth in a series of seven phrases, each of which, excepting our example, contains the demonstrative *zn*/*zʾ*/*hʾ*, a restoration of *zʾ* would seem in order.

5) Finally, then, I cannot accept the absence of a written article on the demonstrative attributes as conclusive evidence that one is not present. If we assume the same origin for the Phoenician article as for that of Hebrew, we must see this *h*-syncope as secondary.[25] I believe that the colonial form *ʾz*[26] represents a second fracture of this same construction, with a different phonological realization influenced by the then developed *ʾaleph prostheticum* on *ʾš*, *ʾb* etc.

## ARABIC

In spite of its early separation from Northwest Semitic, Arabic shares with this group the development of a definite article of similar shape and, I believe, of similar origin. The following particulars should be noted for the classical language:

1) The noun with a definite article occupies an intermediate position morphologically between the unbound (= indefinite) and bound forms:

| | Singular | Plural |
|---|---|---|
| unbound | *malikun* | *malikūna* } |
| "articled" | *ʾal-maliku* } | *ʾal-malikūna* } |
| bound | *maliku-* } | *malikū-* |

2) The demonstrative adjective stands before the noun it modifies, unless that noun is in construct or has a possessive suffix, i.e., is bound:

| | |
|---|---|
| *hāðā l-maliku* | this king |
| *ʾibnu l-maliki hāðā* | this son of the king |
| *malikuhu hāðā* | this king of his |

3) A relative clause after a definite antecedent is introduced by *ʾallaðī*, f. *ʾallatī*, m. pl. *ʾallaðīna*, f. pl. *ʾallātī*:

| | |
|---|---|
| *ʾal-maliku llaðī raʾaytuhu* | the king whom I saw |
| cf. *malikun raʾaytuhu* | a king whom I saw |

25. That is, the *h*- form of the article developed as in Hebrew, presumably when an *h*-syncope rule existed and the *h*-causative had not yet yielded to the *y*-causative, which spread from the negative **ʾīhaqtil* > **ʾīyaqtil* = **ʾī yaqtil*. It was only after this stage that the syncoped form of the article was used more extensively, pointing simply to a wider use of close juncture than we find in Hebrew.

26. While the prosthetic *aleph* on the relative *ʾš* and other proclitic items is explainable by vowel reduction and/or epenthesis, this explanation can hardly apply to an enclitic (or at least postpositive) word like *z*-. If we assume an underlying speech form like **hammalkázzi*, the new fracture and writing as *hmlk ʾz* is not surprising.

In the light of the hypothesis I have presented it is tempting to attribute the Arabic article to the same junctural source, beginning with some such construction as **hāðā + malik-* > **hāðāmmalik-* > *hāðālmalik-*, by dissimilation. The following points militate against this simple solution:

a) It provides no motivation for the loss of nunnation (*tanwīn*) in the articled form.

b) The dissimilation of consonant gemination to *-lC-* with the so-called "moon" consonants, as opposed to the retention of gemination in the "sun" consonants, is difficult to account for.

c) The originally long vowel of the demonstrative seems structurally an unnatural place for gemination to develop, since earlier Semitic appears to have resisted syllables of the *Cv̄C* type.

d) The prepositive position of the demonstrative in Classical Arabic is not reflected in all the dialects; indeed, the postpositive position in the second and third constructions cited under (2) above suggests that the prepositive use may be secondary.[27]

In the long run, following our original hypothesis back a few stages and thence down to Arabic will prove more fruitful, avoiding most, but not all, of the problems listed above.

Up to this point we have assumed the presence of consonant gemination in Northwest Semitic as a phonetic realization of close juncture without speculating as to its origin. I shall now suggest a phonetic origin for junctural doubling itself. The presence of nunnation in Arabic and terminal *-m* in Akkadian on unbound forms ending in a short vowel compels us to see this as a regular feature of the unbound form in early Semitic in general. At an earlier stage of Northwest Semitic than our reconstructions have previously required, the following constructions occurred:

| | | |
|---|---|---|
| 1) | *malikuM* | a king, the king |
| 2) | *malikuM + ðū* | this king |
| 3) | *malikuM + ðū raʾaytuhu* | the king whom I saw |
| 4) | *malikuM raʾaytuhu* | a king whom I saw |

*M* represents the feature yielding Arabic nunnation and Akkadian *-m*; it was phonetically neither **m* nor **n*.[28] In Northwest Semitic *M* was completely assimilated to a following consonant in close juncture, as in constructions (2)

27. For a detailed study of the forms and syntax of the demonstratives in Arabic see W. Fischer, *Die demonstrativen Bildungen der neuarabischen Dialekte* (ʾs-Gavenhage, 1959), especially pp. 46–50, 64–66.

28. *M* is a reconstructional necessity, similar to anceps vowels, where none of the phonemes posited for Proto-Semitic will yield the results found in the attested languages according to normal rules of development. This same *M* can be recognized in the Akkadian ventive suffix (*-am*) and in the locative ending (*-um*), both of which are subject to irregular assimilations, and in the West Semitic counterpart of the former, the short energic in *-an* (as in Arabic). Further study of this phenomenon is required before we can assess the proto-Semitic status of *M*.

and (3) above. The over-all loss of final *M* elsewhere (i.e., before open juncture) led to the adoption of the gemination in close juncture as a distinguishing feature of the juncture itself. Thus, for early Northwest Semitic:

(1) *maliku;* (2) *malikuððū;* (3) *malikuððū raʾaytuhu.*

Our previous discussion takes the development up at this point, assuming that this gemination was extended to masculine plural forms as well. In the forerunners of Classical Arabic, however, *M* in close juncture assimilated completely to the dental and interdental stops and spirants, as well as *l* and *n*, but became *l* before the remaining consonants. This statement is, of course, anachronistic; the first assimilations involved only the initial consonants of the relatively small number of words that could stand in close junctural relationship with a preceding noun. These included, at least, the forerunners of *ðū* and its plural *ʾul-*; schematically:

(1) *malikuM;* (2) *malikuððū;* (3) *malikuððū raʾaytuhu*

The structure of the relative and demonstrative pronouns, even in the classical language, is complex. The common nearer demonstratives have acquired a prefixed *hā* added to bases exhibiting no case inflection except in the dual: m. sing. *hāðā*, f. sing. *hāðihi*; common plural *hāʾulāʾi*. These are closely paralleled by the development in later Aramaic, e.g., Targumic *hādēn*, *hādā*, *hāʾillēn* (in attributive positions). The common farther demonstrative consists of the bases *ðā-*, *ti-*, and *ʾulā(ʾ)* plus *-l(i)ka*, presumably the preposition *la-* (dissimilated between *ā* and *a* to *li-*) with the second person singular pronominal suffix. The preposition *la-* also figures in the reformed relative * + *laðī* (*ʾa*)*llaðī*. The parallel of the Hebrew forms *hallāzeh*/*hallāz* discussed above is obvious. Since the development of these elaborated or analytical forms must have followed the use of simpler forms, which still appear dialectally and are well attested in South Arabic (Southeast Semitic), they do not pose a formal obstacle to our proposed sequence of development. With the change of *M* in close juncture to doubling or *l*, the identity of that form with the unbound form was lost; the positively definite character of the junctural form contrasted with the indeterminate status of the unbound form, with the gradual specialization of the latter as a mark of the indefinite. Because the extension of the newly created article closely paralleled that of Hebrew, discussed above, we shall omit a detailed discussion.[29] Once the

29. It is interesting to note that F. A. Pennacchietti, *Studi sui pronomi determinativi semitici* (Naples, 1968), pp. 77ff., although approaching the problem from an entirely different angle, also regards the construction type **maliku ṭṭayyibu* (surviving in the re-grammatized type *rabīʿu lʾawwali, yawma ssābiʿi* etc.) historically prior to the generalized *ʾalmaliku ṭṭayyibu.*

article appeared prepositively on a noun as a mark of its definite status, the shift of the demonstrative took place in imitation of this construction. Wherever the noun did not have the prepositive article, as in *ʾibnu lmaliki* and *malikuhu*, the demonstrative remained in its original position. The morphologically intermediate position of the articled noun noted above is a result of this form's being derived from the original *unbound* form with the *loss* of -*M*, not from the original bound form.[30]

30. Relevant to our proposal is the fact that the counterpart of Classical Arabic *ʾal* in the ancient dialects varied considerably, both (ʾ)*am* and (ʾ)*an* being noted by the grammarians. See C. Rabin, *Ancient West Arabian* (London, 1951), pp, 34–36. Rabin is certainly mistaken in his view that nunnation was from the beginning a mark of indefiniteness, unless he divorces it completely from the mimmation of Akkadian and Old South Arabic.

# The Converse Tablet: A Litany with Musical Instructions

W. G. LAMBERT

Among Professor Albright's wide Near Eastern interests Assyriology has long had a special place, and it is therefore doubly appropriate to offer here in his honor an important tablet that has been in his possession for many years. It belonged previously to Colonel Converse of the U.S. army, and by a strange combination of circumstances, which need not be gone into here, it passed into new hands.

The tablet measures 155 mm. in height and 100 mm. across, and is a fine specimen of Late Babylonian calligraphy. According to its colophon it was written in Der, and though it is not dated there can be no question that it comes from the period of the Late Babylonian empire or the Persian empire. The scribe who wrote it, Nidintu-Ani, is probably the same scribe who wrote another text of the same genre (*CT*, 42, 12), since they bear the same name and belonged to the town of Der. Unfortunately, this is not quite certain since the father's name on the Converse Tablet is broken off, and there could have been more than one scribe of the name Nidintu-Ani in Der within the relevant centuries. The text of the Converse Tablet is part of a Sumerian liturgical series, with Akkadian translation, for the cult of Nabû, and while other parts of the series have been known previously, this section is hitherto unknown. In addition to its important content and linguistic data, this tablet has the most detailed items so far known of systems of glosses pertaining to the musical presentation of the text.

The liturgical series was known in the ancient world from its first phrase, ukkin.ta eš.bar til.la, "In the assembly a decision was taken." It is listed in the catalogue IV $R^2$ 53 i–ii 31:

| | |
|---|---|
| ukkin.ta eš.bar til.la | ur.sag a.má.ùru ḫu.luḫ.ḫa |
| In the assembly a decision was taken | Hero, fearsome flood |

The first column has the first phrase of the "harp" (balag) section, the second column the same of the eršemma section, see S. H. Langdon, *AnOr*, 12, 202, and J. Krecher, *SKl*, 19[8]. There are both Late Assyrian and Late Babylonian fragments surviving, but they belong to different editions, in that the breaks from one tablet to another occur at different points. Even with the Converse Tablet there is much missing, including the opening section and the whole of the *eršemma* text. The following are the preserved sections in sequence:

i) BM 78878 (S. H. Langdon, *Gaster Anniversary Volume*, pp. 335ff.) obv.
ii) *SBH*, no. 12 obv.
  lines 1–19 restored and duplicated by *BL*, 158 obv.
  lines 14–39 duplicated, restored and continued by BM 78878 rev.
  lines 31–39 duplicated, restored and continued by K 9291 (*BA*, V, 630–31)
iii) *SBH*, no. 12 rev.
  lines 5–9 duplicated by *BL*, 158 rev., which then concludes with catch-line, *šalšu nisḫu* and colophon.
 Converse Tablet: this begins with the catch-line of *SBH*, no. 12, and as its catch-line has: [ur].sag a.ma.ru ḫu.luḫ.ḫa.
 K 10303 (copy given here by permission of the Trustees of the British Museum) duplicates the last few lines on *SBH*, no. 12 rev. and the first six lines of the Converse Tablet, but with recensional variants that are discussed in the note *ad loc.*

There are also four possible pieces, whose placing within the series, if they do in fact belong, cannot be ascertained. K 8399 (*BA*, V, 663), in Babylonian script, has a reverse which could be taken as a duplicate of the Converse Tablet rev. 13–19 with the omitted lines written out in full, but since the obverse does not seem to be duplicated elsewhere, it may be from another part of the series and happens to have the same sequence of places and temples as the Converse Tablet. The other three pieces are *BA*, X, 97, and 98, and K 4836 (unpublished).

The date of composition of this series can only be established from internal criteria. It was composed for the cult of Nabû in the temple Ezida in Borsippa. Since it is only in the First Millennium that Nabû occupied this temple, not in the Second, this litany is presumably a compilation from early in the First Millennium, and the presence of copies in the libraries of Ashurbanipal rules out a later date. The Sumerian grammar agrees with this, since it is not chaotic, but the principle of the nominal bundle is often neglected. Note the position of the gim in rev. 1 and of the ra in rev. 17–18. Prior to his move to Borsippa, Nabû had held only an inferior position in Esagil in Babylon, where he had not of course enjoyed a city cult. With his move to Borsippa, cult texts were needed and existing material was compiled and modified. The importance of the Converse Tablet in this connection is the clear evidence it offers that Ninurta litanies were drawn upon in part. The victories alluded to on the obverse, the capture of the Zû bird, for example, are well known elsewhere as feats of Ninurta (see the notes *ad loc.*). The previously known parts of the series did not make this phenomenon so apparent, but *SBH*, no. 12 twice mentions a very distinctive attribute of Ninurta:

| | |
|---|---|
| dumu šu.mar.gi.a.a.[na] | The son who avenged his father (Rev. 14) |
| ⸢ù⸣.ma sá.sá a.na = *ka-šid ir-nit-te a-bi-šú* | Who won victory for his father (Rev. 26) |

These things are elsewhere[1] said of Ninurta, and refer to his defeat of the Zû bird. Zû had stolen the Tablet of Destinies from Enlil, Ninurta's father, and thereby had put Enlil's position in doubt. By recovering this Tablet Ninurta assured his father's position in the universe. The reason for this assumption of Ninurta's characteristics by Nabû can be suggested. By 1,000 B.C. Marduk, Nabû's father, had usurped the position of Enlil as head of the pantheon. It was natural, then, for Nabû to replace Ninurta. It is uncertain whether the author considered this ecumenically as assimiliation, or whether, like the author of Enūma Eliš, he was polemically minded and wished to remove any prestige that the older god had. The process does not harmonize with Enūma Eliš in any case, since to kill Tiāmat, Marduk had to take over the role of Ninurta as the dragon slayer of ancient Mesopotamia.

The glosses referring to the musical performance are added to the Sumerian (even to the catch-line), never to the Akkadian translation. Similar glosses are known in other Late Babylonian copies of Sumerian cultic texts, but never, it seems, in Late Assyrian copies. Reisner first drew attention to them in some of the texts in *SBH* (p. xvif.), and, more recently, Krecher has commented briefly on them (*WdO*, IV, 277; *RLA*, III, 435, 440) both in Reisner's texts and also in *TCL*, 6, 55–57; *TCL*, 15, 11; and *CT*, 42, 1, 12, 21. In

1. *SBH*, p. 36 30–31; *KAR*, 307, rev. 22, etc.

addition they are found in BM 78878. Reisner recognized two kinds, some concerned with the manner of musical performance, others indicating pronunciation or accentuation. Krecher essentially agrees.

They are often written in small-size signs, like other kinds of glosses, but on occasion this distribution in size is not made clear, so that they are then recognizable only by their extraneous character. Those in the Converse Tablet have been omitted from the transliteration since they are no help to the understanding of the text and to set some of them would have necessitated the cutting of special type. In a few places it is uncertain if a sign belongs to the text or is a gloss: in obv. 10 aka.a.a.ni, one of the A signs could be a gloss, similarly the U in obv. 21, and perhaps the A in é.zi.da.ta.a in rev. 30.

With the new material supplied by the Converse Tablet it is possible to distinguish three kinds of glosses. First, those found only in the left margin and which are plainly instructions on the musical accompaniment. They are meze.lá (rev. 4, 27) and šèm.DU (rev. 5, 28). This pair of glosses occurs again in the same sequence and by two adjacent lines in *SBH*, no. 8 rev. 8–9, and the first alone occurs in *SBH*, no. 66, 49. A related gloss is šú.meze.dib in *SBH*, no. 8, obv. 9 and no. 9, rev. 6. The meze (Akk. *manzû*) and šèm (Akk. *ḫalḫallatu*) are both kinds of drums, often mentioned together in cultic use.[2] The other signs of the glosses are less explicit: lá can mean "diminish" (*maṭû*) or "arrange" (*tarāṣu*), and other things too. DU has a variety of meanings of which no one is particularly probable. dib no doubt means "hold" (*kullu*) here, and the šú might mean "cover" (*kitmu*?). If so, this is an instruction to the player of the *manzû*-drum to hold that part of it termed "cover."

Other glosses consisting of single signs found in the left margin are less clear. RU occurs in rev. 3 and 25 of the Converse Tablet and more commonly elsewhere. KA and BA/MA occur in *CT*, 42, 1, but they are equally obscure.

Altogether more frequent than any of the first category are the vowel signs which make up the second. They are four, A, I, E, and U/Ú, and may occur at the beginning, end, or middle of a line, and rarely they appear in the middle of words. Hitherto, they have been understood as some kind of pronunciation gloss. In fact the system, or systems, if not all tablets with them belong to one, is quite complicated. In some cases they are placed above the line in relation to the adjacent signs of the text, and in some cases below the line. This might be dismissed as of no significance were not contrasting examples of inferior and superior writings found together on *TCL*, 15, no. 11, e.g., line 33. Also combinations of vowel signs occur, such as A.U and E.A. The Converse Tablet has still more complicated combinations, two of the

2. See the Akkadian lexica and H. Hartmann, *Die Musik der sumerischen Kultur*, pp. 98–102.

same vowel signs, one being written on top of the other (henceforth this combination will be called "double"), and, most complicated of all, a few examples of two vowel signs with a third placed superior between them. Rev. 14 offers E.MIN (i.e., the double U repeated from line 9) with a superimposed A between them; and in the middles of rev. 25 and 28 there occur E.A and A.A both with a superimposed superior double U.

The view that this system is some kind of aid to pronunciation is based on the fact that in a majority of cases the vowel sign is the vowel of the adjacent syllable of the text. The difficulty is that there are quite a number of exceptions where the vowel gloss is not that of the adjacent syllable. To take an example from the Converse Tablet, rev. 6–12 have the first half-line ending urú.ni.a, and to each instance a small A is appended. It can be assumed that here the gloss marks some special emphasis on the .a, or some quality of it. But the following three first halves have a small E appended, though they end -na, -ra, and -um. It is totally unsatisfactory to assume either that these vowels were in this context changed to e, or that an e vowel was inserted after them. A similar case is given in *CT*, 42, 12 obv. 16–24, where the second half-line ends .ta, and a small A is appended, but to every first half-line a U is appended, though only one out of the nine cases has a u vowel in the adjacent syllable.

Longer glosses, our third category, seem to be related to the system that uses vowel signs. Some are written within the text, either at the end of lines, or within, or between lines. An important example is:

a.e.e.e.ta.a.e.e.e.a.AN *an-nu-u*
*TCL*, 6, 56, obv. 2

The Converse Tablet offers one similar gloss, and others written in the right margin:

a) *ana* ŠÌR [(..)]x.bi.a urú.šè a.⸢UD.DU⸣ nu.me.a [..) x [x] x u.a
Obv. 28 (gi is perhaps part of the gloss also)
b) é/líl a ku diri *è*[*n*]-*du-u* a.DU nu.me.a *i-lu-u i-lu-u ana* ŠÌR-*ru*
Rev. 5
c) e.e na.ám zé.eb.ba *ana* ŠÌR-*ru*
Rev. 6
d) e.e.ta.a.e.e.a *an-nu-u* a *an-nu-u ana* ⸢DU$_{12}$-*ru*⸣
Rev. 32

The only similar gloss elsewhere is *SBH*, no. 16, obv. 7:

u du a nu ud? [d]a? gul e a ne im du *ana* ⸢DU$_{12}$-*ru*⸣

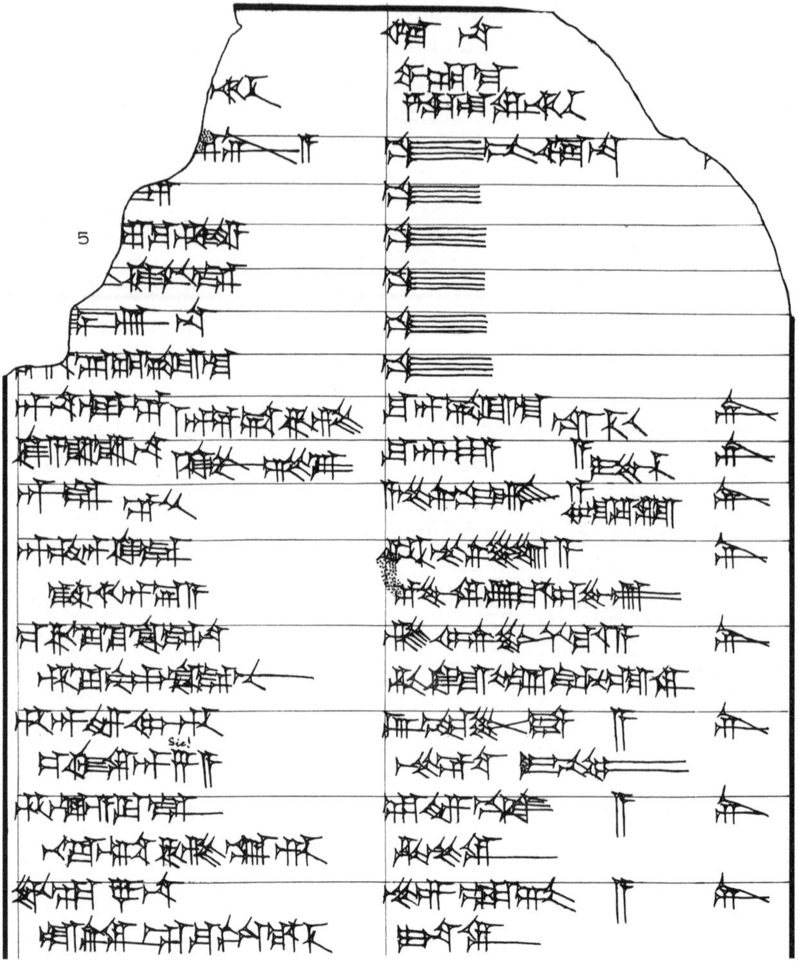


Fig. 1. Converse Tablet, obverse.

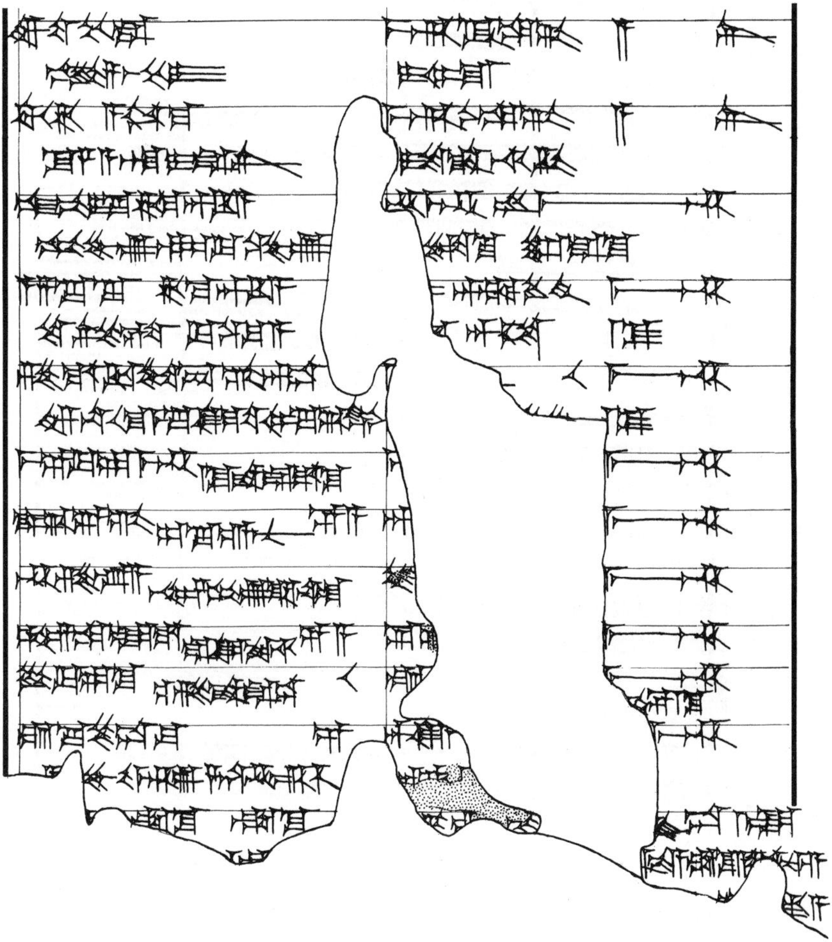

Fig. 1. (continued).

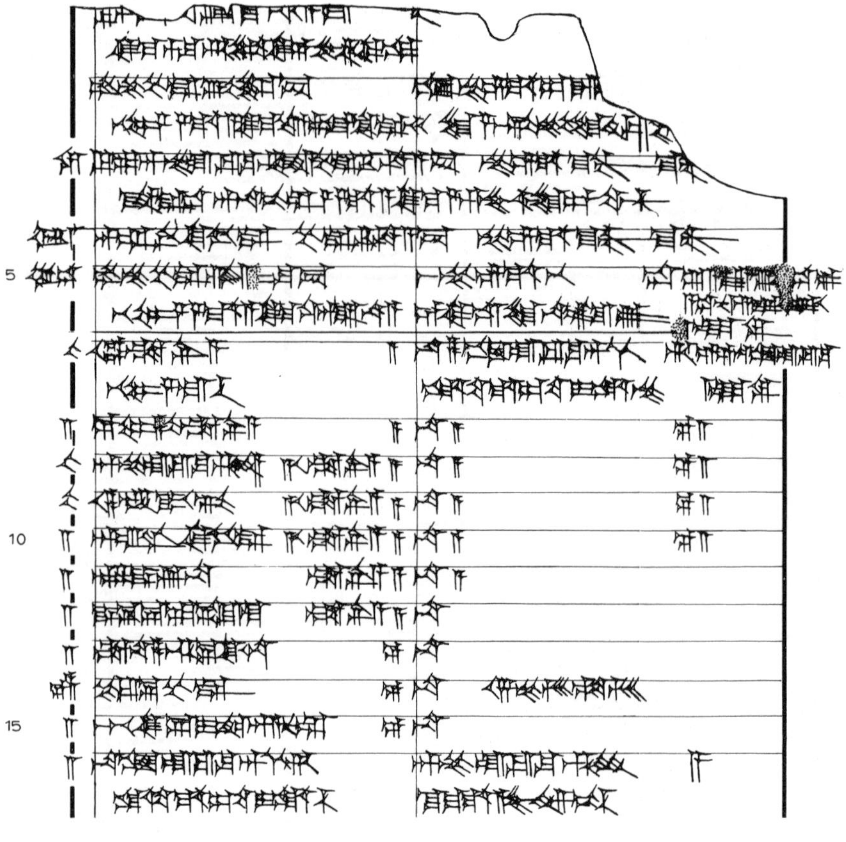

Fig. 2. Converse Tablet, reverse.

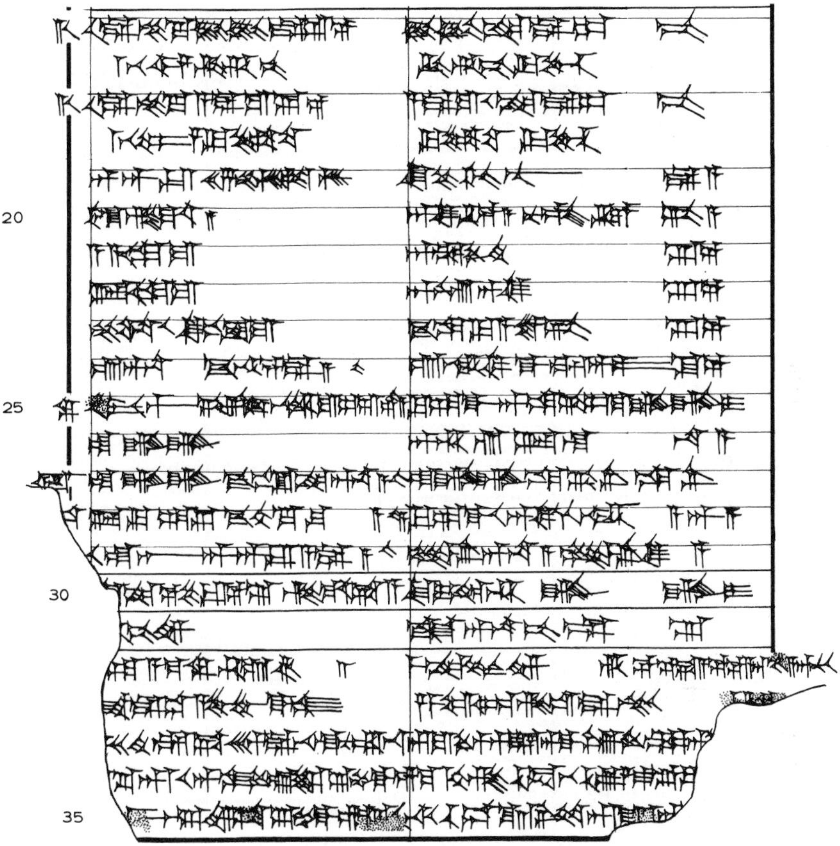

Fig. 2. (continued).

These all contain *ana zamāru* "for singing," and probably the phrase had gerundival force: "should be sung." (c) is the clearest in that nam zebba is cited from the adjacent line. Thus the gloss seems to say that these two words should be sung E.E, whatever that may be. (a) also cites urú.šè from the adjacent line, but the gloss as a whole is not clear. The problem with nam zebba is that in the text there is also a gloss, not E.E, but a double A within nam. Several known Sumerian terms with musical reference appear in these glosses in an Akkadian form: *endû* from èn.du = *zamāru* ("song"),[3] *ilû* from i.lu ("song" or specifically "lament"),[4] and *annû*, not the Akkadian pronoun, but an.na = *elītum* (*ša zamāri*) ("high, of singing").[5] The last one also occurs as an.na in *CT* 42 1, and as *annû* in *TCL*, 6, 56 and *SBH*, no. 16, rev. *CT*, 42, 12, obv. 30 and 33 offer *i-lu-ú/u(-ú) ak-ke-e*, but the meaning of *akkê* is unknown. The same tablet offers two identical long glosses: zag.ga dib. ba.a.ni ér.ra (rev. 21, 24), but their meaning is not clear.

It is frustrating that more cannot be said, but the material has so far yielded few of its secrets. What is certain in some cases, and probable in all, is that musical instructions are being given.

OBVERSE

| | | |
|---|---|---|
| 1 | [íb.bé] | ù.na.[nam] |
| 2 | ...] | pi sag ma [(...)] |
| | [*šá? ug-ga*]*-ti-šú* | *šá ka-ad-ru-ti-šú* [(...)] |
| 3 | [e.lum ur]ú.ni.a | íb.bé ù.na.n[am] |
| 4 | [...] x | íb. |
| 5 | [$^{d}$mu.zé].eb.ba.sa$_4$.a | íb. |
| 6 | [$^{d}$šid.d]ù.ki.šár.ra | íb. |
| 7 | [$^{d}$nà] dumu.nun.na | íb. |
| 8 | ⌜ibila⌝.é.sag.íl.la | íb. |
| 9 | an.na mè.e | ba.an.íl.la.ni |
| | *ana šamê$^{e}$ ta-ḫa-zi* | *iš-šú-u* |
| 10 | ki.a šen.šen.na | ba.an.aka.a.a.ni |
| | *ana erṣetim$^{tim}$ qab-lu* | *i-pu-šú* |
| 11 | an.ra | a mu.ni.íb.gi$_4$.a.ni |
| | *e-liš* | *mi-la ip-ru-su* |
| 12 | $^{d}$am.an.ki.ra | buru$_x$ mu.ni.in.sud.a.ni |
| | *it-ti $^{d}$é-a* | *e-bu-ru ú.ṭa-ab-bu-ú* |
| 13 | $^{giš}$ḫa.lu.úb.ḫar.ra.na | nam mi.ni.in.kud.da.a.ni |
| | *ḫu-lu-up-pa ina ḫar-ra-nu ik-ki-su* : | *dup-ra-nu iz-zu-ru* |
| 14 | mušen $^{d}$im.dugud $^{mušen}$ | sa bí.in.laḫ$_4$.a.ni |
| | *iṣ-ṣu-ru $^{d}$za-a* (tablet: $^{d}$IÁ-*a*) | *ina še-e-tú i-bi-lu$_4$* |

3. See most recently J. Krecher, *SKl*, p. 223.
4. See J. Krecher, op. cit., pp. 148–49.
5. II *R* 30 no. 1 ii 11 (Nabnītu L 181).

| | | |
|---|---|---|
| 15 | en mè.a ur.ra | sag.ní.dúb.a.ni |
| | *be-lu ina ta-ḫa-zi nak-ri* | *ik-mu-ru* |
| 16 | muš.sag.imin.na | mu.un.ug$_5$.ga.a.ni |
| | *ṣe-er-ru si-ba qaq-qa-da-šú* | *i-na-ru* |
| 17 | im.babbar kur.ra | me.ri kin.dug$_4$.ga.a.ni |
| | *gaṣ-ṣa ina šadî$^{i}$* | *i-mi-su* |
| 18 | kušú$^{kua}$ a.nim.ma | me.ri pap.dug$_4$.ga.a.ni |
| | *ku-šá-a ina la-i-ra-ni* | *i-te-et-ti-iq* |
| 19 | íb.bé i.lu ḫa.ma.an.tuku.a | en.me.en lugal.me.en |
| | *qu-bu-ú ag-giš liq-qa-bu-ú* | *[be]-le-ku šar-ra-ku* |
| 20 | a.za.lu.lu ḫa.ma.an.tuku.a | [dum]u.$^{d}$asal.lú.ḫi.me.en |
| | *te-né-še-e-tú liq-qa-ba-a* | *[ma-a]r $^{d}$marduk ana-ku* |
| 21 | zi.da gùb.bu ud.gim ga.an.túm | x [ x ] x U me.en |
| | *im-na u šu-me-lu ki-ma u$_4$-mi lu-uš-lul* | [. . .] x x *ana-ku* |
| 22 | me.e ur.sag.me.en | me.[e. . .].me.en |
| | *ana-ku qar-ra-da-ku* | *[ana-ku. . .-ku]* |
| 23 | ibila kala.ga | $^{d}$[. . .].me.en |
| | *ap-lu dan-nu* | [. . . *ana-ku*] |
| 24 | en zi sa$_5$.a | [. . .].me.en |
| | *be-lum šá-qu-ú šin-na-at* | [. . .*ana-ku*] |
| 25 | gú.un ka.kèš.da | é.s[ag.íl.la].me.en |
| | *ra-ki-is bil-ti* | [. . .*ana-ku*] |
| 26 | urù ur.sag.KU | GIŠGAL [. . .].me.en |
| | *ez-zi qar-ra-du* | [. . .*m*]*e?-ḫe-e ana-ku* |
| 27 | u$_x$.lu še.gub.ba | an.ki.a [. . .].me.en |
| | *a-[bu]-bu: me-ḫu-ú šá tat-šab?* | [*ina*] *šamê$^{e}$ u er*[*ṣetim$^{tim}$. . .ana-ku*] |
| 28 | [ x ] x urú.šè urú.šè | [ x ] x x x [. . .g]e.mèn |
| | . . .]*ana āl*[*i. . .* | |

REVERSE

| | | |
|---|---|---|
| 1 | ur.⌜bar.ra.gim⌝ sila$_4$.šu.ti.a.zu | n[u. . . . |
| | *ki-ma bar-ba-ri le-qé-e pu-ḫa-di-ka* | [. . . |
| 2 | lugal.mu kur.ra dug.sakar$_x$.gim | ara(KA × ŠID) mu.un.da.ab.gi$_4$.[gi$_4$] |
| | *be-lu$_4$ šá šá-da-a ki-ma kar-pa-tum šá-ḫar-ra-ti tu-šá-aš-ga-mu: tu-ḫe-ep-pu-*⌜*ú*⌝ | |
| 3 | ur.sag $^{d}$mu.zé.eb.ba.sa$_4$.a kur.ra síg.máš.a.gim mu.un.da.peš$_5$.peš$_5$ | |
| | *qar-ra-du $^{d}$na-bi-um šá šá-da-a ki-ma šá-rat bu-lim tu-nap-pi-šú* | |
| 4 | $^{d}$šid.dù.ki.šár.ra kur.ra síg.máš.a.gim mu.un.da.peš$_5$.peš$_5$ | |
| 5 | lugal.mu kur.ra gi.min. [t]ab.ba.gim aš mu.un.da.bad.du | |
| | *be-lu$_4$ šá šá-da-a ki-ma qa-an šun-na-a e-di-iš tu-na-as-su-ú* | |

---

| | | |
|---|---|---|
| 6 | umun urú.ni.a | na.ám zé.eb ba.an.tar.re |
| | *be-lum šá āli-šú šim-tam ṭa-ab-tam i-šim-mu* | |
| 7 | e.lum urú.ni.a | na. |
| 8 | $^{d}$mu.zé.eb.ba.sa$_4$.a urú.ni.a | na. |

| | | |
|---|---|---|
| 9 | umun $^{d}$en.zag.ga urú.ni.a | na. |
| 10 | $^{d}$šid.dù.ki.šár.ra urú.ni.a | na. |
| 11 | $^{d}$nà dumu.nun.na urú.ni.a | na. |
| 12 | ibila é.sag.íl.la urú.ni.a | na. |
| 13 | urú.na nibru$^{ki}$.na | na. |
| 14 | še.eb.é.kur.ra | na. 15 mu$^{meš}$ gu$_4$.ud$^{meš}$ |
| 15 | dil.bat$^{ki}$ é.*i-bí-$^{d}$a-nu-um* | na. |
| 16 | na.ám zé.eb ba.an.tar.re | $^{d}$mu.zé.eb.ba.sa$_4$.a |
| | *šim-tam ṭa-ab-tam i-šim-šú* | *šu-ma ṭa-a-bu im-bi-šú* |
| 17 | umun.ra mu.lu.siskur$_x$.ra.ke$_4$ | siskur$_x$ dè.ra.ab.bé |
| | *ana be-lim šá ik-ri-bi* | *ik-ri-bi liq-bu-šú* |
| 18 | umun.ra mu.lu.a.ra.zu.ke$_4$ | a.ra.zu dè.ra.ab.bé |
| | *ana be-lum šá tés-li-tú* | *tés-li-tú liq-bu-šú* |
| 19 | an $^{d}$uraš | ki.še.gu.nu.ra |
| | 25 mu$^{meš}$ gu$_4$.ud$^{meš}$ | |
| 20 | nin zi.da | $^{d}$ki.ša$_6$ nu.nuz$_x$(NUNUZ) ša$_6$.ga |
| 21 | a.a ugu.zu | $^{d}$asal.lú.ḫi.ke$_4$ |
| 22 | ama ugu.zu | $^{d}$pa$_4$.nun.an.ki.ke$_4$ |
| 23 | mu.ud.na ki.ága.zu | gašan.ka.téš.a.sì.ga.ke$_4$ |
| 24 | sukal.an.na gašan.šubur.ra | sukal maḫ.di gal.ukkin $^{d}$enšadu |
| 25 | suḫur.maš sangá.maḫ.ZU.AB.ke$_4$ | ur.sag gal $^{d}$dug$_4$.ga.ab.šu.gi$_4$.gi$_4$ |
| 26 | ad.gi$_4$.gi$_4$ | $^{d}$en.nun.dagal.la.{na} |
| 27 | ad.gi$_4$.gi$_4$ gašan.šud$_x$.dè.an.na | ad.gi$_4$.gi$_4$ dug$_4$.ga.ni.kir$_4$.zal |
| 28 | ama.ur.sag.ke$_4$ gašan.tin.lu.ba | ur.sag gal umun $^{d}$di.ku$_5$.maḫ.àm |
| 29 | umun.ad.ḫal.an.$^{d}$uraš.a.ra | dìm.me.er.an.na dìm.me.er.ki.a |
| 30 | [šu]d$_x$.dè še.eb.é.zi.da.ta.a | ki ne.en.gi$_4$.gi$_4$ |
| 31 | [ki.š]ú.bi.im | balag.$^{d}$na.bi.um.ke$_4$ |
| 32 | [ur].sag a.ma.ru ḫu.luḫ.ḫa | me.lám ḫuš ní ri |
| | *qar-ra-du a-bu-bu gal-tum* | *šá me-lam-mi ez-zi-iš ra-mu-u* |

33 2/3? nis-ḫi ukkin.ta eš.bar.ra til.la nu.al.til $^{md}$*anu*(60)-*le*ʾ*i*(zu) $^{lú}$maš.maš *māru šá* $^{m}$an.gal.dù.nun $^{lú}$bàd.an$^{k}$[$^{i}$-*ú*]

34 x *bīt* $^{d}$*anu*(60) *u an-tum* $^{lú}$dub.sar.é.dim.gal.kalam.ma *ana balāṭ*(tin) *napišti-šú kīma labiri*(sumun)-*šú ú-šá-áš-ṭir i*[*b-ri*...]

35 [ x ] x *ina bīt iltāni*(im.⌜si?sa⌝?) é.dim.gal.kalam.ma *bīt bēlu*(umun)-*ti-šú ukîn*(gub) *qát* $^{m}$*ni-din-tú-*$^{d}$*ani*(60) *māru šá* $^{md}$x[...]

OBVERSE

1 [He is angry], he is furious,
2 ...] ... [(...)]
3 [The revered one] is angry, he is furious with his city,
4 [...]. is angry, he is furious,
5 Muzebbasaʾa is angry, he is furious,
6 Šiddukišarra is angry, he is furious,
7 [Nabû], son of the prince, is angry, he is furious,

8 The heir of Esagil is angry, he is furious,
9 He who raised up battle in heaven,
10 Who made warfare in the underworld,
11 Who held back the flood upstream,
12 Who, with Ea, flooded the harvest,
13 Who cursed the juniper tree,
14 Who caught the Zû bird in a net,
15 The lord who defeated his enemies in battle,
16 Who killed the seven-headed snake,
17 Who crushed Gypsum in the mountain,
18 Who trampled on the shark(?) in deep water,
19 Let laments be uttered in anger: I am lord, I am king.
20 Let the human race be told, I am the son of Marduk.
21 Right and left I will carry off like a storm [...] am I.
22 I am a hero, I am [...]
23 I am the mighty heir of [...]
24 I am the lofty lord, the double of [...]
25 I am he who bears the burden in Esagil,
26 I am the fierce, the warrior,.[...]
27 I am the whining flood, in heaven and underworld [...]
28 [.].to the city, to the city [.]...[...].am I.

REVERSE

1 Like a wolf, that took your lamb.[...
2 My lord, you who made the mountain rumble like a....pot,
3 You, the warrior Nabû, who carded the mountain like animals' hair,
4 Šiddukišarra, you who carded the mountain like animals' hair,
5 My lord, you who separated the mountain like a double reed,

---

6 The lord who decreed a good destiny for his city,
7 The revered one who decreed a good destiny for his city,
8 Muzebbasaʾa who decreed a good destiny for his city,
9 The lord Enzagga who decreed a good destiny for his city,
10 Šiddukišarra who decreed a good destiny for his city,
11 Nabû, son of the prince, who decreed a good destiny for his city,
12 The heir of Esagil who decreed a good destiny for his city,
13 Who for his city, for Nippur, decreed a good destiny,
14 Who for the brickwork of Ekur decreed a good destiny,
(*15 lines skipped*)
15 Who for Dilbat and Eibbianum decreed a good destiny,
16 He decreed a good destiny for it, he called it by a good name.

---

17 Let prayers be addressed to the lord of prayers,
18 Let petitions be addressed to the lord of petitions by:
19 An and Uraš; Earth, where barley sprouted;
(*25 lines skipped*)

20 The faithful lady, Kiša, the charming woman;
21 The father who begat you, Asalluḫi;
22 The mother who bore you, Panunanki;
23 Your beloved spouse, Gašankatešasiga,
24 The vizier of Anu, Gašanšuburra; the lofty vizier who summons to counsel, Enšadu;
25 The Goat-fish, lofty priest of the Apsû; the great warrior Duggabšugigi;
26 The counsellor, Ennundagalla;
27 The counsellor Gašanšuddeanna; the counsellor Dugganikirzal;
28 The mother of the warrior, Gašantinluba; the great warrior, the Lord Dikumaḫ:
29 Lords of the mysteries of heaven and underworld, gods of heaven and gods of underworld.

---

30 This prayer from the brickwork of Ezida.....

---

31 Finis. A balag-song to Nabû.

---

32 Warrior, fearful flood, who fiercely sits in splendour.
33 Second/Third extract of *The Decision was Taken in the Assembly*, not finished. Anu-leʾi, the exorcist, son of Ištarān-bāni-rubê, of Dēr,
34 [.] of the temple of Anu and Antum, scribe of Edimgalkalamma, had this written in accordance with its original and collated it to insure his long life [...]
35 [.].placed it in the north wing of Edimgalkalamma, his lordly temple. Written by Nidintu-Ani, son of.[...]

## *Notes on Obverse*

1–8 The restoration is based on the duplicate K 10303 ([íb].bi ù.na.nam [...]) and on the similar opening of *BL* 16 (íb.bé/ba ù.na.nam). The phrase is no doubt an old liturgical formula, but its construction was doubtful to the editors of the bilingual editions and remains so to this day. *BL* 16 renders the whole phrase *nu-ug-ga-tum-ma*, taking íb as *nagāgu* (it should be *agāgu*, but note *ŠL* 207 2d and Lānu F i 14 apud *CAD agāgu*), na.nam in the usual sense (Delitzsch, *Sum. Grammatik*, §103), and ignoring the bé/ba and ù. K 10303 renders [*ug-g*]*at-su kàd-rat* (sup. ras.) *ana* x [... This takes the .bi as the pronominal suffix (wrongly construed as personal?) and the ù.na as *kadāru*, but it leaves the nam, which is neither àm nor na.nam. The Converse Tablet is obscure. Its first line is the first half-line of K 10303, but it is not certain that obv. 2 of the former is to be restored as the second half of the first line of the latter. The pi sag ma suggests nothing Sumerian, but it could be Akkadian (*pi-ris-ma* "it is a section"? a kind of gloss?). This obscure item appears also in the catch-lines of *SBH*, no. 12. The first line of K 10303 is perhaps to be restored: [urú.ni.a íb.bi ù.na.nam]. The Converse Tablet probably took íb as *agāgu*, and certainly ù.na as *kadāru*, but just how it got its *ša kadrūtišu* is not clear. In such confusion we tentatively take the phrase as íb + e(d) ù.na + (na).nam, since in the present context (but not necessarily the original one) it seems easier to take ib.bé as a finite form.

3–4 Line 3 is restored from rev. 7, and line 4 might be restored from K 10303 as umun.ur.sag.gal.e, though the spacing and traces are not easily reconciled.

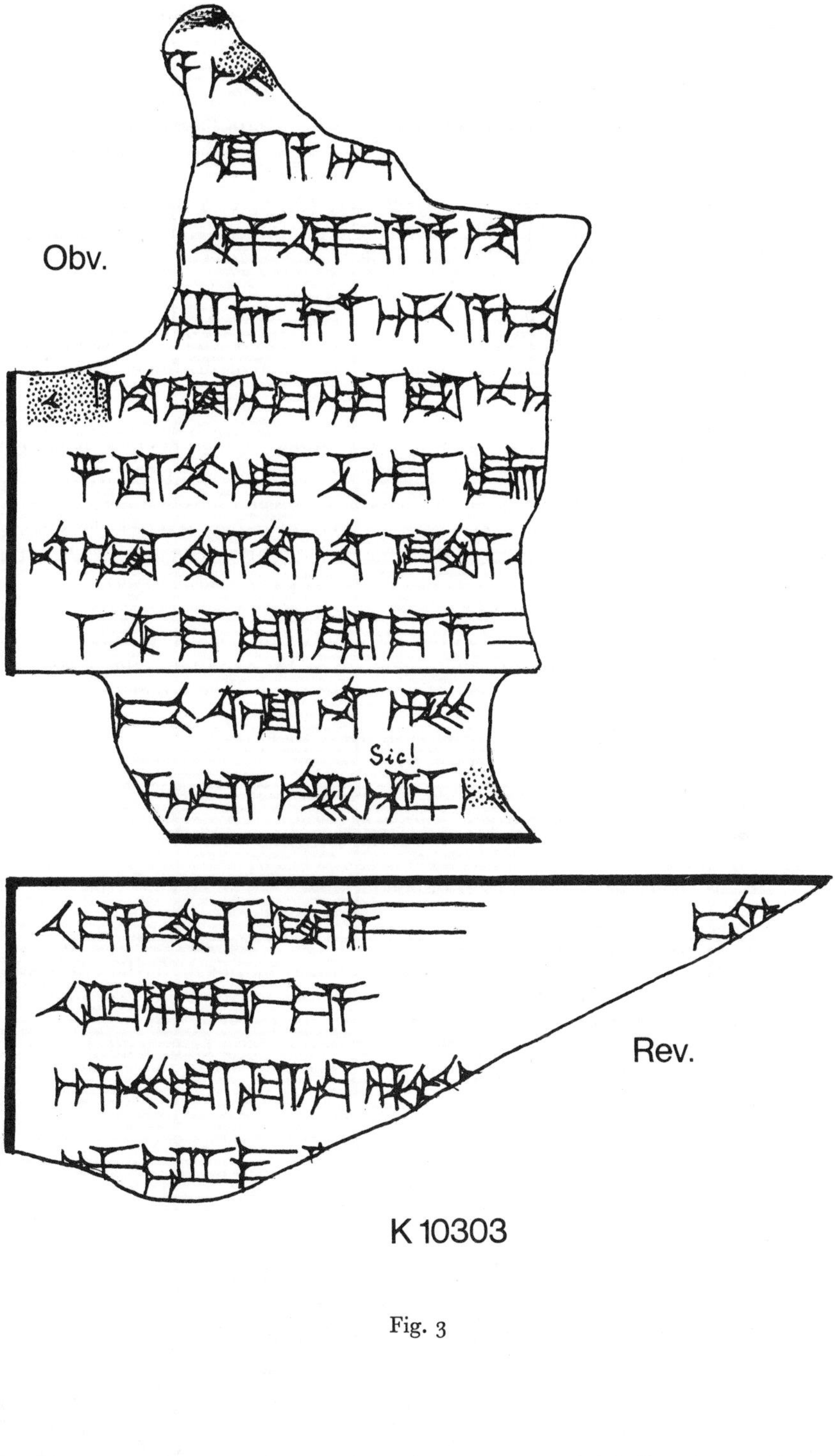


Fig. 3

11 an.ra is probably an error for an.ta perhaps influenced by the following line. The allusion is to a section of Lugal.e (*BE*, XXIX, 2–3, cf. pp. 65–70), also referred to by Gudea (Cylinder A viii 15: a ḫuš $gi_4$.a).

12 Passages from litanies about the flooding of growing crops are cited in *CAD* sub voce *ebūru*. The mention of Ea makes it more specific here, but the allusion is obscure.

13 Note ^giš^mes.ḫa.lu.ub.ḫar.ra.na = *dup-ra-nu* (*MSL*, v, 110, 208), and nam kud = "curse" (*CAD arāru* A), which favor the second interpretation in Akkadian. The allusion is presumably to a Ninurta exploit.

14 This refers to the episode of the Akkadian Zû Epic, alluded to in Lugal.e (*SEM*, 44, obv. 13 = 45, obv. 11) and Angim (*CT*, 15, 42, K 4864 + end). A Ninurta litany also alludes to the episode: mušen ^d^im.dugud^mušen^ im.ma.ni.in.dib.bé.en = *ka-mi iṣ-ṣu-ri ^d^zi-i* (*SBH*, p. 38, 26).

16 The killing of muš.sag.imin by Ninurta is alluded to in Lugal.e (*SEM*, 44, obv. 13 = 45, obv. 11) and Angim (*CT*, 15, 42, K 4864 + restored *WZKM*, 57, $12^2$), but no narrative of the episode survives. Pictorial representations of a hero killing a seven-headed snake-like monster occur on an Old Akkadian seal (H. Frankfort, *Diyala*, p. 478) and on a shell plaque of the same period (J. B. Pritchard, *ANEP*, 671). The creature is referred to in Ālu (*CT*, 40, 24, K 6294 4 = ibid., 23, 33).

17–18 Gypsum is listed as one of Ninurta's victories in Lugal.e (*SEM*, 44, obv. 9 = 45, obv. 7: nì.$bar_x$.$bar_x$.ra) and Angim (*CT*, 15, 42, 16–17: im.babbar = *gaṣ-ṣa*), also a Ninurta litany gives both this and the shark or crab together:

im.babbar kur.ra me.ri síg.ga $dug_4$.ga.na:ni
*gaṣ-ṣa ina šá-di-i i-mi-su*:.*te-mes*
[kušú]^kua^ a.nim.ma me.ri pap.$dug_4$.ga.na: ni
*ku-šá-a ina la-i-ri-a-ni te-ti-qu*: *i-*[*ti-q*]*u*
IV $R^2$ 30 no. 1 rev. 13–16

More details about these episodes seem to be lacking.

27 With še.gub.ba cf. gig.ga.bi.šè še àm.gub.a = *ana ma-ru-uš-ti-šá at-ta-šab* (*SBH*, p. 149, no. 2 rev. 1–2, cf. Witzel, *Tammuz-Liturgien*, p. 270, 85–86). It would seem in both cases the original reading was še $ša_4$ (= *damāmu*, see Krecher, *SKl*, 77–78), but the $ša_4$ was misread as gub and the verb translated as "sit." The wedges following *tat-* in the Akkadian of this line could be those of a badly copied *šab*, but if so presumably *tat-ta-šab* lay behind it in the tradition.

28 Cf. *ASKT*, 17, rev. 1.

## *Notes on Reverse*

2 Cf.:

...dug.$sakar_x$.gim ara(KA × ŠID) mu.un.da.ab.$gi_4$.$gi_4$
...*šá ki-ma kar-pa-ti šá-ḫar-ra-ti ú-šá-áš-ga-mu*
*CT*, 17, 25, 21–22 = 47, 55–56

Thus the first translation is supported, and indeed the basis of the rendering *teḫeppû* is not clear. SAR, read sakar or saḫar, is used for various kinds of pot, see A. Salonen, *Hausgeräte*, II, pp. 357–58. But its meaning is unknown and the simile here is obscure. It is uncertain if kur/*šadû* here refers to the ḫur.sag of Lugal.e. There is much scattered material about battles with mountains, but so far it has not been studied.

3–4 Von Soden, *AHw*, separates *napāšu* "card (wool)" from *napāšu* "breathe," quoting the Middle Hebrew and Aramaic *nps* with the same meaning and the Arabic *napaša* "pick (cotton) with the fingers." These, however, may be loans from the Akkadian, as suggested by P. Haupt in *BA*, V, 471f., and the occurrence of peš$_5$ here as equivalent to *nuppušu* "card" would seem to prove that only one root is involved.

5 A similar line occurs in *The Death of Dumuzi* (*PRAK*, II, D 53, rev. 1 = rev. 20): gi.aš.dù.e aš ba.ra.an.bad.du (cf. T. Jacobsen apud A. L. Oppenheim, *The Interpretation of Dreams*, p. 246, and S. N. Kramer, *Mythologies of the Ancient World*, p. 111). The meaning of gi.aš.dù.e is not altogether clear, cf. *MSL*, VII, 17, 150, with 55, 375.

6 The same line occurs in *SBH*, 55, rev. 18–19, dup. K 10077.

14 The scribal note here and in 19 below refers to the omission of a previously given sequence, as correctly explained by Meissner in 1908 (*OLZ*, 11, 405–8). A stative of *šaḫāṭu* is no doubt implied, but no phonetic writing seems to exist. The missing lines can be restored from K 8399 (*BA*, V, 663) rev. as: ki.ùr é.nam.ti.la, zimbir$^{ki}$ é.babbar, urú.na tin.tir$^{ki}$, še.eb.é.sag.íl.la, urú.na bàd.si.ab.ba$^{ki}$, še.eb.é.zi.da, é.maḫ.ti.la, é.te.me.an.ki, é.dàra.an.na, é.nam.bi.zi.da, é.ur$_4$.me.imin.an.ki, é.EZEN.sag.ús.sa, kiši$^{ki}$ é.dub ba, é.me.te.ur.sag, gú.du$_8$.a$^{ki}$ é.mes.lam; each followed by na. For the temple and shrine names see the notes of Langdon to the parallel series in BM 78878 (*Gaster Ann. Vol.*, p. 339f.) and the articles in *RLA*. The reading of é.EZEN.sag.ús.sa is uncertain, and for é.dub.ba, not é.kišib.ba, see K 9876 rev. 22 (Pallis, *Akîtu* pl. XI).

16 The divine determinative is probably erroneous.

17–18 Cf. *SBH*, p. 29, 16–19.

19 The lacking lines (cf. *SBH*, p. 47, rev. 23, etc.) contained a version of Enlil's theogony leading up to the family and courtiers of Nabû. While parallels can be quoted, no sure restoration is possible, though the first lacking line must have contained $^{d}$en.ki $^{d}$nin.ki, and the last was no doubt $^{d}$íd.lú.ru.gú di.ku$_5$.kalam.ma.ke$_4$, see K 6813 and dup. K 10155.

23 Ninkatešasiga is a well known title of Tašmētum.

25 The suḫur.maš is the commonly attested symbol of Ea. Duggabšugigi occurs in AN = Anum in the court of Šamaš (*CT*, 24, 32, 98 = 25, 26, 36).

26–27 Ennundagalla is a counsellor of Marduk, and Gašanšuddeanna of Ṣarpānītum in AN = Anum, *CT*, 24, 28, 64–65. There is an attested phrase dug$_4$.ga.ni kir$_4$.zal = *šá qí-bit-su mut-tál!-la-at* (*SBH*, p. 38, 24), but here it appears as the name of another counsellor, though it does not occur elsewhere as a proper name.

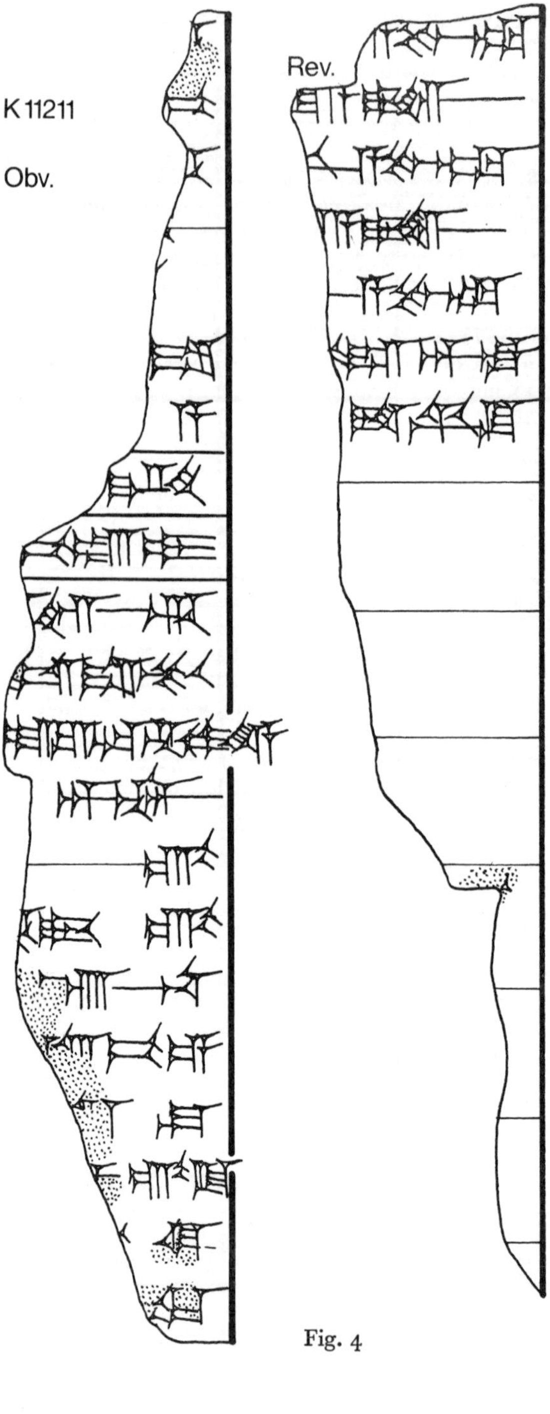


Fig. 4

28 The adjective maḫ.(àm) occurs so commonly with ᵈdi.ku₅ in this genre that it is no doubt to be construed as part of the name.

29 The first half is difficult. Since An and Uraš occur at the head of the list they can hardly appear a second time at its end. Thus ad.ḫal must be joined to them, and their names must here be used for "heaven and earth" (see *AnBib*, 12/III, 71, 3). The problem then remaining is whether a single deity is referred to as umun, or whether all the gods of the preceding list as summed up in this phrase. In either case the .ra must be attributed to a late scribe.

30 Cf. Krecher, *SKl*, 22, 30, 31.

33–35 For other colophons from Der see H. Hunger, *Bab. und Ass. Kolophone*, pp. 66–67. For an.gal = Ištarān see *ZA*, 59, 100–3.

## ADDENDUM

Since the MS. was completed further identifications of related fragments have been made:

(i) K 11211 belongs to the series, duplicates the ends of lines at the conclusion of the Converse Tablet (17b–29, skipping 19b–28a), and offers ends of lines of the beginning of the text of which the catch-line is given on the Converse Tablet. A copy is given here by permission of the Trustees of the British Museum.

(ii) Another fragment almost certainly belonging to the series, but unplaced, is K 13951 (unpublished).

(iii) A duplicate of *BA*, X, 98 (Rm 272) is K 8728 (unpublished), which seems to be part of the same tablet as K 8399 (*BA*, V, 663).

The brief study of M. Bielitz, *Melismen und ungewöhnliche Silbenwiederholung, bzw. Alternanz in sumerischen Kulttexten der Seleukidenzeit* (*Orientalia* 39 [1970]: 152–56) appeared too late to be used. It adds to the Sumerian material two small fragments from Seleucid Warka in copies of Van Dijk and compares similar phenomena in Byzantine texts, but does not contribute anything positive to the interpretation of the Mesopotamian material.

# Punic Art in Italy

SABATINO MOSCATI

THE eminent scholar to whom the present collection of essays is dedicated has brought several essential contributions to Phoenician and Punic studies. Principal among them is the study on the inscription from Nora, with which attention has been focused on the remains of Phoenician–Punic culture in Italy.[1] It is, therefore, our pleasure to present him, as a sign of esteem, with a brief synthesis concerning the discoveries which have recently been made in our country in the field of Punic art, as well as with a preliminary evaluation of the discoveries themselves.

The findings are to be fitted into a vast program of Mediterranean researches promoted by the Institute of Near Eastern Studies of the University of Rome and supported by the National Research Council and the Ministry of Foreign Affairs.[2] The countries in which we are currently engaged in archaeological activities are, from East to West, Syria, Egypt, Tunisia, Malta, Sicily, and Sardinia. In art, the most significant discoveries have been made in the Italian islands proper: in Sicily at Motya, facing Marsala, where we have been conducting excavations in collaboration with the Superintendency

1. W. F. Albright, New Light on the Early History of Phoenician Colonization, *BASOR*, 83 (1941): 17–22.

2. Cf. the writer's, Scoperte archaeologiche nei paesi mediterranei, *Atti della Accademia delle Scienze di Torino, Cl. di Sc. mor., stor. e fil.*, 102 (1967–68): 483–500.

of Antiquities of Western Sicily, directed by Professor Vincenzo Tusa;[3] in Sardinia at Monte Sirai, near Carbonia, where our excavations were held in collaboration with the Superintendency of Antiquities of Cagliari, directed by Professor Ferruccio Barreca.[4]

At Motya we are in the process of bringing to light the *tophet*, an open-air enclosure bordered on one side by the walls of the city, on the others by containment walls, made for the purpose, which show various levels of construction. Several urns containing bones of children are coming to light inside the enclosure; we have also discovered a deposit of terracotta votive masks and almost 300 stelae with figurative representations, often reused in the walls.

Among the votive masks,[5] which have been found in very good state of preservation, we find a male mask (Plate I) belonging to the second group of the Cintas classification of the material from Carthage:[6] the face is marked by deep furrows on the forehead and cheeks, the crescent-shaped eyes are achieved by means of slits, the extremely wide mouth is also cut in the same fashion. The others are female masks (Plate II) and turn out to be, for the most part, similar: they have an Egyptian wig, a band holds up their hair and causes it to fall back behind the ears, the eyebrows meet at an angle of 90° with the lines of the nose; in this case also the correspondence with Carthaginian protomas of the Egyptian type is complete.[7] On the whole, therefore, the Motya masks show a significant identity with the Carthaginian ones, tracing a cultural identity which, as we shall see, is lacking in other aspects of the production.

3. A. Ciasca, M. Forte, G. Garbini, S. Moscati, B. Pugliese, V. Tusa, *Mozia*–I (Roma, 1964); A. Ciasca, M. Forte, G. Garbini, V. Tusa, A. Tusa Cutroni, A. Verger, *Mozia*–II (Roma, 1966); I. Brancoli, A. Ciasca, G. Garbini, B. Pugliese, V. Tusa, A. Tusa Cutroni, *Mozia*–III (Roma, 1967); A. Ciasca, G. Garbini, P. Mingazzini, B. Pugliese, V. Tusa, *Mozia*–IV (Roma, 1968).

4. F. Barreca, G. Garbini, *Monte Sirai–I* (Roma, 1964); M. G. Amadasi, F. Barreca, P. Bartoloni, I. Brancoli, S. M. Cecchini, G. Garbini, S. Moscati, G. Pesce, *Monte Sirai–II* (Roma, 1965); M. G. Amadasi, F. Barreca, G. Garbini, M. and D. Fantar, S. Sorda, *Monte Sirai–III* (Roma, 1966); M. G. Amadasi, F. Barreca, P. Bartoloni, M. and D. Fantar, S. Moscati, *Monte Sirai–IV* (Roma, 1967).

5. Cf. *Mozia–I.* pp. 61–69, plates XLIV–LIII; *Mozia–II,* pp. 28, 38, plate LIII; *Mozia–III,* pp. 27, 37, plates XXX–XXXI; *Mozia–IV,* pp. 44–45, plate XXXVII, I.

6. Cf. P. Cintas, *Amulettes puniques* (Tunis, 1946), p. 49, plate X; C. Picard, Sacra punica, *Karthago,* 13 (1965–66): 12–16, nos. 3–10, 13, figures 3–8, 13.

7. Cf. P. Cintas, *Amulettes puniques,* pp. 34–36, plate VIII, no. 66; C. Picard, *Karthago,* 13 (1965–66): 20–22, nos. 25–32, figures 21–24.

As for the stelae,[8] it is important to point out that they are to be added to the ones previously discovered by Whitaker (120 approximately),[9] forming therefore a considerably large group. Chronologically, they can be dated between the sixth and fifth centuries B.C. They are of considerable importance from various viewpoints, especially as regards technique, typology, and iconography. As for the technical aspect, a stela[10] (Plate III) shows us, for the first time in the ancient phase of this Punic production, a figure which is only painted, whereas the few traces of color which had been previously noticed on other stelae had been considered subsidiary elements of the relief: it is, therefore, probable that several stelae previously defined "with empty niche" were actually painted and not incised and that the fading of the color was an obstacle to understanding their real nature. As regards typology, another unique aspect in the contemporary Punic world can be noticed, i.e., the presence of double stelae: of particular interest is a stela (Plate IV)[11] showing two figures which proceed one toward the other, a fact which suggests a unitary conception of the iconographic theme and brings to mind, for the iconographic pattern, some scenes on Phoenician ivories, whereas no parallel is to be found at Carthage or in other North African sites.

New aspects of the Motya stelae are to be noted, for the most part, in their iconography. First, and generally speaking, there is the abundance of human figures, which are few at Carthage; furthermore, there is an originality of the single themes, in which complex cultural influences and various levels of artisan production are reflected. Several stelae show a female figure (front), its hair descending onto its breast, with hands joined and clothed in a long smooth garment from which only the feet emerge (Plate V).[12] This type of figure is quite rare in Africa, whereas entirely absent is another one attested at Motya, i.e., the female figure which holds a disk to its breast, in a frontal or lateral view (Plate VI).[13] Direct relations with Phoenicia are evident here, and they are confirmed by other iconographies in which a male figure seen laterally appears (Plate VII).[14] Relations with the Greek culture of Sicily are suggested by a few stelae in which the figure is naked (Plate

8. Cf. the writer's, Le nuove stele puniche scoperte a Mozia, *Rendiconti della Pontificia Accademia Romana di Archeologia*, 40 (1967–68): 21–34.

9. Cf. J. I. S. Whitaker, *Motya. A Phoenician Colony in Sicily* (London, 1921), pp. 271–74.

10. Stela no. 189 (numbers refer to the catalogue of the stelae published in the excavation reports).

11. Stela no. 209.

12. Stelae nos. 49–52, 112–13, 165–70, 172.

13. Stelae nos. 118–19.

14. Stelae nos. 175, 179.

VIII):[15] a fact not in harmony with the principles of Phoenician–Punic iconography. Finally, in opposition to the cultured tendencies which evidently operate in the Motya craftsmanship, there seem to be obvious folk art tendencies; or, at least, one can speak of a production with different technical qualities and various social levels, or of differences between workshops: only in this manner can the extreme disparity between elegant and rough stelae, between refined and just outlined iconographies, between contrasting characteristics which are nonetheless unified, be justified.

At Monte Sirai, in Sardinia, we have discovered an important Carthaginian fortified center. The central nucleus of the fortress consists of a large quadrangular tower, built on a previous Sardinian *nuraghe*. Around the tower are several smaller rooms, among which is a shrine abounding in artistic material. A wall, the opening of which is a gate with powerful fortified ramparts, encloses the acropolis. Outside the acropolis, in another part of the mound, there is a temple with an ample staircase leading up to it; at the foot of the staircase a *tophet*, with urns and stelae, has come to light. Finally, there is the necropolis, with tombs cut into the rock, and the remains of a small residence complex. On the whole, Monte Sirai shows us, for the first time, a large Punic military quarter, not on the coast but in the interior of Sardinia, built with the evident aim of controlling the roads leading to the center of the island. It must also be noted that the Monte Sirai excavation has been completed by vast surface explorations which are leading to historical conclusions of great importance, i.e., that the Carthaginians controlled basically the whole island at the height of their expansion.

Evidence of the art of Monte Sirai is supplied, first, by a statue of remarkable antiquity; its body is barely outlined, while its head is accurately designed, with a strong sense of volumes and evident stylization in the rendering of the hair, curls, and ears, the latter reduced to the shape of concentric circles (Plate IX).[16] Considering the general scarcity of Punic statuary, the Monte Sirai piece takes on an extreme importance, especially in view of its particular characteristics, the antecedents of which are to be searched for exclusively in the Near East, particularly in a statue from Tell Halaf and in a relief from Zinjirli.[17] We see here, in conclusion, a further example of the

15. Stela no. 12 and others less certain due to low degree of conservation of the relief.

16. Cf. *Monte Sirai–II*, pp. 53–54, 59–60, plates XXI, XXVIII, XXIX; *Monte Sirai–III*, pp. 108–13, plates L–LI, I.

17. Cf. H. T. Bossert, *Altsyrien* (Tübingen, 1951), nos. 453–54; F. von Luschan, *Ausgrabungen in Sendschirli*, IV (Berlin, 1911), plate LIV.

direct diffusion of iconographical themes from Phoenicia to the islands of the Mediterranean, on which we had focused attention in considering the Motya stelae.

As regards relief on stone, Monte Sirai has provided us with a peculiar head (Plate X),[18] originally sculptured on the wall of a tomb, subsequently detached by unauthorized excavators and finally recovered. Extremely schematical, it has a triangular shape and eyes, mouth, and nose indicated in a rudimental fashion. It is a piece hard to classify and for which comparisons are lacking: it is evidently a folk art product.

The stelae of the Monte Sirai *tophet*, approximately 70,[19] show the predominance of elaborate Egyptian-type *aediculae* and of frontal female figures with a disk held to their breasts (Plate XI). Since the origins of the *tophet* cannot be traced farther back than the fifth century, and the complex reaches down to the first century approximately, it follows that this iconography has all the characteristics of an archaic production: inspired by oriental models (possibly with Sicily as an intermediate passage, as we have seen), it lacks the developments which are characteristic of Carthage in the corresponding period. Another essential aspect of the Monte Sirai production is the important function performed by native craftsmen, owing to whom a part of the stelae take on a decidedly folk art character, detached from the original models: as in a stela where nothing is left of the *aedicula* and the figure has become a trapezoid with thread-like arms (Plate XII);[20] and in another, also without the *aedicula*, in which a schematical female figure is flanked by one of a child (Plate XIII).[21] We can ask ourselves, for the latter case, whether we are in the presence of the extreme stylization of an iconographic theme known to the Greek world, or instead looking upon an ingenuous folk art expression of the Punic rite of sacrificing children.

Going on to the terra-cotta statuary, first let us consider a figurine which was found in a fragmentary condition with a cylinder-like body gradually widening toward the bottom, and a head with globe-shaped eyes and a pointed beard jutting forward (Plate XIV).[22] This last aspect, in particular, refers us to Palestinian and Cypriot models, and fixes a further point of direct connection between the Sardinian production and Phoenician antecedents.

18. Cf. *Monte Sirai–I*, pp. 94–96, plate XLIX.

19. Cf. *Monte Sirai–I*, pp. 30, 65–93, plates XI, XXXVI–XLVII; *Monte Siria–II*, pp. 128–33, plates LI–LVI; *Monte Sirai–III*, pp. 117, 120–22, plates LIII, 1.

20. Stela no. 49.

21. Stela no. 48.

22. Cf. *Monte Sirai–I*, pp. 30, 96–99, plates L–LI; *Monte Sirai–III*, pp. 115–16, plates LIII, 1.

Also in terra-cotta is the mask of a male figure, with stylized curls and a long beard (Plate XV);[23] a rare type, of which only a couple of corresponding and quite fragmentary examples are known to us in the Punic world.

Three bronze statuettes have been discovered at Monte Sirai:[24] the first one represents a seated figure which pours a drink into a cup for himself (Plate XVI), the second one a figure playing the zither (Plate XVII), the third a four-legged animal on a ring. The study of these small bronze pieces is complicated by the nearby flourishing of Sardinian bronze craftsmanship. Generally speaking, it does not seem possible to trace derivations from the environment of the Nuragic people; instead, we can speak of a production with oriental origins and flourishing in a parallel manner, with reciprocal influxes and stimuli, to that of the Sardinian peoples.

As complex and as stimulating is the problem posed by two small bone plaques,[25] one with a palmette incised on it, and the other a male bust (Plate XVIII) with arms folded on its chest and a circular-shaped, schematical head with moustaches and hair in curls, wide nose, mouth or tongue also deformed into a circle. The palmette is a typically Phoenician theme which had wide diffusion in the West; the male bust may have contacts with the so-called Bes, the divine figure, some statues of whom come from Sardinia itself. Once again, Monte Sirai shows us its fundamental characteristics in the field of art: connections with the East, with phenomena of archaic or archaizing art, and local folk art characterizations.

The discoveries in Sicily and Sardinia allow us to pose, and in part to solve, problems which were not perceived, or scarcely so, in the past: the problem of the development of Punic art and of the subsequent diversification of its characteristics in time; the problem of regional articulation, to which are connected the complex phenomena of areas exposed to influences or evolutions to a greater or smaller degree; the problem of the direct ties with the East, from which derive archaic or archaizing factors; the problem of the action of substrata and adstrata, and one can quote as examples the Nuragic influence in Sardinia and the Greek influence in Sicily; the problem

23. Cf. *Monte Sirai–II*, pp. 54, 60–61, plate XXIV; *Monte Sirai–III*, pp. 116-17.

24. Cf. *Monte Sirai–II*, pp. 53, 57, plates XXVI–XXVII; *Monte Sirai–III*, pp. 18, 20, 21, 45, 113–15, plates XXXVIII–XXXIX.

25. Cf. *Monte Sirai–II*, pp. 56, 61–62, plate XXXI; *Monte Sirai–III*, pp. 118–19.

of the different levels of production, i.e., of the craftsmen's workshops, from cultivated art to folk art.

We are in the presence of unexpected possibilities and new mainlines emerging, representing the results of our researches at various points in the basin of the Mediterranean, of the outcome of which, as regards Punic art, we have here given a brief synthesis.

Plate I

Plate II

Plate III

Plate IV

Plate V

Plate VI

Plate VII

Plate VIII

Plate IX

Plate X

Plate XI

Plate XII

Plate XIII

Plate XIV

Plate XV

Plate XVI

Plate XVII

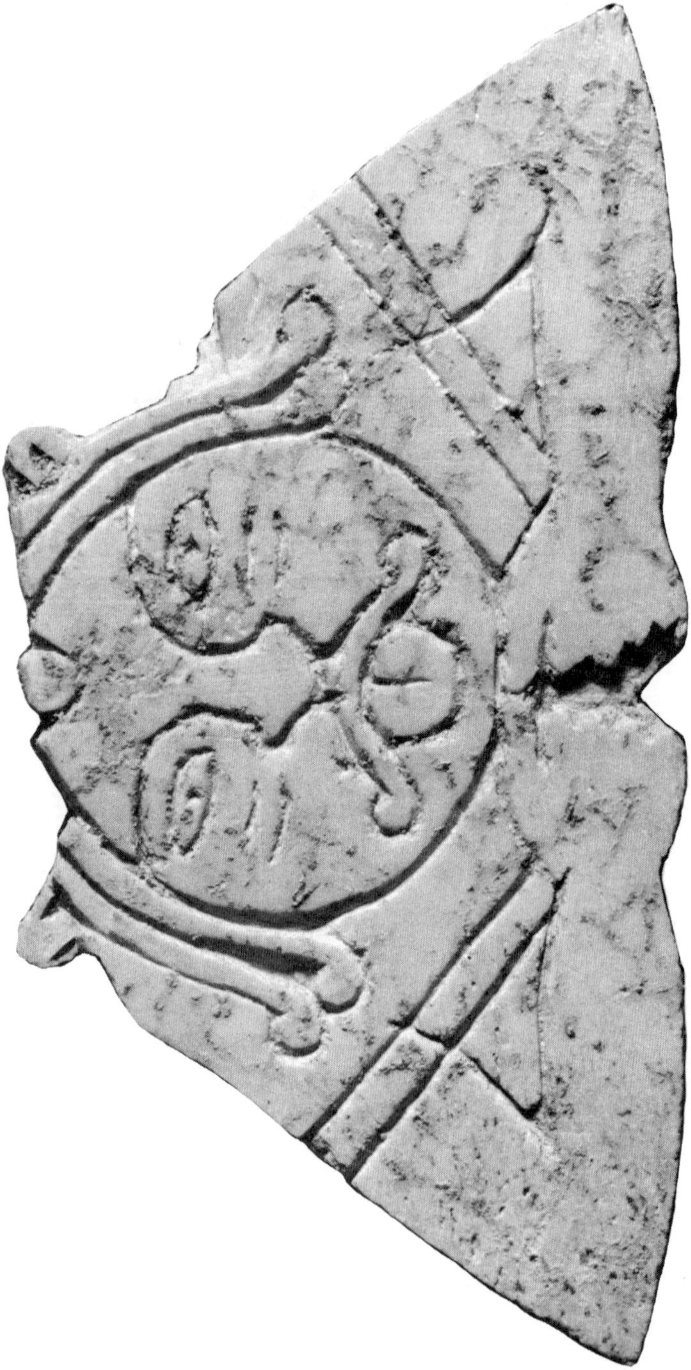

Plate XVIII

# Edom and Judah in the Sixth–Fifth Centuries B.C.

J. M. MYERS

THE history of Edom from the last years of Judah to expulsion from its native land is beset with problems. That old animosities existing between Jacob and Esau were fanned into white heat is demonstrated by prophetic oracles and hymnic outbursts originating in the period noted. While most of these cannot be dated with complete confidence, they do point to unprecedented hostility due to some overt or covert activity on the part of Edom against Judah. The latter's hatred for Edom could hardly have been so intense before the events leading to the collapse of the state, because for the most part throughout her history she had the upper hand. In the wake of her successes vis-à-vis Edom, Israel's early experience with it at the time of the wilderness wanderings (Num. 20:14–21) was played down. Not once is that unbrotherly conduct recalled directly in the course of the later castigation of Edom by prophet, psalmist, or historian. Both Deuteronomist (2 Kings 8:20,22; 14:7ff.) and Chronicler (2 Chr. 21:8; 25:12ff.; 28:17) refer to uprisings of Edom and report that from the time of Jehoram (849–842 B.C.) Edom had been in almost continuous revolt (2 Kings 8:22; 2 Chr. 21:10). Yet the Deuteronomic law warned that "you must not regard an Edomite as an abomination because he is your brother" (Dt. 23:8a); children of the third generation could even marry Israelites.[1]

1. See the discussion on this precept by K. Galling, "Das Gemeindegesetz in Deuteronomium 23," in *Festschrift für Alfred Bertholet* (Tübingen: Mohr, 1950), pp. 176–91.

In the desert period of Israel,[2] Esau-Edom was credited with the possession of Mt. Seir (Num. 24:18), though it may already have been threatened with dispossession of its allotted territory. This tradition is present in all the strata of the Pentateuch (E in Gen. 32:3; P in Gen. 36:8,9; D in Dt. 2:5) and is emphasized in the introduction of Joshua's address at the Shechem covenant celebration (24:4). But then something happened that aroused the ire of the spokesmen of Judah and that recalls the antagonism displayed in connection with Edom's refusal to permit the wilderness wanderers to cross its territory (Num. 20:14–21). The purpose of this paper is to survey the course of events in the sixth–fifth centuries B.C. responsible for their savage denunciation of Edom.

## I. BRIEF SURVEY OF EDOM IN THE EARLY PERIOD

Despite subjugation by David and later kings of Israel, Edom maintained its identity right down through the Neo-Babylonian period. The names of the eight kings of Edom who reigned before there was a king of Israel, are listed in Gen. 36:31–39 and I Chr. 1:43–51. Hadad ben-Bedad of Avith (Gen. 36:35 and I Chr. 1:46) was involved in the Midianite uprising put down by Gideon (Judg. 6:1–8:28).[3] David conquered Edom (2 Sam. 8:13–14), but did not incorporate it into his realm; he simply added it to his possessions by personal union. Hadad, a very young scion of the Edomite royal family, is said to have escaped, with certain members of the court, the vicious act of Joab. He fled to Egypt where he enjoyed the favor of the Pharaoh (I Kings 11:18–19). After David's death he returned to plague Solomon (I Kings 11:25). Early in the reign of Jehoshaphat Edom was ruled by a military governor of Judah (I Kings 22:48),[4] but later on, toward the end of his reign, there is reference to a king of Edom (II Kings 3:9,12,26). Edom seems to have cut loose from Judah in the days of Jehoram. Amaziah (800–783 B.C.) defeated the Edomites and reduced Sela (II Kings 14:7–10 and II Chr.

2. Cf. W. F. Albright, "The Oracles of Balaam," *JBL*, 63 (1944): 207–33.

3. Cf. Albright, *Archaeology and the Religion of Israel* (Baltimore: The Johns Hopkins Press 1942), p. 206, n. 58.

4. I Kings 22:48 is difficult. *wmlk ʾyn bʾdwm nṣb mlk* is usually rendered, "there was no king in Edom, [but] a deputy was king," meaning apparently a deputy of Jehoshaphat. Vss. 47–50 are missing from $LXX^{B}$ but recorded in $LXX^{A}$, Syriac—there was no king in Edom who was ruling. Targum—There was no king in Edom; a military governor was appointed over them for the king. V—nec erat tunc rex constitutus in Edom. For a discussion of the problem see Montgomery-Gehman, *The Books of the Kings* (New York: Scribners, 1951), p. 343f.; A. Sanda, *Die Bücher der Könige* (Münster i. Westf.: Aschendorf, 1911), Vol. I, p. 503; R. deVaux, *La Sainte Bible: Les livres des Rois* (Paris: Cerf, 1949), p. 123, n.b.

25:11ff.). Uzziah-Azariah rebuilt the seaport at Elath (II Chr. 26:2) which was held through the reign of Jotham, as the seal found in the excavations at Ezion-geber attests.[5] But it was regained by Edom in the time of Ahaz (II Kings 16:6; the Chronicler's reference to an invasion of Judah probably refers to the same event, II Chr. 28:17). Thereafter Edom doubtless gained in strength.

The earliest mention of Edom in the Assyrian inscriptions appears in the records of Adad-nirari III's expedition to Palestine (810–783 B.C.).[6] The building inscription of Tiglath-pileser III (745–727 B.C.) refers to Qausmalaku of Edom as one of the kings from whom he received tribute.[7] A Nimrud letter (XVI)[8] tells of a coalition of Palestinian states, led by Ashdod, among which Edom is listed. The letter dates from Sargon II's campaign in 712 B.C. Aiarammu, king of Edom, was one of those bringing gifts and "kissing the feet" of Sennacherib in 701 B.C.[9] Qausgabri, a later king of Edom, was one of twelve kings compelled to furnish supplies for the construction of Esarhaddon's palace at Nineveh.[10] That same king offered gifts and submission to Ashurbanipal[11] who, in his ninth campaign (against Uate, king of Arabia), pursued his quarry into Moab and Edom.[12] There is no reference to Edom in either extant Neo-Babylonian or Persian inscriptions, but there was a king in Edom as late as the fourth year of Zedeqiah (Jer. 27:2ff.). The last mention of Edom in historical literature is I. Esd. 4:45,50.

## II. EDOM IN CONTEMPORARY PROPHECY

It is abundantly clear from contemporary prophetic literature that the Edomites played a significant role in the events that led to the downfall of Judah. As late as Jer. 27:2ff. (the fourth year of Zedeqiah, ca. 594 B.C.)[13] there was a convocation of small Palestinian and Transjordan states—Edom, Moab, Ammon, Tyre, and Sidon—perhaps instigated by Egypt to survey the possibility of a successful revolt against Nebuchadnezzar. The Babylonian

5. See *BASOR*, 79 (1940): 13–15.
6. J. B. Pritchard, *ANET*, p. 281.
7. Ibid., p. 282.
8. H. W. F. Saggs, "The Nimrud Letters, 1952–Part II" in *Iraq*, 17 (1955): 134f., 152f. Cf. also *ANET*, p. 287. But both are broken and the reading cannot be regarded as absolutely certain.
9. *ANET*, p. 287.
10. Ibid., p. 291.
11. Ibid., p. 294.
12. Ibid., p. 298.
13. See W. Rudolph, *Jeremia* (Tübingen: Mohr, 1947), p. 146, and J. Bright, *Jeremiah* (New York: Doubleday, 1965), p. 195, note.

king was occupied elsewhere in his ninth and tenth years[14] which doubtless appeared to the conferees as a good time to lay aside his yoke. The important fact is that Edom was still one of the allied principalities of the west and not yet Judah's implacable opponent. After the appointment of Gedaliah at Mizpah, Jews who had fled to Moab, Ammon, Edom, and elsewhere are said to have returned to Judah to gather the summer crops (Jer. 40:11). Did the alliance of these states break up later or is there another reason why Jews took refuge among them with impunity? Ginsberg suggests that the Phoenician city states and Ammon supported Judah to the bitter end, while the Edomites—and possibly Moabites—did not.[15] If that is so, Jews from Ammon could very well have been permitted to return in the hope of assisting Gedaliah to reorganize Judah, perhaps looking forward to another attempted coup (cf. Jer. 40:13ff.). On the other hand, Jews returning from Edom (and Moab) would, in effect, have been supporting the power with which the latter had recently formed an alliance.

An animosity developed between Judah and Edom after the diplomatic conference of Jer. 27:2 that can be explained only on the basis of a sudden shift on the part of the latter. There is no reference anywhere to a Babylonian campaign against Edom, though Josephus (*Ant.* 10:9:7) reports the subjugation of Moab and Ammon some time in the fifth year after the destruction of Jerusalem (i.e., 582 B.C.). Though admittedly conjectural, it would appear that Edom either joined the conqueror of Judah as an ally or remained deliberately aloof at the critical moment. Whether, as has been suggested, there were Edomite contingents in the army of Nebuchadnezzar[16] is debatable, but some particularly offensive act must have been committed against Judah or else Judean outbursts would hardly have been so impassioned.

The oracle against Edom in Jer. 49:7–22 is composite. There is some Jeremian material in these vss., but it is difficult to identify in view of parallels with other references in Jeremiah and in Obad. 1–8. Moreover, it is possible that the whole corpus of oracles against foreign nations was revised to harmonize with later developments. Whether destruction had already overtaken Edom or not cannot be determined conclusively. It would appear, however,

14. Cf. D. J. Wiseman, *Chronicles of Chaldean Kings* (London: The British Academy, 1956), p. 72f.

15. *Alexander Marx Jubilee Volume* (New York: The Jewish Theological Seminary of America, 1950), p. 364f.

16. This has sometimes been conjectured on the basis of the Syriac reading of Edom for Aram in II Kings 24:2 and Jer. 35:11. But both passages are dated in the reign of Jehoiakim not in that of Zedeqiah.

that the process had already begun or was impending, since the Dedanites[17] are urged to return to the desert for "the calamity of Esau have I brought upon him, the time I have appointed for him" (vs. 8). Cf. also vss. 10, 16b, 17ff. On the whole the passage seems to be a prediction of the impending end for Edom, to be brought about by events already set in motion. But the precise date of the oracle, or even the elements of it belonging to the dicta of Jeremiah, is uncertain.

The Ezekelian oracle on Edom (25:12–14) dates from early in the sixth century, with the possible exception of the last verse which may be a later expansion.[18] The perfidious acts of Edom, whatever they were, had already taken place, although Yahweh's punishment for them had not yet been effected. A second prophecy against Edom (ch. 35) is more difficult to orient because it is closely connected with another (ch. 36) promising salvation for Judah (Israel). The crucial formula is the same in both: "Son of man, set your face against Mt. Seir and prophesy against it" (35:1); "You, son of man, prophesy to the mountains of Israel" (36:1). Included in ch. 36 is a denunciation against those who derided Judah and took over her possessions in the time of her desolation, claiming them as their own. So the Lord now speaks against "the rest of the nations and against all Edom" (vs. 5); they shall all "bear their reproach" (vs. 7). That is the theme of ch. 35, where details are given. As the cities of Judah were laid waste so Edom will suffer deprivation. Edom is guilty of blood and will have to pay the price. The haughtiness of Edom was demonstrated by its presumptive act in claiming both Judah and Israel as a possession. That it "greeted with joy the heritage of Israel" was accentuated by its swift take-over by Edom. While it may still be strong, Edom's time will come. The impression one gets from chs. 35–36 is that it reflects a later period than does the prophecy of 25:12–14. It implies Edom's desertion of Judah during the Babylonian conquest—perhaps active participation in some manner on the side of the invader (35:5). It hints at Edom's taking advantage of the vacuum created by the deportations (36:5) or, at best, the inability of those who remained in the land to defend themselves, though reference is made to Edom's "perpetual enmity" (35:5) —a cliché in Ezekiel (cf. 25:15). It may be that the people of Seir were already being subjected to the pressure that was later to overwhelm their homeland, though that was not so precipitate as was the overthrow of Judah.

The book of Lamentations mentions Edom only once (4:21) but it can

17. On Dedan references in the prophets see Albright, "Dedan" in *Geschichte und Altes Testament* (Tübingen: Mohr, 1953), pp. 7–9.

18. Cf. W. Zimmerli, *Ezechiel* (BKAT, XIII, 8, 9: Neukirchen, 1962), p. 597f.

hardly be doubted that it is in the mind of the author(s) more than once. There is some question as to the exact date of the several chapters. The writer shares the view of Hans-Joachim Kraus[19] that all five poems come from a time soon after the debacle of 587 B.C. According to Jer. 27:3b, Edom was among the states confederate with Judah. Lam. 1:2 informs us that the erstwhile friends of Judah had forsaken her:

> She has not one to comfort her    Of all her lovers;
> All her friends deceived her;    they became her enemies.

Evidently they had much to do with the stance that brought on her downfall.[20] "Her oppressors now looked upon her with glee" (1:7) and those who were forbidden to do so (Dt. 23:4,8) entered her sanctuary (1:10). The neighbors of Jacob became his adversaries (1:17). His enemies rejoiced that Yahweh had brought on him trouble (1:21). Not only did they gape at Jerusalem in mockery but even took advantage of the situation to further their own plans, (3:61) so that Judah's "heritage was turned over to strangers," their "homes to aliens" (5:2). Those left in the land had to pay for the basic necessities of life (5:4). Slaves (5:8) (i.e., the hirelings of the conqueror) were over them and worked their warped will on women and virgins (5:11). The sensitive survivors mourned far more than the ruin of their land, the deportation of the best of the citizens, and the loss of many of their loved ones; they had to endure the expropriation of their land, the horror of personal indignity, and derision on the part of the very people who instigated rebellion or resistance against the Babylonians.

With the exception of Ps. 137:7, the title book of Obadiah is the bitterest invective against Edom in the Bible. Most scholars date it soon after the fall of Jerusalem.[21] The prophet's complaint about the attitude of Edom on that occasion reflects a kind of consensus of feeling on the part of all of Judah's writers of the period. The crucial passage is vss. 10–14:

> Because of wrong [done] to your brother Jacob
> Shame will cover you and you will be cut off forever.
> When you stood aloof, as foreigners plundered his property,
> When aliens entered his gates and cast lots over Jerusalem,
> You were just like them.
>
> Now you should not have looked on in the day of your brother,
> in the hour of his misfortune;

19. *Klagelieder* (Threni) (*BKAT*, XX, Neukirchen, 1956), p. 11.
20. I.e., the treaty of mutual rebellion was betrayed.
21. See e.g., J. Muilenberg, *Interpreter's Dictionary of the Bible* (New York and Nashville: Abingdon Press, 1962), Vol. III, p. 578f.

Nor should you have gloated over the sons of Judah in the
hour of their ruin.
And you should not have boasted in the hour of distress.

Moreover, you should not have obstructed the crossroads to cut
off his escapees,
Nor should you have turned over his survivors in the hour
of distress.

The poet has marshalled phrases and expressions from numerous sources to describe the revulsion felt by the people of Judah over the unnatural attitude of Edom conveyed by perfidy in the hour of disaster. Obad. 1–6 is parallel with Jer. 49:9–16 and there is no agreement on the authorship of the basic material.[22] However that may be, Obadiah's version represents pronouncement of judgment upon Edom primarily because of its arrogance and presumption. Edom boasted of its impregnability, lodged "in the clefts of the rock," its "nest set among the stars," but Yahweh's judgment will find it. Of particular import is vs. 7b with its double-barreled thrust:

All your allies have outwitted you,
Your table-bond companions[23] have set a snare[24] under you—
It is incomprehensible!

Twice (vss. 10,12) Jacob is referred to as "thy brother" (i.e., of Edom-Esau) which relationship the prophet regards as a more intimate bond than any existent between more distant relatives. It was for brothers to support and sustain one another in times of adversity, but such was not the case now. Alliances (cf. the friends and lovers of Lam. 1:2) with others for advantage were entered into and maintained by Edom in preference to relationship between the brothers (Jacob and Esau). Now treaty engagements and table-bond fellowship for purposes of trade and exploitation with its desert (and Babylonian?) friends became a snare for Edom, whose territory was gradually being infiltrated and whose citizens would sooner or later be pushed out of their homeland. Then there is the pointed reference to the traditional wise men of Edom (*ḥkmym*) who, despite their understanding (*tbwnh*), will be outwitted.[25] Note the play on the latter word in the expression *ʾyn tbwnh bw* (= it is incomprehensible)—a *Schimpfwort*. The prophecy of Obadiah gives

22. See the Introductions for the various views expressed by scholars.
23. Reading *ʾanše laḥmᵉka*.
24. Meaning uncertain. Gk. = *enedra* (ambush), V = *insidiae* (= snare, ambush), S = *kmʾnʾ* (something treacherous), T = *tqlʾ* (snare). For various suggestions see Brown, Driver and Briggs, *Hebrew and English Lexicon*, in loco.
25. For another occurrence of the clause *yklw lk ʾnšy šlmk* see Jer. 38:22.

an impression of close proximity to Edom's contemptible behavior but before its expulsion from the homeland. For just as the prophet predicted salvation on Mt. Zion (vs. 17) so he foresaw the destruction of "wise men of Edom and understanding from the mountain of Esau" (vs. 8). The best argument that Edom's end had not yet come may be gleaned from the fact that when it did come later it did not happen exactly the way Obadiah envisioned it (vss. 18–19). Yet with true prophetic insight the day of judgment for the people guilty of such crimes detailed above is predicted. Perhaps the prophet was aware of the insidious movements and involvements destined to vindicate the word of Yahweh.

References to Edom and Seir in Isaiah are all in disputed passages generally recognized as exilic or postexilic in date. Is. 11:14 envisions a time when Judah and Ephraim will be at peace after having co-operated in subjugating Philistia, Edom, Moab, and Ammon who had encroached upon their territory. This appears to be an eschatological piece expressing the hope that Israel reunited will some day reoccupy the land promised to the fathers. No special feeling of hostility against Edom is manifested. The little oracle on Dumah and Seir (Is. 21:11–12) is an enigma. LXX entitles it "an oracle against Edom." If Dumah in North Arabia were meant by the author it is hard to understand why the oracle was not included in vss. 13–17 which deal with Arabia. Probably the importance of the oasis of Dumat al-Ghandel in later times influenced the passage.[26] The mention of Edom with its Bozrah in Is. 63:1 is certainly eschatological, as is evident from the colorful language employed to describe the imaginary character (Yahweh) returning from a punitive expedition. Muilenberg's interpretation is surely correct.[27] It is a vivid portrayal of universal judgment upon the enemies of Israel subsumed under Edom as their symbol. Underlying it, however, is bitter historical experience. Such oracles may reflect something of the time in which they were composed and this one appears near enough to the period of Edom's hostile activity for mention because Edom was still intact.

Joel 3:19 (Heb. 4:19) suggests that judgment had not yet befallen Edom—note use of imperfect tense here. The date of Joel is not quite certain, although there are indicators pointing to the last quarter of the sixth century as probable.[28] Obadiah is echoed, if not actually quoted, at several points[29] from

26. Cf. A. Musil, *Arabia Deserta* (1927), pp. 531–53 and R. Dussaud, *Le pénétration des Arabes en Syrie avant l'Islam* (Paris: Geuthner, 1955), p. 24, n. 6. Dumat al-Ghandel was located at the southern end of Wadi Sirhan, far from both Edom and Judah.

27. *The Interpreter's Bible* (New York and Nashville: Abingdon Press), Vol. V (1956), p. 724f.

28. See *ZAW* 74 (1962): 177–95.

29. Cf. the following: 10a–4:19c; 15b–4:4,7; 17a–2:3c, 3:5; 18c–4:8.

which it could be inferred that the situation with respect to Edom had not changed materially. The designation *mdbr ʾdwm* in the expression *wʾdwm lmdbr šmmh thyh* may be significant, implying movement rather than the more fixed status obtaining since the time of Edom's regaining of Elath in the reign of Ahaz. Zion's rehabilitation had begun and the time for avenging the blood of Judah had arrived when the fortunes of Judah and Edom were reversed.

If the above sequence is correct, the last reference to Edom in prophetic literature occurs in Mal. 1:2–4. Malachi is usually assigned to the first half of the fifth century B.C. The prophet's concern is the justification of Yahweh's love for Israel in spite of the untoward circumstances of the time. He summons history, at least in part, to support his argument. The history of Israel and Edom is subsumed under the names of the eponymous ancestors of each, whose fortunes are said to have been due to Yahweh's acceptance of Jacob and rejection of Esau. But what about the present situation? "I have reduced his (Esau's) mountains to desolation and [given] his heritage to the jackals of the wilderness" (1:3) shows that Edom had by now been expelled from its ancient habitat. This is further confirmed by the remark "Though Edom boasts, we have been utterly beaten down but . . ." (1:4). Note use of perfect tense. It may be that encroachments upon Judah without effective resistance at the time inspired hope in the Edomites that expulsion from their fortresses was only a temporary setback as they had suffered several times before in their protracted history. In due time they would snap back. It appears that the prophet was speaking to the complaint of his fellow countrymen that Edom was enjoying success in claiming for itself former Judean territory while they were going from bad to worse. The point is that Edom has been driven out, and momentary triumph in Judah too will come to an end for "the people with whom Yahweh has always been angry" (1:4).

References to Edom in the Psalms, except Ps. 137:7, cannot be dated with confidence and indeed furnish little additional information.[30] Ps. 137:7 has been regarded with suspicion,[31] but it is quite understandable if Edom was somehow actively involved in the events connected with the downfall of Jerusalem. As such the verse echoes what has been said in Obadiah, Lamentations, and I Esd. 4:45, though only the last passage is specific. It is curious that not a single word is said about Edom in Ezra-Nehemiah.[32] The list of

30. But see L. Itkonen, "Edom und Moab in den Psalmen" in *StOr I* (Tallquist Festschrift) (Helsingforsiae, 1925), pp. 78–82 and the recent commentaries on Psalms.

31. Cf. H. L. Ginsberg, *Alexander Marx Jubilee Volume*, p. 365, n. 49.

32. Attention may be called to Ezr. 9:1 where one of the peoples with whom the Jews are said to have cohabited is the Amorites (all MSS and Versions). The parallel passage is I Esd.

towns in Neh. 11:25ff. would appear to indicate that Judah's territory extended only as far as Beth-zur and that the area to the south and east was no longer in her hands. Edom's control of Judean cities occurred as early as the reign of Darius I (521–486 B.C.) for I Esd. 4:50 reports the Persian king ordering the Edomites to give up the Jewish villages.

What conclusions may be drawn from the scriptural sources about the late history of Edom? (1) Edom was one of the allies planning a revolt against Nebuchadnezzar in the fourth year of Zedeqiah (Jer. 27:2). (2) In the wake of the Babylonian conquest of Judah, Edomites were guilty of some reprehensible activity that incensed the people of Judah. I Esd. 4:45 accuses them of setting the temple on fire. They may have remained aloof from the conflict when they saw the inevitability of its outcome. But that hardly seems enough to elicit the strong statements found in a number of the above noted complaints. They may have rendered some assistance, directly or indirectly, to the Babylonian invaders. Obadiah (14) says they blocked the crossroads, the way of escape for those fleeing from the path of the aggressors. It can hardly be said, without qualification, that they actually joined the army of Nebuchadnezzar, as some have inferred. (3) By the time of Mal. 1:2–4 Edom had itself been dislodged from its ancient habitat of Seir, (4) though the Edomites still appear to have been in their homeland when Joel uttered his prophecy against Edom (3:19). It would appear that Edom was not expelled precipitously; the process may have been set in motion when Nabonidus took over the trade routes around the middle of the sixth century[33] and reached its zenith soon after the turn of the century. It has often been pointed out that such changes frequently take the form of infiltration, and that seems to have been one way by which the Edomites were gradually squeezed out of their fastnesses. (5) The fact that Edom was still present in Seir the last quarter of the sixth century does not militate against its encroachment on southeast Judah soon after the last foray of Nebuchadnezzar in 582 B.C.[34] (6) By the time of Nehemiah, Geshem was in control of both Edom proper and the Edomite territory seized from Judah, since Edom is nowhere mentioned in either Nehemiah or Ezra.[35] Only areas politically involved and whose bor-

8:66 (69) has Edomites (om by S) which may be a reminiscence of 4:45, 50. It may be worth noting that the term Amorite does not appear in I Esdras, nor is there any reference to Edom or Edomites in Haggai and Zechariah.

33. R. H. Dougherty, *Nabonidus and Belshazzer* (New Haven: Yale University Press, 1929), pp. 150ff.; W. F. Albright, *JRAS* (April, 1925): 294ff.

34. See Albright's letter to H. L. Ginsberg in *Alexander Marx Jubilee Volume*, English Section, p. 364, n. 47a.

35. Cf. A. Alt, "Judas Nachbarn zur Zeit Nehemias" in *Palästinajahrbuch* 1931, p. 73f.

ders were contiguous to post-exilic Judah are mentioned—Samaria, Ammon, Arabia, Ashdod. To be sure, there were Moabites in the land of Judah, as attested by the inter-marriages with them protested by Ezra and Nehemiah, but they represented families who migrated under pressure exerted by the desert peoples following Nebuchadnezzar's conquest of Ammon and Moab in 582. Moreover, Moab's border was no longer adjacent to Judah and its land was probably under control of Gesham in the second half of the fifth century.

## III. ARCHAEOLOGICAL CONTRIBUTIONS

Babylonian provincial towns north of Jerusalem and Jewish cities south of Hebron remained relatively untouched by the events of 589–587 B.C.[36] The old Judah territory was taken over by Samaria and Edom, whose advance guard took up residence in the ridge country around Hebron and Adoraim. The more substantial invasion of the former Judean state probably occurred some time after the last Babylonian incursion. On the basis of Josephus (*Ant.* 10:9:7), when Nebuchadnezzar invaded Syria in his twenty-third year (582/1 B.C.) and when Moab and Ammon were subjected and more Jews exiled (Jer. 52:30), it has been suggested an excellent opportunity was afforded for the Edomites to push harder and faster into the area now reduced to a political vacuum.[37] It appears that Edom's disintegration was not due to outright conquest but rather to the convergence of Arab conglomerations which attacked local centers and infiltrated others in the course of trade expansion following the fall of the Neo-Babylonian empire, especially its concentrations at Teima. It may be significant that there seems to have been no sedentary occupation in the land of Edom in the Persian period.[38]

### 1. *Situation at Ezion-geber*

Periods IV and V concern us here. The former was a new industrial city erected on the ruins of the preceding level which had been destroyed by fire. It lasted from the eighth to the end of the sixth century B.C. and was

36. Albright, *BA*, 9 (1946): 6.

37. Mazar, Dothan, Dunayevsky, "En-gedi: The First and Second Seasons of Excavations 1961–1962," (*Atiqot*: *English Series*, Vol. 5, Jerusalem, 1966, pp. 3ff.). Noth (*The History of Israel*, New York: Harpers, 1958, p. 325) thinks the territory south of Beth-zur was ceded to Edom as early as 598 B.C. But one wonders how Edom could then have remained an ally of Judah and implicated in the plot to revolt against Babylon in 594/3 B.C. (Jer. 27:3). What happened to Edom after 582, Noth says he does not know (ibid., p. 292f.). Cf. Aharoni, *BA* 31 (1968), pp. 17f. and Malamat, *IEJ* 18 (1968): 142f.

38. Cf. J. Starcky, *BA*, 18 (1955): 86; observation based on Glueck's explorations; *AASOR*, XV (1935): 138ff. and XVIII–XIX, p. 23f.

composed of at least two phases of occupation. Ezion-geber fell into the hands of Edom toward the end of the third quarter of the eighth century B.C. (II Kings 16:6) and remained in its control to the end of the sixth century. To the first phase belongs the jar stamp inscribed with the name of Qaus ᶜanal, an official of the Edomite king (cf. Jer. 27:2), and dates around 600 B.C.[39] From the second phase of level IV came Ostracon 6043[40] which Albright dates "in or about the first half of the sixth century."[41] None of the names are Arabic while four are Edomite, which would seem to indicate that the land of Seir was still controlled by Edomites at the time. This level then represents the last Edomite settlement at Ezion-geber. Period V was a new industrial development built over the ruins of IV that lasted from the end of the sixth century to perhaps the early fourth century and was under Persian control. That was the period of the Aramaic ostraca, with receipts for wine,[42] which points to the continuance of trade with both Arabia and Greece, as shown by the many Greek sherds. Glueck's excavations confirm the subsequent abandonment of the site when the Nabataean center was established at Alia. It is altogether likely that the population remained ethnically substantially the same in both periods, little affected by the change of government, though by the time Tell el-Kheleifeh was abandoned the community was well Arabized. The vigor of the Edomite trade relationships in seventh–sixth centuries is shown by the pottery situation reported by Glueck.[43] Possibly many Edomite achievements have been transmuted by later civilization.

### 2. *Umm el-Biyara (Selaᶜ)*

In 1933 Gleuck identified the site of Umm el-Biyara with Selaᶜ on the basis of surface pottery,[44] which was later (1934) confirmed by soundings.[45] In 1955 W. H. Morton conducted an exploratory expedition in the area and subsequently reported a profusion of Edomite Iron Age sherds scattered over the entire summit of Umm el-Biyara, with a concentration in the center of the plateau, while the Nabataean, also in considerable quantity all over the place, were most numerous in the northeastern section of the summit.[46] The

39. Cf. *BASOR*, 79 (1940): 13.
40. *BASOR*, 82 (1941): 3.
41. Ibid., pp. 11ff.
42. *BASOR*, 80 (1940): 3–10; 82, pp. 3–11.
43. *BASOR*, 188 (1967): 8–38. Note especially the Minnean jar on p. 23f.
44. *AASOR*, XIV (1934): 77.
45. *AASOR*, XV (1935): 82.
46. *BA*, XIX (1956): 28f.
47. "Fouilles d' Umm el-Biyara: Rapport préliminaire" in *RB*, 73 (1966): 372–403.

preliminary report of Crystal M. Bennett[47] indicates a reoccupation of Edomite structures in the Hellenistic epoch, after their abandonment by the Edomites and before the visible constructions of the Nabataeans on the border of the plateau. The well-arranged constructions show clearly that Umm el-Biyara in the Edomite period was more than a temporary refuge; it was a sedentary installation, even if only seasonally occupied. Interesting enough was the discovery of an ostracon receipt for the delivery of wine and an Edomite royal seal, both of which date from the seventh century. Miss Bennett concludes that the remains of Umm el-Biyara are homogeneous and show no appreciable development, which would mean that the site was abandoned after that, though how or why is not apparent as yet. Meanwhile Glueck[48] observed that nearby Tawilan exhibited the same type of Edomite pottery as Umm el-Biyara, i.e., Iron I–II. No other site yielded so many and varied types of Edomite pottery as Tawilan. It "was the largest Edomite center in the entire Petra area. . . . Situated in the heart of a fertile, well-watered area, which was thickly settled in the Edomite period, and located at a meeting point of important trade routes, Tawilan was one of the most important centers of the Edomite kingdom." (Tawilan is thought to be the Teiman of Am. 1:12.)[49] Nabataean ware also turned up there. But the precise time of Edomite abandonment is certainly not very clear yet. What most of the sites reflect is the fading out of Edom from its Seir home sometime in the sixth century or at least the shifting of its bases of operation.

### 3. *Other Sites in Edom*

Archaeologically speaking, other sites in the land of Edom reflect basically the same situation that prevailed in the above noted places. One of the important northern sites was Feinan (ancient Punon of Num. 33:42) located ca. fifty miles south of the Dead Sea on the eastern edge of the Arabah. Glueck found there,[50] on the basis of pottery remains, sedentary occupation from the thirteenth to seventh centuries B.C. Because of its well-watered surroundings and easy access to iron mines it was an important center which, by virtue of that fact, was continued by the Nabataeans, who generally occupied already established sites. Ten miles northeast of Feinan lay Buseirah (ancient Bozrah)[51] which was a thriving settlement in the Edomite period, mentioned

48. *AASOR*, XV, p. 82f.

49. But identification is rejected by Abel, *Géographie* II (1938): 479–480.

50. *AASOR*, XV, pp. 32–35; *The Other Side of the Jordan* (New Haven, 1940), pp. 68–71.

51. For a description of location and ruins see A. Musil, *Arabia Petraea* II: Edom, Pt. 1 (Hölder: Wien, 1907), pp. 299, 319–21; and Glueck, *AASOR*, XV, p. 97f., who regards it as the strongest city in north Edom, "practically impregnable."

no less than five times in the Bible (Am. 1:12; Is. 34:6; 63:1; Jer. 49:13,22). The rather sparse pottery finds reflect the same history as other sites. Surveys in the Timna valley are too indefinite to draw any firm conclusions, though it now appears that some of the pottery relegated to the tenth century and earlier belongs to a much later period, perhaps to the end of the Edomite age.[52]

Pottery evidence collected by Glueck in his series of explorations is fairly uniform in confining Edomite activity to the periods just noted. The last one is generally put in the seventh–sixth centuries. He now reports that "Archaeological and literary materials demonstrate that the Wadi Arabah was occupied from the time of King Solomon in the tenth century B.C., down to the fifth–fourth centuries B.C. with varying degrees of intensity, and thereafter in the Nabataean–Roman and Byzantine periods."[53] That would take in the period under discussion, but until much more work is done by the archaeologists in Edom we cannot be certain of the precise situation in exilic and postexilic times.

## 4. *Sites in Judah*

Several sites in the Negeb of Judah throw further light on the historical circumstances of our period. Notable are those to the east of Beersheba-Khirbet Gharrah, Khirbet Ghazzeh, Tell Milh, Khirbet Mishash, Khirbet Arʾareh (Aroer of the Bible), and Site 306,[54] all of which were in an area fortified against just such contingencies as transpired at the time of the downfall of Judah. Some were originally formidable fortresses but pottery remains show they came to an end in the sixth century and were never rebuilt. They must have been overwhelmed by invaders from the east, i.e., by Edomites under pressure from Babylonians and then Nabataeans. Khirbet Gharrah and Khirbet Ghazzeh were reoccupied in the Hellenistic period, the latter in the Persian period, but none attained the status of the earlier fortifications.

Of more help here are the excavations at Tell Arad, some twenty miles northeast of Beersheba, where twelve strata have been uncovered dating from EI I to the Mamluke period. Six strata from the period of the Hebrew kings reflect the fortunes of the country throughout its history. Strata VI (last

52. Cf. B. Rothenberg, "Ancient Copper Industries in the Western Arabah," *PEQ* (Jan.–June, 1962): 5–71 and Glueck's study of Edomite pottery from Tell el-Khaleifeh in *BASOR*, 188 (1967): 8–38.

53. *BASOR*, 188, p. 23.

54. Cf. Y. Aharoni, "The Negeb" in *Archaeology and Old Testament Study*, ed. by D. Winton Thomas (Oxford, 1967), pp. 384–403.

of the sixth-century occupation) and V (the Persian period) are of special interest. The city appears to have fallen victim to the pressures released by the Neo-Babylonian invasions of the west in 598 and 589, though there is some question as to the age of the masonry of the Israelite fortress.[55] What is of equal or greater importance is the batch of some two hundred ostraca, half of which are Aramaic and date from the Persian period. Most of them are receipts for oil, wine, cereals, or money delivered to specified individuals. From stratum VI comes the archive of Eliashib containing ostraca receipts for the delivery of bread, oil, wine, flour to designated persons.[56] Among these rather colorless but significant documents was one found in an unstratified locus but belonging to the same time as those of stratum VI. It is a military communication from Arad to Elisha, the commander of the outpost at Ramat-Negeb (cf. Josh. 19:8 = Khirbet Ghazzeh?) and reads as follows: "From Arad . . . and you shall send them to Ramat-Ne[geb by the han]d of Malkijah son . . . and to entrust them to Elisha son of Jeremiah at Ramath-Negeb, lest something befall the city. And the word of the king is with you on your soul (?). Behold I have sent to warn you: are not the men with Elisha, lest Edom come thither."[57] This is the only document so far that mentions Edom and refers to troop deployment in the expectation of an imminent attack upon Arad via its protective fortress at Ramat-Negeb. There was still a king in Judah, but whether it was Jehoiakim, as Aharoni suggests, connecting the ostracon with II Kings 24:2—Jer. 35:11 (see note 16 above) or Zedeqiah is not certain. In either event, Edom was in all probability responsible for the overthrow of Arad.

One other excavation may be considered here, i.e., En-Gedi which was an important settlement toward the end of the Judean monarchy (cf. Ezek. 47:10).[58] Strata V (from Josiah to ca. 582/1 B.C.) and IV (Persian period) are involved here. To judge from the many sherds from Tell Goren V,[59] a flourishing center must have existed there in the late sixth and early fifth centuries B.C. This occupation of the site was a relatively short one and was completely destroyed by conflagration, no doubt by the same forces

55. C. Nylander in *IEJ*, 17 (1967): 56–59.

56. For a discussion of two of these ostraca see *Yediot*, XXX (1966): 32–38.

57. Translation from the transcription of Y. Aharoni in *Qadmoniot*, Vol. 1, No. 3 (1968), p. 104, as follows: *mᶜrd . . . wšlḥtm ᵓtm rmt n[gb by] d mlkyhw bn . . . whpqydm ᶜl yd ᵓlyšᶜ bn yrmyhw brmt ngb pn yqrh ᵓt hᶜyr dbr. wdbr hmlk ᵓtkm bnbškm(?) hnh slḥty lhᶜyd bkm hᵓm hᵓnšm ᵓt ᵓlyšᶜ pn tbᵓ ᵓdm šmh*. See now Aharoni's treatment in *BASOR* 197 (1970): 16–27. Edom is further mentioned in another ostracon from Arad (*ibid.*, pp. 28–32).

58. For a report on the excavations there, see note 37 and *IEJ*, 14 (1964): 121–30 and 17 (1967): 133–43.

59. *En-Gedi Excavations in 1961–1962*, pp. 17–38.

responsible for the destruction of Arad at the same time. Evidence points to an early restoration with a thriving community beginning in the time of Darius I (522–485) and continuing through that of Darius II (424–405 B.C.) after which it went into a rapid decline, a victim of the same upheavals suffered by other areas of Judah, due to nomadic incursions which forced a migration of peoples. In view of the *yhd* stamps it would appear that the people active in the level IV period were Jews, not Edomites. Perhaps the Persian intervention reported in I Esd. 4:50 was effective in forcing their withdrawal from territory north of Hebron or keeping them out of it.[60]

Archaeological discoveries so far reflect the same unsettled and indefinite situation portrayed in the Bible. One definite exception is the Eliashib ostracon which warns against an impending Edomite attack. Perhaps more important, surface and excavational results thus far support the territorial settlement status given by the Chronicler in Neh. 11:25–30. So far, *yhd-yhwd* stamps have not been found outside those limits.[61] On the other hand, Edomite names occur in documents from the time of Darius I, Xerxes, Artaxerxes I, and Darius II (whose mother's name was Cosmartidene, Ctes. *Pers.* 44).[62] Among the families of Nethinim was Barqos (Ezr. 2:53; Neh. 7:55; I Esd. 5:32). That is about as far as we can go at present.

60. Cf. Y. Aharoni, *The Land of the Bible* (Philadelphia: Westminster Press, 1967), map p. 363, and remarks by Albright quoted in note 34.

61. So far only at Jerusalem, Ramat Rahel, Bethany, Jericho, En-gedi, Tell en-Nasbeh, Azekah and Gezer.

62. Cf. H. Zimmern, *Die Keilinschriften und das Alte Testament von Eberhard Schrader* (3rd. ed.; Berlin: Reuther and Reichard, 1903), p. 472f.

# The Scene on the Drinking Mug from Ugarit

MARVIN H. POPE

A DRINKING mug decorated with a painted scene was exhumed in the 24th campaign of excavations at Ras Shamra-Ugarit. The excavator, M. Claude F. A. Schaeffer, first published a photograph of one side of the cup in a preliminary report.[1] A bearded figure wearing a high tiara with a streamer sits on a stool and holds in his raised right hand a drinking vessel. In front of the figure is seen the edge of a stand or table and above the stand part of a large pot. Behind the stool is seen the tail of a fish. The background of the scene is filled in with dots (Fig. 1). M. Schaeffer supposed that the painting represents a sacrificial meal of the god El and he related the scene to a text found near the mug, a text which treats part of a banquet or sacrificial meal (*dbḥ*).[2] M. Schaeffer presented a tantalizing report of the content of the text based on the preliminary study of M. Virolleaud. The chief points were reported to be as follows: El holds a banquet in his house and invites the gods. They eat venison and drink wine to satiety and drunkenness. There arises some sort of dissension involving the goddesses ᶜAštart and ᶜAnat and El goes to his *marziḥ* and drinks to intoxication and then returns to his palace and is confronted by a being with horns and a tail (*bᶜl qrnm wḏnb*) which Virolleaud supposes was a sort of devil, to be compared with the Syrian Rešef and the Babylonian Nergal. It seems to be a

1. "Neue Entdeckungen in Ugarit," *AfO* 20 (1963): 206–16. Photo of the mug, Fig. 30.
2. Op. cit. p. 214, "El als Gastgeber."

Fig. 1. Drinking mug with painted scene, after photo *AfO* 20 (1963): 211, Fig. 30.

case of divine delirium tremens. Still worse, El is beset with diarrhea and enuresis and ends in a most pitiable mess.

M. Schaeffer has since published articles with drawings (Fig. 2) of the entire scene which extend around the mug.[3] In these articles the scene on the mug is more explicitly related to the venerable bon vivant El, whose con-

3. "Le culte d'El à Ras Shamra et le veau d'or," *CRAIBL* (April–June, 1966): 327–38, Fig. 1. Also "Nouveaux témoinages du culte d'El et de Baal à Ras Shamra et ailleurs en Syrie-Palestine," *Syria* XLIII (1966): 1–19, Fig. 1.

Fig. 2. The mug scene as sketched by L. Curtois, *Syria* XLIII (1966): 3. See note 3 below.

viviality is somewhat diminished by the infirmities of senility. This insight fits well with the picture sketched elsewhere of El's latter day condition,[4] but is not the interest of this paper. The text to which M. Schaeffer related the scene on the mug has now been published[5] and the writer has discussed it in another place and in another connection.[6] There is no point in considering the text here since it has no special relevance to the scene in question.

The present concern is to consider certain features of the scene on the mug, especially the new part revealed by L. Curtois' drawing of the entire scene (Fig. 2). According to Schaeffer, the stand in front of the god supports a large plate on which are servings of food, while above, the ceramist painter has sketched a large jar, of which only half remains. The break has also obscured the upper part of a figure who prepares to pour some wine in the goblet of the god (El). Behind this figure there is an equid having the appearance or carriage of a colt or foal. The dots in the background Schaeffer took to represent stars. No mention is made of the fish which appears at the rear of the equid.

At first glimpse of the full scene, there came to the writer's mind a sequence of episodes in the longest of the Ugaritic mythological texts so far exhumed.

4. Cf. M. Pope, *E(l in the) U(garitic) T(exts)* (1955), pp. 32–42, "El's Seniority and Senility," "El as Bull: His Marital Relations."

5. *Ugaritica V* (*Mission de Ras Shamra XVI*). Institute Français d'Archéologie de Beyrouth Bibliothèque Archéologique et Historique LXXX. Ed. J. Nougayrol, E. Laroche, C. Virolleaud, C. F. A. Schaeffer (Paris: Imprimerie National, 1968). Text 1 (RS 24.258), pp. 545–51.

6. In a contribution to a volume of essays in honor of W. F. Stinespring, to be published by Duke University Press.

In the second column of this text,[7] the goddess Asherah, erstwhile spouse of El and mother of the gods, is performing some sort of ritual. She discards her clothing in the sea, puts a vessel on the fire, and entreats or beseeches El:

| | |
|---|---|
| . . . her clothing, the covering of her flesh. | npynh . mks . bšrh |
| She doffed her raiment in the sea, | tmt$^{c}$ . mdh . bym . |
| Her clothing in the river. | ṯn . npynh . bnhrm |
| She put a pot on the fire, | štt . ḫptr . lišt |
| A ewer atop the coals. | ḫbrṯ . lẓr . pḥmm |
| She entreated the Bull El Benign, | t$^{c}$pp . ṯr . il dpid |
| Besought the Creator of Creatures. | tǵẓy . bny . bnwt |

(*UT* 51/CTCA 4, II, 5–11)

Now the puzzling thing is that El is not present during this performance because the text says, immediately following the lines cited above, that Asherah looked up and saw Baal and $^{c}$Anat coming and she became hysterical for fear that some mishap had befallen her children.[8]

7. The Ugaritic Texts are given double citation, first the notation of C. H. Gordon, *U(garitic) T(extbook)*, 1965, and secondly the number assigned by A. Herdner, *C(orpus) des T(extes) en C(uneiformes) Alphabétiques*, 1963. It is not yet practical to switch to Herdner's numbers since the Corpus is incomplete; cf. *JBL* 68 (1966) on the plea for adoption of the Corpus numbers.

8. The episode alluded to here has not been identified with certainty in the Ugaritic mythological texts, so far as I know. There is an allusion to fratricide by Baal in text 12 (*BH* of the original editors, *UT* 75/*CTCA* 12) where we find Baal brought low by a stratagem of El who had sent the divine handmaids of Asherah out into the wilderness equipped with obstetrical paraphernalia—birthstool and swaddling bands—there to give birth to bovine monsters called Eaters and Rippers, with horns like bulls, humps like buffalo, and faces like Baal. The expectation is that Baal will encounter them and, being an avid buffalo hunter (as we learn from text 1, II, 1–12 where Baal takes his bow and resorts to the canebreaks of Lake Šamaḫ, the ancient name of Lake Huleh, which teems with buffalo) will attempt to take them on foot. Although the sequel is fragmentary, the strategem apparently worked for in the middle of column II of that text we find Baal prostrate in a swamp (?) (*mšmš*) with fever in his loins. The reason for this predicament is apparently given in ll. 47–48: "For he wears like a garment his brothers' blood / Like a robe the blood of his kin." The Elkunirsa text, a Canaanite–Hurrian myth in Hittite language, refers to fratricide by Baal. Asherah attempted to seduce Baal and threatened him with her spindle when he refused. Baal went and complained to her husband, Elkunirsa, and reported that beside urging him to lie with her and threatening him, she impugned her husband's potency. Elkunirsa's response to Baal was, "Go, sleep with her! [Lie with] my [wi]fe and humble her!" [So Baal] hearkened to the [wo]rd of Elkunirsa and [went] to Asherah. Baal spoke to Asherah: I have killed seventy-seven of yo[ur children], (yea) eighty-eight have I slain. Asherah heard [this h]umiliating report and was grieved in her mind. She appointed [lame]nting women and she [began] to [lame]nt for seven years." In a later episode there appears to have been a reconciliation between Asherah and her husband and she agreed to sleep with him and Elkunirsa agreed

| | |
|---|---|
| Lifting her eyes, she spied, | bnši.ʿnh.wtphn |
| The coming of Baal Asherah did see, | hlk.bʿl.aṯ}t{rt ktʿn |
| The coming of Virgin ʿAnat, | hlk.btlt.ʿnt |
| The onrush of the Peoples' [Progenitress] | tdrq.ybmt.[limm]. |
| With her the legs [shook], | bh.pʿnm [tṭṭ |
| [Be]hind her loins [broke], | bʿ]dn.ksl [h tṯbr |
| [Above her fa]ce did [sweat], | ʿln p]nh.t[dʿ] |
| [The joints] of her lo[ins] quivered, | tǵṣ [pn]t [ks]lh |
| Those of [her] back grew weak. | anš.dt.ẓr[h] |
| She lifted her voice and cried, | tšu.gh.wtṣḥ |
| "Why comes Mighty[Ba]al? | ik.mǵy.aliyn [b]ʿl |
| Why comes Vi[r]gin ʿAnat? | ik.mǵyt.b[t]lt ʿnt. |
| My Smiters, Or [Smi]ters of my children, | mḫṣy hm [m]ḫṣ bny |
| Destroyers of the Band of my Brood? | h[m.mkly.ṣ]brt aryy. |
| . . . silver Asherah did spy, | [ ].ksp.[aṯ]rt ktʿn |
| Glimmer of silver and glint of gold. | ẓl.ksp.wn[r] ḫrṣ |
| Dame A[sherah] of the Sea rejoiced. | šmḫ rbt.a[ṯrt] ym |

But Baal and ʿAnat explain the purpose of their visit, which is to request Asherah to entreat El to grant permission for Baal to build himself a house. Passing lightly over details not essential to our present interest, there is in the next column a sort of flashback to an episode in which the divine slave girls at Baal's table had done something so obscene that Baal stands and spits in the midst of the assembly of the gods.[9] Then the story returns to Baal and ʿAnat and their call to Asherah to enlist her aid in entreating El. In the succeeding column, Asherah orders her divine lackey to saddle her mount, and she goes off to entreat El:

| | |
|---|---|
| Qadesh and Amurru obeyed. | yšmʿ.qd š wamr[r] |
| He saddled the stallion, | mdl.ʿr. |
| Harnessed the stud ass, | ṣmd.pḥl |

to hand over Baal to Asherah so she could punish him, whether for the insult of refusing to lie with her or for the killing of her children, or both, is not clear. Cf. H. A. Hoffner, Jr., "The Elkunirsa Myth Reconsidered," *RHA* XXIII (1965): fascicle 76, pp. 5–16. It seems altogether likely that both the Ugaritic and the Hittite text have reference to a single complex of common myth. J. Gray treated text 10 in detail (*JNES* 10 [1951]: 146–55), but did not consider the parallels just cited.

9. Cf. *JCS* I (1947): 240f., n. 28. We still do not know what the divine serving wenches did that so disgusted Baal, but it must have been most unseemly since Baal himself was not noted for delicacy.

| | |
|---|---|
| Put on silver harness, | št.gpnm.dt.ksp |
| Golden housings, | dt.yrq.nqbnm |
| Prepared her she-ass' trappings. | ʿdb.gpn.atnth |
| Qadesh and Amurru embraced, | yḫbq.qdš.wamrr |
| Put Asherah on the back of the stallion, | yštn.aṯrt.lbmt.ʿr |
| On the beauteous back of the stud. | lysmsmt.bmt.pḫl |
| Qadesh began to glow, | qdš.yuḫdm.šbʿr |
| Amurru like a star. | amrr.kkbkb. |
| Ahead went Virgin ʿAnat | lpnm aṯr.btlt.ʿnt |
| While Baal returned to lofty Sapan. | wbʿl.tbʿ.myrm.ṣpn |
| Then did she set face | idk.lttn.pnm |
| Toward El at the confluence of the Rivers, | ʿm.il.mbk.nhrm |
| Midst the channels of the Deeps. | qrb.apq.thmtm |
| She penetrated El's domain and entered | tgly.ḏd.il.wtbu |
| The pavilion of the King, Father of Exalted Ones.[10] | qrš.mlk.ab.šnm |
| At El's feet she bowed and fell, | lpʿn.il.thbr.wtql |
| Did obeisance and honored him. | tštḥwy.wtkbdh |
| When El did see her, | hlm.il.kyphnh |
| He spread his gullet and laughed, | yprq.lṣb.wyṣḥq |
| Stamped his feet on the footstool, | pʿnh.lhdm.yṯpd. |
| Twiddled his fingers, | wykrkr uṣbʿth. |
| Lifted his voice and cried: | yšu.gh.wy[ṣḥ] |
| "Why comes Dame Asherah of the Sea, | ik.mǵyt.rbt.aṯr[t y]m |
| Why comes the Progenitress of the Gods? | ik.atwt.qnyt.i[lm] |
| Thou art surely famished, having journeyed. | rǵb.rǵbt.wtǵt [ ] |
| Thou art surely thirsty, having travelled. | hm.ǵmu.ǵmit.wʿs [ ] |
| Eat, yea drink. | lḥm.hm.štym. |
| Eat from the tables food, | lḥ[m] bṯlḥnt.lḥm |
| Drink from the jars wine, | št[y] bkrpnm.yn. |
| From a gold cup the blood of the vine. | bk⟨s⟩.ḫrṣ dm.ʿṣm. |
| King El's love will excite you, | hm.yd.il mlk yḫssk |
| The Bull's ardor arouse you." | ahbt.ṯr.tʿrrk |
| | (*UT* 51/CTCA 4 IV, 8–39) |

10. Cf. *EUT*, pp. 61–81, on the nature and location of El's abode, and p. 32f. on the meaning of *šnm* in El's title *mlk ab šnm*.

Asherah ignored the amorous overtures of her sometime spouse and proceeded immediately to the point of her mission, the intercession for Baal to gain permission to build a house. Again we pass over many interesting details and problems[11] in order to get back to the scene on the drinking mug. The intention is to show that almost every feature in the scene can be related to details in the episodes just cited from the Ugaritic text.

There is no reason to question M. Schaeffer's assumption that the seated figure with the raised cup represents El in a hospitable attitude. But who is the figure behind the stand with the large vessel? The size of the figure is commensurate with that of the seated god and we cannot tell whether it is human or divine. We may, however, safely assume that it is a deity, in view of the manifest mythological character of the scene. The gender of the figure in question is uncertain. There is no sign of clothing on it, but neither is there any discernible raiment on the seated figure. The head of the standing figure is abraded, but what remains shows the Hathor-type coiffure which suggests that the figure is female. (Hair style is, of course, not a reliable evidence of gender at any time.) Turning attention now to the stand and the large vessel above it, M. Schaeffer took the cone-shaped heaps to be servings of food. He remarked simply that the ceramist painter had sketched a large jar above. He failed to notice that the legs of the vessel seem to be resting on top of what is supposed to be food. It would be rather odd to place a pot thus on top of food. It is, therefore, suggested that the mounds between the stand and the pot represent charcoal. All the details thus match the scene in which Asherah removed her clothing, put a vessel on top of the coals, and entreated Bull El Benign.

A word about the terms applied to the vessel placed on the fire—it is called in one line *ḫptr* and in the parallel line *ḫbrṯ*. Both of these terms are Hurrian loanwords designating cult vessels of metal, gold, and copper, occurring in inventories from Qatna, Nuzi, and Alalaḫ, the Akkadian vocalizations being *ḫuppataru*[12] and *ḫuprušḫu*.[13] If the vessel in the scene on our drinking

11. On the estrangement of El and Asherah, cf. *EUT*, p. 37 and n. 8, above, on the Hittite parallel in the relations of Elkunirsa and Asherah. For a different interpretation, cf. A. Van Selms, *Marriage and Family Life in Ugaritic Literature*, pp. 63ff., and the writer's criticism, *JBL* 74 (1955): 293f.

12. *CAD* 6, 238b. Among the inventories of objects treated by Ventris and Chadwick, *Documents in Mycenaean Greek* (Cambridge, 1959), there is *o-pi-te-te-re* (PY 251 = Vn 02.5), which is suggested (p. 330, 402) to designate a lid or cover, cf., *epiṯema*, Homeric *epiṯēma*. The Greek etymology appears to encounter some phological difficulties, while the syllabification *o-pi-te-te-re* is strikingly close to the Akkadian form *ḫu-up-pa-ta-ru*.

13. The vessel termed *ku-ru-su-pa*, Ventris and Chadwick, op. cit. p. 237, no. 207, p. 324, Fig. 16, is a squat globular amphora with three legs on a tripod stand, virtually identical with what is depicted atop the coals of the brazier in the scene on the drinking mug from

mug can be connected with that mentioned in the second column of our text (*UT* 51/CTCA 4, 8–9) we have a pictorial representation of said vessel. For the equid in the scene M. Schaeffer offered no explanation. In the episode which we have cited Dame Asherah of the Sea mounted her ass to journey to the abode of El and carry out the request of Baal and ᶜAnat to entreat El for approval of Baal's desire to build a house for himself. Little can be said about the equid in the drawing, but the designations of the text suggest asinine rather than equine character. One should not, however, press Ugaritic poetic parallelism for consistency in detail, since the text is not even consistent about the gender of the beast; four times it is designated as masculine and once as feminine.

The dots which form the background of the scene were supposed by Schaeffer to represent stars, but they do not exhibit points or other astroid features. The presence of the fish suggests that the dots represent water and this accords with the explicitly attested watery nature of El's abode. Asherah also is connected with the Sea, and, therefore, the fish could be associated with her, but since the scene is set in El's watery domain, it seems more likely that the fish is part of El's environs.

A further detail, which Schaeffer did not discuss, also finds explication in the Ugaritic passage in question. In the upper left hand corner of the scene hovers a bird and this, it is suggested, represents the eavesdropping goddess ᶜAnat. When Asherah set out on her journey to visit El in order to intercede on Baal's behalf, we are told that Anat went ahead while Baal returned to his abode. Nothing is said in this instance about ᶜAnat's mode of locomotion, but in several other passages we are informed that she flies:

| | |
|---|---|
| She lifted wing, did Virgin ᶜAnat, | tšu knp btlt.ᶜn[t] |
| She lifted wing and shot aloft. | tšu.knp.wtr.bᶜp [ ] |
| | (*UT* 76/CTCA 10, II, 10–11) |

When ᶜAnat wished to slay the young hero Aqht in order to get the marvelous composite bow which he had refused to relinquish to her in return for immortality or love, she put her agent Yṭpn in her girdle and hovered among the eagles soaring above the youth as he sat down to eat. She released the aquiline assassin to strike the hapless youth on the head and pour out his life.

---

Ugarit. Ventris and Chadwick cite the Hittite–Hurrian *ḫuprušḫ* in relation to the *ku-ru-su-pa*. The forms of the vessels are virtually identical and the designations are sufficiently similar to suggest common origin.

| | |
|---|---|
| She took Yṭpn, Warrior of the Lady, | tqḫ.yṭpn.mhr.št |
| She put him like an eagle in her girdle, | tštn.knšr.bḥbšh |
| Like a hawk in her scabbard. | km.diy btᶜrth. |
| Aqht when he sat to eat, | aqht.km.yṯb.llḥ[m] |
| Danel's son to dine, | bn.dnil.lṯrm. |
| Over him soared eagles, | ᶜlh.nšr[m].trḫpn. |
| Cruised a flight of hawks. | ybṣr.ḥbl.diy[m |
| Among the eagles soared ᶜAnat; | bn] nšrm trḫp.ᶜnt |
| Over Aqht she put him. | ᶜl [aqht] tᶜdbnh. |
| He struck him twice on the head, | hlmn.ṯnm [qdqd] |
| Thrice above the ear; | ṯlṯid.ᶜl.udn |
| Po[ured out like] a slayer his blood, | š[pk km] šiy.dmh. |
| Like a butch[er to his knees]. | km.šḫ[t lbrkh] |
| His soul expired like wind, | yṣat.km.rḥ.npš [h |
| [Like a breath] his spirit, | km iṯl] brlth. |
| Like smoke [from his nostrils]. | km qṭr.[baph] |

(*UT* 3 Aqht/CTCA 18, 27–37)

One of the new mythological texts recently published in Ugaritica V also mentions ᶜAnat's volatile nature:

| | |
|---|---|
| Then drank ᶜAnat the Mighty, | w tšt.ᶜnt.gṯr |
| Lady of Dominion, Lady of Power, | bᶜlt mlk.bᶜ (7) lt.drkt |
| Lady of High Heaven, [Lad]y of . . . [14] | bᶜlt.šmm.rmm (8) [bᶜl]t.kpṯ |
| Even ᶜAnat, Super Flyer, | wᶜnt.di.dit. |
| She who soars . . . . | rḫpt (9) [ ]rm |

(Ugaritica V, text 2 (*RS* 24.252) obv. 6–9)

ᶜAnat's counterpart in Greek mythology, the winged Athena, also assumed full bird form on occasion.[15]

When Asherah had presented Baal's plea for permission to build a house, and had elicited from El a conditional response which she interpreted as

14. Virolleaud (*Ugaritica* V, pp. 553, 555) renders *kpṯ* as "ce bas monde," assuming that it is not a question of synonym with the preceding *šmm rmm*, "High Heaven," but of antithesis. Accordingly, he appeals to Akkadian *kapašu* and Hebrew *kbš*, "le sol que l'on foule aux pieds." Hebrew *kbš*, however, offers other possible meanings related to assault, sexual and otherwise, which comport with ᶜAnat's violent tendencies. Akkadian *kabāšu*, "be stubborn," is also a possibility. Moreover, it is not clear whether Akkadian and Hebrew *kb/pš* are connected with *kbs*, "tread down," or with a different root *kb/pṯ*. Arabic *kbṯ* which is used of alteration and deterioration of meat offers little help. It may be that Virolleaud's conjecture is correct as to the meaning of *kpṯ*, but pending additional data the matter remains undecided.

15. Cf. Jack Lindsay, on "Birds and Goddesses," *The Clashing Rocks*, pp. 63–69, 404–7.

consent, she praised El for his wisdom and assured him that now Baal would give his rain in season. At the suggestion that Baal should be informed of the permission, ʿAnat sprang into action. Although nothing is said about ʿAnat during Asherah's entreaty of El, the circumstances indicate that she was present and listening to the conversation. She had gone on ahead of Asherah and had eavesdropped on the conversation with El, presumably hovering or perched as a bird, and now, immediately on the conclusion of the matter, without waiting for the matronly Asherah to return as she had gone, riding on her ass, she flew to carry the news to Baal.

| | |
|---|---|
| Virgin ʿAnat rejoiced, | šmḫ. btlt. ʿnt. |
| Thrust (with) her feet and shot (from) earth. | tdʿṣ pʿnm. wtr. arṣ |
| Then did she set face | idk. lttn. pnm |
| Toward Baal (on) the heights of Ṣapān, | ʿm. bʿl. mrym. ṣpn |
| (Over) a thousand fields, a myriad acres. | balp. šd. rbt. kmn |
| Virgin ʿAnat laughed. | ṣḥq. btlt. ʿnt |
| She lifted her voice and cried: | tš u gh. wtṣḥ |
| "Receive glad tidings, O Baal; | tbšr bʿl |
| Thy good news I bring." | bšrtk. yblt |

(*UT* 51/CTCA 4, IV–V, 82–89)

ʿAnat, because of her mode of travel, was the speediest of the deities. In one instance, in the ʿAnat Text, when Baal sent his messengers to her with a request that she hurry to him to hear a secret message, ʿAnat dispatched the messengers with a reference to their slowness and her speed, and the distance to be covered.

| | |
|---|---|
| "Moreover an additional word I will say. | ap. mṯn. rgmm. argmn |
| Go, Go, divine servitors. | lk. lk. ʿnn. ilm |
| You are slow, and I am fast. | atm. bštm. wan. šnt |
| Ugr is indeed distant, O gods. | uǵr. lrḥq. ilm |
| Inbb is distant, O deities. | inbb lrḥq. ilnym |

(*UT* ʿnt/CTCA 3, IV, 75–79)

She then set out and apparently reached Baal's abode ahead of the messengers whose return is not recounted.

The Elkunirsa Myth furnishes an explicit parallel to the motif which is implicit in the Ugaritic myth. There ʿAnat-ʿAstarte, in order to eavesdrop on a boudoir conversation between Elkunirsa and his dissatisfied spouse Asherah, assumed the form of a bird and then flew to Baal to tell what she had learned:

"Anat-Astarte heard these words. She turned herself into an *owl* on Elkunir[sa's] *arm*, (yea) she became a *screech-owl* and perched on his *shoulder*. (There) she overhears the words which the husband and wife speak to each other. Elkunirsa and his wife came to her bed and slept with each other. But ᶜAnat-Astarte like a bird flew off across the desert places. In the desert places she found Baal, and [she said] to him [. . . ]."[16]

The motif of the telltale bird is commonplace in folklore, as reflected in Aḥiqar's words (1. 98):

> Above all you guard, guard your mouth.
> Concerning what you hear, harden the mind.
> For a word is (like) a bird
> Which a man who releases it cannot (re)capture.

in the words of Qohelet:

> Even in your thoughts don't revile (the) king,
> Nor in your bed chamber (the) rich.
> For a bird of heaven may transmit the sound,
> A winged creature tell (the) matter.
> (Eccles. 10:20)

and the expression "a little bird told me."[17]

Every major detail in the scene on the mug is thus accounted for in the first half of the Ugaritic Myth II AB. The seated figure with raised cup is El. The nude (?) figure standing behind the ewer atop the coals on the brazier is Asherah entreating El as described in columns II–IV of the text. The equid, which would ordinarily seem passing strange in aqueous environs, is the mount on which the goddess has just arrived. And finally the bird represents a metamorphosis of the Virgin ᶜAnat, Baal's versatile and volatile sister, who here eavesdrops as in the Elkunirsa myth.

It seems likely that the scene on the cup was actually conceived and executed in illustration of the episode related in the text II AB.

16. Cf. H. A. Hoffner, Jr. op. cit., pp. 76ff.

17. Cf. T. H. Gaster, *Myth, Legend and Custom in the Old Testament* (1969), p. 838. In an African myth the bird was given a crest to distinguish it as a messenger. *Mythology of All Races*, vol. VII, pp. 169f.

Fig. 3. C. F. A. Schaeffer, *Syria* XVIII (1937): pl. 17 and pp. 128–34.

This scene on the drinking cup naturally reminded Schaeffer of similar motifs on a monument which he had discovered earlier, the limestone stela uncovered in 1936 in the workshop of a sculptor of religious images near the temple of Baal (Fig. 3). Schaeffer's identification of the principal figure on this stela as El, the Father of the Gods, has been generally accepted, although there is no epigraphic confirmation. The god is seated on a throne with a footstool; he wears a beard with a curved point and is coiffed with an elaborate tiara decorated with a pair of horns. Facing the seated god is a standing figure coiffed with a high tiara decorated with a uraeus. The lowered left hand holds a pitcher similar to that in the right hand of the standee in the scene on the drinking mug. The raised right hand extends toward the god something which Schaeffer sees as a scepter topped by a bovine head with lowered horns. The standing figure, according to Schaeffer, is the king of Ugarit worshiping the supreme god of the Ugaritic pantheon. The god El receives the king with a gesture of benediction, left hand raised with palm turned out, while in the right hand he extends the goblet to receive the king's drink offering. In the field above the god and the officiant is engraved the winged solar disc which, Schaeffer believes, supports Dussaud's attribution of solar character to El.

There is no reason to doubt that the seated figure represents El in the relief on the limestone stela as well as in the painting on the drinking mug. There are, however, misgivings about the identification of the standee on the stela as the king of Ugarit. The uraeus on the headdress is no assured evidence of royalty, since that emblem is also worn by deities. As for the object in the raised right hand, it is impossible to detect in the available photographs the bovine features discerned by Schaeffer. The writer has shown photographs of the stela to several disinterested persons with good eyesight and the regular reaction has been that the termination of the object held in the right hand appears to be serpentine rather than bovine. There is a break in the painting on the drinking mug, so that it is impossible to tell what, if anything, was held in the raised hand of the standing figure. Moreover, the gender of the standee in both instances is uncertain. The initial surmise of innocent viewers of the stela was often that the standing figure is female. We have already given arguments for the femininity of the standee in the scene on the drinking mug. The similarities on the principal figures of both scenes suggest that we may have merely variant versions of the same motif or episode.

The omission on the stela of various details presented on the mug scene, the stand, brazier and ewer, the equid, fish, and bird, could be attributed to lack of space and greater difficulty of executing such detail in stone.

Whether the scene on the stela is related to that on the mug has no crucial bearing on the interpretation here given to the latter.

# Remarks on the Method of Comparative Mythology

HELMER RINGGREN

THE comparative study of Old Testament ideas and Near Eastern mythology has often been made on the basis of occasional similarities in certain details without asking what place these details occupy in the total structure of each religion. On the other hand, the "patternistic" approach of S. H. Hooke and his followers has been accused—with some reason—of forcing an artificially unified view on religions which are, in principle, different and making similar details mean what they do not actually mean in the context of each religion. Both these approaches seem somewhat inadequate in so far as each of them does not take into account the whole complexity of the problem. For a complete analysis both the details and the way they are combined into a pattern are essential. To exemplify this statement, we shall analyze some of the most interesting cases of similarity in the mythology of the ancient Near East and the Old Testament.

The Gilgamesh Epic first attracted the interest of biblical students because of the story of the flood included in tablet XI of the epic. On the other hand, there are a number of other items which form interesting parallels to biblical texts, though this is not generally observed.

The general theme of the Gilgamesh Epic is the mortality of man; in other words, the aim of the epic is to explain why man is not immortal. In this respect, the epic ranges among the great number of myths from various parts of the world which set out to explain why man is mortal, generally referring to either a crime or a mistake as the reason why man lost his original immortality.[1] There may be some doubt as to whether or not the Gilgamesh Epic is correctly classified as a myth, because it has no certain ritual background. On the other hand, if we accept the wider definition of myth, as used by Cl. Lévi-Strauss and others,[2] it may well be included in that category, since it does explain the present conditions of man by telling a story from primeval times. From another point of view, however, the Gilgamesh Epic is quite clearly a literary work, whose author has utilized a number of earlier Sumerian epics, using what was fitting to his purpose and rejecting material that did not serve his ends.[3]

Brandon has called attention to a number of interesting parallels in detail between the Gilgamesh Epic and the story of the Fall in Ge. 3.[4] These include the fact that it is a woman (a courtesan, Eve) who "seduces the type-figure of a primitive man (Enkidu, Adam) from his original innocence . . . on the course that leads inevitably to death";[5] further, the fact that the seduction involves the giving of sexual knowledge or experience,[6] and the idea that this knowledge makes man "like God" (Gilg. V, iv, 34, "You are wise, Enkidu, you have become like a god," Gen. 3:5, "you shall become like God, knowing good and evil"); at the same time, the acquisition of a certain amount of civilization is involved in both cases (Enkidu learns civilized life and loses his contact with the animals, Adam and Eve discover their nakedness and God makes clothes for them); finally it is a serpent who is the real culprit of the drama; in Gilg. by snatching away the plant of life, in Gen. by setting the whole course of events into movement. A somewhat more remote parallel is provided by the occurrence of the *plant* of life and the *tree* of life respectively.[7] Thus there are a number of details, all connected with one specific problem of human life, which are the same in both stories but have been fitted into a context that is different in each instance based on different presuppositions.

The interesting point is that all these parallels are found in those parts of the Gilgamesh Epic that have no known Sumerian counterpart. In other

1. Cf., e.g., H. Abrahamsson, *The Origin of Death* (Uppsala, 1951).
2. *The Structural Study of Myth and Totemism*, ed. E. Leach (A.S.A. Monographs, 5), London, 1967.
3. S. N. Kramer, *JAOS* 64 (1944): 7–23, cf. R. de Vaux, *VT Suppl.* I (1953): 186.
4. S. G. F. Brandon, *Creation Legends of the Ancient Near East* (London: Hodder & Stoughton, 1963), pp. 131ff.
5. Ibid., p. 132.
6. The problem of the meaning of *daʿath* in Gen. 3 is not solved by this statement. It does not mean to suggest that "sexual knowledge" exhausts the meaning of the term, only that sexual elements are involved. The concept has several other overtones, including that of *divine* knowledge, not accessible to man.
7. It is wrong to treat these two symbols as identical, though they both stand for "life." See my remarks in *JSS* 13 (1968): 298.

words, they belong to a stratum of the Gilgamesh tradition which is definitely Semitic, perhaps even influenced by West Semitic ideas.[8]

The same problem has occupied mythopoeic thought in other connections. In Mesopotamia there is also the Adapa myth which in a very paradoxical way tells the story of a man's prideful rebellion against the divine order and his consequent missing the food of life and water of life offered to him. No particular details remind us of either the Gilgamesh Epic or the Story of the Fall. It represents an entirely different answer to the question of man's mortality, and the whole story is taken up by this one theme.

In Ugaritic mythology, again, conditions are different. The problem is touched upon rather superficially in a context that does not suggest that this is the essential point of the story. In the Epic of Aqhat we are told that Aqhat had been given an especially fine bow, but the goddess Anat got interested in the bow and wanted to have it. But Aqhat refused to give it to her. Even when Anat promised him immortality he insisted that man was mortal, anyway, so that there was no use bargaining about it. This aroused the anger of Anat so that she made arrangements for killing him. This shows that man's mortality was a living issue in Ugarit, too, but it is interesting that the theme was developed in an entirely different context, even as a marginal motif in an epic that placed the main emphasis on quite other problems.[9]

Dealing with the Aqhat Epic, however, we cannot avoid noticing the far-reaching parallelism between this epic and the Baal cycle. Aqhat dies a violent death, just as Baal; the consequence in both cases is that vegetation withers and life declines on earth; and finally, just as Baal's sister Anat sets out to rescue her brother and restore him to life, Aqhat's sister, *Pġt*, makes arrangement to recover her brother and bring him back to life. Unfortunately, the rest of the Aqhat text is lost so that we do not know the results of her efforts. But there is every probability that she was ultimately successful and that Aqhat returned to life.[10]

How is this parallelism to be interpreted? Do the two cycles reflect the same ritual background, i.e., the death and resurrection of the fertility god? Or should they rather be regarded as literary variations of a basic motif, which might, of course, have originated in the celebrations of the fertility

8. It is difficult to decide whether or not this has any implications with regard to the origin of the various parts of the epic and the relative chronology of the mythological elements. Is it possible that some of the mythological elements that the Old Testament has in common with Accadian literature have moved from West to East instead of vice versa, as is generally assumed?

9. A. S. Kapelrud, *The Violent Goddess* (Oslo: Universitetsforlaget, 1969), pp. 72ff.

10. Ibid., pp. 70ff.

cult, but might also reflect more independent creations of the mythopoeic mind? The question is idle, since our knowledge of the cultic life at Ugarit is too limited to allow of a definite answer. But the fact remains: the Baal cycle and the Aqhat Epic are to some extent parallel in that they contain at least three identical mythological elements or motifs, and in the same order. On the other hand, they are combined with other elements in each of the two myths so as to form two entirely different bodies of mythology. For instance, as we have seen, the Aqhat story brings in the mortality/immortality motif, while the Baal cycle takes up the conflict with the sea and the building of Baal's house.

A third kind of myth that is of considerable significance in this context is the cosmogonic complex. In Accadian, Ugaritic, and Israelite texts, the conflict motif, involving the slaying of a dragon, is conspicuous. But this mythological element is differently utilized in the various religions in question. In the *Enūma Elish*, Marduk fights and kills Tiamat and then proceeds to the creation of the universe out of her body. In Ugaritic mythology the episode containing the conflict motif is a battle of kingship. Baal fights Yam, the Sea, and defeats him, thus putting an end to his reign and acquiring kingship for himself. Yam is also referred to as the River (*nhr*), the dragon (*tnn*) and the slippery serpent (*bṯn ᶜqltn*), also as Lotan (*ltn*). Not even an allusion is made to any kind of creation, though, as L. Fisher has pointed out, the acquisition of kingship might even be conceived as a creation in the sense of organizing the universe and establishing its order.[11]

Israel represents, as is well known, a kind of compromise. On one hand, there is a very strong emphasis on Yahweh's kingship in connection with creation, also at times including the fight against the dragon (Leviathan, Rahab, *tannîn*). This is obviously part of Israel's Canaanite heritage. On the other hand, there are several allusive references to *tᵉhôm* (i.e., Tiamat) as the entity defeated by Yahweh in the beginning. But in the creation story of Gen. 1 this motif has been "demythologized": *tᵉhôm* is more or less a lifeless matter; the waters obey God's authoritative word, the sun and moon and stars are not divine beings, but things,[12] and the *tannīnîm* are just one class of beings created by God to live in the water.

These observations raise a problem of methodology in the comparative investigation of myths. It is obvious that certain mythical elements can be present in various mythologies without the myths themselves being identical as totalities. One element—which obviously must be supposed to express a

11. L. Fisher, *VT* 15 (1965): 313ff.
12. Cf. the remarks by von Rad in his commentary on Genesis (Eng. trans. 1961).

certain limited idea—can be combined with one set of elements in one religion and with other sets of elements in other religions. In the case of the ancient Near East it is difficult to avoid the assumption that there is also some real historical connection when one element occurs in two or more places. It seems important for an analysis to break down the myths into small units and to ascertain where these units occur. It is also necessary to pay attention to the way these units are combined with one another, that is, to study the patterns and structures they form together with other units.[13]

It seems to me that in the case of the Near East such a study would not only disclose the structure of the myths in question but also give some hints as to historical processes underlying the growth of Near Eastern mythology. Is it a mere coincidence that those parts of the Gilgamesh Epic that contain units similar to units in biblical mythology are all among those which have no Sumerian counterpart? Do they derive from a common Semitic stock or are they to be interpreted as borrowings from the Western Semites (Amorites etc.)? It is interesting to notice that the conflict motif in the creation myth is also common to the West Semitic and the Accadian myths but absent from Sumerian mythology.

13. Another example of various forms of the same mythic element is provided by the text *RS* 24.245 published in *Ugaritica* V, pp. 553ff. The *verso* contains a combination of passages from V AB II, 31ff. and V AB III, 19ff. Is this a shorter version of the "usual" epic or a different myth utilizing the same elements? Another instance which was not discussed above is the use of the flood motif in (1) the Sumerian flood story, (2) the Atrahasis epic, (3) the Gilgamesh Epic, and (4) the Old Testament.

# The Ugaritic Texts and the Textual Criticism of the Hebrew Bible*

STANISLAV SEGERT

THE never ceasing work on the texts of the Hebrew Bible was in earlier periods restricted by the rather narrow textual basis of the original; this situation led to the frequent use of ancient versions for the reconstruction of the original, as well as to the extensive application of conjectural criticism. To a great extent the change in the approach to the text of the Hebrew Bible was caused by the discovery of new material which could be directly or indirectly utilized for studying the transmitted text.

The manuscripts found in caves of the Qumran region and in other caches in the Judaean desert provided scholars with a Hebrew text much older than those heretofore accessible, in some cases older by more than one millennium. Reliable and relevant results for textual criticism of the Old Testament, based on these manuscripts, were reached by applying methods which had been used with success before to establish the text of the Greek Bible, its New and Old Testaments.

The most important of these results is the application of the theory of local texts to the classification of the Hebrew biblical manuscripts dating from Pre-Christian times, which enabled William F. Albright to distinguish Palestinian, Egyptian, and Babylonian types of Hebrew biblical

* For friendly help in improving his English style, the author is obliged to his colleague in the Department of Near Eastern Languages, University of California, Los Angeles, Professor John B. Callender.

texts.[1] The method used for the Greek Bible gave good results also for the Hebrew Bible.

Textual criticism has been again challenged by the West Semitic texts which are older than any part of the Hebrew Bible. The first Ugaritic cuneiform tablets were found by Claude F.-A. Schaeffer in 1929, their decipherment by Hans Bauer, Paul Dhorme, and Charles Virolleaud was realized on the affinity of their language with biblical Hebrew. Since then many scholars have drawn from them substantial elucidation of words, constructions, literary forms, ideas, and rites of the Old Testament. The results of this research were presented in studies devoted to the Ugaritic texts—often in footnotes—in contributions to the Old Testament lexicography, grammar, prosody, literature, and religion. Even in synthetic studies which evaluated the relevance of Ugaritic texts for Old Testament research the results important to the text of the Hebrew Bible were presented in disconnected samples from various biblical books.[2]

The Ugaritic texts were used as documents of an older Canaanite culture which formed both positive and negative—or polemic—background for the development of Israel in Palestine. From the viewpoint of textual criticism, the Ugaritic material was used in this period mostly to interpret difficult passages. The original meaning of words and constructions which were not known in Hebrew tradition or in the ancient translations were now discovered. In most cases the Hebrew consonantal text was corroborated; its emendations, proposed to great extent on the basis of ancient versions, were proved to be unnecessary.

The application of the Ugaritic material to the Old Testament study has been done by many scholars in different countries. A great proportion of the commonly accepted results was contributed by William F. Albright, in both his pioneering observations and subsequent statements of synthesis.[3] Several pupils of Albright continued this research, using the Ugaritic material for the establishing of text and interpretation of some passages of the Hebrew Bible, mostly archaic poems.[4]

1. W. F. Albright, New Light on Early Recensions of the Hebrew Bible, *BASOR* 140 (1955): 27–33. F. M. Cross, The History of the Biblical Text in the Light of Discoveries in the Judaean desert, *HTR* 57 (1964): 281–99.

2. A bibliography of the relations between the Ugaritic texts and the Hebrew Bible is being prepared by Professor L. S. Fisher in Claremont, California.

3. Cf., i.a., The Oracles of Balaam, *JBL* 63 (1944): 207–33; The Psalm of Habakkuk, Studies in Old Testament Prophecy Presented to Th. H. Robinson (Edinburgh, 1950), pp. 1–18: A Catalogue of Early Hebrew Lyric Poems (Psalm 68), *HUCA* 33/1 (1950–51): 1–39. The most recent synthesis is in: *Yahweh and the Gods of Canaan* (Garden City, 1968).

4. F. M. Cross and D. N. Freedman, The Blessing of Moses, *JBL* 67 (1948): 191–210; Royal Song of Thanksgiving: II Samuel 22 = Psalm 18, *JBL* 72 (1953): 15–21; The Song

The first attempt to apply the results of Ugaritic and Phoenician studies to an entire book of the Old Testament was made by one of Albright's pupils, Mitchell Dahood; it was published in the commentary series of which Albright himself is senior editor.[5] The results of the new approach met with both consent and criticism; some of the critics acknowledged the right of the commentator to challenge the traditional views but did not find it appropriate to surprise the broad public unacquainted with the sophisticated methods of modern biblical studies with their results.[6] The criticism led Dahood to develop his methodical principles, used quite consistently in the establishing and interpretating of the text of the Psalms. The following remarks try to point out some general tendencies, and also trace some consequences to which the use of this methodical approach may lead.

The traditional approach to the Old Testament texts reckons always with the fact that the text of the Hebrew Bible was transmitted by long tradition. Dahood accepts the Hebrew consonantal text as a fixed and reliable basis, which does not need any change or improvement. This approach is generally applied either to autographs written by the author or to inscriptions which remained unchanged from remote times and were not affected by the adverse impact of textual transmission.

It is commonly known that even the author himself can commit some errors in writing his autograph, or he may introduce variants in correcting it.[7] The ancient inscriptions are not free from errors; some of them have been already detected and corrected by the stone-cutters.[8] The errors occurring in the Ugaritic alphabetic cuneiform tablets are of the same character as those committed in transmitting the manuscripts by copying.[9]

The current evaluation of doublets in the Old Testament, e.g., Psalms 14

---

of Miriam, *JNES* 14 (1955): 237–250. Cf. also M. H. Pope, Job (The Anchor Bible, 15) (Garden City, 1965); e.g., pp. XLV, XLVII, 60, 205.

5. M. Dahood, Psalm I, 1–50; Psalms II, 51–100 (The Anchor Bible, 16 and 17) (Garden City, 1964, 1968).

6. It is more than appropriate to keep informed all who are interested in the problems and incertitudes in the interpretation of the biblical texts; no results or even attempts should be concealed; the only point is the presentation, which has to elucidate even the difficult problems in a nontechnical language. Cf. i.a., S. Segert, *ArOr* 36 (1968): 461–62.

7. Cf. F. T. Bowers, Textual Criticism, *Encyclopaedia Britannica 21* (1968), pp. 918–23, esp. p. 918.

8. Cf. A. G. Woodhead, *The Study of Greek Inscriptions* (Cambridge, 1959), p. 9.

9. Cf. S. Segert, *Die Schreibfehler in den ugaritischen literarischen Keilschrifttexten, Von Ugarit nach Qumran, Festschrift für O. Eissfeldt* (Berlin, 1958), pp. 193–212; Die Schreibfehler in den ugaritischen nichtliterarischen Keilschrifttexten, *ZAW* 71 (1959): 23–32. Cf. J. C. Greenfield, *JAOS* 89 (1969): 175. Cf. also n. 12 below.

and 53,[10] is quite consistent with the general, commonly acknowledged principles of textual criticism: "If the unique text is in certain sections degraded to the rank of a variant-carrier, mistakes of the kinds which can be demonstrated in these sections may also be suspected to exist in those sections where we have no check."[11] The variants in the doublets challenged by Dahood are nontypical,[12] but the general principle is valid, even for the Ugaritic texts.[13] The common experience that the deviations affect the transmission of the text from its very beginning applies even for the texts with much shorter and better documented textual tradition. The evaluation of the variants of the consonantal text in the manuscripts from Qumran and Masada will be taken into consideration as they are published and evaluated.[14]

The concentration on the consonantal text as the only reliable basis for the establishing of the wording of the Hebrew Bible has as its corollary the devaluation of the traditions which accompany the consonantal frame, both the pronunciation as it is fixed in the vocalic signs attached much later to the consonants and the ancient versions reflecting a certain stage of traditional pronunciation and interpretation.

On one hand, Dahood admits that it is sometimes necessary to disregard the vocalization, and even the word division;[15] on the other hand, he acknowledges that even in the Psalms there was a strong tradition of prayer and singing which secured the pronunciation.[16] The consonantal text itself was and is not understandable unless it is provided with some vocalization.

The Masoretic Tiberian vocalization is not always consistent with the consonantal text. The Babylonian and Palestinian vocalization systems and the pronunciation reflected in Greek and Latin translations and commentaries go some centuries before the fixation of the pronunciation by the Tiberian Masoretes and at the same time confirm their root in tradition.[17]

The attempt to reconstruct the older pronunciation with the help of the comparative method, especially by using the relatively well known vocalic

10. Cf. F. Vodel, *Die konsonantischen Varianten in den doppelt überlieferten poetischen Stücken des masoretischen Textes* (Leipzig, 1905); Psalm 14 = 53 on pp. 58–65.

11. P. Maas, Textual Criticism (transl. by B. Flower) (Oxford, 1958), p. 15.

12. Psalms I, p. XXI.

13. Cf. F. Rosenthal, Die Parallelstellen in den Texten von Ugarit, *Orientalia* 8 (1939): 213–37; the scribal errors are listed on pp. 215–25.

14. A list of Psalms preserved in the manuscripts from the Judaean Desert is given by J. A. Sanders, *The Dead Sea Psalms Scroll* (Ithaca, 1967), pp. 143–49. "Some variants commend themselves immediately as improvements of the text," Sanders, loc. cit., p. 15.

15. Psalms I, p. xxii.

16. Psalms I, p. xxiii.

17. For the linguistic evaluation of the pre-Tiberian traditions, cf. R. Meyer, *Hebräische Grammatik,* I (Berlin, 1966), pp. 28–30, 33–35.

system of Ugaritic poetic texts, is fully justified. The tension arises wherever this reconstruction goes beyond the "archaizing" of the vocalic elements of words and tries to interpret the words on the basis of their consonantal structure only, while the later added vocalic complements correspond to other forms or even to words of other categories or from other roots than those in the traditional vocalized text. Dahood does not conceal the fact that this approach, which opens so many new possibilities, is a subjective one,[18] he himself rightly characterizes the results as a reconstruction.[19]

The devaluation of ancient versions of the Old Testament is even more conspicuous; they have—according to Dahood—"relatively little to offer toward a better understanding of the difficult text."[20] With the help of the Ugaritic it is possible to demonstrate that the translators did not understand some words, forms, formulas, and constructions. In spite of this general statement, Dahood is quite right in accepting the help of the ancient versions, especially of the Greek Septuagint, if they uphold some of his proposals based on the Ugaritic.[21]

The versions can be more exploited; even the mistranslations can give valuable information about the wording of the original.[22] The stereotyped patterns of individual translations can also help to establish and understand the character of the original text. Some poetical devices, such as the use of the plural instead of the singular, can be imitated in the translation, if there are similar phenomena in the target languages or at least a possibility of introducing them.[23] The study of Greek translations is fruitful in many respects;[24] it has brought about agreement between the understanding of some words in the Septuagint and the results of recent comparative studies of the Semitic languages.[25]

18. Cf. Psalms I, p. xxiv: "choices," "experience"; II, p. xix.
19. Cf. Psalms I, p. 152, and Psalm 24:6.
20. Psalms I, xxiv, cf. II, pp. xviii–xix.
21. Psalms II, p. xviii, cf. note 19 supra.
22. For the limits of this evaluation cf. J. Barr, *Comparative Philology and the Text of the Old Testament* (Oxford, 1968), pp. 249–51.
23. Cf. Psalms I, p. xxv. For the use of a poetical plural in Greek and Latin translations of the Old Testament cf. E. Kamínková, Plural "sanguines" v pozdní antické a středověké latině (in Czech), with an abstract in German "Der Plural sanguines im mittelalterlichen Latein," Listy filologické 80 (1957), pp. 58–61.
24. The attempts of F. Wutz, Die Transkriptionen von der Septuaginta bis zu Hieronymus, I–II (Stuttgart 1925, 1933); Systematische Wege von der Septuaginta zum hebräischen Urtext (Stuttgart, 1937), later dismissed by the author himself, to prove that the Septuagint was translated from a Hebrew original written in Greek letters, have brought as a by-product many interesting suggestions for explanation of Hebrew words on the basis of other Semitic languages. For the most recent evaluation cf. S. Jellicoe, *The Septuagint and Modern Study* (Oxford, 1968), p. 73.
25. For the "Arabisms" cf. J. Barr, loc. cit., pp. 240–41.

In using the versions it will be necessary to distinguish more precisely the establishing of the text and its interpretation. If a translation distinguishes the differences, which in the original are not discernible in the written text itself, but only by its interpretation—as, e.g., the meaning of the preposition *b*-, "in" and "from"[26]—it can be used for confirming the interpretation, perhaps based on ancient tradition, while in establishing the text even the usual meaning "in" has the same value.

The requirements of the new approach to the textual criticism of the Hebrew original are to great extent converging with methods recently used in investigation of the versions. While in the past they were consulted as collections of variants, as testimonies of dissent, they are being studied more in their full extent, for their intrinsic value, as positive bearers of a type of tradition. The relevance of the versions may therefore be increased.[27] The versions can provide, if studied and used in this manner, more positive evidence for flexible and subjective textual criticism.[28]

The manifold relations of Hebrew biblical text to the Phoenician and Ugaritic language and literature are fully exploited by Dahood,[29] the lexical isoglosses,[30] the common or similar morphological features,[31] as well as the common literary patterns.[32] In using the syntactical phenomena it will be necessary to establish the syntactic systems of the languages involved in a more precise manner; the observations presented by Dahood will prove

26. Psalms I, p. xxvi.

27. S. Jellicoe, loc. cit., p. 298, seems to be much impressed by Dahood's evaluation of the versions; his survey demonstrates their growing relevance.

28. Cf. supra, n. 18. A similar situation appears in literary criticism, as the recent traditio-historical approach to the Old Testament is in principle more subjective than the older method of literary criticism; cf. S. Segert, Zur Methode der alttestamentlichen Literarkritik (Quellenscheidung und Überlieferungsgeschichte, *AO* 24 (1956): 610–21.

29. Cf. Psalms II, pp. xv–xvii.

30. Cf. Psalms I, pp. xxvii–xxviii, xli. The Ugaritic equivalents to Hebrew words are given in L. Koehler and W. Baumgartner, *Lexicon in Veteris Testamenti Libros* (Leiden, 1953); they are brought up to date in the third edition prepared by W. Baumgartner, *Hebräisches und aramäisches Lexikon zum Alten Testament, Lieferung I* (Leiden, 1967). The dictionaries of Ugaritic give the Hebrew equivalent: C. H. Gordon, *Ugaritic Textbook* (Roma, 1965), pp. 347–507; J. Aistleitner, *Wörterbuch der ugaritischen Sprache*, ed. O. Eissfeldt, (3rd ed.; Berlin, 1967); for the literary texts only G. R. Driver, *Canaanite Myths and Legends* (Edinburgh, 1956), pp. 133–66. The material from the Hebrew Bible and the Ugaritic texts for the comparative dictionary of Semitic languages sponsored by the Oriental Institute of the Czechoslovak Academy in Prague is prepared for processing on the computer, cf. S. Segert, *Hebrew Bible and Semitic Comparative Lexicography*, Congress Volume, Rome 1968 (Leiden, 1969), pp. 204–11, esp. p. 209.

31. Cf. W. L. Moran, *The Hebrew Language in Its Northwest Semitic Background, The Bible and the Ancient Near East, Essays in Honor of W. F. Albright*, ed. G. E. Wright (Garden City, 1965), pp. 59–84, esp. pp. 67–76.

32. Cf. most recently W. F. Albright, *Yahweh and the Gods of Canaan* (Garden City, 1968), pp. 1–52, esp. p. 31.

valuable for this urgent undertaking, which then will give the basis for evaluating his proposals in a more objective manner.

Textual criticism will always remain an area where the exact science and the art merge.[33] Dahood stresses the possibility of choice.[34] In using Ugaritic and Phoenician material more will be required from any worker in the field, not only as concerns his knowledge of the pertinent languages but also as concerns his discerning and creative imagination.

The ultimate goal of textual criticism seems to be indicated by Dahood in a rather presumptuous way, if his negative statement, that the versions "are not always reliable witnesses to what the Biblical poets intended"[35] means also that he attempts to find *ipsissima verba poetae*. For Psalms 2 and 110 the form and the meaning which they had in the time of their composition in the tenth century B.C.[36] has to be reestablished.

This tendency to seek the original form is appropriate, it perpetuates the humanistic trend "ad fontes." For the Psalms which form individual literary units, the goal of textual criticism coincides with that of literary analysis. Insofar as this textual approach is extended to Old Testament books of more complex character it should be accompanied by an equally thorough and radical criticism of literary form and tradition.[37]

If the goal of textual criticism is limited to establishing a definite textual recension it can be attained now, for the Hebrew biblical canon as the text of the Hebrew biblical manuscripts from about A.D. 100 is close to the consonantal text of the Masoretic manuscripts.[38]

The reconstruction by Dahood goes beyond this canonized stage, and therefore it differs often and strongly from the traditional interpretation. Dahood is right in stressing it and insisting on the originality[39] of his reconstruction; he succeeds in the scholarly attempt to reach the relatively oldest source of tradition.

The traditional view was of value insofar as it is bound to the form of the text in the time of its canonization. This can be observed to some extent in the Jewish approach to the biblical canon, but more in the attitude of the

33. Cf. A. E. Housman, *The Application of Thought to Textual Criticism* (1922; reprinted in: *Selected Prose*, ed. J. Carter [Cambridge, 1961], pp. 131–50). Quoted in B. M. Metzger, *The Text of the New Testament* (2nd ed.; Oxford, 1968), p. 219.

34. Cf. supra, n. 21.

35. Psalms I, p. xxvi.

36. Cf. Psalms I, p. xxix.

37. Of course the use of Ugaritic for the elucidation of the younger books and the prosaic texts will be more limited.

38. Cf. F. M. Cross, loc. cit. (v. n. 2), pp. 287–88.

39. Psalms II, pp. xiv, xxii, xxvi.

Christian church toward its Greek Old Testament; the principle is precisely expressed in the doctrine of the Roman Catholic church, which proclaimed the Latin translation, the Vulgata, as the most reliable textual form. The traditionalist attitude to the biblical text was also shared by a liberal protestant scholar, Adolf von Harnack, who stressed the relevance of the Vulgata for establishing the New Testament text.[40] It is symptomatic of the situation in biblical studies that Mitchell Dahood, professor of the Biblical Pontificial Institute in Rome, attempts to go as far as possible away from the canonized tradition and criticizes the other translations, also based in principle on the Hebrew original, for paying too much attention to the traditional views expressed in the ancient versions.[41]

The problem of the evaluation of the Hebrew Bible for Christians was strongly expressed by Harnack,[42] when he proposed to exclude the Old Testament from Christian Biblical Canon and consider it as a nonauthoritative, but an esteemed and useful historical document. Such an attitude would require a radical textual and literary criticism.

The pioneering efforts of William F. Albright and his followers demonstrate the soundness and fruitfulness of the new approach to the text of the Hebrew Bible, using the data from Phoenician and especially Ugaritic material.[43] The tensions between some results of the new approach and the traditional opinions are healthy and stimulating for further research along this line, which will require higher standards of learning and perceptivity, in order that it may become with every fresh attempt better documented and more creative.

40. A. von Harnack, *Zur Revision der Prinzipien der neutestamentlichen Textkritik: Die Bedeutung der Vulgata für den Text der katholischen Briefe und der Anteil der Hieronymus an dem Übersetzungswerk. Beiträge zur Einleitung in das Neue Testament*, 7. Teil (Leipzig, 1916); Studien zur Vulgata des Hebräerbriefs, Sitzungsberichte der Preussischen Akademie (1920), pp. 170–201: reprinted in *Studien zur Geschichte des Neuen Testaments und der Alten Kirche*, I. ed. by Hans Lietzmann (Berlin, 1931), pp. 191–234. Cf. Metzger, loc. cit., p. 211.

41. Cf. Psalms I, pp. xxvi, xxxix; II, pp. xxv, xxvi.

42. A. von Harnack, *Marcion, Das Evangelium vom fremden Gott* (Berlin, 2nd ed., 1924; reprint Darmstadt 1960), pp. 215–23, esp. pp. 217, 223.

43. This respect to the Canaanite linguistic and literary background of the Old Testament is paralleled in the New Testament research by the growing relevance of the Aramaic background for the study of the gospels and some other books: cf. Metzger, loc. cit., pp. 210, 233–34.

# Some Reflections on the Formation of the Feminine in Semitic Languages

A. VAN SELMS

It was in Jerusalem, in June 1926, that the present author, a very young student then, had the privilege of meeting Professor Albright for the first time. The great scholar, probably at a loss what to discuss with such an ignorant and immature person, told him that he had the hobby of collecting queer and foolish books on scholarly subjects, and he showed him some precious examples. At the present moment, presenting my contribution to the volume in honor of the master, I am beset with the fear that he will consider the following few pages as an addition to his curious collection. Nevertheless, I will take the risk, relying on the mildness of his judgment of the efforts of others.

One of the first things the tyro, when approaching his first Semitic language, has to learn is the fact that all Semitic languages, Egyptian included, have two genders only, masculine and feminine. There is no neuter as it is known in Indogermanic languages. The significant feature of the feminine is the *tāw*, as an afformative in the noun, as a praeformative in the verb. It does not worry the beginner much that the same *tāw* as a praeformative also seems to indicate the second person, whether masculine or feminine, both in the singular and in the plural, and though he may feel some misgivings when learning that in Arabic the feminine plural of the third person imperfect has not got the *tāw* characteristic for the feminine, or that in Ugaritic the masculine plural of the third person often has this praeformative consonant, nevertheless the association of the *tāw* with the idea of the feminine remains an unshakable certainty.

The great masters in comparative Semitic grammar, however, have often remarked that the classification of nouns in a masculine and a feminine group was not part of the original structure of Semitic languages.[1] Some of the most typical words for females and their sexual functions lack the feminine ending.[2] Some animals are called by totally different names, depending on their sex, and the females in such cases are not called by nouns ending on the typical *tāw*.[3] In other cases, both the male and the female are indicated by the same word, without a feminine ending.[4] There are typical masculine notions expressed with the help of the *tāw* ending.[5] A great many feminine words have a "masculine" form, e.g., the words denoting parts of the body that occur in pairs.[6] Many words have a "masculine" form in the singular, and "feminine" in the plural, and *vice versa*.[7]

It is for these reasons that some scholars assume that the classification system in a prae-literary period of the Semitic languages was of a far more intricate character, compared to the systems of some of the Bantu and American languages.[8] It is, of course, doubtful whether we, in trying to reconstruct such a very old system of classification, should still have the right to speak of "Semitic languages," since at such an archaic stage all the typical features of what we call "Semitic languages" were absent. Moreover, it would be extremely difficult, if not impossible, to determine what classes were distinguished at such a stage, and what their characteristics were. Nevertheless, one might ask, e.g., whether the fact that so many words denoting non-domesticated animals have a *bēt* as their last radical could not point to one of those archaic classes. In Biblical Hebrew we have *ᶜaqrāb*, "scorpion"; *ᵓarnèbèt* (Ugaritic *anhb*, Babylonian *annabu*, Arabic *ᶜarnab*, etc.) "hare"; *ᶜakšūb*, "hornviper"; *šaᶜalbīm* (in a place name only, but cf. Babylonian *šēlibu*, Arabic *ṯaᶜlab*), "foxes"; *zᵉᵓēb*, "wolf"; *kèlèb*, "dog"; *sāb*, "a kind of lizard"; *zᵉbūb*, "flies"; *ḥāgāb*, "locust"; perhaps even *dōb*, "bear"; *ᵓarbè*,

1. C. Brockelmann, *Grundriss der vergleichende Grammatik der semitischen Sprachen*, I (1908), p. 404; S. Moscati, *An Introduction to the Comparative Grammar of the Semitic Languages* (1964), p. 86.
2. Brockelmann, *Grundriss*, p. 416f.
3. Ibid., p. 416.
4. Ibid., p. 418.
5. Ibid., p. 420/421; cf. also plural forms like *ᵓābōt*, *ᵓabbāhātā*, "fathers."
6. Brockelmann, *Syrische Grammatik* (1925)$^4$, pp. 42f.; id., *Grundriss*, pp. 422–24.
7. Moscati, *An Introduction*, p. 92.
8. Brockelmann, *Grundriss*, p. 404; De Lacy O'Leary, *Comparative Grammar of the Semitic Languages* (1923), p. 192.

"swarm of locusts"; and *ᶜārōb* (according to *LXX*), "dog-flies." Birds are lacking in this list, and several of them end on a *pē*, as do some words for "to fly" and "wing."

Be this as it may, we find from the earliest period in the history of written Semitic languages the classification into masculine and feminine words. Brockelmann is right when he maintains that this distinction originally had nothing to do with sex as a physical phenomenon,[9] but, nevertheless, we may ask why and when the sexual distinction became preponderant in the Semitic languages. Even if originally it was not a denotation of sex, it became such in the long run, and this use spread over the whole of the language. It attests a preoccupation with sex which to the modern mind, reared on Freud and the techniques of advertisement, is nothing remarkable, but is in reality far from natural. Most animal species have, depending on the seasons of the year, their fixed periods for sexual functions and are not sexually active during the rest of the year. It is only man who has in this respect freed himself from the fetters of the seasons, though in many countries statistics on this subject still show a slight increase in sexual activity during the spring months.

Personal experiences during the last world war, and general observations have taught me that the sexual urge in man is less strong than the will to survive, the urge to continue to barely exist. The daily struggle against hunger and deadly perils forces sexual urges into the background. The whole of human life was such a struggle before man found methods to procure himself food that could be preserved for the meager months. When man passes from the simple food-gathering and hunting stage to agriculture and husbandry, he enters a stage of relative security and finds more time and leisure to occupy himself with things other than the prolonging of his bare existence. From this viewpoint all agriculture and husbandry, primitive as may be, are the first steps to *luxus* and inducements to *luxuria* in all the meanings of these words. The greater life's security becomes, the stronger the occupation with sex will be, as is clearly shown in the realizations of the welfare state. With relative security we fall prey to sexual preoccupations.

So it may be surmissed that the preponderance of the classification according to gender came into being after man had solved the food problem in a passably satisfactory way: after he had learned to raise cattle, to sow and to harvest, and to protect his fields by the building of towns and fortifications. In Jericho the oldest urban civilization which supports agriculture is dated in the seventh millennium, i.e., during the preceramic neolithicum.[10] There

9. Brockelmann, *Grundriss*, p. 404.
10. K. M. Kenyon, *Jericho* (Dutch translation, 1959), pp. 58–60.

is, however, not the slightest indication that the inhabitants of the round houses of oldest Jericho were the ancestors of a Semitic speaking group; the name "Jericho" itself should be explained from a non-Semitic language.[11] It would be erroneous to assign the Semitic classification according to gender to the seventh millennium on the strength of archaeological data in Jericho and elsewhere. We think we have answered the question of why this system of classification became predominant, but we do not dare to assign absolute dates to the process.

More important to us, however, is the question of why the *tāw* became the characteristic of the feminine. It is well known that the same consonant also is the characteristic of the *nomen unitatis*. Whereas, in former times it was thought that the *nomen unitatis* was an application of the feminine gender, Landsberger has made it clear that the *tāw* ending originally indicated a single object out of a natural group. In the herd there were always many more female than male animals.[12] As an example, one might quote Gen. 32:14, the enumeration of Jacob's present to his brother: "two hundred she-goats and twenty he-goats, two hundred ewes and twenty rams."[13] So the chances are great that if one took one animal at random out of the herd, it would prove to be a female. What originally was an indication of one single head of cattle out of a whole flock, in this way became the indication of a female, and the *tāw* an indication of the single individual, became the feminine ending.

Here, however, it is only natural to ask why the *tāw* was the characteristic of the *nomen unitatis*. I am of the opinion that this question may be answered by examining the forms of the personal pronouns in the Semitic languages. In doing so, one has first to eliminate the pronouns of the third person, as, properly speaking, they are not personal pronouns, but rather examples of the *pronomen anaphoricum*.[14] It is then evident that all personal pronouns are

11. To derive the name from *yèraḥ*, "moon" is to indulge into quasi-scholarly popular etymology. It is far more probable that the name of Jericho belongs to the large group of names composed with the element *y-r* which seems to mean "water," cf. Jordan, Jarmuk, Jabbok, Arnon, Jarkon, and even Jerusalem, as proposed in my *Jeruzalem door de eeuwen heen* (1969), ch. 2.; the same element also being present in names like Eridanos, Rhodanus, Iardanos, etc.

12. Quoted after W. von Soden, *Grundriss der akkadischen Grammatik* (1952), p. 74.

13. In the next verse, Gen. 32:15, forty cows and ten bulls are mentioned, but perhaps some of the bulls were (castrated) oxen. It is still otherwise with the asses: twenty she-asses and ten he-asses, understandable when we take into account that the ass was chiefly used as a beast of burden, and in this respect there is not much difference between the female and the male of the species. Also for riding purposes both sexes were used.

14. Von Soden, *Akk. Grammatik*, p. 40.

composed with the help of the preformative *an*, which is also preserved as a preformative to denote abstract nouns in Accadian—words like *andurārum*, "liberation" and *andunānu*, "substitution." If we subtract the preformative *an-* it is clear that the characteristic element in the pronoun second person, all genders and numbers, is the *tāw*. We may assume that having singled out one individual object from its natural group, the ancient hunter said to it: *ʾayyal-t*, "a buck thou art," or whatever animal it might happen to be. We could call such a sentence a sentence of identification, stating the species to which an individual animal belonged. The chance was great that it was a female and so the sentence of identification became the noun for the female individual—*ʾayyèlèt*, "a doe."

Such sentences of identification may seem unusual and superfluous to us, but they were not in ancient times. Calling an entity a name meant to be master of it. By stating the identity between the mental concept of a thing and its outward objective appearance, ancient man conquered reality and brought order to the chaotic mass of his sensual impressions. It might even have meant something more than that: a means of maintaining identity. It is well known that among the ancient Arabs a gazelle might also be the temporary appearance of the demon *ġūl*; there is a story about the poet Taʾabbaṭa-šarran whose name is explained as a remembrance of the fact that once he caught a gazelle and carried it homeward under his armpit (*ʾibṭ*); it was only when he had reached the people of his tribe that the demon revealed itself and disappeared from his grasp. The sentence of identification might be used as a means to prevent such tricky metamorphoses.

In any case, ancient literature presents many examples of the sentence of identification. In the first person it is well known from inscriptions which start with the self-introduction of the king: *Hammurapi lugal kalga. . . . . me-en*, "Hammurapi, the mighty king. . . . . am I."[15] Or in a literary text: *Igigige igigig me-en numunibi*, "The sick-eyed says not 'I am sick-eyed'" meaning: there is none who suffers from eye-sickness.[16] Naming a thing brings it into existence; when a thing is not called by a name it does not exist. As long as "high heaven had not been named, firm ground below had not been called by name," heaven and earth were not there.[17] In the third person, the sentence of identification is typically represented in the dialogue between Enki and his messenger Isimud:

15. L. W. King, *The Letters and Inscriptions of Ḫammurabi*, I, (1898), nr. 58, lines 1–9.
16. S. Langdon, *The Sumerian Epic of Paradise, the Flood and the Fall of Man* (1915), column I, line 22 (*ANET*, p. 38).
17. *Enuma eliš*, I, 1, 2.

He says to his messenger Isimud:
"What is this, what is this?"
His messenger, Isimud answers him;
"My king, this is the 'tree-plant'," he says to him.
He cuts it off for him and he eats it.

And so the dialogue goes on until Enki has eaten eight plants.[18] Even when one is a god, one does not eat any food before having identified it. So frequent were these sentences of identification that the plural suffix for persons, *meš*, is nothing else than the third plural of the enclytic copula, "are they."[19]

The magical implications of the sentence of identification in the second person are very evident in the Ugaritic poem describing the fabrication of the clubs with the help of which Baal will conquer Prince Sea:

Kathir brought down two maces
and proclaimed their names:
"Thy name, thine is Ygrš!
Ygrš, expell Sea!
Expell Sea from his throne,
River from the seat of his dominion!"[20]

By identifying the mace, by giving it a name, it becomes an effective weapon. Moreover, the giving of a name, declaring what an individual or an object is, shows the authority of the name-giver. It creates a strong bond between the name-giver and the person or thing named. Taking into account all these implications of the "sentence of identification" one can understand that the *tāw* of the second person became the *tāw* of the feminine.

There exists, however, a less frequent but, nevertheless, sufficiently attested feminine ending in which the *tāw* is lacking. A great many Ugaritic feminine proper names end on a *yōd*. Baal's daughters are called respectively Pdry, Ṭly, and Arṣy. An alternative name of Ashera is Rḥmy, and a handmaid is called Dmgy. Keret's wife is Ḥry, and Dnils' consort is Dnty.[21] All these

18. S. N. Kramer, *Sumerian Mythology* (1961), p. 57.
19. A. Falkenstein, *Das Sumerische* (1964), p. 37.
20. C. H. Gordon, *Ugaritic Manual* (1955), text 68, 11–13, cf. 18–20. Though Gordon is probably right when he remarks that in the sentence *šmk at ygrš* the independent pronoun is added, as in Hebrew or Arabic, in order to emphasize possession (*Manual*, p. 31), it is possible to translate: "Thy name, thou art Ygrš," cf. Gesenius—Kautzsch, *Hebräische Grammatik* (1896)[26], p. 432: "Uebrigens ist das Pron. separ. in solchen Fällen nicht etwa als *casus obliquus* (Accus. oder Gen.), sondern als Subjekt eines selbständigen Satzes zu betrachten, dessen Prädikat je nach dem Zusammenhang ergänzt werden muss." In the case of our Ugaritic sentence this would be very clear.
21. Gordon, *Manual*, pp. 50f.

names stem from mythological and epical texts, and it may be that they form an archaic element in Ugaritic nomenclature. Nevertheless, they prove that the *yōd* at a certain stage in the development of Ugaritic was a feminine ending. This observation is confirmed by the fact that there is at least one feminine word ending in a *yōd*, apart from the proper names mentioned—the word *nʿmy*, "loveliness," synonymous with *ysmsmt* and *ysmt*, "beauty."[22] As a second example, Gordon mentions *qryy* which he translates "contentious," and Driver "opposition."[23] But the passage ʿnt III, 11, cf. IV. 52, where this word occurs is not very clear to us, and in the corresponding passages, ʿnt IV, 66, and 71, we find the form *aqry*, which is certainly a verbal form. It is therefore more probable that *qryy* is an imperative, parallel to *št* "put down" in the next line, though in view of the absence of *matres lectionis* in the epical texts the second *yōd* is puzzling and the meaning not at all clear.

A direct parallel to the Ugaritic names on -y is the "former" name of Sarah, *śāray*, as distinguished from *śārā* (Gen. 17:15). The difference between the two names is not a difference in meaning, but that between a more archaic and a "modernized" form of the feminine.[24] The Old Testament name is important for us because it proves that we have to pronounce the Ugaritic names as ending on *-ay*: Arṣay, Ṭallay, etc., not as ending on -iya, as Driver presents them. The word *ḥoray* in Is. 19:9, translated as "byssus" in *LXX*, has been adduced as a noun with a feminine ending -ay,[25] but the reading of the Dead Sea Isaiah is a support for the emendation *ḥāwērū*, "they have grown pale," as proposed in Kittel[3] and adopted by Köhler in his Lexicon. Better examples are *gōbay*, "swarm of locusts,"[26] and some words pronounced with an *-è* (originating from *-ay*) as an ending, e.g., *libnè*, "storax-tree," *ʾiššè*, "fire-offering," perhaps also *śādè* (Ugaritic *šd*), though the word, also in its archaic form *śaday*, is construed as a masculine in Biblical Hebrew. In Syriac, Brockelmann has collected seven feminine words with the ending *-ay*, e.g., *salway* "quail," *kūkbay*, "a kind of owl," *tanway*, "stipulation," etc.[27]

In Arabic one thinks immediately of the feminine of the relative form, *ʾakbaru*, feminine *kubrā*, written with a *yā* at the end, which points to a Meccan

22. Ibid., Glossary, nr. 1256.

23. Ibid., p. 51; G. R. Driver, *Canaanite Myths and Legends* (1956), p. 87, nt. 4.

24. The two forms of the name stand in the same relation to each other as Meccan *kubray* to classical Arabic *kubrā*, as mentioned later on in this paper.

25. Brockelmann, *Grundriss*, p, 412.

26. Not to be derived from a root *g-b-h*, as L. Koehler has it in his *Lexicon in Veteris Testamenti libros* (1953), s.v., cf. also *ibid.* (1967)³, but from *gōb*, "locust," Aramaic *gōbā*, cf. *gēbīm*, Jes. 33:4. Here again we have an example of an animal name ending in *b*.

27. Brockelmann, *Syrische Grammatik*, p. 48.

pronunciation *kubray*, which in this case may prove to be closer to the original form than the classical pronunciation with *-ā* as an ending. The rare feminine plural has retained the *yā* even in the classical pronunciation: *kubrayāt*$^{un}$. In view of the regular pronunciation of the ending *-ay* as *-ā* one might ask whether the feminine ending *-āʾu* in words denoting colors or bodily defects, e.g., *saudāʾu*, was originally also formed with a *yā*, though it is somewhat difficult to imagine that *saudayu* should become *saudāʾu*. More certain are three feminine adjectival forms: *alʾūlā*, "the first," *alʾuḫrā*, "the other," and *ḥublā*, "pregnant," all three written with the *yā*.

Having given these examples we do not think it necessary to follow the evolution of this ancient feminine ending in several Semitic languages as sketched by Brockelmann.[28] The facts are well known and anyone may check them. But, just as was the case when we dealt with the feminine *tāw*, we ask ourselves how it came to be that at a certain stage in the development of the Semitic languages the ending *-ay* acquired the feminine meaning. The case is here somewhat more intricate, as we have to do not only with a single consonant but also with the preceding vowel *a*. It is perhaps best first to give our attention to this vowel. In general, the vowel *a* in the earlier stages of several Semitic languages is an indication of the accusative. This, however, hardly applies to our present problem. Why should this type of feminine word have the accusative as normal form, even in languages which, like Ugaritic and Arabic, still have a complete system of declension, with a nominative on *-u*, a genitive on *-i*, and an accusative on *-a*?

It seems to us that there is reason to ask whether at a certain stage in their development Semitic languages (or some of them) have not had a proper form for their vocative. The textbooks on the grammar of these languages do not discuss the proper forms of the vocative; in general it is assumed that the vocative did not exist as a proper and separate case, but as one of the functions of the nominative. It is in Arabic only that one discovers some rather intricate rules for the vocative, and these apply only when a vocative particle precedes, *yā* or *ʾayyuhā*, or the combination of both. In general, the following noun or proper name takes the nominative ending *-u*, but if the person addressed is absent, or the noun is determined by some word or words after it, the noun is put in the accusative, e.g., *yā ġāfilan*, "O careless!" in a rhetorical exclamation, or *yā ʿabda -llāhi*, "O servant of God." There is no reason why the *-a* ending in such cases should be a real accusative; one is rather inclined to assume that we have in the ending *-a* a relic of an ancient separate case, the vocative. This becomes clearer when one takes the word "vocative" in its

28. Brockelmann, *Grundriss*, pp. 410–14.

literal sense: the case used when calling somebody. There is no vowel which lends itself so well to long, protracted calling as the *a* sound. One opens one's mouth wider than in the case of all other vowels; the full volume of breath is used, and one can protract the sound until the breath is spent. In a more primitive society, the vocative is used for calling people; the head of the family calls his wives, handmaids, slaves, children, and animals from a long distance. It is only natural to end the name used on a more or less protracted *a* sound. A typical example is also the Arabic exclamation *yā ʾummāh*, "O (my) mother."[29]

We assume that the *a* sound in the ending *-ay* of the feminine originated with the vocative. Now we have to account for the consonant *y* at the end. Here we might point to a parallel phonetic development in Syriac and Talmudic Aramaic. The feminine anaphoric pronoun *hī* often loses its *h* when used enclitically after a preceding word. In Syriac *mānā hī* becomes *mānāy*;[30] *hādā hī* is pronounced *hādāy*. There is no doubt that in the same way Talmudic *may* (with a short *a*, though often written with an *ʾalèf* as a *mater lectionis*) originated from *mā hī*. It is quite possible that at a much earlier stage in the development of Semitic languages something similar took place, and that the *yōd* in the feminine ending *-ay* is nothing else than the anaphoric pronoun feminine.

We imagine that what happened was that the *pater familias* called from a distance, therefore in a loud voice which led naturally to the ending *-a*, and added a gesture, pointing to the person or animal meant specifically, indicated by the anaphoric pronoun *hī*, if it happened to be a female. His cry was an embryonic sentence, indicating some object and implying that this specific object was meant. One could paraphrase such a sentence as: "n.n! Yes, that is the one I mean!" When explaining the feminine *tāw*, we coined the expression "sentence of identification"; now along with that type of sentence we get what we may call the "sentence of summoning." The same reason which made the *nomen unitatis*, grown from the sentence of identification, into an indication of the feminine (namely, the fact that the big majority of the animals in the herd were females), also had the effect that the sentence of summoning developed into feminine words ending on *-ay*. In the end, the *tāw* ending superseded the *-ay* ending, in the majority of cases; it would be idle speculation to ask which of the two was the older; it is probable that the sentence of identification and that of summoning for a

29. On the consonantal *h* at the end of the exclamation cf. the author's forthcoming paper on "Melisma as an origin of intervocalic *h*," in *Journal of Near Eastern Studies*.
30. Th. Nöldeke, *Compendious Syriac Grammar* (1904), pp. 26, 47.

long time occurred side by side. The sentence of identification is essentially a sentence in the second person; that of summoning is one in the third person; nothing prohibits their side-by-side existence. In some languages, even in very recent times, the third person is used in addressing people, sometimes as a form of polite address (Italian a.o.), sometimes as a means of stressing the inferiority of the person addressed ("er" in the former Prussian army in the mouth of an officer addressing a private). The second alternative is the more probable one in the patriarchal Semitic society.

Having explained how it came to be that both *tāw* and *yōd* became indications of the feminine, we can easily understand the use of both sounds to indicate the feminine in the verb. It is a rather melancholy reflection on human nature that the oldest form of the verb is the imperative. Taking Hebrew as an example, we get the masculine form *q^e^ṭōl* (from *quṭul*) and the feminine *qiṭlī* or *qoṭlī* (from *quṭul hi*). In such instances the *yōd*, which became a consonant in the feminine ending *-ay*, has retained its vocalic character as in the *hī* from which it stems. The process was somewhat more intricate in the case of what is traditionally called the imperfect in Hebrew. Here both *tāw* and *yōd* played their roles. *tāw* in the third person feminine: *tiqṭōl*; but the same *tāw* was also the indication of the second person, *tiqṭōl*, "you kill," and, therefore, in order to indicate that a female was addressed, one had to take refuge in the other means of expressing the feminine, the *yōd* in its vocalic form: *tiqṭ^e^lī*. It is in accordance with the enclitical and anaphoric character of *hī* that the *yōd* as an indication of feminine gender always appears as an afformative and not as a preformative.

In the perfect the same system applies. The third person feminine uses the *tāw*, in Hebrew preserved in the forms with object suffixes: *q^e^ṭālatnī*, etc. In the second person the *tāw* was already used as indication of "thou"; so here the feminine had to be formed again with the help of the *yōd*: in Arabic *qatalti*, in Hebrew *qāṭalt*, but with suffixes the *yōd* is present: *q^e^ṭaltīnī*, etc., and numerous are the forms in the Hebrew Bible where the form without an object suffix has retained the *-ī* in the *k^e^tīb*.[31] It is well known that the pronoun second person feminine in the *k^e^tīb* also often has the *yōd*, pointing to a pronunciation *ʾattī*,[32] cf. Arabic, Syriac, and Geʾez.

In such a way, at least the singular feminine forms of the verb find an easy explanation. It would carry us too far also to treat here the feminine plural

31. Gesenius-Kautzsch, *Hebräische Grammatik*, p. 117.
32. Ibid., pp. 101f.

forms. Other problems, hardly connected with the theory expounded in these pages, present themselves there. In any case, there one also has to take the fact into account that in the herd the majority of animals will probably be females. That might explain the fact, mentioned at the beginning of this paper, that Arabic and Ugaritic, each in its own way, use the same preformative for the masculine and feminine third person plural of the imperfect. On the other hand, one might also ask whether the female ending *-ay*, originating from the "sentence of summoning," might also offer some new perspective on plural endings like Aramaic *-ayyā* and on the gentilic ending *-ī*, *-āyā*, *-āyum*, *-ayya*. But these subjects would carry us far beyond the limits necessarily set to this paper presented in honor of the revered master of Near Eastern scholarship, William Foxwell Albright.

# Amos VI:13–14 und I:3 auf dem Hintergrund der Beziehungen zwischen Israel und Damaskus im 9. und 8. Jahrhundert

J. ALBERTO SOGGIN

## I

Die Nachricht von der Wiedereroberung durch Jerobeam II. der nordöstlichen, traditionell zum Siedlungsgebiet Israels gehörigen, transjordanischen Territorien scheint, aller Wahrscheinlichkeit nach, während des Aufenthalts des Amos in Betʾel eingetroffen zu sein, wie ich u. A. in diesem Aufsatz zeigen möchte. Nach VI:13–14 hat sie angeblich Erleichterung und bald grosse Freude, ja ein nicht geringes Gefühl des Nationalstolzes ausgelöst;[1] nach den bitter-ironischen Worten des Propheten, denn so muss man wohl diesen Text verstehen, waren derartige Gefühle, als er das Wort ergriff, auf ihrem Höhepunkt angelangt.

II Kön. XIV:25 beschreibt uns den Umfang der territorialen Errungenschaften und dieser Text wird von Amos VI:13–14 im Wesentlichen bestätigt: von der "Pforte Hamats" bis an das Tote Meer soll die Wiedereroberung gereicht haben, die am Ende der 760-er Jahre durch Jerobeam II.

1. *BH*[3] und alle Kommentare schlagen die Lesart *l*$^{e}$*lôʾd*$^{e}$*bār* (Ortsname) für die massoretische *l*$^{e}$*lôʾ dābār* vor, welche letztere aber von allen alten Übersetzungen bestätigt wird. Nun liegt aber Qarnayim viel weiter nordöstlich als Lodebar, das also automatisch in die wiedereroberten Gebiete miteinbegriffen ist. Die Erwähnung Lodebars im Text ist also überflüssig. Was der Text wirklich enthält ist ein Wortspiel, wie einige Kommentare und S. Cohen, "The political background of the words of Amos," in *HUCA* 36 (1965): 153–60 mit Recht behaupten, aber gerade ein solches würde durch eine Textänderung abgeschwächt. Also: "Ihr, die Ihr Euch wegen nichts freuet! Ihr, die Ihr sagt: 'Haben wir doch Qarnayim durch unsere Macht erobert!'."

zustande gebracht wurde.[2] Dadurch waren die nördlichen und östlichen Grenzen Israels in einem Umfang wiederhergestellt, der geradezu an den des davidischen Grossreiches errinnerte![3] Eine derartige Nachricht braucht natürlich nicht wörtlich aufgefasst zu werden, als hätte Israel tatsächlich die genannten Gegenden militärisch besetzt; es genügt, dass einige Staaten die Herrschaft des Königs von Israel anerkannten und ihm tributpflichtig wurden. Von einer militärischen Eroberung und Besetzung der Gebiete ist ja ferner in den Texten keine Rede und wir haben keinen Anlass zu glauben, dass sie je in grösserem Umfang stattgefunden habe.[4]

Die Freude des Volkes hatte ihren guten Grund: nicht immer hatte die Lage derartig günstig ausgesehen. Im Völkerspruch gegen Damaskus Amos I:3ff. weiss der Prophet von Greueltaten zu berichten, die die Damaszener in dem von ihnen besetzten Gilead früher begangen hatten; sie müssen sich sogar im Rahmen der damaligen Kriegsführung als besonders grauenhaft hervorgehoben haben. Ja, aus dem genannten Text gewinnt man den Eindruck, dass die Aramäer in Gilead eine bewusst geplante Politik der Ausrottung bzw. der Vertreibung der israelitischen Lokalbevölkerung verfolgten, wohl um in den dadurch entstandenen, leeren Gegenden eigene Kolonisten anzusiedeln. Auch zu diesem Gegenstand möchte ich bald zurückkehren.

Dieses Schreckensgespenst war nun zur Zeit des Auftretens des Amos'

2. Ich glaube beweisen zu können, dass das Erdbeben von Amos I:1, auf das im Buch ein paar Mal Bezug genommen wird, gegen 760 stattfand, sodass Amos Anfangs von 761 ("Zwei Jahre vor dem Erdbeben") in Betʾel aufgetreten ist, vgl. hierzu und für die Ansetzung der Anfangszeit der Regenz Jothams, meinen Aufsatz "Das Erdbeben von Amos I:1 und die Chronologie der Könige Ussia und Jotham von Juda," in *ZAW*, 82 (1970): 117–21. Zu dieser Zeit scheint also die Nachricht von den Siegen Jerobeams II. in Transjordan eingetroffen zu sein.

Für die allgemeinen, in diesem Aufsatz behandelten Fragen vgl. *für Israel*: M. Noth, *Geschichte Israels* (Göttingen, 1954), §19; J. Bright, *A History of Israel* (Philadelphia, 1959), Kap. VI, und M. Haran, "The rise and the decline of the Empire of Jerobeam ben Joaš," in *VT* 17 (1967): 266–97; eine gute Übersicht bietet ferner R. de Vaux, Art. *Israël* (Histoire d'), in *Supplément au Dictionnaire de la Bible,* IV (1949), Sp. 729–77, bes. Sp. 748; *Für Aram*: A. Dupont-Sommer, *Les Araméens* (Paris, 1949), Kap. 3, und M. F. Unger, *Israel and the Aramaeans of Damascus* (London, 1957), Kap. VI–IX. Man vergleiche ferner für beide die Einträge in den verschiedenen Nachschlagewerken; wichtig ist A.M.(alamat) art. *ʾrm dmšq*, in *Encyclopaedia Biblica* I (1954), Sp. 577–80 (Hebr.). Folgende Aufsätze waren mir nicht mehr zugänglich: J. M. Miller, "Geshur and Aram," *JNES* 28 (1969): 60–61 und É. Lipiński, "Ben Hadad II. of the Bible and of History," *Fifth World Congress of Jewish Studies* (Jerusalem 1969.)

3. So richtig schon Jepsen, (S. unten, Anm. 10) und M. Haran a.a.O., S. 266, vgl. ferner die Lesart der LXX. Für die geographischen Probleme siehe zuletzt Y. Aharoni, *The Land of the Bible* (London, 1966), S. 313. H. Tadmor, "The southern border of Aram," in *IEJ* 12 (1962): 114–22, bes.S. 119 hält diesen Bericht für völlig historisch: Jerobeam II. soll es gelungen sein, die Macht Damaskus' endgültig zu zerschlagen. Noth a.a.O., S. 228 findet das ganze problematisch und es verwundert nicht, dass S. Cohen, a.a.O., S. 154 von "Royal boasts" redet.

4. So richtig H. Tadmor a.a.O., S. 119.

angeblich für längere Zeit gebannt. Amos I:4 erwähnt ausdrücklich Ḥazaʾel und Ben-Hadad (wohl der dritte dieses Namens, wie wir noch sehen werden,[5] deren Länder, doch hauptsächlich Damaskus,[6] für die von ihnen begangenen Untaten jetzt heimgesucht worden waren. Durch die Wiederherstellung der eigenen Grenzen in Transjordan und die Unterwerfung verschiedener Aramäerstaaten, schien nun dieses Orakel erfüllt, besonders wenn wir die allerdings aus textkritischen Gründen schwer benutzbare Nachricht II Kön. XIV:28 heranziehen dürfen, nach der es Jerobeam II. gelungen sein soll, sogar Damaskus selbst zu erobern.

Das neugeschaffene Machtbild ist aber bekanntlich von kurzer Dauer gewesen. Es gab zwar keine grösseren Auseinandersetzungen mehr zwischen Aram und Israel, wenigstens soweit wir wissen; die gemeinsame Gefahr schuf wenige Jahrzehnte später ein neues Bündnis gegen Assur, doch es gelang den Alliierten nicht mit dem östlichen Koloss fertig zu werden: zwischen 730 und 720 gab es praktisch keine unabhängigen Gebiete mehr, mit den Ausnahmen von Juda und einigen philistäischen Stadtstaaten, die allerdings in einem Vassallenverhältnis zum assyrischen Grossreich standen. Darin erfüllte sich ein weiterer, prophetischer Spruch gegen Damaskus: Jesaja XVII: 1ff.

## II

Die Geschichte der Auseinandersetzungen zwischen Israel und Damaskus reicht bis in die letzten Jahre des salomonischen Grossreiches zurück, nachdem David ganz Syrien in ein Vassallenverhältnis gebracht hatte. Sie sei hier in ihren Hauptzügen neu aufgezeichnet; wer die Probleme eingehender behandeln möchte, wird auf die oben Anm.2 erwähnte Literatur verwiesen.

Schon I Kön. XI:23–25 berichtet, dass es in den letzten Jahren der Amtszeit Salomos einigen Aramäerstaaten gelang, die unter David verlorene Unabhängigkeit wiederzugewinnen: von Damaskus (txt.emend. nach LXX) und von Ṣobaʾ ist hier ausdrücklich die Rede. Von Streitigkeiten zwischen

5. Im Falle dass die These von W. F. Albright, "A votive stele erected by Ben Hadad I of Damascus to the God Melcart," in *BASOR* Nr. 87 (1942), 23–29 und Nr. 90 (1943): 32–34 zutrifft, nach welcher es nur einen Ben-Hadad vor Ḥazaʾel gegeben habe (für die Melkart-Stele vgl. jetzt *KAI* Nr. 201), wäre der Sohn Ḥazaʾels der zweite, statt der dritte dieses Namens (vgl. unten, Anm.16). Die Frage ist für unser Thema unwichtig, doch ich sehe nicht, dass die Albright'sche Lösung ausser von Unger a.a.O., S. 67, vgl. Anm.33 S. 152 und 8 S. 158f. angenommen worden ist, vgl. H. Donner, *KAI* II, S. 203.

6. Mit den von A. Malamat, "Amos 1:5 in the light of the Til Barsip inscriptions," in *BASOR* Nr. 129 (1953): 25ff. vorgeschlagene Identifizierung von Bêt ʿEden mit *bit adini* brauchen wir uns nicht hier auseinanderzusetzten; sie eröffnet äusserst interessante Perspektiven und zeigt, wie weit sich der politische Einfluss von Damaskus ausdehnte; zu diesem letzten Problem, vgl. unten, den zweiten Teil der Anm. 10.

Israel und Damaskus berichtet I Kön. XV:16–20: auf Anlass von Asa, König von Juda (*ASOR* ca. 913–873, *BJ* ca. 908–868)[7] soll Ben-Hadad I. (Anfang des 9. Jhdts. ca. 880) sein Bündnis mit Baesa von Israel (*ASOR* ca. 900–877, *BJ* ca. 906–883) gebrochen und einen grossen Teil des wegen des Bündnisses nur ungenügend geschützten Nordgebietes Israels besetzt haben.[8] Ben-Hadad II. (*ASOR* ca. 880–842, *BJ* vor 853—ca. 845) gelang es sogar, nach I Kön. XX, bis nach Samarien vorzudringen und es zu belagern. Ahab (*ASOR* ca. 869–850, *BJ*, ca. 871–852) gelang es aber, die Belagerung zu sprengen und ein Jahr darauf Ben-Hadad II. bei ᶜAfeq (am östlichen Ufer des Sees Gennezaret, östlich vom heutigen Ên Gēb) zu schlagen. Darauf folgte eine kurze Periode des Friedens: I Kön. XX:30b-34 berichtet sogar von einem Bündnis zwischen Ben-Hadad und Ahab. Es entstand aber nicht, weil sich die beiden Könige versöhnt hätten, sondern anscheinend um sich gemeinsam dem Drang nach Westen Assurs zu widersetzen: 853 wurde zwischen Šalmaneser III. (*ASOR* 859–825, *BJ* 858–824) und den Verbündeten die Schlacht von Qarqar (*ANET*², S. 279a und *TGI*², S. 49ff.) geschlagen; den Assyrern gelang es zwar, wenn wir ihren Berichten glauben, technisch gesehen, den Sieg davonzutragen, doch nicht, ihn zu praktischen Zwecken auszunützen.[9] Drei Jahre nach der Schlacht von ᶜAfeq begegnete, nach I Kön. XXII, eine Koalition zwischen Ahab von Israel und Josaphat von Juda (*ASOR* ca. 873–849, *BJ* ca. 868–847) dem diesmal in Gilead eingefallenen Ben-Hadad II.; die Verbündeten wurden aber bei Ramot von Gilead verheerend geschlagen und Ahab selbst ward tötlich verletzt.[10] Damit

7. Ich vermerke jedesmal die beiden, heute meistgebrauchten Chronologien: die der "American Schools of Oriental Research," abgekürzt *ASOR*, vgl. W. F. Albright, "The Chronology of the Divided Monarchy," in *BASOR* Nr. 100 (1945): 16–22 und zuletzt E. F. Campbell, "The Ancient Near East: Chronological bibliography and charts," in *The Bible and the Ancient Near East, Essays . . . W. F. Albright . . .*, ed. by G. E. Wright (Garden City, 1961), S. 214–24 (paperback edit. 1965, S. 281–99), und die von J. Begrich, *Die Chronologie der Könige von Israel und Juda* (Tübingen, 1929), weitergeführt von A. Jepsen in A. Jepsen-E. Hanhart, *Untersuchungen zur israelitisch-jüdischen Chronologie* (*BZAW* Nr. 88) (Berlin, 1964) und in den Zeittafeln bei W. Rudolph *Hosea* (*KAT* XIII, 1) (Gütersloh, 1966), S. 271ff., abgekürzt *BJ*.

8. A. Dupont-Sommer a.a.O., S. 33.

9. Ders. S. 34, und W. W. Hallo, "From Qarqar to Carchemish," in *BA* 23 (1960): 34–61, bes. S. 39f. heben mit Recht hervor, dass nur die von I Kön. XX:30bff. erwähnten Umstände die Bedingungen für die Bildung einer israelitisch-aramäischen Koalition stellten. Unsicher ist allerdings Unger a.a.O., S. 67.

10. Nach A. Jepsen, "Israel und Damaskus," in *AfO* 14 (1941–42): S. 153–72, bes. S. 154ff. berichten die assyrischen Annalen von verschiedenen Zügen, in denen Šalmaneser III. gegen dieselben Verbündeten, *Israel einbegriffen* (von mir gesperrt), gekämpft haben soll. Also kann es keine weiteren Kriege zwischen Israel und Damaskus bis 845 gegeben haben. Unger a.a.O., S. 70, bes. Anm. 54 S. 154 erwähnt diesen Umstand, doch nur als eine Möglichkeit. Nun zeigt sich aber, dass die assyrischen Annalen ab 853 bis zur Besiegung Jehus (*ANET*², S. 280) verschiedene assyrische Expeditionen nach Westen, Israel aber nicht, erwähnen.

scheint das Gleichgewicht zwischen Israel und Aram auf Kosten des Ersteren wiederum gebrochen.

Hier müssen wir nun kurz halt machen, um uns schnell einigen chronologischen Fragen zu widmen. Wenn die Schlacht von Ramot mit dem Todesjahr Ahabs zusammenfällt (mit dem oben Anm. 10, gemachten Vorbehalt), so ergibt sich nach den verschiedenen Chronologien folgende Sequenz, *a*) *Schlacht von Ramot und Tod Ahabs*: nach *ASOR* um 850, nach *BJ* um 852; *b*) *Schlacht von ᶜAfeq*: nach *ASOR* um 852, nach *BJ* um 854; *c*) *Belagerung und Entsatz Samariens*: nach *ASOR* um 853, nach *BJ* um 855. Der zwischen den Schlachten von ᶜAfeq und Ramot entstandene, kurze Friede und das darauffolgende Bündnis zwischen Israel und Damaskus haben aber in der *ASOR*-Chronologie praktisch keinen Platz, da sie, wenn auch nur kurz, *vor* der Schlacht von Qarqar, deren Datum 853 feststeht und deren Voraussetzung sie bilden, geschlossen sein müssen. In der Chronologie von *BJ* lässt sich hingegen das ganze gut unterbringen. Ähnlich verhält es sich, wie ich anderswo[11] zu zeigen versucht habe, mit dem Amos I:1 erwähnten Erdbeben, das gegen 760 angesetzt werden und durch das das Anfangsjahr der Regenz Jothams von Juda festgesetzt werden muss.

## III

Eine zweite Phase eröffnet sich mit den beiden Staatsstreichen, die in Damaskus Ḥazaʾel, in Israel Jehu auf den Thron brachten. Nach den biblischen Berichten, vgl. II Kön. VIII:7ff. und IX:1ff., soll der Prophet Elisa an beiden mehr oder weniger Aktiv beteiligt gewesen sein. Während nun

---

Jepsen macht ferner auf den merkwürdigen Umstand aufmerksam, dass I Kön. XXII:40 eine annalistische Notiz wiedergibt, in der der Tod Ahabs mit der für einen natürlichen Tod üblichen Formel registriert ist. Ähnliche Notizen gibt es bei den meisten Königen, was für ihre Glaubwürdigkeit zeugt. Diese Beobachtung wurde, so weit mir bekannt ist, zum ersten Mal von G. Hölscher, "Das Buch der Könige, seine Quellen und seine Redaktion," in *ΕΥΧΑΡΙΣΤΗΡΙΟΝ . . . H. Gunkel* (FRLANT Nr. 36) (Göttingen, 1923), I. S. 158–213, bes. S. 185, gemacht. In so einem Fall kann Ahab allerdings nicht auch in einer Schlacht gefallen sein, vgl. noch Jepsens *Chronologie* . . ., S. 40f. Dieses Problem, auf das weder Dupont-Sommer a.a.O., S. 37f., noch die nach dem 2. Weltkrieg erschienenen Kommentare eingehen (die von Unger a.a.O., S. 72 gemachte Kritik scheint mir ganz ungenügend), ist aber zu wichtig, als dass es nicht erneut und eingehend geprüft werden müsste, was aber in diesem Rahmen nicht geschehen kann.

Die Möglichkeit, dass es Ben-Hadad II. gelungen sei, eine Art grossaramäischen Staat auf föderativen Grundlagen zu errichten, vgl. B. Mazar, "The Aramaean Empire and its relations to Israel," in *BA* 25 (1962): 98–120, bes. S. 106ff., braucht in diesem Rahmen nicht erörtert zu werden. H. Donner, *KAI* II, S. 204, ist dagegen, aber es scheint mir, dass sowohl in assyrischen als auch in aramäischen Urkunden Damaskus oft als führendes Element innerhalb eines solchen Gebildes auftritt.

11. A.a.O. (Anm. 2); ähnlich A. Malamat, *ʾrm dmšq*, Sp. 578.

aber die Aussagen des zweitgenannten Textes durch die anfängliche Einstellung Jehus gegen den synkretistischen und kanaanäischen Kultus, vgl. X:18ff., eine allerdings nur mittelbare Bestätigung erhält, indem durch sie die grosse Wahrscheinlichkeit entsteht, dass tatsächlich prophetische Kreise hinter dem Staatsstreich Jehus standen, ist die Lage in Bezug auf das, was in Damaskus geschah, vollkommen verschieden. Aus der sogenannten "Basaltstatue" Šalmanesers III. (*ANET*², S. 280b) geht nämlich hervor, dass Ben-Hadad II. während einer von ihm verlorenen Schlacht fiel[12] und dass an seiner Stelle Ḥazaʾel "ein Niemandssohn," sich des Thrones bemächtigte. Einen richtigen Staatsstreich, der mit der Ermordung Ben-Hadads II. endete, hat es also nicht gegeben und damit fällt die Beteiligung Elisas von selbst aus.[13] Wenn es aber möglich war, beide Gegebenheiten durch ein angebliches Eingreifen Elisas chronologisch miteinander zu verbinden, so müssen sie gleichzeitig stattgefunden haben, was auch allgemein angenommen wird, und zwar nach *ASOR* um 842, nach *BJ* um 845.[14]

II Kön. X:32ff. berichtet von schweren, von Seiten Jehus erlittenen Niederlagen durch Ḥazaʾel, was wiederum zum Verlust ganz Transjordans führte; ja, sogar Juda wurde einige Zeit später zur Zeit Joaš' (*ASOR* ca. 837–800, *BJ* ca. 840–801) tributpflichtig gemacht. Doch die Bedingung zur Dauerhaftigkeit all dieser Erfolge Arams gegen Israel war, dass Assur nach 853 nicht mehr nach Westen drängen würde. Weil hingegen eine solche Bedingung nicht erfüllt wurde und die Assyrer bald erneut nach Westen drängten, waren die Siege Arams über Israel und Juda von kurzer Wirkung. Unter Adad-nirari III. (*ASOR* ca. 811–784, *BJ* ca. 809–782), im 5. Jahr seines Reiches (807 bzw. 804) erreichte Aram seinen Tiefpunkt: Damaskus wurde belagert und tributpflichtig gemacht (*ANET*², S. 281, *TGI*², S. 53). Um diese Zeit ist Hazaʾel angeblich gestorben, wir wissen nicht ob noch vor, oder erst nach der Belagerung Damaskus': der dort besiegte König wird ja bekanntlich nur mit seinem Titel, nicht mit seinem Namen genannt.[15] Nach de Vaux soll er kurz nach der Belagerung gestorben sein. Die innen- und aussenpolitische Lage Damaskus' wurde hierdurch selbstverständlich äusserst prekär: nach einigen Autoren soll es sogar dem Sohn und Nachfolger

12. Mehr lässt sich kaum aus dem akkadischen Ausdruck *sadāšu ēmid*—"eines nicht natürlichen Todes sterben" folgern; es ist mir deswegen rätselhaft, wieso nach Unger a.a.O., S. 75 der biblische Bericht durch den akkadischen "strikingly" bestätigt wird.

13. Nach Dupont-Sommer a.a.O., S. 38 soll diese Nachricht dennoch historisch sein.

14. Dies wurde richtig schon von Jepsen, 1942, S. 158 vermerkt.

15. So wird heute allgemein das im assyrischen Texte erscheinende *mariʾ* gedeutet, vgl. R. de Vaux, "La chronologie de Ḥazaël et de Benhadad III," *RB* 43 (1934): 512–18 (jetzt *Bible et Orient* [Paris, 1967], S. 75–82) und *ANET*², S. 281, Anm. 2. Nach Dupont-Sommer a.a.O., S. 53 und Haran a.a.O. S. 267 handelt es sich um Ben-Hadad III.

Ḥaza'els, Ben-Hadad III,[16] erst einige Jahre später gelungen sein die Nachfolge anzutreten,[17] nach anderen bleibt das Datum seiner Thronbesteigung völlig ungewiss.[18]

Ein letzter Schlag traf Damaskus durch Zakir, König von Hamat (vgl. dazu die Zakir-Stele, Anfang des 8. Jhdts., *ANET*², S. 501ff. und *KAI* Nr. 202, vgl. bes. A, 4). Das Heer Ben-Hadads III. und der Verbündeten wurde von Zakir geschlagen und Hamat konnte sich von der Herrschaft Damaskus' befreien. Die Schlacht muss kurz nach der Unterwerfung von Damaskus durch Adad-nirari III. stattgefunden haben.[19]

Durch die zeitweilige Beseitigung Arams als politische Macht konnte Israel seine eigene Lage erheblich verbessern, eine Tatsache, auf die vielleicht II Kön. XIII:5 Bezug nimmt.[20] Aber auch diesmal war die Gefahr nicht vollkommen gebannt, denn es scheint nicht, dass Assur seinen Erfolg völlig ausnützte: wiederum gab es sich mit der Tributpflicht und dem Vassallentum der besiegten Völker zufrieden. Immerhin, es gelang Israel sein Haupt wieder zu erheben. König Joaš (*ASOR* ca. 801–786, *BJ* ca. 802–787) konnte in drei Schlachten sein Reich in die traditionellen Grenzen zurückbringen, II Kön. XIII:22–25, und man muss wohl annehmen, dass ein von jeher israelitisches Gebiet wie Gilead dabei inbegriffen war, da unser Text keine Ausnahme vorsieht.[21]

## IV

Eine dritte Phase fängt mit dem Tode Adad-niraris III (gegen 783 oder 782) an. Unter Šalmaneser IV (*ASOR* 783–774, *BJ* 781–772) musste sich Assur an seiner Nordgrenze gegen Urartu[22] zur Wehr setzen und Aram konnte sich langsam wieder erholen.[23] Umsonst versuchte der Assyrerkönig wäh-

16. Darüber, dass Ben-Hadad III. der Sohn Ḥaza'els war, besteht kein Zweifel, vgl. die demnächst zitierte Stele von Zakir von Hamat.

17. Unter Anderen H. Donner, *KAI* II, S. 207.

18. Jüngstens A. Jepsen bei W. Rudolph a.a.O.

19. A. Dupont-Sommer a.a.O., S. 45ff. und H. Donner, *KAI*, S. 209.

20. Ob und eventuell mit wem der dort vom "Dtr." genannte *môšîᵃᶜ* zu identifizieren sei muss hier offenbleiben, vgl. die Kommentare und Haran a.a.O., S. 268; *quot capita, tot sententiae*: es ist oft die Rede entweder von Adad-nirari III, oder von Zakir; doch nach II Kön. XIV:26 käme auch wohl Jeroboam II. in Betracht, obwohl es merkwürdig wäre, ihn vom "Dtr." in so einer theologisch wichtigen Rolle zu sehen. Jeder Erklärung haftet derselbe Grad von Wahrscheinlichkeit bzw. Unwahrscheinlichkeit an.

21. So Jepsen a.a.O. (1942), S. 45ff. und J. Bright a.a.O., S. 238; dagegen Haran a.a.O., S. 267, dessen Argumente mich aber nicht überzeugen.

22. So Cohen a.a.O., S. 158 und der Kommentar von H. W. Wolff (*BK XIV*, 2) S. 183f.

23. Mit diesem Tatbestand scheint H. Tadmor a.a.O., S. 119 nicht zu rechnen und möchte deswegen die von der assyrischen Königsinschrift aus Nimrud bezeugte Südgrenze Damaskus' erst gegen 738 ansetzen. Ich hoffe, die Möglichkeit einer früheren Datierung erwiesen zu haben.

rend der letzten Jahre seiner Amtszeit, Damaskus erneut zu unterwerfen; ja es ist nicht einmal eindeutig, ob die Assyrer angriffen,[24] oder ob es die Aramäer waren, die eine Art von Befreiungskrieg begannen.[25] Es gelang ihnen immerhin, ihre Unabhängigkeit erneut zu behaupten und, nach dem Bericht der Panamuwwa I. Stele (Hälfte des 8. Jhdts., *KAI* Nr. 214), wiederum zu wirtschaftlicher Blüte zu gelangen.

## V

Im Rahmen des assyrisch-aramäischen Krieges gegen das Ende des Reiches Šalmaneser III. lässt sich nun auch der Text Amos I:3–4 gut verstehen. Ein Kampf gegen Norden mit einer im Süden nach den Wiedereroberungen durch Joaš strategisch ungünstig verlaufenden Grenze wäre gefährlich wenn nicht geradezu unmöglich gewesen. So erklärt sich die Invasion Gileads, auf die der Text Bezug nimmt.[26] Sie setzte sich nicht das Ziel, Israel ganz oder teilweise zu bändigen: mit der Eroberung und eventueller Neubesiedlung Gileads war das Ziel erreicht, eine günstige Südgrenze zu schaffen. Der grosse antiassyrische Vorstoss konnte nunmehr beginnen. Wir befinden uns in der Anfangszeit der Regierung Jerobeams II., und in den letzten Jahren Ben-Hadads III. und Šalmanesers IV. Die von den Aramäern begangenen Greueltaten lösten bei Amos das Orakel gegen Damaskus und seine Herrscher aus. Aber zur Zeit, als Amos sich in Betʾel befand, gerade als Damaskus erneut durch eine Periode der Schwäche ging,[27] gelang es Jerobeam II. einen Gegenstoss wider Damaskus auszuführen,[28] dessen Erfolg die im

24. So. A. Dupont-Sommer a.a.O., S. 55; A. Malamat a.a.O., Sp. 579 und M. Haran a.a.O., Sp. 278f.

25. So Cohen a.a.O., S. 158; H. W. Wolff, *BK XIV*, 2 S. 183 nennt es "eine offene Frage" wer tatsächlich angriff, wohl mit Recht.

26. Es scheint mir äusserst unwahrscheinlich, dass Amos I:3 auf II Kön. X:32f. Bezug nimmt, wie man immer wieder hört: vgl. die Kommentare von Fosbrooke (*IB* VI) und A. Weiser (*ATD* 24); ferner H. Tadmor a.a.O., S. 119 s.; L. M. Muntingh, "Political and international relations of Israel's neighboring peoples according to the oracles of Amos," in *Studies in the books of Amos and Hosea* (*OuTWP* Nr. 7–8), ed. by A. H. van Zyl, S. 134–42. Dagegen mit Recht Cohen a.a.O., S. 155 und H. W. Wolff a.a.O., S. 181f. Es muss sich um etwas handeln, dass kurz vorher geschehen war und nicht um die 80 Jahre früher, wenn das Grauen noch andauerte, Ḥazaʾel erscheint dann wohl hier nur deswegen, weil seine neugegründete Dynastie die alte Angriffspolitik gegen Israel wiederaufnahm und fortsetzte.

27. Darin sieht G. Rinaldi, *I Profeti minori*, I (Torino, 1953), S. 137 ein Zeichen, dass Damaskus wiederum geschwächt und deswegen bedeutungslos geworden war, eine Lage, die Jerobeam II. gut auszunützen verstand. Auch nach ihm handelt es sich also um einen neuen Überfall, wie oben Anm. 26 bei Cohen und Wolff.

28. Müsste man deswegen nicht vielleicht doch folgern, das Auftreten des Amos habe etwas länger gedauert als meistens angenommen wird? Diese Frage wird von J. García Trapiello, "Situación histórica del profeta Amós," in *Est. Bíbl.* 26 (1967): 249–74, bes. S. 272 erörtert, doch verneinend beantwortet. Haran a.a.O., S. 279 möchte den Eroberungszug Jerobeams II.

Heiligtum versammelte Kultgemeinde derartig begeisterte. Denn der Erfolg liess sich gut als Erfüllung des kurz vorher vom Propheten geäusserten Orakels gegen Damaskus verstehen. Diese Begeisterung teilte Amos allerdings nicht: politisch hatte sich die Lage nur auf lokaler Ebene etwas zu Gunsten Israels geändert und jene Macht im Osten, der Israel seine Erfolge am Anfang des Jahrhunderts verdankte, stand ja noch immer bereit, ihre Eroberungsziele nach Westen und nach Süden wieder zu verfolgen, wobei sie nicht nur nicht vor den Aramäern, sondern auch nicht vor Israel Halt machen würde. Theologisch hatten sich für den Propheten die Voraussetzungen des Gerichts nicht im Geringsten geändert und die Folgerung, wenn konsequent gezogen, konnte nur die sein, dass Jahwe bald sein Gerichtshandeln in der Geschichte wiederaufnehmen würde.

---

um die Hälfte des 8. Jhdts. ansetzen; doch dies ist nur möglich, wenn auch Amos' Auftreten gegen 750 angesetzt wird, was unmöglich ist (vgl. meinen oben Anm. 2. genannten Aufsatz), es sei denn, man räume mehr Zeit ein für die Dauer seines Amtes.

# Zwei alttestamentliche Königsnamen*

J. J. STAMM

In meinem Beitrag zur Landsberger-Festschrift[1] ging ich auf die Namen der Könige Rehabeam und Jerobeam ein.[2] Es geschah dies in einer kurzen und vorläufigen Weise; so ergreife ich gerne die Gelegenheit, darauf zurückzukommen, umso mehr, als der verehrte Jubilar sich selber verschiedentlich um ihre Deutung bemühte.

## I

*r$^e$ḥăb$^c$am* begegnet im Alten Testament nur als Name von Salomos Sohn und Nachfolger. Der erste Bestandteil des PN enthält das auch in anderen semitischen Sprachen[3] gebrauchte Verb *raḥăb*. Es bedeutet im *Qal* "sich erwei-

* Ausser den üblichen werden noch die folgenden Abkürzungen gebracuht: *AeP* = Hermann Ranke, *Die aegyptischen Personennamen* I (1935), II (1952). Aistl. = Joseph Aistleitner, *Wörterbuch der ugaritischen Sprache*[3] (1967). *AN* = J. J. Stamm, *Die akkadische Namengebung, 1939* (Neudruck, 1968). *HEN* = J. J. Stamm, *Hebräische Ersatznamen*, s. Anm. 1. *IPN* = Martin Noth, *Die israelitischen Personennamen im Rahmen der gemeinsemitischen Namengebung, 1928* (Neudruck, 1966). *KBL* = Ludwig Koehler, Walter Baumgartner, *Lexicon in Veteris Testamenti Libros* (1953). *KBL*[3] = Hebräisches und aramäisches Lexikon zum Alten Testament, 3. Aufl., neu bearbeitet von Walter Baumgartner . . ., Lieferung I (1967). *NPS* = G. Ryckmans, *Les noms propres sud-sémitiques, tome I: Répertoire analytique* (1934). *PN* = Personenname. Die Umschrift des Hebräischen geschieht im folgenden nach *ZAW*.

1. Studies in Honor of Benno Landsberger on his Seventy-Fifth Birthday April 21, 1965 (Assyriological Studies No. 16, 1965, S. 413–24).
2. Loc. cit. S. 418f.
3. Für das Ugaritische s. Aistl. Nr. 2497.

tern" (I Sam. 2:1 von dem gegen die Feinde sich öffnenden Mund und Jes. 60:5 vom Herzen des endzeitlichen Jerusalem gesagt) und "sich verbreitern" (von einem Gang oder Umgang im Tempel), so an der textlich schwierigen Stelle Ez. 41:7. Am einzigen Beleg des *Niphal* (Jes. 30:23) heisst das Partizip *nirḥab* "geräumig," wobei der Weideplatz für das Vieh gemeint ist. Dem *Qal* entsprechend hat das *Hiphil* den Sinn "weit machen," "erweitern." Es gibt dafür 21(20) Belege, von denen mehrere wieder einen übertragenen Gebrauch zeigen mit Beziehung auf den Mund, die Kehle, den Verstand(*leb*) und den Schritt (II Sam. 22:37 = Ps. 18:37). Aber an sieben Stellen steht *hirḥîb* im räumlichen Sinn (Gen. 26:22; Ex. 34:24; Dtn. 12:20; 19:8; 33:20; Jes. 54:2; Am. 1:13). Dieser hat als der alte und ursprüngliche zu gelten, wie er unverfälscht auch im Arabischen zu Tage tritt. Edward William Lane, *Arabic-English Lexicon, Book I/3* (1867), S. 1051 übersetzt das Verb *raḥuba/raḥiba* in den verschiedenen Stammformen folgendermassen: I. "It was, or became, ample, spacious, wide, or roomy"; IV. "He made it ample, spacious, wide, or roomy"; II. "He welcomed him with the greetings of *marḥabān*; or simply: he welcomed him." Es ist klar, dass man für das *Qal* des Verbums im hebräischen Namen allein die I. Form des arabischen *raḥuba/raḥiba* und nicht die wohl vom Begrüssungsruf *marḥabān* abgeleitete II. Form heranziehen darf.[4]

Damit ist erst der allgemeine Sinn des Prädikates in dem uns beschäftigenden Königsnamen gefunden, seine spezielle Bedeutung ist aber noch offen. Bevor sie gesucht wird, ist es angezeigt, die Form des Verbums als Perfekt festzulegen, da theoretisch auch ein Imperativ in Frage käme, wie Albright das einmal erwog.[5] Weil nun Perfekt-Namen im Hebräischen geläufig, mit dem Imperativ gebildete jedoch höchst selten sind,[6] ist das Verständnis der Verbalform nicht zweifelhaft, und zwar nicht im Sinne eines Wunsches,[7]

4. Gegen Montgomery-Gehman, *The Book of Kings* (ICC) (1951), S. 248. Noth, *IPN*, S. 193 zieht das mittelhebräische *raḥab* "freigebig" heran, was nicht nötig ist.

5. So in *AJSL* 44 (1927/28), S. 32, wo er bemerkt: ". . . it was regular in West Semitic to change the imperfect of a verb used in composition to the imperative." Neben das so verstandene *r$^{e}$ḥăb$^{c}$am* stellt Albright ein hypothetisches *yirḥăb$^{c}$am*.

6. Vgl. dazu meinen Aufsatz: "Ein Problem der altsemitischen Namengebung" (Fourth World Congress of Jewish Studies, Papers Vol. I, Jerusalem 1967, S. 141–47, besonders S. 142).

7. So Albright, *From the Stone Age to Christianity* (1940), S. 185 = *Von der Steinzeit zum Christentum* (1949), S. 244. Er übersetzt: "Let (my) People be Widened," bzw. "Möge mein Volk weit werden." Unter Berufung auf Albright übersetzt Alfred Jepsen in BHH III Sp. 1572: "das Volk möge sich ausbreiten." Anders als im Arabischen ist das Perfekt zum Ausdruck des Wunsches im Hebräischen selten und mit der Partikel *lû* "wenn doch!," "o dass doch!" verbunden, vgl. Emil Kautzsch, *Hebräische Grammatik*[28] (1909), §106p (S. 324), §151e (S. 500), und Carl Brockelmann, *Hebräische Syntax* (1956), §8b (S. 6).

sondern einer Aussage, wie es dem normalen Gebrauch des Perfekts im Hebräischen entspricht.[8]

Ausserhalb der Namen gäbe es für *r^eḥăb* (*raḥăb*) nur die Uebersetzung: "Es ist weit geworden," die selbstverständlich auch für den PN möglich ist. Doch kommt für ihn auch eine kausativische Wiedergabe "er hat weit gemacht" in Frage, da bei den Namen öfter das *Qal* anstelle des sonst üblichen *Piᶜel* oder *Hiphil* gebraucht wird, vgl. dazu Noth, *IPN* S. 36. *Qal* anstatt *Piᶜel* haben wir in: *d^elajā(hû)*, *m^elaṭjā*, *p^elaṭjā(hû)* und *palal*, *p^elăljā*, *ʾaelîpăl*; *Qal* für *Hiphil* in *ʾaebjasap*/*ʾaeljasap*, *ʾăbjatar*, *ʾ^azănajā*, *ʾaeljăḥbaʾ*, *ʾaelîšaᶜ* (= *ʾaeljašaᶜ*), *ʾaelᶜad*, *n^ebaṭ*, *p^elaʾjā*/*p^elajā* und dazu vielleicht *ʾaelîp^elehû*.[9]—Mögliche Fälle dieser Art sind auch; *ʾ^amăṣjā(hû)* "Jahwe ist stark" oder "hat gestärkt" (*Pi.*), bzw. "sich stark erwiesen" (*Hi.*); *ʾ^aṣăljā(hû)* "Jahwe hat sich als edel erwiesen" (*Pi.* oder eher *Hi.*, zur Bevorzugung des letzteren vgl. Ernst Jenni, *Das hebräische Piᶜel* [1968], S. 54); *g^edăljā(hû)*, *jigdăljahû* "Jahwe hat sich als gross erwiesen," bzw. "möge sich als gross erweisen" (wieder eher *Hi.* als *Pi.* nach Jenni, loc. cit. S. 46); *ʾlśgb* (Dir. 216) mit dem Bezeichnungsnamen *ś^egûb* (*KBL*, S. 915a) "El hat sich als gross/erhaben gezeigt" (*Hi.*, vgl. Hiob 36,22).

Ob nun in *r^eḥăbᶜam* das Verb intransitiv "ist weit geworden" oder transitiv-kausativ "hat weit gemacht" übersetzt werden muss, lässt sich nicht entscheiden. Beide Möglichkeiten sind gegeben, sie lassen sich aber nicht erwägen, ohne dass zugleich das substantivische Element *ᶜam* mit berücksichtigt wird. Wie in anderen semitischen Sprachen heisst es auch im Hebräischen ursprünglich "Onkel(väterlicherseits)," dann bezeichnet es die nächsten männlichen Verwandten väterlicherseits und schliesslich und vor allem bedeutet es so viel wie Volk, d.h. in Beziehung auf Israel genauer "die Zusammenfassung der Männer zu gemeinsamem Beraten und Handeln, der Männerbund, der verantwortlich ist für den Bestand des Staates im Krieg und Frieden durch Pflege der Wehrhaftigkeit, des Rechts und des Kultes. Er ist der Staat auch dann, wenn dieser eine monarchische Spitze hat."[10] Auf die Tatsache, dass das Hebräische im Worte *ᶜam* einen demokratisch geprägten Begriff für die zu gemeinsamem öffentlichen Handeln berechtigten und verpflichteten Männer hat, werden wir sogleich zurückkommen. Zuvor müssen wir noch betonen, dass in den PN *ᶜam* die alte Bedeutung "Onkel" bewahrt hat, sei es in theophorem oder bei den Ersatznamen in profanem

8. In *AJSL* 38 (1922): 140 hat Albright auch diese Auffassung einmal vertreten mit der Wiedergabe: "He has extended the people."

9. Vgl. zu letzterem *IPN*, S. 32 Anm. 2 und *KBL*³, S. 54b.

10. So Leonhard Rost, *Das kleine Credo und andere Studien zum Alten Testament* (1965), S. 91.

Sinn, vgl. dazu *HEN* S. 418. Ausser *r*$^{e}$*hăb*$^{c}$*am* und *ja/jåråb*$^{c}$*am* sind es die folgenden: $^{\supset a}$*nî*$^{c}$*am*, *j*$^{e}$*qăm*$^{c}$*am*, *jašåb*$^{c}$*am*, *jitr*$^{ec}$*am*, $^{c}$*ammôn*, $^{c}$*ammî*$^{\supset}$*el*, $^{c}$*ammîhûd* $^{c}$*ammîzabad*, $^{c}$*ammînadab* und $^{c}$*ămram*. An diese Reihe darf man wohl die Ortsnamen *jibl*$^{ec}$*am* und *jåqn*$^{ec}$*am* anfügen, da es sich bei ihnen um ursprüngliche PN handeln dürfte.

Wegen dieser Belege läge es nahe, auch in *r*$^{e}$*ḥăb*$^{c}$*am* das Wort $^{c}$*am* mit "Onkel" zu übersetzen, doch kann das nicht ohne weiteres geschehen. Es ist unmöglich, wenn das Prädikat *raḥăb* als normales *Qal* durch "ist weit geworden" wiedergegeben wird. In diesem Falle kann $^{c}$*am* nur "Volk" bedeuten, und der Name lautet: "Das Volk ist weit geworden," eine Auffassung, die ausser von Noth, *IPN* S. 193 Anm.4 auch schon von G. Buchanan Gray, *Studies in Hebrew Proper Names* (*Die israelitischen Personennamen*) (1896), S. 59f. vertreten wurde. Mit $^{c}$*am* = "Volk" als Subjekt und *raḥăb* als Prädikat erhält man einen profanen Satznamen, der, soweit ich sehe, seine einzige Entsprechung im *š*$^{e\supset}$*ar jašûb* des Jesaja-Sohnes hat. Für den Propheten war der Name ein Programm oder besser Ausdruck einer Hoffnung, und aus einer ganz anderen Situation heraus kann der Name Rehabeam für Salomo seinen besonderen Sinn gehabt haben. Was wir meinen, hat Gray, loc. cit. S. 60 in die folgenden Worte gefasst: "it is certainly probable enough that Solomon recorded the national prosperity of his time in naming his son 'The people is enlarged'."

Was der Name festhält, ist somit nicht eine in persönlichen Umständen des Namengebers oder Namenträgers begründete Aeusserung; er hat vielmehr eine allgemeine, den Hintergrund der Benennung ausmachende Lage des Landes zum Inhalt. In diesem allgemeinen Aspekt hat er akkadische und aegyptische Parallelen. Bei beiden ist es das, was man den Hintergrund der Namengebung nennen kann. Für das Akkadische gehören die in *AN* §10 (S. 78ff.) aufgeführten Belege hinzu, darunter die *PN* $^{f}$*Takūn-mātum* "Das Land ist stabil (normal) geworden" und $^{f}$*Tatūr-mātu* "Das Land ist wieder (normal) geworden." Wohl viel zahlreicher sind die Beispiele, die sich aus dem aegyptischen Onomastikon beibringen lassen. Sie finden sich bei Ranke, *AeP* (*Aegyptische Personennamen*) II einerseits in dem grossen Abschnitt "Festnamen" (S. 216ff.) mit Hinweisen entweder auf die allgemeine glückliche oder festliche Situation[11] oder auf eine einzelne Begehung innerhalb des Festes,[12]

11. z.B. "Das Land ist im Feste" MR/NR (*AeP* I, 376/19), "$^{f}$Es ist ein Fest" *NR* (AePT 236/11). Keine Beziehung auf ein Fest zeigen die *r*$^{e}$*ḥăb*$^{c}$*am* besonders ähnlichen *PN* "Es dauert der Friede" *MR* (*AeP* I, 73/21) und "Das Land befindet sich wohl" *NR* (*AeP* II, 328/30).

12. z.B. "Amon ist auf dem See" *NR* (*AeP* I, 29/2), "Horus ist gelandet" *NR* (*AeP* I, 248/21), "Man hat den Apis nach Memphis gebracht" Spät (*AeP* I, 70/16).

und sie finden sich andererseits in der Rubrik: "Politisch-geschichtliche Namen mit Beziehung auf verschiedene Gottheiten" (S. 224 und S. 244f.). Diese gehören erst späteren Epochen (seit der 25. Dynastie) an, in denen Aegypten in den Assyrern und Persern fremde Herren über sich hatte. Auf deren Vertreibung möchte Ranke die *PN* folgenden Inhalts beziehen: "Das Auge des Horus ist (bzw. sei) gegen sie gerichtet," "Gott NN sei stark (bzw. siegreich) gegen sie" und "Möge der Gott NN sie ergreifen."[13]

Wie schon angedeutet, ist die Verwandtschaft von *rᵉḥăbᶜam* = "Das Volk ist weit geworden" mit den erwähnten akkadischen und aegyptischen *PN* nur sehr indirekt und allein darin begründet, dass hier wie dort, wenn auch in ganz verschiedener Weise, die Benennung mit dem Hintergrund zusammenhängt, aus dem sie erwuchs. Eine direktere Beziehung besteht nicht, weil es weder im Akkadischen noch im Aegyptischen ein dem hebräischen *ᶜam* "Volk" mit dem politischen Gehalt, wie wir ihn zuvor im Anschluss an Rost umschrieben, gibt. Im Akkadischen haben weder *awīlum/awīlūtum* "Mensch"/"Menschheit"[14] noch *nišū* "Menschen," "Leute" noch *ṣalmāt qaqqadi* "Die Schwarzköpfigen," was ein poëtischer Ausdruck für Menschheit ist (*CAD* 16 [1962], S. 75), einen entsprechenden Sinn.

Das Gleiche trifft für das Aegyptische zu, wenn man die Worte prüft, welche bei Erman-Grapow, Wörterbuch der aegyptischen Sprache VI (1950), im Deutsch-aegyptischen Wörterverzeichnis S. 176 für "Volk" angegeben sind. Es sind die folgenden fünf: 1. *ᶜšꜣ.t* "die Menge," "die Vielen," "das Volk"; 2. *pᶜ.t* "die Menschen" (im Unterschied zu den Göttern oder zu den Tieren), "das Volk" (im Gegensatz zum Hofstaat); 3. *rḫj.t* "Untertanen," "Volk," "die Menschen" (im Gegensatz zu Göttern oder Tieren); 4. *ḥnmm.t* "das Volk im Himmel" (so in alter Zeit), später "die Menschheit"; 5. *kwj* "das Volk," "die Menge," "die Menschen." Obwohl in der Uebersetzung verschiedentlich das Wort "Volk" auftaucht, so meint es doch nicht wie *ᶜam* den Kreis der verantwortlichen Männer, sondern die zwischen Göttern und Tieren stehende Menge, die Vielen oder dann allgemein die Menschen.

Unsere bisherigen Erwägungen gingen davon aus, dass *rᵉḥăbᶜam* als "das

13. Ueber diese *PN* handelte Ranke gesondert in dem Aufsatz: "Altägyptische Personennamen juristischen und politischen Inhalts" (Beiträge zur Kultur- und Rechtsphilosophie. Gustav Radbruch zum 70. Geburtstag, 1948, S. 244–250). Hier finden sich auch die Belege aus AeP für die in unserem Text zitierten *PN*.

14. Nach, *AHw*, S. 90f. hat *awīlum* in alter Zeit den speziellen Sinn "freier Bürger." Wie mir W. von Soden freundlich bemerkt, gibt es im Akkadischen zu *rᵉḥăbᶜam* keinen vergleichbaren Namen, wohl aber appellativische Sachentsprechungen wie *ummānātu* rapšātu (Delitzsch, *HWB*, S. 626b) "die weiten Truppen" oder *kimtu rapaštu* (*VR*, 44, 21b; *YOS*, 2, 129, 9) "die weite Familie" und *kimtu urappišu* (*VAB*, 7/2, S. 4/5, 29) "der die Familie erweiterte," vgl. dazu Lambert, *BWL*, S. 132, 120.

Volk ist weit geworden" verstanden werden müsse. Wir wiesen aber schon früher darauf hin, dass das *Qal* in den *PN* auch die Funktion eines Kausativs üben kann. Das ergibt für *r$^e$ḥăb$^c$am* die Möglichkeit zu übersetzen: entweder (a) "Der (vergöttlichte) Onkel hat weit gemacht" oder (b) "Er d.i. Jahwe, hat das Volk weit gemacht." Davon ist (a) wenig wahrscheinlich, auch wenn als selbstverständlich angenommen werden darf, dass das Appellativum *$^c$am* "Onkel" mit Jahwe gleichgesetzt wurde. Es ist jedoch zweifelhaft, ob man am Hofe des Salomo auf eine so altertümliche Gottesbezeichnung zurückgegriffen hätte. Für (b) lässt sich der in der Chronik (in einer Levitengenealogie) als Enkel des Mose aufgeführte *r$^e$ḥăbjā(hû)* (I Chr. 23:17; 24:21; 26:25) ins Feld führen; denn der *PN* kann nur heissen "Jahwe hat weit gemacht." Auf *r$^e$ḥăb$^c$am* angewendet, führt das auf einen zu postulierenden Vollnamen der Form: "Jahwe hat das Volk weit gemacht." Das wäre ein dreigliedriger, aus Subjekt, Objekt und Prädikat bestehender Name von einer Gestalt, wie sie wohl das Akkadische, nicht aber das Hebräische kennt. So wird man trotz *r$^e$ḥăbjā(hû)*, das vielleicht nur künstlich und spät nach dem alten *r$^e$ḥăb$^c$am* als eine Art religiöser Korrektur gebildet wurde, auch auf die unter (b) genannte Ableitung verzichten, und es bleibt das schon besprochene *r$^e$ḥăb$^c$am* = "Das Volk ist weit geworden."

Dieser Schluss setzt voraus, dass *r$^e$ḥăbjā(hû)* tatsächlich ein nur sekundär gebildeter und kein wirklich gebrauchter *PN* sei. Das ist möglich, aber nicht sicher; denn, obwohl spät überliefert, kann der Name alt und bei allen Ständen verbreitet gewesen sein. Dann würde das Verb *raḥăb* sich natürlich nicht auf die Ausdehnung des Volkes beziehen können, es müsste vielmehr auf die nach vorheriger Not eingetretene Weite oder Befreiung angespielt sein in einer Weise, wie sich das Ps. 18:20; 31:9 und 118:5 beim Hauptwort *maerḥab* "weiter Raum," "Weite" findet. Besonders sprechend ist Ps. 118:5, wo in den Worten: "Aus Bedrängnis hatte ich Jah gerufen, Jah hat mich erhört, dass ich frei ward" (oder wörtlich: "hat mich in die Weite hinein erhört"), die Worte *meṣăr* "Bedrängnis" und *maerḥab* einander gegenüberstehen.

Darf *r$^e$ḥăbjā(hû)* als echter Name anerkannt und nach den erwähnten Psalmenstellen verstanden werden, so lässt sich auch für *r$^e$ḥăb$^c$am* noch eine weitere Möglichkeit erwägen. Dieses könnte ebenfalls ein alter und schon vor Salomo üblicher Name gewesen sein, der den Dank dafür enthielt, dass der Onkel (gott) in die Weite geführt, d.h. die Not der (kinderlosen) Eltern oder des (kranken) Namenträgers gewendet hat. Salomo würde den alten *PN* aufgenommen und ihn gemäss seiner glücklichen Zeit umgedeutet haben zu: "Das Volk ist weit geworden," wobei er vielleicht von der Praxis der aegyptischen Hintergrundnamen abhängig war, unter denen *PN* wie "Es dauert der Friede" und "Das Land befindet sich wohl" (oben Anm. 11) unserem *r$^{e}$ḥăb$^{c}$am* besonders nahekommen.

Unter den verschiedenen Deutungsmöglichkeiten, die sich zeigten, würde man wahrscheinlich sicherer wählen können, wenn man etwas darüber wüsste, wie Rehabeam zur Thronfolge kam. Leider gibt es dazu nicht mehr als die kurze Notiz in der sog. synchronistischen Chronik S[15] von I Reg. 11:43. Dabei hatte Salomo mit seinen vielen Frauen (I Reg. 11:3) sicher zahlreiche Nachkommen, von denen aber, anders als bei David und Rehabeam (II Chr. 11:18ff.), nichts verlautet. Empfahl sich letzterer seinem Vater als Sohn der aegyptischen Prinzessin (I Reg. 3:1), und hängt das Schweigen unserer Quellen eben damit zusammen?

Gerade Albright hat auch erwogen,[16] ob *r$^{e}$ḥăb$^{c}$am* vielleicht der Thronname des Prinzen war, den er zu seinem ersten Namen hinzu bei der Krönung erhielt. Aber von einem solchen ersten Namen ist nichts bekannt, und der in Aegypten geübte Brauch von Thronnamen lässt sich für die judäischen Könige weder aus II Sam. 7:9 noch aus Jes. 9:5b erweisen.[17]

## II

Jerobeam erscheint im Alten Testament nur als Name der beiden Könige des israelitischen Nordreiches, wobei es sich beim zweiten gewiss um einen bewussten Rückgriff auf den Namen des ersten handelt. Aus der Zeit von Jerobeam II dürfte das bekannte Siegel mit der Aufschrift *lšm$^{c}$ $^{c}$bd jrb$^{c}$m* stammen.[18]

Was zunächst die Aussprache des in *LXX* als *Ιεροβοαμ* überlieferten *PN* angeht, so darf als sicher gelten, dass die tiberiensische Vokalisation mit ihrem *Mataeg* beim ersten *Qamaeṣ* in der Editio Bombergiana[19] auf ein *jaråb$^{c}$am* zielte, wofür auch die Analogie des *PN jašåb$^{c}$am* (I Chr. 12:7) spricht.[20] Rein lautlich ist ferner die verbreitete Aussprache *jåråb$^{c}$am* möglich,

15. Vgl. dazu Alfred Jepsen, *Die Quellen des Königsbuches, 1953* ($^{2}$1956), S. 31.

16. In *AASOR* 21/22 (1943): 67, zitiert bei Montgomery-Gehman, loc. cit. (Anm. 4) S. 248, wo die These Albrights mit Gründen, wie wir sie im Text nennen, abgelehnt wird. Aus dem Wortlaut in *AASOR* lässt sich die Meinung von Albright nicht so deutlich erkennen, wie es nach Montgomery-Gehman scheint. In *JBL* 51 (1932): 85 Anm. 25 nennt Albright Rehabeam als Thronnamen nicht, obwohl er feststellt, dass die entsprechende, von Aegypten entlehnte Sitte in Juda mit Salomo aufkam.

17. Vgl. dazu Hans Wildberger, Die Thronnamen des Messias, Jes. 9, 5b (*ThZ* 16 [1960]: 314–32, besonders S. 325ff.).

18. Vgl. James B. Pritchard, *The Ancient Near East in Pictures Relating to the Old Testament* (1954), Abb. 276 (S. 85).

19. *Biblia Hebraica*, ed. Rudolf Kittel, 1. und 2. Auflage.

20. Vgl. dazu Eberhard Nestle in *ZAW* 33 (1913): 316.

da ein *Qamaeṣ ḥaṭûf* auch in offener Silbe stehen kann.[21] Bei der supralinearen Vokalisation im Targum[22] lässt sich nicht sagen, ob ein *jaråbᶜam* oder ein *jåråbᶜam* beabsichtigt war. Die östliche (babylonische) Ueberlieferung bietet dagegen ein *jᵉrubᶜam.*[23] Im Hinblick darauf wie auch auf die Wiedergabe in *LXX* lässt sich mit Noth, *IPN* S. 247a erwägen, ob *jᵉråbᶜam* allenfalls als die ursprüngliche Aussprache betrachtet werden könne, obwohl gegen ein anfängliches *jaråbᶜam*, das wir vorziehen möchten, nichts einzuwenden ist. Sicherheit wird sich hier nicht erreichen lassen.

Wichtiger als das ist die Frage nach dem Sinn des Namens. Wie allgemein zugestanden, kann sie nicht ohne Berücksichtigung des *PN jᵉrubbăᶜăl* beantwortet werden. Trotz der Deutung, die dieser Jdc. 6:32 erfährt, liegt es nahe, seinen verbalen Bestandteil von *rabăb* "zahlreich sein, werden" (*KBL* S. 868f.) abzuleiten. So findet es sich bei Albright, *Die Religion Israels im Lichte der archäologischen Ausgrabungen* (1956), S. 128, wo er Jerubbaal übersetzt mit: "Baal möge Wachstum geben"[24] und er S. 230 Anm. 59 auch für Jerobeam die Wurzel *r-b-b* "zunehmen" in Anspruch nimmt.[25]

Aehnlich ist es bei Noth, *IPN* S. 206f., dem ich mich *HEN* S. 418 angeschlossen hatte. Auch für ihn enthalten beide *PN* das Verb *rabăb*, nur nicht nach dem Hebräischen in der Bedeutung "zahlreich sein," sondern in der dem Aramäischen und Arabischen geläufigen "gross sein." Noth schreibt: "So würden wir *jrbᶜl* wohl übersetzen dürfen mit: gross, als Herrn möge sich Baal zeigen. *jrbᶜm* allerdings kann profane Bedeutung haben: es mehre sich das Volk."

Um diese Auffassung zu stützen, kann man, wie Koehler, *KBL* S. 401a zu Jerobeam tut, auf die alt-südarabischen *PN Rabbᵓil* und *ᵓIlrabb* (*NPS* I, S. 248a) hinweisen. Während Ryckmans den ersten nicht übersetzt, gibt er den zweiten wieder durch: "'Il est seigneur" ou "Rabb est dieu."

Im Hebräischen hat das Verb *rabăb* das von der gleichen Wurzel abgeleitete *rabā* "zahlreich werden," "gross sein/werden" neben sich. Dieses letztere, auch im Akkadischen vorhandene Verb findet sich ferner im Ost- oder Frühkanaanäischen in dem *PN Jarbi-ilu(AN)* "Gott (El) ist gross."[26]

Im Blick auf diese Parallelen scheint es in der Tat nicht unmöglich,

21. Vgl. dazu Rudolf Meyer, *Hebräische Grammatik* I³ (1966): §11b (S. 55).

22. Nach Alexander Sperber, *The Bible in Aramaic* II (1959), zu I Reg. 11:26 etc.

23. So Paul Kahle, *Der masoretische Text des Alten Testaments nach der Ueberlieferung der babylonischen Juden* (1902), S. 78 (Neudruck, 1966).

24. Im amerikanischen Original: *Archaeology and the Religion of Israel* (1946), S. 112 lautet der Satz: "May Baal give increase."

25. Im Original S.206 Anm. 57.

26. Theo Bauer, *Die Ostkanaanäer* (1926), S. 29 und S. 56; Herbert B. Huffmon, *Amorite Personal Names in the Mari Texts* (1965), S. 70ff. und S. 260.

*j$^{e}$rubbă$^{c}$ăl* durch "Baal ist gross" oder vielleicht "Baal hat sich als gross erwiesen" zu übersetzen, und *jaråb$^{c}$am* wäre entsprechend: "Der Onkel (gott) ist gross" oder "hat sich als gross erwiesen." Weil *$^{c}$am* im zweiten Namen genau an der Stelle des *bă$^{c}$ăl* im ersten steht, muss es theophoren Klang haben. Die von Noth bevorzugte profane Bedeutung von *$^{c}$am* als Volk wäre zudem nur sinnvoll, wenn Jerobeam I zur Königsfamilie gehört hätte, was nach I Reg. 11:26, wo seine Herkunft angegeben wird, nicht der Fall war. Es ist somit durch nichts gefordert, dass das Wort *$^{c}$am* in den Namen Rehabeam und Jerobeam den gleichen Sinn haben müsse.

Trotz alledem kann ich mich der von Albright und Noth je auf ihre Weise vorgeschlagenen Deutung der beiden *PN* nicht anschliessen. Sie hat bei Albright gegen sich, dass sie sich ganz von der Jdc. 6:32 gegebenen Deutung des Jerubbaal-Namens entfernt, und bei Noth, dass sie für *rabăb* eine dem Hebräischen sonst fremde Bedeutung voraussetzt. Hinsichtlich Jdc. 6:32 ist man sich darin einig,[27] dass das *jaraeb bô hăbbă$^{c}$ăl* "Baal streite wider ihn" den ursprünglichen Sinn von *j$^{e}$rubbă$^{c}$ăl* in sein Gegenteil umwendet; denn es gibt kaum einen Namen mit einer gegen seinen Träger gerichteten Aussage oder Bitte. Dennoch ist zu fragen, ob die wortspielerische Umdeutung wirklich so ganz vom Inhalt der Verbalwurzel wegführt. Nach Jdc. 6:32 wäre sie *rîb* "einen Rechtsstreit führen," "rechten" (*KBL*, S. 888f.), was mit der Präposition *b$^{e}$* verbunden "streiten" ("zanken") und auch "anklagen" bedeutet (Gen. 31:36; Hos. 2:4; Jer. 25:31).[28] Von *rîb* aus wäre als Name freilich ein *j$^{e}$ribbă$^{c}$ăl* zu erwarten, doch hängt seine überlieferte Gestalt wohl damit zusammen, dass das Verb *rîb* ein *rûb* als Nebenform bei sich hatte, wie es *śûm* neben *śîm* gibt. *rûb* erscheint im *K$^{e}$tîb* von *tarûb* für *Q$^{e}$rê tarîb* (Prov. 3:30) und in *larôb* für *larîb* (Jdc. 21:22).[29]

Darum zögere ich nicht, dieses Verb *rîb* / *rûb* sowohl in Jerubbaal als auch in Jerobeam zu finden, und zwar in der Bedeutung "die Sache jemandes führen," "für jemanden eintreten." So kommt es gewöhnlich vor im Ausdruck *rab rîb p$^{e}$lonî* "die Sache jemandes führen" (*KBL*, S. 889a), doch kann auch das Verb allein ohne das Substantiv *rîb* diesen Sinn haben, so Jes. 1:17 und 51:22. Der erste der beiden Namen ist dann zu übersetzen mit: "Baal hat Recht geschafft" / "Ist (für das benannte Kind oder seine Eltern)

27. Literatur bei Wolfgang Richter, Traditionsgeschichtliche Untersuchungen zum Richterbuch², 1966 (*BBB* 18): S. 168 Anm. 158.

28. Vgl. Hans J. Boecker, Redeformen des Rechtslebens im Alten Testament, *WMANT* 14 (1964): 54 Anm. 2.

29. So mit Charles F. Burney, *The Book of Judges*² (1920), S. 201; vgl. auch Eugen Täubler, *Biblische Studien. Die Epoche der Richter* (1958), S. 266. Die Ableitung von *rîb/rûb* vertrat auch schon Fritz Hommel in *ZDMG* 49 (1895): 525, vgl. Rud. Kittel, Die Bücher der Könige (1900), S. 99.

eingetreten" und der zweite "Der Onkel(gott) hat Recht geschafft/ist eingetreten für." Um die vergangenheitliche Uebersetzung zu rechtfertigen, berufe ich mich neben allgemeinen Erwägungen, wie ich sie *HEN*, S. 414f. vorgetragen habe, einfach auf die späten *PN j*$^{e}$*hôjarîb/jôjarîb* und *jarîb*, die nicht anders übersetzt werden können als "Jahwe/er hat Recht geschafft." Bei diesen ist, vom Wechsel in der Gestalt der Wurzel *rûb/rîb* abgesehen, nur die altertümliche Folge "Imperfekt + Gottesname" durch die umgekehrte und in späterer Zeit gelegentlich sonst noch auftretende Wortfolge ersetzt vgl. *IPN*, S. 28. Die Wiedergabe der *jarîb*-Namen als Wunsch—so *IPN*, S. 201—"Gott möge streiten," "den Prozess führen" ist durch die Art ihrer Schreibung und Vokalisierung ausgeschlossen.

Die *PN* sagen dasselbe wie die akkadischen mit dem Verb *dânu* gebildeten, von denen als Beispiele gennant seien: die Bitte $^{d}$*NN-dīnanni* "Schaffe mir Recht, o Gott!" (*AN*, S. 172) und der Dank *Idīnanni-*$^{d}$*NN* "Gott NN hat mir Recht geschafft," *Idīn-*$^{d}$*Enlil* "Enlil hat mir Recht geschafft" (*AN*, S. 191f.). von Soden ist *AHw*, S. 167f. gegenüber der hier gebrauchten Uebersetzung von *dânu* zurückhaltend. Wie mir scheint, wird sie bestätigt durch den alten *PN Uta mēšaram* "Ich habe das Recht gefunden" (*AN*, S. 191). Inhaltlich stimmt auch das hebräische *š*$^{e}$*paṭjā(hû)*, *šapaṭ* "Jahwe/er hat Recht geschafft" mit den erwähnten, mit *rûb/rîb* gebildeten Namen überein.

## III

Im Vortstehenden wurden wir dazu geführt, die Namen Rehabeam und Jerobeam nicht nur, wie selbstverständlich, beim Verb, sondern auch beim Substantiv verschieden zu deuten. Dem "Das Volk ist weit geworden" von *r*$^{e}$*ḥăb*$^{c}$*am* steht in *ja/jårâb*$^{c}$*am* ein "Der Onkel (gott) hat Recht geschafft" gegenüber. Das spricht nicht gegen unsere Auffassung, die in der verschiedenen Herkunft der beiden Namenträger genügend begründet sein dürfte. Der aus einem kleinen ephraimitischen Ort stammenden Familie des Jerobeam kann man den Gebrauch des alten theophor verstandenen und mit Jahwe gleichgesetzten Verwandtschaftswortes $^{c}$*am* gewiss zutrauen. Bei Rehabeam dagegen ist es sinnvoll, wenn in der Umgebung des Königs oder durch diesen selber die frühe und spezielle Bedeutung von $^{c}$*am* = "Onkel" durch die modernere und allgemeine $^{c}$*am* = "Volk" ersetzt wurde.

# Inscription d'Anam, roi d'Uruk et successeur de Gilgamesh

R. J. TOURNAY, O.P.

En 1893, H. V. Hilprecht[1] avait publié une petite tablette sumérienne provenant probablement, disait-il, des environs de Babylone. Ce document comprend huit lignes tracées sur l'obvers plat; le revers légèrement bombé est brisé. L'inscription a été traduite par F. Hommel[2] et, à sa suite, par de nombreux sumérologues (Jensen, Radau, Winckler, etc.), notamment F. Thureau-Dangin.[3] En voici la transcription et la traduction:

1 *An-àm* 2 *ab-ba-ugnim* 3 *unu*$^{KI}$*-ga* 4 *dumu Ilān*(NAB)*-še-me-a* 5 *bád unu*$^{KI}$*-ga* 6 *nì-dím-dím-ma libir-ra* 7 $^{d.}$*bil*$_4$*-ga-mèš-ke*$_4$ 8 *ki-bi bí-in-gi*$_4$*-a.*

"Anam,[4] chef des troupes[5] d'Uruk, fils d'Ilān-šemeʾā,[6] ayant

1. *Old Babylonian Inscriptions* (Babylonian Expedition of the University of Pennsylvania), Vol. I, Part I, n° 26 (Planche 15; C.B.M. 103).
2. Dans *PSBA*, 16 (1894): 13.
3. *Die Sumerischen und Akkadischen Königsinschriften* (1907), pp. 222–23.
4. Pour cette lecture, cf. M. Lambert, *RA*, 47 (1953): 37; D. O. Edzard, *Die "zweite Zwischenzeit" Babyloniens* (1957), p. 156, note 826; A. Falkenstein, *Zu den Inschriftfunden der Grabung in Uruk-Warka 1960–1961*, dans *Bagd. Mitteil*, II (1962), p. 35, note 155.
5. L'équivalent babylonien *abbū ṣābim*$^{hi-a}$ se trouve dans la lettre W 20473, envoyée par Anam à Sîn-muballit de Babylone (I, lignes 8, 13, 23; II, lignes 17–18). Voir A. Falkenstein, *art. cit.*, p. 65; M.-J. Seux, *Épithètes Royales akkadiennes et sumériennes* (1967), p. 384. Anam ne portait pas encore le titre de "roi" (cf. A. Falkenstein, ibid., pp. 18, 36); il a régné cinq ans, de 1821 à 1817 environ (ibid., p. 22).
6. C'est-à-dire "les deux divinités exaucent." Pour cette lecture, cf. J. J. Stamm, *MVAeG*, 44, p. 219; D. O. Edzard, *op. cit.*, p. 156. Ces deux divinités sont sans doute celles d'Uruk, An et Inanna.

restauré[7] le rempart d'Uruk, ancien ouvrage[8] de Gilgamesh."[9]

Personne n'a remarqué jusqu'ici que cette inscription ne comportait qu'une titulature suivie d'une proposition subordonnée, comme l'indique le postfixe *-a*, et qu'il manquait la proposition principale. Cependant, Thureau-Dangin traduit: "a restauré." Or, dans deux inscriptions d'Anam publiées par A. T. Clay,[10] on a une proposition subordonnée temporelle: *ud . . . a* (cf. lignes 7 et 9; 10 et 14–15), suivie de la principale: *a-gù-nun-di-dam mu-un-dù*, "il construisit l'*Agunundidam*" (lignes 10–11); et *é-gi$_6$-pàr . . . mu-un-ki-gar* (pour *ki mu-un-gar*), "je fondai l'Egipar" (lignes 16 et 19). On peut en déduire que le revers brisé de notre tablette contenait la proposition principale, attendue après les huit lignes de l'obvers.

Le hasard a voulu qu'en 1966, un second exemplaire de cette inscription ait été acheté par un particulier sur le marché des antiquités à Jérusalem. Je suis heureux de publier ce document en l'honneur du professeur William F. Albright.

Cette nouvelle tablette est incomplète, la partie supérieure manque. On a pris soin de polir et d'arrondir la cassure supérieure pour donner l'illusion d'une tablette intacte. Les cinq lignes conservées sur l'obvers correspondent exactement, pour la graphie et le contenu, aux lignes 4 à 8 de la tablette d'Anam publiée par H. W. Hilprecht. Ces deux tablettes sont taillées dans une pierre identiqueé, un calcaire de couleur crème, sorte de pierre "savonneuse," variété de stéatite. Elles ont la même largeur, 4 cm, et la même épaisseur, 8 cm. La tablette d'Hilprecht a 4,85 cm de hauteur, tandis que la nôtre a 3 cm pour les 5 lignes qui subsistent, ce qui revient au même proportionnellement. Il s'agit donc d'un exact duplicatum. Mais le revers de notre tablette, légèrement bombé, contient quatre lignes jusqu'ici inconnues

7. Littéralement "mis à sa place." Cette expression, courante dans les inscriptions royales, revient dans les deux inscriptions d'Anam publiées par A. T. Clay, dans *Miscellaneous Inscriptions in the Yale Babylonian Collection* (*YOS* I) (1915), pp. 46–47, n° 35, ligne 9, et n° 36, ligne 15. La seconde inscription, n° 36, qui concerne le temple d'Inanna, est reproduite par A. Falkenstein, *art. cit.*, pp. 53–54. L'infixe *-a* interdit de traduire "il a restauré;" on a une proposition complétive subordonnée à sens temporel, sans *ud-* au début.

8. Même expression à propos du temple bâti jadis par Urnammu et Shulgi, et restauré par Anam (n° 36, lignes 11 ss).

9. Génitif implicite. D. O. Edzard (op. cit., p. 156, note 831) lit $^{d}$*Gilgameša-ke$_4$* en restituant le *-a* du génitif. A l'époque néo-sumérienne, dans les textes littéraires sumériens et les textes lexicographiques en ancien babylonien, on a les graphies: $^{d}$*bìl-ga-mèš*, ou comme ici: $^{d}$*bil$_4$-ga-mèš* (cf. A. Falkenstein, art. Gilgamesh, dans *RLA* III, 5 [1968]: 357–58). On sait que le prologue de l'épopée de Gilgamesh glorifie ce héros pour avoir construit les murailles d'Uruk. Notre inscription suppose la même tradition.

10. Voir note 7, inscription n° 35.

Inscription d'Anam, obverse (*left*) reverse (*right*).

(lignes 9 à 12). Les signes sont un peu moins bien conservés que sur l'obvers, mais encore facilement lisibles (illustr.). L'inscription d'Anam nous est ainsi totalement restituée avec son dernier tiers dont voici la transcription et la traduction:

| | | |
|---|---|---|
| 9 | *a nigín-na-ba* | . . . pour l'eau, dans son circuit, |
| 10 | *gu-nu-un-di-da-dàm* | (le canal) qui retentit fortement |
| 11 | *sig*$_4$ *al-ùr-ra-ta* | avec des briques cuites |
| 12 | *mu-na-dù* | il aménagea. |

Ces quatres lignes constituent la proposition principale attendue et se réfèrent à la construction d'une installation hydraulique pour la ville d'Uruk.

La ligne 10 correspond au passage de l'inscription publiée par A. T. Clay et citée ci-dessus: "Il construisit l'*A-gù-nun-di-dam*." Il s'agit certainement de la même installation. L'expression *gù-nun-di-dam* semble être une sorte de cliché littéraire. La 26e année de son règne, Rim-Sin fit dégager le fosse-canal *gù-nun-di* "qui retentit fortement."[11] C'est un nom identique. Appliquée au Tigre et à l'Euphrate,[12] l'expression figure déjà dans le Cylindre A de Gudéa (XXVI, 21); *^dIškur an-ta gù-nun-di-da-àm*, "c'est le dieu Tempête dont la voix retentit fortement au ciel."[13] L'épopée d'Enmerkar (lignes 543–44) mentionne aussi le dieu Iškur "dont la voix retentit fortement au ciel et sur la terre" (*an-ki-a gù nun-bi-di-dam*).[14] Dans le Cylindre B de Gudéa

11. Cf. D. O. Edzard, *Die "zweite Zischenzeit" Babyloniens* (1957), p. 115; p. 178, il traduit "Laut rauschenden Kanal."

12. Cf. A. Falkenstein, *ZA*, N.F. 22 (1964): 78, 88 et 106 (lignes 252 et 257).

13. Cf. M. Lambert et R. Tournay, Le Cylindre de Gudéa, dans *RB*, 55 (1948): 421; A. Falkenstein et W. von Soden, *Sumerische und akkadische Hymnen und Gebete* (1953), p. 163.

14. Cf. A. Sjöberg, dans *ZA*, N.F., 19 (1961): 55–56. Le complexe *nun-bi* est un adverbe; *nun* a pour équivalents akkadiens: *rabû, mâdu, qitrudu*, "grand, nombreux, fort." D'où, pour cet adverbe, le sens de "fortement."

(xv, 9), l'expression s'applique au mugissement du taureau, l'animal du dieu Tempête.

Dans la nouvelle tablette, le postfixe *-dam*[15] est écrit *dàm* (TUM), valeur commune au sumérien et à l'akkadien, mais plutôt rare; on pourrait se demander si on n'est pas ici en présence d'une désinence sémitique, $tam_4$, possible à l'époque d'Anam. Au lieu de la graphie *gù* (KA), "la voix," on a ici l'homophone *gu*. Le sens de l'expression ne fait pas de doute, étant donné les parallèles déjà cités; *di* et *di-da* équivalent à l'akkadien *qabû* "parler";[16] *gù-nun-di* équivaut à *ḫabâbu* "faire du bruit" (en parlant de l'eau) et à *suppû* "prier" (de façon bruyante).[17] Il s'agit donc ici de l'eau qui circule à grand bruit.[18]

La ligne 9 est plus difficile à interpréter; l'expression *nigín*[19]*-na-ba* (= *bi-a*) est ambigüe, car l'antécédent du possessif *bi*, réservé aux êtres inanimés, n'est pas facile à déterminer. Est-ce la ville d'Uruk, nommée au début de l'inscription, ou le canal dénommé "Bruit retentissant"? Dans ces deux cas, l'inscription se rapporterait à une installation hydraulique de quelque importance. Déjà le regretté A. Falkenstein avait rapproché la mention de ce canal de la découverte par les archéologues, au sud-est de la ziqqurat, d'éléments de canaux.[20] D'après J. Jordan, les traces d'un canal (avec murs et restes de briques de la période d'Urnammu) ont été retrouvées à droite et à gauche de la porte de l'est. Mais si *bi* se rapporte au "mur" de Gilgamesh (lignes 8–9), il pourrait s'agir d'un système de siphons d'entrée, qui serait alors bien nommé "Bruit retentissant."[21] Avant la construction du "mur" de Gilgamesh, le Shatt-en-Nil traversait la ville du nord au sud pour séparer

15. Sur cet élément postfixé qui forme certains participes, cf. D. O. Edzard, Das Sumerische Verbalmorphem / ed / in den alt- und neusumerische Texte, dans *Heidelberger Studien zum Alten Orient* (1957), p. 54. Ainsi *dù-dam* "bâtissant."

16. Cf. A. Deimel, *Šumerisches Lexicon*, n° 457, 14 et 67. On a aussi l'équivalent *alâku* "aller" pour *di, di-da, da-di* (ibid., 2 et 67).

17. Cf. ibid., n° 15, 130 et 131; *CAD*, Ḫ, p. 2. On trouve aussi *gù-da* = *šasû* "crier" (*Šumer. Lexicon*, n° 15, 307).

18. Le thème est biblique: "L'abîme appelant l'abîme au bruit de tes écluses" (Ps. XLII: 8).

19. Le mot *nigín* correspond à l'akkadien *saḫâru, seḫertu* "faire un circuit, un tour," "circuit, tour."

20. Il traduit *a-gù-nun-di-dam* "Lautrauschendes Wasser." Cf. Zu den Inschriftfunden der Grabung in Uruk-Warka 1960–61, dans *Bagd. Mitt.*, II (1962): 37; J. Jordan, Drittes vorläufiger Bericht über Ausgrabungen in Uruk (1932), dans *Abh. Preuss. Akad. Wiss., Ph.-Hist.* Kl. 2 (Berlin, 1932), p. 7 (le canal est dessiné sur les planches VII, XIV et XV). Voir A. Falkenstein, *Topographie aus Uruk*, p. 231; R. North, Status of the Warka Excavation, dans *Or*, 26 (1957): 196 et 244; M. A. Brandes, Bruchstück einer archaischen Stele aus Uruk-Warka, dans *JbDAI, ArAnz*, 80 (1965), H. 4, pp. 609 ss (système hydraulique pour irriguer des jardins).

21. Le présent paragraphe doit beaucoup à Melle D. Cocquerillat, spécialiste des fouilles d'Uruk.

Kullab d'Uruk. L'édification de la muraille posait un problème difficile; une brèche pour le canal diminuait la valeur défensive de cette muraille. On pouvait détourner le canal le long de la partie extérieure du mur, mais c'était priver la ville de son alimentation en eau et il fallait renforcer le mur à sa base avec des briques cuites.[22] Or, ce mur était bâti en briques crues, contrairement à ce que déclare la fin du prologue de l'épopée de Gilgamesh (ligne 18) où le poète commet un anachronisme: "Examine le soubassement pour inspecter le briquetage, pour voir si son briquetage n'est pas fait de briques cuites." Par ailleurs, à l'époque néo-babylonienne, le grand canal ne longeait pas la muraille; il pénétrait dans la cité sous le mur, peut-être par un système de siphons, un peu au sud de l'angle est du "losange" urukien. Nous ignorons ce qu'il en était à l'époque de la première dynastie de Babylone; pour le savoir, il faudrait dégager toute la base du mur, du nord-ouest au sud-est et ce serait un travail considérable. Si Anam a fait entrer dans la ville l'eau du Shatt-en-Nil, grâce à une construction en briques *cuites*, comme il est dit à la ligne 11, il a peut-être aménagé un système de siphons d'entrée. S'il n'a pas fait entrer l'eau dans la ville, il a pu aménager le canal extérieur longeant le rempart, en le renforçant avec des briques cuites pour protéger ce rempart. De nouvelles fouilles dans cette partie de Warka apporteront peut-être un jour la lumière sur ce problème encore insoluble.

Dans cette inscription, Anam prend le titre de "chef des troupes d'Uruk"; il n'est pas encore roi d'Uruk, D'après la chronologie proposée par A. Falkenstein,[23] c'est en 1821 qu'il accéda à la royauté. L'inscription est donc un peu antérieure à cette date.

22. *sig₄-al-ùr-ra* correspond à l'akkadien *agurru* "brique cuite au four" (cf. CADA, p. 160). C'est le terme utilisé à la ligne 18 du prologue de l'épopée de Gilgamesh (passage repris en "inclusion" à la fin de la tablette XI, ligne 304).

23. Voir ci-dessus, note 5.

# Erstgeborene und Leviten: Ein Beitrag zur exilisch-nachexilischen Theologie

WALTHER ZIMMERLI

Die neuere traditionsgeschichtliche Arbeit hat sichtbar gemacht, dass sich im Alten Testament feste Überlieferungselemente durch die Zeiten hin durchhalten und durch die verschiedenen Geschichtsphasen hin wandern.[1]

Neben dem Phänomen des geschichtlichen Durchhaltens in kontinuierlicher Weitergabe hat sich dabei ganz ebenso das Phänomen des Wandels und der neuartigen Zuspitzung dieser Elemente gezeigt. Neue geschichtliche Situationen können der Überlieferung einen ganz neuartigen Stempel aufprägen.[2]

1. So ist etwa E. Rohland (Die Bedeutung der Erwählungstraditionen Israels für die Eschatologie der alttestamentlichen Propheten, Diss. Heidelberg, 1956) den drei Traditionskreisen des Exodus aus Ägypten, der Erwählung des Zion und der Erwählung Davids und seiner Dynastie nachgegangen und hat ihren Wandel auf die Bedeutung für die Eschatologie der alttestamentlichen Propheten hin überprüft. In anderer Weise hat S. Herrmann (Die prophetischen Heilserwartungen im Alten Testament. Ursprung und Gestaltwandel, *BWANT* 5. Folge Heft 5, 1965) die prophetischen Heilserwartungen, die von der alten Kulturlandverheissung, dem Bundesgedanken und der Davidverheissung herkommen, gemustert. Und von dem weit über Israel hinausgreifenden Pattern einer Königsideologie her hat die Myth- und Ritual- und in ihrem Gefolge die Uppsalenser Schule eine Reihe von alttestamentlichen Aussagen durch die verschiedenen Zeiten hin zu verstehen gesucht.

2. So hat z.B. die alte Exodusüberlieferung, die nach den durch G. von Rad herausgearbeiteten Credoüberlieferungen ganz allgemein auf die Landnahme hinführte, unter dem Eindruck der Geschehnisse der David- und Salomozeit im Moselied von Ex. 15 eine entschlossene Hinführung zur Zionüberlieferung erfahren: "Du führtest sie (ins Land) hinein und pflanztest sie ein auf dem Berg deines Eigentums, dem Ort, den du dir zur Wohung gemacht hast, Jahwe, dem Heiligtum, das deine Hände, o Herr, gegründet" (v. 17). In ganz anderer Weise hat O. Steck in einem kühnen Versuch, der sich in der Diskussion wohl noch

Die Zeit, welche am einschneidendsten zur Überprüfung und oft zur radikalen Umzeichnung der älteren Überlieferung und Gesetzestradition geführt hat, ist die Katastrophenzeit des Zusammenbruches der Eigenstaatlichkeit Israels, die sog. Exils- und nachfolgende nachexilische Aufbauzeit, gewesen. Im Wetterleuchten der prophetischen Botschaft hat die alte Exodusüberlieferung an der Schwelle der Katastrophe in Ez. 20 eine wahrhaft erschreckende Umakzentuierung erfahren. Aus der Grundlage kommender Gnadenzeit ist hier die Erzählung, von der Exoduszeit zur Ätiologie kommender Gerichtszeit geworden.[3] Im Exil selber hat die Davidverheissung bei Deuterojesaja in 55:1–5 eine revolutionär neue Interpretation und Entschränkung auf das Volksganze erfahren. Und das priesterschriftliche Nachdenken nach der geschehenen Gerichtserfahrung hat der älteren Bundestheologie, wie sie etwa im Deuteronomium erkennbar wird, eine ganz neue Interpretation gegeben. Das in der Tradition fest verankerte Reden von einem "Bund" am Gottesberg in der Mosezeit ist in P hinter der Überlieferung vom Gnadenbund mit den Vätern vollkommen verblasst.[4]

Im Folgenden soll hier ein weiterer Vorgang des Neubedenkens und -formulierens älterer Überlieferung herausgegriffen werden, der das intensive Nach- und Umdenken älterer Ordnungen in der Krisen- und der auf sie folgenden Aufbauzeit sichtbar macht. Dieser Vorgang ist nicht nur dadurch bedeutsam, dass er die tiefen Aporien erkennen lässt, in welche das Bedenken der Überlieferung in der Krisenzeit des Exiles geworfen wird. Er zeigt darüber hinaus, wie in der Lösung, zu welcher sich das nachexilische Umdenken hinfindet, Traditionsbereiche, die von Hause aus nichts miteinander zu tun haben, zu einer ganz neuen Synthese zusammentreten.

## I

Israel kennt schon in früher Zeit die Verpflichtung zur Weihe der Erstgeburt an Jahwe.[5] In Ex. 34:19f. findet sich die Anordnung, dass die opferbaren erstgeborenen Tiere Jahwe gegeben werden sollen. Der nicht opfer-

auf seine Haltbarkeit hin überprüfen lassen muss, in der Untersuchung "Überlieferung und Zeitgeschichte in den Elia-Erzählungen" (*WMANT* 26, 1968) zu zeigen gesucht, dass die Ahab-Isebel-Überlieferung in den ganz kurzfristig aufeinander folgenden Phasen politischen Geschehens der Ahab- und der unmittelbaren Nach-Ahab-Zeit je eine ganz neue Darstellung erfahren habe.

3. Nach Ez. 20:23 fällt Jahwe schon zur Zeit der Wüstenwanderung Israels das Urteil, dass dieses unter die Völker zerstreut werden soll.

4. W. Zimmerli, Sinaibund und Abrahambund. Ein Beitrag zum Verständnis der Priesterschrift, *ThZ* 16 (1960): 268–80 (= Gottes Offenbarung. Theol. Bücherei 19, 1963, 205–216).

5. Vgl. jetzt etwa H. Cazelles, *Suppl. Dict. de la Bible* (1969), Art. Premiers-nés. II Dans l'Ancien Testament, 482–91, dort auch reichhaltige Literaturangaben.

bare Esel wird durch ein Opfertier ausgelöst (*pdh*), oder, wenn kein solches gegeben werden kann, getötet.[6] Jede menschliche Erstgeburt soll ausgelöst werden. Man wird dabei an eine tierische Ersatzgabe zu denken haben. Terminologisch wird zwischen der tierischen Erstgeburt, die als *pæṭær ræḥæm* bezeichnet wird, und der als *bᵊkōr* bezeichneten menschlichen Erstgeburt unterschieden.

Diese terminologische Scheidung ist im Bundesbuch in Ex. 22, 28f., wo zwar die menschliche Erstgeburt als *bᵊkōr* bezeichnet wird, das *paeṭaer raeḥaem* für die tierische Erstgeburt aber fehlt, nicht zu erkennen. Dagegen wird auch hier trotz der knappen Formulierung *bᵊkōr bānǣkā tittæn-lī*, an die sich die Anordnung schliesst, es bei den Tieren analog zu halten wie beim menschlichen Erstgeborenen, der gleiche Modus der Auslösung der menschlichen Erstgeburt vorausgesetzt werden dürfen.[7] Eine Erzählung wie 1. Sam. 1f. kann zeigen, dass es in besonderen Fällen auch in Einlösung eines Gelübdes zu einer Weihe des Erstgeborenen an das Heiligtum kommen konnte.[8]

Eine Opferung des Erstgeborenen scheint diese ältere Gesetzgebung nirgends ins Auge zu fassen. Man hat eine solche für die Traditions-Vorgeschichte von Isaaks Opferung gelegentlich vermutet. Gen. 22 selber führt in seiner Jetztgestalt auf jeden Fall auf die übliche Sitte der Auslösung durch ein Opfertier.

Auch die etwas jüngere Formulierung in Ex. 13:12f.[9] führt wieder ausdrücklich auf die Ordnung, nach welcher die menschliche Erstgeburt ausgelöst wird. Das Gebot ist hier heilsgeschichtlich motiviert und auf die Geschehnisse beim Auszug aus Ägypten bezogen. Terminologisch kann höchstens in 13:15a eine Abweichung von der Formulierung in Ex. 34 festgestellt werden, indem hier *bᵊkōr* auch auf die tierische Erstgeburt angewendet wird. In den umgebenden Versen findet sich aber auch hier die differenzierte Begrifflichkeit für menschliche und tierische Erstgeburt.

Diese terminologische Unterscheidung fällt in der priesterlichen Sprache dahin. In der knappen Anordnung von Ex. 13:2, die Erstgeburt Jahwe zu heiligen, wird die kombinierte Formulierung *kål-bᵊkōr pæṭær kål-ræḥæm* aus-

6. Der Vergleich mit Ex. 23:15 zeigt, dass die Erwähnung der Erstgeburtsforderung in Ex. 34:19, 20abα erst nachträglich in den älteren, geschlossenen Festkalender eingeschoben worden ist. Sie zerreisst den in 23:15 vorliegenden unmittelbaren Zusammenhang von Ex. 34:18, 20bβ.

7. Die Frage von Cazelles loc. cit. 487, ob es bei der "Darbringung" der Erstgeborenen am Heiligtum zu einer sakralen Kennzeichnung derselben gekommen ist, lässt sich leider nicht beantworten.

8. Wird ein solcher als *nātīn* bezeichnet? Vgl. dazu auch u. Anm. 19.

9. Nach Cazelles loc. cit. 487 wäre hier die elohistische Entsprechung zu dem jahwistischen Text Ex. 34:19f. zu finden.

drücklich auf Mensch und Tier bezogen. Von der Möglichkeit der Auslösung ist hier nichts gesagt. Inhaltlich wird die nachexilische Regelung des P erst später voll zur Sprache kommen müssen.[10]

Die vorexilische deuteronomische Regelung von Dt. 15:19–23 redet nur von der tierischen Erstgeburt. Diese wird unbefangen als *bᵊkōr* bezeichnet. Dagegen fällt auf, dass dem Deuteronomium ein Gebot der Darbringung der menschlichen Erstgeburt fehlt. Dafür findet sich in Dt. 18:10 eine scharfe Polemik gegen die Sitte der Darbringung von Sohn oder Tochter durchs Feuer. Vom Erstgeborenen ist dabei nicht ausdrücklich geredet. Die Sitte des Kindesopfers wird als Greuel der kanaanäischen Vorbewohner des Landes gekennzeichnet. Die Darbringung durch Feuer (*hæᶜæbīr bāʾēš* 18:10) wird in der dem Sinne nach gleichartigen Stelle 12:31 ganz unverdeckt als ein Verbrennen (*śrp*) der Kinder im Feuer für die Götter der Landesbewohner bezeichnet.

Man wird angesichts des Deuteronomiums die Frage stellen, ob das Fehlen der Forderung der menschlichen Erstgeburt, die doch in den älteren gesetzlichen Ordnungen so unbefangen erhoben worden war, nicht mit dem Aufkommen der Übung des Kinderopfers, der sich der deuteronomische Gesetzgeber offensichtlich in seinen Tagen gegenübersieht, zusammenhängt. In den Königsbüchern berichten zuerst 2 Reg. 3:27 vom König des Nachbarlandes Moab, dass er in einem Moment höchster kriegerischer Gefahr seinen erstgeborenen Sohn, den Thronfolger (*habbᵊkōr ʾᵃšær jimlōk taḥtāw*) auf der Stadtmauer als Brandopfer (*ᶜōlā*) dargebracht habe. Schwerer zu deuten ist 1 Reg. 16:34. Die Texte erlauben uns kein Urteil darüber, in welchem Zusammenhang und aus welchen aktuellen Neumotivierungen heraus die Übung des Kindesopfers dann auch in Juda Eingang gefunden hat. Auf jeden Fall berichten 2 Reg. 16:3 von Ahas und 2 Reg. 21:6 von Manasse, dass jeder von ihnen "seinen Sohn" (*bᵊnō*) durchs Feuer dargebracht habe (*hæᶜæbīr bāʾēš*). Vom Erstgeborenen ist dabei nicht ausdrücklich geredet. Die zeitgenössische Äusserung von Mi. 6:7 aber, die es als höchstmögliche Steigerung einer Opferleistung ins Auge fasst, dass einer seinen Erstgeborenen (*bᵊkōrī. . .pᵊrī biṭnī*) als Opfer für seine Versündigung darbringen könnte, macht es wahrscheinlich, dass man auf diesem Wege in der Tat auch glaubte der alten Forderung des Erstgeburtsopfers gerecht werden zu können.

Gegen das Kindesopfer als einen Jahwe verhassten Greuel polemisiert auch das Heiligkeitsgesetz in Lev. 18:21 und 20:2–6. Es wird hier als Opfer *lammōlæk* (19:21; 20:2–4) bezeichnet. Da 20:5 von einem Buhlen hinter dem *mōlæk* her redet, ist *mōlæk* wohl nicht als eine Opferbezeichnung, sondern als

10. S. u. Abschnitt III.

die besondere Titulatur des im Kindesopfer Angegangenen zu verstehen.[11] Zwar ist auch hier nicht ausdrücklich von der Darbringung der Erstgeburt geredet. Ist es aber nur Zufall, dass auch in der Gesetzessammlung des Heiligkeitsgesetzes jede Erwähnung der Forderung der Erstgeburt durch Jahwe völlig fehlt?

So dürften denn das Deuteronomium und möglicherweise auch das Heiligkeitsgesetz durch ihr Verschweigen der Forderung der menschlichen Erstgeburt die Verlegenheit widerspiegeln, die sich angesichts des Hochkommens der Übung des Menschenopfers im 8./7. Jahrhundert in steigendem Masse erhob. Hatte die Forderung Jahwes denn nicht in ihrer ältesten Gestalt in Ex. 22:28 klipp und klar gelautet: "Den Erstgeborenen deiner Söhne sollst du mir geben?" Daneben war in strenger Parallele die Forderung zu hören gewesen: "So sollst du es halten mit deinem Ochsen und deinem Kleinvieh. Sieben Tage soll es bei seiner Mutter bleiben. Am 8. Tage sollst du es mir geben" (v. 29). Was konnte angesichts so klarer Formulierungen denn eigentlich ernstlich gegen Menschen gesagt werden, die es mit dem menschlichen Erstgeborenen in voller Strenge ganz so hielten wie mit der tierischen Erstgeburt? Alle scharfe Polemik des Deuteronomiums und des Heiligkeitsgesetzes konnte das leise Unbehagen angesichts der Tatsache nicht aus der Welt schaffen, dass ein klares Gebot Jahwes die Dargabe der menschlichen Erstgeburt ganz ebenso forderte wie die Dargabe der tierischen Erstgeburt.

Dass solche Vermutung nicht einfach danebengreift, wird in den Worten Ezechiels deutlich. Es wurde schon erwähnt, dass bei diesem Propheten, der das Exilsgericht als ein schon 597 mit König Jojachim Deportierter erfahren hatte, bevor es sich dann 587 an Jerusalem bis zum Letzten erfüllte, die alte Heilsüberlieferung vom Auszug aus Ägypten eine unheimliche Umakzentuierung erfahren hat. Aus dem Bericht von der grundlegenden Gnadentat Jahwes wurde hier die Verkündigung der uranfänglichen Schuld Israels. Schon zur Zeit seiner Wüstenwanderung brachte ihm seine Widerspenstigkeit den göttlichen Gerichtsspruch der Zerstreuung unter die Völker ein. Im Anschluss an die Gerichtsverkündigung in 20:23f. aber findet sich der Bericht über einen noch unheimlicheren Entscheid Jahwes angesichts des sündigen Volkes in der Wüste: "Auch gab ich ihnen ungute Satzungen und Rechte, durch die sie nicht leben sollten, und machte sie unrein durch ihre

11. Anders O. Eissfeldt, *Molk als Opferbegriff im Punischen und Hebräischen und das Ende des Gottes Moloch* (1935). Dazu aber auch H. Cazelles, Art. Molok, *Suppl. Dictionnaire de la Bible* (1957), 1337–1346, der 1346 das im Alten Testament vorliegende Verständnis als Gottesname als sekundäres Missverständnis einer älteren phönizischen Opferterminologie (nach Eissfeldt) bewertet.

Gaben, wenn sie alle Erstgeburt (durchs Feuer) darbrachten" (20: 25f.). Hier ist ohne Zweifel vom Opfer der menschlichen Erstgeburt die Rede. Wie in der (jüngeren) priesterlichen Sprache von Ex. 13:2 ist dabei das *pæṭær ræḥæm* auch auf die menschliche Erstgeburt angewendet. Nur an diese kann hier gedacht sein. Auf dem Hintergrund der Aussagen des Deuteronomiums und Heiligkeitsgesetzes über das Kinderopfer wird ohne weiteres verständlich, dass Ezechiel dieses nur als eine abscheuliche Verunreinigung des Volkes beurteilen kann. Das Erschreckende aber besteht nun darin, dass dennoch der Charakter eines Gottesgebotes in keiner Weise abgeschwächt wird. Der Prophet erträgt das Rätsel, dass der Gott Israels diesem ein Gebot gegeben hat, an dem es zu Fall kommen musste. Dieses kann Ezechiel nur auf dem dunklen Hintergrunde göttlichen Zornhandelns verstehen, das sein Volk unausweichlich in noch tiefere Sünde treibt. Der Auftrag Jahwes an Jesaja, sein Volk zu verstocken (Jes. 6:10), ist hier zu der Aussage gesteigert, dass Gott sein Volk gerade durch die Gabe des Gottesgebotes selber, die dieses als sein höchstes Gut glaubte hochhalten zu dürfen, in die volle Tiefe der Versündung hineinstösst.[12] Die tiefe Aporie des Glaubens Israels, welche den Gerichtszorn selbst da lauern sieht, wo das Volk meinte glauben zu dürfen, dass sein Gott ihm den Weg ins Leben weise, bricht hier auf. Wie soll es den Weg aus dieser Bedrängnis heraus finden und den Willen seines Gottes neu verstehen lernen?

Das nachexilische Israel hat den Ausweg aus dieser Aporie zu einem neuen Verständnis des göttlichen Willens in seiner Forderung der menschlichen Erstgeburt auf einem auffallenden Umweg gefunden.

## II

Schon die alten Nachrichten Israels reden von Levi. Die Anfänge Levis liegen im Dunkeln.[13] Ist zu Beginn mit der Existenz eines weltlichen Stammes Levi zu rechnen, der dann in der Katastrophe, die hinter dem Bericht von Gen. 34 zu stehen scheint, unterging und nur noch in der Metamorphose zu einer Gruppe besonders Jahwenaher, zur Kultübung als Priester besonders geeigneter Menschen erkennbar wird? Die Annahme enthält eine Fülle ungelöster Schwierigkeiten.—Oder ist von Anfang an mit einer Gruppe von Menschen (und Familien) zu rechnen, die sich durch die "Levitenregel"

12. Die unheimliche Grenzmöglichkeit, dass Gott selber dem Menschen den "Anstoss" (*mikšōl*) bereitet oder ihn "betört" (*pth*), ist auch in Ez. 3:20 und 14:9 zu erkennen.

13. So auch W. F. Albright, den dieser Artikel zu seinem 80. Geburtstag freundlichst grüssen möchte, in: "Die Religion Israels im Lichte der archäologischen Ausgrabungen" (1956), 124: "Die Levitenfrage ist noch dunkel und verworren."

der Landesbesitzlosigkeit[14] in besonderer Weise von den anderen landbesitznehmenden Gruppen unterschied?

Die Frage braucht hier nicht entschieden zu werden. Es genügt festzustellen, dass nach Jud. 17f. ein Levit schon in älterer Zeit als zum Priestertum besonders geeignet angesehen wurde. Dazu stellen Ex. 32:25–29 und der Levispruch im Mosesegen (Dt. 33:8–11) die Tatsache gegen jeden Zweifel sicher, dass die Leviten eine in besonderer Weise zum Priestertum qualifizierte Gruppe darstellten. So wird man denn damit rechnen müssen, dass in der vordeuteronomischen Zeit an einigen Landesheiligtümern Leviten Priesterdienste taten. Für das Heiligtum Dan scheint das durch Jud. 17f. klar belegt zu sein. Es wird aber auch mit grosser Bestimmtheit vermutet werden dürfen, dass dieses keineswegs an allen Landesheiligtümern der Fall war. Die entschiedene Wendung der deuteronomischen Gesetzgebung, die für ein levitisches Priestertum eintritt (18:1ff.), gegen die Landesheiligtümer (Dt. 12) macht es nicht wahrscheinlich, dass die Träger dieses Kampfes gerade die Inhaber der hauptsächlichen Land-(Höhen-)Priesterstellen sein sollten.

Die deuteronomische These vom levitischen Charakter der Priesterschaft Jahwes hat sich in der Folge durchgesetzt. Die jüngere Zeit kann nur mehr einem Priestertum, das sich von dem Ahnherrn Levi herleitet, Legitimität im Jahwevolke zusprechen.[15] Zugleich aber hat der Umbruch der Exilszeit mit dem, was er an Nachdenken gebracht hat, auch hier zu schwerwiegenden Folgen geführt.

Schon die vorexilische Zeit dürfte bestimmte Differenzierungen der Dienste am Heiligtum gekannt haben. Ez. 44:6ff. lässt nun aber erkennen, dass sich diese Differenzierung mit Wertungen verbunden hat, welche die ganz besondere Signatur jener Umbruchszeit tragen, in der, wie schon Ez. 20 zeigen konnte, die Urteile hart, die Verteilung von Licht und Schatten, von Weiss und Schwarz kompromisslos wurden. Ez. 44:6ff. sind sicher nicht mehr aus der Hand des Propheten Ezechiel selber herzuleiten. In dessen eigener Verkündigung fiel das ganze Volk in allen seinen Ständen (22:23ff.) unter das Verdikt totalen Ungehorsams. Nach 9:6 nimmt das Gericht nach dem ausdrücklichen Befehle Gottes seinen Ausgang bei seinem eigenen Heiligtum (*mimmiqdāšī tāḥēllū*), dessen greuliche geistliche Verwüstung Kap. 8 sichtbar gemacht hatte. Die Sünde ballt sich nach Ez. 8 gerade auch im Jerusalemer Tempel voll zusammen.

In einer folgenden Generation aber hat sich ein gewisses Cliché der

14. So A. H. J. Gunneweg, Leviten und Priester. Hauptlinien der Traditionsbildung und Geschichte des israelitisch-jüdischen Kultpersonals, *FRLANT* 89 (1965).

15. Vgl. etwa 1 Reg. 12:31.

Sündzeit, die Jahwe dann mit dem Gericht des Exils beantwortete, herausgebildet.[16] Was bei Ezechiel selber nur in 9:4 von ferne anklingt, aber nie näher konkretisiert wird, dass da in der Stadt draussen auch Männer sind, "die seufzen und stöhnen ob all der Greuel, die in ihrer Mitte begangen werden," und die dann von der geheimnisvollen priesterlichen Gestalt von 9:2 mit einem Zeichen gezeichnet werden, das sie vor dem Wüten der 6 Rächergestalten in der Stadt bewahrt, das wird in der Folge geschichtstheologisch fixiert. Da waren, so redet eine spätere Zeit von der Phase, in welcher "Israel in die Irre ging" (44:10.15; 48:11), Männer, die standen, und Männer, die fielen. Die Männer, die standen, werden hier in ganz direkter Weise mit dem Kreis der Zadokiden, d.h. der Priesterfamilie in Jerusalem, die sich von Zadok, dem Priester der Zeit Davids,[17] herleitete, gleichgesetzt. Diese werden im Sinne der deuteronomischen These als "levitische Priester" (44:15) bezeichnet. Diejenigen aber, welche fielen, werden in den "Leviten" gefunden, d.h. in den nach der deuteronomischen Regel ebenfalls zum Priestertum fähigen sonstigen Angehörigen der Gruppe Levi ausserhalb der Familie Zadoks. In sehr allgemeiner Weise wird von ihnen gesagt, dass sie sich in der Zeit, da Israel in die Irre ging, von Jahwe weg entfernt hätten, hinter ihren Götzen einhergegangen (44:10) und Israel zum Anstoss zur Schuld geworden seien (44:12). Aus diesem Grunde sollen sie in Zukunft nur die niederen Dienste im Tempel tun, während der eigentliche Opferdienst am Altar den Zadokiden vorbehalten bleibt.

Mit dieser geschichtstheologischen Disqualifikation der Leviten scheinen die Priesterkreise in die Zeit des zweiten Tempels hineingegangen zu sein. Die Auswirkungen derselben sind denn auch durchaus zu erkennen. Unter den 42 360 Personen, welche Esr. 2:64 abgesehen von Sklaven und Sklavinnen und Sängern und Sängerinnen aufzählt, werden in v. 40 ganze 74 Leviten aufgeführt. Die vier Priestergeschlechter, die unmittelbar vorher in 2:36–39 erwähnt sind, umfassen demgegenüber 4 289 Personen. Und noch im Bericht von der Rückwanderung unter Esra ist in Esr. 8:15 erwähnt, dass bei der Besammlung der Rückwanderer sich zwar Priester einfanden, dagegen kein einziger Levit. Durch eine besondere Gesandtschaft werden schliesslich zwei Levitenfamilien mit insgesamt 38 Angehörigen dazu bewogen, sich dem Zuge der Rückwanderer anzuschliessen. Die Disqualifikation der Leviten, die sich nicht nur auf ihre Dienstleistung, sondern nach Ez. 44:6ff. darüber hinaus auf ihre Vorgeschichte erstreckte, hat sich unverkennbar sehr tief eingegraben.

16. W. Zimmerli, Planungen für den Wiederaufbau nach der Katastrophe von 587, *VT* 18 (1968): 229–55, bes. 250–53.
17. Dazu etwa Gunneweg loc. cit., 98ff.

Erneut stossen wir damit auf eine Aporie, die der nachexilischen Gemeinde zu schaffen macht. Kann diese geistliche Disqualifikation, die sich im Zusammenhang mit den Erschütterungen der Exilszeit ergeben hat, das letzte Wort über die Leviten bleiben?

## III

Wieder ist die Priesterschrift, oder genauer, eine jüngere Schicht von Aussagen der Priesterschrift, zu erwähnen. In ihr hat die Aporie ihre Lösung gefunden. Dieser Lösung ist eigentümlich, dass sie zugleich die Aporie, welche das Buch Ezechiel im Blick auf die göttliche Forderung der menschlichen Erstgeburt enthält, aufgreift und auch sie einer neuen Lösung entgegenführt.

Nu. 1f. berichtet von der Musterung des Volkes, das nach P bald danach vom Berge Sinai aufbricht (10, 11ff.). Davon gesondert wird in Nu. 3 von der Musterung des Stammes Levi berichtet. In diesen Bericht sind jüngere Erweiterungen eingetragen worden,[18] von denen im vorliegenden Zusammenhange vor allem Nu. 3:11–13 mit der wohl erst nachträglich aus ihr herausgesponnenen Erweiterung 3:40–51 beachtet sein wollen.

In Nu. 3:11–13 nun ist eine Entscheidung Jahwes zu hören: "Siehe, ich habe die Leviten aus der Mitte der Israeliten heraus genommen anstelle aller Erstgeborenen, die den Schoss ihrer Mutter durchbrechen (*kålbᵊkōr pæṭær ræḥæm*) von den Israeliten, und mir sollen die Leviten gehören. Denn mir gehört jeder Erstgeborene. Am Tage, da ich alle Erstgeborenen im Lande Ägypten schlug, habe ich mir jeden Erstgeborenen in Israel geheiligt. Sowohl Mensch als Vieh, mir gehören sie. Ich bin Jahwe." Die Formulierung gehört in ihrem Sprachtyp deutlich zusammen mit der priesterschriftlichen Formulierung der Erstgeburtsforderung in Ex. 13:2, von der früher schon beiläufig die Rede war. Ihr Plus über jene Formulierung hinaus besteht in der Erklärung Jahwes, dass er sich die Leviten genommen habe, um jenes Gebot zu seiner echten Erfüllung zu bringen. Die leise Inkonzinnität, dass dort die Erstgeburt von Mensch und Tier gefordert wird, was in Nu. 3:13 denn auch wiederholt ist, während die eigentliche Erklärung Jahwes und sein Entscheid es nur mit den Menschen, die nun an die Stelle der Erstgeborenen in Israel treten, zu tun hat, wird nicht weiter beachtet.

Zu achten ist aber auf die innere Verwandlung der Aussage. Was in Ex. 13:2 ein ganz Israel auferlegtes *Gebot* darstellt (imp. *qaddæš-lī*), ist in Nu. 3:11 als erwählender Zugriff Gottes verstanden. Jahwe greift sich dem Stamm Levi aus der Mitte Israels heraus (*waʾanī hinnē lāqaḥtī* 3:12). Der in

18. M. Noth, Das vierte Buch Mose. Numeri. *ATD* 7 (1966): 30f., 33f.

Ex. 13:2 an Israel gerichtete Imperativ (*qaddæš-lī*) wird in Nu. 3:13 in eine göttliche Aussage in 1. Person umgesetzt (*hiqdaštī lī*). Natürlich ist in dieser Wahl Jahwes auch die Forderung eines Gehorsams impliziert: Israel soll ihm die Leviten zur Verfügung stellen. Aber der Akzent der göttlichen Wahl ist doch gar nicht zu überhören. Eine weitere Entfaltung der Pflichten, die diese Wahl für die Leviten mit sich bringt, ist nicht beigefügt.[19]

Mit der Proklamation dieser göttlichen Wahl ist nun aber ein Doppeltes erreicht. Das Erste: Die Schmach ist von den Leviten genommen. Nicht mehr infolge einer Versündigung sind sie zu Dienern am Heiligtum degradiert. Eine göttliche Wahl gibt ihnen das Vorrecht dieses Dienstes. Die volle Würde, die nach dem alten Levisegen Moses und nach Ex. 32:29 auf Levi nach dem alten Verständnis desselben als Priesterstamm schlechthin lag, ist nun auch auf die Leviten nach dem jüngeren Verständnis, d.h. die von den Priestern unterschiedenen Heiligtumsdiener, gelegt. Man möchte von einer vollkommenen geistlichen Rehabilitierung der Leviten sprechen.

Zugleich aber ist darin auch das andere erreicht: Die göttliche Forderung der menschlichen Erstgeburt ist nun ebenfalls wieder ganz voll in ihr Recht eingesetzt. Und zwar in einem radikaleren Verständnis, als es die ältere Zeit gehabt hatte. Dort war ein Tieropfer als Ersatz für die Jahwe nicht gewährte volle Darreichung eines Menschen eingetreten. Der älteren Zeit bedeutete das kein Problem. In der Zeit der Krise im Verständnis der Erstgeburtsgabe aber war die Frage aufgebrochen, ob denn Jahwe in diesem Gebot nicht wirklich die volle Gabe eines ganzen Menschen meine. In der Weihe ans Heiligtum, die etwa in 1 Sam. 1f. zu erkennen war, meinten wir die gelegentlich beschrittene Möglichkeit einer solchen Weihe des ganzen Menschen erkennen zu können. Sie bildet im Grunde auch das Vorbild für das, was nun in Nu. 3:11–13 zu sehen ist. Nur dass hier an die Stelle der gelegentlichen Weihe eines einzelnen die volle Erfüllung in jedem Falle einer Erstgeburt tritt. Durch das Eintreten des ganzen Stammes Levi tritt in der Tat für jeden einzelnen Erstgeborenen in Israel ein ganzer Mensch als Gabe an Gott ein. Das Gebot ist auf dem Wege menschlicher Stellvertretung voll erfüllt.

Die Aufgabe, diese volle Erfüllung nun auch genau rechnerisch nachzuweisen, hat dann der Nachtrag Nu. 3:40–51, welcher zweifellos 3:11–13 vor sich schon voraussetzt und einer noch etwas jüngeren Zeit zugehört, über-

19. Von der Weihe der Leviten reden dann Nu. 8:5–22. Hier sind sie nicht nur in v. 16 als "Hingegebene für mich" (*nᵊtunīm nᵊtunīm hēmmā lī*, vgl. dazu o. Anm. 8) bezeichnet, sondern es werden in v. 16b–18 nochmals die Gedanken von 3:11–13 in gleichartigem Wortgebrauch wiederholt. Da sie im weiteren Textzusammenhang von v. 5–22 aber nicht vorausgesetzt zu sein scheinen, ist (mit Noth loc. cit., 61f., der auch v. 19 noch zu 16b–18 schlägt) in diesen Versen wohl eine nachträgliche Angleichung an 3:11–13 zu sehen.

nommen. Hier wird nun in einem pedantisch genauen Rechnungsverfahren ermittelt, dass die Zahl der 22 273 Erstgeborenen im Israel der Tage Moses fast völlig durch die 22 000 Glieder des Stammes Levi gedeckt wird. Der kleine verbleibende Rest von 273 Erstgeborenen aber darf nach der Anordnung Jahwes durch eine Ersatzgabe in Geld abgegolten werden. In dieser genauen Nachrechnung soll unterstrichen werden, dass die menschliche Ersatzleistung mit einer kleinen Abrundung genau der göttlichen Forderung entspricht. Dass in diesem Zusammenhange auch noch das Vieh der Leviten miterwähnt wird, bei dem dann allerdings die Zählung und der Zahlvergleich unterbleibt, zeigt, dass die volle Regelung von Nu. 3:11–13 die in leiser Inkonsequenz um der Anlehnung an Ex. 13:2 willen ebenfalls das Vieh erwähnte, Ausgangspunkt des Ganzen ist. Der weitere Gedanke, dass sich in späteren Tagen das Zahlenverhältnis von Leviten und Erstgeborenen im Volke verändern könnte, wird gar nicht in Erwägung gezogen. Die Schilderung der Regelung und Berechnung am Anfang muss genügen.

Die priesterliche Darstellung verrät in alledem eine bestimmte Denkweise der "Verrechnung," wie sie im Prinzip ganz ähnlich auch an anderen Stellen anzutreffen ist: Ein Levite wird auf einen Erstgeborenen "angerechnet." Ganz so werden in P etwa die 40 Jahre Wüstenwanderung auf die 40 Tage Kundschafterzeit verrechnet (Nu. 14:34), was wiederum in den 390 Tagen des gebundenen Liegens Ezechiels als Verrechnung für 390 Jahre Sündzeit Israels und den 40 Tagen zur Darstellung der 40 Jahre Strafzeit Judas (Ez. 4:4–6) eine nahe Parallele hat.

Zum anderen aber ist nicht zu übersehen, dass in der neuen Lösung der Gedanke der Stellvertretung von hoher Bedeutung ist—eine Vorstellung, die auch sonst in der exilisch-nachexilischen Theologie eine wachsende Bedeutung gewinnt.[20]

Es sind beachtliche theologische Gedankenleistungen, die auf dem skizzierten Wege im nachexilischen priesterlichen Bereich vollzogen worden sind und die deutlich machen, dass der Glaube der nachexilischen Zeit keineswegs nur von steril gewordener überkommener "Tradition" lebt.

20. Dazu W. Zimmerli, Zur Vorgeschichte von Jes. 53, *S. VT* 17 (1969): 236–44.

# Contributors

FRANCIS I. ANDERSEN
The Church Divinity School of the Pacific
Berkeley, California

HANS BARDTKE
Karl Marx Universität
Leipzig, Germany

M. A. BEEK
Universiteit van Amsterdam
Amsterdam, Netherlands

JOHN BOWMAN
University of Melbourne
Victoria, Australia

J. COPPENS
Universitas Lovaniensis
Louvain, Belgium

MITCHELL DAHOOD, S.J.
Pontifico Instituto Biblico
Roma, Italy

HERBERT DONNER
Eberhard-Karls Universität
Tübingen, Germany

G. R. DRIVER
University of Oxford
Oxford, England

OTTO EISSFELDT
Martin Luther Universität
Halle, Germany

KARL ELLIGER
Eberhard-Karls Universität
Tübingen, Germany

F. CHARLES FENSHAM
University of Stellenbosch
Stellenbosch, South Africa

JOSEPH A. FITZMYER, S.J.
University of Chicago
Chicago, Illinois

GEORG FOHRER
Friedrich-Alexander Universität
Erlangen, Germany

DAVID NOEL FREEDMAN
San Francisco Theological Seminary
San Anselmo, California

KURT GALLING
Eberhard-Karls Universität
Tübingen, Germany

NELSON GLUECK
Hebrew Union College
Cincinnati, Ohio

MOSHE GREENBERG
The Hebrew University of Jerusalem
Jerusalem, Israel

JONAS C. GREENFIELD
University of California
Berkeley, California

E. HAMMERSHAIMB
Aarhus Universitet
Aarhus, Denmark

HERBERT B. HUFFMON
Drew University
Madison, New Jersey

ALFRED JEPSEN
Ernst Moritz Arndt Universität
Greifswald, Germany

ARVID S. KAPELRUD
Universitet I Oslo
Oslo, Norway

THOMAS O. LAMBDIN
Harvard University
Cambridge, Massachusetts

W. G. LAMBERT
Birmingham University
Birmingham, England

SABATINO MOSCATI
Università di Roma
Roma, Italy

J. M. MYERS
Lutheran Theological Seminary
Gettysburg, Pennsylvania

MARVIN H. POPE
Yale University
New Haven, Connecticut

HELMER RINGGREN
Uppsala Universitet
Uppsala, Sweden

STANISLAV SEGERT
University of California
Los Angeles, California

J. ALBERTO SOGGIN
Facoltà valdese di teologia
Roma, Italy

J. J. STAMM
Universität Bern
Bern, Switzerland

A. VAN SELMS
Pretoria University
Pretoria, South Africa

R. J. TOURNAY, O.P.
Révue Biblique
Jerusalem, Israel

WALTHER ZIMMERLI
Georg-August Universität
Göttingen, Germany

THE JOHNS HOPKINS PRESS
Designed by James C. Wageman
Composed in Baskerville text and display
by Wm. Clowes and Sons Ltd.

Printed on 55 lb. Olde Style Laid
by Universal Lithographers, Inc.
Bound in Bancroft Lynene 35200
by L. H. Jenkins, Inc.